# FOOTPRINTS

## A History of the Place We Call Palisades Park

Katy Beck and Marilyn Henkel, Co-Editors
Don Henkel, Photographic Archivist

Bill Potter, Contributing Editor

Marge Roche, Artist

TURNER PUBLISHING COMPANY
NASHVILLE, TENNESSEE

# DEDICATION

## TO MARILYN HENKEL

Those who know Marilyn will understand her deep commitment to this book. She joked once that it was like giving birth to another child, and truly, it was. She worked thousands of hours to pull together the articles and stories contained here, to type them into the computer, design the pages, proof-read time after time after time, and revise based on the opinions of at least a dozen readers. Her husband, Donald, joined in her efforts, drawing together thousands of historical photos, scanning them into the computer, and organizing them for the book.

A common theme throughout this book is the magic of Palisades Park that draws us back year after year, generation after generation. Marilyn first visited the park as a young child and now she watches her grandchildren playing where she once played. Perhaps it was this intangible thread of time, which drew Marilyn through the arduous process of compiling this book. Even when facing difficult health, her overriding concern was to finish this. Her family is extremely proud of her work and grateful for this gift. She has not only made the history of our beloved park tangible and enduring, but she has also left her grandchildren and future generations a legacy that will live far into the future. *Donna Goscinski*

## TO KATY BECK

Katy Beck's love for Palisades Park began in the early 1940's when, as a child, she helped her father design Sundune Cottage. Her childhood summers were spent with family and friends climbing sand dunes, wandering beechwood forests and swimming in Lake Michigan. She has come for 66 years, worked throughout the park, gotten married here, watched her children and her grandchildren grow up here. The fifth generation of Katy's family, too learned to appreciate varied aspects of undisturbed nature amid the abundant rustic beauty of Palisades Park. The latest generations are also starting to see the racial and cultural diversity of the world join the natural bio-diversity of the area.

Katy has endeavored to draw forth meaning through an understanding of human interdependence and connection and its role in the lives, past, present and future, of humanity. Her love of nature and desire to share it with as many people as she can, and her respect for people of diversity, have driven Katy to put down on paper the histories of land and peoples of the area. Her dedication to this project, and her commitment over the twenty-five years in collecting and compiling oral histories and data have compelled her to see this history published. This book binds the fast to the future. It was written so that people who have shared the park over the past 100 years lend a voice to the present and leave a legacy for the future. *Tom Beck*

**Statement of their friendship:**

Marilyn and Katy have been Palisades friends for more than four decades. Just as they once shared summertime picnics and memories on the beach with their children they continue to share this time with their children's children. The making of this history book has been a labor and a love for both of them.

**Turner**
PUBLISHING COMPANY

www.turnerpublishing.com

Copyright © 2004, Palisades Park Country Club

No part of this book may be reproduced or transmitted in any form or by any means, electronic or mechanical, including photocopying, recording, or by any information storage and retrieval system, without permission in writing from Palisades Park Country Club.

Library of Congress Control No. 2004105836

ISBN: 978-1-68162-415-0

Limited Edition

RRH 0 9 8 7 6 5 4 3 2 1

Cover photograph by Nanette Draper Lewis

Dedicated to all the people whose **Footprints** we have followed - who have loved, protected, and been touched by **This Place That We Call Palisades Park.**

# Table of Contents

Preface ........................................................................................ 7
Thanks ........................................................................................ 8
What is Palisades Park? ............................................................ 9
Arthur Quick's Vision ............................................................. 10
Poem: I Am Palisades Park .................................................... 11

## Chapter 1: The Place We Call Palisades Park ..... 13

Poem: A Sand Dune ................................................................ 15
Our Dunelands ........................................................................ 16
Poem: Evening Panorama ...................................................... 19
Principal Stages in Evolution of Great Lakes ..................... 20
Palisades Park – Geologically Speaking .............................. 21
Our Inland Sea – Lake Michigan .......................................... 24
History of Vegetation on the Lake Michigan Dunes ......... 25
Dune Dweller Lives Alone and Likes It .............................. 27
Early Footprints ...................................................................... 28
Interviews
    Lucy and George Bennett ............................................ 42
    Candi Wesaw ................................................................ 44
    Gerald Wesaw ............................................................... 45
Covert Township and the Lumbering Days ....................... 48
South Haven in 1902 .............................................................. 63
Piers at Palisades .................................................................... 65

## Chapter 2: The Early Years (1905 – 1920) ........ 69

Arthur Quick ........................................................................... 72
Palisades Park Opened on the Brandywine ....................... 79
First 21 Cottages ..................................................................... 83
The Sturtevants and Their Lodge ......................................... 84
Robert Ballou .......................................................................... 86
Water Works ........................................................................... 88
Sinks Grocery Store ............................................................... 90
Letters Home .......................................................................... 91
Poem: There Is Pleasure in the Pathless Woods ................ 95
Interviews
    Mary Kay Goodridge .................................................... 96
    Hazel Harper ............................................................... 101
    Ruth Kropp .................................................................. 105
    Vashti Blaney/Mardy Mehagan Mavor ................... 108
    Mardy Mehagan Mavor ............................................. 114

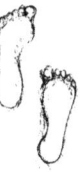

Gwen Miller .................................................................... 121
Mary Lee Tillson ............................................................. 122
Charley Tunecke ............................................................. 126
Betty and Ray Woodhouse ............................................. 130
    Poem: Winter Day In Palisades ............................. 132

Memories
Margaret Abbott ............................................................. 133
Marion Hamilton ............................................................. 135
Anna Holmes .................................................................. 138
Pauline Sauer ................................................................. 141
Virginia Steinbacher ....................................................... 146

Poem: Oh, the Wide Sky ........................................................... 148

# Chapter 3: The 20's .................................. 151

The Story of the Clubhouse ...................................................... 154
The Old Golf Course and its Designer, Tom Bendelow ............. 161
1924 Court Case ........................................................................ 164

Interviews
David Filkins ................................................................... 165
Florence Heitner and Joyce Heitner Lloyd ....................... 167
Betty Householder ........................................................... 170
Jayne Mathias ................................................................. 179
Lou and Thelma Weston ................................................. 184
Betty Wintermute ............................................................ 187

Memories
Virginia Melchert Coleman ............................................. 191
Ray Cooney ..................................................................... 194
Jeanne DeLamarter ......................................................... 195
    Poems: Sea Gulls and Remembered Country ...... 195 & 196
Bill Ferry ......................................................................... 197
    The Tipping Point of Tolerance ........................... 201
Kathryn Welles Goff ....................................................... 203
Margaret Heisel ............................................................... 206
Bill Keehn ........................................................................ 208
Isabel Larson ................................................................... 209
Ginny Peirce Richards .................................................... 211
Margaret Sauer ................................................................ 212
    Poem: Pebbles of the Past ..................................... 213
Mary K. Shepardson ....................................................... 214
Jeanne Welles Sturgeon ................................................... 216

# Chapter 4: The 30's .................................. 221

The Arts Community ................................................................. 225
The Start of the Patter ................................................................ 238
A Race with a Purpose .............................................................. 241
Fishing ....................................................................................... 243
1931 By-Laws and Restrictions ................................................ 246
Tony Canonie ............................................................................ 248

Interviews
Connie Borchert .............................................................. 249
Esther Brand and Peg Ingles Brand ................................ 255

Poem: Reflections on the Family Cottage ..... 256
    Forest Lowrey ..... 257
    Tony Malinowski ..... 264
    Talitha Peat ..... 269
    Bill Potter ..... 275
    Tony and Pearl Sarno ..... 280
Poem: A Heavenly Show ..... 284
<u>Memories</u>
    Katy Beatty Beck ..... 285
    Pat Peat Dusendschon ..... 296
    Marty Edwards ..... 297
    Freida Eldredge ..... 298
    Bert Henderson, Esmah Orcutt, and Clara Strothers ..... 299
    Mary Lou Hession ..... 303
    Nan Draper Lewis ..... 304
    "Old Timer" ..... 324
    Doris Patterson ..... 325
    Paul Schlacks ..... 328
    Jim Williams ..... 332

## Chapter 5: The 40's ..... 335

History of the Circle ..... 339
Signs of the Times ..... 342
Covert Library and Nellie Palmer ..... 344
The Brandywine ..... 345
August 17, 1940 <u>Patter</u> ..... 355
Fires ..... 359
The Covert Fire Department ..... 362
<u>Interviews</u>
    Dr. and Mrs. Joseph Campbell ..... 363
    Mr. Ben Iverson ..... 367
    Helen Packard ..... 374
<u>Memories</u>
    Lori Anderson Dillman ..... 377
    Eleanor DiLuigi ..... 380
    Bill Eldredge ..... 382
    Sally Davis Ellis ..... 384
    Wendy Easterbrook Litterst-Day and
        Judy Easterbrook Coker-Green ..... 385
    Betty Lukey ..... 387

## Chapter 6: The Ensuing Decades ..... 389

Clubhouse Plays ..... 392
<u>Interview</u> : Cecil Burrous ..... 393
Park Resident Managers ..... 400
Loyal Workers in the 50's ..... 403
Tragedy at Palisades ..... 404
The Nine Old Men ..... 407
Past Presidents ..... 408
A Plane Comes Down ..... 409

| | |
|---|---|
| The Monster Down the Beach | 410 |
| Holiday Celebrations | 414 |
| Ethnic Dinners | 421 |
| <u>Memories</u>: Fran Prange and Happy Valley | 422 |
| The Tennis Program | 424 |
| Memorials in the Park | 429 |
| The Pal-Hill Sailing Races | 431 |
| A Toast to Summer Romance | 434 |

## Chapter 7: Lake Michigan: Our Untamed Treasure ... 439

| | |
|---|---|
| The Beach | 441 |
| Lake Levels | 453 |
| Storms | 460 |
| Shore Protection | 478 |

## Chapter 8: Nature Programs .......... 523

| | |
|---|---|
| Our Sanctuary | 524 |
| Through the Eyes of Anne Fuller and Friends | 527 |
| Jack Gardner and Our Trails | 533 |
| <u>Memories</u>: Rob Venner | 537 |

## Chapter 9: Cottages .......... 539

| | |
|---|---|
| Cottage History Chart | 541 |
| Cottage Histories | 555 |

## Afterword .......... 591

| | |
|---|---|
| Changed or Changeless? | 591 |

## Appendix .......... 593

| | |
|---|---|
| The Editors | 594 |
| Future Editors | 595 |
| Cottage Names/Numbers/Owners | 596 |
| Cottage Numbers/Addresses/Owners | 598 |
| Early Sales | 600 |
| Associate Membership List | 604 |
| Photo Credits | 605 |

## Color Photo Section .......... 305

Pages 305 - 320

# Preface

Arthur Quick, the founder of Palisades Park, wrote in the Introduction to his book, Wild Flowers of the Northern States and Canada, that – "from early spring until snow flies" – he planned "to conduct his readers on a weekly hike through the Michigan dunes ... on the writer's own grounds – Palisades Park." Our book, also, will "stroll" through those same Michigan dunes, looking not for "all the Wild Flowers that are in bloom" but for **footprints** from an earlier time - those illusive and fading guides to where we have been and - perhaps - to where we are going.

The editors would assert the importance of keeping the history of the Park alive. Our hats are off to the earlier committee which, in 1984, decided to embark on an oral history project. Many of their voices, as well as the voices of those interviewed, are now stilled. We feel fortunate that their insights were saved. David Baldacci says it well in his "Author's Note" of the novel, Wish You Well (New York, NY: Warner Books Inc., p.x.): "Oral histories ... show appropriate respect for the lives and experiences of those who have come before. And, just as important, they document those remembrances, for once those lives are over, that personal knowledge is lost forever. Unfortunately, we live in a time now where everyone seems to be solely looking ahead, as though we deem nothing in the past worthy of our attention. The future is always fresh and exciting, and it has a pull on us that times past simply can never muster. Yet it may well be that our greatest wealth as human beings can be 'discovered' by simply looking behind us."

This is our story. In 1984 and 1985, a Palisades History Committee met with the intent of updating the previous written history of the Park, Palisades Park Review, 1905-1968. This committee began to gather old pictures and initiated a series of taped interviews of some 23 Park old-timers. Despite the coming and going of various volunteers over the next years, the tapes were slowly transcribed and typed. Certain historical documents were gathered, research continued, new photos discovered. By the end of 1999, the project was stalled. Finally, in the summer of 2000, the present editors teamed up. We collected more pictures, scanned old Patters, elicited the help of and contributions from other Park members, and continued research. We edited the interviews into narratives (maintaining the voices of the interviewees). Marilyn wrote section introductions and several articles. Marge drew her sketches. Don used the computer to scan and organize over 1400 pictures. Katy decided which picture should go where, worked with Don on the color section, and finished her research and writing on the pre-Palisades Park days. Bill produced long articles on various aspects of our beaches - from storms and sea walls to the Brandywine and bridges. Finally, Marilyn typed and then laid out all 608 pages on the computer. Thus this volume came to be born.

We make no claim, however, to give a definitive history of Palisades Park. We cannot be as thorough as Mr. Quick, whose "descriptions apply no matter where in America a flower grows." Our **footprints** will start with a look at the geology of the area and its pre-Palisades Park days – first when Native Americans lived in these dunes and, later, when the area - like so much of Michigan - was the site of a lumbering boom. Then, using the taped interviews and written memories, we will offer some first hand glimpses of the early decades of the Park. We make no pretense of having verified all the information that was shared in the written and oral memories. Indeed, we know there are contradictions, from one person to the next. We are sure the reader will discover inaccuracies in facts and chronology. Our intent is to present the material as simple memories – some more accurate than others – with the hope that they will help us understand both our heritage and our present challenges. Other material, from old maps and minutes to Bill Potter's comprehensive history of the beach, will present a fuller picture of this Park which will soon end its first century.

Palisades Park has remained surprisingly constant through its first 100 years; it has also changed in many profound ways. This history hopes to touch on both. We trust that presenting much of our history in the voices of those who have lived in the Park will (as did Quick's book) "constitute a highly interesting guide to every [Palisades Park] lover, opening up an intimate view that to many people may be distinctly new." So please join us as we follow the trail of **footprints** that tell a part of the story of **this place we call Palisades Park.**

# Thanks

This project was started in 1984 when Betty Householder suggested that an updated Palisades Park History be written. She asked Katy Beck to join her as chair of this endeavor; they formed a committee including Carol and Don Beveridge, Mary Reed, and Dave Livingston. Fran Prange and Mary Lou Tombaugh volunteered to help conduct the interviews. Over the years, Betty and Katy worked to keep the project alive. Betty continued her collection of cottage histories for the rest of her life. We can safely say there would be no 2004 version of the history without Betty's unflagging enthusiasm for the perpetuation of our Park heritage.

---

Special thanks, also, to the following who have helped us by gathering material, typing, sharing old photographs, writing sections, proofreading, and/or encouraging us in many ways.

| | |
|---|---|
| David Beck | Nanette Lewis |
| Joel Beck | Robert McCarthy |
| Kimeri Beck | Mike Mathias |
| Tom Beck | Bonnie Mauer |
| Stuart Bendelow | Amy Mickan |
| Carol and Don Beveridge | Betty Nelson |
| Mary Jo Carr | Nancy Potter |
| Betty Clark | Fran Prange |
| Ginny Coleman | Mary Reed |
| Barb Ferguson | Pearl Sarno |
| Donna Goscinski | Paul Schlacks |
| Ed Gray (Jikewe) | James Sheridan |
| Mary Kilburn | Ron Saiet |
| Janice and Joe King | Barbara Trumbull |
| Marilyn Kleb | Robert Venner |

We would particularly like to express our appreciation to Don Henkel, whose patience, assistance, insights, and photographic and computer skills were invaluable. Without his help there would be no book.

# What Is Palisades Park?

**By Margaret Sauer**
From August 10, 1974 Patter

What is Palisades Park: Ask anyone, of any age. It's <u>sand</u> and <u>trees,</u> and <u>water</u> and <u>breeze.</u> Take away any one of these (go ahead, do it mentally, one item at a time) and what would you have? Well, what you'd have would not be Palisades Park as we know it and love it. The beautiful walks in the woods, the sights and sounds and, yes, the special smell of water – these are all (whether we are conscious of it or not) the setting for all the pleasurable activities of all of us, from the very youngest to the oldest.

We see, we hear, we feel this mass of external loveliness. It soaks into us as if by osmosis, and never again are we the same. What is it that happens to us? Is it chemical, electrical, psychological, spiritual? Why do we come back, year after year, from places as far away as California, and Florida, and Virginia? Why is it so difficult for me to decide to sell my cottage? Why do so many renters or visitors eventually buy or build their own cottage here? It's magical, isn't it? It's a sand-trap! That's what it is! And we can't get it out of our system. Palisades Park is forever a part of each one of us, just as each one of us is forever a part of the world. Nothing is lost.

But yesterday, today, and tomorrow are not forever. What we see hasn't always been here. Where did the sand come from that built our dunes? And what is sand, anyway? Why are the pebbles on the shore so colorful and so interesting and why do some contain fossils? How old are our hills and how old are these pebbles and fossils? The Ice Age – are our big, beautiful, spectacular dunes connected in some mysterious way to the great ice sheets?

> How long were we ridden by glaciers?
> From what rocks were our dune sands shorn?
> Did winds stop howling and wailing
> When primeval forests were born? (MES)

The beauty of Palisades Park is not skin deep. It is above us and it is below the things we see at the surface. The storms, the sunlight, the soil – what influences do they have that are not apparent at the surface? Our past – it goes back, far back, beyond the so-important present. And what of the future? Things are changing. No two days are exactly alike, nor will they ever be. Our Park is part of the past, part of the present, and part of the future. But we see it today; it will not be forever – except within us.

# Arthur Quick's Vision

*Arthur Quick's love for "the place we call Palisades Park" is caught in his own description of his first visit to the area, found in his early brochure, <u>South Haven Palisades Park and The Legend of Thunder Mountain</u> ( pp.24 – 28):*

I had often heard of Thunder Mountain and the large forest surrounding it, with its hills and romantic, shady glens and roads, its wild flowers, ferns and springs of ice cold water; and finally I visited the place. It is six miles south of South Haven, Michigan, directly on the lakeshore. Since the old lumbering days, the place has been known locally as Paulville Pier, but recently the natural beauty of the surroundings has attracted much attention and it is aptly called "Palisades Park." Our launch carried us there easily in a half-hour.

Landing at the old pier, we found a large forest, fronting for a half-mile on old Lake Michigan. A wide, smooth beach was one of the attractions, while upon the bluffs great spreading beech trees, towering pines, and vigorous oaks and sugar maples gave most inviting shade. The bluffs leading down to the beach, as well as Palisades Hill, a high and steep wooded hillside extending inland at right angles to the beach, presented an appearance not unlike the far-famed Palisades of the Hudson.

Thunder Mountain is an oblong wooded hill in the southern portion of this big natural park. About 300 feet high and steep on three sides, it slopes gradually to the lake on the west. From the summit we had an unobstructed view of the country for 15 to 20 miles around, thickly dotted with houses, orchards and groves of timber. Out upon the broad bosom of Lake Michigan we could discern a number of steamers and sailing craft, some of them many miles out. What a site for a modest observatory! And how we wished for a good field-glass.

The general character of the Park is gently rolling, with a few hills, and numerous wooded glens; but best of all is the prodigality of shade. Yet the place is dry and healthful, and with a delicious woodsy odor that is irresistible. Several springs of ice-cold water* were found beside one of the shadiest and most romantic wood roads leading from the old pier to the village of Covert.

There could scarcely be a better place for botanizing than right here in this big woods. Although it was then in June, when most of the wild flowers have disappeared, yet here,

*\*These springs were in our meadow, near cottage #55.*

retarded by the shady woods, were great quantities still in luxuriant bloom and of great variety. Mossy banks flanked by many varieties of ferns and bracken were frequently seen. People living near have told me that earlier in the season, and for about two months, this whole woods and the hillsides are veritable flower gardens. And the song birds – they seem to make headquarters here.

Within a few miles of the Park, nailed to a tree on the edge of the woods, the writer once saw the following notice: "NO HUNTING ALOUD." (sic) The same rule holds in Palisades Park. The forest denizens are safe. The camera owners go on a "still hunt" here, and they frequently make some good shots.

*A Palisades Park wooded dune.*

While not a civil engineer, yet I could readily see that a depression in the land near the mouth of the creek could be transformed into a beautiful artificial lake of about eight acres at very little expense. Evidently this was once a sort of bay, but is now dry, with the creek winding through it. A rustic dam, seventy feet in length, thrown across the ravine a short distance back from the beach, would accomplish this. Several small wooded elevations would remain as islands, and the artificial lake would be bordered on all sides and down to the water's edge by dense groves of pine, beech, and maple, and encircled by a winding, shady drive. This would make one of the most romantic spots in the park, with the clear, cold springs on the banks, heavy shade, and delightfully cool lake breezes. Of the 250 acres in the park, the 130 acre forest fronting the lake is one of the prettiest natural parks to be found in the state. It is always dry, for the sandy soil affords perfect drainage and consequent healthfulness....No wonder Palisades Park is acknowledged by everyone who is at all familiar with the east side of Lake Michigan, as being the most picturesque spot along the Michigan shore. It is a genuine country park. Nothing should be done to mar its rustic simplicity.

# I Am Palisades Park

Author Unknown
From the July, 1963 <u>Patter</u>

I am Palisades Park.

I am sunlight on the water, a mist on the sandy beaches, and the stars.
I am a doorway out of the commonplace into the adventuring experience.
I am a place where youth learns the joy of play without a sting, of fellowship without regrets,
     of creative efforts that weary not, of good times that leave no headache – or heartache – behind.

I am a new purpose for life that will make the years different.
I am noise – and silence with a thrill in it.
I am laughter – and quiet resolution that seeks the comfort of the hills.
I am energy – and the toughness of living service.
I am youth – and the slowly emerging habits that make maturing experience worthy.
I am today and also tomorrow that is being shaped.

I am giver of gifts that pass not away, that time will not chill, that poverty will not quench,
     that riches will not deceive.
I am habits, ideals, ways of living, confirmed attitudes in the soul of youth.

Because I am all these – I invite humanity into fellowship with me.
I am Palisades Park.

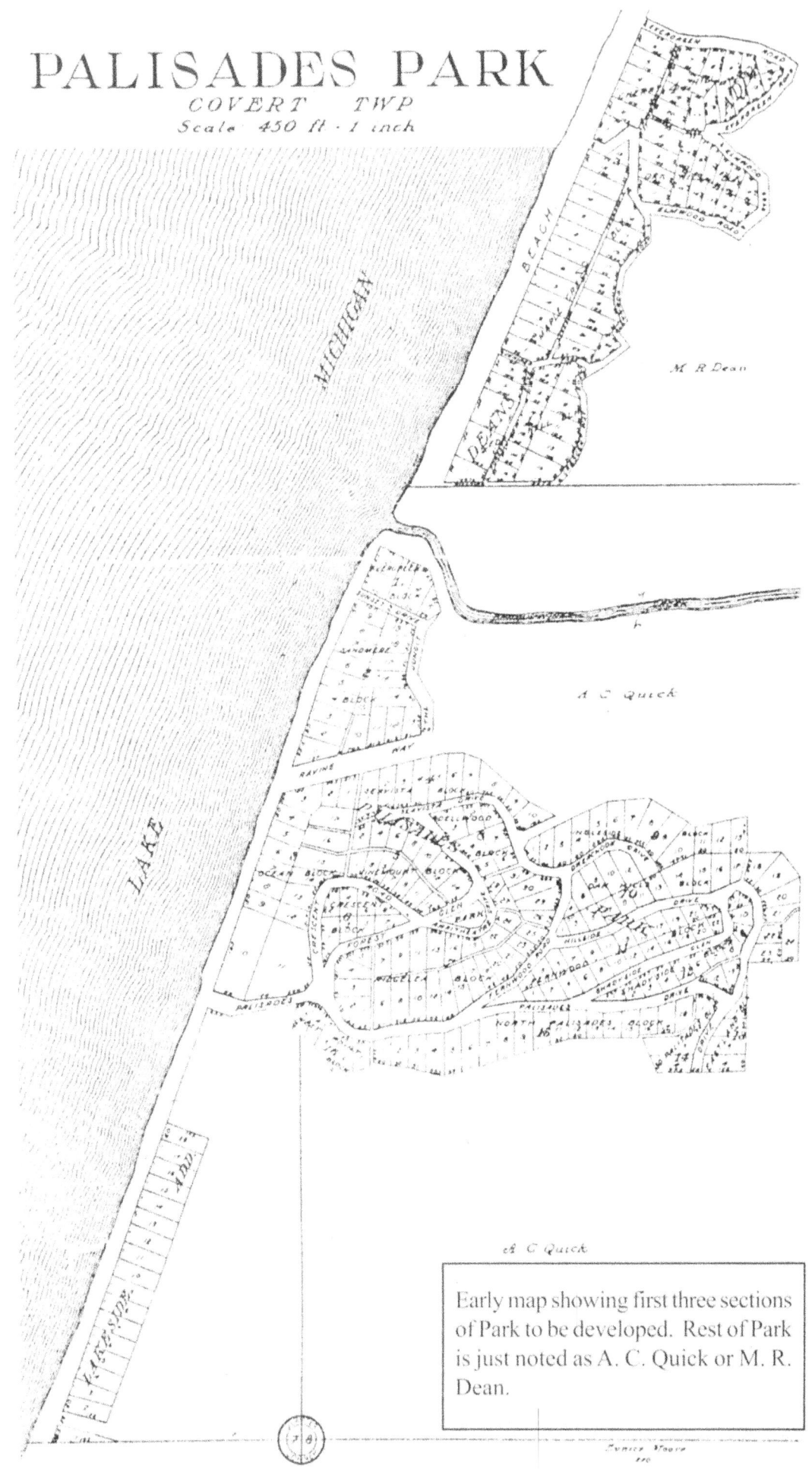

Early map showing first three sections of Park to be developed. Rest of Park is just noted as A. C. Quick or M. R. Dean.

# Chapter 1

# The Place We Call Palisades Park

> Night after night, throughout the millennia, wind and waves resculpt the shore, patterning the sand anew each morning. That may be why each passing stranger assumes his **footprints** are the first.

## The Place We Call Palisades Park

How easy to think a place is "ours" – to believe that this area we call Palisades Park has always been just that, "our Park." Perhaps a certain hubris is connected with knowing and loving a place: familiarity may breed pride and possessiveness. No doubt, in the early days, things were a bit different, but deep in our hearts we may assume that the history of Palisades began in 1905, that things are pretty much as they have always been, that our affection for this spot (and our deeds to its property) gives us dominion. **Footprints** to follow? Complacently, we think of Arthur Quick and the Park pioneers.

The editors of this book, however, would take a longer view. That is why we chose, as part of our title: **The Place <u>We Call</u> Palisades Park.** We want to affirm that this area that has been a Park for almost 100 years has a vast earlier history. Geologically speaking, the dunes on which we stand were formed over thousands of years. Before the first European settlers, Native Americans roamed our shores and fished our waters. (Indeed, some Park members claim they have seen Indian spirits still sitting around their campfires on our shores.) As late as 1796, the area we know as Van Buren County was still considered Indian Tribal Land. Only 30-some years later did it become a County; 27 years after that, Deerfield Township (now Covert Township) was formed. The Park's neighboring towns of South Haven and Covert began to develop. Fruit farming and lumbering became important industries and trees were stripped from the forests. By the late 1800's, a young surveyor named Arthur Quick found and bought 205 acres on the lake, some of which had not been heavily lumbered, and decided to try a fruit farm. It was only with the failure of that venture, as the century turned, that Quick turned to another idea – tourism – and "our part" of the story of this place began.

So the "**footprints**" of our title predate the Park by many centuries. The place <u>we</u> call Palisades has had other names and other uses. The idea of this chapter is to remind us of some of the particulars of those earlier days – and to call us back to a humbler appreciation for what we hold so dear. We have been blessed to have the use of this place for 100 years. Its mystique – its essence – encompasses much more than our limited acquaintance. Hear, then, more of its story.

## A Sand Dune

Child of many centuries –
Born out of the bosom of a Great Lake
And resting on her shoulder;
Sired by the waves and storms of the ages;
Driven, molded and shaped
By the winds of all the seasons;
Pounded by them into great heaps as high as ten houses;
And clothed around in a thick green shirt
Of trees, shrubs and vines –
Thou Mounting Child,
Old, yet ever young:
I seek the aloneness of your bald and curving top,
Tufted about with bunches of grasses and shrubs
Which manage to find some root
In your unanchored sands –
Through which I roll my weary fingers
And wiggle my toes.

Out on your giant sand-pile,
Far from all the din of civilization;
Away from phones, and talk, and everything –
Except your sand, and breezes, and views –
I play again!
I lay my body in the glow of your relaxing sun;
And,
Far beneath the shimmer of your long blue moons,
I forget every duty
But to rest,
And rest,
And dream!

"Written on a hot August day atop a 300 foot sand dune on the eastern shore of Lake Michigan." Author unknown. Discovered and submitted by Marion Keehn to the September 14, 1974 <u>Patter.</u>

**Michigan, a mitten and a shield. The nation's only parcel framed in blue, the blue in turn by green. All carved by Nature's hand. No geometric lines set her off; just miles and miles of shimmering seas and margins of white with sand. (1)**

# Our Dunelands
Compiled by Katy Beck

"The coastal sand dune formations that border portions of Michigan's Great Lakes shoreline represent the largest assemblage of fresh water dunes in the world. The diversification of environmental elements – topographic relief, vegetation, wildlife habitats, and climatic conditions – found naturally occurring within these land forms represents a phenomenon unique to the State of Michigan. Complex natural occurrences … led to the creation of these 'gentle' giants made of sand.

"There are two basic dimensions for this remarkable spaceship we call earth – time and distance. Both are fantastically variable. Distance is the space between two spinning atoms, the length of a person's arm, the span of a continent, the reach of human imagination. Time is the moon's phases, the interval of an ice age, the duration of a sleepless night, the pause between two heartbeats.

"To provide some idea of just how old the earth itself may be, let us set the ages of geologic time against the span of our own 12-month calendar year. By that comparison, if we assume the earth was first formed in the month of January and its crust finally formed about February, the primeval ocean came into being perhaps as early as March, certainly no later than June. By the same measuring device, we would say that 'first life' appeared in the month of August and the earliest fossils in November, dinosaurs had their day about mid-December, and human life did not begin until the last day of the last week of the year. It is humbling to note that the presence of modern society, as we know it, represents but one very small tick on the face of the geologic clock." (2)

Tracing the geological time line back to the retreat of the 4th and last great sheet to cover the Midwest – the mile thick four million mile square sheet of ice known as the Wisconsonian, one can begin to investigate the creation, over time, of the hills, marshes, prairies, and forests of Michigan. The glacier left ice deposited "till," or glacial drift, composed of millions of tons of boulders, rocks, clays, and other mineral particles. Till not only carries a wide variety of sizes in the unsorted debris; the rock materials, having been carried from widely scattered places have great diversity in their mineral makeup. For example, jasper conglomerate fragments, or pudding stone, are scattered throughout Michigan, having originated from north of Lake Huron. Also to be found are erratic or boulder sized rocks from the iron and copper areas of the Upper Peninsula. After the glacial formations, or lobes, retreated, till covered southwestern Michigan at a depth of 200 to 300 feet. As the earth's crust rebounded from the weight of the glacier, water and wind erosion worked on the tons of debris. Waves loosened and carried material into the Great Lakes while streams and rivers carried other glacial deposits into the lakes. A combination of all these forces resulted in the creation of the massive dunes along the Michigan shoreline.

"The **Covert Dunes** were formed in the period from 13,000 years ago until approximately 3000 years ago. Although some dune movements are still present today, the major dune formation took place when the lake level was 25 feet higher than it is today. Because favorable conditions existed - an abundant sand source, the ability of waves to transport sand, and westerly prevailing winds - the sand dunes which formed along the eastern and southern shores of Lake Michigan are unmatched in size, diversity, or complexity of form. The environmental conditions under which the dunes were formed no longer exist; once destroyed, these dunes are not likely ever to regain their present significant size and extent." (3)

"Michigan dune and beach sand is made up predominately of quartz (90%) with other grains of epidote, garnet, magnetite (black sand), hornblende, calcite, ilmenite, orthoclase, tourmaline, and zircon. Human visitors who scuff their bare feet along the band of wet sand near water's edge experience a high, clear ringing tone. It is caused by friction from a special combination of quartz crystals and moisture, activated by pressure from a hand or foot. Thus, the name 'singing sands'" (4).

Wind and waves sorted and deposited the sand into dune formations. Strong winds of 25 miles per hour are needed to move the coarse grains; fine sand movement needs winds of only eight miles per hour and then can be carried long distances in suspension. Thus, wind becomes a good sorting agent.

Sand also moves along the surface of the land, one grain hitting another and causing it to bounce, collide with another grain, jar it loose, and so on – a chain reaction, or saltation, moving the sand inland. Ripples of sand found along the beaches result when the wind is high enough to crease the sand's surface. These form patterns of a gentle slope on the lakeside with a steeper slope to the leeward side. These patterns are repeated on a giant scale in the shapes of the dunes themselves.

"Dunes did not form everywhere along the east coast of Lake Michigan. Even if forces existed to create dunes, the proper geologic formations on the shore had to be present. In Berrien and Van Buren Counties, the retreating ice sheet left many glacial moraines. One was a ridge that extends from near South Haven southerly to the village of Lakeside, Michigan. This gravelly, rocky, low profile ridge is named the **Covert Ridge.** When the Covert Ridge was deposited on the Lake Michigan shore, no dunes could form. When the ridge was deposited inland from the shoreline, dunes could form. From South Haven, the Covert Ridge goes inland and south. Covert is, of course, right on the ridge. The glacial ridge then travels southwest until, at Hagar Shore Road in Berrien County, it rejoins the lake. From there, to south of St. Joseph, the ridge is the lakeshore and no dunes could form. South of St. Joseph, the Covert Ridge again leaves the lakeshore, allowing the Grand Mere Dunes to form. Stevensville is on the Covert Ridge, and the Red Arrow Highway follows it south" (5)

When traveling by boat north from Palisades Park toward Saugatuck, one sees the transition from lake front dunes to the clay deposits of the Covert Ridge clearly delineated. Likewise, a boat trip south will carry one past the meeting place of dunes and clay ridge near Hagar Shore Road. It is well worth the trip to observe this geological phenomenon.

The size, shape, and texture of Michigan's dunes are determined partly by the plant and animal life that is abundant. A short distance from the water's edge is found marram grass, the primary stabilizer of sand in areas where sand is deposited rapidly. It is a rhizomal plant that regenerates from the root system, sending roots down to the water table and then back to the surface to begin new plants. These clumps of grass, with their intertwining root system, hold the sand in place.

The foredunes, or initial topographic rises, continue to foster the growth of marram grass with such added growth as sand cherries – a traditional Palisades Park fruit for jelly making – and little blue stem, milk weed, sand reedgrass, jack pine, ground juniper, goldenrod and cottonwood.

"Mounting the apex of the highest dune ridge places the visitor at the threshold of immense ecological diversification. With time, a rich forest continues to develop in protected areas where human influence has been minimal. In fact, ecologists are convinced that this process has been ongoing for several thousand years. Time has been ample for all types of climatic changes and alterations in the very shape of the land to create a thousand different communities of plants and animals. Each hilltop and depression, meadow, wetland, and wooded setting is its own small, self-contained ecosystem.

"Deep, plunging interdunal valleys bordered by northerly and southerly exposing slopes create a 'mini' weather condition that has resulted in extremely unusual and unique communities perpetuating themselves. Scientists to this day ponder an explanation as to why such systems have developed under such unusual circumstances. The forest floor is rich with wildflowers and is an artist's palette of color during spring months. The protection afforded in this area of the dunes is a haven for songbirds of all types. These niches provide protection from the elements during periods of peak migration, and habitat for the rearing and feeding of young. The naturalist can observe the scarlet tanager, several kinds of woodpeckers, redstarts, chickadees, nuthatches, thrushes, and many species of warblers during an outing to this part of the Lake Michigan scene" (6)

The biological diversity created by the unique formation of the Covert Dunes' unique topographical formation is fascinating. As Chuck Nelson reported in April 1986:

"In a recent half-day, investigation Naturalist Rob Venner and I found seven protected, threatened, or endangered wildflowers in the area to be developed. They were flowering dogwood, climbing bittersweet, Michigan holly, trillium, pipsissewa, false pennyroyal, pitcher's thistle, and lycopodium. The microclimates and undisturbed forest floor render a density and diversity of wildflowers which is outstanding. The most important aspect of the Covert Dunes is the wilderness quality it has retained. Deer, fox, and raccoon trails are more obvious than man's activity in the dune complex. The noise encountered is of birds, winds, and waves. The driveways are few and narrow and are directed by the contour of the natural landscape. Nature is dominant here; it is the prevailing force. What exists now in the Covert Dunes is a very large and complete natural biologically-important dune ecosystem. It may well be one of the largest stretches of fresh water dunes without a major disturbance left anywhere" (7)

"The natural forces that created these magnificent resources can never be duplicated by humans. With all of the environmental values inherent in Michigan's dunes, it is crucial that steps be taken to preserve and protect them for the use and enjoyment of this generation and those to come. The sand dune environmental system is a very special, fragile place – one that deserves our appreciation and protection as a truly unique resource. Michigan is truly blessed to offer such opportunities to those who seek a very special encounter" (8).

## Sources

Kelly, R. W. and Farrand, W. R., The Glacial Lakes Around Michigan: Geological Survey Bulletin 4

Nelson, Charles, Director/Naturalist Sarett Nature Center, Benton Harbor, MI, presentation to Covert Township Planning Commission, April 12, 1986.

Roethele, Jon, Dunes: Pamphlet Reprint by the Division of Land Resource Program, DNR, July/August, 1985.

*References:*

1. Beth Merizon as quoted by Roethele.
2. Jon Roethele.
3. Charles Nelson
4. Jon Roethele
5. Charles Nelson
6. Jon Roethele
7. Charles Nelson
8. Jon Roethele

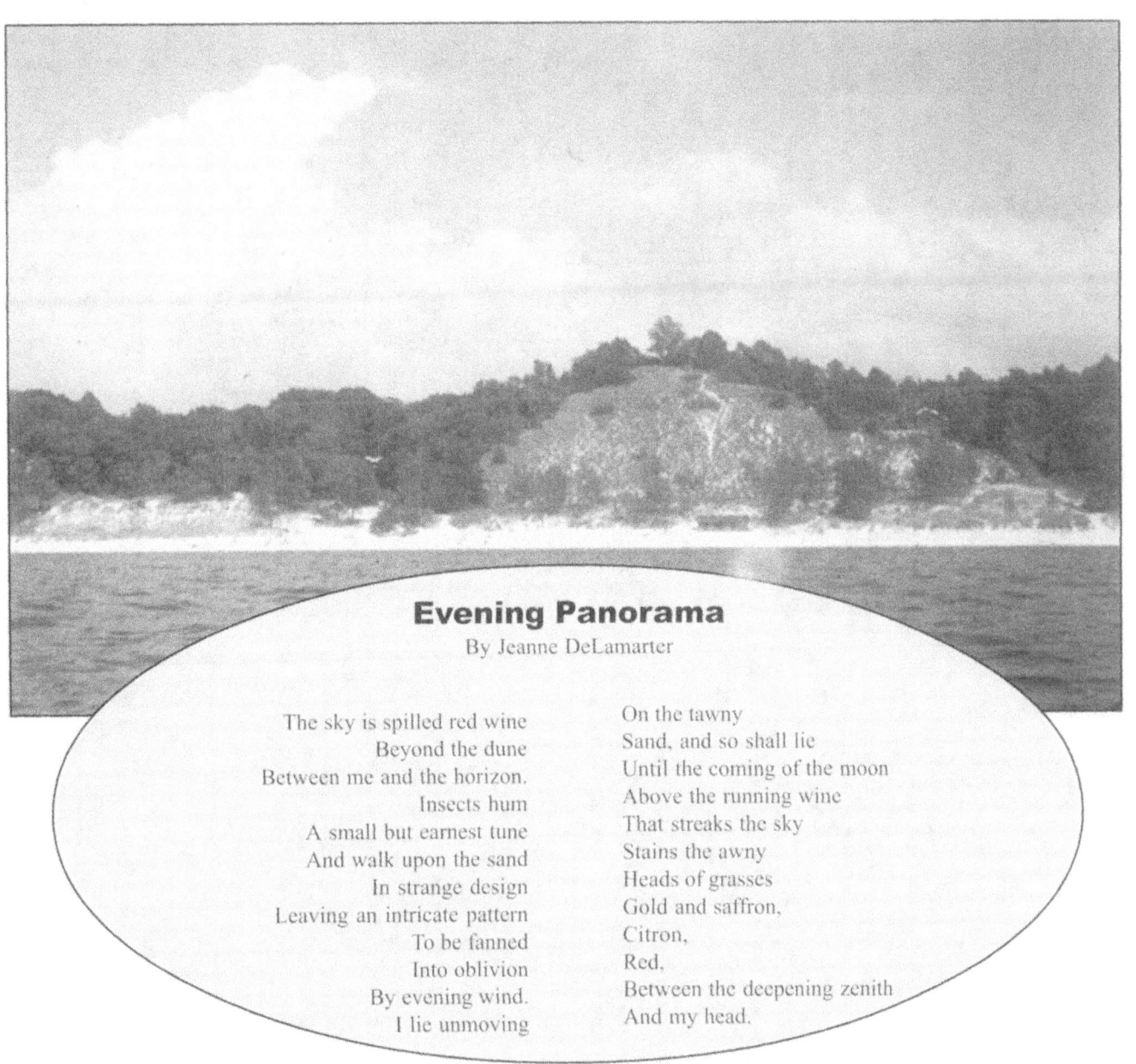

### Evening Panorama
By Jeanne DeLamarter

The sky is spilled red wine
Beyond the dune
Between me and the horizon.
Insects hum
A small but earnest tune
And walk upon the sand
In strange design
Leaving an intricate pattern
To be fanned
Into oblivion
By evening wind.
I lie unmoving
On the tawny
Sand, and so shall lie
Until the coming of the moon
Above the running wine
That streaks the sky
Stains the awny
Heads of grasses
Gold and saffron,
Citron,
Red,
Between the deepening zenith
And my head.

# Principal Stages in Evolution of Great Lakes

| Years Ago | Deployment of Glacier Front | Basin | Lake | Level (Ft. above Tide) | Outlets |
|---|---|---|---|---|---|
| 16,000 | Retreat/halt at Valparaiso Charlotte-Ft. Wayne system | Michigan: Erie: | Early Chicago Highest Maumee | 640? 800 | Illinois Ft. Wayne-Wabash |
| 15,000 | Advance/halt at Tinley Defiance system | Michigan: Erie: | Re-occupied by ice Highest Maumee | 800 | Ft. Wayne-Wabash |
| | Retreat | Michigan: Huron: Erie: | ChicagoEarly Early Saginaw Lowest Maumee | 640 730 760 | Illinois Grand Imlay-Grand |
| 14,000 | Advance/halt at Lake Border system | Michigan: Erie: | Chicago Middle Maumee | 640 780 | Illinois Imlay-Grand (?) and/or Ft. Wayne-Wabash |
| 13,000 | Retreat | Michigan: Huron-Erie: | Chicago Arkona | 640 710, 700, 695 | Illinois Grand |
| | Retreat | Conjectural low water interval | | | East? |
| 12,500 | Advance/halt at Port Huron system | Michigan Huron: Erie: | Chicago Saginaw Whittlesey | 640 695 738 | Illinois Grand Ubly |
| 12,500 – 12,000 | Retreat | Michigan: Huron-Erie: | Chicago Warren Wayne Warren Grassmere Lundy | 620, 605 690, 682 655 675 640 620 | Illinois Grand Mohawk Grand Grand Traverse(?) or Mohawk |
| 12,000 | Retreat | Superior: Michigan-Huron: Low water interval Erie: | Kewanee Two Creeks (Kirkfield) Low water stage | (?) Below 580 (?) | AuTrain/Whitefish (?) Trent Niagra |
| 11,000-11,500 | Advance and halt at Valders system | Superior: Michigan: Huron: Erie: | Filled with ice Early Algonquin Early Algonquin Early Erie | 605 605 Below 572 | Illinois St. Clair Niagra |
| 11,000 | Retreat (Trent outlet still blocked by ice?) | Superior: Michigan-Huron: Erie: | Duluth Algonquin Early Erie | 1085 605 Below 572 | St.Croix Illinois/St. Clair Niagara |
| 10,500 to 9,500 | Retreat | Superior: Michigan-Huron: Erie: | Levels lower than Duluth, includes Minong Post-Algonquin series of successively lower levels to 390 (?) Early Erie, rising levels approaching 572 | | AuTrain-Whitefish and others Trent, Fossmill and others Niagara |
| 9,500 | Final retreat of ice sheet from Great Lakes basins | Superior: Michigan: Huron: Erie: | Houghton Chippewa Stanley Early Erie, rising levels approaching 572 | 360 (?) 230 (extreme low) 180 (?) (extreme low) | St. Mary's Mackinac North Bay Niagara |
| 9,000 to 4,500 | Ice sheet in Hudson Bay area | Superior: Michigan: Huron: Erie | | Rising levels Rising levels Rising levels Rising levels | St. Mary's Mackinac North Bay Niagara |

## Principal Stages in Evolution of Great Lakes (Continued)

| Years | Ice sheet | Lake | Stage | Elevation | Outlet |
|---|---|---|---|---|---|
| 4,500 to 3,500 | No ice sheet on mainland of North America | Superior: | Nipissing | 605 | North Bay, Illinois & St. Clair |
| | | Michigan-Huron: | Great Lakes | | |
| | | Erie: | Early Erie | 570 (approx.) | Niagara |
| 3,500 to 2,000 | | Superior-Michigan-Huron: | Levels falling slightly with pause at Algoma level | 595 | St. Clair Illinois (?) |
| | | Erie: | Modern level | 571 | Niagara |
| 2,000 to present | | Superior: | Modern level | 601 | St. Mary's |
| | | Michigan-Huron: | Modern level | 579 | St. Clair |
| | | Erie: | Modern level | 571 | Niagara |

*The above chart courtesy of the Field Museum in Chicago, IL.*

## Palisades Park – Geologically Speaking

By Anne Fuller

How does one encapsulate the history of this little bit of heaven which we call Palisades Park – the name given to it by our botanist-developer-dreamer, Arthur Craig Quick? Palisades, a tiny dot on the lower western edge of Michigan, a mitten-shaped peninsula capped by a roughly triangular hat pointed to the east at Whitefish Point and bordering Lake Superior with its high Precambrian Pictured Rocks until, running west, the Wisconsin border says, "Stop, the rest belongs to us."

Michigan, our fair peninsula, has a history 2.7 billion years long. Before that we might as well turn to the poesy of the street urchin who was inadvertently dragged into Sunday School one day and heard the creation story. This is how he reported it: "Well, you see, God He got lonesome, He didn't have nothing to do, nor no place to go, so He took a bunch of nothing and He covered it with dirt and He slung it like an incurve, and He said, 'Now dat's de eart.'" (Anon.)

The street urchin was talking about an event eons before the 2.7 billion bottom line of Michigan. All we know is that somewhere in that dim past, the Canadian granitic shield, extending from Hudson's Bay down into Illinois, and the oldest known rock in the world, was thrust up from the center of things. (European explorers really discovered an old world, rather than a new!)

Then there was a long period – millions of years called the Paleozoic (dawn animals) - when this spot on the earth's globe was inundated by warm seas, usually from the east, but sometimes from the southwest – some 57 times, says one geologist – while to the north the volcanic peaks of the Keewenaw area were eroding away to their copper cores and iron ores, and now and then a bit of silver and gold, and perhaps even diamonds. And the eroded sediments were washed into these Michigan seas and piled up layers of useful goodies - limestone, sandstone, shale, salt, oil - for man who was to appear much much later on the scene. The seas were teaming with warm water forms of invertebrate life – sea lilies and corals, trilobites and snails and clams and the chambered nautilus, and finally even fish and then amphibians, and even the first land animal.

So, as many of us were getting "beach-comber-bends" from stooping along the gravelly sands of our Palisades beach back in the low waters of the 60's to search for the circular segments of sea-lily stems, we were picking up antiques from a warm inland sea of probably 350 million years ago. And when during those same years, after a storm, a Palisades Parker came down to the beach from her high dune formed only yesterday, geologically speaking, to pick up any new Petoskey stones the waves had washed up, she was reaching back into those early seas for the fossilized remains of the colonial coral animal, *Hexagonaria percarinata*, designated today as Michigan's state stone.

The time of those early seas came to an end in great earth convulsions and uplift. Then the pages of Michigan history left no records because everything above sea level was eroded away by wind and rain and waves; the sediments deposited elsewhere. We only know what Michigan must have been like and what lived here – elephants and mastodons and saber-toothed tigers – from records embedded in sediments in other areas lying low enough to escape erosion.

The record returns, however, in what the geologists term the Pleistoscene Epoch (Greek meaning *most + new*) some 700,000 to a million years ago when, for some still unexplained cause, the earth turned cold and the ice sheets came down. Four times they came, great mountains of ice over a mile high, grinding, crushing, grabbing and pushing all before it – the mountain tops, the forests, the animals. We know the record best of the last, a Wisconsin ice sheet which had a lobed front crossing our area; it followed only river valleys, the predecessors of today's Great Lakes. It was the scouring action of those frontal lobes, grinding out the old river valleys, which determined the position of this, the largest of all the world's lake systems of today.

When the earth turned warm again and the ice front retreated, our Great Lakes were formed. It is a long and intricate story of advance and retreat as the temperature shifted up and down. In fact, the geologists don't really know whether we are just now in a warm period with the makings of another ice sheet lurking in the north. They, the Pleistoscene geologists, are able to trace the shore lines of 20 or more lakes in the Lake Michigan bed, four of which we hear a great deal about. The first one was Lake Chicago, with its northern shore the ice front. Gigantic piles of glacial debris, called end moraines, confined the melt waters, with varying outlets, over time releasing them to the sea.

If you'd like to "get a feel" of that early Lake Chicago, some afternoon drive west along M43 from South Haven until you reach Glendale. Then turn either north or south and drive through the rolling country of the Valparaiso-Fort Wayne moraine, which impounded those melt waters of the receding glacier. Watch the skyline of the hills. Note its uneven contour, a good indication of a glacial-deposited moraine. That lakelevel was 640 feet, which means the shore line was about 62 feet higher than the 578.7 feet reported in November, 1985.

Two other famous lakes of the retreating ice sheet in the Michigan basin are Lake Algonquin, beginning about 11,500 years ago, when the water level dropped to 605 feet, and Lake Chippewa, with an extreme low of 230 feet about 9500 years ago when the ice sheet had retreated to the Hudson Bay area. I wish some geographer would figure out for me where the shoreline would have been, way out there in the deepest part of the lakebed. Yes, there might have been Paleo-Indians constructing their wigwams way out there on the Chippewa beach, fishing those Chippewa waters and hunting mastodons with their fluted points lashed to wooden spears.

In the ensuing 4000 years, when the waters rose again to 605 feet, the continuing generations of prehistoric peoples could simply retreat before the waves and construct their housing on higher ground. No polluting concrete seawalls or messy fill of auto tires or gabions of glacial boulders to save their dwellings!

Finally, with the ice sheet completely off the mainland of North American, about 4500 years ago, the land began to rise again, released from the great weight of the mile-high ice, and a fourth lake, Lake Nipissing was born.

Three outlets to the sea were exposed and there was great stability for perhaps 1000 years. Enough time, suggested R. W. Kelly, state geologist, to form the strongest and most spectacular shore feature in the entire region. In the eastern Lake Superior area, Nipissing features are found up to 700 feet above sea level. Down here in our area, Nipissing shore evidence is found at 605 feet.

This begins the part of our history which we know and love the best: the story of waves and wind and sand – the building of our famous sand dunes, Nipissing and modern – the longest and highest expanse of fresh water dunes in the world. Because we are in the path of the westerlies, because we are south of the hinge line from above Saginaw Bay to Grand Traverse Bay above which a crustal rebound (still continuing the geologists say, about 1/2 foot per century in the northern Lake Superior region), our southeast shore of Lake Michigan is particularly placed for fabulous dune building.

About 3500 years ago, the stage began leading to the birth of modern Lake Michigan. The geologists credit its birth to the lowering of the lake level. Lake Michigan is considered to be, then, about 2000 years old, when the modern level of 579 feet was achieved.

Each of those historic lakes built dunes of that beautiful wave-washed quartz sand, dried and lifted by the ever-blowing westerlies. Rising first as foredunes parallel to the beach, they then moved inland until new foredunes along the shore blocked the wind and stabilizing plants invaded to serve as sand fences. Always, as I walk the beach and climb the blow-out at the south end of the Park, I ask myself, "Are these dunes moving inward from the present lake shore or are they dunes of earlier lakes?" Most of the detailed studies have been made at the head of the lake in Indiana, a convenient research area for Ph.D. candidates from the University of Chicago, over the last 90 years or so.

But we have one detailed study from right here in the Park, made by our own Margaret Sauer while she worked on an intensive soil study in our dunes for her Master's degree. In her research of the literature, she found that most of our dunes are a part of the Covert Ridge, which is about one-fourth to one and one-half miles wide and has an elevation of about 700 feet. It is part of the Lake Border Moraine and marks the final stand of ice in Van Buren County. She says our dunes are part of the high Nipissing-age dunes that skirt much of the eastern shore line of Lake Michigan.

Margaret's studies of the dune sand development into soil brings us back to our beautiful wooded slopes and ravines, with their spring carpet of wild flowers which captivated our founder, Mr. Quick, near the opening of the 20th Century…. [Whatever size beach, always] we will have our beautiful wooded dunes, mostly of Nipissing origin, our nature trails, our wealth of ferns and wild flowers, and the woodland beasties so sensitively recorded in Anna Holmes's "Memorabilia," (*quoted in full elsewhere in this publication*). As she pointed out, "Palisades Park still offers much, so very much, toward the study of nature and education in all her forms, if only the eye is trained to see, and the ear to hear."

# Our Inland Sea – Lake Michigan

By Don Henkel
From July 1995 Patter

For more than 30 years, my family and I have had the incredible pleasure (and, during extremely high water periods, sometimes pain), of having a cottage on the shores of Lake Michigan at Palisades Park. This body of water often defies adequate description. Its moods reflect our moods. At times calm and peacefully tranquil – often with a gentle lapping of waves – at other times, the awesome force of the storm.

For a greater understanding of the *sea* at our doorstep, I have appreciated the excellent geological insights of Park members like Anne Fuller. (Articles written by Ms. Fuller in the 1960's were reprinted in the August and September, 1994 Patter.)

Recently, seeking more information, I had the privilege of interviewing Chuck Nelson, Director of Sarett Nature Center in Benton Harbor. Significant portions of this article come from that discussion.

Chuck observes that the eastern shoreline of Lake Michigan contains the greatest accumulation of freshwater dunes in the world. He estimates that from nine to twelve separate dune areas exist up and down the shoreline – and Palisades Park is situated in one of these areas, the Van Buren Dunes.

Let's back up a bit. We all know that glaciers formed what are now the Great Lakes, starting perhaps 1 million to 1.5 million years ago. Glaciers advanced and retreated continuously, cutting and filling. The last glacier retreat occurred some 10,000 to 15,000 years ago.

Since then, lake levels have fluctuated greatly. 9000 years ago, those of us with riparian rights on the shore of Lake Michigan could have added eight miles of property to the front of our cottages (about the distance from Palisades Park to South Haven), for the lake level fell 120 feet below present levels. However, 4000 years later, after extensive periods of rain, people like Betty Householder would have owned a lakefront cottage, the lake being 50 feet higher than it is today. Only after some 1000 to 1500 years ago would the lake resemble what we now see.

Since 1918, the U.S.Army Corps of Engineers has measured Great Lakes levels. During that time span, Lake Michigan has fluctuated about five feet between the 1964 minimum and 1986 maximum.

Look closely at our shoreline – and even inland. When boating along the shores of the lake in our area, one sees stretches of clay-like cliffs giving way to sand dunes. Where the glacier deposited debris which formed a significant vertical ridge along the shoreline (called the Covert Ridge in our area, or lake border moraine), no dune could form. The Covert Ridge begins somewhere around Stevensville, follows the shoreline to about Exit 7 on I-196, then turns inland through Covert. Our Van Buren Dune picks up around Exit 7 and extends north through Van Buren State Park.

Chuck Nelson described his search for the exact transition from clay to sand near Exit 7. Walking along the beach, he explained his mission to a cottage owner. "Oh yes," she exclaimed, "I remember that Grandma went down to the beach over there (pointing) to get clay for her facial." And that is the spot. This transition can be noted from the highway when one heads south from Palisades Park along I-196. First one sees extensive dunes on both sides of I-196. When the dunes are no longer visible – around Exit 7 – one passes over the Covert Ridge.

The Palisades Park shoreline is uniquely situated to form dunes. We have the necessary three ingredients:
- plenty of sand (mainly quartz which comes originally from river erosion);
- prevailing westerly winds;
- a flat shoreline where dunes can form.

The other four Great Lakes tend to be east-west in length. Only Lake Michigan has the extensive north-south axis that invites prevailing westerly winds.

Over time, as the lake level receded, shore dunes formed. These were then pushed back in a "U" shape as new dunes were formed. Our Sugar Bowl is an example of this kind of parabolic dune.

Every square inch of Palisades Park rests on a dune – our cottages, roads, tennis courts, trails, woods, and beaches. Our plant and animal life, our weather, and our dunes are all directly related to this inland sea we call Lake Michigan. It is easy to lose sight of the wonder of what we have here.

Imagine, Palisades Park happens to be located on the shores of the largest freshwater system in the world, on a shoreline that contains the greatest accumulation of freshwater dunes in the world. Not bad. How uniquely fortunate we are.

Think about it. Appreciate it.

# History of Vegetation on the Lake Michigan Dunes
## by Leslie A. Kenoyer, Ph.D.
From Quick, Arthur, <u>Wild Flowers of the Northern States and Canada</u>, 1939, p. 473.

Plants grow in societies. We find grouped together those which require the same amount of moisture, the same proportion of sun and shade, the same degree of exposure or shelter from exposure. Nowhere does this social grouping show to better advantage than in sand dune areas. Here we have striking contrasts ranging from deeply shaded ravines to bald sunny exposures. Here, due to the rapid shifting of the sand, new exposures are constantly being made for the occupation of vegetation and old occupied areas are, as constantly, destroyed.

The best development of sand dunes along the Lake Michigan shores is on the east border of the lake. Here the winds, which in our latitude are prevailingly from the west, pick up the sand grains after the waves have tossed them just out of their own reach, enabling them to get dry enough for movement by wind. They are carried to varying distances inland to be dropped as soon as the wind strikes an obstacle which checks its velocity. A piece of driftwood on the shore is sufficient to form the nucleus for a dune. After the dune is started it will itself break the wind sufficiently to enable it to grow. While growing it tends also to move with the wind, since the latter picks up grains on the windward side, carries them over the top, and, its velocity being checked, deposits them on the leeward side of the ridge.

In the course of a few years the wind may have moved our sand ridge hundreds of feet landward from the point at which it originally started. By this time another dune may have started near the shore, and a trough may separate the two. Thus the contour of the sand surface comes to be a series of crests and troughs, not unlike the surface of water waves but on a much larger scale.

As the dune passes through its unsteady formative period and settles down to a stable maturity, different plant associations, in turn, occupy its slopes. Here we might suggest that there is nothing more effective as a stabilzer of sand than a plant cover. Wind cannot get down through a mat of vegetation to lift and scatter the sand on which the mat is growing.

The early pioneer plant society comes on the beach, the fore-dune, and active dunes wherever they occur. This is the sand-grass and herb society. It consists of those hardy pioneers which are able to stake out their claim on unoccupied land and to endure the rigors that such land brings in the way of a shifting foundation and exposure to a hot sun. There are two grasses which are exceedingly successful early settlers in the Michigan dunes: Marram grass and Sand-reed grass....

When the pioneers have settled upon their claim and have given a reasonable degree of stability to the previously shifting sand, they begin to pass out of the picture, yielding to another society, the shrub association. The most numerous members of this group are: Sand cherry, Bailey's dogwood, Glaucous willow, Broad-leaved willow, Hop tree, Climbing bittersweet, Poison ivy, and Wild grapes.

Now that the dune is settled sufficiently to allow slower growing plants to obtain a foothold, trees put in an appearance. The first to come are the poplars. At Palisades Park the prevalent poplar is cottonwood …. Poplars are trees which will germinate and become established only in sunshine. We may look for them always in exposed situations. They are forest outposts that come in to claim the open land for the forest. On some of the dune slopes the sassafras fills a role similar to that of the poplar.

Dune land that is a little older and has been a little longer settled is likely to display another type of plant colony known as the conifer association. The cone-bearing trees are essentially trees of the north. They come into the latitude of southern Michigan only along the lake shores, for it is here only that the summers are sufficiently cool and humid. The dunes of southern Lake Michigan have the following representatives of this interest group: White pine, Red pine, Jack pine, Arbor vitae, Red cedar, Common juniper, and Hemlock ….

Next in order of development we find the oak association. The leading species of oak encountered here are the red, the black, and the white. The oak forest is rather more shady than the conifer, but less so than the beech-maple. On its floor are various shrubs and herbs …. May apple, the true and false Solomon's seal, the maple-leaved viburnum and the witch hazel.

Lastly we come to the most luxuriant of all of our eastern plant associations - the beech-maple forest. In the dune country, because of the favoring humidity from Lake Michigan, hemlock is associated with beech and maple. It is a magnificent forest. One can scarcely realize that these densely wooded slopes were at one time bare sand slides …

The development of a dune is not always a matter of continuous progress from sand-grass to beech and maple. Interruptions and catastrophes will occur. A weak spot in the plant-covered breastworks may be seized upon by the wind. Little by little the sand will be torn away from around the roots, causing herbs, shrubs, and even trees to slump over and die. At the south border of Palisades Park is a large blowout. Acres of woodland and shrub have been destroyed leaving a bare scooped-out place in the sand, a small Sahara for desolation. One can follow the course of the shifted sand and see where it is covering an old established beech-maple forest. So here the wind is proving doubly destructive to plant life, uprooting one area and burying another. The sand here denuded is being occupied in spots by the earliests pioneers, and must repeat the long train of successions.

---

### Arthur Quick's Discovery

Several hundred years ago there were elk in this part of Michigan. At that time one of them met his death in a valley just north of the farm of our good dairyman, Mr. Shepherd. At that time, most of this section was drifting sand, and eventually the sand drifted over this valley, not only filling it but building up quite a dune over the mighty antlers of this fallen elk. Years passed and eventually vegetation formed over this dune, then trees of all sorts sprang up, grew to maturity, and died, while others took their places and grew to large size, and which the writer has seen standing there. Later the trees were all cleared off, the ground planted to fruit trees, cultivated, and thus the wind got another excellent chance to level off the dune and expose the old-time valley. And that is how the writer happened to discover the mighty antlers of the old elk that fell at least a few hundred years ago. They are in excellent preservation, silver-gray with age, and with the skull intact. He is having it mounted and may decide to adorn the clubhouse with it.

-Arthur Quick in an early Patter

# Dune Dweller Lives Alone and Likes It!

*This article is courtesy of The Covert Historical Museum. Unfortunately, the original source has been lost, as has the date; even so, the story of Miss Baldwin is worth telling as we think about our dunelands.*

To resorters and South Havenites themselves, the dunes and woodlands between Palisades Park and town are often just another accumulation of sand and trees. But not to Jessie Baldwin – for the dunes are her home and she loves every inch of sun-bathed timber and billowy terrain. To her, the dunes are "constant and dependable," while the world and its people are "ever-changing." She would do anything to protect her peace-filled sanctuary and preserve its rugged beauty. Now, she is fighting a single-handed battle to prevent the old stage coach route south of town from becoming a public road....

She came here 55 years ago from Evanston, Illinois, where she spent 3 1/2 years at Northwestern University in Liberal Arts School. Today, she wanders the dunes, studying wild life, beachcombing, collecting Indian relics, and enjoying the natural charm of the land surrounding her home, "Hillcrest." A myrtle-covered Indian mound is located only a short distance from her home. The hump in the ground is due to a three-foot layer of burnt clay laid over the grave of the dead Indian, Miss Baldwin says. Other such traces of an abandoned Pottawatamie civilization are also in evidence. And deer, foxes, and chipmunk provide her with constant companionship.... She can tell in an instant that a soft barking noise is not the call of a mature dog or a small puppy, but that of a fox. Or that the high shrill sound that resembles a human giggle is the cry of a deer.

One of her favorite pastimes is watching the blue herons on the beach. They only come early in the morning, she says. She has a stuffed heron in her home with a wingspan of nearly five feet. Another bird she likes to observe is the white owl, a recent immigrant from Canada.

Miss Baldwin lives rugged style. She carries her water from a nearby neighbor's well. Previously, she pumped her own water from an old red pump, but health authorities found her own well had gone bad when they tested it this spring. She figures she'll have to go down almost to lake level to hit good water again.

Although she is getting up in years, she is still active. In fact, she rides her trusty bicycle the ten miles to town and back when necessary. Electricity has not yet found its way into her home, but a portable radio and old-fashioned lanterns provide as homey an atmosphere as anyone dreams of. Sometimes she whiles away her time playing an old pump piano.

But why anyone would want to bring civilization to the dunes is one thing Miss Baldwin can't see. "One of my neighbors has got a television set up here ... that's what most people come here to get away from," she says. She, like other lake-side landowners, is rapidly losing her beach, but she can still remember the days when the beach extended far out and the lake froze over thick enough that it was possible to drive the horse and cutter to town along the slick, icy shore.

Other recollections of her childhood center around exploration of the deserted village of Paulville. There was one farm she and her playmates used to visit in particular, she says. There were peach orchards, old rusted horseshoes, wild blueberries, blackberries, dewberries, and even cranberries, but best of all, an ice-cold spring. Today it's buried beneath the dunes.

Any intrusion on her privacy is a serious thing to Miss Baldwin. She likes people, but she doesn't mind loneliness, and any threat to the hush and serenity of her outdoor cathedral is nothing to take lightly....

Although living with few modern conveniences may sound fatal to those who can't live without knowing what the water temperature is or whether it's going to rain tomorrow, Miss Baldwin finds it no hardship at all. If Thunder Mountain thunders three times and the locusts sing, she knows a hot day is ahead. And she can always tell by looking at the sun set over the lake when to get out the ol' bumbershoot.

Storms on the lake are another thing of beauty to Miss Baldwin. There's nothing more colorful or artistic than jagged streaks of lightning that unzip the sky and light up the beach for miles around, she says. However, she remembers once, when an aunt was visiting her, a freak line squall blew up and the lake was pounding against the shore – the thunder was almost deafening and lightning was crackling overhead. "All of a sudden my aunt screamed and claimed she'd seen a ghost," Miss Baldwin says with a smile. "The horses had gotten loose."

*Jessie Baldwin, looking over Indian grave.*

*Two common problems with writing Indian history. On the one hand, there is a distrust of white historians among Native People; and on the other hand, there is a distrust of native histories on the part of many academic historians. —* Walter Fleming, Missoulian

*One of the problems with so-called Native American history is that it's not really Native American history, it's white history with Native Americans in it.* — David Beck, Missoulian

## Early Footprints

By Katy Beck

*Creation stories and oral histories are important. These stories are the foundation for people's philosophies.* — Walter Fleming, Missoulian

Summarizing the history of Michigan's Van Buren County Indian population runs into immediate difficulties. The two contexts of history differ, Europeans usually constructing theirs around geography and boundaries, emphasizing dates and battles, and American Indians around their oral tradition of legends and stories. Views of leadership hierarchy, land ownership, and laws differ. Oral history that is clear to Indians can be confusing to non-Indians. For these and similar reasons, European historical or missionary writers often have not reflected Indian viewpoints. This, in turn, has led to a lack of trust. Many traditional Indians are hesitant to share their knowledge. This paper hopes to bridge this cultural gap, attempting to give a balanced context while remaining true to Native American oral tradition.

To glimpse the Indian people who inhabited near the shores of the Brandywine Creek, one must remember their view of the continent was not the European view. Stable communities or tribes did not necessarily settle in one specific place. Indeed, Indian people of this region moved constantly, not only for resettlement, but also seasonally within any given area.

In the Palisades Park, Covert, Saugatuck, South Haven, and St. Joseph area, the most familiar Indian tribal name is Potawatomi. However the Potawatomi people, a number of whom still reside in the area, were not the earliest to walk these lands. Indian People have populated the Great Lakes Basin in what is now the state of Michigan since at least 12000 B.C. Paleo-Indians are thought to have migrated into the region as Ice Age glaciers receded.

**The People Shall Continue**: *Many, many years ago, all things came to be. The stars, rocks, plants, rivers, animals. Mountains, sun, moon, birds, all things. And the People were born. Some say, "From the Ocean." Some say, "From a hollow log." Some say, "From an opening in the ground." Some say, "From the mountains." And the People came to live in the Northern Mountains and on the Plains, in the Western Hills and on the Seacoasts, in the Southern Deserts and in the Canyons, in the Eastern Woodlands and on the Piedmonts.* -- Simon J. Ortiz

They were organized into groups of 10-12 people who survived by hunting and gathering. Large animals, including mastodon, roamed the area; smaller animals were plentiful.

The Archaic period of history began in the year 8000 B.C. when the hardwood forests appeared. The People continued to improve their tools and hunting weapons. As the mastodon became extinct, they hunted moose, deer, bear and caribou. People began to settle along the shore of Lake Michigan from 6000 to 3000 B.C.; nuts, berries and other fruit were plentiful and fish became important to their diet. By the late Archaic period, 3000 to 1000 B.C., extensive trade began. Shell products came from as far south as the Gulf of Mexico; copper products were traded from the Keewenaw Peninsula in northern Michigan.

Villages grew and became more settled. Rituals and ceremonies, as well as decorative arts, became a part of their lives. Because plants were plentiful in southern Michigan and the growing season substantial, life was good.

In 100 B.C., the Hopewell - or Mound Builders - reached southern Michigan. Their graves and earthworks can still be found preserved in the state. They left behind Indian mounds of up to 15 feet high and 102 feet in diameter. Many axes, pick axes, and arrowheads have been found in Van Buren County. They are thought to originate with the mound builders, buried in the mounds with the dead. The later Potawatomi and

Ojibway buried their dead under "tumuli" or low banks of earth. The garden beds of the early people were very precise and artistic. Most were of a geometric design, some circular with spokes from an inner circle as in a wheel. Known sites of both mounds and gardens are seen on the archeological map of Berrien, Cass, St. Joseph, Van Buren, Kalamazoo, and Allegan counties. Along the St. Joseph River, for example near Berrien Springs, locations of burying grounds are identified by a circle with a cross within, mounds by a dark dot, and a garden bed by parallel lines.

During the 650 years after 1000 A.D., the Hopewell Culture diminished. The life styles of the Ottawa, Potawatomi and Ojibway were established. Where the prehistoric Mound Builders went is not known, but conjecture is that they slowly migrated south and finally established the ancient Kingdom of Mexico. Cortes, the Spanish invader of 1519, declared them to be as far-advanced in arts and sciences as the Spaniards - except in regards to implements of warfare.

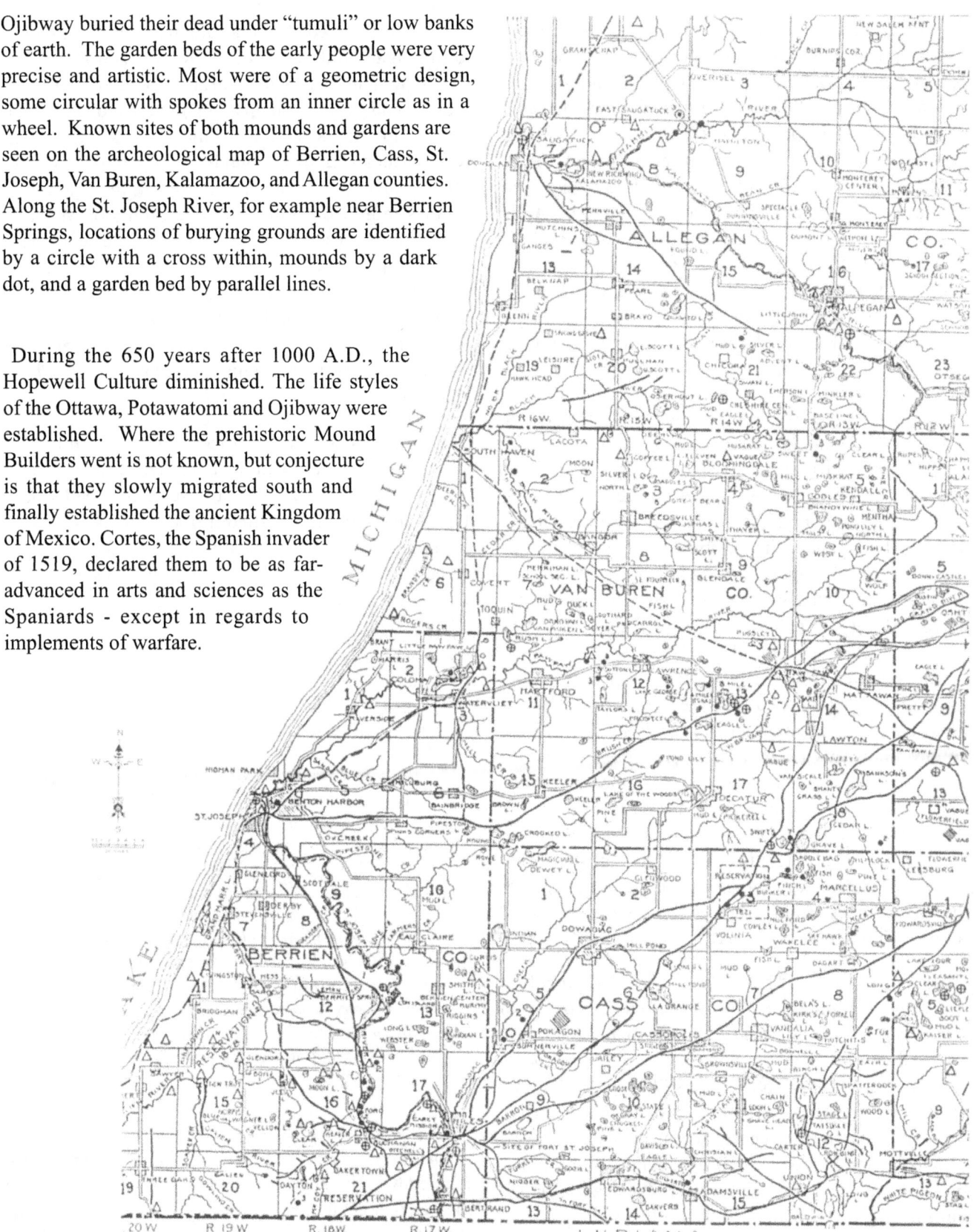

BERRIEN, CASS, ST. JOSEPH, VAN BUREN, KALAMAZOO, ALLEGAN COUNTIES

**Indian Villages along the Brandywine.**
From Hinsdale, Wilbert B., Archeological Atlas of Michigan, Michigan Handbook Series
#4,
Ann Arbor: University of Michigan Press, 1931.

The Native Americans who moved into the Great Lakes Basin in their wake, perhaps a hundred tribes, were all part of the Algonquian language group, the name of which was derived from the *Algonkin* tribe formerly living in Canada, east of the present city of Ottawa. The Ojibway or Chippewa, Ottawa, Menominee, Miami, Sauk, Mascoutin, Potawatomi, Fox, and many others were Algonquian speakers. W. B. Hinsdale suggests that the affiliation of languages is very important; it indicates that at one time in the past, one language was an offshoot of another. They, therefore, may have been derived from the same source. Tribal disintegration and affiliation probably went on constantly due to war among tribes or uniting against common enemies.

According to the traditions of the Potawatomies, as reported by R. David Edmunds, they and the Ottawas and Chippewas all originally were of the same group. They migrated to the Great Lakes area and separated at the Straits of Mackinac by the 1500's. While the Ottawa stayed in that area and the Chippewa tribes moved east in what is now Michigan, the Potawatomi continued to migrate south in what we now call Lower Michigan. They stayed along the plains and eastern coast of Lake Michigan, retaining their roles as Keepers of the Fire for the three united tribes. One historical report dates this southern movement about 1450 A.D. Quite possibly the Potawatomi separated earlier and were settled as a prairie culture known as *Dumwa* in West Central Michigan. However, an Indian view dates the migration as 1100 to 1200 B.C., believing those early people to be related to the later tribal groups. Carbon dating supports the latter. Another date of the migration of the *Nishinabe* (the Indian word for Potawatomi, Chippewa and Ottawa people) to the Great Lakes Basin is *"when food was growing on water."* This refers to wild rice, a food staple.

The people of the Three Fires called themselves *Nishnabek*. Sometimes this is spelled *Nishinabe* or *Anishinabe* depending on the group and source. Historians ascribed the meaning *"True Humans"* or *"First People"* to the name; an Indian definition is *"from when lowered the male of the species."* (Female Indians, they believed, were already here.) Government-accepted words, Chippewa and Ottawa, are different than the preferred Indian names Ojibway and Odawa. Potawatomi is the same in all groups but there are many different spellings. Even today one Michigan Band varies from the rest by doubling the T.

Prior to 1768, epidemics spread through Indian communities; within some tribal communities 75% to 95% died as a result. In 1768 the total population of the Potawatomi was about 3,000. By 1830 they were up to 12,000, possibly reflecting a recovery number. Although villages overlapped, the Potawatomi generally held claim to Michigan lands south of the Kalamazoo River from Detroit west to Lake Michigan and around the shore into Indiana and Illinois, on up along the lake to Green Bay, Wisconsin. At one point in the mid-1600's, the Iroquois, seeking more hunting grounds for fur trading with the French, invaded Michigan. As a result, the Three Fires peoples migrated north across the Straits of Mackinac and into northwest Wisconsin. All lower peninsula villages were completely depopulated. In 1641 the Potawatomi met up with the French and formed an alliance for fur trading. This alliance ultimately involved them in the war against the English. By 1701 the Iroquois were forced into peace and the Potawatomi began moving back to lower Michigan.

The villages of the St. Joseph Potawatomis were scattered. The Potawatomi extended as far north as Ludington, but the Band of St. Joseph itself had villages from Indiana north through Covert and on the Brandywine. Villages usually did not exceed 300 and usually averaged 100 persons, an effective size.

> *Some people fished; others were hunters. Some people farmed; others were artisans. Their leaders were those who served the people. Their healers were those who cared for the people. Their hunters were those who provided for the people. Their warriors were those who protected the people. The teachers and the elders of the people all taught this important knowledge: The Earth is the source of all life. She gives birth. Her children continue the life of the earth. The people must be responsible to her. This is the way that all life continues.* — Simon Ortiz

*Culture means modes of life. It is the sum total of all the activities of a community. All mankind has modes of living. They have motives and habits of thought. They produce and consume. They have family and neighborhood relations. Everything that pertains to existence in and among a group of persons is their culture.* — W.B. Hinsdale

The Potawatomi had an advantage in the cultural pattern of their lives. Their skills of working with birch bark, coupled with their new-found competence in agriculture, enabled them to use the exceptionally fortunate elements of this area to their advantage. Using simple tools for horticulture, they were able to grow corn, beans, squash and melons. They stored foods in pots, baskets, and skin bags. Rich soil along riverbanks and a significant growing season meant excellent crops. Lightweight canoes gave them the ability to carry quantities of trade goods long distances. Added to that was a ready supply of game -- buffalo herds and other large animals; they became less dependent on fish and wild plants than they had been in the north.

> *Grandparents had a part in the extended family and a part in raising the children. Early in the morning or late in the day, they tended gardens, slowly working the earth. They talked to the children who accompanied them. They taught lessons of behavior by sharing legends. The children loved and respected their grandparents and parents seldom had to raise their voices when elders were present.* — Leroy Wesaw

Since they frequently moved, they constructed both summer and winter shelters. The former was of poles covered with bark in a rectangular shape. The winter house, or wigwam, was of saplings fastened into the ground and brought together at the top where they were tied with skin bands. Saugatuck dwellings were described as small bark houses with a fire in the center for roasting game and cooking corn. Heated stones were cooking utensils. More permanent winter dwellings were made in a circular shape, with saplings curved to the center for a frame. The bark of birch, elm, cedar, or basswood covered the frame, as did woven cattails. The villages on the Brandywine were probably summer villages.

In the 1800's both wolves and deer were plentiful; eagles fed on the slaughtered animals that they could find. In the days of Paulville (now Palisades), bears nested nearby in the swamps. In the spring, Indians from Mackinaw paddled down the coast in fleets of canoes, sometimes attached to one another with one main mast and one sail, the wind being right. They made their sugar in the area and captured bear cubs which they took back north. Successful in hunting deer, bear and porcupine, they preserved some meat in birch bark bags, called *Mokokas*, buried them in the ground and took the rest back north for the summer. When returning for the winter hunt, the crop was ready for harvest and food was available for their use.

Indians were frequent visitors to the area, moving up and down the shore, at times in groups of 100 canoes filled with families. Potawatomi Indians came to Cold Springs near South Haven every summer to camp. They picked blackberries and peeled basswood bark for basket making. One settler said her father and other neighbor boys visited the Indian camp, bringing watermelon and green corn. There they learned to build wigwams and make bark rope.

Tanned leather of deer hide was commonly used for clothing. Breech cloth and leggings replaced trousers. Moccasins and dresses were sewn by sinew and fringed by splitting. Bear and buffalo skins were used for winter comfort. Clothing was decorated with paint, shells and stone beads, fossils, and teeth. Porcupine quills were dyed and added. Slowly, colored cloth took the place of skins. Feathers delineated rank. Although they used natural materials, the Indian people had much the same ornaments as Europeans -- earrings, pins, belt buckles, hair ornaments, lockets, silver, bows and fur trim. Women wore their hair in one long braid down the back, while men wore their hair long except during battles.

Leopold Pokagan, a chief from the St. Joseph River, signed three treaties and remained with his followers on small farms in Michigan after the Indians lost their lands. Weesaw was a sub-chief of the Potawatomi in a village on the St. Joseph River. He signed five treaties between 1821-1836. During Pokagan's and Weesaw's days, the girls and women manufactured split baskets. Their finest work was of birch bark, sweet grass, and porcupine quills. The quills were dyed, then woven into the bark in patterns of flowers and leaves. Sweet grass was used for its fragrance. Modern basket makers are working to preserve this traditional craft of black ash split-wood basket making.

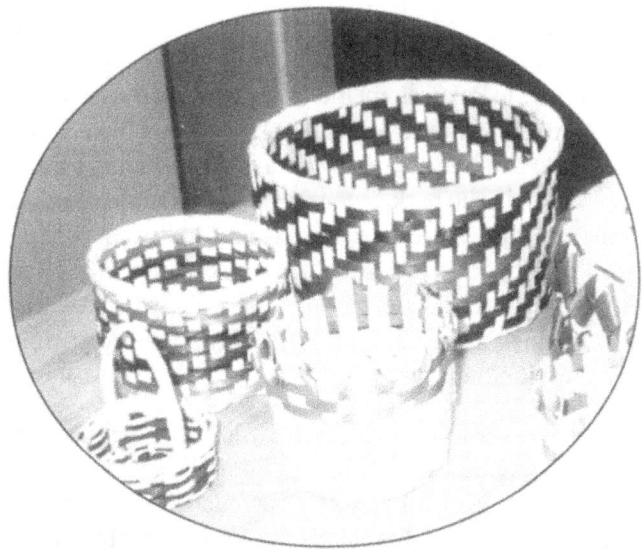

*Above: Open baskets made in Potawatomi Basket Class.*
*Below: Made by modern Potawatomi basketmaker.*

*Antique Potawatomi basket.*

The Great Lakes area has been referred to as the birch bark area. Lightweight bark canoes were of utmost importance in Potawatomi life. They were master builders, unlike the pedestrian tribes (such as the Miami, Fox, Sauk, Kickapoo and Mascoutin) who traveled by foot to escape the Iroquois. The bark canoes were extremely navigable and safe; they were used for fishing and transporting people and goods over long distances. Other tribes had dugouts that were heavier and more unwieldy in the water. One of these can be seen at the Michigan Maritime Museum in South Haven.

Simon Pokagan, Leopold's son, told of a sacred camp ground about a half mile north of South Haven, along the Black River, where the people celebrated the feast for the dead. For six days, they built bonfires along the shore that cast light over the waves. The people feasted and threw food into the fire singing, "We are going around as spirits feeding the dead." The feast was to keep alive the memory of those who died, just as head stones do for white men's graves.

During those days *Nik-a-nong* (South Haven) was a successful manufacturing town. White birch bark was imported in quantity by canoe and buried for trade or manufacture. Birch bark did not decay and was ready to be used for canoes, wigwams, dishes, and hats. It was also used to tie the knot in a marriage. Sugar maple, sold for wampum or buffalo robes, was plentiful. Thus, people lived in this place for generations in ease and plenty.

C.H. Engle, a white citizen of Hartford and administrator of Chief Simon Pokagan's estate after his death, came into possession of several stories,- Indian legends Pokagan had written on birch bark. One story tells the Algonquin Legend of South Haven, mainly using the English translation for the Algonquin words that are interspersed:

*No more for us the wild deer bounds; The plough is on our hunting grounds. Our traditional account of South Haven, given us by our forefathers, was held as sacred by them - as Holy Writ by the white man. Long, long years ago,* Ki-ji Man-i-to *(the Great Spirit) who held dominion over* Mi-shi-gan *(Lake Michigan) and the surrounding country, selected a place at the mouth of* Maw-kaw-te *(Black River) as his seat of government. His royal throne was located on the highest point of that neck of land lying between Maw-kaw-te River and Lake Michigan. This high point of land was called* Ish-pem-ing, *meaning a high place. Here it was that Ki-ji Man-i-to worked out the grand conceptions of his soul. With giant strides he scattered broadcast along the shore, a day's journey northward, a multitude of beautiful stones of various colors, shape and size, that in sunshine outshone the galaxy on high. No such charming stones elsewhere could be found around all the shores of the Great Lakes. He also planted in the forest the most beautiful woodland flowers that ever bloomed on earth and filled all the trees with birds that sang the sweetest songs that ever fell on mortal ears. He also made a neat bow at least ten arrow flights in length and laid it along the beach. He then painted it from end to end with beautiful lines of various hues that outshone the countless stones he had scattered along the shore. While thus at work, a cyclone from the setting sun swept across the great lake. Lightning flashed across the heavens, thunder in concert with the roaring waves rolled their awful burden on the land. The earth shook and hail and rain beat against Him. But he stood in majesty, smiling in the teeth of the storm. At length the gloom clouds rolled away and the setting sun lighted up the passing storm. He then picked up the giant bow he had made, bending it across his knee. Then with his breath he blew a blast that swept it eastward between the sun and clouds. As it stood, each end resting upon the trees, it painted them all aglow, which in contrast with their robes of green, added still more glory to the scene. As he gazed upon its beauty and grandeur, arching the departing storm, He shouted in triumph above the roaring waves saying in tones of thunder, "All men behold my bow in the cloud. See it has no arrow, string or quiver. It is the bow of peace. Tell it to your children's children that Ki-ji Man-i-to made and placed it there, that generations yet unborn when they behold it, might tell their children that Ki-ji Man-i-to placed it there, without arrow, string or quiver, that they might know he loved peace and hated war.*

*The tradition above given was handed down to us by a tribe of Au-nish-naw-be-og (Indians) that lived in Michigan before my people, the Potawatomies. They were called*

*Prairie Tribe, on account of their clearing up large tracts of woodland and living somewhat as farmers. Said to be very peaceful, they seldom went on the warpath. The Ottawas, who had always been very friendly with our people, tell us they drove them out of this country and nearly exterminated them about four hundred years ago. We had a great reverence for their traditions, as we occupied the land of their principal village on the Black River. We named it Nik-onong, from two Algonquin words nik (sunset) and o-nigis (beautiful).*

> *The People of the many Nations visited each other's lands. The People from the North brought elk meat. The People from the West gave them fish. The People from the South brought corn. The People from the East gave them hides. When there were arguments, their leaders would say, "Let us respect each other. We will bring you corn and baskets, you will bring us meat and flint knives. That way we will live in a peaceful life. We must respect each other, and the animals, the plants, the land, the universe. We have much to learn from all the Nations.* — Simon Ortiz

The Indian walked over well-used trails. The Bureau of American Ethnology states that many paths or trails were originally made by deer or buffalo migrating seasonally; some led to water or salt. These trails were extensive; large shells from as far away as the Pacific Coast were found in Michigan burial sites and copper pieces from Michigan in burial sites of Mexico. Besides main trails, hundreds of paths connected villages to hunting and fishing grounds, cornfields, and other villages. The roads from Detroit to Chicago and Grand Rapids to St. Joseph are examples of trails to main roads and important transportation routes. On the archeological map of the counties, the trails are shown as dark or broken lines, as are all the trails from St. Joseph to Kalamazoo and St. Joseph to Waterviet.

Tool makers used a variety of materials. Obsidian from the Rocky Mountains and Ohio flint were important for arrowheads and spears. Chert was also used. Chippers, hammers, and anvils were used to create tools and

POTTAWATTAMIE INDIAN VILLAGE C.F-3.
COPYRIGHTED, 1909, BY J.A. LITTLE.

weapons. The past owner of the Millstone Antique Barn, off of Hagar Shore Road, had a large collection of arrowheads, found along the Brandywine where he wandered as a child. Axes were made from stones found along lakes and streams. With these primitive tools and burning techniques, large trees could be felled. Deer and moose were hunted several ways - - using bow and arrow, running them into water, or setting traps and pitfalls. Dogs were used as coursers. Flint implements with handles were hoes, without were spades. The Indians were good at wood-working; tools such as chisels, gouges, flint blades, scrapers, and copper knives turned out canoes, paddles, digging tools, arrow shafts, pails, spoons and so on. They also built forts, dwellings and fences all with primitive tools.

> *Nevertheless, life was always hard. At times, corn did not grow and there was famine. At times, winters were very cold and there was hardship. At times, the winds blew hot and rivers dried. At times, the People grew uneasy among themselves. The learned men and women talked with each other about what to do for their People, but it was always hard. They had to have great patience and they told their People, "We should not ever take anything for granted. In order for our life to continue, we must struggle very hard for it.* — Simon Ortiz

Since hunting was a major activity of the Potawatomi, stories of hunters often emerged. One centered around a man in the area named old Wapsey. Old Wapsey, an unschooled Indian in Van Buren County, was famous as a bear hunter. He was clever enough to drive the bear near to his wigwam before killing him. He never gave up on a quarry and was so skilled that the other Indians claimed that he could kill 10 bears to another hunter's one.

One story of an old Wapsey bear hunt was shared with C.H. Engle by a Mr. Northrup, a white man who lived near the Indian people for several years. He was awakened early one morning in December by old Wapsey who told him he had treed a bear in a white wood tree nearby. He asked Northrup to bring his gun to shoot him because he had shot his own arrows to the top of the tree and they never came back. When Mr. Northrup reached the tree, Old Wapsey told him to shoot through the heart or the bear might kill them. He shot and his bullet grazed the bear's head causing him to fall from the tree. He began to run. As he passed, Old Wapsey straddled the bear like a farmer would a hog at butchering time. He stuck him in the neck until he fell dying. They found three arrows in the bear, one protruding three inches after passing through his side. Stories of Wapsey interested Mr. Engle enough that he decided to find Wapsey's wigwam. When the elderly Indian found that Engle knew, among others, Pokagan and Little and Big Weso, he allowed him to stay the night. He treated him to a supper of the most delicious soup Engle had ever tasted - finding later that it was made of muskrat.

Wapsey explained his hunting success. He tracked quarry for as long as it took to wear out the animal. He claimed the animals ran in a circle. Taking a stick he drew a number of circles starting at the same point for each. The smallest circle was the path of the rabbit, the next size the raccoon and so on through the fox, wolf, deer, bear and moose. Each started off near the wigwam and, when tired, returned to the starting point. The bear, for example, climbed a tree, waiting to be killed. Wapsey claimed anyone could do it if he followed on and on until the animal tired and returned back. This was the way the Great Spirit made it happen for the Indians who could never have pulled their game home.

The last time Engle saw Wapsey was in July 1893. He went with Chief Simon Pokagan to ask him to answer a request to accompany him to the Chicago World's Fair as he was also the only living Indian who had taken part in the Fort Dearborn Massacre. Wapsey declined, saying they would kill him. He was no longer hunting bear then, at the age of 110; he died soon after.

One day Little Weso went to find Mr. Engle and asked him to go with him on pony back to Saddle Lake to find Joe Kawkee. He was not lost but there was bad, very bad trouble. A white man had said Kawkee had been killed by a white hunter for taking so many deer. Little Weso's perspective was that Joe Kawkee was a good man for killing so many deer (they always shared their game) so he wanted to go check if Kawkee was alive. They reached the wigwam and knocked at the door. Kawkee's wife answered and said Joe was at the spring getting a bucket of water. When Kawkee returned, the two Indians talked in their own tongues for an hour. Engle understood little, but did catch that Kawkee had killed 50 deer, three bears and one wolf in four weeks. The white hunters had stolen five deer and were mad he had killed so many. Engle could hardly blame them. (One role of the Great Lake warrior was to provide for those less able to provide for themselves. Indians hunted for the larger community.) After a delicious supper of deer liver and tongue stew with corn soup, that night they slept soundly on hemlock boughs between green deer skins. Next day, Kawkee said he was grateful they came all that way to see if he was okay and offered them a big buck to take home. Engle and Weso threw the buck astride Weso's pony where Kawkee tied it down securely with strips of basswood inner bark. He tied so tightly, they seemed one. The big horns reached just above the horse's head while the noses sat side by side. In back, the two tails were of about the same length. Weso straddled the buck and after putting on his tall headwear, the result was a double monstrosity. When Engle's horse spied it, he broke into a run and it took much coaxing before he could get within speaking distance of Weso. About a mile outside of Bangor, they met an old man and woman with an old skinny horse and wagon. The horse took one look at the approaching monstrosity and ran into the wood tipping over the wagon, passengers, and a load of pumpkins. The man said the thing was enough to scare the devil himself.

Pigeons were very plentiful. One day Engle was taken by an Uncle Corwin to a camping ground where they pointed out long racks of poles and bark on which they had spread hundreds of dozens of squabs. These were being smoked and dried over a slow fire. They also made squab butter which they claimed was better than cow butter. Wishing to buy squabs at one cent per bird, Engle made a bargain for the Indian men, women and children to catch some for him. They went to a hemlock thicket near the spot where the Packard Mills were later built in Covert. In less than two hours they came back with 210 dozen. The Indian people knew how to hunt the pigeon without depleting their numbers by capturing only squab of a certain age. Late 1800s accounts of millions of pigeons are almost unimaginable. Audubon once computed the number of pigeons in a body flying northward as one billion, one hundred and fifty million, one hundred and thirty six. People in the Van Buren County area would have believed that to be true. Indians called the wild pigeons *ne-ne-og*. Europeans renamed them because they resembled the domesticated pigeons. Pokagan himself described a sighting this way as he camped at the headwaters of the Manistee River in Michigan:

> *One morning while leaving my wigwam I was startled by heaving and gurgling, resembling the sound of an army of horses laden with bells advancing through the deep forests toward me. As I listened intently, I concluded that instead of the trampling of horses, it was distant thunder; and yet the morning was clear, calm, and beautiful. Nearer and nearer came the strange commingling sounds of sleigh bells, mixed with the rumbling of an approaching storm. While I gazed and listened in wonder and astonishment, I beheld moving toward me in an unbroken front, millions of pigeons, the first I had seen that season. They passed like a cloud through the branches of the high trees. Just as the buffalo had gone from the area, within a few years, the wild pigeons were extinct.* -- Simon Pokagon

> *But one day, something unusual began to happen. Maybe there was a small change in the mind. Maybe there was a shift in the stars. Maybe it was a dream that someone dreamed. Maybe it was the strange behavior of an animal. The People thought and remembered, "A long time ago, there were Yellow-skinned men who came upon the ocean to the Western Coasts." The People thought and remembered, "A long time ago, there were Red-haired men who came upon the ocean to the Eastern Coasts." But these visitors had not stayed for long. They met with some of the People and soon they left upon the ocean for their homes.* — Simon Ortiz

While the U.S. Government defined tribe as a specific group of Indians with a council and membership role, the Potawatomi structure was not hierarchical. They were set up to share decision making and wealth by formation of small bands loosely united into a tribe. *Ukama* was the Potawatomi word for leader; it could be used within a variety of groups - families, women, warriors, class and so on. Never, however, was there an *Ukama* who represented the whole tribe. Because of this system of governance, the French, British and Americans found negotiations difficult. Depending on the issue, decisions might be made by families, clans, villages, or warriors. Unfortunately, Europeans sometimes recognized pretenders to this office and made decisions accordingly. *Ukamek* made decisions based on views given in public assemblies; they listened carefully to elders. They could be deposed for excess ambition. Concentration of power or wealth in one individual was not tolerated.

Villages would come together only when treaties threatened their communities or lands. Otherwise, decision-making rested in their individual villages. Kinship was based on male descent. Each clan had a totem or mythological ancestor. This was in the form of a bear, sturgeon, eagle and so on, whose dream devised the power of the clan. More than 42 Potawatomi clans have been identified; undoubtedly more were unrecorded. *Otan*, the Potawatomi name for village, came from the same root word as *totem*, meaning the "*Dwelling place of those who are related as brothers and sisters.*" To the Indian people, it actually meant extended family, at least to cousins, nieces and nephews and beyond. It was here that individuals related day to day. Thus family, clan, and village were most meaningful to the People.

One of the most evil of crimes was violence within the tribal community. Disciplinary action could be public

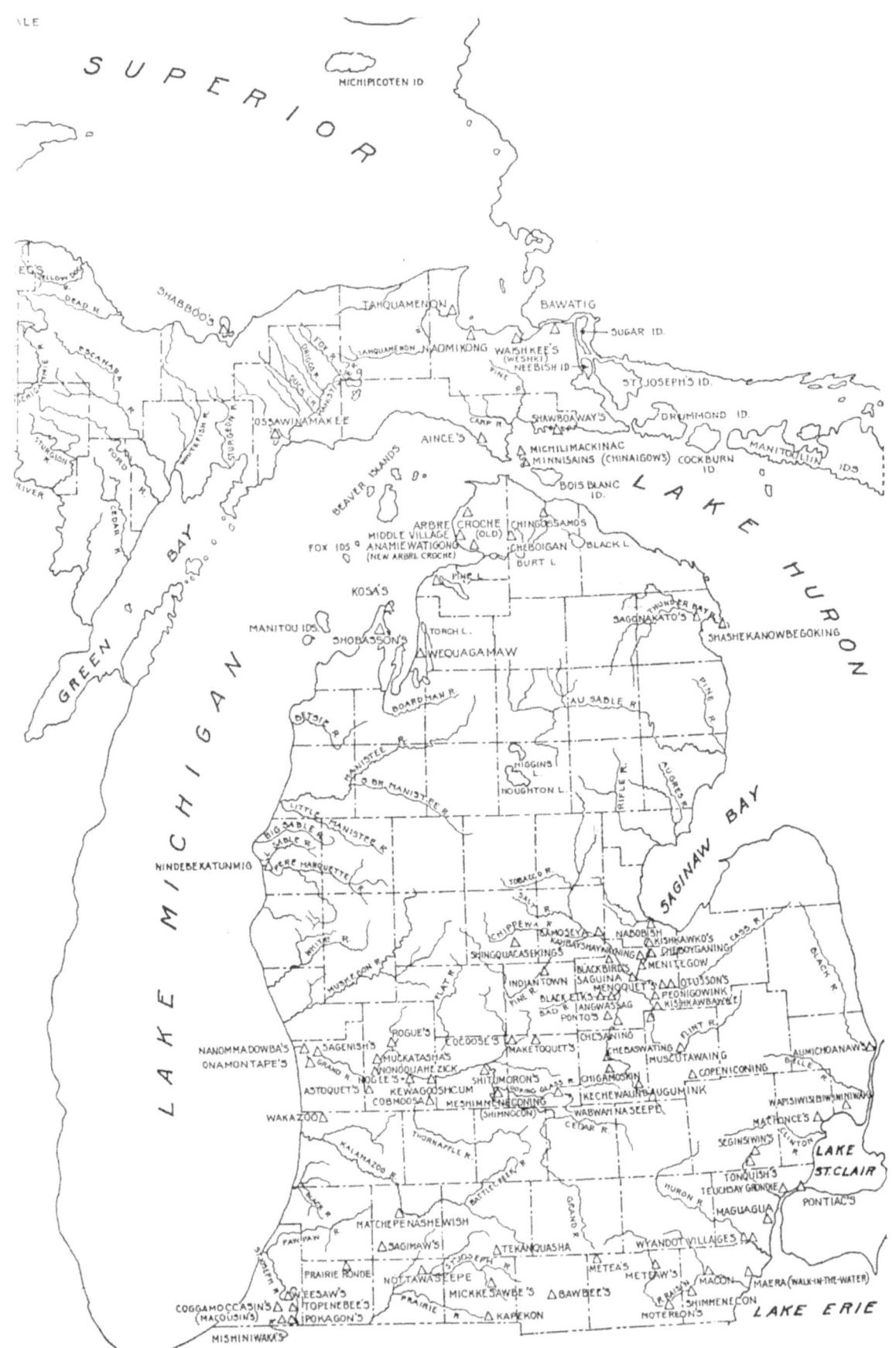

**Indian Villages of Michigan of Which the Names and Locations are Known.**
*From Hinsdale, Wilbert B., Archeological Atlas of Michigan, Michigan Handbook Series #4, Ann Arbor: University of Michigan Press, 1931.*

censure; if that failed to change behavior, the individual could even be exiled. Dissension between groups and within a village was solved by splitting the band into two different villages. Potawatomi did not explain their life through the ages in an evolutionary way. They saw it as an act of creation. This view was the center of the Potawatomi life and is still reflected in the traditional teaching of tribal members. Their spiritual life is an alternative to scientific explanations of life.

All Three Fires tribes had members in their Grand Medicine Society or *Midewiwin*. The people of these societies were highly trained in local botany and knew the use of medicinal plants. Each member collected and had access to the plants; each went through four levels of training to increase skill for curing disease and to gain spiritual insight that - along with herbs - helped cure psychological problems. Poultices, narcotics, and massage were used. Wild cherry and ginseng, still popular today, are modern examples of Indian pharmacy. Some healing was done with plants, some in combination with the supernatural or spiritual world. Modern osteopathy, homeopathy, and Christian Science have ancient roots dating back thousands of years. Medicine men were held in respect; they were thought to invoke both good and bad spirits. John Eichorn, an Odawa now living in Minneapolis, said of their religion: *"The larger society subscribes to the idea that God is God. He can't be trivialized, like an animal, or a tree or a rock. But to Indian people, God is all over. That's why they have respect for the earth. My own idea is that we are all manifestations of God."*

Ed Grey *(Jikewe)* explains the spiritual instruction given to the Nishinabe as the seven gifts of the seven grandfathers; altogether, they bring honor and respect. Still the guiding principles of the traditional people, they are: "To cherish knowledge is to know wisdom. To know love is to know peace. To honor all of the creation is to have respect. Bravery is to face the foe with integrity. Honesty in facing a situation is to be brave. Humility is to know yourself as a sacred part of creation. Truth is to know all of these things." (*From The Mishomis Book.*)

The Three Fires have always been close, according to Jikewe, and are now even more closely knitted. The Odawa was known for its trading ability, the Ojibway for its medicine people, the Potawatomi for its fire keepers.

May Frances Heath, in her early memories of Saugatuck 1830-1930, said her grandfather, who had a trading post, found the Indians peaceful, neighborly, honorable, and courteous. They believed in a Great Spirit who would supply their wants and therefore had no heart for stealing. They kept their promises, were peaceful, and proved to be real friends. When shopping in the trading post of Saugatuck, an Indian woman would have money tied in cloth, according to May Heath's father. He told her how the woman would point to an item; he would show it to her and count out the money for the piece in small change. She would take that and point to another item, while the money lasted. After each item was purchased, she tied up her money, so shopping was prolonged and enjoyed.

Having organized a mission at Rush Lake and Saugatuck, Father Louis Baroux worked for years with the Indian people. He believed converting the Indians to Catholicism of great importance. Deeply involved with the people, he saw many traits in them he thought admirable. He found them to have decorum and dignity; they could serve as models to Europeans. He believed the Indians to have an idea of justice and rights, of falsehood and of truth, a sane judgement, and a desire to conduct themselves worthily in the sight of God. Father Baroux also believed Europeans had treated the Indian with revolting injustice and cruelty, robbing him of his dignity. This led to cruelty given back in return. Rather than learning to appreciate white society, they learned to despise it. They were taught the vices of civilization through white actions. *"When I think of the conduct of the Europeans in regard to these people, I blush at our haughty pretensions,"* Baroux reported to his supervisor in 1862.

> *But now, the People began to hear fearful stories. Strange men had arrived on the shores of the South. Spanish, these men called themselves. They came seeking treasures and slaves. These men caused destruction among the People. The nations of the South were burned by heedless and forceful men. Soon there were other dreadful stories. More men, these with their wives and children, arrived on the Eastern Coasts. English, French, Dutch, they called themselves. They spoke with a fervor that frightened the People who met them. They taught about a God whom all should obey. They said they were special men of this God. Soon the People saw the destruction of their Nations. They soon found out it was the aim of the English, French and Dutch to take their lands. The rich and the powerful of these men formed an American government. They wanted the land because it was fertile with forests and farmland and wealthy with precious minerals. And they wanted the People to serve them as slaves.* — Simon Ortiz

Indians gradually lost their land during the 1800s when British, French and American wars centered around the desire for land and for control of fur trade. From 1654 to 1783, the Potawatomi built up a strong relationship with

France through trade of furs and lesser goods such as maple sugar, corn, and meat. Their relationship was cordial. According to May Frances Heath, the French fur traders had followed rules for their dealing with the Indians.

1. Trade in your own district only.
2. Deal fairly, be friendly.
3. Attend no Indian Councils. Send them no messages with wampum (bribes).
4. Take no liquor of any kind to Indian Country. Do not sell or give to Indians.
5. Try to teach the Indians to live in peace.
6. If one disobeys the above laws, Indians have the right to take and keep any of your possessions they wish.

When the Spanish Crown claimed the interior of North America, the Potawatomi promised to honor that claim. They received tools, weapons, powder, and traps for their furs. They supported the French against the British who sought the take-over of French Colonial Territory.

Trading posts and forts built on major waterways determined the sites of earliest trading-rights conflicts. In Michigan, controlling the straits from Lake Huron to Lake Michigan was crucial for control of the fur trade. A southern route held an important role in canal travel along Lake Michigan, down the St. Joseph River to what is now South Bend, and across the Kankakee River into Illinois.

In 1718, the Potawatomi requested a French fort be built in the lower St. Joseph valley. When St. Joseph Potawatomis sent warriors east to help the French defeat British on Lake George, a combined alliance of tribes overwhelmed the enemy. But the St. Joseph Potawatomi became infected with smallpox and an epidemic took the lives of some pro-French chiefs. The Potawatomi held on to their loyalty to the French as long as they could, despite the European decision that the Lakes were to be under British control. The Potawatomi of the Detroit area finally supported the British, while at the less accessible St. Joseph area, Potawatomies remained with the French, believing that the French would allow them to live in their own way while trading furs; the British wanted the land for settlement.

Chief Pontiac, an Ottawa, led the final great rebellion to hold Michigan as an ally to French traders. Allied with several tribes, he attacked Detroit; the attack failed. In 1760 the French abandoned Ft. St. Joseph. When the Revolutionary War broke out in 1776, the St. Joseph Potawatomi remained neutral, believing they had never ceded land to either France or England. They had worked out a trusting relationship with the French; the English had said they supported Indian rights to the land. But the Indians did not trust the Americans. Following European sovereignty law, the French and British had opposed each other's land claims in order to control trade, not to oppose the native people's land ownership. With threat of European settlement, however, things looked different to the Indians. With the Americans' increasing interest, the St. Joseph Potawatomi decided to join the Detroit Potawatomi to support the British. Chief Pontiac, however, began agitating and enlisting tribes to take over Ft. Detroit. The siege began. The final blow for the Indians came with the Paris Treaty of 1763 when the French and British reached a peace agreement. All during the period, the various tribes had been aiding the British, Americans or French according to indications of possible survival of land holdings.

> *When the People saw these men did not respect them and the land they said, "We must fight to protect ourselves and the land." In the West, Pope called warriors from the Pueblo and Apache Nations. In the East, Tecumseh gathered the Shawnee and the Nations of the Great Lakes, the Appalachians, and the Ohio Valley to fight for the People. In the Midwest, Black Hawk fought to save the Sauk and Fox Nation. In the Great Plains, Crazy Horse led the Sioux in the struggle to keep their land. Osceola in the Southeast, Geronimo in the Southwest, Chief Joseph in the Northwest, Sitting Bull, Captain Jack, all were warriors. They were warriors who resisted and fought to keep the American colonial power from taking their land.* — Simon Ortiz

When the British gained control of the Great Lakes area through the Treaty of Paris in 1783, they persuaded the Indians that the land would still be theirs contrary to what might happen under the Americans. This gave the British control of the fur trade and prevented American/Indian negotiations.

In 1794 the Jay Treaty eliminated all British garrisons from American held territories. Settlers were allowed to remain. Indian people moved freely over borders. Then Americans began to expand. Negotiating with separate tribes, they ensured their occupation of Indian country. Slowly, treaties began to erode the Indian rights to their lands; reservations began to be set up.

When the British fled, the Potawatomi began negotiating with the Americans. Many problems arose for the Indians during the treaty era. The American government often made treaties that took Indian lands by obtaining signatures of people who were not representative of the tribes in question and sometimes not even of that tribe. Later, under the removal treaties, western lands were greatly misrepresented to Indians by descriptions of ideal living conditions.

> *From the 1500s to the late years of the 1800s, the People fought for their lives and lands. In battle after battle, they fought until they grew weak. Their food supplies were gone, and their warriors were killed or imprisoned. And then the People began to settle for agreements with the American government. The leaders of the People agreed to Treaties. The People said they would stop their armed fight. The Americans promised the People they could live on lands they both agreed was the People's land. Upon this land, the People could hunt and fish and have their sacred ceremonies. Upon this land, the Nations of the People could live. The People thought, "The Earth is the source of all life." They knew they must have the courage to continue. The people promised to honor the treaties. The People had to agree to live on reservations. Much of the reservation land was very poor. There were no more buffalo to hunt and the deer and elk were scarce. Many of the People ran away and they were forced back by the Americans. The Nation of the People were weakened. They were broken in united strength.* — Simon Ortiz

In 1803, a treaty at Ft. Wayne set a precedent unfortunate for the Indians. As a result, settlers flooded American lands and spilled over into Indian territory. The Federal government sought to gain as much land as possible. Annuities given for the land were not well distributed; many were not paid in full. The Potawatomi realized that only peace or negotiations were possible from then on. The Americans conceded that the Indians had not been defeated; they had the right to occupy lands until gained by the government through treaty. More than 400 negotiations took place between the government and the Potawatomies; more treaties were signed concerning their lands than with any other single tribe.

> *Soon, more Americans came. They were gold miners, railroad men, outlaws, missionaries, ranchers. They wanted the rest of the land the People had. Treaties were broken by them and the reservations grew even smaller. The Americans sent government agents. They told the People they could not live the way they had before. The missionaries asked the government to put a stop to the sacred ceremonies, the dances, and the songs of the People.* — Simon Ortiz

The government policy up to 1830 had been assimilation or separation of the Indian people. In reality the latter policy did not work. The Indians wished to keep their own cultural ways; new settlers preferred not to have the Indians among them. In the early 1800's John Marshall ruled that tribes were domestic dependent nations with limited sovereignty; - they retained rights. However, in 1830 the Indian Removal Act was passed by Congress; its intent was to give the president authority to remove tribes from their homeland. The law gave the Indian the rights to stay, providing that no tribe could be forced against its will to cede land and move west, but it gave the Indians no power to exercise these rights.

When the Treaty of Chicago was being negotiated, about 8,000 Potawatomis and Americans gathered around Chicago (which was, at the time, still a small village). Of the three groups of Potawatomi, the Michigan group was most strongly against signing the treaty. Chief Leopold Pokagon emphasized the difference in way of life of the Michigan Potawatomi and the Prairie Band. The latter, oriented to long distance hunting and travel by horse, did not object to moving west. Ultimately, the government was forced to negotiate with the Pokagan group separately. Finally they, too, were forced to sign a treaty of removal, both Leopold Pokagan and Wesaw fixing their signature to the document. But Pokagan, who objected to the end, was written into an amendment that allowed his people to remain in Michigan.

For the people who were sent west, the movement has been referred to historically as the *Trail of Death* - an event much like that of the well-known *Trail of Tears* of the Cherokee. Since all of the land was ceded to the government, Pokagan had to use his money grant to purchase property where his people farmed; they could hunt and fish in areas of public domain. For years the Pokagan Band did not receive their allotted annuities. When they finally proved their entitlement, they only received a fraction of what was due.

Between 1830 and 1834, tremendous change came to the St. Joseph Valley. Trading posts of the *Metis* (French/Indian people who for a time, served in the role of intercultural mediators) and the Indians, on which early settlers had depended, were replaced by a large influx of settlers and industrial developers. St. Joseph became a vital transportation route for steamboats and flatboats. A Pokagan Potawatomi named Leroy Wesaw grew up in this area. He remembered picnics on Thunder Mountain in Palisades Park. His grandfather was active here when land was being defended. Following are excerpts from a paper giving his father's version of the wars as handed down orally:

> *Heavy losses in battle, diseases the Indians had no natural resistance to, and the alcohol that was sold to them by traders hastened the decline of the*

*Potawatomi as a cohesive fighting force. In 1812, Potawatomies were fighting on both sides. Brother fought brother, and they were still going to lose their land. This was a time of treaty making and giving up more than they got in return. After ceding all but seven small tracts of land on the banks of the St. Joseph River, the total population of the Potawatomi nation was under 2,000 - - no longer a fighting force. Movement west was rapid now, without the Potawatomi in the way, and these people of the forest and stream were being compressed into smaller areas. A few years before the Potawatomie lost their last land holdings, there were two war chiefs living in a village my forefather came from. They could no longer stand the way of life there, so they took their followers and moved west. They could be traced only as far as the Mississippi because west of the river, called "Indian Territory", was unmapped. But now since Indian tribes are closer than before, it has come to light that living today on the Shoshone reservation are Wesaw and Shavehead - the same names that left the Potawatomie tribe years ago. The remains of the Pokagan Band lived in the lower part of Michigan in several small settlements. They farmed, hired out as farmhands, cut logs in the woods and worked in the sawmills. The government finally gave in to their demands for a land base and established a small reservation to the east of where they lived at the time. They named it Athens. It is still there but is now a very small state reserve. The small band of Pokagan Potawatomies were now landowners, paying taxes on land that years ago was their tribal hunting ground. Their children went to public schools, one-room country schoolhouses or boarding schools in distant cities. It would appear that they had been assimilated into the dominant culture, but if you happen upon a tribal gathering you would smell the traditional foods and hear English used only as a second language. — -Leroy Wesaw*

Evidence is continually being found of Indian life throughout the ages. Some of the latest finds are along the Brandywine. On a tour of the Ross property just west of Covert, a naturalist from Sarett Nature Center explained that the Ross estate was donated to the Nature Conversancy and Sarett given the responsibility of overseeing it. When the land was given, the idea was to preserve rare plants. The evidence of Native American life was not known. This entire area was Indian land. All through here are Indian finds. Most were on the east side of the sand dunes, but as sand is continually moving, these finds are now often discovered in the sand. Native Americans walked along the lake to the side of the sand dunes on a very good trail. Where they walked and disturbed the land with grazing animals, blowouts evolved 100-plus years ago. Present blowouts were previously flatter lands with trees, grass and plants. When sand moved in, blowouts took place and finds were uncovered. A blowout does not necessarily need to be a large sand hill. It can have a wide flat area of land. Wind whiffing through forms an unstabilized dune. The dune continues to move until stabilized with plants. Whenever new blowouts appear, one may find fire rocks and other evidence of habitation along the Brandywine.

*Ross Property dunes, site of an old Indian village by the Brandywine Creek.*

The Brandywine area is now lined with dry land along its banks, but was much marshier before drainage creeks were formed; the river wound around through the marshes. Waterfowl and huge sturgeon came upstream. It was a fine area for food gathering. Consequently, the land was continuously settled. The earliest artifacts found are from the prehistoric Middle Woodland culture. Rocks for cooking or boiling have been found. Sharp edges have been chipped off with tools. These rocks probably had been piled up and left by the glaciers at the Covert/Valparaiso moraines, although some archeologists suggest they were collected from the lake. These rocks contain moisture in them and can blow up. If that is all one has, however, one uses them. Some sandstone rocks have been found; they appear to have been changed by fire.

Today the Pokagan band continues to survive and grow in this area. They are working to educate their youth to traditional beliefs and cultural ways of their ancestors. The Band won federal recognition as a nation on September 25, 1994.

The long history of the land we enjoy today at Palisades Park includes remarkable people who lived here in harmony with the land for many centuries, fought to retain it, and are still present in the area today. While we think of Palisades Park as a small piece of land with clear boundaries, the people of the past had a more communal land use; however, they lived here on a permanent and seasonal basis just as we do today. The Odawa from as far away as the Keewenaw peninsula had permanent villages along our shore for hunting, gathering and journeys for trade. Those from the St. Joseph Potawatomi stayed in the area permanently. Their **footprints** preceded ours in these woods and on these sandy shores.

> *The government agents gathered the children. They took the children to boarding schools far from their homes and families. The children from the West were taken to the East. The children from the East were taken to the West. The People's children were scattered like leaves torn from a tree. At schools far from home, the children were taught to become Americans. They learned to be ashamed of their People. The People went to schools. They went to Christian churches. They served in the American Army. Some even almost became Americans. But they were still the People. They farmed and raised livestock. They made and sold crafts for a living. Nevertheless, the People were very poor. There were no jobs on the reservations. Even though they didn't want to, many of the People had to leave. They were moved by the government into cities across America: Oakland, Cleveland, Chicago, Dallas, Denver, Phoenix, Los Angeles. They worked in factories, on railroads, in businesses, even for the government. Often they were discouraged and their families suffered in the cities. They struggled hard for their lives. — Simon Ortiz*

## Bibliography

Barous, Father Louis. An Early Indian Mission: Facsimile Edition, 1862.

Benton-Benai, Edward. The Mishomis Book: Hayward, Wisconsin, Indian Country Communications, Inc. 1988.

Clifton, James A. The Pokagans 1683-1983 Catholic Potawatomi of the St. Joseph Valley: Boston Mass, University Press of American, 1984.

Clifton, James A. George Cornell and James M. McClurken, People of the Three Fires: Grand Rapids, MI, Inter-Tribal Council, Michigan Press, 1986.

Edmunds, David R. The Potawatomi - Keepers of the Fire: Norman, OK, University of Oklahoma Press 1978.

Eichorn, John (Odawa), Interview: Minneapolis, MN and Berrien. Odawa.

Ensign, D.W. & Co. History of Van Buren Counties: Philadelphia, Press of J.B. Lipincott Co. Philadelphia, 1880.

Grey, Ed (Ojibway): Fennville, MI.

Hinsdale, W.B. Primitive Man in Michigan: Ann Arbor, MI, University of Michigan, Museum.

Ortiz, Simon. Missoulian Newspaper - September 20, 2003, The People Shall Continue: San Francisco, CA, Children's Book Press, 1977. Now in public domain.

Sarett Nature Center naturalist

Tanner, Helen Hornbeck, Editor. - Atlas of Great Lakes Indian History. Norman, OK: University of Oklahoma Press, 1987.

Vogel, Virgil. Indian Names in Michigan Ann Arbor, MI, University of Ann Arbor Press, 1986.

# Interviews

## Lucy and George Bennett
Peshawbestown, Michigan

George Bennett, an Odawa from the Grand Traverse Band of Michigan, and his wife Lucy, a Sioux from the Brule Band of the Dakota, are dedicated to building Indian self-sufficiency through small businesses and housing development. They graduated from NAES College in Chicago, a Native American college. George was previously chairman of his Band. The Grand Traverse Band has attained federal recognition. Its reserve is entirely within one county.

One tradition of the Odawa society involves community service as recompense for wrongdoing. Lucy shared an example of some children playing in a flower box and destroying the flowers; their service was to plant flowers at the church for the community. The flowers became a symbol. Every Sunday the children are reminded by seeing how well the flowers are doing. Soon they began to think of them as "our flowers."

Requirements for becoming a medicine man, according to George, include being at least 30 years old and having been brought up in the Indian way with medicine in the family. This responsibility differs from one location to another. Medicine men have great respect for medicine men in other tribes. The medicine man must select someone to follow him, possibly a son or a grandson or someone studying to be a doctor. The medicine man, thinking ahead, will take the younger person with him to identify plants and their locations and uses.

Odawa undoubtedly passed through the Palisades Brandywine area. They made migration trips, hunting and fishing all the way to Chicago. If one looks at old maps, one can find their camps along the way. Most of the people who migrated had campsites. They would actually put away their food and take time to dry food and preserve it so they would have it on the way back. They would take enough food between camps, knowing exactly how many miles they would be traveling. George's great-grandfather was part of the migration group going to Chicago. His grandfather worked cutting trees, finding enough work with that and in local orchards that his people could remain on the peninsula. Lumber on the entire peninsula, including hard woods, was cut until it was lumbered out.

When George's mother got to the 8th grade, her grandmother pulled her out of school. The school was not allowing her traditions and she was losing many of them. The government schools tried to control the environment by sending children to schools far from home and not allowing them to speak the language; supposedly this was to help them become assimilated. George's grandmother was a very strong woman and disciplinarian. This was her homeland and her people were very concerned with education. She began a school at a little wooden schoolhouse. Everyone went there. George went one year; then for economic reasons, he was sent away to boarding mission school the next year. At the mission school, the classes were taught by nuns. They spoke the language of the Indian children, but were actually taught the Catholic religion. George became an altar boy. Even though taken from his culture, people, and language, he learned discipline. When he transferred from the boarding school to public school, he was actually a grade and a half ahead of students in that public school. As a young man, George went into the Navy, getting away from his people. But an Indian never, ever actually gets away from his culture; he is always identified as Native American.

A treaty in 1855, to acquire the Odawa land, meant settlement for $15,100,000. Indeed, a number of treaties were designed to take the land from Indians; they had to take the amount of money offered and the money received was invested. For 30 years the Odawa tribe still had not seen their money. The money built up to 35 million dollars with interest and all. The tribe is trying to set up an annuity program with the money. They want to put at least half the money anyway into long-term investments to provide continuing benefits. Many people are in a desperate situation without jobs, but if the money is divided up, $4,000 each would not be too helpful.

George's great-grandfather was part of negotiations for one treaty. The Indian nation in those days was under control of the War Department, so military men came out to negotiate. As George tells it:

*Our names were hard to pronounce by the military. The way things are in the military, reaction to things they didn't know would be to kind of react belligerently. Hyphenated long names that are hard to pronounce to them didn't stand for anything. In our culture we go through periods when we have three or four different names based on things that happened in our life. When born we get a name, when we reach boyhood we get a name, as we grow up like a young warrior we get a name, when a young man we get a name, if something happens in our life and we do a great deed we get another name. And that's the way we work it in our culture. We have naming ceremonies. So in the old days, when the military were coming in touch with our people to enroll them or add their name to the tribal role, in order to pronounce those Indian names, they changed the names to something common. A lot of common names are still used by Indian families today.*

*At first we were allowed to chose any name we wanted. Oftentimes in our culture this was an opportunity to have a very festive occasion. But what happened was the military soon sat down and asked, "What would you like your name to be?" Some common name - like Smith, Jones, whatever. So the military said, "You come back in two weeks and we'll have a name for you." So people went back and had a big celebration and decided on a name they'd like to have. But when the military came back each Indian stepped forward and announced who he was. They ended up with about 15 giant surnames. That really threw a monkey into the whole military works. They said "No, no, you have to go back to select something different and unique. You can't have the same surname." So guess what happened next? It just happened that my great-grandfather met a lumberman. His name was Yanot. When asked if he could use his name, Yanot was very honored. He allowed him to use it. When the military came back again, all the people had different names. If you look on the role now, his name is on there - Yanot. My mother's maiden name is Yanot but now they spell it Yannot.*

*I saw my father only two or three times - the last time in the Navy. He told me he was proud of me. In life experience there were good times and there were rough times. What is good about my life looking back - 'I've gone past my own expectations, from where I've come from. There comes a time when you have to look back. In terms of working with people, I've tried to be the best that I can be in terms of giving them guidance.*

*All this time, the People remembered. Parents told their children, "You are Shawnee. You are Lakota. You are Pima. You are Acoma. You are Tlingit. You are Mohawk. You are all these Nations of the People." The People told each other, "This is the life of our People. These are the stories and these are the songs. This is our heritage." And the children listened. The parents said, "This has been the struggle of our People. We have suffered but we have endured." Listen, they said, and they sang the songs. Listen, they said, and they told the stories. Listen, they said, this is the way our People live. All across America, the Nations of the People were talking. The Cheyennes in the cities and the Navajos in the country. The Seminoles in Los Angeles and the Cherokees in Oklahoma. The Chippewa in Red Lake and the Sioux in Denver. Everywhere, the People on the reservations, in small town, in the large cities, they were talking, and they were listening. They were listening to the words of the elder People who were speaking. "This is the life that includes you. This is the land that is yours. All these things that were pushed away from us and broken by the American powers and government, they were alive and we must keep them alive. All these things will help us to continue." Once again, the People realized what was happening to the land. They realized it was the powerful forces of the rich and the government that made the People suffer. — Simon Ortiz*

*Examples of firestones.*

## Candi Wesaw

Pokagan Band of the Potawatomi

*Candi Wesaw is the daughter of Martin and Viola Wesaw. Martin is the cousin of Leroy and Gerald Wesaw. Her job is Cultural Associate for the Education Department of the Pokagans. Following are excerpts from a program she directed for training Pokagan Band Potawatomi staff.*

Based on our own creation story and oral history by our elders, we believe southern Michigan, parts of Illinois, Wisconsin, northern Indiana, and western Ohio have been our homeland since the beginning of time. The Pokagan Band of the Potawatomi Indians is a sovereign nation. The premises of sovereignty includes authority by self-governing states and determination of decision by their people, themselves. The Pokagan Nation functions independently with self-government under Federal Law. They operate as a sovereign government establishing laws, policies, and procedures on behalf of and with our tribal citizens to govern our land, administration and citizens.

The mission of the Pokagan Band of Potawatomi Indians is to respectfully promote and protect the culture, dignity, education, health, welfare and self-sufficiency of our elders, our youth and our families and our future generations while preserving mother earth. We develop real jobs to give our people a better way of life, keep the band and office economically independent from federal and local government, allowing the band to fully exercise its sovereignty.

Today there are eight Potawatomi nations, four in Michigan, one in Wisconsin, one in Kansas, one in Oklahoma and one in Canada. They were different villages of Potawatomi that the government divided into different places. All of them have different chapters on what happened to them and why they ended up where they are today. All share links to important historical events that affected all of us like treaties and the Trail of Death, which is the Potawatomi removal story. The Niles/South Bend area near the St. Joseph River, the Dowagiac area, and the Hartford area along the Paw Paw River are our largest population centers to this day.

One of the reasons Pokagan and his followers were allowed to stay in the area was because most of the people had converted to Catholicism and were adapting to permanent villages with wood frame houses.

*Candi's Education Department also has a film in which various members of the Pokagan Community share their views. Some of their views follow.*

**A citizen:** "To most people we are invisible, yet parks, streets, names of townships and cities are borrowed from our language."

**Tom Topash - a youth**: "People could only hold on to their culture if it did not affect children. They had often been forced to attend boarding school. They didn't want their children to go through that. They needed to create a home environment so children were part of the larger culture."

**Julie Stauffer**: "Mother didn't learn the complete language. Folks didn't teach them. They sent children to the wood shed when catching them talking among them-selves. So they (the next generation) didn't put that on their children."

**Mrs. Daugherty:** "Grandfather was a medicine man. It is a very simple religion. Traditional ways were taken from us. It really gets to me because this is a country founded on the same thing."

**Tom Topash**: "We respect teaching of the past. Our culture was damaged for a while but didn't die; some were around to retain the culture. Some, like me, come together to fulfill our identity and learn about culture. This is accomplished in a beautiful way."

*Gerald Wesaw holding a decorative piece.*

# Gerald Wesaw
Pokagan Band of Potawatomi, Brother of Leroy

Today Rogers Lake Campgrounds in Dowagiac is the central meeting place for the Band. Most everything is there now. Two years ago we began to try to get all services on site. The Education Department is about the only thing not on site. We have treaty rights for fishing. Although the government has said we can go fishing and hunting any time we want, the Conservation Department is now taking care of it and the Pokagans don't go by that. They buy licenses like everyone else. But once we have established our own land at Scott Lake we can fish like we want. The tribal government likes to observe the season limits; otherwise all would be gone. Some make a business of fishing, especially up north. And I don't have a problem with that. In the 50s some men I worked with were still netting perch in nets left out and gathered up later. Some sturgeon still live in a lake north of here.

In recent years, the People have been trying to bring the Three Fires Groups together. The Ojubaway, Odowa and Potawatomi meet yearly. I attended one meeting about two years ago. The meetings centered around fishing rights and land issues. We are now working to get land in trust. When a tribe gets land in trust, it governs that land. To do so, we have to prove many things to the government.

We have our own court that operates within land held in trust. We selected a judge and several appellate judges last year. We have a police captain at Rogers Lake, so we have started our own police department. They can function as the law. The tribe has signed an agreement in Berrien County and are working on it in Van Buren County so the tribal police can function as the law anywhere in the county, as long as they have property there. They function like the state police, the agreement being set up so the law enforcements can work together.

My dad did not talk about the family too much to me. Leroy was five years older. Grandma Wesaw died when I was just a kid. She didn't speak English. Maybe Dad opened up to her more when she was alive. Potawatomi is the language. My Dad understood the language, but after Grandma Wesaw died there was no one to talk to, so the children did not learn the language.

> *Some elements of tribal history can only be expressed in the Potawatomi language. I know my native tongue but am impeded in discussion of these because I am no longer adept enough to converse at length about abstractions.* — Leroy Wesaw

My father, Thomas, was born in 1890 in Toquin and grew up there. Grandfather Thomas died just before or soon after his son Thomas was born. He had lived during Indian land settlement and Indians being sent west. I was born in Hartford. Genevieve, my older sister, graduated from there. One of the family graduated from South Haven schools.

My dad ran into some problems in the early 1900s. He got a janitor's job. His boss had him go out and wash windows and the water froze on the windows. So dad quit - he didn't take that. The union tried to get him to go back and fight for better conditions, but he didn't. The union, at that time, was on the side of the working man. There was strength there.

Cousin Martin's family lived in Grand Rapids. I believe there was an Indian Center there or pow wows. So they probably got more involved in Indian affairs there. Leroy did a lot of things in earlier years. He worked on the railroad, drove a truck. (In later years he received a college degree at NAES College in Chicago.) When his family moved there he became involved in the Indian Center. So if you are interested in the Indian Center your interest will be the Indian way of life. I had always been interested in the Indian community, but not involved. I was not around cultural teaching. I got a job at 17 and life centered around job and raising my family. My activities were mostly of the white world, like judo with my kids when they were younger - 10-15 years old. When my children were growing up, there were not powwows like today. This weekend there will probably be three powwows within 50 miles of here.

I have always been Indian first - never claimed to be anything else, but I worked in a white world. But I was still an Indian while working at Whirlpool.

Dad was married to a French/Indian woman. We couldn't track her family back. She died in '36 and Dad never remarried. He did well to raise us alone. He told his wife he'd never have a stepparent for his children, the way he grew up. In the winter of '38 or '39, Leroy and I went up to Harbor Springs to a Catholic boarding school. Leroy was in Jr. High and I was in 2nd or 3rd grade. I stayed one year and I felt I got a better education there than here. But Leroy really didn't like it and ran away. Harbor Springs School was quite large. It was right in town. Better food than at home - it was the 30's and times were hard. The first night there we didn't eat. The next day we got two pieces of bread and Karo syrup (they had their own bakery) and coffee or tea with milk. One dish they called hash. I think it was made from stuffing only, but I liked it because the flavor was good. They also served mashed potatoes and beans. We really looked forward to Sunday when we had a traditional Sunday dinner. We'd get two apples in the afternoon donated by farmers, of apples they couldn't use. I felt bad when Leroy left. There was a high school boy who looked out for me. I was 8 or 9. Younger kids slept on one side of a dormitory room and older boys on the other with a doorway between. A nun had a room upstairs. Girls and boys had their own dormitory. The school had Indians from different tribes.

My son, Matthew, has been active with the Pokagans all along. His lifetime goal all along has been to work to help the Indians. He is a retired state trooper and involved in politics a lot. He received an eagle feather and asked me if I would make him a cedar box to display and preserve it. That was how I got back to being active in Potawatomi affairs. The box turned out to be quite the thing so that is what I began to do, make cedar boxes.

Jason, Grandson to Gerald and Cookie from the second son Mark, is really involved. He works at the Education Office in Dowagiac. He is a potter and has been working in Ed Grey's workshop. He is also a singer on the drum. I began to make drums. The first was of plywood with hide. It takes 2 men to carry it. Jason's group plays it at the powwows and when this year they had a ground breaking for the elders housing they played a drum song there. They play for various Pokagan occasions. They played recently when there was a blessing of eagle feathers - a ceremony of young people who received eagle feathers from the government. At that they used the drum I made out of cedar. It is a light drum. Jason talked about how you can sing with a hand drum. He helped me string my first hand drum; since then, I have made a lot of hand drums. The braid on the back of the white cedar drum is what my father taught me when I was real young; it looks like weaving. Drumming gives a rhythm of song that fits the dance.

*Above: Pottery, wood box, and drums made by Wesaw family. Below: Hand drum*

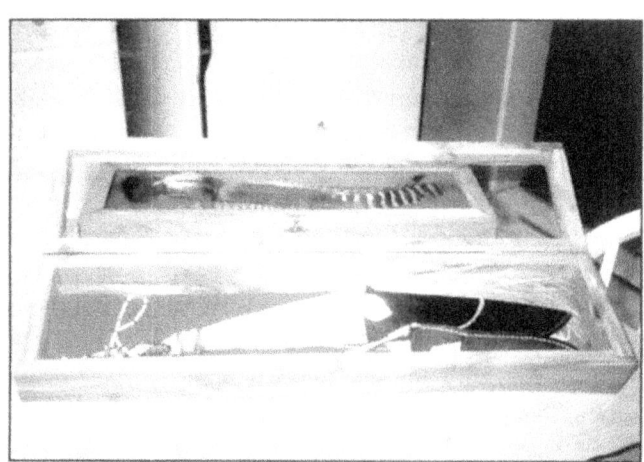

*Wesaw box for holding special artifacts, including eagle feather which legally can only be owned by a Native American.*

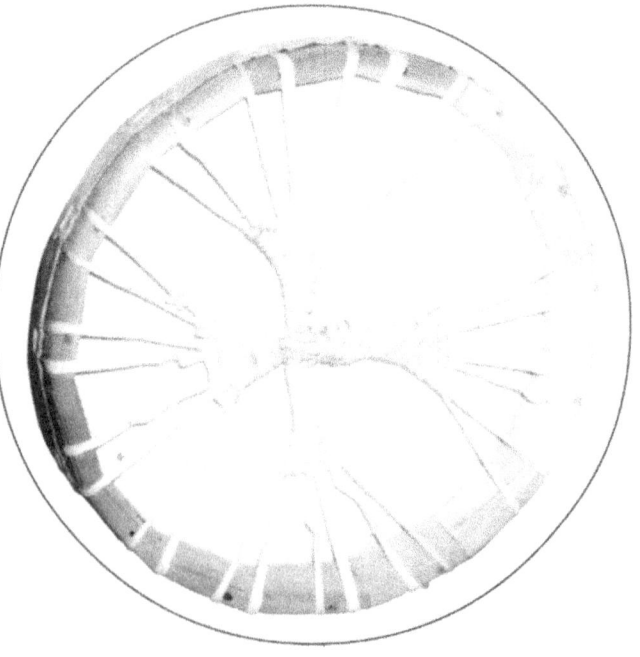

There is a sneak-up dance that reflects hunting, a grass dance for stomping grass down. You dance with the beat of the drum. The vibrations represent the heartbeat. In the fancy dance, you dance as fast as the drummer drums. Another hereditary craft being practiced and passed on is that of basket making from split wood. Cookie and I have both made a basket. A Miss Rapp was a master basket maker. Some baskets have sweet grass added to it.

To get advice about how to handle things in traditional ways, I go to an elder, Mr. White, who gives traditional and spiritual advice. John Warren can do the same, although he is younger. They explain about uses of sweet oil and tobacco. Tobacco is used in ceremonies as well as sage, to purify with smudging. I grow my own sage and sweet grass. Sweet grass is not to be sold. It can be shared by giving it away.

> *The People looked around them and they saw Black People, Chicano People, Asian People, many White People and others who were kept poor by American wealth and power. The People saw that these people who were not rich and powerful shared a common life with them. The People realized they must share their history with them. "We shall tell you of our struggles," they said. "We are all the People of this land. We were created out of the forces of earth and sky, the stars and water. We must make sure that the balance of the earth be kept. There is no other way. We must struggle for our lives. We must take great care with each other. We must share our concern with each other. Nothing is separate from us. We are all one body of People. We must struggle to share our human lives with each other. We must fight against those forces which will take our humanity from us. We must ensure that life continues. We must be responsible to that life. With that humanity and the strength which comes from our shared responsibility for this life, the People shall continue." — Simon Ortiz*

# Covert Township and Its Lumbering Days

By Katy Beck

Palisades Park is located in Covert Township in Van Buren County. The development of specific places, such as Palisades Park, within Van Buren County are, of course, tied up in the history of the entire Southwest Michigan area and need to be seen in context. The County of Van Buren, coming late into government organization, remained isolated and sparsely populated. By looking at the record of County development, one can see when the Township of Covert itself, of which Palisades Park is so much a part, finally developed.

| | |
|---|---|
| 1796 | Governor Cass of the Northwest Territory proposed that all of Michigan and some of Ohio, Indiana, and Wisconsin be named Wayne County. The Van Buren area was excluded as it was still recognized as **Indian Tribal Land** by the U. S. government. |
| 1815 | Michigan was organized as part of Wayne County, excluding Van Buren area. |
| 1821 | Topenabee and Wesaw were part of a group of 53 Indians signing the **Treaty of Chicago** relinquishing most of the land. This affected nine of today's counties and parts of others and this area was named **Monroe County.** |
| 1829 | **Van Buren County** was set up. It included Van Buren and Berrien Counties in a five county court system. |
| 01/16/1837 | Michigan was granted **Statehood** and became the 26th State of the Union. Van Buren County was given all rights over municipal affairs. Seven of today's townships were included here under the name **South Haven Township.** |
| 1856 | The Board of Supervisors organized the county into 18 townships including **Deerfield Township (now Covert Township).** |
| 1876 | An act of legislation by the state changed the name of Deerfield Township to **Covert Township.** |

It was thought that there were too many Michigan places named Deerfield, but with the name Covert, the meaning remained the same. It suggested a time when deer roamed unharmed in the forests, a "covert" being a hiding place for deer.

Settlement of European immigrants began slowly. Roads in the area were little more than trails and were nearly impassable as a result of storms, snow, and felled trees. A 30 mile trip to a mill in Niles could take 7 to 14 days. Roads, therefore, were needed to attract settlers. In 1818, the first steamboat to sail on the Great Lakes arrived on Lake Michigan. With the opening of the Erie Canal in 1825, about 300 passengers per day arrived in the eastern part of Michigan. Meanwhile, by Act of Congress in 1825, a road was started from the west end of Lake Erie to Chicago. This "Old Chicago Road," constructed over an earlier Indian route, was the first thoroughfare crossing Michigan; it was completed in 1836. Settlers passed on this route westward to Van Buren County. By 1834, the Territory of Michigan had a population of 60,000; thoughts turned to statehood.

*Below: Constructing the road between Covert and the lake.*

As late as 1857, the road up the lakeshore was still no more than a trail. It was along this road that a combine – a machine to harvest and thresh grain – and several people got lost in the hemlock forest while walking from South Haven to Paulville (the settlement that preceded Palisades Park). Settlers who arrived in the 1800's discovered good soil for agriculture, especially fruit, corn, and wheat. They lived, often assisted by the remaining Indian people, by farming, hunting, and fishing.

Liberty Hyde Bailey, the well-known botanist who was born in South Haven in 1858, wrote to Arthur Quick*: "The 'Bluffs,' as we called the dunes in the early days,

*Quick, Arthur, <u>Wild Flowers of the Northern States and Canada</u>, 1939.

were favorite exploring grounds for me as a youth; I thought they must contain more mysteries than any other place. The strange plants on the windy sands and in the dark swamps behind, the birds, the animals fascinated me."

Farmers' tools included a "bar share plow," "wooden toothed barrow," hoe, and sickle. Horses tramped the grain to winnow it. Flour condition, therefore, was poor – it was mixed with dirt and there were no facilities to clean it.

Survival was the way of life of these first pioneers. Around St. Joseph, the forests held game; fish were in streams and lakes. Robert Beatty, in a reminiscience of pioneer days in South Haven, told of thousands of wild pigeons coming overhead – no end to them. Men could kill them by throwing clubs at them or netting them. By the next year, they were almost extinct.

Although there was usually a plentiful supply of fruits and berries, frost or sandstorms could be cause of near famine. Beatty remembered cleared land with peaches and other fruit farms all along the lake. Once he saw sand blown so it covered peach-loaded trees, the branches resting on the ground.

In 1845 a stagecoach statute was enacted by legislature. Roads for stagecoach lines were authorized, provided they were laid on the most direct and eligible routes. These crooked and angling roads were mostly changed later. Roads were still crude when, in 1849, a stagecoach road opened which, according to A. C. Quick, went through Paulville (now Palisades Park). In an early Patter, he wrote: "When the lumbering days were here, just after the Civil War, the old stagecoaches used to run from South Haven to Benton Harbor and on to Chicago. They crossed the Brandywine near the far end of our old golf course, hit the hill just a few feet east of our double tennis court, and so on, winding in and out between the dunes. This old road up the hill by the tennis court is still there and very steep, but somehow they managed to climb it with their four-horse teams. Our ice truck still comes down that way sometimes to save time."

The Central Railroad depended on stagecoaches for safety and comfort in transmission of passengers from its western terminal. Therefore, coaches were used between Paw Paw and St. Joseph, Dowagiac, and Territorial Road in Van Buren County. A description of an early stagecoach was found in the Kalamazoo Gazette, January 5, 1947. Jim Kenney drove a coach between South Haven and Watervliet that serviced passengers, did errands, and delivered mail. He developed his own coach model that could survive sandy, muddy, and stony roads. His coach was lightweight but made of sheet iron with a canvas roof. This resulted in a strong coach, one that would ride out the bumps. His wheels were six feet in diameter with wide treads to reduce sinking. He put this extra wide, long body on resilient springs. He also placed the driver's

*"Kalamazoo" Stagecoach.*

seat inside the coach, enclosed with doors having isinglass windows. It could seat 20 passengers who were kept comfortable by being enclosed by doors with isinglass windows and a canvas drop to keep out the cold. To warm the feet, he installed a charcoal burner that had a stovepipe out the side. This was an extremely innovative coach, far different than the European or East Coast coaches. Eventually, the expansion of the railroad lines ended the stage era.

In 1848, the legislature enacted a plank road law authorizing companies to occupy county highways and streets in villages. Paw Paw was the closest terminal to Palisades Park of one of these major roads. However, smaller ones were in evidence where sand hills made wheeled transportation difficult. One such section led from Covert to Paulville on a hill just east of what is now Blue Star Highway. Despite a plentitude of lumber, plank or corduroy roads were not a big success.

*The Old Plank Road*

When settlers arrived in the area and cleared the land for farming, they had little use for the logs they felled. Generally, they used the wood to make rail fences, corduroy roads, barn scaffolding, and shanties, using black walnut and choice "white wood." The clearing exacted a high cost of labor. Soon, however, because of vast stands of white pine in the state, lumber barons became involved in logging and Michigan became a leading lumber-producing state.

The lumbermen often pioneered regions of the state. "Cruisers," or estimators of standing timber, competed with government surveyors for being the first white men into lands that were ceded by Indians. Thus, frontier industrialists helped establish the pattern of settlement. The small towns in the interior of the state that were totally dependent on logging did disappear.

In 1843, the first settler of the Deerfield Township area entered a homestead claim for 160 acres. In 1853, Matthius Farnum built a small water power mill on Section 8 on the Brandywine, near the mouth of the creek. With that development began a long period when Covert life became inextricably woven into that of what is now called Palisades Park. Names of early settlers began to emerge and their familiarity lasted well into the 1900's – names such as Packard, Spelman, Rood, Gunsaul, Shattuck, Iverson, and Sarno.

Matthius Farnum moved to Benton Harbor, but on his Brandywine site, in 1857, a steam mill with upright saws was built under the direction of a settler named Paul. The settlement surrounding this venture was named Paulville. Boarding houses were erected for the choppers.

According to Arthur Quick, a huge timber dam was set up along Brandywine Creek about midway of the former golf course. "It formed an extensive lake for impounding water in which thousands of logs were stored, waiting for the big sawmill to carve them up into building material." He stated, in a 1939 <u>Patter</u>, that the foundation of this big mill was still there, as well as hollows that marked the cellars of cabins and the boarding houses for lumbermen. Some logs from the dam were found in the Brandywine years later. Quick wrote, "The dredge that straightened the course of the Creek a dozen years ago, lifted out all the large logs that were used to form the dam. Those had been covered with earth and water, preventing decay, and the logs were lifted out by the dredge in as fresh condition as when placed there about 100 years before. The big pine logs were taken to the sawmill, cut into planks, and these planks were made into window sills that are now in quite a number of our Palisades cottages, as good and sound today as any made from freshly cut timber."

*Flooded Brandywine made "Lake Palisades." 1973.*

*Old map showing Paulville at the present site of Palisades Park, south of South Haven.*

Liberty Hyde Bailey, in his previously quoted letter to A. C. Quick, said reference to Paulville brought back "rollicking memories." In 1871, Bailey had sailed from Ludwig pier, at the end of the Brandywine, on a lumber schooner. He returned in the 1920's to visit the scenes of childhood. He remembered Paulville where once he went to find blackberries. In the old golf course, he rode his horse to the site of the lumber buildings where he could hitch the animal to the peak of one building buried in the sand. The Brandywine was still pure enough to take a drink.

It made sense to build mills on the waterways connected to Lake Michigan, as the lumber barons needed ingenuity

*Palisades Pier. 1905.*

to get their wares to market. Lake travel was, by far, the most advantageous. Paul, expecting to use waterpower for his upright saw, met failure. Lumbering is a year-round business and only spring season saw enough water dammed up from the Brandywine for regular use. According to John Spelman of Covert, the mill was moved, the boarding house was burned or rotted, and piers were washed away. Exactly when this happened is not clear.

Other stories have survived concerning the failure of Paul's mill and shady dealings by the lumber industry. One claimed an agent from the east, sent to view a vast forest being sold by Farnum, was so drunk he was shown a small tract of pine from various angles all day, to make him think it was a vast tract of pine. He was bamboozled and overestimated the amount of timber to his eastern company. Another story said he was shown hemlock, instead of pine, and didn't know the difference. Robert Beattie tells of lumber shipped to Bangor from the north, which was improperly accounted for. The cheating of the woods boss - who had already disappeared with his pay - was discovered when the wood ran out too early. Beattie says the man eventually was lost off of a boat in mid-Lake Michigan - his stealing bringing him to a bad end. For whatever reason, Paul's sawmill was not a success.

Hawks and Lambert then came to Covert from Niles, in 1867, and brought an upright steam sawmill into the village. They hauled lumber to Paulville by horses and oxen and – according to one source – used the pier that Paul had built. In 1868, they sold their mill to Packard,

*Hawk and Lambert Mill in Covert.*

Sons and Co. In 1867, a second mill, called North Mill, was built by Wm. O. Packard, Joshua Packard, and Oren Shaw, on section 2SE 1/4. Lumber from there was hauled by team to Paulville Pier. A third mill was also built, as well as a wooden railroad from Covert to Paulville and a second one from North Mill to Ludwig Pier in South Haven Township.

The height of the lumber era in Michigan was 1860 to 1880. In 1860, no lumber dealers were located in South Haven or Covert, with only one in Bangor and two in Watervliet. By 1875, five were listed in South Haven, seven in Bangor, and Packard Sons and Co. in Covert.

Packard Sons and Co. acquired thousands of acres of land for a supplement of timber. They ran three mills and two horse railroads with two substantial piers and also owned a general store during the height of the lumber era. The two mills in Covert were capable of cutting 4,000,000 ft. of lumber per year, while the North Mill site had an even greater capacity. The hamlet at North Mill included a Spelman store, a pickle factory, and a railroad station.

One George Beattie worked in the Covert sawmills as a boy peeling hemlock bark for tanning hides and curing leather. He remembered the shanties that sprang up all around the Village of Covert. One of the sites was located just about at the intersection of I-196 and the Covert road. The shanties were located just to the southwest, before reaching the location of the future Blue Star Highway.

Mr. Spelman said that oak, white ash, hickory, elm, and some pine and white wood were cut. Some beech was also cut for shavings to make vinegar. Firewood for

*Packard Mill in Covert.*

*Woman going to Packard Hamlet store.*

*Above: Shanties near Covert.*
*Inset: Lumbering tools used in cutting and skidding logs.*
*Below: Lumbermen at work.*

*Above: Team skidding logs.*

*Right: Log-transporting tool pulled by horses, discovered in the Palisades meadow by Cecil Burrous.*

*Below: July 30, 1899 picture of lumbermen in Lawrence, MI.*

heating purposes was also shipped from Paulville. S. H. Shattuck, who at age 15 was drawing sawdust from North Mill to Ludwig's Pier, was able to list 20 varieties of lumber scaled that year.

In the forests, the cutters or sawyers were so expert that they could fell a log in the exact spot they indicated. They used axes and cross cut saws. Before cutting a tree, they placed logs crosswise to the tree so when it fell the log could be sawed without dulling the saw in the dirt. Logs were transported more than one way. The lifting of logs onto log "boats" was done with chain and horsepower. When a log fell onto a boat, the horse team pulled it to a bobsled where the log would be rolled. This was called "skidding the logs." When enough logs were skidded, the teams were hitched to the bobsled and they were off. The boat was returned to pick up the next log.

Another method of transporting was by the horse drawn tramways. This eased the movement of the logs over sandy or swampy roads. Mr. Spelman recalled that the rails were of hardwood placed into grooves sawed into the ties and then wedged. The cars had iron flanged wheels and axles. The wooden flat beds projected over the wheels. When the horse came to a steep grade, other horses were stationed ready to give temporary assistance up the hill. Brakes were used on a downgrade. That way, roads did not need to be leveled. According to Arthur Quick, "The old tram road passed within fifty feet of the old spring (in Brandywine meadow behind Joneses cottage) and a wagon road passed it on a hillside terrace just above where the main road now passes; so this old spring with its clear cold water was known for miles around by woodsmen and pioneer settlers."

In an 1873 South Haven Sentinel article, Ludwig's Pier is described extending 300 feet into the lake, with 600 feet of dockage. Vessels could be loaded from both sides in six to eight hours. Arthur Quick, quoted in old Patters, described the Paulville Pier this way: "The old loading pier at Paulville stood some 40 rods into the water. It was 50 feet wide. It held four team tracks and a clear space for the piling and handling of the lumber for loading onto lake steamers. Beech and oak pilings topped with heavy planking formed the body of the pier. The tram tracks are all 'ribbon tracks.' In winter months, these piers were loaded with cordwood and logs to hold them against the destruction of waves and ice." Millions of feet of lumber and logs, tons of tan bark, and thousands of shingles were loaded on the lake freighters each summer. Much of this material went to Chicago, especially after the disastrous 1871 Chicago Fire.

The Covert area escaped from the massive fire in Michigan on October 8, 1871- a fire so broad in scope it resulted in more devastation than either the Chicago or Peshtigo, Wisconsin fires that happened at that same time. Perhaps ten or more deaths in Michigan were attributed to the fire, while in Wisconsin, with a fire fed by hurricane-force winds, over 1000 people died. One of the worst droughts on record for the northern U.S. set up conditions for the holocaust in Michigan. Fire moved from St. Joseph to Manistee and most of Holland, Michigan was lost. Lumbering mills and wooden side walks burned and over 1000 people in Manistee became homeless. The thumb area of the state was hardest hit. Somehow the Paulville/South Haven area survived. Robert Beattie remembered that in South Haven, in 1871, lumber was stacked high on the Black River for rebuilding after the Chicago Fire.

Smaller sailing vessels were used to carry the cargo. They carried lumber, fruits and vegetables, flour – and passengers. Sometimes boats had to wait for enough wind to catch their sails. During a severe windstorm, the

---

**In the center of our present golf course there was once quite a settlement of cabins and a large boarding house to care for the men working in the forest and in the sawmill located on the adjacent stream, where a dam had been built. Where these cabins stood, we now find small areas of a dense growth of Bouncing Betty and Cypress Spurge, clumps of lilac and snowberries, old-fashioned red and yellow roses, and nearby - in the 'rough' near the creek bank - a thrifty little grapery of Concords.... This all tells a mute story of the early pioneers, coming west with ox teams, settling in a new country in the midst of dense forests, miles from other settlements and bases of supplies; but bringing with them plants, flowers, and fruit cuttings endeared to them in their eastern homes.... What stories may lie back of these mute evidences ... though the principals have passed on.**

*From Arthur C. Quick's Wild Flowers of the Northern States and Canada, p.202.*

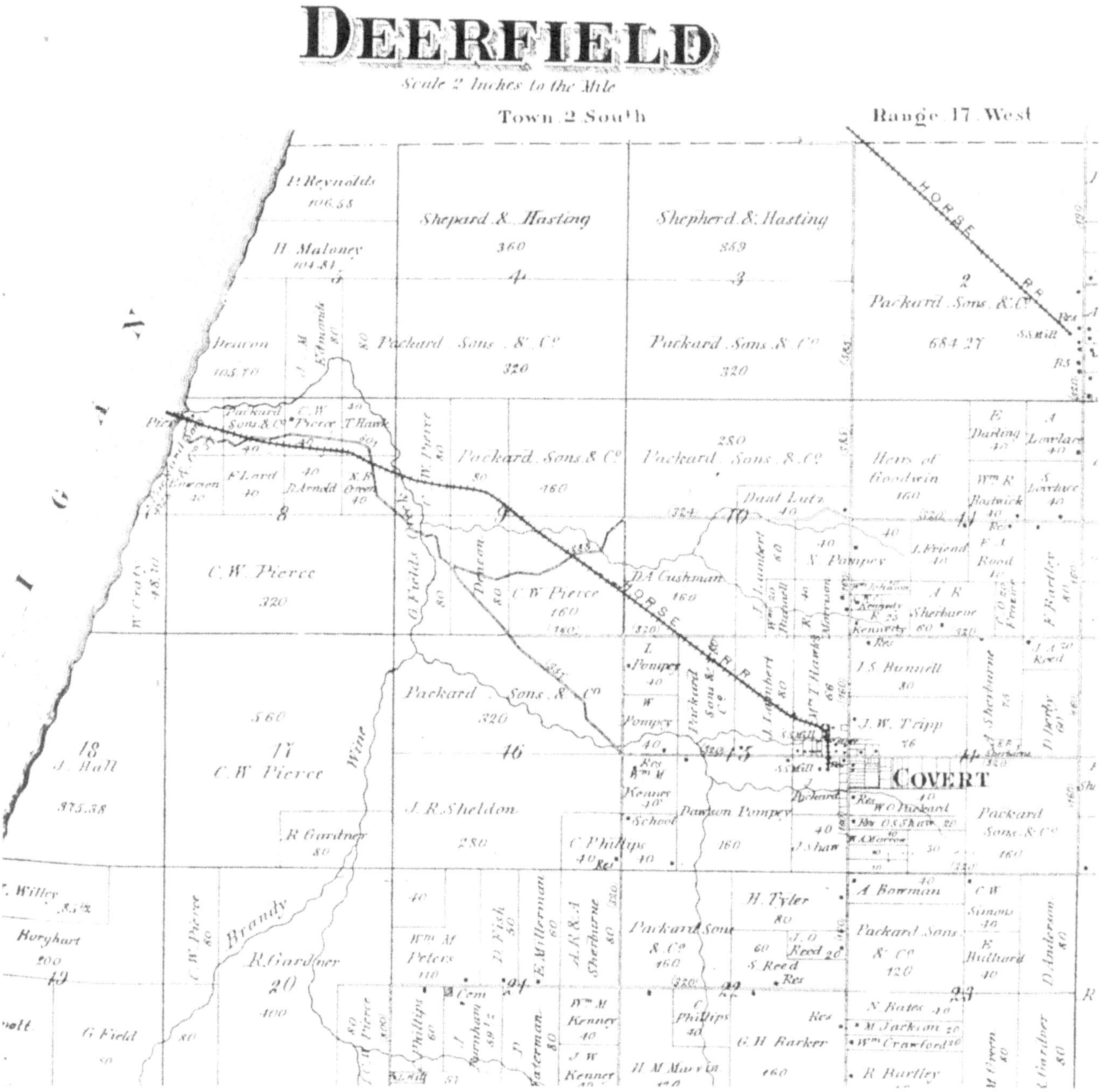

# DEERFIELD

*Scale 2 Inches to the Mile*

Town 2 South — Range 17 West

*This map showing the Horse Railroad between Covert and the Brandywine Pier was made under the direction of D. J. Lake, C. E., based on an actual survey. It was printed in the <u>Atlas of Van Buren County</u> dated 1873, published by C. O. Titus.*

*Right: Scene in a Covert sawmill.*

schooners were usually anchored well out in deep water. Some of the oldest settlers remembered that at least one ship went down at the Paulville Pier, having been lashed to the pier at the onset of a sudden blow and, thus, unable to get loose to seek safety in deeper water. The old anchor of the boat now sits in the Circle at Palisades Park.

Much press has recently gone into the search for the Chicora, a ship that went down near our area in 1895 and has never been located. The following eye witness story of its floundering was told to Irving Pershing, a newspaperman.* In 1895, 16 year old Henry Goss, who lived on a farm at Paulville one mile inland from the lake, was out during a terrible storm, bringing a load of corn from Bangor to his farm. He arrived about 9:00 p.m. After supper, when he went out to tend his horses, he heard a fog horn from north of Paulville Pier. He believed it was a steamer in trouble on the lake. He and his mother went down to the pier. Out in the lake, beyond three tiers of icebergs, they heard the whistle plainly again. About every ten minutes for one hour the whistle repeated. The last sound was different – more like a gurgle or the sound of engines exploding. No one believed his story until hundreds of barrels of flour washed up on the beach. The Chicora sinking took place just as the telegraph was coming into use. As the story was breaking, daily reports came from different locations around the shore, from Holland to Chesterton, Indiana. When the ship is finally located, some of the unanswered questions about what really happened that night may be answered.

*Source: Lane, Kit, <u>Chicora: Lost on Lake Michigan</u>, Saugatuck Maritime Series Book 3.

*North Mill picnic c. 1900.*

Certainly lumbering was an important industry in Michigan. Five of the first 28 governors were lumbermen. However, there are differing perspectives on the legacy it left the state. One interpretation suggested that our white pine and hardwood forests "are now man-made deserts of fire-blasted stumps and slashings." On the other hand, the romance of the changing times, from lumbering to farming, was caught by Edwin Barnum's poem at a Paw Paw Association meeting in 1873, excerpts from which read:

> I've seen the sturdy axmen, with well directed blow,
> Attack the mighty forest and lay the monarchs low.
> I've seen the hungry fire consume your heaps of logs
> And seen the ditcher's spade remove the marshy bogs;
> And here upon the openings, no timber in the way,
> I've seen the patient oxen move on from day to day.
> The sod was quite unyielding, the roots were tough and long,
> To draw the heavy "breaker," the team it must be strong.
> Sometimes eight yoke of cattle were tethered in a row,
> Their march across the breaking was powerful, but slow.
> The steady watchful driver made each perform his toil;
> The father held the plow that turned the virgin soil,
> For he had early learned that by the plow to thrive
> Himself must either hold, or take the whip and drive.
>
> Thus by your patient labor and well directed skill
> You have subdued the county and conquered it at will;
> Have swept away the forests, removed the stumps and stones,
> Torn down your lowly cabins and built your stately homes;
> Have planted fruitful orchards whose tops now kiss the breeze,
> Have made our pleasant highways and lined them well with trees.
> Have drained the stagnant marshes and bridged the brooks and rills,
> Threw dams across our rivers and built thereon our mills.
> As said an ancient prophet, although 'twas said in prose,
> You have removed the bramble and planted there the rose;
> Cut down the noxious thistle, removed the ugly thorn,
> And planted out the fir tree, your dwellings to adorn.
> We know your task was arduous and troubles thick and fast,
> We welcome you as victors; you overcame at last.*

*Printed in 1912 <u>History of Van Buren County.</u>

*A.S. and Mrs. Packard, their residence and saw mill in covert.*

The people who settled Covert - and the Packards who made a success of their mills during the prosperous era of lumbering - can be credited with the growth of the village. After lumber, of course, the village did not die. Many settlers were already involved deeply in growing and shipping fruit. Stores had grown up, beginning with the first store in the first building erected by the Packards. It was a two-story building with a basement and is now the library and historical museum, with its extraordinary collection begun by Pearl Sarno.

The lumbering families tended to come from the Northeast, as far as Massachusetts. Packards, Spelmans, Roods, and Shaws were among the earliest. But people of many different backgrounds emigrated or settled in the Covert area: Polish, American Indian, Italian, Scandinavian, Jewish, German and Black. The latter were integrated into the society in an exceptional way. They were included in the economic, political, and social fabric of life in Covert. For example, from the beginning in the 1860's, schools were important and were fully integrated. Prosper Phillips, a black citizen, built the first school. When the school population was large enough, it was organized into six districts and Paulville School on Section 9 was among them. At one time, Pearl Sarno's father was director of that school and she attended there. Eugene Phillips later was to build many of the Palisades Park cottages.

Socially, the entire population interacted. Not all abolitionists in the North who fought for the end of slavery wished to see intermixing of the people socially. But in Covert it happened. In 1896, Plessy vs. Ferguson legislation officially set up segregation and Indiana, Illinois, Michigan and Ohio were the frontiers for the idea in the Midwest. But not in Covert. The black population was scattered throughout the township so every white family had a black neighbor. The very year that Plessy vs. Ferguson went into effect, a Covert black man won a lawsuit against a white man, even after the case went to the Michigan Supreme Court. Blacks were elected to important positions in Covert at the very time discrimination laws were being enacted elsewhere. Several blacks were counted among the prosperous of the village; they were a force economically. Much of this can be attributed to the forcefulness of the blacks who came there; credit can also be given to the abolitionist reading materials promoted in the schools. The mail carrier for Palisades Park, Phyllis Burton, says the feeling of neighborliness across ethnic boundaries still exists today.

Fruit farming was significant at the end of the 1800's. In 1949, John Spelman recalled, "My first contact with the blueberry industry in Covert was when I was a boy eight years old, living in the parsonage at Covert. One morning when we were eating a late breakfast, an Indian, I think his name was Wesaw, came to our door with a basket nearly full of huckleberries for sale. My father wanted the basket; in order to buy the basket, he had also to buy the huckleberries. The basket was made from one piece of elm bark and here is the basket, 62 years old."* When he grew up, Spelman discovered that the sandy acidic soil was perfect for growing the local wild berries, so he went into the business. In the 1930's, he became the King of Blueberries. In 1953, he sold his cropland to an adjacent farm and the owner became the largest blueberry grower in the U. S. Spelman also had seven stores. One, for awhile, was at the railroad station stop in Packard. Fruit from the entire area was processed and shipped from there. Covert became one of the largest fruit producing centers in the fruit belt. The Sarnos were another family who settled in Covert and were known for their fruit farming. Grandma Sarno had a farm wagon. She used to say, "This is fresh; I picked it myself." Later, she had a small stand; later still, that was enlarged.

Genevieve Rood Bentley, whose grandparents arrived in Covert among the earliest settlers, remembers that after her parents moved to South Haven, she was allowed, in 4th grade, to walk to the KLS & C station downtown and pay 10 cents for fare to Covert. Being let off at the depot, she walked to the family farm to visit. "The best part of that was stopping at Iversons' farm adjoining the south border of the family farm. Iversons made ice cream which they delivered by wagon to Palisades Park. Mrs. Iverson would make me a little cone on a tiny waffle iron, then shape it and fill it for me."*

Mr. Quick gained an interest in growing an orchard when he bought the land that became Palisades Park. He gave up after harsh weather brought failed crops. Indeed, in October of 1906, many fruit farmers lost their entire crop. On October 8th there were green leaves on the trees, sap in the wood, and no frost. On October 9th, six inches of snow fell; by the next morning it was eight degrees above zero. Many trees were killed and others injured beyond recovery. The Covert Fruit Company, of Packard, Rood, and Spelman, lost all of the apples they had purchased that were on the trees. Those on the ground were saved by a covering of snow. According to Genevieve Rood Bentley, nearly all the peaches in Michigan froze. Many large fruit farms just disappeared. By then, Arthur Quick had turned his attention to building a summer settlement, rather than farming.

Genevieve Rood Bentley said, "Palisades Park resort area was on Lake Michigan, three miles west of the farm. There were two hotels – Sturtevant Lodge and Ballou Inn. The surrounding area had many private cottages. Mother and Aunt Clara each had a 'lot' in the Park. I remember going there as a family equipped to spend the night, taking two-quart zinc-topped blue mason jars of lemonade and 'ginger ale' (water flavored with powdered ginger and sugar). It was exciting to see Mother cook over an open campfire. In those days, there was a lot of driftwood on the beach. My delight was to climb to the top of a dune and come flying down taking great strides. It was in a meadow, just before the ravine entrance to the Park where I saw my first airplane. It looked just like the picture of Kitty Hawk. One of the cottages at the Park, named Fern Hill (#68), was where we spent our honeymoon. Since my siblings had come from far and wide, we had a family reunion there the second day." *

In the early days, many visitors to Palisades arrived from Chicago via the Fruit Belt Line, a train that stopped in Covert and was a connection to boats in South Haven. They often hooked up with Shattucks in Covert, for a ride through sand hills to the Park. In 1910, there were seven regular trains per day, from June 1st to the end of October. By 1920, this changed to six per day, with only three or four in the winter. Roads improved and cars were more common. By 1938, only three freight trains passed through; after several years, the depot closed.

The Park was described in the 1912 History of Van Buren County in this way: "Abrupt and picturesque hills line the shores, some almost worthy of being called mountains. Indeed, one of them bears the name of "Thunder Mountain" from which tradition has it that, in an early day, strange sounds emanated resembling subdued thunder about which weird tales are related. It is said that the vicinity was at one time a rendezvous for counterfeiters and other criminals, but these stories are probably all imaginary ...."

Arthur Quick referred to the Thunder Mountain at Palisades as one involving Indian lore. It is quite possible that the Thunder Mountain south of Palisades is the authentic Indian site, being one of the most significant hills along the Van Buren lakeshore. As to criminals in the area, Palisades Park has known its share.

Several parks and resorts developed along the western edge of Covert Township, with its wide beaches and dunes. Linden Hills, which property was bought by Drs. Vaughn and Gunsaul in 1900 from delinquent taxes, dates its opening to 1903. Palisades Park, which had been acquired by Quick in 1892, announced its incorporation in 1905. Covert Township Park began development in 1924. Pearl Sarno camped there with her family each year and it is used regularly today for camping and scouting trips. Forest Dunes evolved south of Covert Park. For years, a

*Covert Museum files.*

store on the highway there was frequented by all of the lakeshore people

In later years, John Spelman's memoirs stated that "Covert Township's greatest wealth today is no doubt the dune country along Lake Michigan – the summer homes and resorts of Palisades Park and Linden Hills. The name Palisades Park, however, became well known in Michigan, not for natural beauty, but because of harnessing the atom for electricity by what will be known as Palisades Consumer Power Plant."

It is good to stop and think about all of the extraordinary people who had a part in developing the lakeshore, and the interesting, hard-working, and diverse people from Covert who have remained involved with Palisades Park over the years. It is no wonder the early Park people so enjoyed and admired all of those with whom they were in contact. The latter were an important and integral part of the Park's summer world.

*Map c. late 1800's showing "Lumber and Wood R.R." between Covert and Ludwig Pier.*

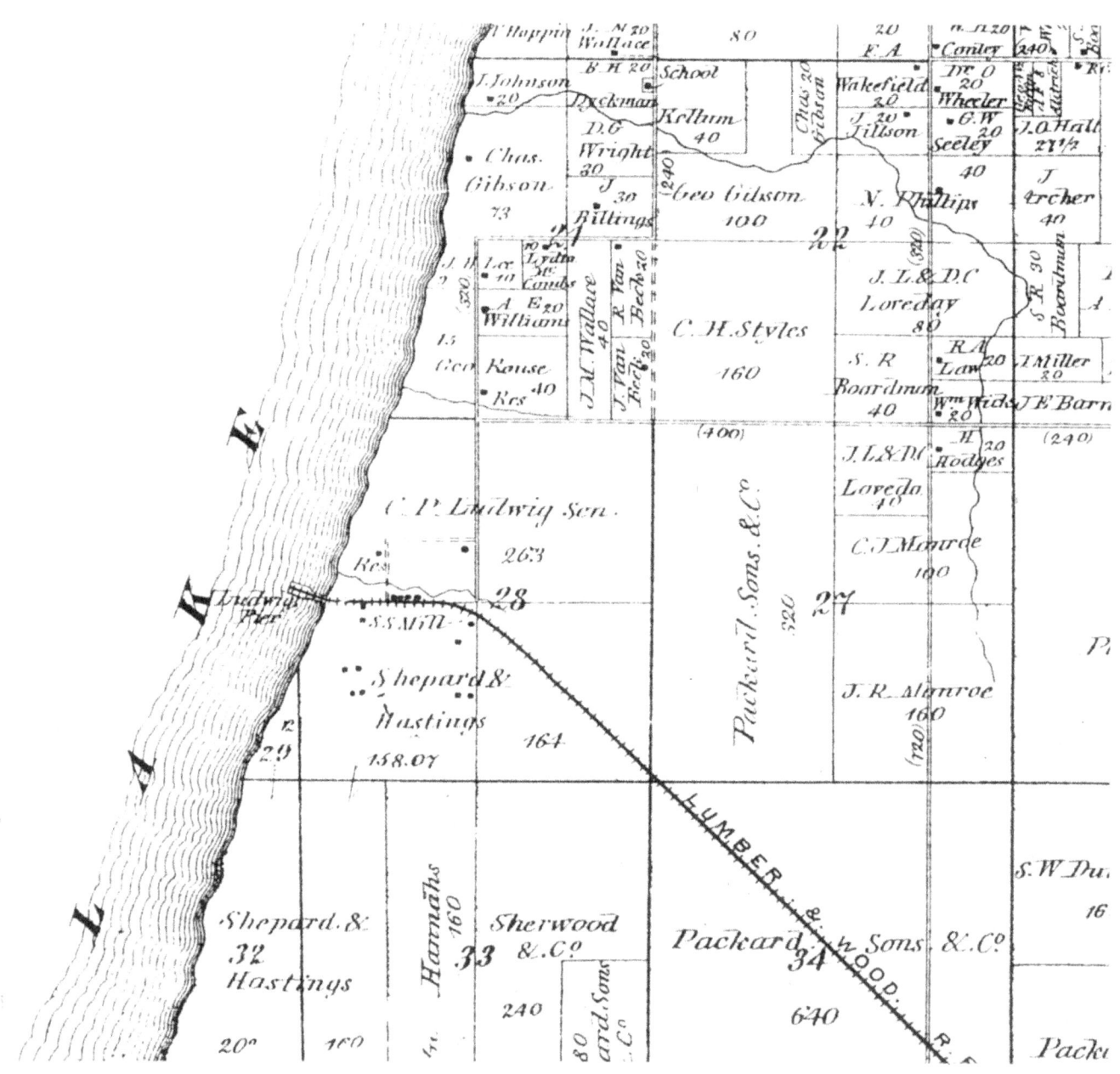

> As late as 1893, the village of Covert still resembled a typical lumber town. Most of the houses were small and carried nature's own decorations of moss and lichens on their exteriors. Only one lone house sported a coat of paint. The old sawmill was in occasional use still, and there were several stores with their inevitable potbellied stoves, nail-keg seats, and cracker barrels; here was enacted daily and nightly the rustic scenes that we occasionally see in the movies today.
>
> - A. C. Quick

## Sources for Previous Article

Beattie, Robert, <u>History of the Beattie Family and Memoirs</u>, Covert Historical Museum.

Bentley, Genevieve rood, <u>Memoirs of a Lady in a Hurry:</u> Personal Unpublished Paper from the Covert Museum files.

Cox, Anna Lisa, <u>A Pocket of Freedom: Blacks in Covert, Michigan, in the Nineteenth Century.</u>

Covert Museum files.

"Covert Pioneer Turning 95," <u>The News Palladium</u>, Benton Harbor, MI, date unknown.

Flagg, Vivian, <u>Outline of Covert History as Compiled by L. L. (Vivian) Flagg</u>: Personal Unpublished Papers from the Covert Museum files, Spring, 1969.

"From the Michigan Lumberman," <u>South Haven Sentinel</u>: August 30, 1873.

<u>History of Berrien and Van Buren Counties Michigan</u>, Van Buren History Section: D. W. Ensign Company, 1880.

Lane, Kit, <u>Chicora Lost on Lake Michgan</u>, Saugatuck Maritime Museum Series, Book 3.

"Michigan Yesterday," <u>The Michigan Laker</u>, date unknown.

"Packard Sons and Company," <u>The News Palladium</u>, Benton Harbor, MI, date unknown.

<u>Palisades Park Review, 1905-1968.</u>

Quick, Arthur, <u>Wild Flowers of the Northern States and Canada</u>: 1939.

Rowland, O.W., <u>History of Van Buren County, A Narrative Account of its Historical Progress, Its People and Its Principal Interests</u>, Vol. 1: 1912.

Sarno, Pearl, <u>A Look At Covert's Heritage</u>: 1976.

"South Haven Roadways Trace Trail History," <u>Herald Palladium</u>, Benton Harbor/St. Joseph, October 18, 1992.

Spelman, John R., Personal Unpublished Papers from the Covert Museum files.

Stieve, Jeannette, "Robert Beattie 1845-1924, <u>Pioneer Days in South Haven.</u>

Titus, C. O., <u>Atlas of Van Buren County Michigan</u>: 1873.

Tripp Family: Personal Unpublished Paper from the Covert Museum files, April 22, 1924.

Weissert, Charles A. "Area Man Had Streamline Previewing Travel of Today," <u>Kalamazoo Gazette</u>, June 5, 1947.

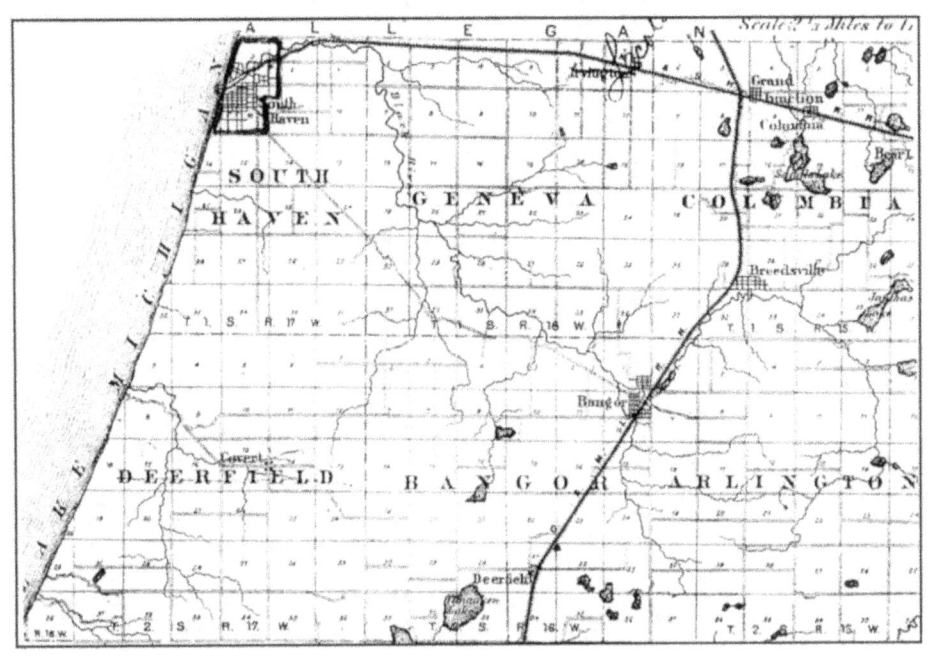

*Early roads during Deerfield Township days - showing none along lake shore and one between Paulville and Covert. From 1873 <u>Atlas of Van Buren County.</u>*

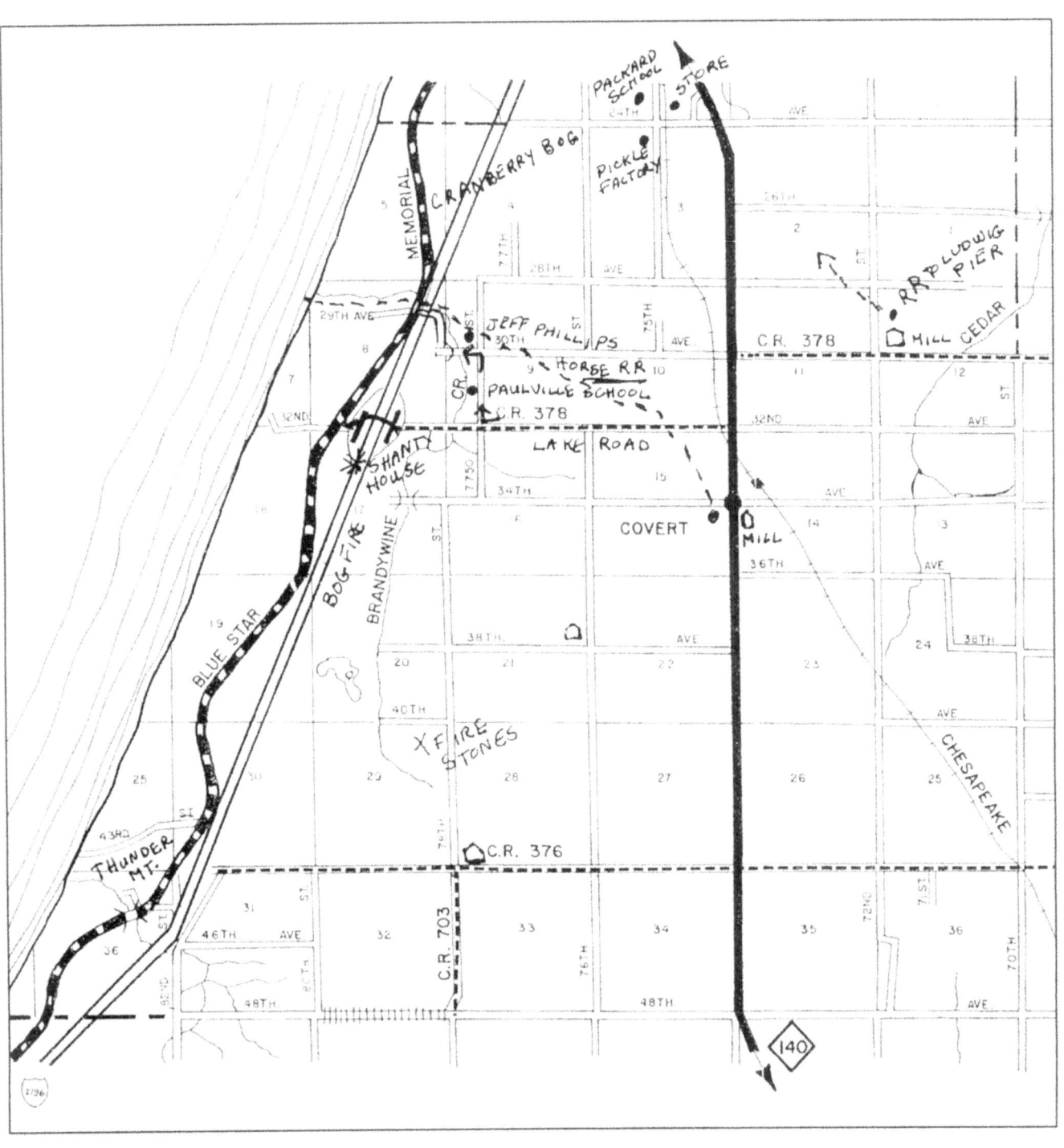

# Then and Now: South Haven of 1902 and 2002

By Becky Burkert, Editor and General Manager
South Haven Tribune, September 29, 2002, p. 3B.

What was life like in South Haven 100 years ago in 1902? If you look at the numbers, not much different than today. A glance at early records indicates that the town had 4000 residents, versus the 5500 who live here today. There were architects, attorneys, barbers, resorts, dentists, banks, bakeries, factories, schools, and churches – just like today.

But a closer look tells a much different story. For instance, a number of the ravines that one time existed in town, such as the one located just east of the Center and Phoenix Street intersection of downtown, no longer are noticeable. Over the years, many of the ravines over the city's streets have been filled in. Although you could use the steel Dyckman Avenue bridge to get from the south side to the north side of the city, a quicker method was to hop on a ferry boat.

Churches – though they bear the same name from 100 years ago – are now located in different buildings, including St. Basil's, Hope Reformed Church, First United Methodist Church, First Congregational Church, and First Baptist Church.

The electricity and phone services we take so much for granted were relatively new for South Haven residents in 1902 …. [they] weren't introduced to the city until 1895. Nobody in 1902 owned a car, then called "horseless carriage." Hitching posts for horses were the norm on downtown streets. And although the city had an assortment of businesses downtown, they were quite a bit different from today's stores. Back then downtown businesses included two confectionery shops, ten drug stores, six "dry goods" stores, four furniture stores, an ice house, three hardware stores, three feed shops, three liveries, a mason, two music shops, three newspapers, a planing mill, four photographers, several ship carpenters, four shoe repair shops, four tailors, a spa, eight real estate agents, and restaurants. In all, there were nearly 500 businesses operating in South Haven in 1902, and more than 150 resorts, many of which consisted of rooms let by home owners (similar to today's small bed and breakfast inns).

In 1902, people seeking recreation could go to one of two bowling alleys – the Brunswick Billiard Hall and Bowling Alley, corner of Phoenix and Kalamazoo Streets, or Lakeside Bowling Alley on Williams Street ; attend a play at the Selkirk Opera House at 419 Phoenix Street or the Leighton Opera House on Phoenix Street; dance at the Dunkley Pavilion at the foot of Kalamazoo Street; listen to the Citizens Marine Band at French's Hall on Phoenix Street; swim in Lake Michigan; canoe on the Black River; or go sailing on a pleasure boat on Lake Michigan.

The streets fronting the Black River – Water and Williams Streets – were much busier than today in terms of businesses. Lumber yards, boat docks for the large steamers from Chicago, and the Pierce-Williams Company fruit packaging plant lined the streets along the south side of the Black River. On the north side of the Black River, the Michigan Central Railroad depot was the site of much fruit shipping as farmers brought wagon loads of fruit to ship to markets in other cities and towns. Fruit was also loaded at the various docks along the Black River channel destined for Chicago markets.

*Above: Phillips Grocery Store in South Haven c. 1918*

*Below: Train in South Haven area c. 1918.*

**SOUTH HAVEN BEACH FUN c. 1910.**

*Paulville Pier pilings remaining in the water by Sturtevant Lodge c. 1920's.*

# Piers

By Bill Potter

## Paulville Piers

Two piers at Palisades Park (then called Paulville) were built in the 1870's – 1880's to load lumber from the saw mill operations in the Paulville and Covert areas into sailing vessels for transport to Chicago and Milwaukee. One pier was located in front of what today is the Old Pier cottage (#45), and the other in front of what later became Sturtevant Lodge (now Master Lodge #53). After lumbering ceased, the piers were no longer used and they deteriorated rapidly.

An excerpt from the January 1, 1940, Benton Harbor News Palladium describes the huge size of these piers, extending some 660 feet – over two football fields or 40 rods – out into the lake:

> The sturdy, water-worn piles standing in the shallow water directly in front of Sturtevant Lodge are mute evidence of the days when this place was known as Paulville and several boats were loaded each day during the shipping season with lumber, shingles, and tan bark from the forests and mills of Covert township. This loading pier, in use during the 1870's and 1880's, was built some 40 rods out into the water. It was 50 feet wide, held four tram, or horse railroad car tracks, and a clear space 12 feet square for the piling and handling of the lumber in loading. Beech and oak piles topped with heavy planking formed the body of the pier. To save it from the destruction of winter storms, it was heavily loaded with cord wood and logs. Much of the material shipped from Paulville went directly to Chicago. The breakwater at Michigan City was built from 12 by 12 white wood timbers, ranging in length from 12 to 36 feet, cut in the forests of the township.

Arthur Quick, the founder of Palisades, described the lumber operations in more detail on page 50 of his classic book, <u>Wild Flowers of the Northern States and Canada</u>, printed in 1939:

> Sixty to eighty years ago this entire country inland was heavily timbered. A large part of this particular township was owned by Senator Alfred S. Packard, from whom we purchased the Palisades Park tract. He had large lumbering interests hereabouts, a sawmill here on the creek (Brandywine) and others back inland a few miles. A wooden-rail, horse tramroad ran from the mills down to the lake front here, which was then known as Paulville Piers. These two piers ran out into Lake Michigan, and here the sawed lumber was loaded onto small sailing schooners, after having been brought down over the tramroad on cars drawn by one horse.

The untreated wood pilings and superstructure didn't last long without constant rebuilding, due to rot, storm damage, and ice damage. Only the submerged pilings endured through the years, and were still visible and a hazard to boats well into the 1940's.

*Chart by Bill Potter. Three piers drawn to scale.*

## Palisades Pier

In 1910, another – narrower, 8 foot wide, and much shorter – pier was built at the Clubhouse Beach. Palisades Pier served visitors arriving from and departing to South Haven by motor launch. The pier's deck was made in short sections which were removed during the winter months to prevent their destruction. Pictures suggest that these sections did not fit together evenly; the result - although apparently a popular place to sit and stroll - as well as a needed docking spot for the south Haven boat service - looks somewhat wobbly.

*Remnant Paulville Pier pilings. Sturtevant Lodge Pier closest. Old Pier cottage Pier in background. c. 1913.*

*Palisades Pier c. 1913.
Remnants of the two Paulville piers
can be seen in the background.*

This pier was not always usable, as described in the News Palladium, January 1, 1940, article:

*"COVERT, Dec. 30 -- 'Man over board?' shouted R. D. Hempy, seated at the oars of a row boat which was bringing tourists from the launch, running from South Haven to Palisades Park, on a day when the lake was too choppy for the usual unloading at the pier which stood on the shore just west of the club house. The "man" in question happened to be a lady who preferred standing to being seated, as she had been advised. The sudden grounding of the boat toppled her into shallow water at the very feet of A. C. Quick, manager and promoter of the park, who was assisting the guests as they came ashore. The lady was quite unhurt except for a thorough ducking and a resulting attack of hysteria.*

*"This amusing incident occurred back in the early 1900's when Palisades Park was in its infancy insofar as resort development was concerned. Since that time, it has been made the most accessible, well-developed summer play ground on Covert township's lake front, with R. D. Hempy and A. C. Quick still active in park affairs."*

*Closeup of Paliasades Pier showing the removable deck sections. c. 1913.*

# Chapter 2

# The Early Years
# 1905-1920

*1903 - Orville and Wilbur Wright make the first airplane flight;
1905 - Arthur Quick starts South Haven Palisades Park Company;
1908 - Henry Ford introduces the Model T; 1912 - Titanic sinks;
1913 - 16th Amendment to the Constitution gives Congress power to levy income taxes;
1914 - World War I begins; 1918 - World War I ends.*

*Arthur Quick reading in the "tent camp." Probably 1906. Julia Quick remembered camping that year; only one cottage had been built and that was Treetops.*

## **The Early Years**

Palisades Park started with Arthur Quick. So, too, does this section, introducing the man and, through some of his written documents, the initial development of this area. Early pamphlets flesh out some of Quick's plans for this new venture. Nine interviews, supplemented by written memoirs and letters, give personal glimpses of the neophyte Palisades Park.

Julia Quick, Arthur Quick's daughter, was ten the year she and her family put up their tents on the ridge where the Richmond/Owens/Brand cottages now stand. The Quicks spent that first summer in Palisades. The year was 1906, the 205 acres of the Park having been incorporated the previous August. Remains of the deserted lumber camp were still to be found in what was to become Palisades Park's golf course. It was in that same year that plans for the First Subdivision, about 20 acres in size, were drawn by Quick and Olaf Benson and Company, of Chicago.

Originally, the Park was called the South Haven Palisades Park Company. Arthur Quick served as President, F. S. Cable as First Vice-President, Charles D. Spaulding as Second Vice-President, Edwin C. Wyman as Secretary/Treasurer, and Harrison M. Parker as Chair of the Executive Committee.

Although in its first year Palisades housing was limited to tents, a building boom of sorts soon got underway. Lots and stock were sold. Starting with Treetops - the first cottage built by the Reverend Shreck, from England - and the cluster of buildings around the Circle, a small community began to evolve. Ballou Inn, then a rooming-boarding house, and its two neighboring cottages, Graystone and Oceana, were built by the Robert Ballou family. They molded their own cement blocks, using gravel from the beach. The Sturtevant family built four cottages as well as their Lodge. The careful plans that Mr. Quick drew, aided by Olaf Benson of the Chicago Park District (and designer of Chicago's Lincoln Park), meant roads and paths could be opened – and more cottages built. Although travel to Palisades was slow and difficult, early vacationers were generously served by local craftsmen, merchants, and farmers.

According to the August 2, 1952 Patter, there was "quite a substantial pier just below the Clubhouse road … used for entry by boat for several years, until better roads were built leading into the Park. It ran out into the water about 40 feet. The top was built in sections and each fall it was taken apart in sections," then pulled ashore with a team of horses.

Private vs. public pathways were a concern from the beginnings. Although Mr. Quick's walkways – intended for common use – were on the map, they had not all been developed immediately. Access to many cottages was limited and no doubt the issue of who could walk where was raised more than once. A 1915 agreement made among the owners of four lots near the water tower designed a path "for the exclusive use and benefit of the owners and occupants of said lots." That the agreement, which then reiterated that the path "shall not be made a public path," was drawn up legally suggests some early concern about property rights – though the history of the Park offers numerous cases in which boundaries have been treated lightly. Unfortunately, such questions are still at issue in 2003.

The interviews mentioning these early years at Palisades Park share many common images – Mr. Hempy and his horse-drawn wagon jingling down the beach; Tony Canonie, ice slung over his shoulder, whistling his way up to a delivery; children squealing as they crossed the swinging bridge over Brandywine Creek; finely dressed men and women promenading down the boardwalk to the Clubhouse on the beach; the golf course with its oiled sand greens; and the ever-present Mr. Quick, a maestro whose baton gave rhythm to the Park and directed its every harmony. How noteworthy that, of the 23 people interviewed in the mid-80's, ten had roots dating back to the first decades of Palisades. Although each interviewee had special reasons for his or her long love affair with the Park, all seemed to be drawn by its beauty, sense of community, and wholesome family atmosphere. The stability of these early families has enhanced a sense of tradition at Palisades; their heritage has been passed from generation to generation and from oldtimers to newcomers. Hear, then, some stories of the early years.

*Another group camping at Palisades. c. 1906.*

# Arthur Craig Quick

**In grateful memory of Arthur Craig Quick, 1864 – 1946. He loved nature. He developed and preserved this beautiful wooded Lake Michigan Duneland for us and for Posterity. Enjoy the beach, the lake, the breeze, the wild flowers, wild life and trees, the trails, the dunes – for all around a wonderful vacationland is found. Palisades Park Michigan, 1960.**

*Found on the bronze plaque in the Circle.*

Arthur Quick – the originator – surveyor, botanist, engineer, businessman, writer. Who was this man who started Palisades Park? A dreamer? A legend? An enigma? To many current Palisaders, he is a symbol – a memory to be admired despite its haziness. From those who knew him, a clearer picture arises. All agree with Pauline Sauer: "Arthur C. Quick - Park founder, owner, and long-time manager - was the central figure in the Park from the time he founded it until his death in the 1940's."

Certainly Arthur Quick was a dreamer. Many of the early documents advertising the Park give testament to his dream. In a first year sales brochure, South Haven Palisades Park Company, he wrote a "General Prospectus" outlining his plans for development of the new resort area. In it, he envisioned a clubhouse, hotel, pavilion, cottages, dam lake, boat house with boats and launches, bathing houses, a yacht club, and spring houses. Additionally, he promised cement walks, swings, rustic seats and bridges, an observation pavilion and flagstaff on the summit of Thunder Mountain, steps up Thunder Mountain and Palisades Hill, golf, tennis, ball grounds, and a shelter house with lockers. (This brochure also includes some ideas he would veto in his Park, such as "Sunday business," "saloons," or "trashy amusements.") Clearly, his dream was detailed and ambitious.

The legends surrounding Arthur Quick are many. Some remember him as a gentleman – a patriarch, though friendly and helpful. " We used to go up to the Clubhouse Saturday nights and he was always the host. He danced with all the ladies. He was very much the gentleman."

(Brand)** "I can remember Mr. Quick walking around with his navy or black suit on and a hat that was very dressy and a black tie that was very dressy. He was a patriarch." (Kropp) "Mr. Quick was always friendly and helpful, even bringing supplies to my brother who was out there occasionally in the spring or fall. Mrs. Quick was also very pleasant, gracious, and sweet, though she was hard of hearing. Kitty Wisson, Mr. Quick's second wife, was another friendly person who visited frequently with my mother." (M. Sauer)

"Quick was a great engineer and a fine Christian man. He had his whole life in the Park. He bought this thing and he had his own ideas how he wanted to develop it. You might not like it and I might not like it, but he persisted in it and he got it; he was the caretaker. He did all the work that the present manager does. He had no regular help. He prepared the roads. He did everything. He was wiry. He had Hempy when he needed a man. Hempy had a scraper to push the sand out. The place behind the hotel would fill up with drift sand. That's how they made that parking space. Quick's main job was to keep the roads up. He spent a lot of time doing that. He had help when he had to have it. It all came out of his pocket. The public didn't own any part of this Park. He had to do the selling and everything else, right on his own." (Lowrey)

"He did a great job modernizing the Park. When we got here in '33, there was running water – good water – all over the Park and electricity and telephone. We had septic tanks and inside toilets – everybody. There was no outside toilet within range of our cottage that I remember. Quick saw to that. There might have been only one light in the middle of the season, but we had a bathtub in the house. It wasn't very big, but I wasn't very big, either, so it worked out ok." (Lowrey)

His love for and knowledge of wildflowers can be seen in his book, Wildflowers of the Northern States and Canada. Its format – the reporting of flowers found on his weekly walks through the Park – suggests the time and care he took to nurture this Wildlife Sanctuary. "Mr. Quick was a very fine person - a naturalist, a botanist, and a business man. He kept beautiful flowerbeds in the cement-bordered beds at the Circle, or main business area, by Sturtevant Lodge, Ballou Inn, and the ice cream parlor. He also had some lovely flowerbeds in the Ravine after it was cleared of trees in preparation for being damned up to form a small lake for boating and canoeing. Mr. Quick was a fine botanist and knew all of the wildflowers in the Park." (P. Sauer)

*\*Quotes in this article are from interviews printed in full elsewhere in this volume.*

*Possibly Arthur Quick strolling on a path through the woods.*

Tony Malinowski recalls that Quick presented him with a booklet, which had been "printed on a limited basis" for Park residents. "It described the varieties of trees, shrubs, flowers, etc. – [even] squirrels, rabbits and other such creatures including skunks and possums and raccoons, warning residents to discourage 'em by keeping garbage containers sealed." Unfortunately, such booklet has not been found.

"Mr. Quick was a remarkable man, very intelligent. His book is an outstanding text. It was used over at Western Michigan in botany classes. He also wrote a genealogy of the Quick family, that went way back to Holland in the 1600's. Innovative recordings in it get away from the stereotype of genealogy. He just made it seem, even though you weren't a member of the Quick family, they became your family as you read it. The same way with the flowers of the area here: when you got in that book and read it, it was just fascinating. He didn't just tell about the flowers, but also the habitat. He wrote it by the week. He'd say, 'The first week in May, such and such is in bloom, and if you wander up the hill you'll find some other kind of plant …' and he did this every week. He told about things to see when you take a walk. He bought this land over here originally, after the turn of the century. And then, of course, he cleared some of the land, encouraged other people to come, and gradually cottages got built, and the Hotel. He was a good manager. There wasn't anything high-falutin' about him. He wanted people to come here more or less as a family group, to keep out rowdyism and that sort of thing. People could come up here with their family and just enjoy each other. He wasn't much on dress, though – he was shabby. He could dress formally, but as he wandered around the Park, he just fit himself into it and dressed accordingly. One who didn't know

*Sketch of Arthur Quick's cottage, now called Sp'eyeglass #85.*

him would think, 'Who is that character?' But he was far from a character. He was a very intelligent man." (Campbell)

But there was another side to this man. Ever the businessman, he was a supersalesman, persistent in courting future customers, especially first-time visitors to the Park. If a sale were to be made, he would be there. Presently, the Park is concerned about a limit of 200 cottages. However, an early map of Palisades shows that Mr. Quick had planned much more development. Forest Lowrey, referring to the divisions on that map, guessed "there were 800 or 900 of them, maybe 1000." And, continued Lowrey, "He would put a house on every lot – and did, on every one he could sell." The crowded area of early cottages built just behind the Circle attests to that. Bill Potter recalls that he was "a sly fox" in business matters. He certainly counted his pennies. As Tony Malinowski remembers, "He watched his pennies. He always told me, 'Hey, save your pennies.' Wait, how'd he say it? 'It makes a lot of cents to make a dollar.' I always remember that. Very good." Ruth Kropp remembered that "he had Joe Putz pull all the nails out of the boardwalk for the winter, and he'd save all of them, and the next spring Joe would use them over again." Tony Sarno, who spent several summers working in the Park, remembered him as "all business."

In his dignity, he must have been somewhat unapproachable. Tony Malinowski remembered a farewell party given to honor Tony's departure for the Navy. In the excitement of the moment, Tony surprised Mr. Quick with "a big Polish hug" – and speculated that "no one had ever hugged him before." Even losing his false teeth at a Clubhouse dance didn't alter his dignified demeanor, according to Ginny Coleman.

Tony Malinowski's letter to Betty Householder, dated October 16, 1987, starts where Tony started, with his gladiolus blooms, and brings life to the picture of Mr. Quick, as follows: "Our old farmhouse in Covert is where, while in high school, I'd plant gladiolus – cut and bundle the blooms and peddle them to Park people. Some even asked for glad bulbs [and] I'd oblige, mailing them in the fall. All this made me quite an entrepreneur – a word I hadn't learned until a few years ago – until Sir Quick caught up to me. He was furious that someone – a kid at that – was peddling goods without his permission; he had a great dislike for any peddlers, especially those of a certain nationality. That stopped my business – which would have stopped anyway, because I was to be in college the next year and had visions of making "real" money to pay for it. Quick's granite heart had a crack in it; when I told him of my future plans, he sent me to see Del Jones….[who] tolerated me for four years, plus one more right after WWII …. During all those years, my association with the Quick man were infrequent but memorable (to me) occasions…. He knew every resident, names of all, even the children, their home towns, their occupations, their quirks. Too, he talked about his trees, shrubs, plants, grasses, even insects (he knew their seasons, their areas – some thrived in high places, some in low). His park was his life; he was its supreme commander. Above all, he was a lonely man – probably fearful of damaging his image [as] the stern policeman and overseer of His Park. Though he scowled and scolded often, he loved everyone and everything in his domain."

Not all of Quick's ideas worked. The golf course was ended in the Depression. Lake Palisades was never dependable and, though there was at least one boat house, providing a place for boating never really materialized. Once, to keep cars out of the Park, he proposed that everyone buy small pieces of a parking area out by the tennis courts. Walking was to be the norm.

Frustrated that Linden Hills people used the Palisades boardwalk, he once erected a barbed wire fence to block their access. In <u>Linden Hills: A History of Covert Resort Association 1979</u> (p.11), Inger C. and Alex B. Claney remember this conflict. "We walked to Palisades each day to get the mail at the old Ballou Inn and maybe an ice cream cone (5 cents). In the beginning we came by train to Hartford, changed there to the Fruit Belt Line to Covert.

*Picnicers hiking to the lake on sand road. 1912.*

From there the Shattucks transported us and baggage, originally by carriage and later by car, to Palisades.... From Palisades we walked on a twenty-inch board walk carrying our luggage. Mr. Quick, the Palisades promoter, wanted to sell his lots so he did not like us Covert Resorters using his road and boardwalk. He finally created a barbed-wire fence at his south property line right down to the water's edge. This didn't last long – the wire was cut several times, the posts pulled up. He finally gave up."

His rules were to be followed. This was HIS Park and it was run HIS way. "If someone had a party on a Saturday night that he didn't like, that was kind of loud, he'd turn off their water. That brought them down on their knees." (Kropp) "We kids, when we were young and playing around the Park, would see Mr. Quick pop up when we didn't expect him. He'd keep his eyes on things. He'd patrol the park. In the later part of the year, he'd have his 32 rifle to shoot squirrels. He didn't like the squirrels damaging the trees." (Woodhouse) Paul Schlacks recalls Mr. Quick arriving just as Paul's father was unloading his groceries – which included some cases of beer. Mr. Quick would talk and talk – quite possibly aware that he was delaying the unpacking of the "forbidden spirits." Bert Henderson even tells of the secret poker games (which no doubt included liquid refreshments) in the basement of his present cottage, out of the oversight of the disapproving Mr. Quick. "He kept order in the Park and he loved it. He wanted it a certain way. He would have had a fit at some of the things that go on today. The erosion, and the kids running up and down the banks. He'd never let you do that. He was quite a character." (Tillson)

"Mr. Quick was always the old bear of the Park, and yet he was very, very nice. There were always kids who would try to cause him grief and trouble. He'd try to keep the gate down so that we'd have water in the Brandywine or up so we wouldn't, and some kids would do whatever he didn't want them to do. If he wanted the gate down, they'd put it up. Finally, he chained it and they got hacksaws and cut the chain. Mr. Quick was so patient with these kids, yet he'd be so mad at them. You'd look at him and you'd be scared to death of him because he looked so stern. He dressed formally, too – you always saw him in a coat and tie and vest and hat. He wasn't mean or anything – it was just the way he looked." (Borchert)

He was a man caught up in the prejudices of his day. Palisades was to cater to white, Protestant professionals, preferably connected to education, the arts, or business. All others were to be discouraged in – if not denied – their quest for access. Early ads proclaimed "No Hebrews." Rumor had it that "No Catholics," though not written, was another rule – or "No Italians." Several stories in the interviews illustrate this attitude that by today's standards would not be acceptable. Of course, as

*Quick's daughter Julia*

"He had a beautiful daughter, Julia. At one of the house parties (at the Wards) when we came up, all of the boys wanted to be the beau of Vashti's sister, Marian Ward. One of the boys fully expected that Marian was going to be his partner for the occasion and Marian was all signed up with somebody else. So the boy turned to Julia. He thought she was quite pretty and had really quite a nice time with her. They would go out on the beach, you know. He had the funniest things to say about Mr. Quick going out with the lantern and trying to find them. They were always dodging him." (Mavor)

One trait about Mr. Quick can be surmised– he didn't like to have his picture taken. Evidence? Amid the many old photographs we have discovered, we have found so few pictures of this man

So who was Arthur Quick? A man who loved this area, he remains somewhat of an enigma. Not quite the naturalist/environmentalist that we would have him be, more of a developer than we want to admit, a bit of a dictator, very much caught up in the prejudices of his time, but nonetheless the guiding spirit who made this place into his own image and to whom later generations owe much.

times have changed, both racial and religious barriers have relaxed. Indeed, the present day barrier seems to be more a financial one, as cottages are increasingly outpriced except for those who are relatively wealthy.

Perhaps because Mr. Quick was such a central figure in such a small community, he engendered his share of gossip. Mardy Mehagan Mavor remembered the time of his second marriage: "The Quicks had a cottage up on the hill, just beyond Treetops. Now called Sp'eyeglass #85. Well, if you think this whole Park wasn't in an uproar of gossip when Mr. Quick married Kitty Wisson (after the first Mrs. Quick died). She had been an old maid around the Park and we couldn't believe it. That time we had the cabaret, the tables were sold way in advance. It was shortly after Kitty had married Mr. Quick. She came up to the Clubhouse at 7:00 and said that she had come to the party. I asked if she had a ticket, and she said no. I said, 'I'm awfully sorry, but we are just sold out to the last inch of space and I don't have any place that I could really put you.' She replied, 'I am Mr. Quick's wife, and I'm coming to the party.' Well, I didn't want to get in wrong with Mr. Quick, after all, so we made a place for her."

*Cover of reprint of Arthur Quick's book.*

## Palisades Park Sketches: Do You Remember When?

*Arthur Quick, Palisades Park founder, excelled as both historian and writer. Besides his two books – one on wildflowers and the other on the genealogy of the Quick family – in the 30's he wrote a series of articles for the <u>Patter</u>, detailing some of the history of this area. These have been reproduced elsewhere, but give such valuable insight into the early days that we repeat two of them here.*

### From July 29, 1939 <u>Patter</u>
### Palisades Park Review 1905 – 1968

When the lumbering days were on here, just after the Civil War, the old stage coaches used to run from South Haven to Benton Harbor and on to Chicago. They crossed the Brandywine near the far end of our old golf course, hit the hill just a few feet east of our double tennis court and so on southwards, winding in and out between the dunes. This old road up the hill by the tennis courts is still there and very steep, but somehow they managed to climb it with their four-horse teams. Our ice truck still comes down that way sometimes, to save time.

That big old ash tree, some fifteen feet in circumference, in back of the garage and in front of the Ewing-Steele cottage*, years ago sheltered a barn at the foot of it; but the sand has blown in around the tree to such an extent that the barn is entirely buried. There may be some buried antiques there. Who knows?

*\*Now Golden cottage #48.*

When we first knew it, the oak tree by the hotel dining-room door was a little sapling. Right east of it, there was a high sand hill where the hydrangea mound now is, and directly beyond that was a deep bayou extending under where the garage now stands and quite up to the soda emporium. That high mound of sand was moved over into the bayou and leveled off much like it now appears.

We have photos taken before anything was built here showing the hillside where the Greystone and Ballou Inn stand, and all of the trees at the foot of this hill had all their bare roots exposed, the wind having blown the sand out from under them. These were later covered with sod.

Other early photos show our hills literally covered with the beautiful white blossoms of the trilliums in early May; but visitors who do not understand wild flowers, especially trilliums, have plucked the flowers each spring until now the hillsides in the older sections of the Park have seen a few trilliums left. The trillium is especially sensitive, and

*The "big old ash tree" - one of the biggest in the state of Michigan -is still there, by cottage #48, albeit missing some limbs.*

*Mr. Quick would be delighted to see the trillium in bloom each spring.*

when the flower is pulled off, the plant rarely survives. Everyone should remember this and help conserve this most beautiful of our numerous species of wild flowers.

Years before the steel bridge and dam were built, we had a curious cable bridge, 150 feet long, swung across the creek, suspended from large trees on either bank. On the two heavy cables, cross timbers were bolted, and on these, planks were laid lengthwise of the bridge, forming an excellent footbridge. It was the hugest kind of sport to get out in the middle of the bridge and make it sway side to side and up and down. Many similar bridges are still in use in our eastern states, spanning deep gorges and turbulent streams.

*The Palisades Pier.*

**From August 12, 1939 Patter**
**Palisades Park Review 1905 – 1968**

As mentioned in a former article, we built a substantial pier just below the Clubhouse road. This we used for several years until better roads were built into the Park. The pier ran out into about ten feet of water. The broad eight-foot top was built in sections and each fall we took this apart in 8 by 16 foot sections and pulled them ashore with a team, piling them up out of reach of high seas.

On one occasion, we carried a nice lot of passengers down from the South Haven steamer, but the sea was so choppy that if we had tied up at the pier the launch would have been badly pounded against the pier. Consequently, we signaled to Mr. Hempy to run a rowboat out to the launch so we could land the passengers in that way. All went along nicely until the last load. One of the ladies in the boat decided it was safer to stand up than to sit down as she was advised. Consequently, when the boat struck the beach and stopped, Mrs. Lady went headlong into the blue. It happened that the writer was standing on the beach, right where the boat touched, and of course, he could not refrain from the gallantry of reaching out his hand to pull the lady up on her feet. This he accomplished without even stepping into the water, but the lady, hysterical to a high degree, screamed and hugged his neck until he was thoroughly soaked from the wet clothing. Later she could not be convinced that she had never been in danger of drowning, but declared she was in water up to her neck and that the man in question had saved her life. That was almost the worst hugging he ever got.

The dam, as you know, now controls the flow of Brandywine Creek. This should withstand quite a water siege for the foundations are 13 feet below low water, and extending 125 feet long, it juts into the bank at either end for quite a long distance. Before this bridge was built, we used a cable footbridge, but wagons were obliged to ford the stream. The terrace roads throughout the park, as well as Ravineway, out to the tennis courts, we built from logs built up, one on top of another, slanting inwards, with sand filling in between and behind the logs. When completed, the surface was covered with clay and gravel to form the hard surfaces we now drive over.

Some of the old-timers in this part of the country, who would just as soon hunt "bee trees" as work, were adept at the pastime. They would crouch in a field of wild flowers or buckwheat, waiting for a bee to gorge himself with nectar and then carefully watch the exact direction the bee took on his flight for the home tree. The hunter would then advance along that precise line for quite a long distance and here wait for other bees to fly along that line towards the same home tree. In this way, the hunter would eventually spot the hollow tree in which a large colony of bees were storing up food for the winter. This tree he would mark as his property and later on, at night, he would cut down the tree, cut it open, and haul the honey home in a tub.

Several years ago the bees discovered a tiny opening in the siding of Oceana Cottage #91 that led to a large space between the roof and the ceiling of the porch. Late in the fall, the owner had an experienced bee man take out part of the ceiling and what a sight greeted them! Row after row of honeycomb was methodically hung between the joists and three or four very large dishpans full of comb honey was taken out.

When we built our 12,000-gallon concrete reservoir on top of West Summit, the concrete was mixed down on the shore at the foot of the hill. A wooden rail tramway was built up to the summit, and a logging car with flanged wheels carried the concrete up the hill, being propelled by Mr. Hempy's big team attached to 750 feet of rope cable that ran over pulleys at the top of the hill. When empty, the car ran down gently by gravity, being retarded by the rope dragging uphill through the sand. One day, a young suntanned fellow on the job suddenly decided he wanted to go "below decks." He jumped onto the empty car and before anyone could jump to the brakes, his weight carried the car down the incline of 150 feet in just about three seconds, sending him head-over-heels another fifty feet into the lake. The rest of the day, he was nearly three shades lighter in color.

*The Brandywine Creek.*

# Palisades Park Opened on the Brandywine

*Palisades Park Opened on the Brandywine* is the title on the front page of the South Haven, Michigan, <u>Daily Tribune</u> of August 15, 1905. It goes on to say, *"The latest addition to South Haven's resort places is Palisades Park, a beautiful tract of land comprising 250 acres with a frontage of half of a mile on Lake Michigan. It lies six miles south on the lakeshore, at the mouth of Brandywine Creek, a beautiful little stream which flows through the grounds, and comprises one of the most naturally beautiful pieces of ground anywhere along the lakeshore. The former owner of the land and the president of the newly organized and incorporated Palisades Park Company is Arthur Craig Quick."*

An early promotional brochure, <u>Palisades Park on Lake Michigan</u>, written by Mr. Quick, describes the beauty of the area:

> Palisades Park takes its name from the high and beautifully wooded dunes and bluffs that confront the lake shore at this point. These dunes straggle off inland a half mile or so in the most careless manner, winding around, joining together, separating again, losing themselves, and finally making their way back again to the shore apparently augmented in stature and ending at the lake side in towering palisades and miniature mountains. Other ridges run around in complete circles, enclosing deep, tree-lined bowls a hundred to five hundred feet across. Still other ridges form horseshoes enclosing amphitheaters.

> With such a groundwork plan of the Palisades before you, just imagine the hundreds of beautiful spots in the park. Numberless glens and ravines, romantic and shady; nooks with a wealth of ferns and wild flowers; ivy-covered trees and banks; wild grape bowers; winding ridge-like crests of the numerous palisades that momentarily give you the most unexpected surprises by opening up wide vistas of lake views or miles of surrounding country or outlines of distant bungalows on neighboring hills. Another moment you catch a glimpse into some deep valley, where, nestling in the cool shade, you spy the wide-eaved, red-roofed bungalows of others of our summer friends."

This brochure also offers a clear statement of Quick's intent to leave Palisades Park in a natural state. He says, *"Our way of building a country park is to **let it alone**. Nature is a capital designer. Our method has been to leave Palisades Park just as Nature made it, only intruding enough to make it all accessible. This we have done by laying out, grading, and improving miles of winding drives and paths and byways that follow the natural contour of the hills and valleys, picturesque in their apparently utter wantonness of purpose."* No doubt those who travel the Palisades winding "drives and paths" for the first time would agree with their "utter wantonness of purpose" – as well as their picturesque qualities.

Quick's plans for Palisades are explained further in the General Prospectus of an early advertising brochure, <u>South Haven Palisades Park Company</u>. In "The Whole Proposition in a Nut Shell," Quick wrote:

> This Company was organized to develop - as a quiet, exclusive summer residence community -

this beautiful 250-acre natural park and forest, fronting a half mile on Lake Michigan. A cool, shady, restful spot; all its wild and rustic features will be retained. In a secluded spot, aside from the noisy resort centers and attendant annoyances, it will readily attract the best classes of people. It is to such people only that we offer an opportunity to become stockholders or lot or cottage-owners in this residence park and enterprise.

Quick's elitism (looking for "the best classes of people") is apparent. He asked: "Are you one of those who have been looking for us – for a quiet, exclusive, picturesque spot for a summer home or an outing … free from the annoyances of transient centers – a place with moral and social surroundings that make it a pleasure and a comfort to live there?" The document goes on to illustrate his business acumen:

By special arrangement a stockholder may at any time exchange his stock, at par, for any of the lots on the Company at the current selling prices. The by-laws provide for the safest and most conservative management. The Company cannot incur indebtedness of any sort beyond funds appropriated by the stockholders and in the treasury for such purposes. In fact, the organization and all the plans of the Company have been made with the advice and counsel of the men of character composing the Advisory Committee, and we believe the Directors will carry out these plans to the letter.

The park, lots, and grounds for golf and other sports will be laid out by Mr. Benson, the well-known landscape engineer, who designed Lincoln Park, Chicago, and was its superintendent for many years. Lots will sell at good prices, and together with profits from rents, concessions and other sources, will pay stockholders good dividends. It is an investment where you can see it. The stock is fully paid, non-assessable, and this Prospectus will demonstrate that there is a *handsome profit* (and many summers-full of quiet enjoyment to those who go there) in becoming a stockholder *now*, while this *ground floor proposition* is open.

R. J. Spelman, a leading citizen of Covert, in his notes written on the development of Covert Township in the late 30's, explains the role Palisades Park has played along the Township shoreline of Lake Michigan. These notes, found in the Covert Historical Museum, state:

One of the bright spots in the development of Covert Township are the summer homes along the lake. Credit for this should be given Arthur C. Quick, who bought considerable acreage in Sec. 8, in 1893, adjacent to Lake Michigan, where Brandywine Creek flows into the lake and where Paul's Mill and Farnum's were located and the pier extended into the lake. He incorporated this land into the Palisades Park Association. He had the wooded part platted and had the roads and lots surveyed so that each lot in the subdivision could be built upon and was accessible to laid out roads.

Mr. Olaf Benson did the platting. He laid out Lincoln Park in Chicago. The proceeds from the sale of lots was used in building roads, putting in a water system, and other improvements. At the present time there are 130 summer homes, a hotel, a store, post office, and a garage; also an ice cream and soft drink stand, a clubhouse and a golf course and tennis courts. The homes are owned most by Chicago people and some of the people live there all winter.

One of the local South Haven luminaries who blessed the concept of Palisades Park was Liberty Hyde Bailey. The July 24, 1976 Patter, in an article on Park history, reminds us that *"Liberty Hyde Bailey was the great Cornell University botanist, born and memorialized in South Haven, in a house across the street from the hospital. He roamed this duneland even before it was a lumber camp."* The following excerpts are from Bailey's letter to Arthur Craig Quick, the founder of Palisades Park.

*Looking east at dunes. Note lack of vegetation on sand.*

Your letter with reference to Paulville and Ludwig's Pier brings back rollicking memories. It was sixty-eight years ago (1870?) that I sailed away from Ludwig's Pier to the big round world, going in a lumber-loaded schooner to Milwaukee. The "Bluffs," as we called the dunes in the early days, were favorite exploring grounds for me as a youth; I thought they must contain more mysteries than any other place. The strange plants on the windy sands and in the dark swamps behind, the birds and other animals, fascinated me. A few years ago I went back again. I lay alone under the pines on the sand, with bearberry and other low things, and slept. My first school essay was an account of a blackberry trip in old slashings near Paulville; and years afterwards, returning from far journeys, I horsebacked to the place and hitched my beast to the peak of a building buried in the sands, and drank from the waters of Brandywine Creek …

Your enterprise to make and to keep a reservation for nature lovers fascinates me. I hope you will have abounding success.

*Below: Marvin Slide, a popular hike down the beach. 1908.*

*This map was found by Betty Nelson. The first 21 cottages are marked with a black square. They are identified on the following page.*

# The Twenty-One Earliest Cottages

*One of the earliest maps of the Park – which, unfortunately, is undated – shows the 21 original cottages in Palisades. Those cottages, with the names of the present owners and present cottage numbers are below:*

| Names on Map | Now Owned By / Cottage Name | Number |
|---|---|---|
| Browning | Tom Flynn /Slieve Liag | 152 |
| Klein/Miller | Henkel /Bonnie Dune | 150 |
| S. T. Baker (later Henderson) | Schwartz/Shortridge/ Hermitage | 120 |
| S. Baker (called Hi-Lo) | Trezise /Bozeman | 108 |
| Log Cabin (Zoz?) (called Hemlock) | Goeppinger /Blueberry Hill | 113 |
| Drs. Vail and Hedger | Ferry /Up Country | 65 |
| Lewis | Gustafson | 107 |
| Nelson | Nelson | 76 |
| Dr. Bergman | King/Mailander /Buckeye King | 77 |
| Rev. Shreck | Rudmann /Treetops | 83 |
| Rev. Shreck | Coleman /Old Pier | 45 |
| Dr. McCollum | Master /Master's Lodge | 53 |
| Sturtevant Lodge (1st building) | O'Brien /Castlemaine Kerry | 52 |
| Dr. Smith and Louella Ballou Smith | Dinnin/Forsee/Huffine - Graystone | 89 |
| Robert Ballou | Flynn /Ballou Inn | 90 |
| Robert Ballou | Connor /Ambivalent | 91 |
| Ward | Tillson /Vashmar | 92 |
| Baker | Site of King /Hong Kong Hilton | 95 |
| Holmstrom | Mathias /Crest Haven | 96 |
| Ewing | Golden /Better There Than Here | 48 |
| Cota | Haude /Owl's Nest | 47 |

---

**It is interesting to note that two of these still are owned by the original families – the Ward/Tillson cottage, built by the present owners great-grandparents, and the Nelson cottage, still owned by Nelsons. Indeed, we have discovered <u>20 Five Generation Families Presently in the Park</u> – families who have vacationed at or owned property in the Park over the span of five generations. They are: Beck, Brand, Bendelow, Carr, Davis (Casa Loca), Goff, Hamilton, Henderson, Hession/Heisel, King/Mailander, Kropp, McCarthy/Foley, Nelson, Peat, Plain/McWethy, Potter, Stanger, Tillson, Williams, Wintermute. In the Brand family, the five generations can be traced two ways – through both John's and Marian's families.**

*Lodge and guests on railing. 1914.*

# THE STURTEVANTS AND THEIR LODGE

*Mrs. Sturtevant (right) and unknown visitor.*

One of the earliest buildings in Palisades Park was the lodge built by Ezra Thompson Sturtevant and his wife. Ezra, who in his younger days lived in Vermont where his father was an entrepreneur, received a common school education. As a young man he evidently became a druggist and, at 20 years of age, opened a store at Woodstock, Vermont, with his brother. They continued this business for five years. Then, Ezra's restless and unsettled spirit caused him to travel into many parts of the country. He became a druggist in Wisconsin, a ranch owner, a pie manufacturer in Chicago, and finally a resort owner at Palisades Park.

At one time, in Chicago, Ezra had a "squatter's right" claim to the land on which the Tribune Tower now stands. In the course of his travels, he went as far west as Seattle, Washington, from which point he planned to go prospecting for gold in Alaska. However, he was persuaded not to proceed. He was an opportunist; his many activities prove his considerable ability but his restlessness kept him on the move.

Sturtevant was a fine man morally, a member of the Masonic Order and a Christian Scientist. He was kind and generous and managed to keep his family together through many locations and changes in business enterprises. After his death, his widow Clara carried on the resort hotel business at Palisades Park until her death. In later years she was assisted by the daughters by her first marriage.

Following is an interesting quotation from an advertising brochure for the Lodge: "*A BEAUTIFUL, quiet home-like lodge situated on Lake Michigan. Forty-five rooms opening on wide verandas. Large double and single rooms; also connecting rooms. Cottage rooms in*

*Ezra Thompson Sturtevant*

*Clara Harriet Logan Sturtevant*

*connection with the lodge. Excellent table board – home service.* **Rates for board and room: $8.00 to $12.00 per week. Day rate $1.50. Table board $6.00 per week.** *If possible, write in advance for reservations. Open June 1st to October 1st. Situated 6 miles south of South Haven with frontage on Lake Michigan. Fine sandy bathing beaches, boating, tennis; dancing and cards at private country club.*"

The Lodge, with 224 feet of lake frontage, was passed to the Sturtevants' nephew, Del Jones. Jones sold it to Virginia and Ralph Wenham in 1957. In 1972, when the Wenhams tried to sell, Claude Mann, a local realtor, found the fair market value of the property at $50,000. In a letter to Donald Goodwillie, the then Park attorney, Mann said: "*It is my opinion these buildings have seen their usefulness and should be torn down. I would think it almost impossible to secure insurance coverage for fire and liability at a premium you could afford to pay on this type of property. There is a very limited number of private bathrooms to serve the approximately 42 total rooms …. The lake frontage is not protected by a steel sea wall; however there are some wood structures that offer some protection on a very limited basis.*" Possibly because of this assessment, the property was subsequently split, the lakeside building sold to the David Livingstons and the old dining room sold to the O'Brien family. The Livingstons later sold to present owner Lynne Master.

# Pioneer Resident and Builder, Robert G. Ballou

*One of the earliest and most influential families at Palisades Park was the Ballou family. Starting with a nearby boarding house during the lumbering era, this family built some of the first Park structures. Ballou Inn, with its store and post office, became a key element in our Circle. Robert Ballou's story, as told by his daughter, granddaughter, and nephew, was told in the Palisades Park Review 1905 – 1968 and is repeated here:*

Palisades Park history would not be complete without mention of Ballou Inn and its owner and builder, Robert G. Ballou. It was among the first places built on the Circle. At first, Ballou Inn was a summer home with only five bedrooms and the living quarters below, but – like Topsy – it grew. Mr. Ballou, being a contractor and builder, stayed in the Park early in the spring and late in the fall, building many of the early cottages, including Arthur Quick's. For that reason, he was the first caretaker and made the rounds, checking on the cottages after the owners had returned to their regular homes. But as the number of cottages increased, a full-time caretaker was employed.

As time passed and cottagers came earlier and stayed later than the regular season, they came to Mr. Ballou's to borrow a little sugar, a few eggs, a quart of milk – for there was no store nearer than South Haven. Thus, Mr. Ballou got the idea that a store was needed, and the next year he stocked a few things as a convenience to the Park people, especially fresh fruit and vegetables in season.

Next, the Park people were dissatisfied with the mail delivery, for it had to be brought over from the box on the main road where the R.F.D. carrier had left it. Sturtevant Lodge personnel or the Shattucks would bring in the mail when they brought people in from the trains at Covert. A Post Office was needed ; it became a reality when Mrs. Ballou took the Civil Service Examination and was appointed as the first Postmistress in Palisades Park. The Post Office was located in a part of the grocery store where it continued, over the years. At first it was inside, but later was moved out onto the enclosed porch with the inspector's approval. After Mrs. Ballou, Mrs. Georgia Underwood, who owned a cottage just outside the Ravineway entrance, was Postmistress for a long time.

Mrs. Packard took over in 1940. She had rented the store several years before that, purchasing the building in 1960.

Over the years, Mr. Ballou had enlarged the Inn building by putting on a third floor and making 13 bedrooms in all. He also enlarged the kitchen and built on a dining room, principally to provide an eating place for the cottagers and guests for Sunday dinners, although all meals were served throughout the week. Mr. Ballou saw to it that only fresh fruit and vegetables were served. Many people wanted to come early in June and stay late in September, and Sturtevant Lodge usually only opened about June 20, when the college girls could come to wait on tables; it closed right after Labor Day.

Mr. Ballou was always lending a helping hand to some cottager in distress by either doing for them, himself, or getting in touch with someone who could take care of the emergency or whatever was needed. To keep Palisades Park in its natural unspoiled beauty – and not to pick the wild flowers so they would go to seed and thus grow and bloom another year – were obsessions of both Mr. Quick and Mr. Ballou. Many a time, Mr. Ballou would come home and tell of seeing the first anemone or Jack-in-the-Pulpit. In the fall, he would say, "I saw the first flock of geese heading South; we must be going to have an early winter." In the spring, "Today I heard a flock of geese going North; it won't be long now before the water warms up." He was a friend to everyone and his love of the Park and what it meant to him are some of his daughter's precious memories. *Written by his daughter, Adelaide Ballou Beshgetoor.*

*Added by his granddaughter, Eleanor B. DiLuigi:*
We first stayed at Ballou Inn during the summer of 1941. It badly needed painting, so Dad purchased the paint, ladders, brushes, and turpentine and enlisted Andrew, Shirley, and me into the intricacies of scraping, puttying windows, sanding, and painting. We had never done anything like this in Argentina. Dad would wake us up every morning by banging on a pan and calling, "Rise and Shine! I want to see you hopping!" We would get up – he and the cook had a great breakfast prepared for us – and then we had to help him until about 1:00 p.m. He kept on working, but the afternoons were ours to vacation and enjoy the beach. We gradually got most of that place painted. It was an enormous wooded cottage/hotel with a large living room, dining room, and porch, 13 bedrooms, and a store and Post Office on the first level. When Dad left to begin his new job at RCA in Camden, NJ, he arranged for me to have a job as a waitress at the Inn where I was paid $5 a week, plus tips, for seven days a week. Dad paid me another $10.

*Mr. Ballou's nephew, Robert O. Barker, added more detail, explaining the five generations of the Ballou family who worked in and enjoyed the Park. He said:*
According to my grandmother, Charlotte Barker, 87 years old, about the 1870's, my great, great aunt, Mrs. Louise Carpenter, ran a "Boarding House" at the Brandywine "Park." It is believed that sometime after that, several cottages were buried under the dunes, just north of the Brandywine, time unknown.

Our second generation, early 1900's, built a cottage at the Circle, now known as the store and Post Office. My Aunt Grace Barker Ballou ran the Inn while her husband, Rob, as a contractor, built many of the present-day cottages.

My dad, Cecil Barker, actually lived with my aunt and uncle at the Ballou Inn, in the summers; that was the third generation. Then my dad married in the 20's and they stayed at the Inn. My folks tell of how I used to sleep in a cradle out on the big porch after I was born (1932). So I was the fourth generation. Helen Packard then bought the cottage from the family during the 1950's. I spent one summer, 1950, working and staying at Sturtevant Lodge. After getting married, we started renting in the Park. Since we have two children, they represent the fifth generation.

*Current picture of Ballou Inn, now owned by the Flynns.*

## Water Works

No bigger challenge faces Palisades Park as it ends its first century than what to do about its antiquated water system. More and more cottage owners are putting in their own wells to provide year-round water. Dishwashers, clothes washers, and hot tubs add stress to our septic systems. The central water system pipes are clogging and all too often producing impure water. Breaks in the system are common. Pressure is often a problem. As Bert Henderson, past president (1996 – 97), suggested, "We have stretched our system to the maximum and probably our septics as well."

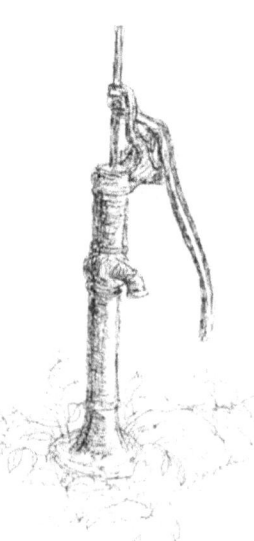

While Park members are struggling with solutions to this situation, they are faced with the enormous expenses each proposal entails. At the July, 2001, membership meeting, suggested solutions ranged from one to three million dollars, or up to $15,000 per cottage. After considerable study, in 2003, the members voted for a less expensive option, choosing to replace the pipes - but keep the seasonal well water we have had since 1916. The implementation of the new piping system will not start until after this book is published.

The fact is that, from the beginning, water expenses have often been on the agenda – though the difference in cost estimates is rather overwhelming. Early pictures suggest that the initial water tower – a relatively small, freestanding structure, was someplace near the Brandywine, behind Sturtevant Lodge. As the Park grew, so did demands for a more adequate supply. The earliest maps show a proposed water system on the dune where it now exists. One can guess that moving to this location was an early and important priority. Within ten years of the start of the Park, a plan to do so was underway. Arthur Quick's letter, written on September 7, 1916 to Margaret Sauer's father (and reproduced in the August 10, 1974 Patter), explains the financing of this proposed Water Works:

> Just a word regarding the progress of the Water Works System and subscription loan. We wish to complete the water system this fall and find we are $2000 short of the amount needed. As the Company is not allowed to incur indebtedness, I have offered to take over about $6000 worth of lots that is due me in dividends on my stock, and

*Early water tower.*

mortgage these lots to a group of lot owners who will subscribe to this $2000 loan. The lots are to be selected by the Finance Committee of the lot owners.

We have already secured subscriptions to the pledge below, totaling nearly $1500 in amounts of $50 each. ... We are asking these as well as those already on the list to increase their loans to $100 if convenient and to set the date of payment by September 20th ... We need $800 by September 20th to pay in advance for the pipe, $500 by October 20th for expense of laying pipe and putting in the wells, and $700 by February 1st for engine and pump.

The Water Works Committee will greatly appreciate your cooperation in this much needed improvement that will greatly facilitate the sales of property next year, as well as building work.

*Our present pump house above the Clubhouse Beach.*

So, in 1916, a $50 or $100 loan from 30 or 40 people saved the day. In 2004, would that we would be so lucky!

*Two views of work on the Covert water line that was brought to the Park gate in the spring of 2003.*

# Sinks Grocery Store

A Reminiscence by Carl D. Sink
From August 10, 1965 Patter

*Carl D. Sink was the last owner of Sinks Grocery Store in Covert, which he sold in November, 1964. The store had been started by his father, N. S. Sink, in 1906. Early Palisades vacationers bought many supplies from the Sinks' horse-drawn grocery wagon. A year after Carl Sink retired, he wrote this reminiscence for the August 10, 1965 Patter:*

Delivering food to Palisades Park in the early 1900's was far removed from the present day of cars and trucks. The horse and wagon made it a whole day's experience, slowed down by the roads of sand and clay. However, we didn't mind as we didn't know any other way. We took orders one day and delivered the next. The orders consisted not only of food, but also kerosene and gasoline for lights and cooking; pots and pans from Mr. Gunsaul or Mr. Eisenlohr's Hardware Store, and wicks for kerosene lamps or cooking stoves. If anyone needed an item from any of the Covert stores, we delivered it free.

I still feel sorry for the team of horses pulling the wagon down to the sandy beach by the Covert resort now called Linden Hills. We never stopped for a coffee break. Even for lunch, we ate (only) between cottage stops. Our lunch usually was topped off by a delicious pie bought from Mr. Shepherd, the milkman.

We had to be young and in good physical condition to take a five gallon can full of kerosene in one hand and a basket of groceries in the other and run in the sand to a cottage on the beach, back from the wagon road. We were always welcomed by our customers as we were the only supply line from the outside world. We were just young boys in our early teens trying to do a job.

*Early sand roads.*

*City of South Haven c. 1908*

## Letters Home

*Betty Nelson provided this series of letters from one of the Nelson relatives, young Gertrude, written home while she was vacationing in the Nelson cottage in 1914 and 1915. The letters are such treasures that they are quoted below. They are full of swimming and sunsets, collecting bugs and cooking lessons, picnics and church activities – the Nelsons were one of several Palisades families active in the Linden Hills Swedenborgian Church. With no television or radio in those days, much time was spent reading. One senses a touch of homesickness, also, and real concern for the beloved and ailing "Meemo." The first letter, mentioning an "awful" train ride and a worse boat ride, makes clear the difficulties of travel at that time.*

**Palisades Park, July, 1914:** Dear Mama – After taking that awful train ride we had a nice auto one to Palisades. When Aunty Annie met us then we went and saw the new porch and dressing room and really you would be surprised to see how much that (taking the) curtain away improves its looks. Here is a rough sketch of the looks of the new porch. We were not able to eat very much at South Haven so we had a lot left over, and Aunty Annie poached eggs and served on toast and I was so hungry that I ate three, and counting the one I ate at South Haven I ate four eggs yesterday. Aunty Adah thought Bea would be very sick on account of throwing up so much but she is all right today. We started on deck of the boat but when it got rough Aunty Adah got a stateroom. She said when she came in and saw me I was as pale as the pillowcase although I did not throw up at all. After we all got tucked into bed we felt better and today are all well. Aunty Selma read six stories to us when we were in bed. Now all the work is done. Dorothy and I made the beds. We are both writing at the foot of West Point. The lake is very smooth. I will write again soon. From your daughter Gertrude. P. S. Kiss them all around from me.

**Palisades Park, July 14, 1914:** Dear Papa – Thank you very much for the nice letter you sent me. It has been chilly today and last night both. We had had chicken and today Aunty Adah was going to make chicken salad out of it so I watched her and now know how to make it all but the mayonnaise. Aunty Selma gave Dorothy and me a cooking lesson this morning and tomorrow we are going to make breakfast all ourselves. This morning John and Bud Vos came over to play and really Buddy is the cutest little fellow. Oh! How Lois would love to play in the sand here, where she could make cakes to heart's content. I am in a club at Covert Resort, Grace Graham is the president. The little boys who sell around here are very generous and we got a quart of lovely red raspberries for fifteen cents from one of them while Aunty Selma said in town or Glenview (I don't remember which) she paid a quarter for not half that much. We were all glad to hear that Marion was going to help dear Mama. Is Meemo well again? Tell her I will write to her soon. Last night a ship or rather a sailboat saw the light in the window of the house (of) a man who lived on a hill and thought it was the South Haven light house and almost came in here. That is all I know about it but I don't see how he could think so here in such shallow water! We were so glad to hear from home. Aunty Adah and Aunty Selma put up some curtains which add so much to the looks of the room. Aunty Annie and Uncle Seymour are enjoying the new porch so much! Aunty Selma is reading "The Scarlet Pimpernel" and enjoying it very much. She is almost through.

*Nelson cottage porch.*

The chipmunks around here are very tame. And now I will close with love to all from Gertrude.

**Palisades Park, July 20, 1914:** Dear Mama – I do hope dear Meemo is better. Aunty Annie and Uncle Seymour are going home and we will miss them sadly. It is a very hot day today and we were in swimming over an hour. Last Thursday our club met at Edith Wunsches and we had ice cream! After it Willy Hake rowed us down to see the wreck or ship but we just got there in time to see a tug hauling it away. My hair is sopping wet. Aunty Emelia wrote that you might have a girl today. The lake is glassy smooth and here we need never go over on a rough day. We are watching the boat come in. There are a lot of motorcycles going past. We are going down at five to flash to Aunty and Uncle and we are going to bring our supper and a book we are reading (which is "Ronald Bannerman's Boyhood"). It is very interesting. Mr. Reed made a lovely shelf in the kitchen and so they moved up a kind of wash stand so Aunty Annie gave us the other for our dolls. Marian Ward is teaching dancing lessons for a quarter a lesson so WE DID NOT GO!! Aunty Annie has a glass chime which is very sweet. Beatrice is going to be the boy of the house. She is going to be called "Tomey." Mrs. Elise Carter (formerly Miss Elise Wunsch) and Mr. Carter, her husband, were in church last Sunday. Friday there is going to be a Friday class supper and all Tuesday Mr. and Mrs. Cline and Mr. Gladish are going to teach Bible lessons. Dorothy and I have cooked six breakfasts. (Tell Papa.) Mr. Ballou insulted Dorothy and I when we went down to get ice cream. He said "You don't look as if they starved you up there!" Aunty Selma sends her love joined with us all. With love from Gertrude.

**Palisades Park, July 21, 1914:** Dear Aunty Emelia – Thank you for your letter. We all enjoyed it very much. I am writing in bed Tuesday morning. Last night we had a marshmallow roast and it was right in front of Fields. Now a few days before, John Vos had hurt his eye badly and wore a piece of cotton on it which stuck out behind the bandage and after all the marshmallows were gone, the little boys stuck their sticks into the fire and got them on fire and played they were torches. Mrs. Vos made them stop and all but John's had gone out so Mrs. Vos told him to stick it in the sand or water but he said he would blow it out. Now I was not looking but soon everybody screamed "Duck your head in the sand, John" and others, "John is burning!" I turned quickly around and saw that the cotton bandage was flaming up. Everybody threw sand at him which bewildered him so his mother went and ducked him in the sand and the fire went out. Of course poor John was terrified and they brought him in to Field's cottage. Harriet Field went to the Clubhouse for Dr. Earnest Wunsch who came quickly

*Swedenborgian Church picnic in the dunes.*

as possible and bandaged John up. Mrs. Vos asked him, "John, do you know who took care of you?" and John said, "God." When Mrs. Vos asked him if he was ready to go, he said, "Yes Mother dear." Aunty Adah went down to see how he was this morning and Mr. Vos said he was pretty badly scorched so they had thought of going home but had thought it better to go to South Haven to a doctor who took care of him when he broke his arm. Ask Aunty Annie if they saw the mirror flash. And now I will close with love to all from Gertrude.

**Palisades Park, July 29, 1914:** Dear Papa – Aunty Emelia arrived yesterday and she told us all about the reception which was lovely. Tell Mama that we are enjoying all the goodies she sent to us. It is lovely and cool today and I think we are going in for a dip. I wonder how dear Meemo is getting along …. John and Buddy Vos can hardly wait for you to bring Hubert and Gerald. Saturday or somewhere around there Aunty Adah bought an Indian basket for picnics. John Vos's face is much better and will probably be well when Hubert and Gerald come. We have all written to Aunty Sophie today.
Aunty Selma is going to teach Dorothy and I to make pancakes. The lake is streaked in different shades of blue which is very pretty to look at. We had corn for dinner which we bought from a little boy who was selling it. It was very good. Aunty Annie bought a little chime for down stairs which she hung in the middle of the dining room table, but yesterday Dorothy and I filled the fern baskets so Aunty Adah took them down (the chimes) and put a fern basket up there which looks better by far. Then she put the chimes over by the window nearest the steps and now it catches the wind fine. Miss Adah W. gave Dorothy, Bea, and me a tablet of drawing paper. Wasn't that nice of her? Now I will tell you something about

*Group of Nelsons enjoying the water.*

our club and it is this. The club is formed for the purpose of getting a new piano for our new church meeting house and now between fees and promises we have thirty something dollars but of course that is not enough so it would take an age to get the piano. Some people are going to buy it so they can have it soon so we will pay them for it when we can raise the money. And now I will close, with love to all and loads to Meemo from Gertrude.

**Palisades Park, August 1, 1914:** Dear Meemo – How are you today? I hope you are much better. According to Dorothy's and my wishbone you are well and up. A few days ago Dorothy and I caught a walking stick and "alcoholed" him. He was not perfect as one leg was gone. A few days ago Dorothy and I found a locust on a door downstairs. Leddy Philip is up at our house helping get ready for Creda and Bona and she is very nice. She said she had three little fatherless boys to support as their father had been drowned two or three years ago.

Last night we went to Friday class and to a picnic also. Mrs. Bergman gave an entertainment and we had to miss it as we were at the meeting house. Sunday we are going down to the hotel for dinner and are all looking forward to it. Yesterday Aunty Emelia, Dorothy, Beatrice, and I went down to the beach and wore our swimming suits. First Aunty read to us and then we went to go in swimming but booooo!!!! the water was icy so we had to keep coming out and rolling in the sand. When I come home be prepared to see a brown, tanned girl. Beatrice is getting much fatter and is no longer skin and bones. And now I will close with love. I hope you are better, Gertrude.

*Dorothy Nelson's plate, earned when she was a very sick young girl at the Nelson cottage. She was quarantined in part of the living room and given a plate whenever she was a "good patient."*

*Nelson living room.*

*Visitors to Sturtevant Lodge in early years.*

**Palisades Park, August, 1914:** Dear Mama – (Monday) We are expecting the Glens today and hope to see them at five. Aunty Selma is sick in bed, which is thought to have been caused by taking cold. Yesterday was Sunday and we went to the hotel for dinner, and my but it was fun. George Hoeck has been selling his postals here today. (Tuesday) The Glens are here and my but they are lovely young ladies too. Aunty Selma is not feeling quite herself yet but is much better. Yesterday they came at four thirty or around then and all but cousin Margret were sea sick and Cousin Margret teased them so. We three girls are coming Saturday if the weather is nice and the lake smooth. Last night we and the Glens and Aunties went to see the sunset and it was perfectly lovely. We are going to have corn and chicken for dinner. Dorothy, Aunty Adah, and the Glens are at Two Oaks. And now I will close, with love from Gertrude. P. S. I am glad to be coming home.

*The final letter, dated one year later, indicates that Gertrude, this time, had money for the 25 cents dance lesson – as well as the money for the Indian wares. Might she have arrived with $1.00?*

**Palisades Park, July 21, 1915:** Dear Mama and Papa – Dorothy and I have just come home from a dancing lesson. We enjoyed it very much. It only cost a quarter an hour, and I am sure we learned one dollar's worth. Such a busy day as it is! We took dancing, entertained company, did our work, and will go to Miss Emily's class, and then to the picnic. The folks came yesterday. (A secret, do not read aloud.) I bought 70 cents worth of Indian stuff. Don't you call that living up to the holes between my fingers? I was so ashamed of myself that I could have died. It is a beautiful day, sunshiny yet cool and pleasant. We will go in swimming at 3:30 p.m. Aunty Emelia, Dorothy, and I went out and got some ferns and planted them in baskets for cousin Philo's arrival. We also visited the real Boy Scout's camp. The Scouts under Mr. Smith are camping at the Burnham's old camp. They come up every now and then to borrow things. I finished the "Lightning Conductor" and am very pleased with it. And, oh wonder of wonders, will wait four days before I begin Frickels. Dorothy is doing well in her reading. Thank Beatrice for her letter and give my love to everybody. From your bankrupted uneconomical spendthrift.

Dear Miss Emma – I received your postal and like it very much. We use our dish aprons a lot and Aunty Emelia has fallen in love with them and wants you to make her one. We often wish we had taken your advice and brought our coats. And now I must go to dinner. Love from Gertrude.

P. S. Later – We heard about the fire. Do tell someone to write us about it.

*Circa 1913.*

There is a pleasure in the pathless woods,
There is a rapture on the lonely shore,
There is society, where none intrudes
By the deep sea, and music in its roar:
I love not man the less, but Nature more ...

By Lord Byron
As published in the August 10, 1974 Patter.

# Interviews

## Mary Kay Goodrich
Interviewed by Frances Prange
August 31, 1984

I've heard through the years that Mr. Quick wanted the Park populated with professional people – artists, musicians, teachers, doctors, attorneys, and the like. So in the Chicago area, Mr. Quick went to the American Conservatory of Music. There he met some of the faculty: my aunts, Katherine and Angela Baker, Leo Sowerby, and Arthur Olaf Andersen. My aunts retold the beauty of the sales pitch to their brothers, my father John and my uncle, Samuel Taylor Baker, who then came to Palisades, in the summer of 1906, and camped out on the dune right above the lots where they eventually built the family cottage.

My family, the Bakers, included my grandmother, Katherine; my father, John; my aunts, Katherine and Angela; my uncle, Sam; and my mother, Florence. They built their cottage on lots 7 and 8 in the Oceana Block, in 1907. That is where the Hong Kong Hilton now stands. Somewhere around 1910, my Uncle Sam came over from Chicago and built Hi-Lo (#108), which he sold to the Gervais family, May and Lucian Gervais, and the Hermitage (#120), which he sold to Mr. Henderson. When I first came to Palisades Park, in the summer of 1915, I was nine months old. I spent entire summers here until I got to be a teenager. When I was young, my mother and father would only come for two weeks here and a week there, but I stayed with my aunts all summer and they had charge of me.

In February of 1927, the Baker cottage fell into the lake. Mr. Quick and his helpers were really wonderful, though; they did all they could to save it. They cabled it to those large trees up on the bluff, but nothing helped. It took three days for it to finally - just gradually - fall on its face. All the treasures were lost – including the rosewood piano and the brand new, mahogany-lined canoe, which I was just old enough to take out myself. Through friendship and the fact that my family were among the first property owners here, Mr. Quick gave them a woods lot, back in Palisades Hill Block, where they built our present cottage in the spring of 1930. We eventually sold one beach lot to Bill Heitner and one to Art Warner; we knew we'd never build on them again.

*A happy group joins Mary Kay Goodrich (right) . c. 1930's.*

*Baker cottage after the storm.*

Charles Goodrich and I were married August 27, 1938. We continue to enjoy and appreciate the beauty of this incomparable Park.* Our children, Gary and Kathleen, spent entire summers at the Park, as has our granddaughter, Taylor Louise. She is the fifth generation Palisader. There were very few children in the Park, as I remember, and when I was very young, we were to be seen and not heard. We used to play on the "shimmy bridge." Mr. Quick was always nearby, wherever we were playing, to be sure that we didn't go off a trail, run down a dune, or pick a wildflower. Betty Holmes Woodhouse and her sister Joan (who were older than we were) would join Mr. Henderson's nephews, Alan and Harry Summer, and form a group of seven or eight of us to go on hikes through the woods. Alan and Joan would be the leaders because they were the older ones.

Betty's father had a telescope, which he took to the beach every night. I can remember being held up, night after night, to look through the telescope. He would tell us about the Dippers and other important stars. It was a big event for me. Usually when the whippoorwill would call from the bluff up above, saying, "Time for bed," I was called inside, but I got to stay up on the nights we looked through the telescope.

At the beach cottage, the dining room table had a large center leg. To me, this was a magic table with a magic leg; every night, at sunset, a surprise lump – candy or some kind of treat – came up under the tablecloth at my place. No doubt my aunt did this, but as I got a little older, although I tried to peek around the door, I never caught anybody putting anything under the tablecloth. Yet it was there every night. That really is one of my fondest memories.

As children, we had Bunco parties at the Clubhouse on Friday nights. That was the first and only organized thing they ever had at the Clubhouse for children back then. They had marvelous prizes: beautiful flashlights and wonderful things like that. I do remember sometimes going

*In 1996 they sold the cottage to Ken and JoAnn Gryzwa.

*The Baker cottage on the beach, at right, site of present Hong Kong Hilton #95. Baker cottage was washed into the lake in late 1920's and not rebuilt.*

*Angela Baker (second on left) and her class at the Dramatic Arts of American in Covert. c. 1911.*

on organized hikes, all day picnic affairs, and campfire parties where we'd sing all evening. I loved to watch the ladies, in their long white dresses, and the men, who <u>all</u> wore white trousers, parade down the boardwalk, all dressed up for the Saturday night dances – they really used to dress up. Seeing them and listening to the music was just a marvelous experience.

I remember sitting on the steps beside big pitchers, waiting for Mr. Shepherd to come and deliver the milk and his other goodies – fresh fruits and butter and eggs and vegetables. He even had flowers. Once, when I was very little, some Indians walked down the beach. It was a family – I'd say there were no more than four or five of them. Someone in my family purchased what is called a "sweet grass" basket for me, from the Indians, and we had that for years at the beach cottage. It wasn't large, but it was beautifully made. I have an idea the Indians were Pottawatomi, but I don't know where I get that idea, unless it's the Thunder Mountain story.

Going to Covert to shop at Sinks Grocery Store was a very big deal. We'd stock up for a whole week, if possible, because transportation wasn't that good and we could not walk that far. Then we'd go to an ice cream parlor in Covert, run by a Swedish woman and her mother. In the very early days, people would order meat from the Ballous who would go into town and pick up these meat orders for many families. When we would go up to get our order, there would be no names on the packages, so we just took the package we thought was ours back to our cottage. Well, sometimes people had ordered a large roast because they were expecting a lot of company (in the instance of my family at one time) and they unwrapped it and had half-a-dozen frankfurters and maybe two chops and a little bit of cheese, or something like that. Then everybody would rush back to the store at the Circle and exchange packages. I remember hearing that often.

In the early, early spring, we sometimes had the joy of staying at Ballou Inn. There would be huge blocks of ice still on the beach, but we had heated rooms and the food was wonderful. In the summer, we went to the Inn for some meals and, in later years, to Sturtevant Lodge.

Joe Putz was a man of all trades, just a handyman; his sister, Mary, would clean the cottages. Every year they brought us a gift of four quarts of strawberries at a time. We would have a huge, old-fashioned strawberry shortcake. We'd eat the entire four quarts at a sitting; that would be the whole meal – we couldn't eat anything else with it. That was something we'd look forward to.

We came by train, to Watervliet, or by boat, from Chicago to South Haven. Either way, we were always picked up by Mr. and Mrs. Shattuck. How their cars changed through the years. I remember my grandmother being lifted off the train on a chair – not a wheelchair, just a chair. I suppose the Shattucks brought the chair over in the wagon and carried her that way down to the Park. And those four miles were a <u>long</u> way.

Mr. and Mrs. Phillips were wonderful workers. She would clean and she was a marvelous cook. Of course, he was a builder as well as a handyman of all trades. They put a name up over some little houses they had, and they called it "Phillips's Colored Resort." Mr. and Mrs. Hempy collected the garbage with their wonderful team of horses, Mrs. Hempy wearing her big sunbonnet with the floppy brim.

Our iceman was Charley Tunecke. The old icehouse used to be down where the parking lot is now, just east of the Circle. Charley would cut the ice in the winter and store it in all this straw; it was very clean. Tony Canonie was a very young kid, I would say about eight or ten years old, when he first started helping Charley with ice. We'd hitch a ride on the back of the wagon and Tony would chop off little pieces of ice for us to suck on.

Where Forest Dunes is now, down the Blue Star Highway, a man by the name of Tompkins owned a gas station. That was always a stop before we left for Chicago, to check up on our gasoline and anything else. Mr. Tompkins could fix anything that was wrong with our car.

Some of my fondest impressions are of the beach. I played for hours, building sandcastles and all kinds of imaginative things. The beach was about a block wide, and the sand literally burned the soles of my feet because it was such a long way to the water. Watching storms come up on the lake used to excite and fascinate me. I was taught to swim with the old-fashioned canvas waterwings; I remember those well. Sometimes I'd run down the boardwalk to get the mail and get slivers in the bottom of my feet.

*Mr. Shattuck and son Karl. Covert. 1914.*

From the time I was a wee one, I dearly loved the time spent playing on the rosewood square piano. It broke my heart when it turned into matchsticks when the beach cottage went in the lake. Betty Holmes and other friends loved to climb over the store stairs. We played a lot in the gazebo. That made a wonderful playhouse. It was in the fork of the road, right near Mrs. Ott's cottage. It was quite large and a beautiful place.

One family story I heard repeated through the years dates from around 1909. The family expected guests, from Chicago, who were to arrive by launch from the South Haven pier to our pier, at Clubhouse Beach. My Aunt Angela tied large red bows on her big toes and walked out on the pier to meet the guests, but there was not a soul she knew on the launch. She lived with that story in the Park for a long time. She thought she had made a fool of herself, but everyone else thought it was very funny.

Chuck served four years as secretary of the Board, from 1957 – 1962, when Henry Prange was president. In later years, I was very active in Clubhouse affairs – our style shows and plays. I directed three plays. The cast presented me with a little kitten that we had for 15 years.

Chuck and I treasure our collection of postcards and photos dating from 1906. I'd like to read you one, dated two days after we were married, in 1938. I wrote this postcard home to my parents. "Dear Folks: Arrived all OK at 1:00 a.m. and had a delicious dinner at the Spa on the way. The weather is glorious and the cottage looks beautiful – three bouquets of flowers. Mr. Shepherd came this morning and presented me with a huge bouquet of gladiolas because he had known Mrs. Goodridge since she was a baby." I thought that was so sweet that I remember it to this day. Mr. Shepherd was a dear.

*One of the old gazebos, probably built by Mr. Henderson.*

*Collection of old Palisades Park postcards.*

*Hazel Harper. 1985.*

# Hazel Harper
Interviewed by Katy Beck

I first came to Palisades in high school days, to house parties – quite a lot of them. My name then was Hazel Bruce. When I came up to those parties, I wasn't interested in anything but our little teenage group. And swimming. I didn't play tennis, but the others did. And so I didn't know about the names of neighbors at that time.

My family visited Pottawatomi (#154), then owned by the DeSouchet family, who had built it and the cottage south of it. I went to Lewis Institute – that's part of Illinois Tech now – and so did the DeSouchet children. Around 1918 it was, and the DeSouchets had been at Palisades a long, long time.

In the early days, Mrs. Shattuck ran a sort of livery service, with horses and a two-seated conveyance. She would pick up visitors in South Haven. Of course, the roads were not very good coming out here. Mr. DeSouchet would take the wheelbarrow down to the hotel and meet visitors with their luggage. That's how they got their luggage from the Circle to their cottage. That was a long walk. People didn't mind going a little distance in those days. And the boardwalk was kept in good repair, you know. Mr. Quick was very particular about that.

I later married Clifford Harper. His parents, Mr. and Mrs. Thomas Harper, had built this cottage (#166). Mr. and Mrs. Harper belonged to a dancing club in Chicago with the DeSouchets, and they came over to visit, across the lake on the boat called The City of South Haven. The DeSouchets were always very generous with their cottage. That's how Mr. Harper happened to build this one. In fact, Mr. Harper's sister designed the cottage. She had read a book, <u>Seven Peas to Bald Pate</u>, and in the book was a balcony. When Aunt Docia knew that her brother was going to build a cottage, she remembered the book; that's why there is a balcony here. In those days, there was no air conditioning, you know, and it got very hot on the beach, at Pottawatomi, and didn't cool off until later in the evening. Mr. Harper kept looking up at the ridge and thinking how nice and cool it must be. There were no cottages up here, no road. Mr. Quick came quickly when he knew there were guests that might be interested in property. Mr. Harper bought the two lots up here. I think they started building in about 1929. They had to have horses drag the road – make the road – before he could build.

At the time, Mr. Quick was very anxious to sell some lots up on the bluff, so other people would see the possibility. And they did, very quickly. About two years after Mr. Harper built this one, Heisels built theirs (#164). And then the Drapers after that (#165). And VanRipers, who were next to the Heisels – the one Joys are in now – Enchanted Hill, it used to be called (#162). It changed hands several times. Later, the Paulsens built the little one that the Kirks are in now (#161). The Bob Burkharts were the last to build (#167). Mrs. Chamberlain had the cottage the Masons are in now (#168). To get to it, there was no road so they had to walk down the beach to Campbells (#171) and then go up that way. That was another long walk.

*Cliff Harper. 1942.*

*Picnicers enjoying Clubhouse Beach before Clubhouse was moved.*

Things were very nice. Ballou Inn served meals, you know, and so did Sturtevant Lodge. We used to go down, sometimes, for a meal when we had house parties. And sometimes we'd go down after the meal, to see if there were any pies left that we could buy. The Ballous ran the Inn until her health gave out. They were a very nice couple.

We sometimes went to the Clubhouse when it was on the beach. Mr. DeSouchet was one of its founders. He and a group of men built it and owned it. We mostly stayed in our end. Social life has changed here a great deal. Most of our social life was in our cottage, with our friends and relatives – Harpers had a lot of relatives and they were all here. We had a lot of things going on in the cottage and not much time for outside. But now, of course, there are always planned activities, like the Crafts and the Ladies' Night Out. All pretty new. Like all older people, I don't like the changes quite so much. I am still used to the activities of the people, my guests and family, who visit here; that's my main thing. I don't participate in the other things.

We didn't have to go shopping in the early days. We lived luxuriously. Taft and Burton, a store in South Haven, came Monday and Friday and took our order for the next day. They always managed to bring things for the weekend. Then there was, God bless his heart, our milkman, Mr. Shepherd. He had not only milk, but the top of it was just rich cream. And then, on weekends, he would have chickens and flowers and homemade ice cream which his wife made. I think he had butter, also. We had everything brought to our door. We were much better off than now. No shopping, because no roads to get any place. Even when we had roads, they were not like they are now. We were apt to get stuck in the sand. But we really just lived luxuriously.

Nobody had electricity. We had two chimney-like things in the bathroom and kitchen for hot water. And a Bunsen burner oven, I think they called it. And then we had the fireplace; it was quite large and kept us warm. We cooked using kerosene, on two burners. And we had kerosene lamps in all the rooms. I have some of them upstairs that I saved. Some I have taken to the white elephant sales. Not too long after the cottage was built, we put in electricity. We had a phone right away, with the long and short bells. We'd have to listen, be very alert, because we wondered, "Was that three long and one short, or was it …?" And we'd forget, you know. Mrs. Harper had it over there in that corner and it was a busy phone because they had a lot of relatives, all very close.

*Garage on Blue Star Highway at entrance to Linden Hills. c. 1930.*

*Two unidentified workmen on the beach. All cottage and road building materials had to be carried by horse and wagon for several decades.*

Charley Tunecke and Joe Putz worked for Mr. Quick. Joe is gone now. Charley was our very good, faithful friend. Of course, he worked hard for Mr. Quick, but we found any time we'd come up here, maybe late at night, you know, and something wouldn't be working, we'd call Charley. And he came right away to help. Charley also had the Standard Station out on the road. I think he leased it to the Knapps for a short time, though I'm not too sure about what happened. And then there was another young couple, Gene Howe and his wife; he finally went to work for Whirlpool. They lived back of the filling station. He and his wife made pottery and sold it, as well as running the filling station. He was very ambitious. He worked hard, with all the pottery. And then, of course, he bought the fruit from the farmers and sold that, too, at the gas station. He had a big truck out there, filled with things. That was very handy. Finally the Nicholses bought the station; it became a store.

The ice was delivered twice a week by the Canonies We got our icebox loaded about Monday and then the ice would last until about Friday, unless it was terribly hot. Sometimes it was down to almost nothing by the time we got through with the week. The Canonies were a wonderful family; the parents had the ice house. They supplied us with our necessities, ice and wood, and I know in an emergency, they would have brought us anything.

They were always so helpful. There were two or three boys, but Tony was the one that usually brought our ice and that we knew best. Such a nice person, he was. And the nicest thing happened to him. Tony did himself proud and learned a great deal in the Army. So wars do some good things. What he learned he used out in front, to put in seawalls. I think Forest Lowrey was responsible for some of his training. Forest wouldn't be talking about it, but we think, just in the background, he did help. Tony was a hard worker, and now you find his name all over the world.

Of course, Tony has been very wonderful to Charley Tunecke, very fond of him. Everybody was fond of Charley. Wonderful, happy disposition and he loved Palisades and he loved the people here. He has never forgotten them. Tony, you know, is interested in raising race horses. I presume he trains them and follows their races. Now, he has practically retired from his other businesses, and he has Charley over frequently for dinner. In fact, Charley lived there with them for awhile, when the children were little, and helped with things. Now Tony has given Charley a racehorse. A colt. And they are going to train it. Charley told me immediately and I could see what that meant to him, to have his own race horse. The Canonie children are all very, very devoted to him and he thinks dearly of them, also.

*Stairs to Harper cottage; Keith Kline on stairs. 1939.*

I remember Mrs. Overhuel, a very busy business woman, and Helen Packard, who was here many years. Helen was very faithful. She was the Postmistress as well as running the store, and she did a tremendous job. I hear from her every Christmas. She is in a retirement home in South Haven. She was very business-like, really did everything just right.

I knew Del Jones just vaguely, though the DeSouchets knew him real well. When we went down to the hotel, we always visited with him, but we didn't really know him personally. I think he inherited the hotel from his aunt. He was not the original owner.

Rudy Weber was fantastic. He built most everything around here, including this cottage. Charley and Joe Putz helped; they were both employed by Mr. Quick. Rudy built most of the cottages in the Club. And then he worked for us – for all the Harpers – for a long time after that, doing any building that we needed. We could call him as he went by, and he would come in and help us out. It is too bad he is not available for a conversation because he would really know everything about Covert and ev-

erything here. He volunteered for the Covert Fire Department.

A few years ago, Pauline and I were coming back from South Haven and we saw smoldering on the bluff on the narrow street opposite Nicholses. Just a small portion. We went into the store to call the Fire Department but Mr. Nichols said that he had already called. Cecil was there and he had it under control before the Fire Department got there. In my whole life, I never saw anyone work as fast and hard as Cecil did. He had all that path that you see all the way to the top. Cecil did every bit of it. He just dug furiously and got the fire smothered. Every time I go past there, I think that was so wonderful, how Cecil did that by himself. We watched and it never once got out of control. It burned up that way and he got it stopped. It was a tremendous job.

Cecil always worked for me. In fact, I'm grateful to him. I wouldn't be here if it wasn't for Cecil. When my husband died, I thought I couldn't possibly manage this alone. It would be too expensive and it would be impossible for me to keep it up. I was born in an apartment and always lived in one and was used to being able to call the janitor, you know. I was going to Canada to visit some relatives after the funeral, and they insisted that I not be here alone. So I thought I would stop and tell Cecil to fix up the cottage and sell it. Cecil was around the Park some place. Well, I didn't want to see the cottage, so I went down looking for Cecil and got stuck in the sand. Then I knew I really <u>would</u> have to see Cecil. Pretty soon he came along and got me out of there, and talked to me. It seemed possible that, with his help, maybe I could try to keep the cottage. I wasn't too sure about it, but I told him, well, get it open and do whatever's necessary to be done, and I would try it for awhile and see. Without Cecil I wouldn't have done that; I wouldn't know what to do. I'm eternally grateful to him. Tell him that, too.

# Ruth Kropp

Interviewed by Frances Prange
August 27, 1984

The first year we came to Palisades, probably 1916, I was just a year and a half old. We stayed in Hemlocks (#113), which was owned by Ann and Ralph Holmes and, later, by their daughter, Betty Woodhouse. It had no inside plumbing and no lights, so we had to use a privy and kerosene lamps. Down at the corner, near where Alice Ott lived, was a pump for water. My mother and the lady with her were both pregnant, so they couldn't carry any heavy loads. They brought my uncle, who was 15 or 16 at the time, to carry the water from the pump. How my folks got here I'll never know – somebody must have told them about Palisades. But my grandparents, the Hubert Stoddards, came over to visit them and fell in love with Palisades and bought the property that the Beyers now own (#135), back in the woods.

I had four brothers. As children, we lived back in the woods at Grandpa and Grandma's cottage. We had to go home the middle of August because that's when Grandpa came up for his vacation and he wanted to be alone and to have quiet. I don't blame him. Dad came on weekends and we used to pick him up at Watervliet, at the train station. He left the car at the station since my mother didn't drive. This was before the time of licenses, and when my brother was 12 years old, he used to drive the car over to the station and back. My parents always stayed at my grandparents' cottage; they never built a cottage.

We children used to have most vivid imaginations. We went up on Thunder Mountain hill and played in the roots of a tree or down on the beach, building cars in the sand. We didn't need to be entertained. When we first came here, my mother loved to read – that was her diversion – and she would get on the porch with a book and tell us to go play. We would go running down to the beach and then come back and say, "What do we do now, Mother?" She'd say, "Look kids, if you don't make up your minds to entertain yourselves, we're going home; I might just as well be at home as trying to read up here with all of you screaming on the porch." We'd play tennis every morning from 9:00 or 9:30 until noon and go to the beach every afternoon. There were miles and miles of beach – it was beautiful! We used to play baseball on the beach. When the weather got cold, we sat behind the pump house.

*Sunning behind the pumphouse.*

*Ruth and Ray Kropp. 1953.*

I often visited the Circle. Our entertainment was to get a chocolate coke at the Soda Bar, for a nickel apiece. We'd watch Mrs. Sturtevant in her old rocking chair as we sat on the steps by Ballou Inn and waited for the mail to come in. That was the best part of the whole day, was the mail. They didn't have any children's activities at the Clubhouse when I was a girl. At that time, the Clubhouse was rather a decadent place; it really was. Once in awhile I used to go with Mrs. Ward to her bridge parties, just because Grandma went.

I invited Ray up when we were seniors in high school. He brought a friend with him; they both stayed at the hotel for a weekend. I got his friend a date with Weensie Borchert. Of course, Ray and I took off and left the two of them, and Weensie said she would get the friend home to the hotel. She did, but then, to be polite, he had to walk her home to her cottage, back in the woods. He'd get her to her house and she'd say, "Do you think you can find your way back to the hotel?" He'd say, "I doubt it," so she'd go back to the hotel with him. Anyway, that was the beginning. Ray and I went out to play tennis the first morning he arrived. He had never played tennis in his life and I had played all my life and wasn't a bad tennis player, but he beat me terribly. That was before breakfast. He always kidded me about the fact that I had to be nice to him. After breakfast I beat him.

After Ray and I married and started our family, we didn't come to Palisades until Judy was about eight. We rented what was then known as Sunnyside, now the Colb's Cozy #115. We always laughed about it because "Sunnyside" had no sun at all. We rented that with the Lotts family.

In about four years, we bought property up at the north end by the Brandywine, near the Welleses. But the beach was eroding at that time and the property didn't seem very good for building. Mrs. Knapp, the caretaker's wife, talked us into looking at property at the south end. She had a long strip on the lake, not in Palisades at the time, but she said all we would have to do to be members was to buy another piece of property in the Park. When we looked at it, Ray said he wouldn't buy unless Palisades would promise to annex us to the Park. They did, so we built in 1951 and we have been here ever since.

Rudy Weber, bless his heart, built our cottage. He worked on many of the cottages. On Sunday morning, he used to come over here in a fresh pair of bib overalls, all clean, walking up the driveway with the Chicago Sunday paper. He'd come in and Ray would say, "Come on Rudy, and have a cup of coffee." He'd say, "Oh, no, I've just had coffee ... Well, alright, just a little one." So he'd come in and take his clean red bandanna and fluff it and put it down on the chair and sit on it. Then he'd tell us the same stories every week. On Sunday morning the children would just disappear. At the end of the year, he always came with his board and sat at the table while Ray told him what had to be done in the wintertime on the cottage. He could do anything. He'd write on the board what he had to do. I still have one of his boards with all its notations. He and his wife, Millie, were our very dear friends. We always had a get together with them. They'd come over here in the truck and

*Rudy Weber 1954.*

have dinner. Rudy liked his bourbon. Once a year, in the fall, we'd go to his house and have dinner there; it was like Thanksgiving, with hot biscuits and turkey and gravy and mashed potatoes. It was always hot in his house and we'd eat so much.

I remember Joe Putz. He was a handyman and a jack of all trades. Joe, as a child, had had polio, I think, and one of his arms was deformed. What he couldn't do with that one short arm was amazing. He was very artistic. In fact, our sign out in back, "Retreat," was one Joe carved. It is hanging on an old brass bedpost that he straightened out and painted black. Because the smell from the septic tanks he often worked on was so terrible, we always talked to him outside. Joe collected everything; he saved everything. When he died, Rudy Weber was appointed by the township to go into Joe's house and take out what was valuable. He said that he'd never seen such a conglomeration of junk. Joe had collected newspapers and piled them up, one on top of another, and slept on top of them. He saved pennies in a jar and they had all melted together.

My brother John's wife was a Shepherd. When I was a kid, Mr. Shepherd used to come around in his flat wagon with the milk cans; we used to come out with any size pitcher and he'd pour his milk in. I don't think it was pasteurized, either, just raw milk. We would let the cream float to the top and Mother would use the cream on her cereal. He also sold cakes and pies and cookies and such, made by the farmers' wives. I remember Charlie Tunecke's mother. She wore a horse blanket for a skirt. We kids would try to get the watermelons out of her garden. She would come out at night with a shotgun and shoot at us.

We used to have a fashion show with Polly's (a store in South Haven) every year. When Jeanne DeLamarter was here, we had one-act plays; I was in those. Didn't Mary Kay Goodrich direct one of those? One time we had a mystery and needed ears in a jar, so I got a potato and carved ears out of the potato. Once I played the part of an Indian. Mikey Mathias – who at that time was real tiny – wore somebody's big sombrero and all the audience could see was the feet and the sombrero walking across the stage. We used to build the props. It was a lot of fun. I remember my daughter was in the hospital one time with an emergency appendectomy; I practiced my lines for one of the plays while I stayed in the hospital overnight.

Ray was one of the Nine Old Men. They incorporated into a group and put up all the money to buy the property that Julia Quick Hill was going to sell to some real estate group in South Haven. They kept the property for several years and the Park eventually took it all over from them.

Ray was on two Boards, in the 50's and 70's. Back in the early times the annual meetings were on Saturday night. People would go to cocktail parties and get all liquored up and fight with everybody at the meetings. Ray decided that was enough of that. He said he didn't want to go to any more fights – he could fight at the office all week. So the meetings were changed to the morning, which was better. People had a good night's sleep and didn't fight with each other.

*Rubbing of a Shepherd bottle.*

*Deck of Kropp Cottage #178, "Retreat"*

# Mardy Mehagan Mavor and Vashti Blaney

Interviewed by Mary Louise Tombaugh and Frances Prange. August 27, 1984.

V: I'd like to tell how I first came to Palisades Park. Mr. Quick used to call on my father in Chicago and try to sell him lots. My father finally thought, "Well, I'll end these calls by going over and seeing the property, and then he'll realize that I'm not interested." So Father came over with Mr. Quick, and he <u>liked</u> it, and he bought a lot and built a cottage. So that's how we started coming. Mr. Phillips built the cottage. His wife used to do our laundry.

M: One of the Phillips grandchildren was a red-haired little child and they named her Vashti. Mrs. Ward clothed that child.

V: That's my only namesake! Anyway, Mardy always came with us in the summers. I think we first came in 1907. I was about eight years old, and it was quite a trip in those times. We took a train from the Grand Central Station in Chicago, and then we changed trains in Hartford, Michigan, and got on the Fruit Belt Line to Covert. In Covert, we were met by Mr. Shattuck in a horse-drawn bus that had two planks on the sides. All of our belongings were sent by train, in trunks, since we came for the whole summer. Those are my first recollections. Later, the bus became mechanized and it was drawn by an engine instead of the horses, but in the beginning, that's the way it was. Of course, there were very few cottages here then. There was Sturtevant Lodge. Our cottage was right where it is now (#92). It was much smaller. In the beginning, it was just sort of on stilts; then they made a room downstairs. Later Mother and Father added on to it; later still, the Hal and Mary Lee Tillson enlarged it. I had one sister. We had always gone away in the summer because she had hay fever. We used to go farther north, but she got along pretty well here.

M: When we would change trains from the New York Central train, we'd get on the Chicago Lake Shore and Kalamazoo - an impressive name but the funniest little train you ever saw. It had horrible red plush seats that hadn't been cleaned since they were manufactured. The cinders that came out of the engine were probably about as big as marbles; they'd come showering down on us. Anyway, there were several stops between Hartford and Covert; it was really a fruit belt line, its main business to take the fruit to South Haven where it would be shipped by boat to Chicago. Oftentimes there was quite a delay and we'd stop by a station. Everybody on the train would get out and sit on the grass and chitchat; then they'd have

*Vashmar, the Ward cottage #92 on the beach. Now owned by the Tillsons, Mrs. Ward's great-grand children.*

*The Covert Depot. Note buggy in background.*

*First building of Sturtevant Lodge on right;
Cota cottage #47 (now Haude's Owl's Nest) on left;
Rev. Schreck's cottage #45 ( now Coleman's Old Pier) in back.
1910.*

the things unloaded and the conductor would come along and say, "Now come on. You all have to get on the train." And away we'd go. Well, the first time I came over here alone, I believe I was a freshman in high school. I'd been in a convent and the sister superior had lectured us very seriously about men, warning us to be careful not to be picked up and to beware of anything at the other end of a cigar. So I got on the train and this young chap came and sat down next to me. I thought, "Shall I do as the sister superior said or shall I be pleasant? Well, he'll be getting off someplace so what's the difference?" So we rode into Covert, chatting a bit, and he got off in Covert. I thought, "Well, I'll lose him here, anyway." Heavens no! He got into Shattuck's buggy and rode all the way to Palisades with me, chattering like a magpie all the time. Turned out it was Bert Henderson, whom probably everybody at Palisades knows and a most affable somebody. Of course, he loved people and was a great talker, but he certainly had me scared to death for awhile.

V: I only remember a few early cottages - the Henderson cottage (#120) and Treetops (#83) and Sturtevant Lodge. We didn't have a kitchen in our house so we took all of our meals at the Lodge. The Sturtevants rang a bell at 8:00 a.m. and if you weren't there in five minutes, you didn't get breakfast, so we were just breathless every time we went over. And then the same thing at noon and at night. Dinner was at 6:00 p.m., wasn't it?

M: Yes. It was such fun for the children to get over there early enough to ring the bell. We just vied with each other in order to get over there first.

V: The Lodge, then, was just the part that later was the dining room. There were some bedrooms above that. One time we were having breakfast and Mr. and Mrs. Miles were up here visiting my mother and father. Mr. Miles was very particular; he was cross before he had his breakfast. So he was eating, and – all of a sudden – Elise Wunsch, who was staying in one of the rooms above, upset her washbasin. There was no running water, you see. She upset her washbasin and the water came pouring down on Mr. Miles's table. He was like a wet hen!

M: The meals were very simple and very little. I mean, the helpings were not large. Particularly later, when Del Jones, the son, took over.

V: Everyone used to tease him and say, "We're still hungry, Del." He'd say, "You've had plenty." Oh, he was a funny old man.

M: In the hotel, in the early days, the partitions didn't go all the way up; they went within about a foot of the ceiling. Originally, Swedenborgian* people became interested in the Park – there were several of them who were the original settlers here. They had services at the Lodge. We knew a young Swendenborgian minister, a very personable young man who was a lot of fun, and one day we "pie-crusted" his bed while he was out swimming. Well, the next morning we were standing around just eager to see who he would blame it on, and he never said a word to anybody. We were so deflated; all our fun amounted to nothing at all.

V: Miss Gare and her mother used to put up a little temporary house in front of the hotel, where they slept; they took their meals at the hotel. The Wunsches built about that time, the cottage Colemans have now. That was a tiny cottage – just a living room and two bedrooms. At first they stayed over the Lodge dining room; it was Elise Wunsch who tipped over the water. Otherwise, there was almost nothing here. The Clubhouse hadn't been built. We spent our time on the beach and in the lake.

M: And then they put up the tennis courts; we lived on the courts. The two courts on the south side of the road were put in very early. Tennis was really the great thing.

V: People came to the cottage and we entertained. We didn't need to get any groceries since we didn't eat in the cottage. Occasionally we'd walk to Covert and sometimes to South Haven. The beach was beautiful.

M: We picked wild strawberries on the hill, and raspberries and blackberries. I can remember filling buckets, going over the hill from the Clubhouse.

*A Swedenborgian Church was built between Linden Hills and Palisades Park.

V: When we were teenagers, Mother insisted we were in the cottage at 10:00 at night.

M: Vashti's sister, Marian, who is Mary Lee's mother, was my dearest friend. Mr. and Mrs. Ward, they were just darlings and took me under their wing; my mother was not living. Marian and I were such good friends that when they'd go away in the summer, they'd take me along, which was wonderful. Anyway, they would invite twelve young people, six boys and six girls, to come over and stay for two weeks at the cottage. We had our meals at the hotel, $5.00 a week for three meals a day. Of course, the evenings were long; we could go out on the beach after dinner and stay, but if we weren't in the cottage at 10:00, we were not invited back the next year. Mrs. Ward was always sweet and darling and she wasn't a disciplinarian, but when she said something, why, we listened. I can remember one night when I was over here with my later husband. We were out on the beach and we were tired from playing tennis and swimming. We went to sleep, and we woke up at three minutes to ten. I'm telling you, we came down that beach like a cyclone, to be sure to be in that cottage before 10:00. She didn't care how long we stayed up, but we were back in the cottage. One of the chaps who usually came along with us was an excellent amateur pianist; he knew everything and he played by ear; it didn't matter what we suggested – he'd play and we sang. We played games and we had much fun.

V: Later, when the Clubhouse was built, we used to go down there in the afternoons, sometimes, and turn on a Victrola and dance. Or play ping pong. We used it a lot, day and night. Adults used it too. Well, it was a smaller group of people; it wasn't divided into adults and children.

M: When the Clubhouse was built, of course, it was down on the beach. Then they moved it up on the hill. When the Depression came along all of the members dropped out of the Club except four couples. Mrs. and Mrs. Ward were among those four couples. The Clubhouse stood vacant then for quite a number of years and children were getting in and vandalizing it. Well, by that time I was grown and married and had my two children. Mrs. Ward said one time, when I was over here, "How would you like to come and stay in the

*A postcard showing the Park's early tennis court.*

*The Clubhouse on the beach.*

Clubhouse? You don't have to do anything but just be there so children won't be coming in and damaging it." So we did and we had the most wonderful time. Of course we didn't go over to the Lodge to eat. We had a two burner electric plate that I cooked for four on, and we kept house. We had one bedroom. There was a double bed that was out on the stage and two single beds in the bedroom. But we managed just beautifully and it was fun.

We had, of course, an icebox there and Tony Canonie would bring the ice. Many times I'd be in bed on the stage when Tony would come, but he wasn't embarrassed and neither was I. I put out the sign for 25 pounds of ice or 50 pounds. When I put out a 25 pound sign, he always brought 50, and when I put out a 50 pound sign, he always brought 75. One time my younger boy, who was small, said, "Tony, my mother only wants 50 pounds." Tony said, "Will you be quiet? This is for your mother." He was such an interesting character. I remember being up here with Mrs. Adams, who was Catholic. I went to church with her in South Haven and, as we were coming out of church one day, all of a sudden we felt these great bear arms coming around our necks and he said, "Here are two of my girls." That was Tony; he was just a sweetheart.

V: There were a great many Swedenborgians around here, and also in Covert Resort. Linden Hills was called Covert Resort.

M: They put in a golf course down here. Mr. Bendelow, one of the most prominent golf course architects in the country, laid out the course here**. Of course, there were sand greens and the fairways left much to be desired, but we'd go down there and play. There was a lot of goldenrod around, and poor Marian – who had hay fever, you know – would sneeze and cough and carry on. There were millions of grasshoppers. The course started right when you come in off the highway and went all the way down to the tennis courts.

V: There were eight holes. But they couldn't keep it up because it needed so much water.

** *The Bendelows still own his cottage #74.*

*Hole #9 on the old golf course.*

M: On the 4th of July they had a baseball game between the married men and the single men. Once when little Sue Sweet (DeButts at that time) was about nine or ten, a little tom boy, although she was the cutest looking little curly headed thing, she wanted to umpire the game. They said all right and I can still hear her coming out in this ringing voice: "Three strikes and you're out!"

Mr. Hempy always came over to watch. Then, after they had the game, they'd have a driving contest on the golf course. Somebody said, "Mr. Hempy, don't you want to play golf?" "I never played golf," he said. "Well, come on, we'll show you how." So he picked up a club and he wound up and he made the most fantastic drive that went way down the fairway. Everyone gasped! "Well, this is nothing," he said, "I don't know what's so hard about this game." So then they said, "Do it again; you have to do it three times." Well, the next two times he absolutely whiffed; he never hit the ball at all. He realized there was more to golf than met the eye.

The Hempys used to clean up that garbage wagon once a year and get all dressed up in their best clothes and come down and call on Mr. and Mrs. Ward. In their horse and buggy. They had the two horses that drew the garbage wagon. Molly was the white one. After Mary Lee's mother had passed away, we'd come over here. Our son John and Mary Lee were about three, I guess, and Mr. Hempy used to let them get up on the horses and ride around while they collected the garbage. They'd come back smelling like a rose, believe me.

V: One time they used to have horses to rent.

M: We have pictures of the children, about seven or eight, riding around the Park. There was a barn here then, where the garage was.

*Mr. and Mrs. Hempy collecting garbage with their horse and wagon. 1946.*

V: When we got a car, the trip to Palisades took <u>forever</u> on those roads. From Chicago, we had to go through Gary and Hammond and Whiting - all those railroad tracks – and we would be delayed by trains. One time we were taking some fruit home and by the time we got home the peaches were just mashed; they were hot. Oh, it was just dreadful.

M: My husband enjoyed Palisades. We used to leave the house in LaGrange about 10:00 in the morning. In those days, there was no trunk space in cars; everything had to be on a luggage rack on the running board. We couldn't open the door on the driver's side. We'd have the two boys and the dog. Since there were no kitchen facilities or bedding at the Clubhouse, I had to bring all the kitchen things and all the bedding plus the children's clothes and toys and equipment of various and sundry kinds. That all had to be packed on the car. We always had a dog. We'd stop just the other side of Gary for a picnic lunch and we'd get here about 5:00 p.m. When they first began running buses from South Haven to Chicago, they black-topped the roads, but they made the blacktop very narrow. There really was just room for the bus; the edges were all jagged. They didn't even them off like a curb, you know. And the buses would come roaring down the road. It was up to you to get out of the way.

V: Another thing – we used to hire a launch to come over, sometimes, from South Haven. The original posts in the water now are from way back, from the logging camp and lumber days. But then we did have a dock that went out. It was high for the launch. I'll never forget a friend of my mother's was here, and she was very large. Well, to get her on the boat - she got in all right when we were going to South Haven, but to get her out was a different matter. It took several men to pull her onto the dock. We used to go over to dance in South Haven, and one night we went over by launch. Coming back, a storm was beginning. Mother said, "I don't think we had better try to go back, do you?" and the man who was running the launch said, "Oh, I think we can make it all right." Well, we started off, and you know how storms come up on the lake. Mother was responsible for all of these children, and people were down on their knees praying. It was that bad. We finally got here and Mother was so thankful because she thought this was going to be the end of all of us.

M: Mr. and Mrs. Ward were both marvelous bridge players. They taught me how to play bridge. I used to go up to the Clubhouse shivering in my timbers when I played bridge with Leo Sowerby and Mr. and Mrs. Ward.

V: I remember Mr. Shepherd and his beard.

M: Yes. I'll tell you another character here in the Park, Mr. Gervais. He used to come around to all the cottages and deliver from the store and he was about as big as a match – I don't think he had a dime's worth of flesh on his whole body. He always wore the same green sweater, even if it was a hundred in the shade. Well, he ran an old Ford, the tin-lizzy kind you know, and one time when he was coming around on the "In" road, he went over the side. He came out of that unscratched, I think, or not badly hurt, anyway.

V: I didn't appreciate Mr. Quick at all. He planned the roads and was interested in Nature, and he wrote that book about wildflowers, but to us he was just a character.

M: Mrs. Quick was very sweet and very deaf.

V: She was very retiring.

M: Speaking of characters in the Park, do you know about Archie Allen? He was the postmaster here and the post office, at that time, was in the Soda Bar. He and my husband and Ernest Wunsch used to get together and have fun. They had gambling machines here at the time – slot machines. The word would come that the "law" was on the way out and they'd scurry around and get those machines out of the way so everything was pure and simple by the time the lawmen arrived. Anyway, for some reason or other, authorities became very suspicious of Archie, so they came up here and raided his cottage and found a complete setup of counterfeit money. He'd been making it and they caught him.

V: He spent years in jail.

M: One of the things that I remember happened at the North Shore Pavilion, in South Haven. We went up there. My husband-to-be (this was when we were engaged) was a very good dancer and they had a dance contest. We won second prize, which was a two and a half-dollar gold piece. We started that as our "nest egg" for our married life.

*Right: Mardy and Gilby Mehagan, 1941.*

*Below: The South Haven Dance Pavillion.*

*Mardy in 1945.*

# Mardy Mehagan Mavor
Interviewed by Katy Beck
August 14, 1986

When we first came, we took the train to Covert and then Mr. Shattuck met us. He had a private delivery business. He would come and pick us up with his horse and carriage and bring us to the Park. Well, it was kind of like a bus – it had seats across. Then he would go back with a wagon and bring our trunks, piled high. When the Tin-Lizzies came in, he bought a Ford.

There was a very artistic group of people who first came up here. They were really quite choice. I don't know why such people as Olaf Anderson came to the Park. Leo Sowerby came because of Olaf Anderson. Leo used to compose up at his cottage. He had a neighbor who didn't appreciate his composing, so she would turn her Victrola on and try to outdo him in sound. They really had a very funny thing going there; all the people in the Park who knew them appreciated what was going on. He was in a cottage on the right side of the road and Mrs. Brown was on the other side of the road. He had a studio, you know – he had his cottage and then he had a little sort of an annex to it, a small cottage that was his studio. It was quite close range so she could hear it, and she didn't enjoy it. She'd turn up the Victrola as loud as she could and then he would bang on the piano as loud as he could, trying to outdo each other. He was probably around his 30's then.

I never owned property here. But I visited. We were with Mildred Adams for a good many years. She would come from California and she had no way of getting over here, so we would meet her at the plane or train or whatever, bring her over, and then stay with her. She stayed where Gwen Ott is now (#106). After my husband retired, the cottage needed a lot of things done to it. He was handy at painting and that sort of thing, so he came over and did that for her.

One of the funny things that happened – I've referred to Bert Henderson, the type of person he was … well, he was in school with my husband, University of Chicago, so they knew each other. Bert was walking down through the woods and my husband was out in the yard raking leaves, and the "no-see'ums" were just terrible, so he had on a hat as protection against the bugs. Bert Henderson walked by and thought it was Mr. Hempy and called to him, "Hi, Mr. Hempy!" My husband was ready to cut his throat. Mr. Hempy was an old man - the garbage man, you know - so this wasn't any great compliment or anything. Bert's father was the only person who stayed in the Park in the winter, as I understand it, so he kind of kept his eyes on things. I don't know whether Mr. Henderson was paid or not. Did anybody ever mention the furniture that he made? There's still quite a little bit of it that I see. He would go off into the woods and get branches, about two or three inches in diameter, with interesting shapes. And he would make furniture - chairs and swings and tables. A lot of people had it, because,

*Leo Sowerby (right) and Robert Jordan doing some "monkey business." 1927.*

you know, in the early days, almost all of the furniture in the cottages came out of the attics. There wasn't anything very fancy in the way of furnishings in the good old days.

Another family from the early days was the Manierres. I remember when their cottage was built (#148). I think it cost $5000. Everybody was horrified at the price. And, oh, it had a great big living room. It was really a very nice cottage. One of the Manierre girls eventually bought Mr. and Mrs. Ward's home in Riverside. That was rather interesting. They also had a place over on Paw Paw Lake. Jack Manierre was quite a successful lawyer. They were very good bridge players, and very active in the Clubhouse. The Clubhouse, then, was mainly for adults. The main thing that went on for the children was Bunco. Bazaars were a very important part of the money that was raised for Clubhouse expenses. And plays. Sometimes we would put on a couple of them each summer, if we could get people who wanted to give up time at the tennis courts. This was before I was in the Clubhouse, but after it was up on the hill.

The Wards, of course, were Mary Lee Tillson's grandparents. When we had house parties at Mrs. Ward's - six boys and six girls, one of them quite a pianist – we would put on skits. Her house parties would do that. Mrs. Ward was the hub of the Clubhouse activities. She didn't participate, but she saw to it that whatever people could do, they were brought together to do it. Every year Mrs. Ward would have a big card party. She would invite all the guests at the Hotel and people in the Park and have a luncheon for them at the Hotel so all the people would get to know each other. That's how the Otts came here, and that's how the Adamses bought their cottage here. That's how the DeButts came – it was through Mrs. Ward's hospitality. They had just been staying at the Hotel; when they realized the Park people were so pleasant, why it interested them into buying property to build a cottage. Mary Lee Tillson's father, Cady, was an architect. He designed and built the cottage where Replogles and MacDougals lived – (#173) - and it was called the Mary Lee. You see, when Mr. Ward retired, they bought several cottages here in the Park. They had Tree Tops (#83), Brown Jug (#153), Mary Lee, and their own Vashmar.

Mr. Ward – William Henry Ward – was the traffic freight manager of New York Central Rail Road. One of his friends, a Mr. Markman, was a vice president of the company. The Markmans were people of considerable means. They were interested in the Park and bought the cottage that the Baers own, right behind the Wards. (#91) Well, the restrictions here – I don't know if they can still uphold those – but no Jews and no colored were allowed to buy property. Come to find out, Mr. Markman was Jewish. Life was so unpleasant for them here that they kept their cottage for one year and sold it the next. Which was a shame; they were lovely people. But they were not included socially. In early years, the people who rented Treetops had a colored maid and so did the people who rented Sandbox; the maids couldn't go swimming until after dark. Of course, the stupidest thing the Park ever did was to deny Tony Canonie a cottage in the Park. We wouldn't be having these beach problems if he were here. He would see that things were in ... that was his business. But the Park didn't want Italian Catholics, at that time. One woman was on a soapbox about how Irish Catholics were taking over the Park. That's part of the history of the Park, but it was the history of the whole society, of the country.

*A Ward house party. 1911.*

Another early family was the Gervais family. They are on a list of 1917 members of the Park. He was very tall and lean and sort of sepulchral, you know – undertakerish. I don't recall his wife very much, but she was an invalid and she didn't get out into circulation. She must have been a very pretty woman, because their daughter, Julia, was a very beautiful girl.

A Mrs. Brown, who was part of a rich family from Chicago, built the Mooney cottage (#82) and moved up here from her great big house in Chicago. She brought the most beautiful Oriental rugs and china and silver and linen. That cottage was just – well, it wasn't Hearst's Castle, but it had similar things in it. She and Mrs. Ward were good friends, so I was up there with them and had an opportunity to see the house. Mrs. Brown was the one who paid for the cement steps to the Clubhouse. Well, when she died, the cottage was sold. The Enoses bought it, lock, stock, and barrel, for $5000. Those Oriental rugs in there were priceless, and the silver and china. The Enoses had it for many, many years. Then they sold to the Mooneys.

One story about Mrs. Brown. One of the entertainments that we put on in the Clubhouse had boys all dressed up like ballet dancers. We had the greatest time making tulle skirts for them, and band-brassieres. Somehow or other, they all got wigs. They were having this great performance ballet dancing. And, of course, gladiolas are a part of Palisades Park and we had two beautiful bouquets of glads, one for each side of the stage. The boys went through their dances and they were so carried away with the enthusiasm of the audience that they picked up the vase of gladiolas, all dripping wet, and threw the flowers out into the audience. They landed in Mrs. Brown's lap. She was not too thrilled over the whole things. She was sort of the patroness of the Clubhouse. It was a great mistake to have thrown it at her.

*"Ballet dancers" - glads in hand!*

Oh, I wanted to tell you something about the Bishops. They would come up here from St. Louis for the summer, you know, and Helen had a maid. Helen knew that when she got here, she wouldn't have any time to grocery shop, so she'd bring up food that would take care of the family. The maid cooked a turkey; she got up early so it would be ready to go when the family was ready to go. Well, it's a long, hot trip from St. Louis. When they got here, they had Charlie Tunecke help them unload. The turkey was in the roaster and he carried it in; all the way there were drippings of turkey juice. When he got the turkey into the cottage, they realized it had spoiled. It smelled to high heaven. All that horrible odor, greasy smell, was all over on the rug and on the floor. It took her all summer long to get that odor out of there.

Forest Lowrey and my husband were fraternity brothers and that's how I really got to know him. Of course, Marion Skinner, his wife, was in Marion Ward's wedding party, and I was a part of that too. I've known Marion a long, long time.

There was a great rivalry between Ballou Inn and Sturtevant Lodge. In the Inn, the dining room was on the second floor and the rooms were up above that. Mrs. Ballou served meals that she thought were better than Sturtevant Lodge meals. The first Hotel had a little store that was funny. They had one of those glass counters, you know. They sold cigars. I can still see Mr. Sturtevant back there with his cigar. He was a nice man and helped a lot. Mrs. Sturtevant was the aggressive hotel keeper, really. He just sort of did what she said. When I first came, both the Hotel and Ballou Inn were here, and I don't know anything before that.

Ballou Inn served meals to its guests, but the Lodge let people who lived in the Park come there to have their meals. The Wards were the Lodge's meat and gravy because they had their cottage full all summer long and they ate three meals a day at the hotel. But when Mr. Ward retired and put a kitchen in their cottage, Del Jones – that's the Sturtevant's nephew who was running the Lodge by then – wouldn't let them come over there and eat because they weren't taking three meals a day there. I thought that was a very strange reaction. Of course, Del was a crabby old thing. The kids loved to tease him. His brother, Art, was a darling. All the young people just loved him. But Del had a sort of abrasive attitude. Oh, Ernest Wunsch and Mr. Ward would just devil the life out of Del at the hotel. They'd say, "Well, you didn't serve enough," and come back for seconds. They were just kidding, you know. They would tease the life out of him about the food, about the fried potatoes that they had every morning. They were sure the potatoes were done once a week and scraped off the plates to come back from Monday to Saturday.

*Sturtevant Lodge when second building was complete, but women still wore long dresses. c. 1915?*

In the early years, the Lodge rooms were partitioned. We had a little wash stand and a place to hang clothes. There was about a two-foot clearance up at the top where it was open to the ceiling, like a partitioned dormitory. The bigger part of the Lodge must have been built between 1912 and 1913. No, it would have been before that because they had a little boardwalk that came from that new part of the hotel down through the sand for us to get to Mrs. Ward's cottage when we came for house parties. A funny thing happened when we were here one year. One of the girls at the house party dropped her watch. It came off and she wasn't aware of it, but she knew she'd had it when she went over to breakfast. Then it was gone. When we came back the next year, a bunch of us were standing there kicking up the sand between the boards, and we kicked up a watch. Wasn't that something?

There was a road coming in as far as the Circle, just like it is now. It hasn't changed a bit. I don't think they sold lots in the Park until they had all the roads ready, because people couldn't get in to see the lots. I remember there were always roads. We walked down here, you know, when I was young. I first came in 1907. Mrs. Overhuel ran the store. She really carried very nice things. Swift and Company would bring their trucks with good meat and all the various merchants' cereals and crackers and cheese and that sort of thing. The store was very nicely stocked. The farmers around here would bring their produce – berries and vegetables and things like that – so you could get absolutely anything you wanted at that store. It is really too bad that chain-store living has become such a part of people's lives. These places that carry tennis shoes at the grocery store – everything from pins to automobiles – have really killed off the small grocery.

The garage came long after the big part of the hotel was built. It was here when I was in the Clubhouse in the 30's. I guess there was an ice house there, come to think about it. And then they built the brick garage. The icehouse was on that property. The ice cream parlor was not here when I first came. That came quite a bit later. It was first built as a cottage, but for awhile the mail came there. Archie Allen was Postmaster. He went to jail for counterfeiting. He lived in the cottage across from Tree Tops, Valley Haven. The counterfeiting was in the basement.

One of the most interesting cottages in the Park is the Edwards cottage (#163). I don't think too many people know about it. Mr. Edwards got all the plans together, then built a little log cabin to scale of the size of his cottage. He ordered the lumber for that, down to the last piece of what he was going to need. He designed it, did all the drawings and that sort of thing. Their living room has a great big compass painted on the floor – very interesting.

*Compass on the floor of Tree House #163.*

The Clubhouse was first on the beach. In fact, Gilby and I did some courting there. That would be 1915 and 1916. By 1920, it was moved up on the hill. They wanted a little more space and since property on the hill was available, they decided it would be better to have the Clubhouse in the woods. Oftentimes they would have something going on and, in bad weather, it was difficult to get to it, on the beach. Up on the hill, people could get there by car.

*Old postcard of Clubhouse after it was moved.*

*Mardy in 1990.*

All of the Clubhouse members, the wives, would work like beavers all winter long and make all kinds of beautiful things. Once a year, they would have a sale up at the Clubhouse. One year they raised $700, a vast sum in those days. That was remarkable. But the ladies did beautiful handiwork of all kinds. Very interesting. We had that every summer for years. That was what funded the Clubhouse, really, yes.

Once at the Clubhouse, we put on a performance called Cabaret. We sold one hundred tables. Can you imagine getting a hundred tables in that Clubhouse? We served food. I was the manager and I tell you, I was never so tired in my life when that was over. Anyway, Connie and Weensie Lowrey dressed up as cabaret girls and Bill DeButts dressed up as Diamond Jim Brady – with a diamond stickpin and all that. We persuaded Jeanne Best to let us bring her beautiful miniature piano down to the Clubhouse, and they wheeled that all around to the various and sundry tables. People requested the song that they wanted, and – for a dollar – Weensie played the song and they both sang. We raised a fabulous amount of money.

We had a costume party one time where we dressed up in anything we wanted. I was very disappointed because the Otts, who had always supported me in my endeavors at the Clubhouse, had said they weren't coming. Their excuse was they didn't have any costumes. Well, about the middle of the evening, while there was a lull in the dancing, somebody came storming up onto the porch and here the whole Ott family came dressed up as the Yokum family. Alice was Mammy Yokum, Dorothy was Daisy Mae, all of them with great big clubs on their shoulders. At the end of the procession – it was just like a bunch of little ducks coming in – was little Jackie with his stick over his arm. Well, they were a smashing success! I've loved them every since, and here, I thought they had let me down. Hoddy Clark was really a very famous artist, a portrait painter, and we got enormous sheets of wrapping paper and she helped make murals on the walls of different characters here in the Park. The murals were raffled off. Hoddy used to do some lovely portraits of the children around here.

A New York theatrical director came here when we put on <u>Candida</u>. I think his name was Mr. Timmons. Jayne Mathias had the leading part. In the middle of the performance, Mr. Jones (who was Dr. Matthews's father-in-law) got up and said, "I think this performance should be halted. I don't think that this is anything that the people of Palisades Park should be subjected to." Well, everybody in the audience was simply furious. They halted the play and Mr. Timmons came out on the stage and said, "Well, Mr. Jones, what do you think is objectionable about it?" "Everything," said Mr. Jones. "Well," Mr. Timmons said, "do you think you could do any better?" And Mr. Jones replied, "Yes, I think I could." And so they put the curtain down and he came up on stage and talked to the characters for a little while. Then, as they said their lines, he'd correct them. Then, when the curtain came down in the end, Mr. Timmons came out and asked, "Is this a better job?" Everybody gave J. Harry Jones a standing ovation because he put on such a wonderful act. People had been so furious at him and then in the end – but nobody knew that they were going to do this. The cast had never leaked a word. It was a very hilarious occasion.

Mr. Quick wanted to introduce square dancing when I was up there at the Clubhouse. We had a funny orchestra that came from Covert, a violinist, piano, and drum, which was just perfect for square dancing. He sent to Detroit and got all the books about square dancing and came to the Clubhouse and said, "Mrs. Mehagan, can't we do something about this?" I couldn't interest any of the young people in square dancing; that was the last thing in the world they wanted to do. Two years later, the whole country was going crazy with square dancing.

When we were first asked to stay at the Clubhouse, we weren't paid. Mrs. Ward was the one responsible for it and she just said, "Would you like to come up with the children and stay all summer?" It was a place to stay and we helped her out really, to care for it, when she had been so nice to me. It turned out to be just great. I ran the Clubhouse, let's see – well, it was during the Depression, the last of the 20's and the early 30's. I did it for several years, before Palisades Park took over the Clubhouse. They decided that they wanted to have some type of activity and they asked if I would do it. Then after the Depression, when people began to get on their feet a little bit financially, the Park decided the Clubhouse couldn't be run as a private membership thing – people were not interested in that sort of thing anymore – so the Park decided to buy the Clubhouse. It became property of the Park. It had first been owned by the members, twelve in all.

*An earlier - and shorter - interview took place August 27, 1984, conducted by Mary Louise Tombaugh and Frances Prange.*

The Swedenborgians are a religious sect – I presume you would call it a denomination. I don't know what exactly their philosophy is, but it is Christian. They were very strong here. Many of the people here – the Nelsons and the Sengenbergers – were Swedenborgians. They would have services at the Clubhouse every Sunday. By the late 30's, the Clubhouse had regular vespers. I was a soloist at the Sunday evening services in the early 20's.

We often shopped at Sinks store in Covert. He had wonderful meat there. Mr. Sink was a funny old man. Of course, you know why he went out of business? When the State put in the tax on food, he couldn't be bothered by keeping track of the tax at all. Finally, the government got after him. At the time, his sons were in the business with him; they finally figured out, somehow or another, figures that were acceptable to the government, but Mr. Sink no longer had any part in the store. Another one of the reasons why they almost went out of business was some of our people never paid their bills. It was the same way with the white people in Covert; they were taking advantage of him. When the Depression came on, you know, the town was taken over by colored people and his business picked up; they paid cash for everything. His business was back in running order. Quite a reflection, I thought.

Although most fun things here in the Park revolved around the water and the tennis courts, once a year we'd

*The Vespers service was a regular Sunday evening event during many summers.*

have a hayride. We'd go up to South Haven and dance, and then come back on the hayride. It was fun. Frequently, we walked to South Haven. When the automobile came in, that changed things. You could get out of the Park and people could go shopping and that's when there was a wonderful market in South Haven near McDonald's. Ken was the butcher there; he had beautiful meat. Eventually, he established his own store out near the Catholic Church. That didn't go so well.

The Iversons used to have a farm in Covert, down the road. Later, they bought property over at Paw Paw, with a very nice house. The vegetables they sold would be washed and arranged beautifully. They looked like someone with real skill at arranging things had put them all together in an eye-appealing way. It was all so good. Mrs. Iverson would give you lovely flowers. She knew I loved lima beans; I'd always get the first ones. One summer, I was leaving the first of August and I said to Mrs. Iverson, "I hope you have some lima beans for me before I go." I went over there the day before I left, and she had a little envelope. She had found one pod with three lima beans that were ripe enough for her to cook, and she cooked them for me. Oh, they were darling people. Lovely. Do you remember the strawberry jam she used to make for 50 cents a quart? They never had livestock on their farms, or grew field corn or anything like that. Only vegetables, as far as I know. Mrs. Iverson worked like a galley slave, too. She'd be out on the farm. One time I went there and she was a block away, picking beans. They had a big clientele and when we'd go home, we'd load up – when the Bishops went home, they had a BIG carload of melons and corn.

Mary Putz would bring these beautiful boxes of raspberries, arranged in rows with three little green leaves on top, for 25 cents. She and Joe would bring all kinds of vegetables; she would tootle through the Park with her basket and sell her things. She was a little "tetched." Joe Putz would come and do anything, anytime you wanted, day or night. He had a crippled arm; one was smaller than the other. Once we were at Helen Bishop's after we'd all been swimming. We were having a little sundowner, and old Joe Putz came along the boardwalk and came up and joined us. "Here are my girls," he said. Well, the group of people who were available to help with the cottages – Joe Putz and Charlie Tunecke and Warren Knapp – they would do anything in the world to help you. Mr. Knapp was especially good with plumbing when the roots of the trees would get in the way. "Them poplars. Them's just a nuisance," he'd say.

The hill by Buckeye King used to be covered with wild strawberries and blackberries. The berries were the pits to try and pick, but they were good. We'd just pick all we wanted to. Then cottages were built there. One was owned by a Mrs. Peach; it later burned. That was a long time ago, before I was married. It's the only really big fire that I remember here, except the McQuigg's.

*The Park cocktail party July 2, 1994, was a celebration for Mardy's 100th birthday.. Indeed, that July party ever since has been named in her honor. At that first party, she was serenaded with the following two songs:*

---

(To the tune of "Daisy, Daisy")

Southside, northside, all around the Park,
There goes Mardy, walking from dawn to dark.
She knows every path and byway
From lakefront to the highway;
The folks she meets
She always greets
With her typically cheerful spark.

Oh, how lucky, having our friend around!
In her presence, comraderie will abound.
With slightest of instigation
There's lively conversation;
She listens well,
Has stories to tell,
What a jewel of a friend we've found!

(To the tune of "Let Me Call You Sweetheart")

You helped to settle Palisades, long years ago,
As a girl you had such fun, you loved it so.
Started up the Clubhouse, set the social tone –
First creative chairman that the Park has known.

Then you brought your family to join you here,
Adding to our history, year after year;
Generations passing on their values, and
Love for nature's beauty, forest, lake, and sand.

Tell us all your secret, oh dear Mardy, do,
How to reach one hundred and stay young like you!
We know you found the "fountain" celebrating age:
Just look at you, our model, our centenarian sage.

---

*At her 100th birthday party, Mardy greets Betty Householder.*

*Miller cottage #185.*

# Gwen Hautau Miller
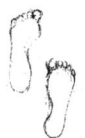
Interviewed by Betty Householder
August 28, 1984

I was about 10 or 11 the first time I came to Palisades Park to visit my aunt and uncle, about 1919, driving in one of those big clumsy Studebakers. As we came down Ravine Road, my mother was so terrified that when we came to the Y, we all had to climb out of the car and let Father go up the hill alone. For some reason, we didn't come up after that for quite awhile. We went to inland lakes, but Lake Michigan was much more thrilling. In 1934, and for several summers after that, we rented a cottage from Mr. Quick. He was so enthusiastic about the flowers and trees and what the Park meant.

My parents, Mr. And Mrs. Allen Hautau, purchased a cottage at the south end of the Park in 1945, just at the end of World War II (#185). Mother was Gwendolyn Louella; she is one of the four girls on the front of the South Haven history book. Our cottage was called No Man's Land because we weren't part of the Park until several years later. In fact, from Beck's cottage south to Linden Hills was called No Man's Land. Father bought a lot next to the Owens cottage and we paid dues on that, which gave us the right to ride through and use the Park. Ruth Kropp knows the year we became part of the Park because it was they who promoted the idea, shortly after they built. We had had our water from Linden Hills, a direct line, but when we came into Palisades we were hooked up to Palisades water. Linden Hills wouldn't give us water anymore.

We and the Egberts and the Hamiltons were the only ones down there. Mrs. Hamilton's father, Mr. Palmer, was an interesting old man from Chicago. He loved the lake. He'd get off the bus at Linden Hills and walk, and we'd see him when he came down the beach with his little suitcase.

Mrs. Ballou had a tearoom we ate in, on the second floor of Ballou Inn, where later there was a store. The hotel was running full force. We stayed largely at the south end of the Park, though in the 30's we had fun with bridge in the Clubhouse every week. The ladies were rabid players. Mrs. Ward and Mrs. Mehagan ran it. All three of my children grew up here. They went to the Clubhouse for something, but it wasn't as organized as it is now. One time our son decided to bring the champion tennis player from LaGrange High School up here for the Honor and Glory tennis tournament. However, in the tournament he got wiped out by a 13-year-old boy. That was a family joke ever since – what good tennis players we have had up here.

All the arts people who came here in the early years were interesting. My daughter Margot once met a girl in California. She seemed familiar but the two could never figure out where they had met. Years later we sent Margot an oil painting of the Park and this girl came over with her little daughter who said, "That looks like Palisades Park." They discovered, of course, that was where they had met. It was Betty Householder's niece. Of course Margot lived at the south end and the friend near the Circle. They figured they'd met each other at the Soda Bar.

In the deed to our cottage, we find that it was built by a pianist. If you can imagine, in those early days – she must have built it in the early 1900's, as soon as the Park started – she had her piano dragged down the beach. When we bought the cottage, it still had that darling little upright piano in it. One of the interesting names on the deed was Genovese. We found that the Internal Revenue had liens against him. There is some question in the title on this. They must have been running rum in prohibition days from this last cottage on the south, over to Chicago. With our children, that used to be a big game; we'd talk about the rum running and my boys would dig out in the sand dunes, hoping to find a pure copper still in the hills out there. After Mr. Genovese, another owner was in trouble with the Internal Revenue. Although the cottage was built by a very artistic woman, its history has certainly been varied.

*G. F. Palmer, early Park member who owned Cherry Hill.*

## Mary Lee Tillson
Interviewed by Betty Householder
September 11, 1984

I first came to Palisades Park in 1919, the year I was born. My grandparents, William and Mary Ward from Riverside, Illinois, came every summer starting in 1907 or 1908, with my mother and Aunt Ti, their daughters. I think Mr. Phillips built the cottage in 1907, but we're not sure. How he built it, I don't know. I don't think he had any education or anything, did he? I remember my grandfather saying that there were many cottages built the same year they built this one. Ballou Inn was here and the Lodge was built about then.

My grandparents came to the Park on the train. I know for awhile we came to Watervliet, when I was little. Mrs. Shattuck would meet us in that little taxicab and whisk us over for the summer. We came when school was out and stayed until Labor Day.

We took all our meals at Sturtevant Lodge until I was well into high school. My grandparents started eating over there because there wasn't a kitchen in the cottage. There was sort of a little icebox; there must have been a sink, but there wasn't a stove. So we had all three meals at the Lodge. Breakfast, lunch, and dinner. And we had to be there between 7:00 and 7:30 a.m. for breakfast, 12:00 and 12:30 p.m. for lunch, 6:00 and 6:30 p.m. for dinner, and that was it.

Grandmother played a lot of bridge. There were many bridge parties at the Clubhouse; adults used the Clubhouse more than they do now. I've been reading my mother's diaries from when she was up here. They went dancing at the Clubhouse every night, I think. Must have had a Victrola.

Dad was a good tennis player. He used to win tournaments at St. Joe, too. In fact, I still have a cup that he and his friend from Oak Park won – they were always going over to South Haven and winning tournaments there, too. It was fun, competing in other towns. It kept the communities together, too. We knew people over there.

I don't remember Mr. Ballou too well. We never ate there. It was more like a boarding house, as I remember. They served meals to their boarders, but I don't know as

*1909 on the beach - old seawall and remnants of old pier apparent. Note clothing; even on a cool day, these people look warm!*

they let outsiders come in.** The Ballous and various relatives of theirs ran the store.

Archie Allen ran the post office. I'm sure you've heard about him. The post office, most of the time, was in the store, but when he was doing his counterfeiting, it was in the Soda Fountain. (Later, Archie Allen was arrested by Internal Revenue.) Mr. Quick must have owned the Soda Fountain; his daughter and granddaughter ran it many years. They made the best chocolate milkshakes. They didn't serve food over there then, just ice cream.

We played cards over there or at the Lodge. We'd play Michigan Rummy all day long on rainy days, on the porch of the hotel. I was thinking about all the people who used to come up and stay at the hotel and eventually built cottages – the Otts, and I'm sure the deButts did, too. The Hagies and Ginny Melchert started there, too, before they bought. And the Wunsches. Life seemed simpler then, maybe because there weren't as many people and there weren't cars in the Park. We never went out of the Park.

*The Circle c.??*

There were funny old cars out there in the Circle, yet we used to play baseball every night. Del Jones's cousin, Frank Sturman, was a semi-pro baseball player, and he rounded up all the kids every night. The outfield was over in Flynn's front yard, and home plate was right there where those benches are, in front of the hotel. I don't know why we didn't break windows. We were little; I don't suppose we hit the ball that hard. And then we'd play hide-and-go-seek after that, in the dark, and prisoner's base at the Brandywine. We'd rocket down the

*\*\*This seems to contradict other interviews in which meals at the Inn were remembered.*

hotel porch. I don't know why we didn't expire before Del Jones, the Lodge owner, did! But the madder he got, the more fun it was to tease him. I didn't ever do too much to him, but people did put firecrackers in the toilet. He had those slot machines in there, too, in the office. They were illegal. He'd get the word the police were coming, and he'd put them in his bedroom off the office. He always had one or two slot machines – a nickel and a quarter one. We used to deliver telegrams for him. That was our big money-earner. We got 25 cents if we went to Linden Hills and a dime for Palisades. Nobody had phones so that was the only way people could keep in touch.

I liked everything about coming to Palisades. I played tennis. We had a routine – out to the tennis courts every morning and to the beach every afternoon. Allen Ferry all but put himself through college – well, that's an exaggeration – selling lemonade. He was Bill Ferry's brother, more my age. He'd come down from his cottage with a great big cooler thing. He'd make real lemonade every day and sell it. He kept a tab because nobody had any money on the beach. Then he'd collect it later. He really made quite a bit of money. The Ferrys had a good cottage to have a party in, because they had that great big porch all around.

My goodness, parties ended at 11:00 p.m. then, just as they're starting now. We had to be home or Mr. Quick had a fit. He'd be down on the beach looking for us. He was always very kind to me, though he was a gruff sort of a man. In his later years, he wasn't very well. When he married Kitty Wisson, he was sort of an old grouch then. But, as I look back on it, he was really a wonderful person.

I remember Mr. Hempy with his garbage wagon and Mrs. Hempy sitting there beside him, holding the horses. My grandfather always got such a kick out of him because he'd call him Will and my grandfather called him Mr. Hempy. He'd come home and he'd say, "How did that happen?" Of course, we didn't have much garbage because we ate at the hotel. He was manager for awhile before Mr. Knapp came in. Clare, Mr. Knapp's older son, ran the gas station. Squeak, the younger one, died in the war.

Tony Malinowski worked at the Lodge for several summers. I think he was a journalism major at Western Michigan, and he worked at the desk at the Lodge. Now I have no idea whether Mr. Quick ever hired him – I don't ever remember him as the director of anything. Well, maybe he ran the tennis tournaments. Somebody had to run them, and he was the type who liked to organize things. He was good at that. He was the one who started the Patter. Well, Jayne Mathias and I really started it. We used to just tack something up on a tree. We thought up "Strolling Through the Park." Then Tony decided it should be a little paper of some kind. He thought of the name "Patter." It was nothing like it is now; it was just a little gossip thing. It was fun.

*Tony Malinowski c. 1940's*

Later on, when Mrs. Bishop and Jeanne Anderson got involved, they made it more of a paper. They bought a mimeograph machine and made it of more interest to everyone. They had an office on top of the garage. It was hotter than Hades. They were always working late at night. Then they'd take the mimeograph machine down to the Brandywine and wash it right in the Creek when they were through with it. You could hardly read the paper when it came out. Oh, they were good, those Patters were. It is wonderful now, though. It has held the Park together. If you know people, you're more tolerant of them than if you don't know them at all. And there's a lot of interesting stuff in the Patter that you wouldn't know otherwise. It keeps the rumors down, for one thing. Of course the Patter didn't go during the war years – it just stopped.

The half-mile swim was pretty loosey-goosey in the beginning. The idea was to prove to yourself that you could swim a half-mile. Somebody always won, but that was very minor. Mr. Lowrey's idea, when he first thought of the race, was for our own safety, to show we could swim that far if we ever had to. We had canoes and rowboats, but there weren't many speedboats. Some people had motors for their canoes and just putted around. Nobody got into water skiing until much later.

The old swinging bridge was scarey but fun. We used to swing in the middle of that bridge, just like everybody else. Sometimes we'd go up the trail to Old Baldy, where Consumer's is now. Or south to Marvin's Slide, an area which now has been built into homes. We did that about once a year because it was quite a hike. And we would go to South Haven once a year also. It was a beautiful walk. It's sad we can't get through anymore. We slept out on the beach at least once a year – and

*Marvin's Slide c. 1905*

wondered why we did it, at 4:00 o'clock in the morning when the sand would get hard and cold. I still go swimming before breakfast sometimes. That's one thing about living on the beach. It's hard to think about living anywhere else because it's so convenient here.

The lake has treated us badly over the years. Although not when you consider how old our cottage is. We have had a big wide beach from time to time. The first seawall was built in 1929. My grandfather came (after the big storm) and found the water lapping at the front door. It wasn't standing there, but if it was a little bit rough ... that was when the Bishop's cottage and the Von Rosen's had everything washed out from under them. So the water did get really high before, many times, but I think that was the highest. That was when Mary Kay Goodridge's cottage, the Baker cottage, was washed out. Since then, I think we've put in two more walls of some variety. Two wood and one steel.

I remember the posts from the old pier, but I don't ever remember the pier. One summer we had just a beautiful summer, with hardly any bad weather. We had a diving board on the posts where it was deep; that was fun. It seemed to stay there all summer and didn't get washed out. We used those rafts with the tubes and they were fun, too. But of course, we could pull them in and they were no problem on the beach. At that time, everyone used to swim here, in the Circle. Then for awhile we all went down to the Clubhouse, and then for awhile everyone came back here.

One time, George Bishop and I had to pretend we'd drowned. Julia Quick's husband – I don't remember which husband she was on, Mr. Pond, I believe – he thought it would be interesting to see how fast the Coast Guard could get down here. For some reason, he wasn't allowed to do it as an experiment; some of us had to act like we were in trouble. He told George and me to go out in the canoe – you know how you get out there and you don't think you're as far as you really are, and my grandmother was such a worrier, pacing up and down. Well, we tipped over in the canoe. Mr. Pond was up on top of the hotel, and since he saw us go over in the canoe, he called the Coast Guard in South Haven. They got down in seven minutes or something like that. But they didn't know – we knew, but they didn't – that it was a put-up job. They kept trying to do artificial respiration on us, and we kept saying, "We're all right; we're all right!" Well, they got us in and it was funny, but I think my grandmother and Mrs. Bishop aged twenty years by the time they got us back in. Mr. Pond was satisfied. Now I guess there isn't any Coast Guard in South Haven. They relay calls to St. Joe.

I don't suppose I knew the kids from the south end so well. People stayed pretty much where they were. I still don't know too many people on the north end, on the other side of the Brandywine, except for the ones that have been here forever.

For a few years the Bookmobile came in. Betty Householder started that. They came into the Circle, but they lost so many books and we had to pay them so much money, in the end it got less economical and they had to cut it out. It was always something we'd look forward to. That was very nice. It was from the Paw Paw Library, a county thing. People would forget to return books and renters would take them home and there was no way for the Park to retrieve them. But all the kids in the Park came for books and they would get any book you wanted. I miss that and the store and the post office. But their closing couldn't be helped. They just weren't economically feasible.

*The remainders of Palisades Pier posts. Vashmar on right.*

*Entrance to Vashmar today.*

*Charlie Tunecke and Cecil Burrous. 1985.*

*1937 picture of Brandywine and old boat house.*

# Charley Tunecke

Interviewed by Katy Beck and Cecil Burrous
August 25, 1985

I was the old originator. I carried stakes for A. C. Quick. He was president of the Park. He owned about 260 acres and then he turned back 100 acres and kept 160 acres and built Palisades out of that. Built the roads. He drew plans for people for cottages and he built them and figured out how much lumber, nails, and plumbing for each cottage – everything that was in there. He figured out and told them what the cost of the cottage would be. Eugene Phillips built 67 cottages with his own hands. I helped with the surveying. I was only about 15 or 16 years old, so I carried the stakes, see? A fellow was doing the surveying - he laid out Lincoln Park in Chicago. Benson, his name was. He and Mr. Quick laid out all those roads in there and all. Mr. Quick helped a lot on that. He was right on the job when they were doing the work, see? He figured out that when he laid out those roads, he took that dirt from the side hill and just pushed it over. So there was no need to carry sand. He followed the hill quite a bit. Mr. A. B. Palmer laid out the plumbing in the Park. He was Frank Palmer's brother.

Mr. Quick was president of the Park – the old originator. A. C. Quick. He did most everything himself. He used to work to midnight up there in his cottage. He lived across from the hotel up there. He could see all over. The first cottage that was built there was for Reverend Schreck. He came from England. And A. C. gave him that place to build a cottage. What was the name of that? Treetops (#83). That was the first cottage built. Mr. Quick gave him that lot to build on. Before the Quick's cottage was there. Mr. Quick built that garage and he built a boathouse, too, a long boathouse near where the garage was, by the Brandywine. I used to keep my horses in there, in the boathouse. At noon, when I got through working with my team, I put them in the boathouse. That's where the marsh was. It was built right into the marsh. The Brandywine Creek wound around there with a bridge across the creek.

The old icehouse was where you come out of the woods. There was a road, just as you came out, and it turned left. It went aways, made a turn, and came straight down hill and there was the icehouse. Remember where Warren Knapp used to keep his horse over there? That was the icehouse. Where he stored his hay was the icehouse. But Dave Vanderboegh and Cecil tore the icehouse down. It was full of sawdust. Hempy used to keep his horses in there. And Vern Underwood used it for his riding horses last. Anyway, I used to get ice wherever I could.

*Mrs. Schreck - English owner of the earliest cottage built in Park, Treetops #83.*

Sometimes I made it off of Paw Paw Lake or another lake. Sometimes, I'd make it from Lake Michigan if the icebergs were just right. If there was a wide space between the bergs, there would be a flat space of water and then that would freeze and I'd get ice off the lake. We'd drive right out onto the lake with our sleighs and just pick up the ice. We used handsaws. And after awhile, I got what they called a snowplow, see? It had six prongs. One was just a little ways down. The next was a little deeper and then a little deeper. Maybe cut the ice down about six inches. But we always kept the horse on the hard part of the ice so it didn't get on where we cut with that machine. And then I had what we called a needle bard. It had a round handle up here. And I'd just get that with the needle bard, and spin it off the rest of the way. And then we had to make a little channel where the ice would go. It would go up on the chute and onto platforms and then onto our sleighs or whatever was there to haul it away to the icehouse near the Brandywine. We kept the ice about a foot away from the outside of the building. We'd cover it with sawdust, about 12 – 14 inches between each one of the layers. We had a little more sawdust to about three feet deep on top. Then I'd get marsh hay and put on top of that. I'd put on 90 to 120 ton of ice, for the whole summer. Oh, I had a lot of help. Eight or ten fellas helping me. One time I had about ten or twelve teams haul ice from Paw Paw Lake. We had a string of teams. We'd carry it on the sleighs. What we called firing racks. We'd fill them right up. We could haul a big load. I'd carry maybe six, seven ton of ice on a sleigh. We cut little poles about that big around, put them under the sled runners so when we took off, sometimes, they'd freeze right to the ice. Then we'd get going right to the icehouse. I took care of ice for Palisades Park and Linden Hills. It would last the whole summer. Sometimes I'd have one or two layers left over, but not very often.

R. J. Hempy and I hauled clay with teams, too, for the Park roads. We had to dig the clay out. We'd even have to dynamite it! It was from Covert. Before we got there in the morning, we'd put that dynamite in the oven and then stick a big hole in there, about as big as your finger. We'd put a cap on the fuse and poke it in the cap, maybe six-foot long, and then we'd run away and wait until it goes off and blows the clay loose. We had shovels and we'd shovel it on our trucks. And haul it to Palisades, with the horses. We had about ten or twelve teams hauling the clay. We put the clay down. Then in the spring, we'd go down to the lake when there was an east wind. That would bring out the gravel like in windrows. And that was pure gravel. We'd put the gravel on top of the clay and that went into the cracks of the clay and made it strong. I hauled a good many loads of gravel. They used to haul gravel out of there up to Covert and all over. They overdid it. There was a fellow east of Covert, used to come over. And when it was all sandy, they used to holler at their horses and cuss like everything. People found fault with that. They went to Quick about it and he forbid 'em any more gravel.

Walt Derby was a fisherman in those days. They had a big boat – a row boat. One day they went out in the lake. They had a cement block with a long rope and when they pulled that block up – I think it was Scott – he didn't think very much about it and let the block just drop down. It went right through the bottom of the boat. The ole man says to him, "You set right in that hole and start bailing water." And they come to shore and they made it. He thought pretty quick, didn't he? They caught perch and whitefish. But those days are gone now.

We had, one time, a little pier we built there, coming down from the Clubhouse straight to the lake. See, the Clubhouse used to be on the lakefront. They moved it back. I widened that road right up to Schlack's cottage. We cut all those trees. Remember Ley Struble? He swamped that out for us. They asked me who to get and

*Mr. Hempy and his team ready to go to work.*

*Clubhouse on beach with Palisade Pier visible on right.*

I said he was a good woodsman. He swamped that out so they could move the Clubhouse through there. They added on quite a bit to the Clubhouse after that. The Clubhouse was on the north side of the road, see? Quick built a little pier there. He was going to have boats come in. But it never panned out. At first, a launch from South Haven used to come down. Chicago people would come to Palisades that way. They would put them on the launch in South Haven and bring them down to Palisades. Then Shattucks used to have a livery stable. Quick used to get that taxi service and he'd drive it clear down from South Haven. He'd get me to drive that team. They were wonderful horses. One day, I touched one like that, and I come pretty near to having a run away. Man, that scared the living day lights out of me. I'll never forget that! They were ready to go! I never had horses that good. I had plenty of horses after that. I had a riding academy down there after awhile.

A fellow named Wilson, in Palisades Park, was a pretty good friend of mine. There were several of us who wanted the corner (on the Blue Star by the entrance to the Park) – that lot right there. So I think Wilson was on the Board, too. He says, "Charley, I'm going to see that you get that lot." I guess Quick wanted it too. I offered a little bit more than he did, and I got it. I'll never forget that. I built a gas station there. I ran it for awhile. Then Tony Canonie took it over. Later, Mr. Knapp rented it from me. He lived in that Monroe cottage down there (#63). Gene Howe rented it for a few years, too, and had a fruit stand out in front. Finally I sold it to Fred Nichols. When I delivered ice, I'd have some left over, so I built that little icehouse by the gas station, and I'd have three or four cakes in there. I'd pack sawdust on both sides and the top. And the people would come in , like late Saturday night. If they wanted ice, I'd go get them a piece of ice and take it down to the Park and fix them up. I didn't have to go clear to South Haven to get it.

*The gas station at entrance to Park.*

I knew the Sturtevants. Frank Sturtevant. Mrs. Sturtevant was a baker. She baked her own bread. She was a little bit of a woman. She'd pitter patter across that little ole restaurant, hotel, like that. She was a worker! They built that hotel. I'll tell you who built that – that same carpenter, Eugene Phillips. He built all of that. Then they put up a nice big hotel facing the lake. You remember Cliff Morgan, Dale Morgan? They lived in Covert. They built the new hotel. Cliff was a shrewd builder. He passed on and Dale Morgan took over and finished it. And the garage too. Mrs. Sturtevant built a little cottage right back of her place. They called that "Where the Light Hits." They left the Lodge to Del Jones, who ran it by himself and then married Blanche. I guess she wore the pants after that. She ran the dining room and it was run just so. Those waitresses would line up and sit. She knew when all the people got there and looked around the tables and the chairs and everything. She'd give the signal and the waitresses got right up and started waiting on the people. Boy, she was the boss. Del didn't have much to say then. He was kind of a back number.

*Mrs. Sturtevant and a tall guest!*

They tried to make a lake out of the Brandywine. They built the bridge and had that dammed with a swivel wheel. They'd raise and lower it. A couple times I saw it filled with water. One time, they said they'd stock it with fish. But that never occurred. It grew up like a marsh.

Forest Lowrey was a wonderful man. One time he sent me $700 and I took Tony Canonie in as a partner; we went out in the oil business. He was in the office of the Pure Oil people. But we never had any luck. We built one well west of Covert once. And another one across the road. We went down 1900 feet – no luck.

Mr. Henderson stayed here all winter in the Hermitage (#120). Then he moved out of the Park, right straight back where you make that turn. He lived there a good many years. I could see his cottage from my house up on the ridge. His son was a minister, Norm Henderson. And Bert Henderson sold bonds. And Dave, he went into show business. He'd take a barrel full of water and he'd make a dive and go right into that barrel. No kidding. He was a wonderful boy! Mr. Henderson – uh oh. He'd take a little tea once in a while. And he had a horse named Topsy. A little grey horse and he'd ride that and he'd fall off of it! Too much tea!!

Mrs. Abbott, her first husband was a fellow by the name of Lobenstein. I think he was Jewish. See, they didn't sell to Jews, remember. They had 90 by-laws and you had to live up to those by-laws. But on account of Mrs. Abbott being such a wonderful person, they let her come into the Park, even though she was married to Lobenstein. He was a wonderful fellow, though. He was a real guy. He was full of fun. He was kind of the making of the Park. Mr. Quick made all those by-laws and you had to live up to them.

Another Jewish Park member, in the early days, was Leo Lowenthal. I got myself into trouble there a little bit. He bought a cottage from a fella by the name of Root. Root didn't like the cottage he had built so he sold to Lowenthal and there he was. Dr. Vaughn and Charlie Gunsaul were the owners of places down there, in Linden Hills. They come down there and shut off the Lowenthal water and came to me. They forbid me to give him ice or to have any dealings with the Lowenthals. It went along for a few days. But I didn't pay no attention. I took them ice. He had a mother there, see, and I felt sorry for him. I'd seen the family, see? I said, "Look it here. I'm going to give them people all the ice they want, and I'll give them water, too." I gave them water in jugs, see? Leo was a veteran and he went to one of the veterans he knew. So a few days after that, here came the fella and he says, "I'm a veteran of a foreign war, see? Do you know Lowenthal?" I says, "Yes." He says, "He's a veteran, too. From now on you give that fella whatever he asks and you tell me who is running this business." I said Mr. A. C. Quick. He went to Quick and he straightened him out, too. There was no more trouble. That was because Mr. Lowenthal was a veteran of a foreign war. They might have kept an Italian from buying in the Park, but that went for everybody … languages … and Lowenthal, you know, they were going to kick him out, too, but they had war veterans in here to straighten them out, and he was a wonderful guy.

### Charley Did It
by Judy von Rosen
From August 1, 1953 Patter

Charley, do this; Charley, do that. There is no doubt about it. Charley Tunecke is a mighty busy man around this Park. Charley has been a Palisades handy man for several decades. He began his career as water boy, hauling water for the men who were clearing away brush for the new roads. He handled the water works for 15 years, and assisted in laying the first water mains. Park folks have had 20 years of faithful service from Charley as iceman. Charley put in the flowerbed by the hotel, therefore making the "curve" of the Circle. Older families remember how Charley hauled clay and gravel to make the Park roads. The Brandywine bridge is a credit of Charley's too.

Now that the tennis tourney is over, have you thought of the wear and tear those courts have taken? Charley helped lay the courts many years ago. Many of our cottages were Charley's work. He ran the steam engine (which was stored in the old Garage) for making the seawalls. One activity that Charley is proudest of was when he picked wild flowers to enter in the big festival back in Mr. Quick's days, and came out with first prize. Just about that time was when Leo Sowerby wrote a song about Charley. If anyone remembers the title of that song, let us know…. No argument about it, Charley did it.

*Dee Prange enjoys the petunias in circle Charley made. Picture 1950.*

## Betty and Ray Woodhouse

Interviewed by Betty Householder
August 28, 1984

I first came to Palisades when I was about a year old, the summer of 1916. My parents were Ann and Ralph Holmes. Mother was a nurse at Mary Thompson Hospital in Chicago and Dr. McCullum and Miss Vincent, the head nurse, brought her up here. Mother vacationed in the Park a summer or two, and she loved it so much that she wanted to come back. She and my dad had their honeymoon up here. A few years later, they bought Hemlocks, the cabin we still have.* It had been in use a number of years. It was one room to begin with, which was brought in from Phillips Corners, we understand. Cecil tells us that he thinks that it was the headquarters of the lumber company at that time. He may know more about the origins than we do. We have enclosed the porches to make it more comfortable.

We came by boat a few times in the early days. The Shattucks would meet us in South Haven with their horse and buggy. Sometimes we took a train – the Pere Marquette - to Bangor. Later on the Shattucks got a Ford and we would come in by car with them. We stayed all summer without a car. There wasn't a store here at that time. For groceries, Mr. Sink would come in from town and bring meat or take an order and bring it back. He also had vegetables. Mr. Shepherd was here; he'd bring the milk and pour it into our milk cans. Of course nothing was pasteurized. Ray and I came up here on our honeymoon; when Mr. Shepherd discovered we were newlyweds, he came in with a little bouquet of flowers for us. I thought that was sweet. I remember him bringing fruit and vegetables, especially berries. We picked berries, also. Mother was a marvelous cook so we had all kinds of goodies. She cooked on a kerosene stove. We had no electricity; I remember cleaning the chimneys of our kerosene lamps. We got water from a pump right down below the cottage. An old hand pump – the pipe is still there. Of course we had an outside washhouse. I'm not sure about mail. Dad came weekends and maybe he brought the mail.

The woman who brought in pies and baked goods was Freda and we called here Freda Roller-Eyes. Her eyes kind of rolled around in her head when she talked; we kids were fascinated by that. She carried her baked goods in a basket and went from cottage to cottage. That is the way we got a lot of things. She had a farm somewhere nearby – probably came in with horse and buggy.

As a kid I used to walk to Thunder Mountain. I guess the Indians named it – we could sometimes hear it thunder, on perfectly clear days. We felt the tremor, too – one time a small earthquake even shook the dishes. We also walked to the other Thunder Mountain, five miles down the beach.

The roads, when we first came, weren't too good. They are in the same places, though, essentially. Some of the old ones aren't used any more. I can remember the Canonie brothers hauling truck load after truck load of stoney clay that they put on to hold the roads, especially after a rainstorm when they were rutted a bit. The

*The cottage has since been sold to John and Kathleen Goeppinger who renamed it Blueberry Hill #113.*

*Outside of a remodelled Blueberry Hill, showing remaining log wall.*

Stagecoach Trail was originally just that – a trail for stagecoaches. By our time, Mr. Hempy would come down Stagecoach Trail with the garbage. He'd dump it in the meadow back by the creek. We have walked another branch of the Stagecoach Trail with our kids. It comes out by Forest Dunes. It is not well defined any more. Off season, when our store was closed, we sometimes walked to the Forest Dunes store, which was open all year, for supplies. We marked the trail with tin can lids painted red. Amazingly, some places we could still see wheel ruts on the trail. Amazing to think the old stagecoaches came that far into the dunes. Stan and Cecil say every year they pull out kids who try to drive it. So it is still an interesting trail.

*Forest Dunes Store, open all year, on Stagecoach Trail.*

Mr. Hempy lived by the gate in the Courthouse #61. He used to referee the 4th of July ball games all the time. Mr. Knapp built the Gatehouse. Later on he retired on a little farm near Covert. Charlie Tunecke took care of the horses, down by the creek, in the woods. Oh, were there a lot of flies! The icehouse was down there too. When Mr. Henderson was up here winters he built a lot of things. The original sign for our cottage, Hemlocks, was made by him out of bent twigs and tree branches about the size of your thumb. He made all the outdoor garages, also, with branches. And a summerhouse near Otts #106.

We came up sometimes in the off season when ice was on the lake. The boardwalks would be in a pile for the winter and snow fences put along the beach. The winter here was really fascinating. Such a stillness about it.

There wasn't much social life as such, except at the Clubhouse. We just roamed and took sandwiches when we went hiking. We walked to South Haven every year. Sometimes we would stay for a movie, but Daddy or Mother would come down and meet us to bring us home so we didn't have to walk back. That was always fun.

One summer I went to Campfire Girl Camp down the pike, about four miles north of here, right on the lake. I was so homesick – I'd have rather been here at Palisades where I had more freedom.

An Indian tribe - I can't remember the name - lived somewhere outside of Covert and they made beautiful woven baskets. They would bring them around from cottage to cottage, carrying them on their arms, all kinds, from big picnic baskets to anything you'd want. We always had some of their baskets in the cottage. They didn't wear Indian garb when they came into the Park, but we did visit their village one time and we have a picture of them in traditional outfits.

When they first started the Park, they had slabs of cement up on the hill where George Boyles's cottage is (#99) below the Clubhouse. Tents were set there. That was probably way, way back. We had a lot of beach then in front of that tent area – with several dunes in front of it. Later on, fishermen used to come down in the evenings and fish right off the dunes there. I think there was a pier down in our area where the excursion boats from South Haven stopped at Palisades.

*Two inside views of Blueberry Hill, showing the retention of the original log wall. The original cabin was moved to its present site shortly after Palisades Park was opened; it shows up on the map of the earliest 21 cottages.*

## WINTER DAY IN PALISADES

Blasting cold, chipping the mind
        With shards of pain
Sand ripped from the face of the dune
        Slinging bitter stings
Shifting ice wind, frosting
        The senses
Only the heart remembering
        Is warm.

*By Robert M. Woodhouse, 1968*
*Published in the July 16, 1969, Patter.*

# Written Memories

*Jeep on beach. Sandbox #175 and boarded up Abbott cottage #174 in background.*

## Margaret Abbott
### "Memorabilia II"

Written about 1967 when she was 78 years old.

My family has been coming to Palisades for 57 years spanning five generations. I first came with my grandmother, Mrs. Charles A. Allen, to visit her son, Charles, in 1911. He built his cottage in 1910. It was called El Dor Mar after his three daughters, Elizabeth, Dorothy, and Margaret. They had outside plumbing and their chic "facility" was called the Alhambra (Spanish Castle). When they put water in the Park, Uncle Charley covered the Alhambra with excelsior and gasoline and all the neighbors on the beach came to see the burning of the Alhambra. We all cooked with blue flame kerosene stoves, and the fried potatoes, cooked on the blue flame, were always the best.

For several years, my father and mother, Mr. And Mrs. Harry C. Knisely, rented a cottage. I remember one time when my sister had a boy friend sleep in the downstairs bedroom. Somebody forgot to empty the pan under the ice box and he was soaked the next morning. That rented cottage burned down many years ago.

For several years after my first husband and I were married, we stayed at the hotel. In 1925, we built our cottage, Lehigh #174. We paid for our cottage with Lehigh Valley stock; hence the name, Lehigh. Our daughter Ann was a baby at the time. We had seven happy years here. My husband died in 1932 and in 1933 I married Tom Abbott. We are still enjoying Lehigh.*

Rudy Weber built our cottage; he is a good builder and a fine man. Mr. Harry Wildt has done many fine things for me through the years, as well. When we built, there were no roads through the woods and Charley Tunecke, from Covert, hauled all the wood for the cottage down the beach. As a young man, Charley lived with his mother and he had a strict upbringing. He was a handyman in the Park. We would always see him with his monkey wrench on his way to fix somebody's plumbing.

The Coate's cottage #173, next door to us, was built by Mrs. William Ward and was called The Mary Lee. The original lumber came out of the old Riverside Golf Club in Riverside, Illinois. The Oasis #171, where Mr. and Mrs. Joseph Campbell live, is a very old cottage built by the Sengenbergers. Mrs. Sengenberger was quite an artist; I have a nice watercolor she gave me.

The cottage in back of Campbells, # 170, was built by Judge Sproul, a Congressman. His son, Wilfred, used to come each summer until it was sold to the Nelsons. The Beck's cottage, Traylside, #177, was originally owned by Mr. Spelman, who had a nice grocery store in South Haven. Mr. and Mrs. William DeSouchet, a fine family, owned Pottawatomi, #154 and Point of View, #155.

I can remember when the Harding cottage hung on the cliff, north of the Brandywine, after the big storm of 1930.

I remember the Clubhouse on the big beach. We used to have beautiful dances and minstrels and bazaars at the Clubhouse. We also had dances in the old dining room at the hotel; I can still see the man playing the fiddle. When Leo Sowerby first came to Palisades, we would go and sit underneath his cottage and listen to him practice the piano. It was a treat.

Mrs. Jessie Filkins, an old timer, and I were always friends and we would walk all through the beautiful woods and over the bluffs together. I often played golf on our Palisades golf course; it was nice, though a bit sandy. Mr. Quick kept it up.

*After Tom's death, Margaret sold the cottage.*

In about 1926, the fishermen used to come in front of our cottage. They had a big old wooden boat which they left on the beach. The men would row out and set their nets. They would bring their families, and the wives would cook their supper on the beach. I can still see their coffee pot on the fire. Later the men would go out and bring in the nets and have many beautiful fish; they would sell us a whitefish. It was a very picturesque scene. Often I would have to get up in the middle of the night and go put out their fires.

We had many beautiful boats passing in those days. The mail boat, called the *Glenn*, always looked attractive lit up at night. We also used to ride in a boat on Lake Brandywine, where there were boats to hire. Years ago, we could rent riding horses; there were many beautiful bridle paths through the woods.

Mrs. Manierre, an old timer, was a great walker. She was always getting up hiking parties; we had many good hikes. We often walked to Covert and back. Covert had a fine hardware store, called Eisenlohr's, and, of course, we all loved Mr. and Mrs. Sink and their sons Darl and Carl, who owned the only grocery store. There was a darling little ice cream parlor and the hotel on the corner was known for its good pancakes.

We all liked the Canonie brothers – Pete, Sam, and Tony. They brought the ice around. Del Jones ran Sturtevant Lodge. He was a bit tight, and they used to kid him and tell him how thin he sliced the meat. Ballou Inn was across

*Three-board boardwalk on Clubhouse Beach. 1964.*

from the lodge. One of my Uncle Charley's daughters had a Russian Wolfhound, and one Sunday the Ballous had all the chickens prepared for Sunday dinner and somehow that dog got in the kitchen and took off with several chickens. Later Uncle Charley got a bill from the Ballous. In front of Ballou Inn, there was always a horseshoe game going on, with real horseshoes.

I just want to say "Thanks" to Mr. Quick. And to say Cecil is the greatest and we should be thankful for him.

*The inside of Theodore Eisenlohr's Hardware Store in Covert.*

## Marion Hamilton
Memories written to Betty Householder in 70's.

In 1910 - or perhaps 1909 - Mr. Arthur C. Quick approached my Aunt Fanny Palmer in regard to buying a lot at Palisades Park which he described as a beautiful wooded area on the shore of Lake Michigan in the dunes near South Haven. He said he owned a good sized-piece of property which he would like to make into a resort for a selected group of owners who wanted a quiet place to enjoy nature without the noise and hubbub of so many resorts. He was approaching teachers, doctors, lawyers, ministers, and others who would be interested in that sort of place and who would keep it that way. My Aunt Fanny, her two sisters – Louise Palmer who was a visiting nurse in Chicago and Anna Palmer who was the family homemaker – and their mother Eliza Lydia Hunt Palmer, all living together in Chicago, became very interested and visited the area. They came to South Haven by boat (the old City of South Haven which later was taken to Spain and used in wartime service and sunk in World War I, according to what I have heard). They then had to take a horse and buggy to get to Palisades. They were delighted with the place and bought four contiguous lots in the woods in 1910. They hired Mr. Ballou to build their cottage, which they named Whippoorwill (#125) because of the great number of birds of that name which filled the night air with their constant cries of "Whip poor Will." My aunts had frequent visitors – teachers, doctors, nurses, and ministers – some of whom also bought property in the Park.

My father, George Frank Palmer, their brother, brought my mother and me to visit Palisades in 1910. I was eight years old and I haven't missed a summer at Palisades since. To me, Palisades has always seemed a fairyland of beauty.

When I was in my preteens, I brought friends over and we explored every inch of the Park. I learned to swim in that little hole near the bridge and I learned to dive off the spring board built on the decaying piles in the water just off shore near the old hotel and Ballou Inn. Long before Mr. Quick had developed Palisades Park there were two good-sized piers in front of where Sturtevant Lodge and Old Pier Cottage were later built. Lumber-carrying lake boats docked there for loading. (They must have been pretty small boats as there was no real harbor.)

When I was growing up, the basement of Ballou Inn was used as the post office; Mrs. Ballou was the postmistress. The coming of the mail was the most exciting event of the day. Usually, some member from each cottage arrived when the mail was due, packing the place, wall to wall, with people.

A much smaller Clubhouse was down on the beach about 200 feet from where it is now. We children who were not yet old enough to dance loved to peek through the windows. The grown-up young ladies put on their best dresses and danced to a real live orchestra hired from South Haven. I remember how I kept my eyes glued to two young ladies who I thought were the most beautiful I had ever seen. One was Julia Quick and the other Marion Ward; I never was able to decide who was the more beautiful. They were entirely different types: Julia was the delicate calendar-girl type, looking very fragile, and Marion the athlete – graceful, strong, the kind you picture with a tennis racket.

*Marion Hamilton in canoe by Clubhouse which was still on the beach. Pre-1920.*

*Sophia Meyer, on burro, and Mathilde Meyer Bruninga. 1917.*

## Addendum by Marion's daughter, Jean Hamilton Keller.

But there were other things to do beside looking at grown up young ladies with envy. There were burros to ride, kept in Brandywine pasture. They could be rented for 25 cents an hour and we rode them all through the Park. Aside from swimming, riding the burros was the most fun.

I remember the golf course when it really was in use. My father invested in some clubs though he never was much of a golfer. One day he put his club to good use and killed a rattlesnake on the course. It had rattles on its tail. However, I have never seen a rattlesnake since in the Park.

The ice cream parlor, now a private cottage, was very well patronized. At one time, Julia Quick took over the running of it. She had been attending classes at the Art Institute of Chicago and she made the ice cream parlor very attractive. She also served a most mouthwatering chocolate soda! The Holmstrom boys also ran it shortly after or shortly before Julia had it. It was a very popular spot. I become nostalgic thinking about the Circle in those days; Sturtevant Lodge and Ballou Inn were always full and things seemed humming.

Mother worked an extra year after retirement to buy a used motor home. She and my dad planned to travel south in the winter and spend summers at Palisades. The motor home, which we called "the bus," was big and ugly, with a gaping hole gouged in the right front fender. It was also high; my dad got a power complex driving it, demanding – and getting – the right-of-way on any road. This included the Park roads. The "bus" was so wide, it was almost impossible to pass on the narrow Park roads. Daddy always waited and made every on-coming driver back up to a spot wide enough to pass. At night, the sight of a huge monster with bright staring eyes would intimidate, startle, or scare even the bravest of drivers. So the Park Board made the rule: <u>No RV's in the Park</u> and Daddy had to park outside the gate and walk in.

*Marion's "Grandma Palmer" in buggy watching construction of a beach cottage. Mrs. G. F. Palmer, Marion's mother, behind.*

Mother was given a lot by her parents, George and Erminie Palmer, as a graduation gift. After she started working as a social worker in Chicago, she had Seagull Cottage (#181) built on that lakefront lot. My two sisters, Judy and Jerri, and I spent summers there. We swam in the Brandywine, where Mother had learned to swim; we hiked south to Marvin Slide and north along the beach to South Haven. We waited for Mr. Sherman to deliver milk and followed Mr. Hempy and his horses as they collected the garbage. We walked to the circle and bought milk and bread from Edith and Mrs. Packard, and waited eagerly for the 4:00 mail delivery to the Park Post Office. I spent my honeymoon at Palisades in 1952. As my sisters and I moved around when we grew up, Palisades was more home than anywhere.

Concerned that at her death we would have problems about who would use and take care of the cottage, Mother resolved the issue in a typical Marion Hamilton way. First, she persuaded Dad to buy the Carpenter cottage #182 when it was for sale. It is now Grapevine Cottage. Then she was bequeathed Whippoorwill Cottage, once owned by her aunts and then by the Owens family. It had no electricity or running water. Mother made a deal with the Park Board; she would install electricity and water and maintain the cottage if they would forgive the unpaid back dues on Whippoorwill. So she did and they did.

Now Mother was happy – she had a cottage to leave each of us. The Board, however, became anxious. Was she a real estate tycoon, buying up cottages to rent and to wait for appreciation? So they made another ruling: **No One Can Have More Than Three Cottages At a Time.** Mother was through – she didn't have any more children – but as far as I know, the 3-cottage limit still stands today.

*Building sand castles. 1909.*

*An early sand road.*

# Anna Holmes

From *Palisades Park Review, 1905–1968*

I think it was 1905 when I first saw Palisades Park. It had been a long, tiresome trip from Chicago on the excursion steamer to South Haven, then a train ride on the Fruit Belt Line to Covert, and from there in a buggy drawn by two horses. The roads were just wagon trials really, and we had to get out of the vehicle at times while the horses strained up over the sand dunes.

After we crossed the road, now the Blue Star Highway, a stand of stark, bare peach trees came in view. A heavy frost had taken its toil. The Ravineway was a cool, reviving tunnel of green. Our driver let us out at Sturtevant Lodge, the end of the line. The Lodge at that time was the building used now for the kitchen and dining room. Dr. McCollum's and Miss Vincent's shore cottage was a few lots away, closer to the water's edge. The building was not completed, but habitable, so we moved in. There were four of us: Dr. McCollum, Miss Vincent, a student nurse from Mary Thompson Hospital, and me. For me, it was a spot of complete enchantment. The bird songs, the refreshing lake breezes, and bathing seemed primeval to a city girl. There was not much hiking through the woods at that time, as brambles everywhere tore and grabbed at legs and clothing.

During this time I met Robert Ballou, a genial man who was building cottages and later, in 1907, built his own store and dining room, which he called Ballou Inn. As time went on, the cabin was put up, and each succeeding year, more cottages were erected. We had no running water or electrical current, but we loved this unusual relaxing atmosphere. Carrying water from the old camping area, then later from a community pump paid for by four cottage owners, did not dismay us. Filling oil lamps, or cleaning glass chimneys was no chore, and using outside toilet facilities no inconvenience.

Robert Ballou was as enterprising as he was good natured and provided means of entertainment as well as food and other necessities for the summer folk. Bob Ballou rented out a pair of burros, by the hour, for a nominal charge, and these patient, sure footed animals carried their passengers, bare back, over all the trails, to the delight of their riders. Mr. Ballou had chickens, which roamed the area where the garage and parking lot are today. My husband, Dr. Ralph Holmes, was an avid chicken eater and on weekends, when he could leave his practice and spend some time with his family at Hemlocks (#113), our cottage, the visits were not complete without chicken dinners, so Bob Ballou and my husband would start on a wild chase after a terrified,

squawking fowl. The poor chicken did not have a chance and the hapless bird would be presented to me, limp and bloody, feathers and all. Starting from scratch it was, and not at all to my liking. From that time, if I ever had an appetite for chicken, it left me never to return.

Ballou had a cow which pastured around the grassy open spaces outside the Park entrance, I recall. One evening Bossy appeared outside our lean-to door, waiting patiently for someone to relieve her of the burden of milk she was carrying. Our youngsters scattered in search of Bob, and he came soon and led Bossy away to be milked. A pressing job had detained Bob and delayed his rendevous with the cow at full udder time.

Five generations in my family and countless friends have enjoyed and loved Palisades Park throughout the years. We hiked, swam, played tennis, picnicked on the beach around a drift wood fire, studied the stars through a telescope, became bird-watchers, and delved into biology in all its forms. During the early years in Palisades, the woods were dense with large trees and heavy undergrowth. This condition caused a dampness, which encouraged the growth of moss and all forms of life which flourished in such an environment. Turquoise and gold lizards were like shining jewels when they came out from under rocks to sun themselves on a rotting log. There were large hairy jumping spiders which dragged heavy water beetles to their lairs, winning over the desperate clinging of the beetles to rough bark. In early spring, there were wonderful days searching for dragon fly nymphs in marshy spots along the Brandywine and watching the development of polliwogs to the full grown toads which would rim the lake, in the evening, during the summer months, to soak themselves in the gentle lapping of the waves.

Looking forward to spending a week at Palisades, when school was out in the spring, helped us through many an arduous winter in Chicago. The many spring flowers – hepatica, squirrel corn, dutchman's breeches, adders tongue, trillium, and countless others – welcomed us. The thrilling, ecstatic bird choruses, during the early June and July mornings, were well worth waking at dawn to hear. What a joy it was to wander through the woods, nibbling tender sassafras leaves and wintergreen blossoms. A drumming would halt our progress, and as we moved forward with caution, a ruffled grouse, on a stump, beating his wings to attract a female, would come in view, then

*A good time in the lake.*

disappear in a whirr of wings at our approach. Adventuring farther, we would stop when an unexpected huckleberry bush at our feet, or a beautiful tanager in branches above, met our eyes.

Our excursions varied as time went by and our children grew old enough to join us on our field trips. On one ramble, my young son and I found the outlines of the lumber camp buildings above the Brandywine, along what was at that time part of the golf course. The logs lying on the sand were crumbling to dust and, as we surveyed the lay-out, we gathered nearly a one pound coffee can full of what looked like hand made square nails. Then years later, when grandchildren came along and grew old enough to start out on their own explorations, we found bird points and arrowheads north on the beach and called certain spots, where these treasures were found, "Arrowhead Gulch" and "Pirates' Gulch." On one hike, the boys found – much to their joy – fulgurites, which are grayish rough tubes, formed when lightning strikes the sand.

Early one summer we were treated to a rare sight. Fifteen luna moths had lighted on the outside of the screen on the porch. A wonderful, beautiful sight it was. There must have been a female among the cluster, as our books on moths and butterflies informed us that a female luna deposits a milky substance which attracts males of this species from miles away.

During the period when our daughters and son were growing up, we left Chicago for Palisades as soon as school was out and stayed until September, when it was time for school to open. Many an evening at dusk, we would count as many as a dozen whippoorwills calling to each other. The wood thrush would also fill the twilight air with its lovely flute-like notes.

Palisades Park has changed so much in so many ways since the early years of its existence. Gone are the whippoorwills, the spine tingling call of the loon in the dead of the night, and the graceful flight of herons at sunset. There are still a few wood thrushes in our woods and I hear them blowing their flutes at dusk and on dark days, if I reach Palisades early enough in the season. Palisades Park still offers much, so very much toward the study of nature and education in all her forms, if only the eye is trained to see, and the ear to hear.

# From August 13, 1955 <u>Patter</u>
By Anna D. Holmes

It was in the year 1907 that Dr. Josephine McCollum, Miss Mary Vincent, and I – for the first time – came to Palisades Park. We left Chicago on the steamer, City of South Haven, and at South Haven took a train, the Fruit Belt Line, to Covert. At Covert a farmer met us in his two-seated buggy drawn by a team of horses. The trip from Covert to Palisades was long and tiresome. Half a day it seemed – to go 4 and 1/2 miles. The road was just a buggy track and the narrow wheels of the vehicle bit deep into the sand. Several times along the way, we got out of the buggy and climbed the dunes which the horses could not make with their human cargo.

Later, a small launch plied between the Park and South Haven, carrying passengers to and from the lake steamer. The "Peanut" docked at a pier which ran into the lake a little south of our main blowout. The little boat bobbed merrily along on these trips, except on rough days when persons going back to Chicago had to find other means of travel to South Haven.

These days, it is a simple matter to reach Palisades Park. Paved roads and automobiles have shortened the time to just a few hours instead of a whole day's travel from Chicago and its environs. The liquid notes of the wood thrush in the evening, the sunsets across the lake, the canopy of green which offers such restful coolness on hot days are all worth the time and distance to come to this enchanted spot. Some folks travel many miles each summer to partake of a generous Creator's bounty.

# PaulineSauer "Recollections"

August, 1986
Sent to Betty Householder

I first came to Palisades in 1917, when I was just one year old. My parents heard about the Park from some Chicago friends of ours. We rented Munro Lodge, on the south side of the road at the entrance to Ravineway Drive, just before the hill rises and the ravine descends. We used to park our car under the two beautiful tall white pines in the level area west of Munro Lodge, at the foot of our hill. I understand those trees are now gone. Later my parents built a cottage part way up this hill. They oriented the cottage so we had a view of Lake Michigan from our front porch. This, of course, involved trimming and topping some trees elsewhere on our property between the front porch and the lake. Mr. Phillips and his son Jeff, of rural Covert, very nice black men, were the builders.

When I was too young to remember, an aunt and uncle came to visit us at Munro Lodge. By mistake, instead of finding Munro Lodge, the first cottage on the south side of the road before Ravineway Drive, they entered the first cottage beyond the Forks, on the south side of the road. Since the cottage was open and no one was home, they assumed we were all at the beach. Seeing a basket of grapes, sugar, kettle, and jars in the kitchen, my aunt decided to surprise us by making grape jelly, which she did. Right after she finished the jelly, they discovered they had entered the wrong house. They hurriedly left and inquired of someone where we lived. They finally found us, but we often wondered what the residents of the first cottage thought when, upon their return, they found some strangers had entered and made the grape jelly. My aunt and uncle were too embarrassed to go back and tell them. They had, of course, not disturbed anything else.

We first traveled to Palisades Park on a boat, from Chicago's Navy Pier to South Haven. Mr. Shattuck met us with his taxi and drove us to the Park. After 1920, when we had our own car, an open Dodge touring car, we drove from Chicago, a ten-hour trip. As highways and cars improved, we were able to make the trip in much less time.

We loved the countryside with its woods, lake, birds, and wildflowers; the peace, quiet, and relative solitude of nature meant relaxation. Favorite pastimes included swimming, hiking to Thunder Mountain or Old Baldy, wiener roasts on the beach, playing tennis, picking dewberries on the golf course and blackberries along Brandywine Creek, bird-watching with field glasses and the National Geographic bird book at 4:30 or 5:00 a.m., and watching sunsets and stars. This profound interest in nature, nurtured and encouraged by my parents and inspired by Mr. Quick and his knowledge of wild flowers, led ultimately to my career as a field biologist with an M.A. in botany from the University of Michigan and a Ph.D. in Nature and Conservation Education from Cornell University.

Our social life was very informal. We visited our friends at their cottages, and they visited us at ours. There were no organized activities - we didn't need any. We learned

*Crowds boarding The City of South Haven to cross Lake Michigan to Chicago. On dock in South Haven.*

from Mother, early in life, to develop our inner resources and make our own good times. My brother and I would sometimes sit in the evening darkness on our front porch overlooking Lake Michigan and create stories. One would start with "Once upon a time…" and, after a few paragraphs, pass the story to the other, who would add to it as he/she went along; the story developed as it passed back and forth between us. A playground was across the road north of the Clubhouse; it consisted of a few swings on a metal framework, a teeter-totter, and a slide. The area was well shaded by trees.

*Old postcard of playground near the Clubhouse. The swings and slide are barely visible through the trees.*

The roads – how different from today. They were sandy, dusty, and used more by horses and wagons in the early days. Stage Coach Trail never was much more than two wheel tracks with grass and sedges between the tracks. At Munro Lodge, Dad spread Dowflake, a salt, on the road to keep down the dust. Made by Dow Chemical Company, it drew moisture from the air and kept the road damp. Damp road, no dust after cars drove by. Now the roads are wider and more heavily graveled. There are also many more miles of roads in the Park.

People got around in the Park mostly on their own two feet. For a while in the 1920's and 1930's, there was some horseback riding for fun. The Park Board put a stop to that because of dust raised and the hazard to people walking on the roads with small children. In the 30's and later, some young people got around the Park on motorcycles, thus shattering the peace and quiet formerly enjoyed by others.

In the 1920's, we bought most of our groceries in Covert from Sinks Grocery Store. Mr. Sink was such a pleasant gray-haired man, with a very large brown mole on his temple. He always gave us each a small piece of Colby cheese from his big wheel of cheese under glass. We also got other supplies from Eisenlohr's Hardware Store. Before returning from Covert, we would stop at the local dairy for a gallon of real, genuine buttermilk for eight cents, for which we provided our own clean gallon jug. This thin, watery buttermilk was the most delicious I have ever tasted. It was the real thing, the watery residue from the churning of butter.

After the new highway was opened, when Dad was with us, we did most of our shopping in South Haven, at Niffenegger's Meat Market, the A & P, Woolworth's, and Hale's. During July, when my Dad and his car were not here, we got our meat and some groceries at Ballou Inn, or my brother rode his bicycle to South Haven for groceries.

*Postcard showing rutted sand road.*

When we built our own cottage in the mid-20's, we had indoor plumbing, with all necessary fixtures, installed immediately – and felt very modern, as that was not common in the Park in those days!

For years, laundry was done in large galvanized laundry tubs on a bench in the back yard. Mother and the hired girl would hang the laundry to dry in an opening in the woods across the road.

Up the hill at our own cottage, we managed to find a few places to stretch clothes lines where the sun could dry the laundry. After a few years, we sent laundry to South Haven; a laundry there serviced the Park on a regular schedule. Eventually, of course, commercial laundromats became available in South Haven and also in Benton Harbor, and we patronized them.

We had an icebox in the early days. Since our house is not visible from the road near Ferrys (#65), we would go up our path and tie a sign to a convenient tree indicating when and how much ice we needed. I believe the ice was delivered two or three times a week. The icehouse was down an obscure sand road near the beginning of the Ravine, and we always were under the impression that the ice was harvested from the adjacent Brandywine creek in winter and stored in the icehouse for summer use.

In 1949, when we got a new electric refrigerator in Chicago, we sent the old one to Palisades. The movers picked it up in Chicago and delivered it to our cottage for a total bill of $6.00! Amazing, even in those days. And what an improvement an electric refrigerator was! In time, of course, we got a frost-free refrigerator.

We first used kerosene lamps and candles. They never created any hazards; children in those days grew up learning to be careful around these light sources. In a few years, we had our cottage electrified; we enjoyed this modern convenience.

> **Running the household differed in many ways from today. We had a pump in the back yard, elevated and reached by cement block stairs, which pump was our main source of water. Some water dripped down to the cooling room "spring house" below, accessible by a small wooden door beside the stairs. This "spring house" was where we kept food – milk, butter, meat, vegetables, and fruit – to cool. Even after we moved to our own cottage, since Munro Lodge was seldom rented, we would keep our large watermelons in the "spring house" to save space in the icebox. In addition to the pump in the yard, we also had a small pump at the kitchen sink. Later, we had a water storage tank in one corner of the stone garage to the southeast of the cottage. This was up near the ceiling, and Dad would try to keep it pumped full of water so we could turn on a faucet at the kitchen sink. Just south of the garage was the outhouse.**

Charley Tunecke was the earliest serviceman I remember. He delivered ice, collected garbage, and maintained the roads. He was strawberry blond, tall, and brawny – my idea of what a cowboy looked like. Charley later built his service station at the intersection of the Park road with the Blue Star. Thus, he was the first and last person one saw upon arriving at or leaving Palisades.

Joe Putz used to control the rope at the Forks on weekends to maintain the privacy of the Park for those who lived there or rented cottages. He also assisted with general maintenance of the Park. He liked to carve and paint boats. We bought one of his 3-D pictures of a sailboat with a rope picture frame.

Mr. Shepherd was the milkman. He was tall, blond, and slender, a local farmer, and looked like the traditional pictures of the Good Shepherd. His personality, too, was consistent with what one would expect of the Good Shepherd. He was, of course, very well liked by everyone. He came daily with his horse and wagon, bringing large cans of milk, cream, butter, and eggs. We would have our pitchers clean and ready, and he would pour milk from his large can into a metal quart pitcher and from that into our containers. After we

*Mr. Shepherd delivering his milk.*

moved up the hill, I got a half-gallon aluminum milk pail filled with candy for my mid-July birthday. After removing the candy to another container, we used this pail for our milk, placing it behind a large tree near the foot of the hill every morning so Mr. Shepherd could fill it on his rounds. Later he delivered the milk to our house. In his last years, he delivered milk in glass bottles embossed "H. L. Shepherd, Covert, Michigan" or something like that. I had some of his bottles here in my basement for some years, but, since I can no longer find them here, I assume I may have returned them to Margaret to donate to a local historical museum.

Freda Haertling, a sweet, middle-aged lady (who seemed elderly to us children, of course), always seemed tired; she badly needed to earn some money to keep going. She came every Saturday, going from one cottage to another, selling fresh vegetables and fruits, dressed chickens, eggs, and her home-baked pies and cakes. She lived in the area, of course. I think she lived alone, had no marketable skills, and depended on Park sales in the summer to keep going. Like others, she too came, at first, with horse and buggy.

While we were in Munro Lodge, some Indians came several times a summer to sell their baskets, birch bark, porcupine quill, and beaded souvenirs. I believe we still have a few of the things we purchased from them. Where they came from, I really don't know.

The Ballous, very nice people, kept the Park store. They also had the Post Office, and for many years we had the same mailbox - number 17. My sister Margaret was born in 1921. When she was just a little tot, one day we suddenly realized that we had not seen her for quite a while. In panic, we scattered in all directions, hunting for her. Finally, our "adopted" grandmother, Margaret's godmother and namesake who was living with us at the time, reached Ballou Inn just as Margaret was reaching up to hand Mr. Ballou her nickel as he leaned over and handed her her order, a "choca I-Kee-Koe" (chocolate ice cream cone). With it, he gave her a big smile, as she was perhaps his youngest customer. As the name "Ballou Inn" implies, there was an inn where they rented rooms, above the store and Post Office. The Inn dining room was across the stone steps, in an adjacent stone building.

Other interesting people in the early days included Leo Sowerby and Eric DeLamarter, two of Chicago's most distinguished musicians, who had cottages near the south end of the Park. The Whitney Trio, of radio fame, also had a cottage, but I never really knew them. Dr. Ludwig Fuerbringer of St. Louis, president of the Lutheran Church – Missouri Synod, was an elderly widower and a close relative of one of our relatives. He spent a few weeks every summer at Sturtevant Lodge. He loved swimming in Lake Michigan. Dr. Martin Pfotenhauer, Dr. Fuerbringer's successor as president of the Synod, also came later with his family. They only spent a few weeks in summer and never became permanent residents.

*Ballou Inn*

As far as I know, Mr. Henderson was a cottager rather than a Park employee. He seemed quite elderly from the earliest time I knew him. He seemed to spend quite a bit of time at the Park and enjoyed making several tree branch, rustic gazebos. One was at a fork in the road beyond the Clubhouse, near Happy Hollow (#104). I understand this is now gone. Another one still remains near Villa Memdadh (#86). He was a pleasant, friendly man and added much to the woodsy atmosphere of the Park with his gazebos, in which one could sit down and rest a bit and enjoy the scenery and the birds. His cottage was back farther in the woods than most, near Cooney's Ye Nooc (#121), near the start of Thunder Mountain trail.

*A gazebo nestled in the woods - possibly the one mentioned above - one of several in the early years.*

At first, we had a relatively wide sandy beach for the whole length of the Park. Then in early November, 1929, a devastating storm smashed the lakefront, wrecking practically all of the beach cottages. We drove over a few days later, on Armistice Day, to observe the effects of the storm and were absolutely appalled at the devastation we saw. Walls were smashed in, furniture twisted and strewn about, roofs collapsed. Indescribable and hard to believe, it left a lasting impression on me. If I had not actually seen it, I could not have imagined anything so terrible. Fortunately, our cottage was back in the woods, so was spared. The Lake level has been high ever since then.

One of my most vivid memories was of the Northwest Airlines plane crash over Lake Michigan, opposite the Park. It was midsummer, and the plane encountered a terrible thunderstorm. In spite of the pilot's urgent pleas to be allowed to go to a different level, the air traffic controller refused to allow this, insisting that the pilot remain on his established course. Shortly thereafter, lightning struck the plane; it went down over the Lake. There were no survivors. For days, bits of the plane, luggage, and human body parts washed up on shore and were turned over to the Coast Guard.

Another dramatic memory was the considerable excitement, one Saturday night, when one of the two cottages at the top of the Forks burned down. Everyone was alerted in case the fire would spread, which – fortunately – it didn't. The burned cottage was never replaced.

A swinging bridge crossed the Brandywine Creek just west of the dam. It always made me nervous; I was glad when it was replaced by something more solid that didn't move. The dam across the Creek created a small lake for boating, canoeing, and fishing. However, the area became a breeding ground for mosquitoes. Splashing and "swimming" in the Brandywine was fun. While we were little tots, in July, Mother and our hired girl would take us across from the cottage and through the woods to play in safety in the Creek's shallow waters. In August, when Dad was at the Park, we would go to the beach as soon as we were old enough to walk there.

I vividly remember getting up at 2:00 a.m., about 1920, to stand out in the road to look at a comet. Dad said he would not live to see it again, but if we children lived to be 75 years old, we might. Now I'm trying to find out from our University astronomers what comet is coming again around 1990.

*Innes Welles on the "swinging bridge" across the Brandywine. c. 1922.*

ARTHUR C. QUICK AND HIS WIFE—CATHERINE V. STRYKER, AND DAUGHTERS. I-1428

## Virginia Steinbacher,
### Granddaughter of Mr. Quick

Letter to Betty Householder,
February 23, 1985

I think I'd best begin by explaining where I fit in the picture of Palisades Park, since it appears that I am the unknown quantity.

At the time of Mr. Quick's death, I was awaiting orders to join my husband overseas after the war. I knew that with the military life ahead of me, I would have very little opportunity to ever spend any time at Palisades Park, so I sold out my interest in the Park to Julia, my aunt. This may account in part for the fact that I am remembered by only a few of the "old-timers," if any. It would appear that Julia never bothered to correct the impression that she was Mr. Quick's only daughter. My mother, Laura, was nine years older than Julia.

My mother married Hayward Tracy of South Haven in 1913. I was born in 1914, and, so far as I know, I spent every summer of my life at Palisades Park until 1932.

My mother and dad operated the Soda Fountain, as it was called in those days, every summer until 1926. That year my dad had a job that made it impossible for him to spend the summer there, so it was just my mother, with my not always too willing help – I'm afraid I much preferred to be on the beach or tennis court to helping in the soda fountain.

The summer of 1927 proved to be a tragic one. In the middle of the night late in July, my mother was stricken with terrible pain; she sent me up to my grandfather's cottage on the hill to get help. I'll never forget how frightened I was climbing that long, long flight of steps up the hill. Dr. Vaughn was called from Covert; my mother was taken to the hospital where she died on July 30. At her request, my grandparents took me, since my father had practically deserted us.

With my grandfather's help, I kept the soda fountain open the rest of that summer, and then, the next year, took it over on my own (with his supervision) through the summer of 1932. During those years I had little or no time to take part in any social life, but I did manage to get to the beach every day – that beautiful beach that is no more! It breaks my heart to see what has happened – it's almost unbelievable!

I have little to add about the early years that hasn't already been mentioned by others. Wonderful people helped my grandfather make Palisades Park the beautiful haven that it is – Charley Tunecke, Joe Putz, Mr. Hempy, and who could ever forget Mr. Shepherd with his beautiful beard. And his lovely flowers – I never see a beautiful bunch of glads that I don't remember him! And I can still remember Tony Canonie with his cheerful smile when he'd deliver ice to the Fountain.

I remember walking the golf course with my grandfather and helping him plant acorns at selected spots. I wonder if any of those acorns ever grew into mighty oaks?

I have one minor correction in the history of the Post Office. For some reason that I can't remember, the Post Office was moved to the Soda Fountain for two years when Archie Allen was Postmaster, and I became his assistant. I'm not sure of the years, but it must have been about 1929 or 1930. Cal Lehman was Postmaster the last year or two that I was there.

After my marriage in 1933, I rather lost touch with the Park, although I was still close to my grandparents. My grandmother died the summer of 1935 and eventually my grandfather went to live with Julia, with whom he was living at the time of his death. I wanted him to live with me, but I'm afraid my three young sons were a bit too much for him.

My husband went to work for him at the Park in 1939 and, much to my delight, they became very fond of one another – Grandfather had strongly opposed my marriage. Ray, my husband, was with him until he was called to active duty in World War II. Possibly some people might remember him – Ray Steinbacher.

I really can't add much more to this history. My major objective has been to set the record straight – I think my mother deserves that much.

*The Soda Bar, so closely connected to the Quicks through the 40's.*

*From Oh, the Wide Sky!*
*A Volume of Southwest Verse*

*By Jeanne Delamarter Bonnette*

*As published in the August 9, 1969 Patter.*

### OH, THE WIDE SKY!

Oh, the wide sky!

Like a bird on the wing
Or a kite on a string,
Something, something
Inside me rises, is lifted
Into the far blue air.

Where
Would I go
If I could, up there?

What music
What colors,
What fragrances
Would be my delight
Far, far up in the bright
Blue heaven?

Oh, to fly high
In the wide sky!

*Above: Local entrepreneur with produce to sell. Lodge in background.*
*Below: Note water tower in this vintage postcard.*

149

THE BRIDGE, PALISADES PARK MICH.

*Above: Old postcard of "The Bridge" - swinging, that is.*
*Below: Old cars crowd circle - looks like 4th of July! Or is everyone heading toward the Soda Bar to buy that "Ice Cream Soda"?*

# Chapter 3

# The 20's

1920 - 19th Amendment ratified giving women the right to vote;
1923 - South Haven Lighthouse electrified; the Charleston becomes popular dance;
1924 - Van Buren State Park formally dedicated;
1927 - *The Jazz Singer* is first talking movie; Charles Lindberg completes first solo flight;
1929 - first Academy Awards; first car radio; stock market crashes.

## The 20's

Palisades Park rather by-passed the Roaring Twenties. Growth took place in that decade, to be sure, but the Park was still as proper as it was primitive. Mr. Quick was often seen patrolling the Park, wearing coat and tie. His rules imposed a Prohibition in the Park regardless of national policy. Admittedly, alcoholic beverages were often spirited into cottages when Mr. Quick wasn't looking, though Paul Schlacks remembers his father grumbling that Mr. Quick had the uncanny ability to show up for a lengthy conversation just as Mr. Schlacks wanted to unload his beer from the car. Ladies with white gloves and hats called on possible tenants to determine their "suitability" for renting. The Clubhouse, newly expanded and moved to its present location, presented theatrical evenings. Several professional musicians who owned property in the Park arranged concerts. Mr. Hempy's horses still carried much of the heavy building materials down the beach. Tony Canonie brought ice for the iceboxes. Del Jones inherited Sturtevant Lodge in 1923. And a "splendid horse-drawn steam fire engine" sat regally in the Park garage.

We do not have records of when the dam and car bridge replaced the old "swinging bridge," but the August 2, 1952 Patter tells us that "the dam, constructed to control the flow of Brandywine Creek, has foundations 13 feet below low water and extends 125 feet across. It was so designed to hold back the waters for a yacht basin, for many years a Park dream project. Before the bridge was built, a cable footbridge was used – swinging in the air every time a person ventured across. Kids considered it high adventure to cross on windy days, while parents got grey hair over the prospect of the cable snapping. Mr. Hempy had to ford the creek to get his wagon across."

The decade had its share of problems – one major tragedy being the loss of three beach cottages in the 1929 storm. In one case, the family rebuilt a cottage in the woods and sold the lake lot many years later. In another, cables were used to prevent total loss; in the process, the cottage was moved from one side of the Brandywine to the other. Apparently the Park was involved in a 1924 Circuit Court lawsuit trying to stop the defendants from digging and removing sand and gravel from the Park beaches. However, because the road to the beach had existed and been used by the public since 1851, the Judge ruled that Palisades be "enjoined from interfering with or obstructing the free and full use of said highway by the public for any highway purpose." Indeed, the road to our Circle remained a "public road" until the closing of our Post Office some decades later.

Ralph Nelson, previous owner of Heart's Haven (now Sandpiper #170) shared his "sure recipe for catching perch in the mid 20's" - which he calls his "Big Fish Story." Supposedly he filled a burlap bag with rocks for weight and edible garbage for bait. The bag was tied with string attached to a fishing "bobber" float and taken out about 200 yards to deep water. The bag was dropped overboard and left for a few hours. When he would return for his "reward," he would find multiple fish as two or three hooks had been placed on each line. So much for high tech fishing!

In "Remember When" (July, 1964, Patter), an unnamed "oldtimer" listed favorite activities from his or her early days in the Park. Although horses were seen in the Park through the 40's, the article's mention of the golf course dates these memories to pre-Depression years. Yet the last items sound very familiar to present day vacationers. Playing on the Brandywine Beach, sleeping out, running down the dunes, crossing the bridge are as popular in 2002 as in the 1920's! Here's the article:

---

*Remember When?*

*As kids, we loved to go horseback riding. We'd sit by hours and watch the horses go in and out from the stables which were housed in back of the garage. Remember that wonderful horse odor!*

*As kids, we loved to ride on the back of the horse drawn ice wagon that went through the Park every day. Charlie would give us kids pieces of ice to suck.*

*As kids, we played "at golf" on our nine hole sand golf course. Remember how much fun it was to putt on the sand greens? There was a big fuzzy "welcome" foot mat tied to two strings that we'd drag around the sand green to remove foot prints so we could putt. Fun, wasn't it?*

*As kids, we'd all meet on the beach by the Brandywine to play Prisoner's Base.*

*As kids, we had an annual tradition to hike south to Marvin Slide, to hike north to South Haven, to hike to Peter Pan Trail sand dune on the north end of the Park, and to sleep on the beach all night.*

*As kids, we'd take our weekend guests to the Water Tower Observatory, to run down the sand at the Sugar Bowl, and to take the broken down bridge trail to the tennis courts.*

# THE STORY OF THE CLUBHOUSE

*A personal view of the early Clubhouse years comes from Mardy Mehagan Mavor. Mardy, who started visiting the Park in its first decades, both lived in and directed activities for the Clubhouse in the 1930's and 1940's. In recalling her experience for the July 18, 1980 Patter, she told of the inception of this private Club (the original "Palisades Park Country Club") which was owned and organized by individuals within the community and independent of the Park itself. Her article, "Recollections of the Clubhouse," follows:*

For most of the 75 years of activities at Palisades Park, the Clubhouse has been the focal point. Originally, it was organized as a private club with Palisades Park residents only being eligible for membership. Mr. and Mrs. William Ward (Mary Lee Tillson's grandparents), Mr. and Mrs. Charles Allen, Mr. and Mrs. DeSouchet, and Mr. and Mrs. Ernest Wunsch were among the founders. The original Clubhouse was built on the beach and remained there for several years. Money was raised to run the Club by most successful bazaars each summer and the ladies worked all winter creating lovely things for the sale. Dances were held on Saturday nights with a "fiddler," a piano player, and a drummer from Covert. This provided toe tapping music. Mr. Ward was an excellent dancer and well known cotillion leader; each summer, the highlight of the season was a beautiful party, with favors for each dance number - all directed by the cotillion leader, Bill Ward, affectionately called "Uncle Willie Ward."

*A picnic by the Clubhouse on the beach.*

Palisades was blessed with well know musicians who owned cottages in Palisades. Among them, Leo Sowerby, composer and organist; Eric DeLamarter, assistant conductor of the Chicago Symphony Orchestra and his wife, Rose, who was an accomplished pianist; and Olaf Anderson, head of the Harmony Department of the American Conservatory of Music in Chicago. Thanks to their contacts, many famous musicians came each summer and gave beautiful concerts in the Clubhouse.

It became apparent during the 1920's that the Clubhouse needed to be enlarged to include a stage. So property was acquired on the hill back of the original site and the Clubhouse was moved there. There were many fund raising benefits, supported by everyone in the Park. One such was repeated for several years – a sort of vaudeville performance with the outstanding talent in the Park making up the program. The highlight each time was the "Men's Ballet Chorus Line" made up of the young men in the Park in short tutus and padded bras, dancing in elephantine grace to popular tunes of the day. Other activities were some excellent plays directed by Mr. Timmons, a well-known New York theatrical director. George Bernard Shaw's "Candida" was one of the most successful. Then there was a musical where Jayne Tyrrell (Mathias) and David Moore danced in the leading roles. During the early days, activities for adults were the primary functions, with weekly bridge parties in the evening and occasional luncheons. But Min Ward saw to it that the children had their share of fun when she established and directed the weekly Bunco Parties. These are precious memories for many of the present cottage owners who are grandparents today.

During the Depression, all but four couples dropped their membership in the Club and it was closed for four years. Mrs. and Mrs. Ward remained in charge and while the Club was closed, there was some vandalism. They decided

*Expanded Clubhouse moved to its present location.*

to ask Mrs. Gilby Mehagan, who had spent part of each summer as the Ward's house guest, to bring her two sons – John and Gilby – and stay in the Clubhouse for its protection. This plan was in effect for two years, when it

154

was decided to renew activities there with Mr. and Mrs. Mehagan in charge. Financial conditions improved and the Palisades Park Association decided to buy the stock of the few remaining members. Mrs. Mehagan was offered the position of director and continued in this capacity for about ten successful, fun-filled years.

One of the memorable features during the Mehagans' reign was the Sadie Hawkins costume party. The entire Ott family came as the "Yokum Family," carrying clubs, even to little Jackie Ott, age 5. Hoddie Clark, the son-in-law of Olaf Anderson, was a well-known artist; he drew large cartoons and murals that decorated the walls. These bore slight resemblances to the popular cottage owners, but were auctioned off after the party for sizable sums. Another and perhaps the largest and most successful party was a cabaret dance. A hundred tables were set up and sold at four dollars a table. The entertainment was provided by Connie Borchert, Weensie Bishop, and Bill DeButts. They were dressed in gaudy western vaudeville finery. The highlight of the program was provided by the generosity of Jeanne DeLamarter Bonnette, who owned a rare and beautiful small, upright piano. With promises of handling it with "tender, loving care," she allowed it to be transported to the Clubhouse, where it could be pushed around from table to table, and for a slight or generous fee, Connie and Weensie and Bill would perform requested numbers in their inimitable style.

As we all know, times change. The automobile made it possible for cottages to be filled with outside guests. Interest shifted from the Park for entertainment farther afield. The accent changed to more children-oriented activities and a new era began. The Clubhouse is filled with happy memories for young and old and the moving spirit of dear Mrs. Ward, without whose dedication and enthusiasm none of this would have survived, is still remembered with affection and appreciation.

## Articles of Government

The Articles of Government under which the Clubhouse had been started were found in a pamphlet loaned to the editor of the Patter by Lou Weston and reprinted in the July 18, 1980 edition. Until the Clubhouse was sold to the Park in the 1930's, membership was held only by those who paid their dues.

### Articles of Government

Article I - Name: The name of the organization shall be "The Palisades Park Country Club."

Article II – Object: The object of the Club shall be to promote the Social Development of Palisades Park, to erect a Clubhouse or Pavillion, which shall be for the purpose of providing a general meeting place for club members. The Clubhouse shall be used for religious services and entertainments of such character as may be approved by the Board of Governors.

Article III – Membership: Owners of property in Palisades Park shall be eligible for regular membership. Each regular membership shall entitle the holder to the privileges of the Club for himself and his family. The initiation fee for regular membership shall be $35.00 and may be increased or decreased by a majority vote of the Board of Directors. Associate memberships … for visitors in Palisades Park will be issued subject to approval of the Board of Directors on the following basis: Season membership - $20; One month - $10. … Such an associate member will have no vote at the annual or special meetings of the Club, nor will he be qualified to hold office in the Club organization.

---

**House Rules**

**No intoxicating liquor will be permitted on the Club premises.**

**The Clubhouse will not be open after twelve midnight.**

**The Clubhouse will be devoted on Sundays to religious service.**

---

## Early Presidents of the Clubhouse

The presidents of the Palisades Park Country Club, from 1915 – 1927, are listed below. Minutes from the annual meetings exist for each of those years. We also have a report of the "House Committee" as early as 1913; the building had to have been completed by then (or earlier). Whether presidents were elected before 1915 we do not know.

| | | |
|---|---|---|
| 1915 | Charles Allen |
| 1916 | A. C. DeSouchet |
| 1917 | A. W. Fleming |
| 1918 | A. W. Fleming |
| 1919 | D. A. Anderson |
| 1920 | E. J. McCarthy |
| 1921 | Martha Braun |
| 1922 | Seymour Nelson |
| 1923 | Dr. A. W. Stilliaus |
| 1924 | Alma Nellis |
| 1925 | Leo Sowerby |
| 1926 | Leo Sowerby |
| 1927 | Mrs. D. A. Anderson |

## A Look at Early Minutes: An Overview

The origin of our Palisades Clubhouse is somewhat dim. Although Quick's original plans included such a structure, exactly when it was built and by whom, or how it was first financed are not clear. Some of the interviews in this volume suggest that a few families initiated the project, certainly with Mr. Quick's blessings. Built on the beach sometime before 1913, the original "Palisades Park Country Club" was not a part of Mr. Quick's "Company." The Club had its own membership, by-laws, budget, activities, and rules. The land was leased – from whom it is not clear but possibly the Company – until seven lots on the bluff were purchased from Mr. Quick. In 1922, the building was moved to these new lots and gradually expanded to its present size. Many details of its early history are to be found in existing minutes of Annual Meetings from 1915 – 1927 and treasurer's reports from 1919 – 1938.

Those early minutes provide several consistent themes. Always they included an election of officers and of the Board of Directors, sometimes the naming of, or reports from, committee chairs. Throughout, key decisions were referred to the Board for action; activities to the committees for planning. These activities included social evenings - usually Saturday dances with live music; Wednesday card parties; the almost-annual bazaar which, with dues, provided the needed funding; and Sunday church services. Dances and card parties were limited to members and their guests plus guests at the Hotel; Sunday services were open to all. Members (for 25cents) and others (for $1.00) could rent the facility when it was not otherwise in use. The 1918 report on the August card party reported 12 had been present, $2.00 received, and $1.50 spent. The party was deemed "successful as far as it went, but it was a cold night and as there was a beach party being held on the same night, the attendance was small."

Care of the facility was also high on the agenda. Apparently the Clubhouse was to be kept locked, with each member having a key. One wonders how well that worked. As early as 1913, Mr. Wunsch warned of the need for care in the use of the player piano. Members were asked "not to use the pedals too vigorously" and younger children were to be kept away from the piano "unless accompanied by an older person." Routine maintenance was always a problem – from painting and construction of a platform stage to need for a caretaker, the topic came up each year. Screens were called for in 1919, plus "new dance records for the player piano." By 1923, needs for paint, a new roof, windows, and "making the house mouse proof" were all cited as important. By then there was talk of replacing the player piano – which later was repaired, instead.

Starting in 1920, efforts to move the Clubhouse to its present location began. Negotiations over the purchase of the seven lots were intense. The Park turned down a $700 cash offer and countered with $1000. The Club refused that and offered $800 cash, also turned down. Finally, an agreement of $200 a year for seven years, with no interest, was reached. Meanwhile the Club vacillated between the move and enlarging the building in its beach location. A bigger porch, kitchen, and dressing rooms were paramount in the plans. By the 1921 meeting, an estimate of $1500 was given for moving and enlarging; since the funds were not available, the decision was postponed.

Meanwhile, negotiations were taking place to bring electricity into the Park – and into the Clubhouse. Lines were to be run from St. Joseph to Covert and the Park could tap into those lines. In 1922, the Clubhouse was finally moved, lights were installed, and the cement stairs up to the building were built, apparently a gift from one of the Club members. The next year, a 20-foot addition on the north end and 12x20 on the east was contracted – to include a stage and dressing rooms. "Plumbing was to be of the best." This would cost $1200 and Mr. Quick would do the work. The Club had $500; a loan for $700 at 7% interest was secured by a note signed by four members.

*2002 Annual Meeting in Clubhouse*

Through the years, dues were often discussed – and raised. In 1917, dues were $5.00 per month, for families or individuals. By 1918, the War impacted dues with a 10% fee "due as a war tax" to cover the shortfall caused by remitting the fees of "anyone now in the Armed Services." Guest dues for 1920 were raised to $10 a season; initiation fees were $35.

Membership criteria were another continuing debate. In 1919 it was decided members must be "elected" to membership. New members were voted in "having completed the necessary requirements." In 1923, property owners in Dean's Addition - the area north of the Brandywine - were denied membership since the Addition was not yet a part of the Park. Mr. Quick was quoted as saying that admitting them "would not be in the best interests of the Park." Minutes of that same meeting suggested that if the Club decided "to invite (as) members those we wish," they would "thus keep out undesirables." One wonders what "undesirables" were threatening the membership lists.

One sad and embarrassing episode covered in the minutes did, indeed, touch on Club members' definition of "undesirables." On August 2, 1919, a special meeting was called; fourteen were present. The chair stated they were "assembled today to take some action that would be for the welfare of the Park." It seemed that "Mr. Ballou had rented his cottage to a family of Italians which did not tend to uplift the Park." Further, "a number of Hebrews were coming into the Park and something ought to be done to stop such things." A Mr. Walters "had brought the Hebrews here in his auto." A seven member committee was formed "to call on Mr. Ballou, Mr. Walters, and Mr. Quick regarding the objectionable features." The committee was to "see if they could not remedy same for the future." Further, they asked that Mr. Quick "should have a constable posted at the entrance on Sundays and holidays to keep out undesirables." Finally, "Mr. Ballou should clean up his front yard and put lattice work around it to cover up the unsightly appearance of same." Well! That was quite a meeting! Oh, that we could find some follow-up to those visits of what seems – at least from this vantage point – to have been almost a vigilante committee. Certainly this was a group sure of their "standards" and determined to adhere to them. We do know, from both our interviews and other early documents, that the anti-Hebrew policy was official for years. The anti-Italian policy, though more subtle, is also documented. It is interesting to note that one year later, as the then-president ended his term, his closing remarks included this passage: "We must assert the community spirit if we desire results and benefits commensurate with our ideals of what a summer colony should give. We come to this beautiful spot to rest and play! Not to fuss and fume and find we are spending our vacation with rankling thoughts in our minds." Perhaps his "ideals" included exclusions of religious and ethnic groups. Or perhaps the committee voted upon above had, indeed, led to "fussing and fuming" and "rankling thoughts."

The Treasurer's Reports give us lists of names of the dues-paying members - not everyone at Palisades at the time, but surely an accurate list of many. Expenditures flesh out activities – lighting and care taking, music rolls and orchestras, paint and prizes, fireworks and playing cards, excavating and trimming trees, tables and chairs, piano tuning and repair, printing and insurance, kerosene and cleaning. The Depression Years records tell a sad story. The "approximate budget for 1932-33" included $449 in expenses (electricity, taxes, insurance, repairs, postage, and prizes) and $343 in income ($10 dues from 24 members and receipts from plays, concerts, and parties); thus the Club faced a deficit of $106. By 1935-6, the membership list was down to 18 members. The next year the members were given a special assessment of $2.50; only four members could pay the $15 dues. Apparently the few members struggled on for another few years, though activities were curtailed. That leads us to the next step in the story of the Clubhouse.

## The Purchase of the Clubhouse by the Park

The official vote for the Park to purchase the Clubhouse from the original group of owners came in 1939, at a special meeting called by the Board. For a few more years, Mrs. Mavor directed the activities. As she noted, however, the focus of Clubhouse activities was shifting. Adults, who now often had cars at their disposal, sought entertainment "further afield." Gradually, a program for children evolved. By 1952, interest in such a recreational program for children was high enough that Betty Householder instituted the "Clubhouse couple" – for many years, a young couple from Western Michigan University who lived in the Clubhouse and provided leadership for a variety of youth activities. That practice has continued.

Apparently the negotiations between the "Palisades Park Country Club" (as the Clubhouse – owned by several families - was then called) and the "Palisades Park Improvement Association" (which represented all the cottage owners) took several years. A September 4, 1937, memo from Mary B. Ward, President of the Club, and Hubert H. Stoddard, Secretary, to the Improvement Association, agrees to let the Association operate the Clubhouse for two years, "provided they agree to assume and pay all operating expenses … and any repairs to the

*Cast of a Clubhouse summer musical.*

*Boys Chorus Line*

building deemed necessary to keep the same in good condition." It continues to stipulate that "it is not too much to request that during this two-year period ... the Improvement Association ... provide some form of entertainment – parties, recreation, dancing – for the Palisades Park property owners at least once every week from July 4th till Labor Day of each year." Believing this trial period "will demonstrate that the establishing of a general recreation center will be for the best interests of the entire community," the Club hoped for a "permanent transfer" of the Clubhouse and a future purchase that would be "fair with the pioneers who have invested their money in this property at a time when a Clubhouse was badly needed and no Company funds available with which to build it." Apparently this memo was put to a mailed vote of the all owners of property in Palisades Park.

We assume the trial went well, because two years later, in 1939, the extant correspondence is about the financing of the purchase. Although Club President Ward hoped for a $5000 selling price to be repaid in five years, the agreement was not so generous. A special meeting of all members (in good standing) of the Palisades Park Improvement Association was called for September 2, 1939, to vote on the following:

> RESOLVED, That the proposal received from the Palisades Park Country Club, through its President, be and is hereby accepted covering the purchase of the Clubhouse and seven lots owned by the Club, at a price of $4500, payable in yearly payments of no certain sum, without interest, final payment to be made not later than September 10th 1947.
>
> BE IT FURTHER RESOLVED, that the annual membership fee of each cottage owner member of the Association be increased in the amount of $5.00 and the annual membership fee of each lot owner member of the Association be increased in the amount of $1.00 for such period as may be necessary to discharge the obligation incurred for the purchase of said Clubhouse and property; and that said additional annual membership fees from each member be ear-marked, set aside, and on each succeeding September 20th, beginning with the year 1940, the total accumulation from this source shall be paid on the purchase price of said Clubhouse and grounds until the obligation is paid in full.

Park residents – young and old – can be thankful that the membership in 1939 approved this resolution and saved the Clubhouse for future generations. Everyone at Palisades is invited to use the facilities. Plays and revues, vespers, bridge parties, fashion shows, weddings, annual meetings, musical programs, and lately slide shows are some of the events held in the Clubhouse. Through the years, the programming has changed to include more activities for children and fewer for adults. "Clubhouse couples" have long provided leadership and popular events – Capture the Flag, sleep-outs, carnivals, and competitions, became established. Although its uses have changed somewhat over the years, it is still a popular and busy hub of activities and an asset to the Park.

## Recent Years
## Memories of Maureen Schlacks

Sand castle building contests, kick-the-can, field olympics, teen night out, and movie nights. These are just a few of my memories from my early years in Palisades. The walls of our cottage are filled with my brothers' and my ribbons from shuffle board tournaments, egg tosses, and stone-skipping contests. The Clubhouse is where I made all of my childhood friends, and where my bond with my cousins grew stronger. I loved packing a lunch and going on hobo hikes through the trails of Palisades. I loved dressing up for the costume parties, going on scavenger hunts, and working at the carnivals. The sleep-outs, however, were my favorite events of the summer. My brother and I would be sent to the Sugar Bowl carrying our sleeping bags, flashlights, and snacks – full of energy – only to return home the next day, dragging our sleeping bags behind us, still half asleep at 6:00 a.m. It's what happened in between those two times that made the sleep-out so special. We would run around the dunes for hours, tell secrets, and repeat our rituals. We would make s'mores while listening to all of the ghost stories about Palisades Park – the same stories that were told to our parents and the same stories that we'll tell to our children. Well after the sun set, we would begin to hear sounds from the top of the Sugar Bowl – the same sounds that we waited for every sleep-out, the sounds that frightened us but made us go looking, the sounds of the teenagers on a mission to scare us just as they, themselves, had been scared by another generation. Just as we would, in turn, try to frighten those younger than us. These memories will stay with us our whole lives.

> The Clubhouse is all about tradition. The tradition of Wednesday night Bingo and Bunco games. The tradition of Friday morning capture-the-flag, and Friday night movies with fresh popcorn. The tradition of ping pong, shuffle board, and badminton tournaments. All of these traditions were what made me want to run the Clubhouse when I became older. I wanted to continue the activities and nature crafts I enjoyed so much when I was a kid. I ran the Clubhouse for four years, and in those years, I watched many children come to love the Park as much as I do. I tried to teach them about the beauty of Palisades, the wonders it holds, and how to preserve them.
> - Maureen Schlacks

## Adult Programs in Later Years

In keeping with Arthur Quick's vision of Palisades as a haven for artists and their endeavors, recent years have found both musical and visual programs presented for the Park members.

From 1994 on to the present, a popular musical evening has been provided by Steve Heavrin and his quartet, Soundcheck. The quartet features two men and two women plus two guitars. They have performed in coffee houses, banjo conventions, weddings, and as concert openers near Steve's home in Trenton, MI. Usually the Soundcheck members make a weekend of it, visiting the Heavrins and enjoying the pleasures of Palisades. In recent years, they have been joined by the Friends duo of Bob and Dennis. These musical evenings have been a big treat for Park members.

Beginning in 1997, and each year thereafter, Don Henkel has organized and presented a mid-August photographic program of interest to Park members and their guests. The most popular program was in the millennium year, 2000; titled "Yesteryear at Palisades Park," it presented vintage slides of the Park from twelve "oldtimers." Bill Potter, assisted by John Sentgerath and Don Henkel, made a video of this program, copies of which were later sold. The seven programs have been:

1997: Themes in Outdoor Photography by Don Henkel
1998: Palisades Park slides by Katy Beck, Nan Lewis, and Don Henkel
1999: Michigan's Beauty by Rob Venner and Lighthouses by Don Henkel
2000: Yesteryear at Palisades Park – Katy Beck, John Brand, Kay Goff, Don Henkel Bill Keehn, Nan Lewis, Doris Patterson, David Peat, Brad Piper, Bill Potter, Sally Schlobohm, and Shirley Sentgerath
2001: Pictorial History of South Haven (video) and Palisades Park Photo Quiz by Don Henkel
2002: The Story of the Eastland by Jerry Foust and America the Beautiful by Don Henkel
2003: Park History Publication Preview by Marilyn Henkel, Katy Beck, Bill Potter, Marge Roche, Don Henkel

**Themes in Outdoor Photography**

*Tom Bendelow, designer of our golf course, and friends enroute to Palisades Park. c.1920*

# Tom Bendelow and the Palisades Park Golf Course

A golf course, advertised in his earliest brochures, was part of Mr. Quick's initial plan for Palisades Park. Unlike some of the other rather grandiose plans that Quick first announced, the dream of a nine hole course became an early reality when Tom Bendelow, a well known golf course designer, laid out our course in the area beyond the manager's house out to the Blue Star Highway. Born in Scotland, Mr. Bendelow worked for A. G. Spalding and Brothers, a sporting goods manufacturer headquartered in Chicago. Mr. Bendelow had begun, in 1893, designing golf courses - first in New York, then in Chicago, and finally all across the U. S. and Canada. Of course, at Palisades he built a sand course, quite unlike the manicured courses we expect today. Here, sand greens were oiled and swept clean with a mat on a chain after each use; the tee was made with a mound of wet sand, for which a bucket of sand and another of water were provided.

In return for the work he did at Palisades, Mr. Quick gave Bendelow several lots in the Park and Bendelow built "Balgownie," a cottage near the Clubhouse, which is still owned by his family. The cottage name came from the name of a bridge in Aberdeen, Scotland, where he had courted his wife, Mary Ann. She was from a well-to-do farm family. The status of Tom's family, who ran a small pie shop, didn't exactly please Mary Ann's. Tom was working for the Aberdeen newspaper at the time, and his future father-in-law could see right away that he would never be a farmer. So the bridge became the special and secret meeting place for the young couple, whose romance was opposed at home. In 1892, shortly after their marriage, Tom came to this country. Mary Ann and their first child, Mae, followed the next year.

In New York, Bendelow first worked for the New York Herald. One day the paper received an ad from the Pratt family – of Standard Oil fame – asking for someone to teach them golf. Tom answered the ad and got the job. He was successful in his instruction and was asked by the Pratts to design a course for them. That started his illustrious career. Soon he was hired by New York City Parks Authority to redesign and expand to 18 holes the Van Cortlandt Golf Course, this country's first public course. Thus began a lifelong interest in public courses; he hoped to open the game to a broader, less affluent, public. Among other innovations, he was the first to establish tee times. His success in New York led him to Illinois, about 1901, where he was to design over 100 courses. No doubt his connection to the Chicago Park District led him into contact with Olaf Benson, a park designer for the Park District who also laid out Palisades

Park for Arthur Quick. We assume this connection led Bendelow to Palisades Park. Altogether, Bendelow designed over 600 courses, including Illinois's Medinah Country Club and the nearby Kalamazoo Country Club. Medina recently published its history, complete with pictures of Tom and references to his golfing career.

Bendelow's daughter Mary Ann (Mae), who was born in Scotland, married the artist Frederic Mizen who later decorated the cottage. Bendelow also had two sons - Ernie, who had a publishing house in Chicago, and John. John's son Jack may be remembered at Palisades for his tennis prowess; he was the Junior Honor and Glory champion in 1939 and the Senior in 1943. The elder Tom Bendelow died in 1936, and the ownership of the cottage passed to his children and then to Ernie's son, a second Tom and his wife Shirley. Shirley still owns it.

In the September, 1996 Patter, Betty Householder told of her memories of the Old Golf Course:

*The Tuesday, August 15, 1905 edition of the South Haven Daily Tribune features the opening "down on the Brandywine" of another resort in the South Haven area – Palisades Park. Much glowing prose is devoted to extolling the present and planned features of "one of the most naturally beautiful pieces of ground" in the area.*

*The article assures all readers that "golf and other sports" will be laid out, and continues to describe the grandiose plans, many of which never came to fruition. However, the Clubhouse and tennis courts have served Palisades well, and at one time there really was a golf course!*

*In my early days at the Park (I started coming here with my parents, John and Mary Gardner in 1921), a "sand greens" golf course was located at the back of the baseball diamond. While I don't remember exactly, I'm almost sure there were no more than five or six holes. The "greens" were actually sand – when playing the course, one checked out a small doormat on a chain which was used to drag out any marks or footprints on the "green" after playing a hole.*

*The course was too short to use a driver, so a 3-iron was the club of choice. Players moved from the tee along the fairway, which was rough by today's standards. Once on the "green," out came the putter, and the balls left tracks in the sand. The whole "green" was then smoothed with the little pad.*

*In later years, my sister Janette (Gardner) King and I used to take our parents down to the Park golf course to practice in preparation for their weekly Thursday outing to play nine holes at Glenshore Golf Course near Saugatuck and lunch at the Showtop Restaurant.*

*The old sand greens course was never much of a success and money and energy went instead to the improvement and upkeep of the tennis courts, a decision heartily supported by the Householder family!*

Apparently, for awhile there was a Palisades Golf Association, of which George Graham Wilson was one of the founders. Wilson was the grandfather of Kathryn Larsen Harriman, owner of The Highlands #78 until 1999. Wilson's son-in-law, E. E. Larsen, was the designer and engineer of the dam and bridge across the Brandywine.

*The old golf course*

Vashti Blaney remembered that the golf course had eight holes, although a picture we have shows a flag for hole #9. Mardy Mavor suggested that the course had problems from the start – from the rough fairways to an abundance of goldenrod – thought to be a bane to those who have allergies - and grasshoppers. Nonetheless, golf remained popular at Palisades through the 20's, though maintenance and adequate water were always problems. During the Depression years, the cost became prohibitive and the course was gradually abandoned. Later, as roads improved and other nearby golfing sites expanded, the Park saw no need to revive its course. Two 1939 letters from Arthur Quick tell the story of the ending of the golf course. In the first, to Mr. Hubert Nelson, Quick asks for a "vote on the matter of disposing with the golf grounds. It is a white elephant as it is, and I cannot keep on carrying the expenses. If we sell it, it will, I insist, remain under the control of the Palisades Park Company and be subject to the same restrictions as the rest of the Park. I think there is enough money among the park people to buy it in and hold it as an investment if I have a definite proposition to put up to them and have enough time to put it over." The second letter is to the Directors of the Palisades Park Golf Club, G. A. Clark, A. W. Stillians, S. G. Nelson, and L. L. Gervais. Here Quick was more specific about the problems of the course and his hopes to sell:

*It is generally conceded by the members of the golf club and many others that with so many really good golf courses within easy driving distance of Palisades Park, it would be useless for our club, with the thin soil on our course and the necessary expense to keep it in proper fertility, to try to keep up our course or put any further expense on it.*

*Consequently we have before us the question of making some use of this land or disposing of it; for there is no money forthcoming from the members of the club for the yearly overhead expense – taxes and interest on the $700 mortgage that we assumed.*

*There seems to be no way of utilizing this land in any way that would bring in an income to cover these expenses, and as I have personally, for some years, paid these expenses, and hardly feel like continuing the practice; therefore, it would seem advantageous to dispose of the land if it can be done, and in a way that would relieve the members of further expense, and also perhaps return to them what they have paid in for memberships. With this in mind I have done a bit of scouting around with the view to finding a purchaser. Results have been encouraging, not at all. Especially so, because I have had no definite proposition or terms to present. With that object in mind I am now asking our Directors, in this letter which is being sent to all of them, for their views on the matter, and if no other plan than <u>selling</u> is suggested, then if they are willing and agreeable ... to grant to any acceptable customer a two-year option to purchase for say $6100 (the value of our total memberships), provided purchaser agrees to assume the $700 mortgage, and also assume the $1100, which is the amount we agreed to pay the Palisades Park Company for the equity ... and during these two years pay the current taxes and the interest on the $700 mortgage.*

To the best of our knowledge, no buyer was found and the land ultimately became part of the property of Palisades Park. Was it part of Quick's estate, willed to his daughter and later purchased by the Nine Old Men? We do not know, though a future historian could find out. In 2001, two barns, several tennis courts, a boat storage area, a ball field, a basketball court, and a Park dump share this land with thousands of cacti, whose yellow blossoms blanket the fields every June. Two trails wend their way out to the Blue Star Highway, leading a few stalwart walkers to explore the area. Most Palisaders probably drive past the area and give it little or no thought, content in the certainty that it will never be developed.

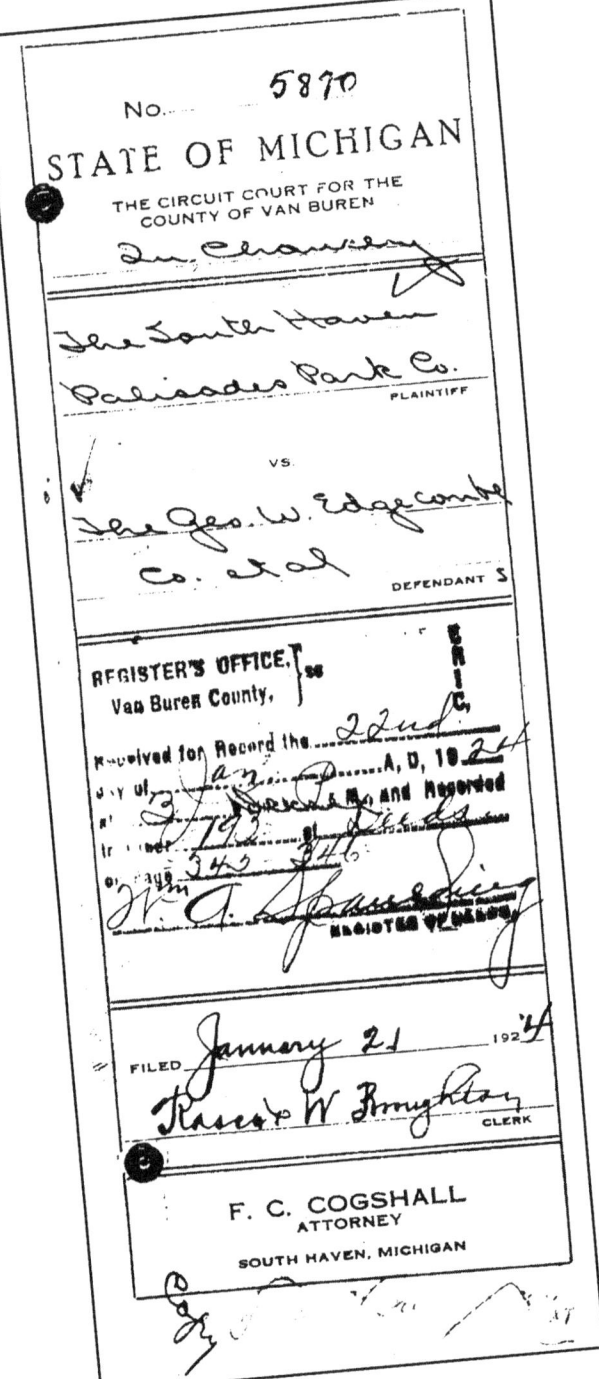

## 1924 Court Ruling:
### Park Road to the Beach Must Remain Open to the Public

*Last page of Court Document*

The documents for this 1924 lawsuit show that Mr. Quick and his Company went to court to stop the defendants - the George W. Edgecombe Company, Herbert L. Daggett, Ray Miller, and Roscoe Emery - from "entering upon the beach fronting said subdivision" and digging and removing sand and gravel from the beach. "The removing of such sand and gravel was causing damage to the plaintiff in that it tends to destroy the beach and to remove the lateral support therefrom."

However, the court replied that "ever since the above highway was established it has been worked, kept open, and suitable for public travel; ...that the public used said highway for all necessary purposes, as well as a public road to the waters of Lake Michigan until a short time before the filing of the bill of complaint in this cause." Therefore, "the public has the right to travel over and along the same, and that the plaintiff be and it hereby is enjoined from interfering with or obstructing the free and full use of said highway by the public for any highway purpose."

# Interviews

*wicker chair from the old Filkins' cottage*

## David Filkins
Interviewed by Betty Householder
September 3, 1984
Also letter and documents sent
from David to Betty in 1994

My grandparents, Arthur and Jessie Filkins, first came to Palisades in the summer of 1925, to the Dean cottage*, up on the hill next to where they later built. My grandmother's older sister rented that cottage. When my grandparents came here to see how the sister was doing, they found that she just hated the place and wanted to go home. She thought this was the most desolate spot on earth! Originally from North Dakato, where my grandmother was born, she was a teacher and had wanted to get out of the city; she had asked the principal if he knew of a reasonably priced place. He had recommended Palisades Park. She didn't like it, but my grandmother (Jessie Filkins) loved it. She sat on the hill and said, if they ever had a cottage, that would be the spot. My grandfather went down the next day and bought the lot, May 1st, 1926. The title insurance policy was issued for $300. The cottage was built in 1926 for an additional $800 by Rudy Weber and Charley Tunecke of Covert. All of the building materials were hauled along the beach by horse and wagon.

*\* One of the cottages destroyed when the power plant was built.*

Arthur's children - my father, Edward, and my Aunt Jean - spent all or most of their childhood summers in the Park. They enjoyed some of the other children then in the Park - Ginny Pierce (Ginny Richards), Elizabeth Gardner (Betty Householder), the Welles children (including Kay Goff and Peter Welles's father) – all members who were part of the Park in the 20's and 30's. My grandfather apparently went to an old factory in Chicago that was throwing out old conveyor belt and asked if he could have it. He somehow got it over here. He used it as a walk. It got awfully hot and slippery to walk on.

Originally, everything north of Eldridge's cottage was not part of Arthur Quick's Palisades Park. The north part of the Park, up to what is now the riprap of the power plant, was "Dean's Addition to Palisades Park." This includes lots which now belong to Eldridge, Goff, Cooney, Steiner, Vandersalm, Roche, Potter, Canonie, and Welles. In early years, there was some friction between residents of Dean's Addition and Mr. Quick, since Dean's Addition residents were not members of Palisades Park but they used the

*Mrs. Dora Dean of Dean's Addition c. 1920*

roads of the Park. Eventually, this was settled by having Dean's Addition residents purchase lots in Palisades Park proper and pay the appropriate annual dues. All of the older cottages in the Addition still have lots somewhere else in the Park. In most cases, the lots are poorly located because they were the least expensive lots available, purchased only to qualify for membership.

Dean's Addition to Palisades Park also included three cottages which no longer exist. They were on a small dune overlooking the beach further north, where rubble and debris and the remains of an old sea wall can still be seen. The three cottages belonged, from north to south, to the Millikens (later Jocelyn and Scott); to my grandparents, Arthur and Jessie Filkins – Bonnie Doone; and to the Deans (later Olsen and Chambers) – Sea Breeze. These three cottages were taken over by Consumer's Power Company when they got permission to build the power plant in the 1960's. Although none of the cottage owners wanted to sell, the power company was able to compel the owners to sell by invoking the legal principle of eminent domain. The cottages were torn down or moved in 1969. My grandmother was still here then; she came up for her last visit and passed away two years ago (1982) at the age of 98. She sure loved it up here, and so did my dad. He loved the beach and the tennis courts. Everyone still knew him as Bud Filkins, though I never knew him as that. Father only came up once, for two weeks, after we lost that cottage.

We rented the cottage behind Stan's for one year. Our family was away from the Park from 1970, the year after Bonnie Doone was torn down, until 1982, when our daughter Jessie was born. After two generations of the Filkins family spending their childhood summers at Palisades Park, I couldn't imagine my child (soon to become children) not spending her summers the same way. We purchased our lot from the Vandersalms and built our cottage in 1983. The area in which our cottage and the Henry's cottage are located is not part of Dean's Addition nor is it in the original survey of Palisades.

*Mrs. Filkins and David c. 1970. Their cottage was removed when the power plant was built.*

One interesting document I have is a letter from Canonie Excavating Company dated May 9, 1952. The same erosion problems existed in 1952 as have existed often, since, and lakefront cottage owners had to build seawalls. However, in 1952, a seawall only cost $18 per linear foot. It was wooden with steel bolts holding the posts and boards in place. Several years ago, when the lake was high, that wall built in the 50's was exposed.

*Aerial view of the Palisades Nuclear Power Plant. 1985. The Plant bought and destroyed the Filkins cottage in the 1960's.*

## Florence Heitner and Joyce Heitner Lloyd

Interviewed by Betty Householder
September 5, 1984

In 1926, I came to Palisades Park as guest of my "to be" sister-in-law. She and a group of friends had rented the Browning cottage (#152), which was being moved to a higher location on the next lot on the beach. It wasn't finished, so her friends rented Cherry Hill (#144) instead and wanted us up for the weekend. Bill, my sister, and I were leaving to go home on Monday morning – we had to be at work at 8:00 a.m. – and early in the morning we drove around, and around, and around the Clubhouse. We didn't know our way out! Bill had come in 1920, before we met, with a friend who went to Armour Institute, now ITT, in Chicago. The friend had rented Balgownie (#74) and they came up for a weekend. They came up in a Ford, and Bill said it shook and rattled all the way. It took <u>forever</u> to get here.

In those days we had to go over through Covert; Rt. 31 wasn't yet built. We kept coming up at different times and renting the Wilson cottage, which is the cottage that Katherine Harriman now owns (#78); her mother, Isabel Larson, is the daughter of the Wilsons. Isabel was the first to bring myrtle into the Park. Everybody else has transplanted some from that area. Her father transplanted many ferns around the cottage. There was a wooden garage that Mr. Henderson had built and the most interesting furniture in the cottage. I loved the brass beds, and all the old wicker furniture, too.

After Joyce was born, we used to rent Miss Miller's cottage on the beach, Bonnie Dune (#150). But we continued to rent the Wilson cottage for weekends. One Decoration Day weekend, when Bill, my husband, was walking down the beach and passed another Mrs. Wilson, Jayne Mathias's aunt, she told Bill the O'Malley cottage was for sale (#98). It was owned then by the Kirby family . He came back to get me and we went up and peeked in the front windows and the screen door on the back porch. We went home and called the people and bought the

*Gulls on North Beach. 1937.*

cottage. That was in 1948. We had looked at Sunset (#88) the cottage the Householders later bought, and told the owner, who was talking about selling, that we were interested in it. After we bought this one, the owner called us and told us she had decided to sell. We told her we had already bought one. That was when the Householders bought it – that 4th of July weekend.

I don't know much about Mrs. O'Malley. She was from Chicago. When she became ill, the house was going to be put up for sale, and the nephew – Bill Kirby – was given first chance to buy it. He had it about five years and decided to move to California. That is when we bought it. It was built in 1928 – 1929, after the Baker cottage went into the lake. We had to get some kind of release or clearance from I don't know where, because the Indians still owned the land. It had to be cleared through some Indian tribe. It took one year to be cleared, when we bought it. George and Myrtle Boyles built the same year we bought (#99).

In the early years, we drove over often. We came and watched when the first seawall was being built by Tony Canonie. We saw the wreckage of the Baker cottage that had gone into the lake in front of us, in 1928, and of another cottage, on the other side of the Brandywine. The latter didn't go in all the way and was moved back to shore. Perhaps that was the Harding cottage. After that beautiful storm we had in '73, our wall was cut off, and then this cement thing was put on top. I don't know who constructed it. We had everything in – the forms were in – and then the storm came. We had a well down there and we lost that. We lost almost all our grass down there. So did George Boyles. Every time the lake was rough, the area behind the breakwater filled with water and kids swam in there. You couldn't keep them out. Betty Householder remembers telling George Boyles at the Annual Meeting that the water behind the breakwater was a public nuisance and he might be sued if some kid dove in and broke his neck. She thought a lawyer had ruled that it was an "attractive nuisance." George sold his cottage soon thereafter. We put sand in – brought it in, carload by carload – to solve the problem. The Owens family bought from George and put in thousands of blades of dune grass after the sand was replaced. We did too; we put in fencing to hold the grass and hay on top of everything. One beach fire down there in front of us was horrible. We sat out here with buckets of water and we were scared to death the grass would catch fire. The people next door were renters and they were having fits about it, too.

I don't know how many people know that they used to have a band on Saturday nights at the Clubhouse. When we rented up at the Harriman cottage, we could hear the band. We never went down to join the fun, though. We were only renters, then. I don't think they still had dances by the time we bought.

We used to watch the Half-Mile Swim race out our front. This cottage, when we bought it, had two small windows there and two small windows here, and where you're sitting was the end of this sunroom, as they called it. We first put in one picture window and had a small window on each side. Then we decided to open the whole thing up, so we had another picture window put in two years later. We have loved it ever since. We added fans, too. The porches were here but they had canvas roll-up awnings. Joyce and Ross decided it would be nice to enclose the porch with these – awning windows, what do you call them? – so we did. Joyce's husband started the deck in '78 and Cecil finished it in '79.

It's hard to say what we loved best about coming here. We just simply loved Palisades. The lake. We had a beautiful wide beach when we first came. And we loved the woods. We have enjoyed our motor boat and canoe and sailboat. Joyce had her group of friends – Haven Best and Judy VonRosen, Mary Householder and Nancy O'Brien, Nancy Neubauer Menconi and her sister Barbara, and Nancy Campbell. That was about it for the high school group. There weren't as many kids here then as when Joyce's children came along.

Joe Putz was such a dear. He helped put in our well; when the water came in, we thought we'd struck oil, we were so excited. Charley Tunecke used to come down with a lantern and take care of the water and the old pump house. He and Joe were very good friends. We would come up early in the spring and late in the fall; that's why we had the well put in. Joe would bring big milk cans of water for us. He was good to us. The day that he died, we had been up here, and Bill couldn't remember whether he had drained the faucets when we got back to Chicago. He wrote and asked Joe if he would look and see, and Joe took the postal card that Bill had sent for him to reply, and said that he had done it. And then we got the news, later, that that was the day he died, in his truck. Bill came up to see what he could do. Joe must have had a heart attack, because he ran off the road.

We never stayed at the Hotel but we used to come up on weekends and stay at the Ballou Inn. We went there for meals when we rented Kitty Wisson's cottage, Fern Hill (#68). Their chicken dinners were delicious. This was before Joyce was born. We did our shopping at Sinks in the beginning, and somebody came around with vegetables to sell. Sometimes we got vegetables at Iversons' farm. Kitty Wisson was a spinster, a librarian in Chicago, I believe. She was retired when we met her. She owned Fern Hill and Oceana. When his first wife died, she married Mr. Quick. They lived in South Haven.

Mr. Quick was alive when we first came, of course. He was always on the go around the Park, and he sure did try to sell Bill, when we used to rent; he sure did try to sell him lots. I can remember the roads being maintained by Quick. Mr. Hempy and his horses brought gravel from the beach. He would take the horses along the beach, and every once in awhile he'd have to stop and do a little clean-up job; but remember, he used to go down to pick up the garbage. I don't know who helped him. Of course, Knapp used to have the service station out there, where Fred Nichols later lived and had his store and restaurant. Which way did it go … Knapp had the station after Tony Canonie, is that right? One time we were renting Cherry Hill, just a weekend, I think, over Memorial Day, and it was so doggone cold out on the porch. Cherry Hill was for sale. Tony brought a couple up to look at it and I said, "It isn't always this cold up here. We've got a wind coming out of the north, northeast, and it's <u>very</u> cold today." He looked at me and said, "Do you know what it is out at the service station? 98 degrees!" And we were freezing up on the porch!

*Postcard showing Graystone #89, Ballou Inn #90, and Oceana #91 . c. 1932.*

## Betty Householder

Interviewed by Katy Beck

My name is Betty Householder; my brother was Jack Gardner and my sister was Jeanette Gardner King. My mother and father, John and Mary Gardner, brought Jeanette and me to walk through Palisades Park on Labor Day, 1921. Then Mrs. Filkins had my sister and me over to the Park to stay two weeks at her cottage at the north end. From that time on, we began to come every summer. We rented. We had Pottawatomi once; the upstairs loft was awfully hot in summer. It has changed so much now. Then we were in the Little Brown Jug and, later, Clark's cottage, which is now Pat Roche's, near the Brandywine. And we rented next to McWethy's cottage.

When we were real young, we would come to Covert by train, from our home in Riverside, Illinois, and Mrs. Shattuck would meet us with the horses. She'd bring us over here, unload us, and get us into the cottage we were renting. We brought a trunk and we stayed all summer, once we came. My father came by train on weekends; he also had two weeks of vacation. Later on, when we had a car, we met him at the train in Bangor. We met him every Friday night and took him back every Sunday. Of course, at first we went to the Palisades store, because we were just stuck here - all of us women, who didn't have cars, didn't have husbands during the week, and had all the kids. We bought all our groceries at the store, here at the Park. When we had a car, we went to Sinks for a lot of groceries. A lot of people went there. Mrs. Plain – Mrs. Doris McWethy Plain – thought that Sinks was the best place to buy groceries in Covert. But a lot of people insisted on going to South Haven. After awhile, people began comparing prices and, of course, Helen Packard's things were two cents more because she had to drag them in and drag them out. When people got to comparing, they began buying things in South Haven. I remember Mrs. Packard very well. I was up and down there, half a dozen times a day. Every time she had goods that were going to spoil, she knew I had a big family here and asked me if I wanted them, half price, so we got melon and lettuce and all these vegetables that were spoiling.

*Betty and Frank Householder, 1953*

When I was young, we played Prisoner's Base (it's like Capture the Flag) every night on Brandywine beach. Life around the circle was gay. Sometimes we played hide and seek in the dark. Oh, that was very exciting. Running around all the cottages and nobody seeming to mind. We were all in at 10:00 p.m., though. I remember my children fussing because one girl in the Park could stay out as late as she wanted to. I said, "Well, maybe her folks just don't care about her so much." Mary felt better after she knew we cared about her.

We went to the tennis courts every morning. That was a ritual. 10:00 a.m. – 12:00 noon, we went to the tennis courts. And my folks used to watch us play. It would be cold on the lake in the morning, but warm at the courts. Then we came home and, after lunch, everybody had a nap. Then at 3:00 we went to the beach. Every afternoon. We had a real ritual. At 3:00 I'd get the old Buick and I'd get my folks up there with their inner tubes and umbrella and beach towels, and I'd take them down to Mary Lee's corner there and let them off at the sidewalk. Then I'd go and park the car, that old Buick, in the parking lot and go down and set up the umbrella and the towels. We'd sit in our chairs until 5:00. If they went in the water, they used the tires to keep them steady in the water, 'cuz sometimes there were stones. They swam until 5:00 when I'd go get the car and we'd come up. My mother went swimming the year she was 84. She died the year she was 85. She still was going swimming, when it was calm and the water was warm.

In August, we had all those lovely plays – adult plays. Jeanne Anderson was one of the directors and Mary Kay Goodrich was the other one. We had all these one act plays. My mother was in one and Frank was in several and I was in one. At the end of the summer, just before Labor Day, we always had a skit at the Clubhouse that the Clubhouse couple put on. But the kids wrote the script. Teens wrote down by the Brandywine, you know. They all sang. That was fantastic. And all the parents came to see their kids.

*Clubhouse play. 1953.*

When we stayed at the hotel, before we bought our cottage or rented, Mrs. Gates was there with her two boys; she always brought a lot of games which we played after dinner, in the hotel living room. Her boys were very well behaved. She had games and they didn't fool around. Mr. Wunsch lingered in the dining room and he had candy for all of us kids. He always passed out candy for all of us. In later years, he passed out candy to all of my children, too. He and the Wards ate all their meals at the hotel. Oh, we thought that was wonderful.

The hotel served a beautiful breakfast, you know, with all the bacon you could eat, and hot rolls. Oh, Mrs. Wenham was a wonderful cook. And of course Mrs. Jones was, too. The cook that was in the kitchen was Melzora Johnson – wasn't that her name? She made wonderful pies. When Jones sold the hotel, he brought a picture up to my mother, so we have that old picture and nobody knows who painted it. It's a Grandma Moses thing. My mother always put on it "artist unknown" because she didn't want people to think she did it – it's not her style. It shows the hotel and our cottage and Mary Lee's cottage and Sankes' cottage. It was painted a long time ago, before Bishops' and VonRosens' and the rest of the cottages were ever built. At least, the artist didn't put them in.

My folks played Bingo at the hotel. It was against the law to do that but nobody knew it. There were slot machines, also. You put in money and then it came out oranges and apples. They kept confiscating the machines, but then the next year Del seemed to have them back. Oh, that was really kind of daring for everybody. We thought we were real wicked. Poor Del Jones. The kids just ran him ragged. They wanted to use his toilet – there was no other toilet down there in the Circle area – and he said no, they couldn't and then they'd put peanut butter on the toilet seat. Oh, they did all kinds of horrible things in the public toilet. He was the kind that yelled at them, so it made it fun for them.

Mrs. Steele and Mae Sanke and Mrs. Prange (who was in Bittersweet (#51) at that time) and my mother played canasta every night. Those old ladies! Mrs. Sanke had one of the early cottages, built in 1907 by the Ballou family at the same time they built Ballou Inn. It is in many early pictures, along with Ballou Inn. When Mrs. Sanke got old and feeble, I had to go down and sleep with her for a week because she was sick. Right down here in the cottage Ted Baer owns now. (#91) The toilet, I remember, was down on the second floor and we slept on the third floor, which was a nuisance. We had pots up there. Every morning I had to empty those pots. Mrs. Steele owned what is now the Golden cottage (#48). Once she picked up a hitchhiker coming up here. Remember that? He threw her out of the car and took her pocketbook and keys and left her on the side of the road. So from that time on, we were advised never to pick up a hitchhiker. She had felt sorry for this kid and she picked him up.

*Oceana #91.*

What my folks liked was the boardwalk. They could walk up and down there. They walked every single night after dinner. In those days, we walked everywhere. Once a year we went to Marvin Slides, down south. We hiked there. And once a year we went to where Consumer Power now is, to a great big sand dune back there. We called that Peter Pan Trail. Once a year we hiked to South Haven. Somebody met us in a car and brought us home. That was a once-a-year thing we always did. People in those days really walked around and hiked more than nowadays. We had beach fires, and once a year, we slept on the beach. My father moaned because it was hard sleeping on that beach, but we kids always liked it. The whole family slept down there so we could see the stars. Of course, when the Clubhouse couple started coming in 1952, they took over that sleeping out. They took the children to the Sugar Bowl. Then the parents didn't have to do that. So we were relieved of doing that like my folks had to do with us. But it wasn't so crowded then; there weren't that many people.

I got married in 1940 and had three daughters, so we didn't come up very much then. During that time, my folks stayed two weeks at the hotel and had all of us come over there if our children were three years and up and were toilet trained. Then Del Jones would have us at the hotel. He didn't allow babies. So the first year, Annie couldn't come. Mary, Sally, and I and my sister, Jeanette, and her daughter, Caroline, came. The little ones weren't allowed.

*Mary, Sally, and Annie Householder. 1953.*

Then Mary Lee Tillson, when they built that sea wall, couldn't come up, so we rented her cottage for the month of August and Weensie Bishop had us the month of July. The next year, we had the Ward cottage (Mary Lee's) for the whole summer. We took off the shutters and Mary Lee took $50 off the price of the rent. She paid for the paint and I rolled down paint in the bedrooms. We had a real good time.

The 4th of July that year, 1948, I was sitting on the beach and Blanche Knapp, Mrs. Warren Knapp, sat down there and said, "Betty, there's going to be a nice cottage for sale. It's going to be on the bulletin board on Monday. It's the one right up the hill, above us." So my father and I went up to see it the next morning at 11:00. We liked it so well, we went down and got my mother and brought her up and she liked it, also. That afternoon, we gave the owner a check. In 1928, my folks had bought a lot at the north end. They were always going to build, but we had to go to college, so they didn't ever build. And in 1948, we found this already furnished place. All the lovely wicker furniture was here. The owners were daughters of Mrs. and Mrs. Jessie Shuman and granddaughters of Mr. and Mrs. George Monroe who built the cottage in 1910. George Monroe was a state senator from Joliet, Illinois, in 1890. The cottage dining room furniture was built in the Joliet prison, in Illinois. I understand the Monroes also built that little white cottage by the gate -- the one Mr. Hempy used to be in. They used to come up here with their chauffeur; he always lived out at that gate cottage and would drive for the Monroes, care for them, cook for them, and what not. Our cottage was named Sunset when we bought it. Mrs. Monroe built it too close to the front because she wanted to save two pine trees. So that's why it has been falling down the hill, all these 75 years. It was built too close to the edge. She had two lots here, too. Plenty of room. But she didn't want to cut down any trees. It was always two stories – always up and down. The house has a trap door which was always very attractive to children. We can enter the downstairs rooms - three bedrooms, a porch, and a bathroom - from either side of the house, but when it's raining we go down the trap door here in the porch floor.

I don't remember much more about Mrs. Knapp except she was very pleasant and quite plump. She came to the beach and sat on the seawall there, in front of Mary Lee's cottage. She was Mr. Knapp's secretary and she took all the messages to help him with things. She helped some other folks find their property, too, like the Kropps. We remember him scraping the roads every weekend with that scraper he had behind his horses. He and his sons ran the gas station for awhile. One son was Clare; the other was killed in the service.

Across the walk from me, Mrs. Edee's cottage was built about the same time by Mr. Phillips, the Covert contractor. He built a lot of cottages. Mrs. Pierce Jensen was Mrs. Edee's daughter; she inherited the cottage. Then my sister, Jeanette, bought it. Now the Robins family owns it. When Mrs. Edee died, Mrs. Jensen's brother and sister had all the furniture put out on the lawn to be auctioned because he was not interested in coming to Palisades at all. So they put it out, had an auction, and nobody bought anything. They put it all back and Mrs. Jensen got it. She had wanted the furniture and everything, but he seemed to want part of the money from the sale. The Jensen children lived in Iowa. It was a long way to come. The boys were very active when they were here. They made their own rowboats, and they had canoes and loved it. The grandchildren came for quite awhile.

There were horses down by the Brandywine, where that parking lot is. There were flies galore. We went horseback riding by renting horses in Covert and went back and forth. But the horses down at the Brandywine belonged to people in the Park. Mr. Underwood had two horses. He let kids ride them around the golf course. He was a barber in South Haven and lived where the Guirls now live.

*Potter girls visiting horse corral by Broken Down Bridge.*

We knew Joe Putz the best. He helped my father do everything. He and my mother laid out our patio and all our yard and our sun deck out there. He helped my father put four Sears Roebuck jacks at the bottom of the cottage and jack it up to keep it from falling down the hill. His sister, Mary, was here, too. He was friendly as the dickens. He had one withered hand, you know, from infantile paralysis when he was two. But it didn't seem to make any difference; you hardly ever noticed it because he did everything – he did <u>everything</u>! And in the winter, he made these darling pictures, you know, in picture frames with – oh, like a fireplace out of little pieces of wood, sticks like match sticks. He did beautiful work. He made rustic signs for people's cottages. It was fun to know him.

We were scared to death of Mr. Quick. He was quite imposing. When we ran on the bank, he told us to get off. As kids, we were pretty much afraid of him. He wanted us to stay on the path. He didn't want us to run on the hillsides. We couldn't pick the wildflowers, either. His daughter, Julia Quick, ran the Soda Bar. Mrs. Sanke's daughter ran it one year and the Roaches, for several years. They all stayed there, the whole big family. There were no gaming machines in there then. It was a tight ship. It was noisy, but it wasn't like it is now. No electronic noise.

Once a year, we would go way out to the garbage dump, my sister and my brother and I, way at the end of the golf course by Brandywine. In the spring, my mother would insist we go out to get ferns for our lot. So we got carving knives to dig way down by the roots and bring them in and put them on the lot. It was against the rules to take anything out of the Park, but we could move things from the garbage dump to the lot if we wanted to beautify it. It was very fertile there.

I remember Tony Canonie as the iceman. They kept the ice here in the Park in sawdust, near where the horses were. They had a great big storeroom - the icehouse – full of sawdust and great big chunks of ice that they would get every year.

The garage was primarily for the lodge guests and people at the Circle who didn't have parking spaces after the cars began coming in. Mrs. Bishop, the VonRosens, and Art Warner all had their cars in the garage. They kept the plows and equipment that Mr. Knapp used in the garage, too. The thing that got pulled along the road, the old, old scraper, must have been bought when horses pulled it, I imagine. Lots of times, the roads were like a washboard, you know; it was awful.

*Palisades garage.*

I remember when my girls wanted to go to a movie in South Haven once a week. That was always traumatic for parents, seeing them drive off and getting them back safe again from on the highway.

The Clubhouse became more prominent. When I first came here, they had teenagers running it. And then they had teenagers sleeping in the Park on the porch. In 1952, when I was teaching at Western, I suggested that I hire a college couple. So from '52 on, I hired all those recreation couples. Don and Marge McIlvride were the first ones, in 1952. He was a minister. He wouldn't allow Bunco because he wouldn't have gambling. Or Bingo. He was back here just last week, to see what the Park looked like. He lived in that little bitty shack that Carl Anderson had for his hideout because there was no apartment for the couple then. So I took him over to Meadowcrofts – it's their cottage now (#128) – and he just couldn't believe how beautiful it looked. It still seemed the same when they came up Ravineway – they recognized the tennis courts and they went to the Soda Bar and wanted to know if I was still here. Sharon Kirk was there and she said, yes, go right up the stairs. There was a note on the dining room table saying I was at the tennis courts, so they came on down to the courts. They just wanted to see the Park, they had had such a good time here. They were here on their honeymoon, see. Most of the time we got people who were here on their honeymoon and then they had free room. They didn't have any place to live, so they lived here.

*1952 Clubhouse couple, Don and Marge McIlvride, at work.*

We were upset when Mr. Lowrey burned the meadow. And we were upset when the road went in just north of the meadow – on our favorite path, you know, that had been on the edge of the water. Then we could walk to the bird sanctuary and the tennis courts. Colleen and Bob Schlacks now own the Muckenhirn's cottage (#34). Mr. Muckenhirn had friends from all over the world that sent him all those lovely trees. That's why there's still an olive tree down there and really unusual trees from all over the world. My brother Jack knows what all the trees are. Oh, it's gorgeous; it's all terraced with slats. All walks from the Brandywine go up to that house. One of the Muckenhirn daughters was a nun and she'd go, with her habit, way to the North Beach and take the habit off and swim, when nobody was looking. She was a neat lady. Everybody liked her but we all felt sorry for her. Mary Ellen was her name. Chuck and Eddie were her brothers.

We used to have Vespers in the Clubhouse. Mrs. Dinsmore, who lived in one of those houses out beyond Cecil, knew my father was superintendent of the Presbyterian Sunday School in Riverside, so she enlisted his help. My mother had to do the flowers, because she was an artist. So she got all these flowers – glads – and we fixed them every single Sunday. I don't know what denomination Mrs. Dinsmore belonged to, but she was very religious. When my children were little, she wrote out Bible verses for them. Of course, the Gardners and the Householders all had to come to Vespers and sit in the front row. We had to swell the attendance, because there weren't very many people there. Bill Ferry preached off and on, and she had people come from all different churches all over the South Haven area, a different minister every time. She paid them money. After Mrs. Dinsmore went, Virginia VanBeuren ran them. She was the treasurer. We still had them as long as my folks lived. And then we only had one a summer, and we had Bill Ferry do that one. Finally, we gave them up because not enough people came. But we still had money in that memorial fund. Virginia said we might as well use it for something worthwhile. So many people went to South Haven Memorial Hospital on emergencies that we gave money to them, every year. It wasn't much – only $50. We finally got rid of all the money by giving it away. The hymnbooks are still up in the Clubhouse. Somebody would always play the piano and we always sang and she passed out Bible verses. She usually had a soloist. Esmah Orcutt played the harmonica always; she did a beautiful job. She was one of the Hendersons – Bert Henderson's cousin. She owns Hermitage (#120) with Bert right now. She's here the month of August.

The Park is changing. We were pretty much professional people in the beginning. Artists and teachers and musicians. Now it is just everybody as the Park gets bigger. It is more diverse, especially in interests and educational background. There are more rich people than there used to be – although several of the pioneers were quite rich; they were most generous with their money, although they didn't let others know about their money. You know, Mr. Lowrey did all these wonderful things with his money – bought all the trophies for the half-mile swim and paid for the first Patter and the first recreation director. And the Bishops paid for the tennis courts, paid for having colored sand, or whatever you call it, put on the tennis courts so they didn't glare. All those things without people doing anything about it, or even knowing about it at the time. Well, the people who used the courts knew about it. And then Benny Bishop bought all those beautiful fireworks on the Fourth of July, along with the Wenhams and, later, the Peats. People used to contribute – give them $10 every time they had fireworks. But now all that's gone. We've lost a little bit of community spirit. It's because the Park is larger; there are so many people. That's why we've made a desperate effort to keep the Patter up, because it got to be so that people didn't know who their neighbors were. And we felt if they knew their neighbors, they wouldn't be so apt to criticize them. If they knew them personally. Another thing, we thought that if something were written in black and white, it was more apt to be the truth than just gossip. So then it got to be the official arm of the Board and they put official notices in the Patter. It got to be an official paper as well as a teenage gossip column.

When we lost the beach, we started the Ladies' Crafts, which has been fun for the ladies. We used to walk up and down the beach and see everybody in front of their own cottages. Now we can't do that. Then there's all the tennis players, you know. I'd still be down at the courts playing tennis instead of at crafts, if I didn't have sore knees and all this arthritis. But the senior citizens - like Betty Wintermute and Ruth Kropp and myself, all of us who used to play tennis - are now in Ladies' Crafts. When it rains, we get all the tennis players to come to Crafts. Meeting every single Tuesday, from 10:00 a.m. – 12:00 noon, we do have a communication network set up from the north end to the south end. And then we have our own little cottage walk, because each time we meet at somebody else's cottage.

Mr. Quick was the boss and he said when decisions would be made. Now everybody feels that they have a say in things. They do as they please, pretty much, now. Of course, it was awfully hard to enforce the rules. Mr. Quick used to do it himself, but now, who does it? Just like sororities – they've gone out of colleges because they couldn't enforce the rules. The girls wouldn't do the things they used to do.

Kids are still interested in the Soda Bar as a gathering place for them. But they aren't as interested in the outdoors as we used to be. They don't make up their own fun any more. So many of them watch television. The way we used to play games and make up our own fun, they don't do that anymore. When we had the Clark cottage, we'd carve soap at night, to make animals. Remember all those things? Everybody did those soap animals out of Ivory soap. The little rabbits were darling. We used to make all those stone animals and we collected stones and beach glass and made tables and did all those handicrafts using outdoor things. We don't do that now unless someone in the household really makes an effort to do so. It was fun.

A lot of people at the south end never knew the people at the north end. Even nowadays, people don't get back and forth. At the annual meetings they see each other, but that's all, and a lot of people don't come to those meetings. Many just stay in their cottages and don't get out at all; they come over here for a retreat. They don't want to socialize.

Kids used to read a lot. We had that Bookmobile that came for years. When I was at Western, they came there and I said, "Why can't you come to South Haven?" They said, sure, they could, it was part of their territory. So

*Betty in 1997, wearing her button necklace craft project and ready to teach another.*

they came over here in front of the Soda Bar and the girls told children's stories. And it was fun. Then they lost so many books – because renters would take them and they'd go home – that the Women's Clubhouse Committee would have to subsidize them every year. $25 to pay for all the books that were in cottages that they never got back. And then the committee didn't have the funds to do it anymore, so the Bookmobile just stopped coming. It came from Paw Paw. If you go to the Covert library, you can get your books for nothing. Otherwise, you pay $5 in South Haven. It seems that teenagers don't read like they used to. And I think they are staying out later than they used to, at night. Now my grandchildren beg because it is so and so's last night and he can stay out until midnight. For a 13 year old, that seems awfully late, but that's what most of the kids do now. After Labor Day, they had all those fancy parties in the Sugar Bowl – with chariot races and all that. It was the college kids who came back. That was a party just for college kids that the younger people never even thought of going to. They looked at it from a distance or waited until they got to be that age.

Of course, people come and go and you can't help that, I guess. Now we have 13 cottages for sale, which – if you take 10% of our 184 cottages – that's not too bad, I guess. That's the natural turnover for any club in the summer. With all the old-timers leaving and selling their cottages, things change. But Ravineway is still the same, coming in. The land remains the same and the people and society change. After all, we're the caretakers of the land. And what we don't do, then our kids don't benefit from. We lose a beach and that's tough. I don't know – if anything ever happens to the beaches, the cottages below can never be rebuilt. The Army Corps of Engineers won't let you rebuild if anything happens. I suppose if the lake goes down, we'll build walks down into the water, over the top of the walls and riprap. The children are diving off the stones out there and making the best of it. The Park manager, Stan Severinghouse, has a burlap plank that kids go out on, down in front of the Circle. So they are managing. The other day, a little girl got bruised when a wave came up and she got hit against the stones getting out, but it was just part of the day. The children take it in stride better than the old-timers.

I remember when Dunlap Harrington got hit with a horseshoe. They used to play horseshoes right in front of the store. There was a pit there. After dinner, when we went to the hotel, all the hotel people played horseshoes. In fact, there were some very good players. Anyway, one night, Dunlap picked up a horseshoe when someone else was throwing. He had this big scalp wound and, of course, it bled like everything, which scared us all to death. He went to the ER and got it sewed up.

The Harrington boys rented Mary Lee's cottage once, a long time ago, for three weeks. We were down there together. And one night we had bats in the cottage. They came down the chimney. And so we all put towels on our heads and got tennis rackets – and, of course, the more we swatted at them, the wilder they got. So that was a wild night.

Posts from an old pier remained in front of Mary Lee's cottage, and we tried to put a diving board out there. This was in the 20's, before I graduated from high school. I graduated from high school in '28, so it must have been '26. I was a junior in high school, I think. We decided to have our own diving board so we got out there with sticks and we put one on the posts. Someone lost the hammer, I remember, down at the bottom on the sand and we dove and dove and dove – but it had just disappeared.

We never went to Ballou Inn. We always went to the hotel. But I remember hearing the old-timers tell about it. The most exciting thing was when we came into the Park, to see the beach from the Circle, you know. We'd all come down there and they'd have petunias in all the beds. Mr. Hempy planted them and Del Jones watered them, all summer. So here were those great beds all full of flowers. Nowadays – well, Mary Lee took her turn for a long time and the people in the Circle watered them.

*Garden in Betty's memory in the Circle.*

We had a beautiful, long beach. Our feet would get hot, you know, which would never happen nowadays. We had to have beach shoes to walk the beach, because it was so hot and it went way out there. Once in awhile, we'd see big steamers in the lake, but they were generally out of sight. They didn't come this close because of the sandbars. Once or twice, we went to South Haven on a big boat and we went to Benton Harbor from Chicago on a weekend, after the Park was closed. Once we went and had a terrible storm. We went early in the morning and spent the whole day in South Haven on the beach. When we went to go home, it was rough. Everybody was sick. We had come from Chicago – Navy Pier. We'd spent the day on the beach with a picnic lunch and our bathing suits and towels and the whole works. When we went back, it was rough. Usually, that was a big treat for people to do that.

We didn't have all the Sunfish when I was a kid. We had sails on canoes, with boards that hung out over the side – what do you call those to balance it? – so we wouldn't tip over. The Jensen boys had those boards on, so then we all had tippy sailboat-canoes. Almost every year, somebody would build a raft and we'd have a raft out there that we'd sit on and dive off of. Nobody worried about us. Every storm would blow the raft up to the beach and it would get covered with sand and then the big kids would dig it out and drag it out into the water again. It was made on great big oil tanks with boards on the top. But nobody drowned and nobody got hurt. Even though you got pushed off, nobody got hurt. But about ten years ago, somebody had a raft at the Brandywine and someone said, "Do you know you're responsible if anybody gets hurt?" and so he dismantled it and took it away. The kids were having so much fun with it, but he just couldn't take the chance of having somebody hurt and being sued.

We always went blueberry and strawberry picking. My mother insisted on canning everything up here. I hated it. Oh – peaches and pears – we went and bought them and did 24 quart jars. So we'd do all the canning here and take all of the jars home with us. It was a real chore. Kids hated it. I decided when I grew up, I was going to buy everything at the grocery. We made strawberry jam by the ton. But the blueberries, we generally ate.

In 1940, when I got married, we always came across the road straight across from the Park. At the corner there, towards Covert, there was a big sand dune. Every time we'd come over from Kalamazoo, our boxer dog would get up as soon as he'd see that sand dune. He'd just perk up his ears. That's where we got sand for our sandbox, every year. We knew that man and asked him if we couldn't have sand, so every fall when Mary and Sally and Annie were little, when we went home we'd stop and get sand for their sandboxes so we had that for another year, at home. In those days, Labor Day was something. I mean nothing happened – I mean the activities all ended on Labor Day. The Honor and Glory tennis tournament was then and all the parents were waiting, with the cars all packed and everything, for the kids to get through with the tournament so they could go home. They were lined up. The Westons and the Neubauers and all of them were lined up. They got the kids out of the tournament. If you never played tennis any other time of the year, you played in that last tournament. Now only the good players are in it. Although we are getting better this year because Vickie Ferry had a lot of newcomers and the old-timers played with eight year olds and they did a very good job. They just mixed them up. And it was fun. They didn't play to win. It was a real teaching situation. They tried real hard. The eight-year-olds, when they got with the thirteen year olds, tried real hard. So it was fun again. Well, things come and go. But I think it's a perpetual struggle to keep the values up, don't you think? A lot of us have to keep working at it all the time.

One value that can be perpetuated at Palisades is the time you have over here with your families. That's the main thing. A cement for families. I think that I got to know all my brother's children by being over here – and my sister's children, my nieces and nephews – it can be an extended family for a lot of people. Even though they came from California and Florida and New York, they all came for their three weeks. My brother came from New Jersey and then he came from Houston, always for his three weeks. No matter where he was, he came. That was one of the things he always did in the summer. So we never could go anywhere – I've never been to Norway or Sweden – we always came to Palisades. But we got to know each other. For a lot of families, it was their get-together time, their extended family.

*Kids on raft, which has come to shore. Ray Lewis remembers a raft built by Dr. VanRiper in the 40's. The sport was for the Linden Hills kids to steal it - and for Palisaders to steal it back. Note in picture, the S.S. Roosevelt on horizon.*

*Jody Rogers and Tom Beck roasting marshmellows. 1967.*

Another Palisades value would be the wholesome activities, don't you think? I mean, we didn't do town things. Movies weren't predominant. We liked things like beach fires. And friendships. I wrote people and had friends from different cities all over the United States instead of just my town. I have more friends over here – if I went home to Riverside, I wouldn't know anybody. But here, it's Mary Lee and all these people I grew up with that are still here and still come back. Of course, here I go out at night every night. When I'm home, I don't dare go out, even in Kalamazoo. Here, I walk home at midnight, after playing bridge, and think nothing of it. I feel safe here still. I don't feel like I am going to be accosted. We have hardly ever locked our cottages, from Memorial Day to Labor Day. A few things have been taken, over the years, but we have generally always caught the people and it has been pranks and kids wanting pin money or something to drink or candy money. Wasn't anything serious. I had the old carpenter that built our sundeck up here last year and my granddaughter drove up here with her aunt and she told the carpenter, "I prayed all the way up here that I'd get here." She's 15 – and to think that she prayed all the way coming up was amazing. She never told us that, but she told the carpenter. He said, "My, she likes the place, doesn't she?" But she's never been anywhere else, her 15 years, in the summer, except here. Jack's son, Peter Gardner, this is home for him because he lived in New Jersey and Houston and then Switzerland and England and Kenya. Palisades is his roots. For a lot of people, it's continuity. Jeanette's granddaughter wrote a cute little poem about always coming here and she prayed that her folks wouldn't sell the cottage so she wouldn't get to come back. It was a cute thing ... in the Patter several years ago ... Caroline Barber. It was a cute thing about how she always thought about how much fun it was to be here. So I think the values are still here, but sometimes we have to look for them.

One positive change has been our feelings about excluding others. I remember once when Mike Mooney brought some priests to the Park and one was black. People had never seen blacks in the Park before. And so one man got up at a meeting and asked how come we were having beach parties with black people and somebody else got up and said that he was playing with firecrackers to talk about things like that – that we didn't talk about things like that, so they hushed him up. That was the end of the conversation. But the person who recorded it in the Patter, the reporter who attended the meeting, printed it. Then the people who owned houses in Chicago were scared to death that the black people in Covert would read our Patter and burn their houses down. They thought that they would take it out on them because they were not allowed to come in here – they would take it out on them in their homes in Chicago, in retaliation. Because it had been printed in the Patter. Oh, it all blew over. And since that time, there have been all kinds of people here. This year a black lad from St. Louis came up and made friends with everybody. What was his name? Cornell. Black as the ace of spades. And friendly. Came to say goodbye to everybody. He was very nice. Visiting in Toplofty. So that was a change. To have him come for just a week and make friends with everybody in the Park and have him be accepted was a big change from a time when we had "Gentiles Only," you know, on the hotel sign. Of course, in South Haven it said "Hebrews Only," too, so everybody just took it for granted that you went where birds of a feather flock together. Covert Park was for black people and Van Buren Park was for white. Now both are populated by everybody. So that has changed over the years. One Jewish family decided they didn't want to come in because they didn't feel comfortable enough. But they were allowed to come in, the Board voted to let them come in. We had a big discussion in the Board meeting (I was on the Board at that time) whether we voted how we personally felt, as an ambassador, or whether we voted as our constituency wanted us to, as a representative. People voted different ways. Some people voted what they thought their constituency wanted; others voted what they thought they were elected to do, what they thought best. So there was a difference of opinion in that very meeting. But the meeting did allow the Jewish people to come in – though they chose not to come. They'd gotten the feeling already that there might be some problem. We now have quite a few, today. Most of them are mixed marriages, so that's made it easier for some people in some ways, over the years.

## Jayne Mathias
Interviewed by Betty Householder
September 14, 1984

I first came to Palisades in 1924, to my family's cottage, Cresthaven (#96). My grandmother bought the cottage from people by the name of Holmstrom, who, incidentally, also built Hi Brazil, the old Ochsenschlager cottage (#159). My grandmother's two daughters were Catherine Wilson and Alice Tyrrell. They and their husbands owned the cottage and had my brother and myself and my two cousins, Hal and Bert Wilson, all here together. In later years – I can't exactly remember when – my mother and father bought out the Wilsons and I inherited the cottage when my mother died. When we first came here, to my earliest memory, there were only about 28 to 30 cottages and there was nothing on the front ridge at all. What is now the Osth's cottage (#75) was not here. The Ott's cottage (#106) was not here but Bendelow's Balgownie was (#74). And of course, Quick's (#85) and Munro Lodge (#63). And Edee's (#87) and Larson's - which didn't belong to Larsons; it belonged to (her mother) named Wilson, a school teacher (#78). That's about all I can remember around here. Many cottages really were on the beach. The Clubhouse was here. So that when we first came out of our cottage, it was all just sloping, rolling dunes, and we would just come out of the house and go right through the dunes to this enormous white sand beach. The stairs were here. We'd come out and go down the stairs and right through the dune, right where the Heitner (now Richmond) and McNamara cottages are. I remember when the Heitner cottage was being built. I couldn't have been more than nine years old and Bob Ott and I would sneak in there, to play. He fell through some tar paper stuff and broke his leg, so he was in a cast all that summer. He later married Gwen.

We came every summer. Never missed a summer. It was just great. My parents always said it was an investment in health. We got out of school in early June, and we would come then. The trip took forever to get here. I think it was eight hours or something. We lived in South Shore. It was just an incredibly long trip. When we got here, we stayed, because there was nowhere to go and few people had cars. The family car would go home. We were here, so we made our own fun and our own entertainment. Nobody was here to do it for us. No activities director. There was very little happening at the Clubhouse and the activities were entirely different than we have now. We had Bunco – Mary Lee's grandmother, Mrs. Ward, was the Bunco Lady. And we had dances and plays. Dr. and Mrs. Tieman, from the East, had a dramatic school – he was a drama coach – at Terryton on the Hudson. She taught esthetic dancing, interpretive dancing, and they always had a couple of their promising students here with them. They would put on plays. They stayed in the Heitners' cottage. Very interesting people. I was in several plays as well, when Jeanne Anderson directed them. Not too many, because I was so much younger than the people who were in them, like Helen and Mary Anderson, Bud Johnson, and Jack Ott. It was fun! Really, a lot of fun!

*Mrs. Hohman, Mrs. Smith, Jayne Mathias, Mrs. Anderson Clubhouse play. 1953.*

On the weekends, when we were teenagers, we'd go over to Crystal Palace, in Paw Paw. We bought tickets for ten cents a dance. There were always more girls than boys. We'd go over there and the boys would dance with each one of us. The big bands all played there. Hal Kemp, Glenn Miller, they were all over there. It was a big deal. We'd sometimes have a turn about and we'd wash cars to get the money to take the boys to the dance. But there weren't so many people then. We'd go to each other's cottages and have parties. Most of those consisted of cokes and maybe popcorn. We played games, like Sardines and Murder. We had fun. We played a lot of cards – Michigan Rummy – but, you know, times were different.

It was the Depression years. A lot of the boys couldn't get work. My brother worked for Charley Tunecke; he took care of the horses. We used to have riding horses up here. They were saddled out at the tennis courts and kept by the Brandywine, in an old horse barn. My brother tended the horses and rented them for Charley, saddled them and did all that kind of stuff. We rode around the golf course and through the Park and, many times, we went on the beach. Most of the time, we were asked to stay in the area of the golf course. Of course, the highway was not in, so there were a lot of roads we could ride on. I think Charley had four horses. Mr. Hempy and Mr. Underwood had horses, too, but not for riding. Sometimes they let kids exercise them, though. They were kept in back of Stan's house (#58). People object to dogs on the beach but they should have been around when the horses were here. Betty Householder's sister, Jeanette, fell off and sprained her wrist one time, going up and down the beach on a horse. It didn't seem to hurt much but she didn't dare tell her mother, because she wouldn't have let her go again. Lessons were 25 cents for a half hour and 50 cents for an hour.

You have to remember how long ago this was. There was no electricity or telephone. One time, my brother was taking the horses to water, riding bareback through the woods, when a branch caught his lip and cut off half of his lip. It was just hanging there by a thread. Because we couldn't get a doctor, there being none in the Park and no way to get to a hospital, my mother sat up for two nights and a day, holding that lip in place. And it grew back. You could hardly see the scar. The doctor said if she had ever gotten anywhere to be stitched, there would have been a big scar.

My brother worked for Archie Allen, the postmaster. He took care of the Special Delivery letters and stuff like that. Kids all got paid to deliver Special Delivery letters. 25 cents. We used to get paid for delivering telegrams that came in to Del Jones at the hotel – ten cents for delivering the telegram here and fifteen cents to Linden Hills. But let me tell you, we didn't get paid by Del. He wrote on the envelope, "Please pay messenger ten cents." So the person who got the telegram would have to pay. Some of the boys in the Park had summer jobs helping build US 31 when it was going through. Not the highway we know today. It went straight across from Ravineway toward Covert, a winding, fun road. In the 60's they closed that road because of I-196. Now to get to the highway, we have to go a mile south.

We used to have a lot of beach parties too. You know, Mr. Quick was everywhere, checking on things. No matter where we were, he would pop up. Believe me, we were never safe. My parents used that as an admonition: "Don't you try to do anything or Mr. Quick will get you!" He came up and down the beach at 10:00 p.m. But there was no electricity and folks weren't going to keep kerosene lamps going, so kids went home. Mr. Quick had rules and we obeyed them. It never occurred to us not to. But it wasn't a police state. I cannot remember the first Mrs. Quick. I know that she was here, but she didn't walk around. I can't tell you what she looked like. I don't ever remember seeing her. After she died, Mr. Quick married Kitty Wisson, who owned Fern Hill. He put in that walk that goes across the hill so that he could get from his cottage to hers, without much trouble.

Activities centered in the home. We couldn't cook a pizza. We cooked with kerosene and popped corn in the fireplace. It was an entirely different way of life – very primitive. We always had running water, of course. But nobody had hot water. Everybody heated water on the stove and believe me, it was difficult. We bathed mostly in the lake. When people had little kids, trying to do laundry was very, very difficult. But nobody seemed to mind. It wasn't because it was so terribly long ago. After all, there were many, many resorts that had everything. But Palisades was rustic and wonderful, a complete change from our mode of living at home. Just wonderful. We threw away all the cares of the city and came. No telephones. Nothing here was that far away. The Park wasn't spread out like it is today.

We didn't go to the hotel very often, for dinner, though we did go on occasion. Not like Mary Lee's family. They did that every night, but we didn't. We played tennis and rode horses and had beach fires and swam, just everything was my favorite pastime. The only playmate I was close to who is still here is Mary Lee. Of course, Connie was here, and Ginny Coleman. The Borchert girls were here and Shirley Adams. Her family owned Gwen Ott's cottage. And I think that was all of my gang. Mary Kay Goodrich was here, about my brother's age, maybe a bit younger.

There was no road system like today. The roads were just clay, you know. Like rocks, really. We didn't have a road in front of our cottage. There was no Crescent Drive in front of our cottage and just a path behind us, to Householders. Mainly we shopped at Sinks, in Covert. Mr. Shepherd came around and sold things. As a matter of fact, I have one of his old milk bottles. It says: "One Quart Liquid, H. L. Shepherd, Registered Covert, Michigan." Now what kind of cover did this have on it? Cardboard? I can't remember. It is heavier than lead, too. Mr. Shepherd sold milk fresh from his farm, heavy with cream, and flowers and fresh vegetables and fruits. Mr. Hempy was the garbage collector. He came with his horses, you know, and picked up the garbage. I can't remember whether he came up or we had to bring the garbage down. I didn't have to do that. I remember Joe Putz very well, with his withered arm. He carved the most beautiful bird houses and all kinds of things. And he sat at the road on the weekends with a rope and didn't let anybody get through that didn't belong here. He knew everybody. But there again, there were so few people. We guarded the gate then even more so than now, because Joe knew everybody and he was particular about who got into the Park.

Tony Canonie delivered the ice. We had an ice card that we used to have to put out on the porch to show whether he was to bring 25 or 50 pounds of ice. Tony's brother, Pete, was the first ice man. They worked together. Charley Tunecke had the gas station out on the Blue Star. In later years, when Pete didn't deliver the ice, he worked for Charley out at the gas station. Fred Nichols later bought that property. The ice house was near where the horses were kept. Ice blocks were covered with bales of hay and straw. They used to cut it and bring in up.

The lake level has come and gone. It took away the Baker cottage, in 1928, and then it receded. It was such a gorgeous beach for so long. It seems now that we lost it all of a sudden, although I'm sure that it wasn't. I remember those jetties going out. Then one year the jetties were covered with sand. It was lovely. Then, before we knew it, it was gone.

I have a vivid memory of the night the cottages burned down over here, where Buckeye King is. I was very young. My brother and Stan Berg were coming home about 10:00 p.m. and I was in bed. They saw the smoke and flames

*Poles to which Joe Putz attached ropes to keep strangers out of the Park, located on Fernwood Drive.*

*Ravine Way to Circle was then a public road.*

and they awakened whoever it was, the lady who was in there, and got her out. How they were able to, I don't know. There were two cottages there, and they both went. Of course everybody was scared green! The fire department came. We were all awakened to get out of bed and be alerted to get ready to leave. The fire started to spread. But the Covert Fire Department came and got it under control. The cottages were burned beyond repair.

Very few people remember that we used to have a tennis court right below my cottage, in the hollow across from the Clubhouse. That was a playground and, at the end of it, a clay tennis court. It wasn't maintained too well, so it sort of went by the wayside. But my brother and I used to go down there and play. And Bill DeButts would play – just a few people from the few nearby cottages.

*A stroll through the woods in the early years.*

From August 16, 1980 Patter

*Mike Mathias was one of those honored in the recent pageant at the 75th Anniversary Dinner on July 19, 1980. He was listed as a contributor to the history because for many years he staged the Labor Day week-end extravaganzas termed "Orgies." He also originated the Homecoming weekends – with a parade and games and chariot races with Greek togas, etc. – held in late September or early October when many families returned to close their cottages before the water was turned off.*

*Excerpts are from a letter from Mike to his mother, Jayne, which was delivered just before the Pageant started.*

" …. Personally, I'm kinda proud that you were among those chosen to control PPCC's 75th Anniversary celebration. It's a pride, however, that is only matched (or perhaps exceeded by) overwhelming gratitude; gratitude for the 30 summers I enjoyed with your blessing and patronage, gaining a sense of wonder, joy, and awareness of the sensuality of nature – from the sound of a June-bug pinging against a porch screen to the smell of an August beach fire trapped in September's sweater – from the razor sharp touch of a single grain of sand on a clean sheet to the subtle taste of a stick in a marshmallow, medium rare. For the opportunity to see beyond the

*Park's 75th birthday party.*

pavement to the gravel, past the walls to the sunset, and above the neon to the stars, I thank you.

Let me thank you as well for remembering me in the pageant. To have my name included on such an honorable list of Park notables is truly a privilege. It does seem ironic, however, that I would be mentioned as a contributor to Palisades, when, in fact, it is really Palisades that has contributed so much to me. If I have managed to do anything of consequence for the Park, anything of value to be stored in a memory bank, gathering interest against a winter day, it was because **I** owned a debt. Not to a person so much, or a thing, or to the physical place itself, but to a spirit – **The** spirit – that makes the place what it is. The faces **of the** Park, the faces **in the** Park, change continually and forever, but that amorphous "whatchmacallit" remains unblemished from generation to generation. Look around you tonight and feel the energy, the excitement, the creativity, the caring, the love … that's not **part** of the Park, it **is** the Park … Palisades has known the power and unification of the **"Force"** decades before "Star Wars" made it a household word, and it is to this spirit, so much a part of me now, that I have tried to offer some small effort.

Many out there tonight may not really understand what is going on at this anniversary, what it really means. To them, it's perhaps just a dinner party with entertainment. That's O.K. and certainly is in keeping with fine, established Park traditions. But many more have a much deeper sense of celebration for the Park's first three quarters of a century. So many of us did our real growing up on these shores, in these woods, on the front porch of the Soda Bar; more growing up, perhaps, during a few too short weeks of summer vacation than in years of urban schooling. A first romance, a first kiss, a first beer, first friends, all those bittersweet traumas that hallmark the wondrous, formative years of life. Yes, many have grown up in the Park; some may have grown out; but the real magic is that no one grows old.

I wish there was some way I could make a really profound statement of a lasting nature on this occasion, but Peter Ferry playing Joe Putz is a tough act to follow. Once again, a thank you is in order for being placed on the park honor roll in such hallowed company. It's unfortunate that time and production costs don't allow for the mentioning and well deserved recognition of other contemporaries in the audience tonight, whose names even now are synonymous with various Palisades institutions. Families of people who by their examples, lifestyles, personal efforts, and loving concern for past, present, and future generations have helped preserve the unique character of Palisades. All those who have striven to keep intact all the love, friendships, and time honored traditions of PPCC that have been with us for the last 75 years, protecting one little square mile of Never-Never Land from modern mayhem and dingy routine, may I propose a salute, a tribute, a toast … Let all raise their glasses, their voices, and their hearts in community homage to "the Guard at the Gate." Love and thanks, Mike

*Jayne Tyrell and two Wilson cousins - Hal and Bert - with Gordon Tyrell, Jr. (in car) and Alice and Gordon Tyrell. c. 1930.*

*Mathias tennis enthusiasts. 1957.*

## Lou and Thelma Weston

Interviewed by Mary Lou Tombaugh and Frances Prange
August 27, 1984

We came to visit Palisades together while we were in high school. Thelma came over prior to that. Her parents had friends over here, in the Nelson cottage (#76), and they used to come over to visit them. Also, she came from Hartford every year and spent a week in the Smith cottage (#148). She was in grade school then. She has been around Palisades for many years. It was in the 1920's when she first came.

After we had been married twelve years, in 1944, we contacted Julia Hill; she sold us the lot that we picked out. In 1945, we started building, but we had a problem. Because it was just after the war, we couldn't buy any cured lumber. So we decided to go with a treated cedar log which we located in Detroit. Our contractor over in Decatur came over and built the cottage, Sugar Hill (#69), now owned by the Kolehmainens. We were lucky that Julia Hill really watched the construction going on. We were in Chicago when she called us one day and said, "You have a problem over there. There's a timber right through your fireplace and they put the concrete right over it." So we tore over here and looked and sure enough, that's what they had done. We had to tear out the whole fireplace and rebuild it from scratch. That gave us some serious thought because we had carefully picked out those stones from all around and placed them where we wanted them in the fireplace. It was quite a long procedure, getting those particular stones where we wanted them. We stayed in that cottage for 23 years. Our neighbors were Alice Ott, who lived with her sons Jack and Bob, and Mildred Adams. Next door to us were the Woods and, later, the Ericksons. We were a very social group and there were many parties which we enjoyed.

Thelma stayed the whole summer and Lou came weekends by train. Thelma would meet him in Watervliet or Benton Harbor or Bangor. Lou did do some driving, too, but that was toward the latter part. Thelma didn't go back until after Labor Day. We'd wait for the Honor and Glory Tennis Tournament. We almost hoped our daughters would get beat when they were playing, hoping they'd get out of there so we could go back to Chicago. We'd get the car all packed on Labor Day; it would be about three o'clock in the afternoon and we'd still be down there, sometimes until seven or eight, waiting for them to complete their game. We knew the traffic would be bumper to bumper all the way back to Chicago.

After our first grandchild arrived, the cottage grew too small for us. We sold it and bought our present cottage, in 1967, from the Kluenders. We actually bought it from Bethany Mission, a retirement home in Wisconsin. It had been deeded to them by Kluenders. We moved in and started to remodel it, and we're still working on it. We wish we knew more about its history. Rudy Weber was one of the original builders. He built several cottages and always told us that this was one of the first cottages he built in the Park.

Thelma was chair of the Clubhouse Committee several times. We used to have plays – Jeanne DeLamarter was active in that. We also had children's activities, fairs for the children. And style shows. That was quite an interesting thing; just before it was time for the girls to go to college, one of the places in South Haven would come in and put on a style show for us. We also had bridge nights, once in awhile. Betty Householder hired the Clubhouse couple. She and Frank would bring them over from Western U.

*Alice Beatty in Clubhouse styleshow. 1952.*

Lou served on the Board for ten years - as treasurer, vice president, and president. When he was president, the first thing we did was to change the collection of the garbage, from horse and wagon to public contractor; this has been very successful. Prior to that, Mr. Knapp and Charlie or Joe Putz would go around in the wagon two days a week. They took the garbage and dumped it in a spot out in back of the tennis courts. You can imagine what that was like – full of rats and stuff. When Bill Heitner was president, we went out and got a big crane and buried all that stuff. That was one thing. Then, when Henry Prange was president, we had another problem. We needed to get the CCR's signed. CCR means "Covenants, Conditions, and Restrictions." Henry worked with a lawyer over in Hartford. Finally, they got them drawn up and Henry had about 70% of them signed when Lou came on. Lou had to get the rest of the owners to sign. We finally got 95% to sign so the CCR's were effective. That was very important at the time.

It was during Lou's time as president that the nuclear plant came to the front. We had many meetings with members of Consumer's Power. Lou used to call meetings in Chicago and they'd come over there and we'd get the Board together. We had a lot of compromises on both sides; one of the things that came out of the meetings was that Palisades could continue to use our north beach as long as we kept it clean. Also, through our efforts, they installed the cooling towers, which prevented the warm water from being discharged into the lake; that would have affected the ecology of the lake. Lou spent all his time one term on that. We had all kinds of meetings, but we didn't get all that we wanted. He used to get calls at midnight, in Chicago, saying "Let's do something about it; let's fight them." The language wasn't always very good, but he got the message. We were going to hire a

*Palisades Power Plant before cooling towers. 1970.*

lawyer, at one point, to fight the plant. But that was absolutely impossible to do. Of course, it took hours and hours of our time, but it was really important.

We knew Tony Canonie and his wife, Georgia. After the war, he was able to buy surplus war equipment machinery to start his business. He got the contract to do seawalls, here, and road contracts all around the country. Helen Packard ran the store and the Post Office. She retired to South Haven and is now active in a senior citizens group there. The Soda Bar has always been a place for the teenagers and youngsters to go. It gave them something to do.

Warren Knapp was caretaker when we first came here. But he wouldn't do anything except collect garbage. Charlie and Joe did most of the work. It got to the point where Warren was doing more work on his farm than he was in the Park. Henry and Lou had quite a few meetings on that. Finally, we had to ask him to retire. Charlie Wolford worked for Mr. Knapp. One time the Board had a problem with him about reporting his time right. Henry and Lou went over, one morning, to Covert and got him out of bed. We went around in circles. With that smile of his, we couldn't pin him down, but he insisted he was working these hours and wasn't getting paid for it. Warren denied it, but eventually we compromised and paid him for part of it. We never knew for sure who was telling the truth. We didn't have any more trouble after that.

That was the time we were looking for a new manager. We had been over in Linden Hills and talked to Cecil Burrous. He was doing a real nice job over there. We talked to Henry about that. Cecil seemed to be a man who could really do the job for us if he were interested. Henry got in touch with him and hired him. But in order to do that, we had to build a place in a hurry out here by the gate. The Park gave Cecil the lot, and Cecil got busy with his father. We never saw a house go up so fast. One reason we were interested in Cecil was that we were having a lot of trouble with our roads washing out. Drainage was bad. He had done a pretty good job over in Linden Hills, by putting in gutters. Henry bought a mixer and Cecil went to work and put in our gutters and they work well. They still do, if they are cleaned out. Cecil worked in South Haven in the winter. He had to provide his own equipment. The Park rented the equipment from him. His salary was low. David Vanderboegh made $1.25 an hour and Cecil made about double that. Yet he seemed glad to come here. It was an interesting era – never a dull minute.

Palisades was a wonderful place to have friends come and visit. If we had neighbors who wanted to come up, they could stay at the Lodge a couple of weeks. We could get meals there when we wished, by making reservations. Very good meals, if we didn't wish to cook. We would take our guests there. We miss it very much now. We enjoy Palisades or we wouldn't still be coming back from San Diego. It kind of grows on you.

*Warren Knapp and Charley Wolford. 1951.*

# Betty Wintermute

Interviewed by Katy Beck
August 16, 1984

I first came to Palisades when I was three, 58 years ago. We rented Pottawatomi (#154) and Breezy Nol (#155), next door to the Seymours. Today Pottawatomi is owned by the Duesings and Breezy Nol is owned by the Bushmans. My parents, the Egberts, rented 15 years and then stopped for four years, during the war. In 1946, we rented Mar-Jo-More (#164). That year, we went down and bought Dr. Woodard's cottage (#183) which we still own. My folks thought that all children should be raised up here; Cindy was two years old and John nine months. We've been here ever since. The cottage was built in 1921, I think. The people who built it owned it only two years and then sold to Dr. and Mrs. Woodard. The cottage was called, then and now, Breezy Hollow. The Woodard boys came back after we had been living here about 15 years; the only thing they were disappointed about was that we had taken the grand piano out of the living room. It was a very small living room. We had a pot-belly stove and a grand piano in there, and that was all we had in there. We added a back porch so now we have three screened porches.

I can remember when we all had to park down here, at this end of the Park, or at the Clubhouse, and walk to Pottawatomi. It was exactly the same distance, one way or the other, and we lugged all our suitcases and groceries to and from. We had wheelbarrows; we'd take them up and leave them where the car was and use the boardwalks.

*Area behind Cottages 152 (Flynn) and 151 (Patterson) before the present road was built.*

*Betty and Ray Wintermute. 1961.*

Sam Canonie brought the ice, and that was one of our pet things, to ride the ice wagon out to the tennis courts. It was an open truck. Sam kept a canvas on to keep the ice from melting. One day I rode all the way out to Forest Dunes. My father was bringing guests up and here was his daughter, sitting on the ice wagon at Forest Dunes, which was kind of a tavern at the time.

Mr. Shepherd delivered the milk but he had to stop because so many people – renters and owners – never paid their bills. I just could not believe it. He said it was so hard to keep up, you know, when people moved out and moved in. He would leave a milk bill but the next person would pick it up. Of course, it was getting more expensive, as time went on, to deliver. He was a minister, I think, in Hartford. He was married with two kids when he was delivering milk for us. This was his summer job. He was just a real nice man. Don Goodwillie was our laundry man from the South Haven Laundry. That's how he got introduced to the Park, originally, driving the SHL truck.

People didn't have hot water. That was the biggest thing we ever had when we bought this cottage: we put in a hot water heater. It was just like heaven! No more boiling water for dishes. I had babies up here, with diapers and formula. We had a shower in the cottage, but I don't think my kids took a shower once a week. They were in the lake all the time; they washed their hair in the lake. Their kids come up from the lake and then, into the shower. They're in the shower in the morning and I think, holy cats, they're going to rub that skin right off their bodies.

My parents had learned of Palisades through friends at home. Bill Seymour lived a block from us and Mardy Mehagan two blocks. Mardy was a friend of the Wards and Mary Lee Tillson; the Wards are among the very early people in the Park. Mardy used to run the Clubhouse with her husband, Gilby, when I was about eight. The Clubhouse used to be more adult-centered. Adults had something going on every evening up there, lots of bridge parties. I really don't know what all went on up there. Later it was more child-centered, with a lot more ping pong tournaments and baseball; it was artsy-craftsy. Of course, we had a lot of beach, so much that we were busy playing on the beach all day – volleyball, tetherball – all beach activities. This was in the 30's. We had the pump house and pipes all out into the lake, so we used to do all sorts of stunts on the pipes, hanging by our knees. But we didn't spend much time at the Clubhouse. Teenagers ended up at north beach, but we had beach all up and down so we were all over. We'd sometimes walk to South Haven on the beach. We could go south to Marvin Slide for the day. It was almost the same thing my kids did; that made it special.

At that time, each family came to Palisades in its car, but then the husbands would go back to Chicago in some of the cars and the women would carpool. Mrs. Mehagan, Mrs. Seymour, and my mother had one car among them, and then the men came up on the weekends together. That was a long trip – five or six hours. No expressways. Our trunks, filled with bedding, came by train over to Covert and the Canonie boys would bring them over to the Park and put them in our cottage. We had running boards on the cars, and we'd pile all our suitcases on the running boards. It was a whole day's trip up here. That I can remember, because I hated that drive.

We used to go into Covert for groceries. Everyone dealt at Sinks. They came three or four families to a car. At night, we always had free movies in Covert, where the fire station is now. A church there put up a screen and showed all these Shirley Temple movies. We would go over in George Bishop's car and watch the movies every Friday night. That was a big deal. That was our entertainment. Of course, George Bishop had maybe the one car out of the 20 teenagers in the Park. Almost all our entertainment was done in the Park. The adult entertainment was done in the Park, also. It was nothing really planned. People just knew each other and would get together for something, maybe at the Lodge. The hotel had a lot to do with that, you know, with that pretty deck and the meals there. And the store. I miss that. I mean, it's getting to be a Park of weekend people.

Our electricity was out whenever anything blew between here and Michigan City. But we made do. Sometimes it was out for four or five days; sometimes we had a roast in the oven. Mrs. Edwards had bottled gas and we could always manage to get the half-cooked food done. I don't remember grills, either. I don't think we had grills. We had the fireplace. We cooked out over our own campfires, but not on a grill. We had lots of beach fires and all the beach in the world. We slept on the beach. We would have a sleepout like they do in the dunes now, but we would sleep right in front of our cottages. My brother was in scouting with the Seymour boy; they built a lean-to and slept out one whole summer, in back of Seymour's cottage. That was up for ages. We used to all take turns sleeping out there. Another thing I can remember is lying on the floor and listening to "Lights Out." Everybody would get in one cottage and listen to "Lights Out" on the radio, with all the lights out. It was scarey. Of course, we all liked radio. It was so much better for imagination than TV.

Cottages have changed. Oh, my goodness. In the first place, it makes me sick – I see all the screened porches going. There are very few cottages with screened porches anymore. Of course, we didn't have hot water when we rented, and cottages were a lot smaller. I mean, they've just built around them. They used to be really rough. In Pottawatomi, when we had a storm, we had to sit in front of the French doors because they just blew wide open. Very few of the cottages are recognizable since they have been remodelled. It was good to see one recently that was still more or less like the old cottages, enlarged a little, but still cottagey. So many are houses.

*The Swedenborgian Church located at the north end of Linden Hills, almost within view of the Wintermute cottage.*

The only early neighbors I remember are the Dawsons and the Youngs. I remember the (Swedenborgian) church in Linden Hills; that was still there, on the north end of Linden Hills, almost within view of our cottage. Elizabeth Phillips worked for me until two years ago. Her husband, Jeff Phillips, built the Seymour cottage and quite a few others. They lived in Covert. Elizabeth died two years ago and she must have been 83. My children were her grandchildren – she worked for my folks when I was a little girl. She was a part of my family. Harry Wildt was a carpenter who did a lot of repairs and handy work. He built porches. When we were building our new cottage, Cecil suggested I talk to the fellow laying our chimney. I did and his name was Wally Wildt. I said, "I knew you years ago." He said, "No, that was my father. Harry Wildt was my grandfather." He's in the same line of work. Lives in South Haven. One of Harry's sons works in South Haven but has been around the Park a lot. He must have been ten when his father first came here and he always worked here. He's a funny guy. Quite a character. Of course there was old man Hempy, the garbage man, with his horses down on the beach. People just don't believe that.

The only caretaker I remember is Warren Knapp. The Underwoods were here – they had a place out by the tennis courts. They had horses, back behind Stan's house. That was kind of out of bounds for kids. Today, of course, with all the nature walks, everybody knows every inch of the Park, which is great. I didn't really know Mr. Quick. All I remember is being scared of him.

I hear the Clubhouse doesn't have the kids it used to. The girls have to play baseball and the boys have to do crafts. My kids went down there every morning religiously, and they all met and had a great time. But that is the car situation again, where mothers are going to town and taking the kids to do this and that. I think the car is what has changed the Park the most. It has changed every place, not just the Park.

Everybody went to the Honor and Glory tennis tournaments. Mrs. Lowrey was there with her camera. I remember being out there all the time. That was true, even when my children were growing up. It was where everybody met. Part of the socializing of the Park, more than it is today. Now it's a group of tennis people, serious about their tennis. But I still go out and watch and spend half my day there every day. There are a lot of people who don't play, but I think there are a lot of newer people who don't play and don't go out. They do what they like to do. But the Park is more tennis-conscious than it's ever been. We have more courts and they are all busy. They're all kept very well. So many people, years ago, went to play golf. My folks were golfers and the men all had their courses up here. I don't even know where they went to play golf, but I remember them going out in the morning to do so. My husband and the boys play in Paw Paw, but I'm trying to think where my father played. I would guess it was South Haven.

We used to do a lot of horseback riding up here, too, just north of South Haven. We rode the beaches. And my kids rode, too; I used to go shopping and leave them at the stables for an hour. Maybe they went on trails, I'm not sure. Now, the price of horseback riding is high. I get kind of upset with the car situation, where they have to go out of the Park. The cars are the same at home. Anywhere you are, all these kids with their own cars. They drive down to the South Beach where they have their parties – they used to walk and now the parking lot here is full of cars. People seem like they can't walk from here to the Soda Bar or the North Beach, because they have a car and it's convenient to drive. But that's every place. Kids are kids. Well, our kids had all the paths over to the tennis courts. We used to have a contest. John could get from our cottage to the tennis courts faster than I could drive it.

The lake level has gone up and down. It's much higher now, and things have to be done to protect our cottages. But I'm one of those people that don't think we can put walls up and hold back that lake. We had to put up a wall – but that lake wants to do whatever it wants to do and it's going to do it. I have no doubt of that. There must have been a big problem in the war years, when we didn't come up. Somewhere in that time, the pumphouse with the pipes was washed out and they had to build a new one part way up the hill. That was the first I saw the lake come up. But it went right back out again. Later, we had to put in our first breakwall. And I can remember that, eventually, it was completely covered by sand. We didn't even know where it was. We rolled our boats up on rollers, right over the top of the wall.

We had a boat for water skiing and we could bring it right up on the beach and be safe. For awhile, we could even do that on the south beach after we put in the second breakwall. Now, we're lucky if we can even sit on the beach. John hasn't had his sailboat out for a year. We take our big boat into South Haven and launch it there.

> **One of my worst memories was of Bobby Seymour drowning. I was there and I'm the one who called Mr. Seymour and ran to the hotel .... I was eleven and Mother and Mrs. Seymour were in Saugatuck....**

One of my worst memories was of Bobby Seymour drowning. I was there and I'm the one who called Mr. Seymour and ran to the hotel … not the hotel, the Circle … I was eleven and mother and Mrs. Seymour were in Saugutuck. It wasn't a wavy day. A little cloudy water, but … Mother and Mrs. Seymour had senior high school girls that helped in the cottage and we were all to play in the back of the cottage. Nancy Seymour and a little girl who was renting in Little Brown Jug (#153) wanted to go swimming and they snuck down the front, and then Bobby – who was five then – followed them. They carried him out to the sandbar. He said he wanted to come in and this girl started carrying him in and - he could walk, I mean it was not over his head – but he started fussing and she let him down. He must have fallen and hit his head. That's all they could figure out. But instead of picking him up, they went out to the sandbar and they ran up and down the sandbar, shouting, and then they forgot where they had dropped him. They had to form a human chain. I think it was Sam Canonie who found him. Everybody came, but they didn't know where they had dropped the child. I don't remember who told me to go down and call my father in Chicago. I ran the boardwalk all the way down and said, "There's a drowning!" People asked if it was in the Brandywine. Someone screamed. Someone – I don't know who it was – gave me money and I called and they called the Coast Guard at the same time. Then, when they found him, they took him to the hotel and put him on the pulmotor, but that didn't help. The other Seymour children stayed with us when the parents went home for the burial. They only lived a block from us at home. That was the first year they had owned that cottage. They kept coming over the years, but Mrs. Seymour never went on the beach, for almost 15 years. They felt it was very important to keep coming; they had three other children. Oh, I can still almost see and feel that. My mother and Mrs. Seymour met my father and Mr. Seymour at Tony Canonie's gas station, and told them what had happened. It is such a vivid memory. It's probably the only unhappy time I had here. It's so different from everything else that went on here. As a kid, I didn't know what older kids were doing and the problems they were having.

My husband had spent a lot of time in Michigan, where he was stationed during the war. He hated the place. But he's grown to love it now. All of the grandchildren love it as much as my kids do; they spend as much time as they can up here. In 1977 or '78, we built our second cottage, called Generation Four #184, when my mother died. We took her money and built the cottage. Her ashes and my father's ashes are scattered in the front of the cottage, so all of us can be here at the same time. In the little cottage there was just no way for all 16 of us to stay. Each family gets the lower cottage for two weeks. The rest of the time, they visit us in the new one. The new cottage is sort of winterized. The kids come in the winter and ski, but we have no well. They have to learn to rough it. I'm not going to put in a well for them – they have it too easy as it is!

---

 **Written Memories**

## Virginia Melchert Coleman

August 20, 1985
Aged 61

Palisades Park! The name was magic when I was a little girl in the 20's and it is magic now. It was (and is) synonymous with golden summer days, blue lake water, awe-inspiring storms, and good friends – people I saw only in the summer, and yet, they have remained close to me all of my life. Palisades brought us together each year and renewed and strengthened the bonds between us. Where else could I know families where I have known the grandparents, parents, my own friends, their children, and now, their grandchildren? Five generations! Surely that is unique in America!

I was born in 1923 and my first year at the Park was in 1924. My parents, Ernest and Margaret Melchert, and my sister, Jane, rented the Harding cottage, which stood at the Brandywine about where the Jennings cottage is now (#18). Even then, that was a dangerous spot and in 1927, or thereabouts, that cottage was washed away. The only way to reach it was by crossing the "swinging bridge," a foot bridge which swung in the wind

*The old "swinging bridge" and the Harding Cottage, later moved to the other side of the creek as # 39.*

or with the passage of people across it and gave terrifying vistas of the swirling Brandywine water below between its floor boards.

After the Harding cottage went into the lake, we stayed at Sturtevant Lodge for three weeks every summer. We always dressed up for dinner, and all the clothes for a family with two daughters necessitated bringing a steamer trunk. My first memory of the Lodge is of Grandma Sturtevant sitting in a rocking chair on the downstairs porch, looking like Whistler's Mother with a long dark dress and a lace cap and shawl. Del Jones (Delno) was the hotel proprietor; his wife, Blanche, cooked and looked after housekeeping. Del was about 5'7" with black hair and horn-rimmed glasses. He never seemed to change. His hair never greyed and he never got fat or feeble. He always retained the mien of a stern frog, to me. His wife, Blanche, was round and blonde and looked like a 1920's movie actress. She ran a tight ship and more than one cook left in high dudgeon because she ran afoul of Blanche. The waitresses were all college girls who came for the whole summer and worked long hours for next-to-nothing. The "rising bell" was a small bell rung by one of the waitresses walking up and down the porches at 7:30 a.m. Breakfast was from 8:00 a.m. to 8:30. If one arrived at 8:34, it was too late and he was turned away. Lunch was at 12:30 p.m., dinner from 6:00 p.m. to 6:30, announced by a dinner bell. I loved waiting outside the dining room door before dinner so I could have a chance to ring the bell. The food was family style, the portions small, but usually we could have seconds - except for dessert. My father had a running battle with Del about the meager proportions of pie! After dinner, the men adjourned to the hotel office and Del brought out the dice cup for a game of Indian dice. No one could lose more than a dollar, but if five or six played, the winner could come away with $5.00 – a not insignificant amount during the Depression.

The first job to perform after arriving at the Lodge was to pump the drinking water. Each room was provided with a small stoneware pitcher and bowl and a large jar in which to empty the washing water. The women's bathroom (no tub or shower) was upstairs; the men's was downstairs. The only tub was in the annex bathroom. Almost everyone took a bar of soap – floating Ivory – to the lake to perform their ablutions. Water from the bathroom tap was not safe to drink, but pump water was all right. The pump was located just outside the dining room, across from the Soda Fountain. The Lodge had

*Lodge waitresses in uniform.*

electricity, but most cottages depended upon oil lamps and kerosene stoves and iceboxes.

The personalities of the Park seemed more definite then than now. In retrospect, it was a time of innocence. People understood honesty, honor, and integrity – and lived by their precepts. The most important person in the Park, of course, was Arthur Quick. He was already an old man when I first knew him, and was, unquestionably, an autocrat. Tall, cadaverous, unsmiling, he was an object of fear to a little girl. What he said, went. If he didn't approve of your buying a cottage, there was no possibility of buying one. No liquor was allowed, even after Prohibition ended. No Jews were allowed, and there was a sign on the Lodge and at the entrance to the Park so stating. South Haven was predominantly Jewish in the summer, but not Palisades.

Another personality was Mr. Hempy. I never knew his first name; he was always called Mr. Hempy. He collected garbage and raked the beach with a wagon and two stout draft horses which he kept in a barn near the Brandywine. The gas station out on U. S. 31 was owned by Charley Tunecke who was also a man-of-all-work, ably assisted by Joe Putz. Joe knew the location of every septic tank and all the water pipes in the Park. On Sunday, he sat at the fork in the road in his old car, with a string stretched across the road to keep out undesirables. He had a withered arm and was minus fingers and lots of teeth, but he was always smiling and working hard. A fine man. He lived with his sister, Mary, who was always dressed like a Sears Roebuck version of Queen Mary, with a flowered dress and beribboned hat - finished off with bobby sox and high tennis shoes.

An arbiter of Park society was Mrs. William Ward, Mary Lee Tillson's grandmother. When we first considered renting a cottage, Mrs. Ward and several ladies came to call to consider our suitability. They wore hats and gloves, and it was terribly important to make the right impression on them and to receive her imprimatur. She ran the Bunco parties for the children at the Clubhouse every Wednesday night. Nothing would have kept us from those parties. When I consider that today's Park children of that age are drinking (et al) on the Village Green until two or three in the morning, I mourn for that innocent time when we had so much fun while our families knew where we were and what we were doing.

Tony Canonie started out by helping Charley as an iceman. When he was seventeen or eighteen years old, he lugged the ice under a canvas cover. No one had electric refrigerators. The icehouse was in the woods, near the broken down bridge. Later, after Prohibition, my father

*Tony and Marialyce Canonie*
*August, 1943*

would ask Tony to join him in a drink. Tony never forgot that, and many years later told me, "Your father never treated me like a WOP." Surely that was "bread cast up on the waters," because in 1973, when our cottage almost washed away, it was Tony Canonie with his giant company and expertise in building sea walls who put in a new wall for us. The first sea wall he built was in 1946-7, when he first got out of the Sea Bees. He meant to succeed and he did. I remember that he had his appendix out on a Friday and was back in the icy October waters working on Monday. To me, Tony has always epitomized the American Dream – hard work, talent, and a desire to succeed.

All of our milk came in those days from Mr. Shepherd's farm. Of course, it was un-pasteurized, and though people glamorize the good old days, that milk, fresh as it was, caused a gastric intestinal disorder for me, called by us "Palisades-itis." The only known cure was castor oil, a difficult remedy when the bathroom was down the porch from my room at the Lodge.

Palisades Park looked much the same in my childhood as it does today, I am glad to say. There was a huge garage where the Village Green is now. It housed a splendid horse-drawn steam fire engine. The swinging bridge across the Brandywine was replaced by today's bridge, which had locks and dammed the river into a lake known as Lake Palisades. A picture of me as a little girl, walking on the road, looks exactly the same as a picture of my grandson on the same road. Although changes must occur, I can only hope that the spirit of the place remains the same.

*Addendum: In a phone conversation with Marilyn Henkel, Ginny recalled the following incident with Mr. Quick.*

We used to have dances in the Clubhouse – with live bands – and everyone came. Once, when I was a teenager, I was dancing with my then boyfriend and my parents and their friends were sitting on the porch watching – and perhaps enjoying a drink or two. Mr. Quick arrived and my father greeted him with "How are you, Mr. Quick?" – accompanied by a hearty pat on the back. At this, Mr. Quick's false teeth popped out and skittered across the Clubhouse porch floor. A quick scramble on hands and knees, everyone patting into dark recesses under the chairs, produced the teeth, which were promptly put back in place. The dignity of Arthur Quick was not to be disturbed by such a matter. My mother, however, was *sure* that we wouldn't be accepted after that fiasco.

# Ray Cooney
## "Memorabilia"
June 25, 1973 Patter

When I was just seven years old, I came to Palisades Park for the first time. My aunt, Lillian Irene Cooney, had graduated from Chicago Normal Teacher's College and some time after that her mother, Sadie Cooney, purchased the cottage for her as a sort of gift. The cottage was named "Ye Nooc" (Cooney spelled backwards). Years ago, when someone was passing, he snickered and said, "Teachers live there and don't even know how to spell Ye Nook."

The first trip to Ye Nooc was long and interesting. Grandmother and Grandfather, Aunt Lillian, and I started from Chicago. We took a big boat across the lake to St. Joseph. We stayed overnight in a hotel. The next day we took a bus to Covert and then hired a taxi to bring us to the cottage. Today the same trip takes less than two hours.

At this end of Route 1, in the woods, were the following cottages: The Hermitage #120, Whippoorwill #125, Fleming #123, Elk's Lodge #118, the Lewis cottage #119, and a cottage near Whippoorwill that burned down. We cooked on a kerosene range and kept warm with a beautiful wood stove. Pete Canonie brought us ice and Charley Tunecke kept us supplied with cords of cut wood. Mr. Shepherd, the farmer from Covert, brought us fresh milk, vegetables, fruits, and huge strawberries.

After our first trip here by boat, my father, Raymond, Sr., generally drove us here. It took him about four hours in the "Overland 90" and then the 1924 and 1926 Nash. If we went home on Sunday, it generally took us six hours because of a big tie-up in Gary. As soon as school was closed for the summer, we would come to Palisades and stay until about Labor Day. When Grandmother retired, she would at times stay until Thanksgiving. Uncle Frank Cooney and I were with her and would chop and cut wood for the stove. We often melted snow for additional water. Away back before we had inside plumbing, we would get our water from the Hermitage pump. It is still standing there!

Almost daily we would take a short cut through the woods to the grocery store and pick up our mail. I can still see Georgia Underwood's smiling face. Remember the Whitney Trio? The sounds of the beautiful string instruments floating through the air? Remember the Warren Knapp family and the gas station on Blue Star Highway? We used to call Warren "Knapper." Remember some of Mr. Henderson's branch art work? There is still some of it in the Park.

Remember old Mr. Hempy and his horse and wagon? He used to live in the Court House by the tennis courts. My wife and I will never forget him. We were coming here for our honeymoon in October, 32 years ago (1941). That night it was raining and somehow in the night the wheels of my Buick got off the road and bogged in the ditch almost across from Hempy's house. Since it was late and impossible to get the car out, we took a suitcase and a few groceries and walked to Ye Nooc by way of a back road that goes up south of the Gate House. The next day, Mr. Hempy hitched up his horse and with a big "Ha ha and haw haw" pulled us out. He thought it was pretty funny!

*The City of South Haven.*

## Jeanne DeLamarter
(Mrs. Arthur E. Bonnette)
In September 5, 1959 Patter

There are others besides myself, and it would be interesting to learn what they recall, who have spent most of their summer lives in Palisades Park. When I first came here, I was eight years old. Ballou Inn was where the store is now, rooms were available, and dinners were 50 cents each. Sunday and chicken dinners, she said apologetically, she had to ask 65 cents. There was no store – we usually shopped at Sinks in Covert, and the post office was where the Neubauers hold forth today at the Soda Bar. The postmaster fell upon unfortunate ways and ended up in jail.

The Park had no electricity and depended upon the strength and enterprise of Tony and Sam Canonie for ice delivery. We cooked on kerosene stoves and used kerosene lamps for light. Frozen foods and ice cubes had yet to be invented. Highway 31 did not exist, so we took the train to Watervleit and got someone to drive us to the Park. We had a friend, Mr. Earl Walters, who taxied us in his Star touring car.

All this makes the writer sound pre-war – take your choice of wars. During the Second World War we had no grocery here for the duration, after having had Mrs. Overheul's store for a few years, but Julia Quick Hill did sell bread and milk only, in what is now the Soda Bar. This helped some in our eternal quest for food during the nuisance of gas ration cards.

After a recent night rain, gentle and dripping in the soft dark, I heard, for the third time in my life here, the Indian Drums. This is a feeling-and-a-sound, all in one, and everyone who loves the Park experiences it sometime. It is a legend and a truth, being an echo of the past days lost in history when our beach and our woods belonged to other peoples. It is a link in a great chain, and without it, we – when it comes our time to leave – would not have our place in the chain.

Sadly enough for us, it is now our time to depart. We can never forget the enchantment that is Palisades Park, and would never try. "Theotherworlde" is truly what it has meant to us, and we bid you all adieu with affection. We hope you keep the Park lovely in reality as we will in memory. Au revoir!

Sea Gulls

The sea gulls whirl, and deftly land,
Like ballet dancers on the sand,

Settling neatly on their toes
In graceful but defiant rows.

Proud, imperious, and still
They nod to empty air, until

All suddenly they spread their wings
And leave the strand to minor things.

By Jeanne DeLamarter
August 29, 1953 Patter

## Remembered Country

By Jeanne DeLamarter
From July 24, 1981 Patter

The sapphire, the emerald,
The foamwhite toss
And beat of Lake Michigan,
The brisk breeze coming in
And with it the gulls
Wheeling and soaring.

These are still there
Though I am not.

You
And the others
Are not there either

And yet
The interlocking winged' circles
Of love
Still wheel and soar
In the rich azure
Of remembrance.

# Bill Ferry
## "Some Memories of Palisades in General and Up Country in Particular"
1986

Sometime in the fifties we renamed this old cottage (#65) "Up Country," quite simply because we had always said to one another, "Let's go up country," whether from Chicago or Wichita, from Sandusky or Parkersburg. When we first came to Palisades in the summer of 1926, it was known as "The Snow Cottage" because it had been built by Ruth Vail Snow, a Chicago doctor, sometime in or shortly after 1911 - the earliest date on the Warranty Deed which records the sale of lots 18 and 19 in Oakhill Block in the First Subdivision of Palisades Park to Ruth Vail Snow by The South Haven Palisades Park Company. Incidentally, a letter from Arthur C. Quick, dated December 5, 1932, indicates that at the annual meeting that summer, it was voted to drop the words "South Haven" from the corporate name and to change the corporation from a profit-corporation to a non-profit corporation. Gradually, "Snow" became "Oakhill" (after the name of the block), until our renaming the cottage in the 50's.

Our legend has it that Mrs. Snow and Mrs. Brown, sisters and both Chicago doctors, built twin houses along this high ridge which parallels the main entry road to the Park, the only two cottages on the ridge at that time, with a path between them along the top. The cottages were of similar construction, although the Brown cottage, (#82) was considerably larger. Both were constructed of cement block molded here in the Park by Mr. Quick and his crew, using local sand and gravel; they used wood above, of course, with great, wide porches. In our case, the body of the house upstairs was 24' x 24' in exterior measurement, completely surrounded by full-length screened porches, six feet wide on three sides and ten feet on the front. Beneath that front porch, on the north paralleling the main road, and giving us a magnificent view of the lake over the valley of the Brandywine, stood our kitchen, dining room, and "maid's room." The past tense means only that the "maid's room" has long since been converted into a den or study with a picture window which, along with the removal of one interior wall, gave us clear view of the lake while dining. We stand on the second highest point in the Park, we were always told, exceeded only by Observatory Hill and proven by the fact that the steps leading upward to our cottage from Fernwood Drive (Route 7) are on Park property designed to give a lovely view of the lake to those who would venture up them in those early days. The view is now lost to the great oaks and pines, beech and sassafras which cover our dunes. Outhouses must have been in order in those early days, but by the time we arrived in 1926, the southeast corner of the porch had been converted into bathrooms. Until the early 30's, however, kerosene lamps still gave us light; an aggravating kerosene heater gave us hot-of-a-kind hot water; and a very tempermental kerosene stove – courtesy of Sears Roebuck and Co. – graced our kitchen. Our only heat came from a central fireplace upstairs, set in the dividing wall between a spacious living room and two bedrooms, seldom ever – then or now – slept in. The porch provides sleeping space for all of us, with a 50 year old rollaway double bed becoming the master bedroom on the wide front porch each night. (It still does!) A massive pot-bellied, wood and coal burning stove did (remembrance prompts) fill half the living room in those early days. The original shakes still give unique character to our ceiling, sloping upward to the chimney throughout the house. The drainage system in those early days was to lay cement walks around the house, under overhanging eaves, and let her run. Ultimately, but not until sometime in the 50's, gutters were installed to keep this old "house built on sand" from settling downward on the steep side of the dune, a minor form of erosion compared to that suffered by the lakeside cottages in recent years. A "snake path" runs back and forth down that steep side of our dune, carved out across the years by Dr. Sauer who owned the cottage just below us, giving us easy access to Ravine Way and the tennis courts.

*Bill Ferry on an early tennis court.*

In 1926, the two courts on the south side of Ravine Way were all there were. Sometime in the 30's, the single court was built, paralleling the fairway of hole number six of the old golf course. We loved that old course - nine holes, winter rules, sand greens and all. The "greens" were oiled and dragged daily by Mr. Hempy or Joe Putz. More later about "the country gentlemen" who kept the Park in order in those years, under Mr. Quick's vigilant eye. That sixth hole ran a hundred yards or so, a gentle "mashy" shot, from just opposite Cecil's home to the rise on which our children's playground now stands. We teed off on hole one about where the path leads down to the "broken down bridge" – so named when it was broken down and one scrambled across the Brandwine on fallen logs. Between holes two and three, a dog-leg which took us all the way down to where Park rubbish now finds its way, all except the most serious players stopped to pluck blackberries and think of Elizabeth Barrett Browning and God. Hole four ran along the "new highway" to the road across from Fred's.

That "new highway" was a masterpiece of engineering, we thought, destined to be a four lane super thruway from Chicago north. We resented the encroachment of civilization it foreboded as it became one of the most heavily traveled and hazardous highways in the Midwest. Until that new, wide US 31 (now the Blue Star Highway) cut the edge off the old golf course, it was from the rise above fairway number four we caught our first wiff and sight of the Park, at the far end (it seemed far, then) of the dirt road, four miles in from Covert and what was then US 12. Covert, Sinks Grocery in particular, was our chief shopping center. The Park had its own grocery store then, of course, and a Post Office and two thriving hotels – Sturtevant Lodge and Ballou Inn – around the Circle. A wide, sand beach stretched out 100 yards (or was it 200?) beyond 1985's rip rap. Remnants of an old pier, used to ship lumber to Chicago at the end of the century, still held a diving board far out in deep water. The "new garage" was built sometime in the 30's – parking permits $10 a month  - where the Village Green now provides a center for our village life. Charley Tunecke's stable stood where our Continentals and Toyotas now park. Yes, we were of "the horsey set" in those years, vying with one another to ride Charley's horses to water in the Brandywine, either down through the underbrush which then stood below the parking area or out to the broken down bridge.

Charley - red-headed  Irishman who was never called by his last name – was Mr. Quick's right hand man. Later, he moved his stable back into the old broken down bridge area, next to the old ice house. Still later, he owned and ran a gas station at the Park entrance on US 31. "Ice" makes me think of Tony Canonie, who started his illustrious career, as founder and President of the Canonie Construction Company, delivering ice throughout the Park and keeping some of us from falling off Charley's "nags." Two gentlefolk named Hempy and Mrs. Hempy were resident caretakers way back then (in what is now the Branding cottage #61), Hempy dragging the roads with his team of horses, Mrs. Hempy tending her flower beds with loving care.  Joe Putz, general assistant and man-of-all-works, knew every pipe and cesspool in the Park; he manned the chain across the roadway up into the Park proper (Route 1) every Sunday, often accompanied by his sister. Ravine Way could not be blocked then, at the present gatehouse, since it was a county road leading  to a U. S. Post Office. I remember Mr. Shepherd, too – bearded, dignified, taciturn, reputed to have resigned his college professorship to deliver our milk because of failing health. There were other, later, "persons of note" who made our pleasant way-of-summer life possible here in Palisades, but these come first to memory, along with Arthur C. Quick. Mr. Quick really did seem to always have a mantle of gnats about him as he walked the Park of an evening or early morning. He – may his name be revered – and the Hempys were, to our knowledge, the only year-round residents of the Park (or nearly so) in those "long, lost days beyond recall." Perhaps "Old Man Henderson" should be included.

Other memories flood in as I look backward over nearly 60 years of summer living here at Palisades. For most of us, summer work in other places during college years or distant jobs or the war broke the pattern, for awhile. But in the end, many of us came back, with our own children and our children's children, to find the Park amazingly unchanged, in spirit if not in buildings, Brandywine, and beaches. The Brandywine runs, of course, where it always ran, always brandywine in color. Some of us remember well that flimsy-feeling, swinging footbridge just west of the present bridge and dam, which alone gave access to the north side of the Park. Old Baldy, down that way beyond Consumers Power Plant, was our favorite place to hike and picnic or swim in the buff. A very substantial road continued up and around and over a very substantial dune where the present road ends, at the Jennings cottage (#18). Some of us remember working on a cottage far back on a dune, lakeside of that road, during high school days – helping to roof it at fifteen bucks a week. We also remember a cottage washed away in an early rising of the lake and particularly ferocious spring storm. We did not then believe that one day that great wide beach of ours would all be gone.

But back to Brandywine. We used to paddle and push an old canoe up it, as far as we could go, through thick, swampy underbrush. At night, ten thousand frogs formed a mighty chorus and loons cried out like damsels in distress; great blue herons lived in the branches of those three tall pines which towered over the valley. Although Arthur Quick's dream of Lake Palisades never quite became reality, we bemoaned the passing of frogdom there; the burning off of all that brush made for a very sooty summer up our ridge. However, liabilities turned gradually into assets as the meadow came into being, thanks to Forest Lowrey.

*Untamed Brandywine before it was cleared for the meadow.*

Organized social life was limited in those early years, limited but creative. Dr. Tieman, trained in the Moscow Art Theatre (owner of cottage #98) where he served borsch on occasion to any who could stomach it), directed some amazing theatre in the Clubhouse, including Shaw's <u>Candida</u>, with consummate skill. Musical evenings featured Eric DeLamarter, Leo Sowerby, and the Olaf Andersons – and some of us remember one hilarious evening of music and dance featuring our children and grandchildren of various ages, the theme song of which was "High Hopes." Vesper services were part of our summer regimen for many years, for half the summer at least, arranged by Mrs. Dinsmore, Virginia Van Beuren, or Esmah Orcutt. The Gardners helped, Betty

Householder was always "generalissimo," and Mrs. Brand played the "grand" piano. All of this was at a time when there were not yet three cars in every driveway and it just wasn't that easy to reach the Red Barn or church in town or handy supermarkets. Dancing at the old pavilion in Saugatuck (burned down many years ago now) or at a similar pavilion on Paw Paw Lake highlighted our summer high school age activities in those years, along with the same-old-forever beach parties far into the night (when beaches were still beaches at Palisades). Always, for some of us, of course, tennis was Palisades, even then when two courts were all we had and our only coaching was by father or uncles who had never had any professional coaching either.

May we end this brief personal early history of our family in the Park by playing "The Association Game," with our associations given in parentheses. For example: Del Jones – (the grouchy former owner of the Lodge). Try The Hundred Steps – (dark and frightening when we first mounted them, on very short legs, in the fall of 1925). Helen Packard – (long Postmistress and manager of the store in what is now the first floor porch of Flynn's cottage). Benton Harbor – (that thriving, larger city nearby where we went on special days to do our shopping in a wide selection of busy downtown stores clustered around the Hotel Vincent). The S. S. Roosevelt – (luxury [?] lake liner on which we first came from Chicago, docking just west of the Black River Bridge in South Haven). Sunset – (the way the sun sank nightly into Lake Michigan – Copernicus notwithstanding – as we used to be able to see it from our porch before all those little trees grew so tall, as little trees are apt to do in sixty years).

*Burning of the Saugatuck pavillion. Date?*

*Bill Ferry in 1957.*

# The Tipping Point of Tolerance: A Palisades Legacy

By Marilyn Henkel

"It's hard sometimes to put your finger on the tipping point of tolerance. It's not usually the big headlines and the major stories. It's in the small incremental ways the world stops seeing differences as threatening." So says Anna Quindlen, in "The Last Word: The Right to Be Ordinary" (Newsweek, September 11, 2000, page 82). Palisades Park has, in its history, many instances of intolerance. However, no doubt following our larger society, it has also slowly moved - in many "small incremental ways" – to cease "seeing differences as threatening."

The evidence is there, however; our records give proof of intolerance. An early postcard, advertising Sturtevant Lodge, says:

> A beautiful, quiet home-like Lodge, situated on Lake Michigan. Double and single rooms; also connecting rooms, opening on wide verandas. Excellent table board – home service. Open June 15th to October 1st. If possible write in advance for reservations. No Hebrews.

Again, one of Mr. Quick's sales brochures continues the bias against the Jewish population:

> Property Fully Restricted: Saloons and public drinking is forever barred. All building plans are approved by the Directors, thus insuring an attractive, though not expensive, class of cottages....We are using the greatest care in selling only to desirable people of good moral and social standing, exclusively Gentile, and this restriction insures our always having good neighbors.

To be sure, one explanation for this early intolerance can be seen in the large number of "Jewish only" summer resorts in nearby South Haven. Palisades Park was not ordained to become one of those. However, the comment on "good neighbors" stretches beyond such concerns. Were non-Gentiles considered "bad" neighbors?

As such attitudes usually go, the concern for "good" neighbors spilled out into intolerance in other directions. Even as late as the mid 40's we find, in old minutes, the Park Board discussing paying "colored" help 75 cents an hour as against paying "whites" $1.00. Whispers of blackballing certain ethnic groups were heard throughout the Park. One interviewee (who asked to remain anonymous) recalled the time that one of the early workers in the Park, well beloved by all, was refused membership. She said:

> It was very unfortunate ... I really don't know about it because I didn't go to those meetings, but he cleared all that Brandywine, you know, and worked very hard to do that, and then he decided he'd like to have a cottage here. Down at the north end. He loved Palisades, in his early days at work here. I don't even like to talk about it, but I hear that he was blackballed at a meeting and wasn't permitted to buy in the Park, which was a very sad thing .... Because I knew him, I was hurt for him.

A May, 1963 letter, from the Board of Directors to the members of the Park, presents a newly revised set of By-Laws to be voted upon at the July, 1963 meeting. Section 4 starts: *"Realizing the paramount importance of protecting all our members against possible re-sale to prospective residents not compatible to the membership majority...."* One can only surmise that the issue of race and religion still was the benchmark of "compatibility."

However, one of those "tipping points" that Quindlen mentioned can be found in the Park history of 1967. In that year's August Patter, Bill Ferry wrote an answer to a question raised in the Annual Meeting of letting "hoodlum Negro elements" in the Park. Bill responded, in an article he called "In Praise of Discrimination," reproduced on the next page. It is worthy of consideration before one reads any further in this history.

**In Praise of Discrimination**
By the Reverend Bill Ferry

A "dynamite-loaded" question at the Annual Meeting has been lying uneasily in my mind ever since, demanding answer. That question was whether, in the light of rumored attempts on the part of "hoodlum Negro elements" to infiltrate our summer domain through the acquisition of property to the north or along our road, we should not confront this menace at its source, namely with our own members who might be unwise enough to invite Negro guests to their cottage or to our beach. The real question is the meaning of discrimination. For Webster defines that much belabored word as "the faculty of distinguishing nicely."

I would hope that all of us here at Palisades would be wise enough to discriminate between hoodlums and gentlemen, in the good, old-fashioned sense of that latter word, without regard to religion, race, skin pigmentation, or previous condition of servitude. By a gentleman I mean the man of intelligence, culture, good manners, sensitivity, justice, and integrity as opposed to the narrow-minded, uncultured, boorish, arrogant, unjust, dishonest man – to say nothing of morals or religion from which these virtues largely derive. None of us has any brief for hoodlums of any race, but by the same token I happen to know some Negroes who have all the characteristics of the gentleman, so defined, and who would be welcome in our home at any time, whether in Chicago or at Palisades. The occasion has not arisen for us here, but I want the record straight so far as we are concerned.

A long time ago now, when our elder son, John, was "six or seven or eight" - to quote South Pacific's "You Have To Be Carefully Taught" – he came from the clubhouse one day with a report that the Bookmobile was in and that the librarian had been reading aloud to some thirty of our then children. "Do you mean," we asked, "that one poor librarian read to all thirty of you, all at once?" "Oh no," he replied, "we were divided into piles and one librarian read to each pile of kids."

**May I suggest that one of the major problems of our time is our tendency to think of people in piles and that this is discrimination of the wrong kind, wherever it is found. The right kind is to "distinguish nicely" between people within piles, on the basis of individual character. As I understand it, this is both the American way and the Christian way, and I have no reason to believe that we at Palisades Park are exempt from either.**

May I suggest that one of the major problems of our time is our tendency to think of people in piles and that this is discrimination of the wrong kind, wherever it is found. The right kind is to "distinguish nicely" between people within piles, on the basis of individual character. As I understand it, this is both the American way and the Christian way, and I have no reason to believe that we at Palisades Park are exempt from either.

And now? Certainly not an integrated Park, but we are well past the early intolerance. Japanese and Native American, Filipino and African American, Chinese and Paraguayan owners, children, and grandchildren give evidence that we are indeed moving away from seeing differences as threatening. By 2025, who knows?

# Kathryn Welles Goff
## The Welles Cottage

February, 2002

In 1914, newly-weds Claude and Ines Welles were living in Rogers Park, Illinois. One of their neighbors was Dora Dean. As they became acquainted, Mrs. Dean told them about her property adjacent to Palisades Park on the eastern shore of Lake Michigan in the dunes. In the next few years, as their family grew to four – Emerson, Leonard, and the twins Jeanne and Claude, Jr. – Claude and Ines became more and more interested in Michigan as their summer home where the children could enjoy the sand and the lake. Claude had always had a dream of building a summer home for the family and this seemed to be the perfect opportunity.

They purchased a lot in Dean's Addition, one of the first lots sold north of the Brandywine Creek. There was no bridge access from the south across the creek except for a suspension bridge, which was for pedestrians only. This was no deterrent to these enthusiastic young people. They simply hauled building materials on foot across the creek, and with some help from Mr. Ballou, who built and managed the Inn on the Circle in Palisades Park, built the cottage which is now the Ark #7. In 1920, during the period of construction, the Welles family stayed in a cottage next to the garage owned by the Ewing family (#48).

Claude Sr., who was employed in Chicago, spent all his weekends and vacations commuting to Palisades, building the cottage for his family. With no electricity on the site, all the work had to be done by hand. The children helped by gathering large rocks from the beach for their father to use as facing for the fireplace. (That fireplace was rebuilt out of brick in later years when the foundation below it required reinforcing.) It wasn't long before the family was able to occupy the cottage, once the well and outhouse had been installed. Lamps were kerosene fueled. By the time their fifth child, Kathryn, was born, they were comfortably settled in the cottage. Before long they had inside plumbing and electricity.

My father's occupation, as Executive Treasurer of Marshall Field and Company, must have been confining to him, so he was eager to vent his energies on weekends in Michigan, where he always had a hammer in his hand. How excited we would be on Friday evenings when "Pop" arrived at the train station in Bangor with hugs and small gifts for each of us.

The building of the cottage continued. There were always improvements under way, tearing out and rebuilding, never seeming to finish completely. During the summer of 1929, when the lake began to threaten the shoreline and cottage, my father had a concrete wall constructed in front as a barrier. That very autumn was the big storm that caused all the beach cottages except ours, to the north of the Brandywine, to be undermined. My mother, a devout student of the Bible, named our cottage the Ark and that it is to this day, surviving other severe storms and beach erosions. The concrete wall has settled gradually since then, but is still in evidence behind the steel wall which was constructed in the early 70's. The cottage was partially undermined during the storm in 1929. With the help of Mr. Ballou, my father added the kitchen and dining room under the cottage to support it, creating room upstairs for another bedroom and inside bathroom. In 1963, the roof was removed and replaced with the present chalet design.

As the family grew and took summer jobs in Chicago, the cottage was rented for several weeks each summer, until all the children were married. Then each family took its two week vacation in the Ark. Though my parents settled in California after my father retired, they would return to Palisades for a few weeks each summer as long as they were able. We laughed when my father would fill a spare suitcase to carry rocks back to California on the airplane to polish in his lapidary tumbler, bringing them back the next trip for us to see the results. His love for the cottage as a place to "play" (in his own way) and to watch his children and grandchildren frolicking on the beach never waned. Now his great-great-grandchildren are learning to love that same cottage and the beauty of the area that we all enjoy. Thank you, Mother and Pop, for giving us this treasure.

*Above: Welles cottage #7. 1929. Below: Welles cottage's view south of the Brandywine. Swinging Bridge still in use.*

*Kathryn Welles Goff on steps to The Ark 1929.*

*Kay's early memories of Palisades Park include the following rich images – involving all her senses:*

… Mr. Quick's presence "patrolling" the Park, though not in a threatening way
… Picking wild grapes, sand cherries, and bittersweet back on the dunes to Mt. Baldy
… Coming out of the Brandywine with the leeches on our legs
… Pollywogs hatching along the creek
… Changing the channel of Brandywine Creek
… Mr. Hempy's garbage wagon surrounded by flies on the beach in front of the cottage
… Handsome Tony Canonie delivering chunks of ice for our ice boxes
… Mr. and Mrs. Shepherd delivering milk that was so rich that the top milk could be whipped and used for topping for the strawberries they also grew and delivered
… Waiting for the mail truck, morning and afternoon deliveries at the Circle to the Post Office (which was originally in the Soda Fountain, then Ballou Inn, and even in the Lodge dining room)
… Dinner at the Sturtevant Lodge dining room – what a treat!
… Yelling as we ran through the Garage to hear the wonderful echo of our voices
… Conveyor belts for pathways on the north end of the Park – slippery and blistering hot!
… Irene Milliken's wedding outside their cottage
… Little Mary Householder (now Fleming) sitting prettily on the steps next to the store, smiling and talking to shoppers
… Betty Householder's infectious enthusiasm
… Watching the Aurora Borealis in the northern sky – awesome and breathtaking!
… Beach fires at the Filkins beach; falling asleep and being carried home to bed by one of my brothers
… Thick callouses on my feet and running down the rocky road in front of the Peirce cottage without wincing
… Removing almost daily boardwalk slivers from our feet
… Mr. Knapp, caretaker, delivering luggage and groceries by tractor north on the beach to the Milliken and Filkins cottages
… Watching the "big kids" playing football on Brandywine beach – Bill and Sue DeButts, Jack Gardner, et al
… More recently, the clearing and mowing of the meadow, more orderly and cooperative membership meetings at the Clubhouse, and improved boardwalks
… Organized nature walks, flowers in the Circle and Village Green, parties on the Village Green, and the restoration of old cottages. She hopes to perpetuate the natural beauty of Palisades, to encourage friendliness of members, and to restrict commercial development.

*Kay Goff's painting of The Ark.
1955.*

*The Heisel cottage "MarJoMore" #164.*

## Margaret Heisel
In July 18, 1980 <u>Patter</u>

In 1928, my husband, Elmore, and I were going for a trip around Lake Michigan. A friend said, "Be sure and spend a night or two at Palisades Park, Michigan; it is a beautiful spot and you will just love it. The food at Sturtevant Lodge is delicious; there is a nice beach which the children will love." So 52 years ago we sent a telegram to the Lodge and they wired back that they could take care of us. We found it a delightful place to stay, loving the woods and the sandy beaches and the songs of the beautiful birds. Instead of going around the Lake, we stayed at Palisades for 16 days. Mr. Quick took us all through the Park (the Grand Tour). The northern part was just beginning to be developed beyond the Brandwine, by the McWethys and Crawshaws. We loved the southern part of the Park with its dunes. We decided to buy a lot on the ridge where we had a wonderful view of Lake Michigan and its sunsets, from our front porch, and of the woods, from our dining room and back porch. We liked having the road with easy access to the cottage, for groceries and luggage. So, in the spring of 1929, we built our cottage (#164). Our only neighbor was the Harper cottage, built in 1927. The children had all sorts of names for the cottage. Their Dad suggested Marjomore, a combination of all the names; we all liked the idea.

The builders asked if they could do anything special for us. So they built our dining room table with extension leaves to seat fourteen people. We have a "larder," a closet near the dining room. In the early days, the roads were poor so my husband would order canned fruits and vegetables from Sinks Grocery in Covert, in cases of 24, which were delivered to the cottage and stored in the larder. Mr. Shepherd, who lived nearby, would come two or three times a week with milk, cream, butter, and berries. He was always dressed in blue and white pin-stripped overhauls. He had a beard and our children said, "He looks like a picture of Jesus" – which was really true.

We became acquainted with a family, the Iversons, who lived beyond Covert, about three miles on a gravel road, the first house beyond the octagon house. We always drove over on Sundays and they had three dressed spring chickens for us plus a five gallon can of home-made ice cream – any flavor we wanted. We also bought home-made catsup and strawberry preserves. We still visit them in their present beautiful home on Little Paw Paw Lake.

We had a Cris Craft motor boat for six people – the first one at Palisades. Mr. Quick said we could keep it at Brandywine. He put pilings out into the lake to make a channel, but they all fell into the lake. Brandywine changes its course every night or so, so we often had to dig our boat out and eventually kept it at the South Haven water garage.

We were fortunate in having good water from the first day in Palisades and for years paid for the water each month. There was no electricity in the early years so we had gasoline lamps on the wall and kerosene lamps for the four bedrooms. My husband felt the lamps were dangerous so we had to keep a bowl of sand by every lamp. The lamps had delicate mantles. Charley Tunecke owned the ice-house and the Canonie boys delivered 150 pounds of ice twice a week, filling our refrigerator full.

We were saddened by the death of my husband on October 13, 1930. He always had said he had built the cottage for my pleasure, so we have continued to come all these years. We had the first telephone at the south end, as my husband needed it for business. After his death, I had it removed and I sold the boat.

We had a wonderful Clubhouse which was used for parties. I remember one party in particular, given by Mrs. Ward (Mary Lee's grandmother), where I won first prize. We all enjoyed the golf course, nine holes. It was really a "stubble field" and was finally dropped as people would rather play elsewhere and it was so expensive to keep up. It was real work to play there.

Before my husband died, he designed and had Mr. Henderson, who loved to work with sassafras wood, build a luggage rack for each bedroom and a log holder for the fireplace. Mr. Henderson made a small table for me as a gift, out of one of the last pieces of white pine for the top and sassafras for the feet.

We are 255 miles from home (Peoria, Illinois). At first it took us 13 hours to drive to Palisades. We usually had a blow-out or two. Then, as the roads improved, the time was shortened to five hours. Marjomore is now owned by my daughter, Mary Lou Heisel Hession, and my son, John. Fifty-one great years we have had our cottage in Palisades Park.

*Three examples of furniture made by Mr. Henderson and still found in the Heisel cottage - a luggage rack, above left; a log holder, below left; and a chair, above right.*

## Bill Keehn

My earliest recollections of Palisades Park go back to when I was six years old, or – to put it another way – to the summer of 1928. My parents, Roland and Marion Keehn, brought me to the Park, along with some good friends, Bert and Bea Francis and their daughter Patty. Patty and I got along well, but she didn't get sunburned. I DID, and it was not compatible with my woolen swimsuit. We stayed at Sturtevant Lodge; our rooms were on the second floor, in the middle of the south side. Opposite my room, however, was another bedroom precariously clinging to the veranda. Its presence spoiled my view, and its occupants could witness me when I would go down toward the bathroom, around the corner of the veranda. The building wasn't insulated very well; I recall it being drafty. It looks much better now.

Some of the people to whom I was introduced in the early years still come to mind. Mr. Hempy was perceived as the Park Manager, a "jack-of-all-trades" and a man respected by all. His horse and wagon were a wonderful sight. I would see them up on Thunder Mountain Road, and then at the Circle, and then on the beach. He and Joe Putz kept the Park running. They were both generous and cooperative men.

Mr. Ernest Melchert (folks called him "The Mayor") was, to me, something of a tutor. He and my father were acquainted through Oak Park/River Forest activities. Mr. Melchert loved the dunes, and many times the three of us would hike the woods and the dunes, especially north of Palisades. He was knowledgeable about nature and had a skilled eye for the beauty of the landscape, being a great artist. His favorite medium was etchings. He was president of the American Etching Society.

One of my favorite activities was to visit the horse corral in the woods across the road, just west of the baseball field. I loved "Old Suzy" and would ride the bridle path that paralleled the north side of what is now 29th Avenue and around the area of the old golf course. To my great disappointment, this activity was stopped. Another activity that came and went was archery. It didn't survive very long, but could perhaps return.

The Circle, with its hotel, brought folks together. Del Jones had bingo parties; he also had, I believe, three slot machines. Gathering on the benches under the arbor along the hotel walk, people would chat before and after meals in the Annex. Other groups gathered at the Clubhouse for movies, cards, and musical home-grown entertainers, such as The Tillson Gang. On Sunday evenings, Reverend Bill Ferry would conduct Vesper Services – a time to share while surrounded by the wonders of nature. Finally, I recall my greatest thrill was competing in the Sunfish sailing races – Palisades Park vs. Linden Hills. Memories piled upon memories have created the ambiance that has brought our family back, year after year, to Palisades Park.

*Sturtevant Lodge and vintage cars in the Circle. c. 20's.*

# Isabel M. Larson

In Palisades Park Review 1905 – 1968

The "Highlands" cottage (#78) was built in 1913 by Mr. Phillips who built many of the early cottages in Palisades Park. (Mr. Phillips had been the carpenter for the company that lumbered in this area.) We have been told that all the lumber had to be pulled up the hill by horses; (it was then little more than a sandhill, with only a few trees). My parents, George Graham Wilson and Catherine J. Wilson, bought the cottage from Valentine Scheppers in 1924. It included an 80-foot well and a cold cellar. They named it "Hi-Up""cottage and began to remodel it. Walls were moved out, the front porch enclosed, ceilings lowered, wallboard installed on interior walls, the kitchen redone, and an indoor bathroom added. (Rudy Weber did some of this work as he was then employed by the man who did the remodeling.) Wood stoves and kerosene lamps were the order of the day.

In 1926 Mr. Wilson bought lots from the Shepardsons, the Seators, and the Bruckers - for a total of five - and undertook to landscape them. The hillside was terraced with huge logs that Mr. Hempy hauled up with his team. Charley Tunecke brought in loads of dirt and Joe Putz's father helped with the work. Ferns and evergreens were planted on the hill and the hollow down at the curve of the road was filled in, raised, and planted. Grass did not grow well, so Mr. Wilson brought in the first myrtle in Palisades – large rolls of it – from Allegan, Michigan. He built a waterfall on one side of the slope and planted a garden down by the garage with flowers, varieties of cactus, and a martin house. This was screened from the road by shrubs and small boulders were placed along the road as a border. Mr. Henderson did the rustic wood designs on the garage. Retaining walls along the road were put in by Mr. Wilson, at Mr. Quick's request.

George Wilson was one of the original members of the Palisades Park Golf Club, and he and Dr. Stillian of "WoodThrushWood" spent many afternoons on the golf course. The family came to the cottage in all seasons and several times had Thanksgiving dinner here. Such trips were a real adventure in those days as getting mired in mud or sand three times between Covert and Palisades was not unusual.

The Wilsons were often visited by their daughter, Isabel Larson, and son-in-law, E. E. Larson, who brought their daughter, Kathryn, to the Park when she was four months old. A sailboat owner, Mr. Larson agreed to donate plans for the dam across the Brandywine Creek which originally was to create a lake with boating facilities. These plans were later modified to reduce costs, but some original features, such as a fish-ladder, were retained. Mr. Larson acted as engineer during construction.

Mrs. Larson, daughter Kathy Harriman, and grandsons Sandy and John Harriman, still look forward to Palisades each summer, the boys having been brought to the Park when they were two and three months old respectively. Recent improvements to the cottage include a downstairs family room, a patio, and the new name, "The Highlands."*

* *The cottage was sold to John and Patricia Hoskin in 1999 and extensively remodeled in 2000.*

*Selling produce on the beach.*

*The bridge as seen from Ravine Way.*

*Below: Brandywine Bridge with the sluice gates used to create Lake Palisades.*

# Ginny Richards
## Miscellaneous Memories

I Remember …

I rode with Mrs. Hempy while Mr. collected the garbage. My brother, Andy Peirce, was dating Jane Healy at the time and it drove him "nuts" –

Tony Canonie delivered ice to Mrs. Milliken and Mrs. Filkins at the north end of the Park. It was a long walk, and if he got sand on the ice, he had to go back and get a clean piece –

The road at the north end was one way going down behind the "ice palace" (#190) and it was a race track! Beware if you came up the wrong way –

Andy Peirce and John McWethy built a boat that was so heavy it sank –

The swinging bridge over the Brandywine was all we had to get over to the north side. It was very shaky –

When Crawford's cottage (next to The Ark) was about to be washed out, cables were put around it and it was moved up hill. Starks bought it, then Fredians –

North of our road was Dean's Addition. Mrs. Dean lived back of Cecil Burrous.

Fun picnics on the Brandywine Beach entailed card tables, blankets, hot dogs, s'mores, sand and "snipe hunts." Have you ever been snipe hunting? All you need is a flashlight and a brown paper bag -

*Above: Brandywine Beach showing steep road that came down hill. The road was later washed away.*
*Below: Typical family picnic on beach c. 1930. Matthews family.*

*Old postcard showing the swinging bridge.*

# Margaret Sauer

Letter to Betty Householder
August 31, 1986

In the 20's and 30's, people were always very friendly, greeting each other when passing and exchanging a few comments. As the population of the Park increased and changed and more renters came in, some people seemed to become more distant and aloof. The Park also became noisier and evenings were not so quiet as previously.

Mr. Ballou had the very best chocolate ice cream cones, which I knew about almost before I could say "choca I-kee-koe."

Mr. Shepherd, who sold milk, gladiolas, and sweet corn, was always smiling, gracious, courteous, and spic and span in his light blue overalls with fine white stripes and his light blue or white shirt. He was lanky, with a slight forward tilt of the upper back, as he carried his produce and climbed the paths from one house to another. His first name was Henry. One time after leaving our place after a delivery, my mother called to my brother, "Henry!" Mr. Shepherd heard, and thinking my mother was calling him, turned and came back. We were all surprised, because we never called him anything except _Mr. Shepherd_.

My father's vacation was the month of August. Since he had the car, we stocked up well when he brought us out right after school closed in June. Sometimes he mailed us a package of food. At that time, in the 20's and early 30's, it took ten hours to drive to Palisades from Chicago. So in July, when we ran out of food and supplies, my brother would go by bicycle to Covert, and, after the highway was built, to South Haven, and load up with what we needed. For a while the Greyhound Bus took the new route, and we could go to South Haven that way. We also shopped at the Circle grocery store where Mrs. Packard and Mrs. Underwood were always smiling and helpful.

*Main street of Covert, location of many popular stores used by early Palisades summer residents.*

The stores I remember in Covert were Sinks Market; Eisenlohrs' Hardware, the next store north of Sinks, J. R. Spelman and Company, the lumber, millwork, coal, fertilizer and feed store across from Sinks; and the creamery near the railroad tracks, with its delicious buttermilk which was cool, thin, tangy, and tart. The pool hall a few doors north of Sinks had signs saying "No cursing, no swearing, no gambling" – and they had good ice cream cones! Shattucks' Livery was across and to the north of Sinks. Dr. Vaughan was the Covert doctor who attended the Palisaders.

Our two favorite South Haven shops were Niffenneggers' butcher shop, south across from the bank (recently an art shop), and MacKenzies' Bakery. The Bakery had the most delicious rye bread until about ten years ago. I still keep trying to find it, but they either changed bakers or the recipe. Today's is no match.

Our family loved the tranquillity of unhurried living surrounded by the peace and beauty of nature. We enjoyed Lake Michigan – swimming, sunbathing, examining beach pebbles, cooking at beach fires, and long walks along the north shoreline. We often walked in the woods, listening, studying the vegetation, and discovering new sights. We picked wild blackberries, sand cherries, and – in autumn – wild grapes. We watched every moment of sunsets and the emergence of stars. We listened to the sounds of birds, insects, rain, wind, and waves. At summer's close, we felt nourished and refreshed in body, mind, and spirit.

---

Pebbles of the Past at Palisades Park
By Margaret E. Sauer
In September, 1988, Patter

These are the things I remember the best:
Watching the sun going down in the west;
Watching the moon as it moves through the trees;
Sounds of the night on a whispering breeze;

Whippoorwill's warning, a little owl's screech,
Seagulls and sandpipers on the north beach;
Hot dogs and marshmallows, campfires' soft glow,
Stars up above and on waters below;

Cardinals calling and wood thrushes' trills
Echoing joyously over the hills;
Sassafras, wintergreen, needles of pine,
Bracken and brambles, wild grapes on a vine;

Pockets with pebbles, and sand in my toes,
Billowing clouds when a northerly blows;
Flashes of lightning and thundering roars;
Wave after wave on the shimmering shores;

Glorious sun on the sands where I lie,
Space without time, and in it am I
Content to do nothing, content just to be
One with the earth and the sky and the sea.

## Mary K. Shepardson
### "Early Days of Palisades Park"
From August 1964 <u>Patter Special Edition</u>

Our clan, the Donohues, Van Beurens, and Shepardsons (three sisters), has been coming to Palisades Park for over forty-five years. Getting to the Park was quite an adventure. From Chicago we could come by boat to Benton Harbor or by train to Watervliet. If we weren't in a hurry, we could stay on the train to Hartford and change to the Fruit-Belt train to Covert. Mrs. Shattuck provided the taxi service from any of these places into the Park in her faithful Model T Ford. She would load us in – baggage and all – and we'd chug through the sandy road to the cottage on the hill.

There were two hotels at the circle, Sturtevant Lodge and Ballou Inn. Energetic, peppy little Mrs. Sturtevant and her daughter, Mrs. Dusenberry - and in later years, her nephew, Del Jones – managed the Lodge. Mrs. Ballou took care of the Inn and store. Both places served meals. It was fun to hear the two dinner bells ring.

Mr. Quick's daughter ran the Ice Cream Parlor. The Post Office was in that building – with Mrs. Allen and later her son in charge. Mrs. Shattuck brought the mail and picked up mail – and passengers, if anyone wanted to go to Covert to shop at Sinks Grocery, or the Variety Store, or eat at the Star Hotel on the corner there.

The Circle was brightly lit at night with Delco electric lights, but the rest of the park was dark – except Mrs. Brown's big cottage with Delco lights, too (#82). Lanterns or flashlights were a necessity for walking through the woods; without them was impossible in the dark of the moon. Full moonlight helped a little. The cottages were so far apart, the cheery soft glow of kerosene lamps in the windows made only a small path of light. Plumbing was

> **The cottages were so far apart, the cheery soft glow of kerosene lamps in the windows made only a small path of light. Plumbing was "Chick Dales" style with the traditional Montgomery Ward Catalogue.**

"Chick Dales" style with the traditional Montgomery Ward Catalogue. We drank well water the first few years.

The Clubhouse was much smaller but housed many activities – card parties for adults, bunco for children, a church service every Sunday. Rev. Norman Henderson and Rev. William Ferry were frequent speakers. Mrs. Manierre, Mrs. Ward, and Mrs. Schlacks were responsible for many of the Club affairs. Mr. Leo Sowerby and the Whitney Trio (radio artists) gave benefit concerts for the Club.

In the earliest days there was a long dock out into the lake, down in front of the Clubhouse. A wiggley narrow suspension bridge was the only way across Brandywine – except the bridge way back in the woods near the old ice house. The ice was cut from Brandywine and stored in the icehouse in sawdust until the cottagers came. When the Park progressed to running water, the pump house was on the beach. We used Lake Michigan water then. One year the lake came up and washed out several beach cottages; it took the pump house, too.

The Golf Course provided good exercise – hunting the ball under black berry brambles or in chipmunk holes. There was a lovely view from the various trees. Mr. Bendelow had hopes of a good course but the expense of upkeep was overwhelming.

The Park was Mr. Quick's dream. I believe he knew and loved every inch of it. He had fascinating scenic trails all through the Park – some lined with rustic fences, each named and marked and easy to follow. He walked miles through the woods, enthusiastic about showing lots to prospective buyers. Many of today's roads were paths then, but he had a vision of what the Park could become. He would even draw up house plans suitable for certain lots, and show how the road could be brought in. He loved the wild flowers and trees and tried to protect them. We owe Mr. Quick many thanks for planning so well for our happiness.

There were many interesting people who made life more pleasant for us. "Dad" Henderson, caretaker many years, was an artist in making rustic benches, fences, gates, etc. of sassafras. Joe Putz could fix most anything – plumber, carpenter, jack-of-all-trades. Sundays he guarded the rope that closed the road up into the woods. He would let cottagers through, but outsiders could only go down to the Circle. He and his father helped Mr. Quick plant the lovely willow trees around Lake Palisades, trees Mr. Quick brought from Wisconsin. Joe's sister, Mary, helped clean cottages in spring, ready for occupants.

Mr. and Mrs. Hempy, with horse and wagon, cheerfully collected the garbage – others days Mr. Hempy drove down on the beach to the water's edge to get loads of gravel for the roads. Mrs. Hempy always had a cheery word for everyone. Mr. Shepherd, in his Ford truck, brought milk and whipping-rich cream in big shiny milk cans – and vegetables and flowers. His glads and asters were especially beautiful. Freda also came through with vegetables. She spoke with an interesting accent. What was it? Mrs. Stearns made delicious candy for sale – in her cottage, way back in the woods. Charley Tunecke drove through in his horse drawn wagon with chunks of ice; Tony Canonie was his helper as a boy. It was hard, sometimes, in hot weather, to squeeze enough ice into the refrigerator to keep it cold until next time the ice came around.

Once a year, the Indians went through the Park selling their gay baskets.

I wonder if there are still snakes around? We used to see them often in the woods. Whip-poor-wills sang every evening and the bull frog chorus was delightful. Enough reminiscing! The Park is precious to us all.

At the Forks, Palisades Park, Michigan.

*Swing by The Ark: David Early, Claude Welles, Jr., Robin Early, and Jeanne Welles Sturgeon in kakhi playsuits. 1926.*

# Jeanne Welles Sturgeon

**A Story of the Ark and Its Beginnings
Told by One Who Was There From the Beginning**

In 1920, with their family of four ranging in age two to seven, Claude and Ines Welles had a dream of building a cottage on the shores of Lake Michigan. In 1921, that dream started to become a reality with the acquisition of beachfront property north of the Brandywine; soon the building began. Claude and several local workers erected the structure and moved his family into the cottage while it was still open to the elements, before the windows were installed. Never mind that electricity was not available, nor running water, nor indoor plumbing. This scenario was undaunting to the couple, both having grown up in homes without electricity and modern plumbing.

One way of getting to southwestern Michigan was by boat. A steamship company would ferry people from Chicago to Benton Harbor, then on to South Haven in the morning and back in the afternoon, two or three times a week. Because of the difficulties of car travel, the steamship line did a good business. The vessel, The City of Benton Harbor, passed in front of the Cottage about a mile offshore. As I saw it come into view, it seemed to loom large, like an ocean liner. It was a large boat — large enough to carry several hundred passengers. As road conditions improved, boat riders dwindled, and so, by 1930, many of the routes were eliminated, and the steamer no longer passed in front of the Park.

The car trip from Evanston to Palisades Park took several times as long as it does now because of poor country roads and frequent tire trouble. Tires hadn't yet been developed to hold up under poor road conditions. Our seven-passenger Stutz, outfitted with two extra tires, was loaded up inside and out. Suitcases were strapped to the running boards. It was so full, I had to sit atop a suitcase. Leaving after breakfast, we would have our picnic lunch in a park in downtown Gary and then continue on our way. The long trip was sometimes prolonged by a flat tire or blowout, so it could be suppertime before arriving at our destination. In those early years there were only two trips a summer, one to get the family there for the season and one to bring us home when school started.

Aside from wading, a footbridge was the only way to cross the Brandywine. Those unfamiliar with its "swinging" would slowly and cautiously make it to the other side while the rest of us walked and sometimes ran on it with perfect balance. We thought it great fun to cause it to undulate as much as we could! Sadly, in 1927, when we arrived in June, we saw the Swinging Bridge was gone and a much-needed modern bridge had been built to accommodate both autos and pedestrians. I am sure many like us who had enjoyed the uniqueness of the Swinging Bridge also felt its loss.

*A view of the swinging bridge. Early 20's.*

Papa's first project after moving in was facing the fireplace with large stones collected on the beach. Taudie (my twin) and I were very young, but we toted stones, one by one, up the long flight of stairs to help our Papa who was busy doing the cementing. The finished project was a beautiful stone fireplace, a conversation piece for many years until, in the 60's, when it was knocked down and a new unit was positioned in the corner and faced with brick.

One of the realities of cottage living was having to deal with the ever-present mouse. Use of traps controlled the problem during the summer, but opening up in the spring revealed the little creatures had taken up residence while raising their families. Would that they had brought their own bedding, but no — they had gnawed into the mattresses to get at the soft filling for their nests! The routine of opening the cottage was enough of a chore without having to clean out all the mess they made. Mama, in desperation, tried hanging the mattresses from the rafters at closing time. While that worked, it was an impractical solution and so, when a new product, D-Con, came on the market, we used it to rid us of that wintertime nuisance. In the summer, occasionally a single little beastie could still be seen scurrying around on the rafters. We were so accustomed to it that we hardly bothered to notice.

Mr. Shepherd, a local dairy farmer, would bring his unpasteurized products to the Circle to sell out of his truck. Taudie and I were entrusted with the errand of fetching the family's daily milk supply. Together, we brought our milk pails to the Circle and Mr. Shepherd filled them from a large old-style milk can. His overalls, long gray beard, and kindly manner made a lasting impression on this four year old.

In the beginning, perishable foods were placed close to the cold pipes under the outdoor pump. This method of cooling had to suffice until an icebox made a most welcome addition to the kitchen. Ours was a wooden box the size and shape of a small refrigerator standing about five feet high. The ice compartment held a chunk of ice about 18" x 18" x 24". As it slowly melted, it kept the food inside the box cool. The melting ice dripped into a tray underneath and, of course, needed emptying regularly. The iceman delivered ice regularly too. Tony Canonie, who is well known for having had a very successful business career, was an iceman when he was a young man in the 30's. By that time we had an electric refrigerator. The icebox had become history for us!

Park "rules" bring back memories of Mr. Quick, the founder of Palisades Park. He was a tall, distinguished-looking gentleman, never casually dressed, and well past middle age at the time of these observations. "DO NOT PICK THE WILDFLOWERS" was posted on signs throughout the Park, and Mr. Quick, in his austere manner, seemed always on the lookout for offenders. To a child five years of age, that made him an intimidating individual. Later, I realized he was only striving to preserve the pristine beauty of the Park he founded. Another rule was boldly advertised at the entrance into the Park. On a large sign, "GENTILES ONLY" could be seen from the road. Meant to discourage Jewish would-be members, it also was reflective of society's attitudes. For example, one weekend when Papa invited a friend, who happened to be Jewish, to be his guest, he cautioned us children to keep that information private. We did what we were told without question. That memory has made me well aware of how far society has come in the acceptance of people of all races. Thankfully now we are free to openly enjoy the company of friends regardless of race. In the early 30's, that large sign was replaced by a smaller one, "PALISADES PARK MEMBERS ONLY."

Until the late 60's, the beaches were unblemished by commercial developments of any kind and the natural beauty of the tall dunes bordering these beaches was an attraction to vacation-bound nature lovers like us. In those early years before the restrictions of rules and/or fences to protect the erosion of the tall sand dunes, we were totally free to climb the dunes and feel the exhilaration when running back down afterwards.

*Peter Welles. 1952.*

*Joan Welles Laner ringing the dinner bell at The Ark. 1956.*

Our favorite dune and one to which we often hiked, Mt. Baldy, was located about a half mile into the dunes. The hike began just north of the Milliken Cottage, the last one on the beach, now near the south edge of the Power Plant property. On the trek to Mt. Baldy were a series of small dunes, one very steep, and then a stretch of desert-like terrain. In this area, Mama would pick sand cherries, a sparsely-growing wild berry she found on little bushes. They were inedible but made pretty good tasting jelly. Picking them became an annual project for the family. Usually, though, we would be on our way to Mt. Baldy, which was the last and highest dune on the top of which we would have our picnic lunch. (In later years that was where wild grapes grew plentifully and we made a production of picking them, as they made wonderful jelly!) By that time we were more than ready to return to the beach to enjoy those cool lake breezes and go for a swim.

One important little structure, the Outhouse, or "privy," was located on the southeast corner of the property. One hand pump was located at the kitchen sink. The outside hand pump was directly behind the Cottage a few steps up from the back walkway. In about 1925, the primitive "one-holer" was replaced with a flushable toilet (still in the outhouse). Adjacent to the outhouse was a large barrel-shaped holding tank, open at the top, to catch rainwater and the pumped well water, which served to flush the toilet. Emerson and Leonard's regular chore was to pump the daily supply for the tank, not a small task, as the hundreds of strokes required to maintain an adequate water supply demanded a certain amount of strength and endurance! I pitched in to help — once! I soon realized I couldn't pump much before running out of steam! After a couple years of this, an electric pump was installed, eliminating the need for hand pumps and the holding tank which were then removed from the property. Later when the kitchen was converted to a bathroom, the outdoor plumbing was moved inside and the outhouse was taken down. In about 1945, the Park made their water available and the electric pump was discarded.

A hot water heater was acquired some time in the late 30's, but until then, a very large spouted aluminum kettle filled with water was kept on the stove ready to be heated for dish washing and the small hand-washing chores. As children, we thought our neighbors were living in pure luxury with a bathtub in their cottage. However, we had never wanted one. After all, how could we need a bath when taking daily dips in that big bathtub, Lake Michigan? Regardless, the adult view prevailed and a shower was installed.

Until electricity became available, kerosene lamps were used. They were better than no lighting at all, but not much better! The glass chimneys smoked up and often needed washing, and the fuel needed replenishing regularly. The light they gave was inadequate for reading or close work. Because those were adult activities, only Papa and Mama were well aware of the great improvement electric lights made in our lives there!

The kerosene stove also produced sooty smoke. Later, the clean-burning gasoline stove took its place and all considered it a great 'step up.' By that time, I was doing some cooking. In hindsight, I believe safety was traded for clean burning; we were totally unaware of its ever-present danger while blissfully using that stove. How fortunate we were never to have had a conflagration while preparing meals. We also had a new innovation called a "Waterless Cooker;" the size of a stove, it had three deep wells, each fitted with a removable pot. To generate heat for cooking, stone discs, twelve inches in diameter and four inches thick were heated on the gasoline stove burners and then lowered into the wells by means of a hand-held hook. The uncooked food was then placed in the pots and their lids clamped on tightly. They, in turn, were lowered by means of the hook into the wells to rest on the hot stones and the stove was closed, allowing the heat to generate steam inside the pots, which cooked the food. We had many great meals from that method, but when the electric stove replaced the gasoline stove in about 1934, the waterless cooker was seldom used and was soon discarded.

In the 20's, we disposed of trash and garbage as best we could. Our older siblings used the shovel daily to bury what was not burnable. Later, an old-timer known only as "Hempy" did odd jobs in the Park and collecting garbage was one of them. His appearance alone made him a memorable figure. He was tanned and wrinkled in spite of the tattered wide-brimmed straw hat he always wore, and he could be seen anywhere in the Park with his wagon and pair of horses. Mostly I remember him with Mrs. Hempy seated next to him in his horse-drawn wagon moving slowly up the beach, pausing at each cottage to pick up the waste. Plastic bags were nonexistent then so you can imagine the stench and flies that surely followed that wagon. Mr. Knapp took over the job in the 40's, using a tractor to get him up the beach, collecting along the way. Now a waste management company provides the service, and while it certainly does the job more efficiently, I treasure the memory of old "Hempy' and his horse-drawn wagon and Mr. Knapp and his tractor.

Around 1924, when we weren't in our bathing suits, Taudie and I lived in our 'khakis.' The color and name were reminiscent of the World War I soldiers' uniforms. The little one-piece playsuits were comfortable and sturdy and didn't show soil, a perfect choice of playwear for that environment. We wore 'khakis' for several summers and I never tired of them. On the other hand, those awful woolen Jantzen bathing suits were in fashion for years before someone finally designed swimwear in more comfortable fabrics. I will always remember the clammy discomfort of that slow-to-dry woolen suit when pulling it on for the second swim of the day. Nowadays, owning at least two suits is the norm, but no one considered it back then.

From the moment we arrived at the cottage, our shoes came off for the summer. We went barefoot on sand, gravel, and stones — and boardwalks. Our feet were toughened to all but the splinters from the latter, but we learned how to remove them using a needle and became quite stoic handling the pain from the occasional deeply embedded splinter.

One summer, a courageous lady, Edna Witsiep, along with her five children, came and took care of all ten of us, ages three to fifteen. It was a full cottage and a bit chaotic, but much fun! Edna was a very relaxed person and there were few rules. One time, we decided to try to stay awake all night. We had the Victrola playing all those Roaring Twenties tunes, like "We're in the Money" while we enjoyed games of all sorts. I think along about 11:00 I curled up in a big chair and closed my eyes (just to "rest" them). The next thing I knew, it was morning. I was still dressed, but in bed. I must have walked there in my sleep. Little attention was given to sweeping out the tracked-in sand. Being young, I didn't notice or care how sandy the floors became, but I suppose Edna would sweep at least before Papa and Mama came for a weekend. Edna kept us fed, and that was all that mattered to us.

The once wide beach became narrower every year as the lake moved close to the dune on which the cottage was built. In the spring of 1929, a cement wall, eight feet high, was poured at the base of the dune, spanning the width of the property as a protection from the advancing Lake. When the family returned home that year, the beach had narrowed to no beach at all. Later that fall, the first Big Storm eroded the sand from under half of the cottage, leaving it precariously close to falling into the lake, a fate that had already claimed many beach cottages. Without the cement wall there to weaken the force of the waves, our cottage surely would have gone too; that wall plus quick action by Mr. Ballou (of Ballou Inn) saved it. Stilts supported it until a room could be built in the empty space where the dune had been. That room became the kitchen and dining area and the vacated rooms above became the bathroom and bedroom. In later years, after a couple more Big Storms, since our cottage was still standing, it was aptly named The Ark by our mother, who read the Bible daily.

One day, an American Indian in tribal costume, feather headdress and all, came to the door selling his handmade baskets and trinkets. I had never seen an Indian, except in a silent movie where the natives were depicted as hostile foes. In contrast, he seemed nice and peaceful. He was from a remnant of the Potawatomi tribe living in

*Three cousins - Lindsay Goff St. John, Joan Welles Lanier, and Anne Sturgeon Frenchick - with parasols. 1960.*

the area, trying to make a living. A toy canoe acquired that day became a permanent part of the Cottage décor.

Much later, as an adult, while I was visiting with a neighbor, Mrs. Filkins, on her porch, we observed a man approaching on the beach boardwalk dressed inappropriately in his business suit and hat, carrying a briefcase. Sensing it was serious business, I left to allow them to converse in private. Little did I know that the wheels of progress were turning that day and the company that man represented was soon to mar the pristine beauty of our shoreline to the north. He offered her a fair price for her cottage, informing her the property was to be condemned, thus making it an offer she couldn't refuse. That fall (1969) we watched sadly as her "Bonnie Doone" and the Milliken cottage went up in smoke. Only then did it hit me that the Consumers Power Company was there to stay.

Papa was, besides a loving father, primarily a businessman. He would arrive weekends in his business suit, looking very dapper wearing his straw hat and carrying a cane, which was the fashion of the day. He would come by train to Michigan City, transferring, I believe, to another train bound for Bangor where he was met by someone from the Park. Thus, he was able to avoid the long, tedious trip by car. Besides his suitcase, he always carried a treat for the family. Once it was peanuts in the shell, but usually it was candy — as much as he could carry!

Though Papa spent most of the time on weekends enjoying his hobby, carpentry, I never felt neglected. In fact, his hammering was like music to my ears as it meant Papa was present. I adored him and he loved us all. Sundays he would devote time reading the "funnies" to Taudie and me, while each perched on the arms of a big chair with him sitting in between.

If Papa was "king of his castle" (and he was!) Mama was the "power behind the throne." They made a good team, though their personalities sometimes clashed. Strong willed and always possessing the courage of her convictions, she was primarily a dedicated Bible-reading churchgoer. Her radiant smile and hearty laugh indicated how much she loved fun. She encouraged games of all sorts: board games, parlor games, and card games. Also, she saw to it that we had music. The hand cranked Victrola played all the popular tunes of the day plus operatic arias as well.

Mama was Papa's biggest fan and always expressed praise for his accomplishments. That side of her personality was never more apparent than at the Ark where one project after another was in progress. A remarkable example of this occurred late in Pop's life when he would not be expected to undertake such a project, but with help, he enclosed the living room rafters with decorative lumber, thus making her wish for a finished ceiling come true. She enthusiastically approved.

The Cottage was built to house the original seven, but when the in-laws and grandchildren came along, the family count expanded to twenty-two. Getting together in the Ark demanded a certain amount of cooperation for a positive experience. In order to work it out harmoniously, each member exhibited a good-natured willingness to follow a plan, which sometimes involved sacrifices. Teenagers gave up their privacy by sleeping on cots in the living room. Families with smaller children doubled up in bedrooms. The women carefully planned the meals and their preparation was divided equally. Until the remodeling gave us the second bathroom, sometimes the children and grownups alike would have to line up waiting to use the facilities.

Papa and Mama created their summer home mainly for their family's use, probably never dreaming that their later years would be so greatly enriched spending time there with their beloved grandchildren, and even several great grandchildren. Their enlarged family, gathered around the dining table, delighted them and the tasty meals pleased everyone. All cooperated to make it a happy time for Pop and Nana; consequently, we have many happy memories from the years when we congregated at the Ark.

*Emerson, Leonard, and Kathryn Welles in their homemade boat in Lake Palisades. c. 1928.*

# Chapter 4
# The 30's

1931 First South Haven Blueberry Day; U.S. 31 opens from South Haven to Benton Harbor
1932 Franklin D. Roosevelt elected president during the Great Depression
1932 Amelia Earhart 1st woman to fly solo across the Atlantic
1934 Dionne Quintuplets are born in Canada
1936 Golden Gate Bridge completed
1937 First feature-length Disney movie, *Snow White and the Seven Dwarfs*; South Haven Casino burns
1939 *Gone with the Wind* and *The Wizard of Oz* are released; Germany invades Poland.

*Famous composers Leo Sowerby and Eric DeLamarter, both of whom owned cottages at Palisades Park, were contributors to the Park's music heritage.*

## The 30's

The 30's brought continued growth to the Park. Route 31 was completed, from Benton Harbor to South Haven, making travel easier. A 1938 map of the Park, reproduced on the back of Mr. Quick's stationery in a letter encouraging further building, showed over 125 cottages in place; eight had been completed during the previous season. More cars could be seen in the Circle – as were evening games of baseball and Capture the Flag. Kids waited outside the Lodge for a chance to deliver a telegram – at five cents per delivery, to be paid by the recipient and spent on an ice cream cone. Sandcastles built on the beach were washed away by the waves of The Roosevelt as it brought passengers to South Haven – with kids betting on whose castle would stand the longest. Horseback riding and horseshoes were popular sports. Although facilities remained both "rustic and simple" – no hot water often meant bathing in the lake – electricity was reaching many of the cottages. Shopping done outside the Park was probably done at Sinks, in Covert. Young people enjoyed the dance pavilions in nearby towns.

Of course, the Great Depression had its effect. Vacation expenses were often first to be cut by families in financial troubles. Jobs were hard to find; teens looked for odd jobs within the Park. One owner, however, later commented how pleased she was to have invested in property, not the stock market, since the former held its value during this difficult time. Another plus was the drop in taxes. Records of George E. Duwe (cottage #137) show his taxes fell from $33, in 1932, to $18.91, in 1940. Either way, quite a bargain in today's terms!

The arts community was flourishing, true to Mr. Quick's original intent – with concerts and plays in the Clubhouse and composers at work in their cottages. Resident artist, Wilbur Peat, was often seen painting or working with driftwood. Aileen Bennett ran a Music Camp in the mid-30's, headquartered at Ballou Inn. One participant of the Camp remembered that Park real estate ads of the time still specified "Gentiles only." Happily, though, as a young Jewish student at the Camp, she "was never questioned." *

*In letter written by May Kaplan to Pearl Sarno, dated May 8, 1966, found in the Covert Historical Museum.*

Tragedy struck one Park family around 1934, with the drowning death of their small son. Given unguarded beaches and Lake Michigan's at times treacherous waves, the Park is fortunate that this is the only recorded drowning of a member, although in the late 70's, an older teenage guest also lost his life in the waves. With swimming safety in mind, Forest Lowrey instituted the Annual Marathon Swim in 1939, hoping that participants would be assured that they could, indeed, swim one half mile in any emergency.

The Clubhouse, which was all but closed during the Depression, was bought by the Park in 1939. Each cottage was assessed an extra $5.00 in dues for some years thereafter, to pay for the purchase. 1939 saw the birth of both the Half-Mile Swim and The Patter. The Honor and Glory Tennis Tournament had been started in 1937.

The Park government was changed in this decade. The Articles of Association of the **Palisades Park Improvement Association**, signed by Arthur C. Quick, president and treasurer, William H. Ward, vice-president, Dora Heuermann, secretary, and Thomas O. Browning, was presented to the State of Michigan on June 27, 1931. The membership was asked, in a December 5, 1932, letter by Arthur Quick, to vote at the following summer meeting to approve the change to a non-profit corporation, incorporated under the General Corporation Laws of Michigan, as a "corporation not for pecuniary profit." The South Haven Palisades Park Company would be no more. All cottage owners would be members of the Association. Quick would retain his ownership of the Company; according to the new By-Laws, he would also serve as President of the Association. By the end of the decade, that, too, changed with the election of George E. Duwe as the first President. Arthur Quick then had the title of Secretary.

There are hints, throughout the interviews, of crime-related events in our otherwise pristine Park. An arrest for counterfeiting, a well known gangster hiding in one of the cottages, rumors of a still in the dunes, another gangster named on a cottage deed, slot machines in the Lodge. Perhaps these don't add up to anything – or perhaps, with its proximity to Chicago and isolation, the Park had unsavory connections for a few years.

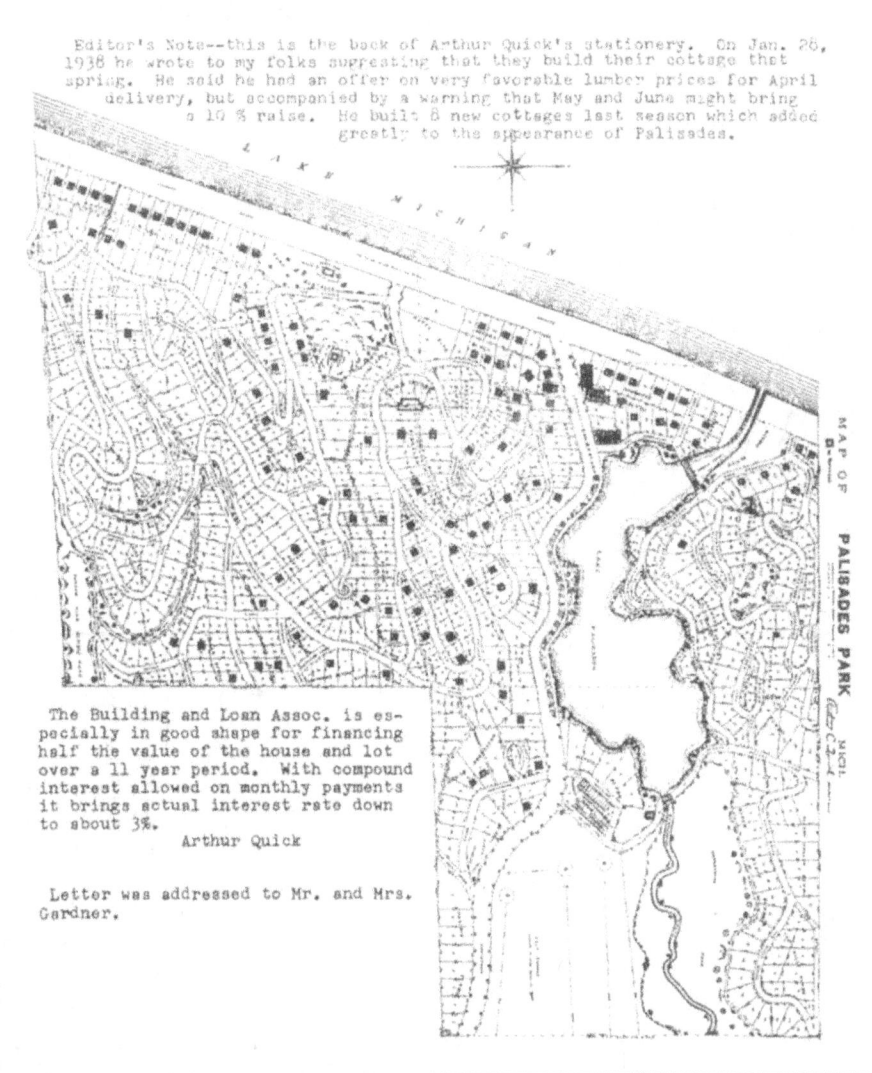

*Betty Householder provided this 1938 map, printed on the back of Mr. Quick's letter to her parents, Mr. and Mrs. Gardner, showing the cottages that were then built. The letter, dated January 28, 1938, suggested that the Gardners build their cottage that spring. Quick had an offer on "very favorable lumber prices for April delivery" but warned that "May and June might bring a 10% raise." He built eight new cottages the previous season, which "added greatly to the appearance of Palisades."*

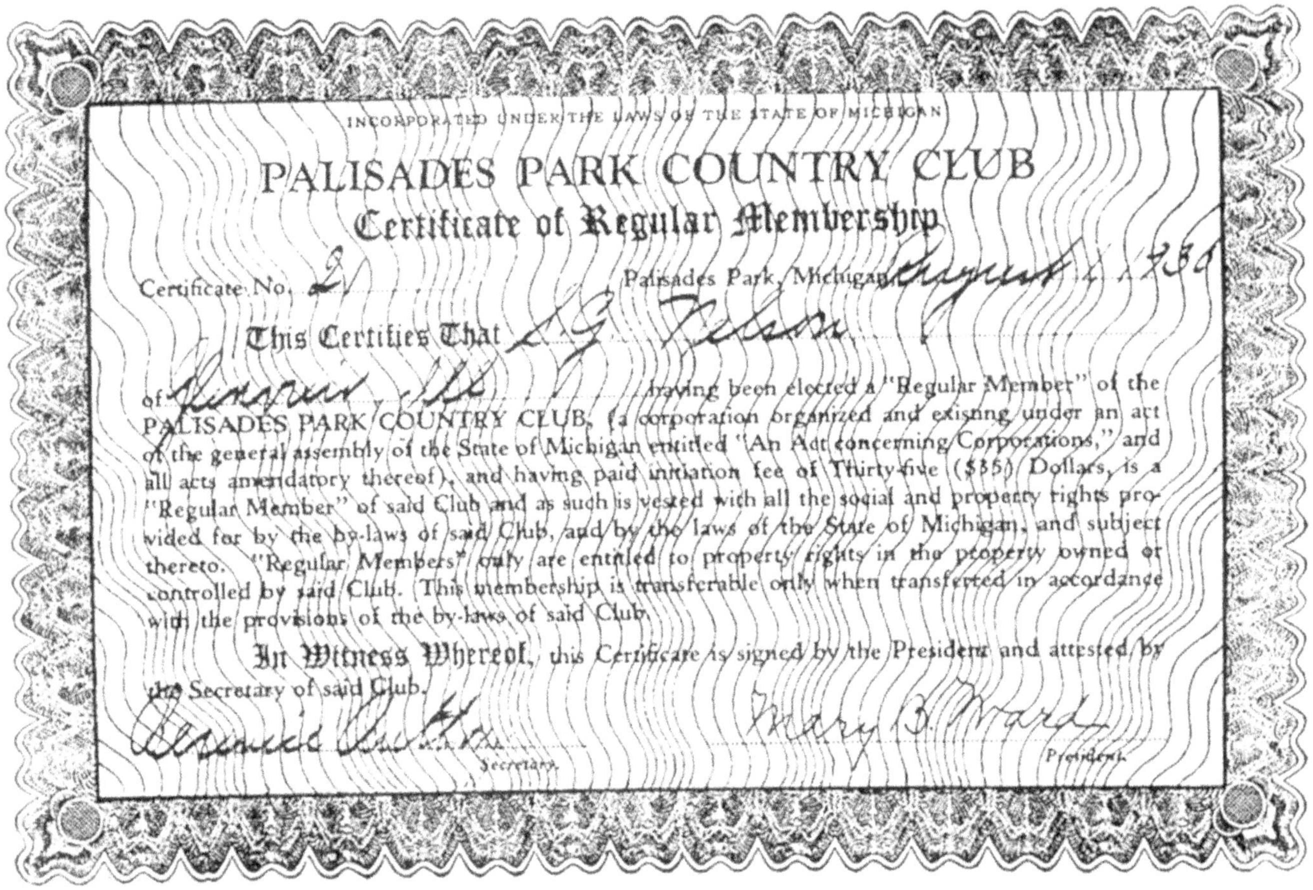

*This 1930 membership certificate, made out to S. G. Nelson and signed by Mary B. Ward, indicates an "initiation fee" of $35 had been paid.*

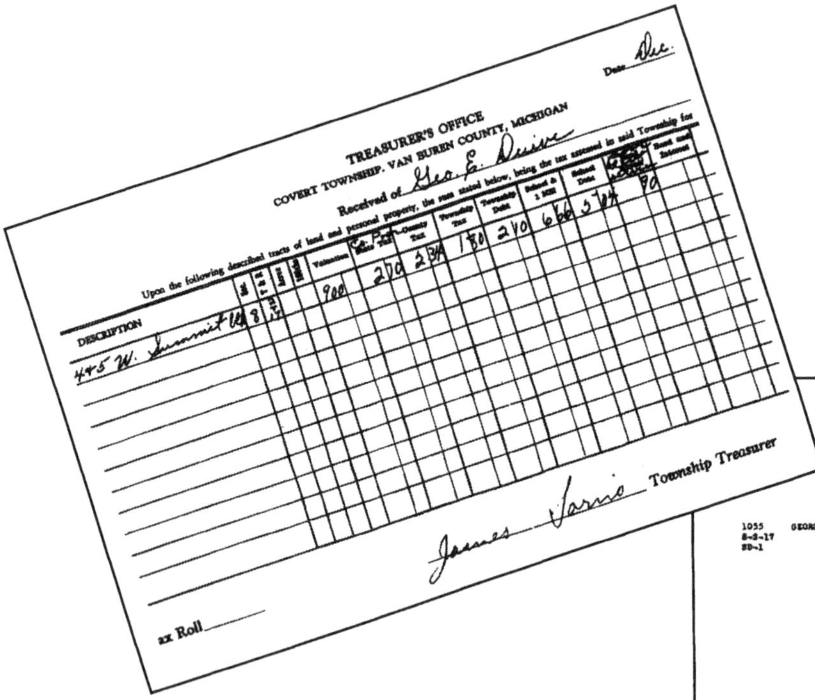

*Two tax bills dating in the 30's: in 1936 the bill was $21.76 and in 1938 it was $20.54. Both on the George Duwe cottage #137.*

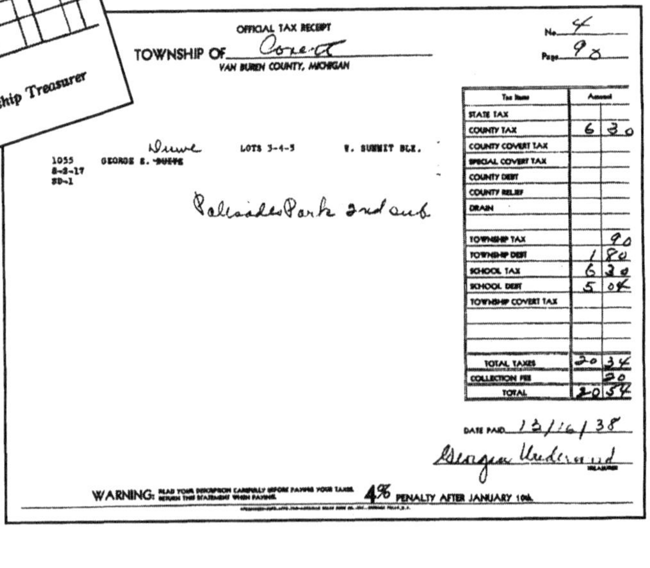

# The Arts Community

## Introduction by Margaret Roche
August 3, 2003

As I set out to do the sketches for the Park history, I walked the roads and paths and looked with a new eye at our cottages. I was the fly on the wall. My observations took me beyond the casual, cursory glance at a door, flowers, or window treatment. I saw delightful folk art everywhere – creative messages telling about the artist's pleasure to be here. When I was asked by the editors to write something about Park artists, past and present, I said, "I can't name them. There are too many and I might leave someone out." But I do need to mention one artist, long passed but fondly remembered. She is Mary Gardner, mother of Betty Householder, Jack Gardner, and Janette King. I distinguish her here because of the dozens of little oil paintings of early Palisades Park that adorn the walls of Sunset cottage(#88). What a legacy to leave for her grandchildren and great-grandchildren who still come there.

We are all artists as we walk the beaches, stroll the roads, hike the trails, and ruminate on our porches and decks. Finally away from our schedules, appointments, and to-do lists, we get down to the real business of living. Maybe we compose a poem or a short story, write a journal or autobiography, creatively frame our memories on our walls or in a book. There is that little sketch of the cottage, painted many years ago, framed and hung in that special place over the mantel. Our beaches, porches, and woods are the places where we seem to make our most sincere statements about who we are. Somehow, with time to meditate and contemplate, our creative spirits soar and each new idea or project gives life to another. A painted stone, a poem, a beach glass vase, painted furniture, a memory quilt, and unique wall paintings all give voice to our love of Palisades Park.

The muse beckons and we answer with a poem, a song, a painting, a dance, a renewed love of life.

*Both paintings on this page by Mary Gardner.*

# Leo Sowerby (1895 – 1968)

*Part of Mr. Quick's original dream for Palisades Park was that it become a community of artists, musicians, and other professional people. To that end, he aimed early sales campaigns at such institutions as the American Conservatory of Music in Chicago. He was successful enough that through the early decades of the Park's history, several esteemed musicians owned cottages at Palisades. One of those was Leo Sowerby. At the age of 22, Sowerby was the guest of Olaf Anderson who then owned Trumbull's Set Point #147. Sowerby liked the Park so much, he stayed for over 50 years. Mardy Mehagan Mavor and Vashti Blaney, in an interview on August 27, 1984, remembered Leo as follows:*

*Portrait of Leo Sowerby c.1930's.*

Mardy: One of the most illustrious residents of Palisades Park, of course, was Leo Sowerby, who has become recognized the world over as a famous composer. He lived in Grand Rapids in his boyhood. There is a musical organization in Grand Rapids called the Saint Cecilia Society, which is very active and particularly interested in young musicians. My father's cousin was president of the St. Cecilia's Society when somebody brought to their attention the fact that Leo had great potential, even as a young boy. So the Society gave money for him to be sent to Chicago to study under Olaf Anderson. Olaf Anderson had a cottage here. Anyway, after he had been at the American Conservatory for some time and was very successful in his composing (that was what he specialized in) and organ (he was an organist), he was sent to Rome to study. He is the only American, to date, that won the Grand Prix in Rome for his compositions. Well, he came back here to the United States and was immediately drafted into WWI; he was sent down to Rockford and put in charge of the horses in the stable. Vashti's sister's husband was a captain at the time, as was Marion Lowrey's brother, and Leo made the request that he be allowed to join the band and so he was allowed to. Well, the two men were coming up here to Chicago to spend the weekend and picked up the newspaper. The headlines on one of the pages said, "Leo Sowerby Is Coming to Chicago." A symphony which he had composed was being premiered by the Chicago Symphony Orchestra. Well, these two young chaps were simply aghast. One turned to the other and said, "I just made that fellow First Class Musician today!" Well anyway, Leo ended up by going to Europe and being the head of the band of General Pershing. Since then, the Chicago Symphony Orchestra has played several of his compositions. Once, he was interviewed and asked how he ever dreamed up such strange, unusual, and interesting harmonies in his compositions. He replied, "Mr. Borafsky, you have no idea what the flies of Palisades Park can do to a piece of paper!" Of course, everybody got a laugh out of that. When he was in Rome, he bought a bathrobe, a flowing robe that looked exactly like the Pope's robe – sort of gold colored – and, with his flaming red hair, he came strolling down to the beach with this bathrobe flying in the breezes. He was such a funny man.

Mr. DeLamarter, who was assistant conductor of the symphony, had his cottage here also. With two such fine musicians, when I ran the Clubhouse, we used to have the most beautiful recitals over here on Sunday afternoons. We had the opera singers from the Chicago Opera, in the good old days. Mr. DeLamarter's wife was a very fine musician also; she gave beautiful programs. And we had some of the most famous pianists.

Vashti: I saw one of Mr. DeLamarter's scores one time. He was noted for having the most beautiful musical scores. Leo used to compose up at his cottage, but he had a neighbor who didn't appreciate his composing and would turn on her victrola. Finally, he asked Mother and

Father if he could come down and use the piano that they had and compose at their cottage. Father came in one time, after he had been swimming, and said, "I think I'll just put a few little dots in there." Leo said, "Don't you dare!"

Mardy: When Leo was the organist and choir master of St. James Cathedral, he used to bring his choir up here on the 4th of July weekend. Some of them would stay at the Lodge and some up there on the hill with him. They had a very good and gay time. They used to have a lot of fireworks on the 4th; it was really very gay. At midnight, the choir came out on the bluff and sang "The Star Spangled Banner" and I have never heard anything so thrilling in my life. That beautiful choir with those wonderful voices.

Leo Sowerby a lot to build a cottage on which he did the very next year. He also had a little guest house which he called his studio, although he had the piano that he composed on in his own cottage. He bought the cottage behind him, the Brown Derby, which he rented to the Burt Hohmans every single year until they bought it in 1965. Sowerby is well known all over the world for his wonderful choir music. He is Director of the Choir Masters School at the National Cathedral of Washington, D. C., a nondenominational school. He has received many honors – the Prix de Rome, the Pulitzer Prize, honors from the Queen of England, and last year a commission to write masses for the Catholic Church. When he was 71 years old, the St. James Cathedral honored him by having a concert and playing all his compositions. At the end of the program, the

*Sowerby with his choir on the Palisades Park beach.*
*c. 1930's.*

### *The August, 1967 Patter continued Sowerby's story:*

Gen and Burt Hohman had a farewell party for Leo Sowerby last week in honor of his being in the Park 50 years. At the age of 22, he came to visit the Olaf Andersons and liked it so well he stayed all summer. The Andersons taught at the American Conservatory of Music in Chicago. In return for services Leo had performed for the Andersons that summer, they gave

orchestra playing the works gave Leo a standing ovation. He always brings a protégé with him to the Park who writes down the compositions as he composes them. He loves Palisades Park. He was terribly concerned about the looks of the beach this year, as it was cluttered with junk. He left last week to go to a convention in Canada, where he was the visiting artist.

*Bernie Fissinger shared her Sowerby memories in a note written July 22, 2000:*

My family began renting The Chalet, on Route 9, in 1965. At that time, we were up the hill a bit from the two cottages which were owned by Dr. Leo Sowerby. My husband was one of Leo's students at American Conservatory and studied composition under Dr. Sowerby's tutelage. One of Leo's cottages was a one-room affair, called The Studio. One of my vivid memories of Sowerby was his ability to make a "killer" martini. Leo would often talk of his using the lake for bathing and shampooing. Often our evenings were spent with Gen and Bert Hohman, our in-laws, and Leo's friends from Chicago. This was before he moved to Washington, D. C. He was always an inspiration to my husband and spending time with him in the summer was a true delight.

*Sowerby composing in his cottage at Palisades Park.*

After Sowerby's death, the Leo Sowerby Foundation was started. Its goal was "to arrange for the preservation, promotion, publication, and dissemination of the music of Leo Sowerby; to facilitate access to musical scores, documentation and iconography pertaining to the life and work of Leo Sowerby; to assist and encourage performers, organizations, and scholars interested in the performance of Sowerby's music and the study of his life and works." In their pamphlet, Francis J. Crociata, president of the Foundation, said: "As we approach the celebration of his 100th birthday, musicians and their audiences are ready to make a place in their hearts for the long overlooked and taken-for-granted American lyrical composers of this century. Leo Sowerby is among the greatest of these." The city of Chicago honored his 95th birthday by proclaiming May, 1990, as Dr. Leo Sowerby Month.

---

## PIANO RECITAL
– BY –
### Leo Sowerby

*Palisades Park Club House,*

*August 1921*
*8:15 P. M.*

### PROGRAM

I.
- Novellette
- To a Water Lily ......................... MacDowell
- Arabesque, E Major
- Arabesque, G Major ...................... Debussy
- Notturno ................................ Grieg
- May Time ............................... Arthur Olaf Andersen

II.
- Gay But Wistful
- Colonial Song
- Country Gardens ......................... Grainger
- Lento .................................. Cyril Scott
- "If I Were a Bird" ..................... Henselt
- Ballade, A Flat Major .................. Chopin

III.
- The Cuckoo
- Lord Rendal  (Three folk tunes from Somerset)
- My Man John
- Fisherman's Tune ....................... Leo Sowerby
- Money Musk

---

### Sowerby's Connection to Palisades Park

1910 – 15-year-old Leo Sowerby moves to Chicago to study at the American Conservatory of Music with Arthur Olaf Anderson, who owned a cottage at Palisades Park.

1916 – Sowerby finishes his first popular work, "Comes Autumn Time," and it is performed two days later by organist Eric DeLamarter at Fourth Presbyterian Church. DeLamarter also owned a cottage at Palisades Park.

1917 – Sowerby builds a cottage at Palisades Park on property given to him by Arthur Olaf Anderson.

1918 – Sowerby's 1917 work, "A Set of Four; Suite of Ironics," is first performed by the Chicago Symphony Orchestra, beginning his 25-year relationship as a composer in residence. It is dedicated to Eric DeLamarter.

1927 – Sowerby is appointed organist and choirmaster at St. James Cathedral and serves until 1962.

1942 – Arthur Olaf Anderson's cottage is purchased by Karl W. Anderson, who had joined the St. James choir in 1930.

1948 – Karl Anderson marries the former Jeanne DeLamarter and begins using the DeLamarter cottage, "Theotherworlde."

## Eric DeLamarter
## (1880 – 1953)

*As Mardy Mavor mentioned previously, another composer who came to the Park in the early days was Eric DeLamarter, the Assistant Conductor of the Chicago Symphony Orchestra.*

Eric DeLamarter – composer, conductor, pianist, organist, and cellist – spent most of his musical career in Chicago. His major positions were as assistant (later associate) conductor of the Chicago Symphony (1918-36) and as organist and choirmaster of Fourth Presbyterian Church (1914-36). He also taught at Chicago Musical College and served as music critic for the Tribune.

DeLamarter was a friend and Palisades Park neighbor of fellow Chicago musician Leo Sowerby. He and his second wife Alice built a cottage called Hillcrest (#136) in 1927 (now owned by the Beveridges). In 1939, several years after Alice died, Eric deeded the cottage to his daughter, Jeanne DeLamarter Best.

Eric retired from his Chicago activities in 1936 but often returned to Palisades Park. He later taught and conducted in Michigan, Texas, and Los Angeles. His talent and striking appearance got him a job in at least one movie. In the 1946 drama "Humoresque," in which John Garfield plays a violin virtuoso and Joan Crawford plays her usual femme fatale, Eric can be seen conducting the orchestra for Garfield's climactic performance near the end of the film.

When DeLamarter's daughter Jeanne inherited the cottage, she decided it needed a new name and she called it "The Other World." She subsequently married Karl Anderson, becoming the stepmother of the Anderson kids – Steve, Lori and Carol. Jeanne moved to New Mexico in 1959 and reluctantly sold the cottage. After another twenty years, Carol Anderson, now Carol Beveridge, and husband Don became the fourth owners of "The Other World" so, in a sense, it is "back in the family."

Some memories of daughter Jeanne DeLamarter, a published poet, are included elsewhere in this volume as are some of her poems.

*Wilbur Peat painting at Palisades Park.*

## Wilbur Peat (1898 - 1966)

Wilbur Peat was, for many years, the "artist in residence" at Palisades – at least in August each year. Born in Chengtu, China, of Methodist missionary parents, he came to Palisades in 1929, building his cottage in 1932. Ever after he spent the summer weekends and the month of August at Palisades, often spending his month on landscape paintings. He created about 100 paintings of scenes in Palisades – lake, forest, and cottage views. Most of those pictures are owned by his family.

Mr. Peat was Director of the John Herron Art Museum in Indianapolis from 1929 until his retirement in 1965. His tenure was the longest for any director of an American art museum. He authored five books and many articles on Art and Architecture. The art exhibitions he organized were internationally recognized.

Palisades Park was an important factor in his life and provided a much needed change of scene and a chance to relax from his busy professional life.

*Portrait etching of Ernest Melchert*

## Ernest Melchert (1890 - 1970)

According to his daughter, Virginia Melchert Coleman, Ernest Albert Melchert had a challenging childhood. Born in Chicago March 11, 1890, to Fannie and Albert Melchert, he had three almost-adult sisters. His father, a Commodore in the U. S. Navy, died from injuries inflicted by gun-runners off the coast of Florida. Ernest was six months old. Money was tight for the widow and her family, and the situation approached desperation when two of the older daughters developed tuberculosis. The sickness necessitated a move to Albuquerque, which was really the only treatment available for TB. Thus, when Ernest was 13, he took his six-month-old nephew out west on the train. The trip took a week – with no formula, no Pampers. The baby cried the whole time. A nightmare journey. The family later moved to Colorado Springs. After one year at Colorado College, Ernest returned to Chicago and went to work for the Chicago Paper Company, where he stayed for 40 years.

Before the move to New Mexico, Ernest had studied at the Art Institute and Vogue Wright. His tuition was paid by one of his teachers who saw that he had promise. One of his classmates was N. C. Wyeth, who remained a lifelong friend. As a boy of about ten, he visited Palisades with a friend (Frederick Mizen, a renowned portrait painter) and stayed with the Bendelows. Later he, with his mother and sisters, visited PPCC and stayed at Ballou Inn.

Ernest married Margaret Duster in about 1915. As they began their family, they continued to vacation at Palisades, first at the hotel and later in their own cottage. Over the years, they had become good friends with the Wunsch family. In 1942, the elder Mr. Wunsch died, at about the time that the Melchert's 26-year-old daughter died. Partly as family therapy to deal with their loss, Ernest bought the Wunsch cottage, Old Pier (#45). The cottage is still owned by his daughter, Virginia Coleman. Evidence of his art legacy can still be seen throughout the cottage, in wall panels which he painted, and in pictures on the wall.

He remained at Chicago Paper to earn his living, but he never gave up art, eventually gravitating towards etching. Etching is a very demanding art form requiring drawing perfection. Everything etched onto a copper plate comes out backwards in the print; it needs almost perfect "draughts-man-ship." Ernest became a member of the Chicago Society of Etchers and was, for many years, its president. During his tenure, etchers from all over the world showed their work in Chicago and the movement became known as the "Chicago School."

Virginia Coleman enjoys telling stories about her father. One story is about the anchor now found in the Park Circle, in memory of her son Bucky (Melchert's grandson). Ernest found the anchor on the beach in front of Kavanaugh's cottage (#51) after a storm washed away the sand covering it. He put it by his cottage. Apparently Mr. Quick thought it belonged to the Park and took it from Melchert's cottage and put it in the Circle, starting a bit of a tug-of-war. Ernest, sure the anchor belonged to him by right of his having found it, hauled it back to his cottage. It was Virginia and her husband, Randy Coleman, who – years later - finally returned it to the Circle. Another family story Virginia shared was of Melchert's boxing ability. Ernest was an amateur boxer, champion of the printers' league. When he was in his mid-30's, he was challenged by Paget Cady, Mary Lee Tillson's father who was an Ivy League boxing champion, to a match on the Brandywine. A rink was set up and the match took place by torchlight. Melchert won. He later insisted that any boxer coming up through the ranks of workers would be able to beat someone coming up through the Ivy League.

One of Melchert's most valuable works, Lone Pine, was based on a pine on the north beach, since destroyed by the power plant. Much of Melchert's work is now in the permanent collections of the Art Institute of Chicago, the Smithsonian, and the New York Metropolitan Museum. He was a fellow of the Royal Society of Etchers in England. In 1995, a Chicago dealer mounted a one-man show which was opened by a Vernissage attended by many prominent Chicagoans. Several of his first-place prize etchings were of drawings made at Palisades Park. He died on May 19, 1972. His ashes were scattered at Palisades.

*Above: Mary Gardner painting of Palisades;*
*Below left, Ernest Melchert etching;*
*Below right: Display at a Park Art Fair.*

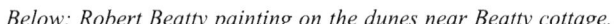

*Above: A Robert Beatty painting.*

*Left: Wilbur Peat's pictures on display at a Palisades Art Fair.*

*Below: Robert Beatty painting on the dunes near Beatty cottage.*

*Scene in a Clubhouse play. 1953*

## Clubhouse Plays

*For awhile, drama held its sway in the Clubhouse. Jayne Mathias recalled the following:*

"Dr. and Mrs. Timmons, from the East, had a dramatic school – he was a drama coach – at Terryton on the Hudson. She taught esthetic dancing, interpretive dancing, and they always had a couple of their promising students here with them. They would put on plays. They stayed in the Heitner's cottage (#98). Very interesting people. I was in several plays as well, when Jeanne Anderson directed them. Not too many, because I was so much younger than the people who were in them, like Helen and Mary Anderson, Bud Johnson, and Jack Ott. It was fun! Really, a lot of fun!"

## Musical Programs

Musicians have continued to enrich the Park with their programs. Jim Williams's grandfather, J. Harry Jones, was organist at the Welsh Presbyterian church in Chicago and guest conductor of the Chicago Symphony. His son-in-law (Jim's uncle) owned cottage #157 (now G'Sell).. Two interviews mention the Whitney Trio concerts. Apparently members of this radio trio spent summers at Palisades. As Marge Roche mentioned earlier in this chapter, the list goes on and on. In the 70's we were entertained by Rick and Steve Brill's Combo and by the Tillsons; in the 80's by Bill Trumbull's quartet (plus Janet Kolehmainen); in the 90's by Steve Heavrin's Soundcheck combo; in 2003 by Patty and Howard Beyer.

*The Tillsons entertain at the Clubhouse in 1976.*

*The Brills and their group, Magpie, entertain in the dunes.*

*Free To Be You and Me - a musical put on by Clubhouse kids in 1976.*

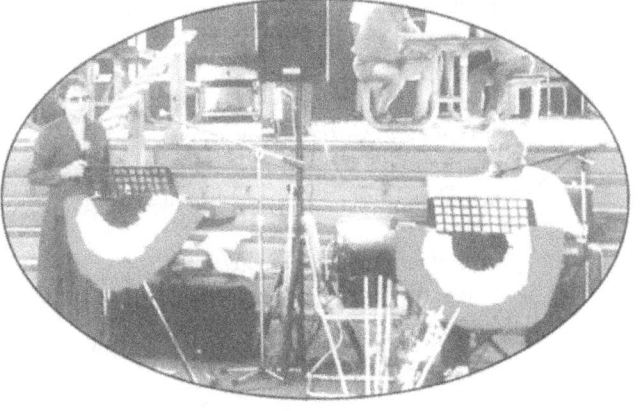
*Patty and Howard Beyer entertaining on the Village Green. 2003.*

## The 1996 Friendship Quilt

During the winter of 1994-95, 48 women in the Park completed squares commemorating Palisades Park. The techniques varied, but after the squares were bordered with two shades of green, the results were a loving tribute to many aspects of the Park. The quilt was raffled at the 1996 Betty's Club auction. Marilyn Henkel wrote the poem below based on each square. It was published in the September, 1996 Patter.

### A Tale Told By A Quilt

Beach umbrellas and bonfires,
Sailboats in the sun,
Sand and sky and water ...
Children having fun.

Golf, bingo, and tennis
Weddings to celebrate,
Cocktail parties at sunset,
The guardhouse at our gate.

Beautiful flowers through the seasons -
Trillium blooming each May;
Butterflies adding their colors
To a perfect summer day.

The woods in the Park so stately -
Firs and oaks so high -
And the willow by the meadow
Which sways as children go by.

Our cottages each so special -
Set Point and Upside Dune
And Richard's Roost and Sandpiper,
Each name plays a wonderful tune.

The cottage list is quite lengthy
From Little Brown Jug on the beach
To Masons' cottage beside the dunes -
A treasure trove found in each.

Some good times to remember:
Stan roasting his pig one year

Or a row of rustic mailboxes
That used to bring us cheer.

Blueberries in abundance,
The South Haven lighthouse so red,
Watermelon on the Fourth of July -
Bright colors through summer are spread.

Palisades has its own wildlife:
The stately herons that soar,
Gulls and hummers and grosbeaks,
Little black squirrels and more.

The dunes in the Park are a treasure
With their ever-shifting sand -
A geological wonder
From the time Lake Michigan began.

Our Soda Bar has a long history,
Each summer it beckons us all
For ice cream and burgers and parties
Too numerous to recall.

Labor Day games with their logo
Remind us that summer can't last.
The October beach with its flotsam
Hints of good times that passed.

So here's to Palisades glory -
Our quilt tells its story in part.
From the Park's creative women
It shares an affair of the heart.

*Marge Roche*

## Artists

Nor have artistic endeavors been forgotten in recent decades. To mention a few, they include:

- Bob Beatty and Phyllis Butcher Hartzler with their painting;
- Marge Roche, with her sketches and sculpture;
- Nanette Draper Lewis, Don Henkel, Lucie Tillson and Katy Beck with their photography;
- Wendy Anderson Halpern, with her children's books;
- Laverne Ankenbruck with her quilts (which inspired the two friendship quilts made by many Park members).

These and many others have continued to find inspiration at Palisades. Of recent note, Butch Haude runs the foundry that put the DaVinci horse together for the Grand Rapids Meijer Sculpture Gardens.

*Right: Amy Beck Micken using a potter's wheel on deck of Beck cottage.*

*Below: Sculpture by Marge Roche, on her deck overlooking Lake Michigan.*

*Nancy Potter, Kay Goff, Laverne Ankenbruck and Marilyn Henkel piecing the Quick Anniversary Quilt. The quilt contains 30 wildflowers, designed by enlarging the wildflower sketches in Mr. Quick's book. Each wildflower was traced, colored, and embroidered by different women in the Park. There are also 16 bugs and butterflies. Hand quilted during 2003 - 4, the quilt will be raffled at the Park's 100th anniversary celebration in 2005.*

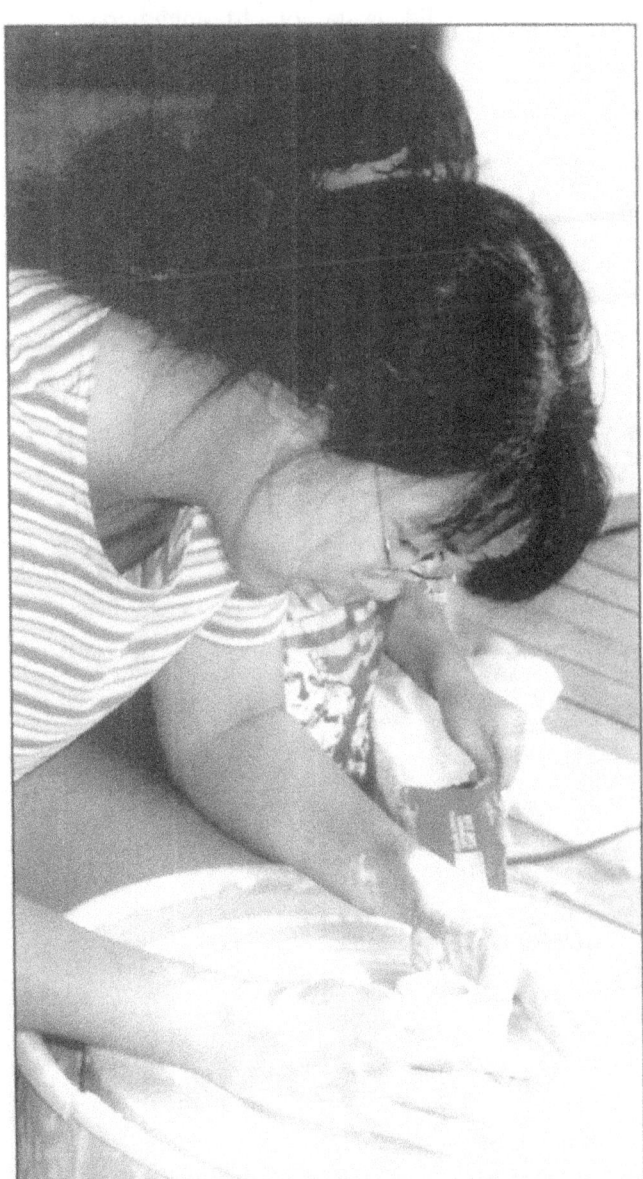

# Tom Venner's Primitive Pottery – A Palisades Success Story

*In the 60's and 70's, Tom Venner, now Dean of the Arts Department at Eastern Michigan University, started his career in pottery by experimenting with clay he found on the beach. After molding it to the desired shape, he "fired" it directly in the sand.*

*Tom Venner grew up at Palisades Park. Before his family built their own cottage, in 1965, they spent many summers renting. Thus, from a very young age, Tom spent every summer in the Park. For several summers he and his brother ran our Soda Bar. Presently a well known sculptor, Tom credits at least some of his lifelong interest in ceramics to a project he completed on our beach. Here is his story.*

In the summer of 1973, Tom began a project that was intended to put the finishing touches on an undergraduate degree in art from Alma College. Little did he know that the project would be the start of a life-long pursuit.

*Tom at work on Soda Bar deck. 1973.*

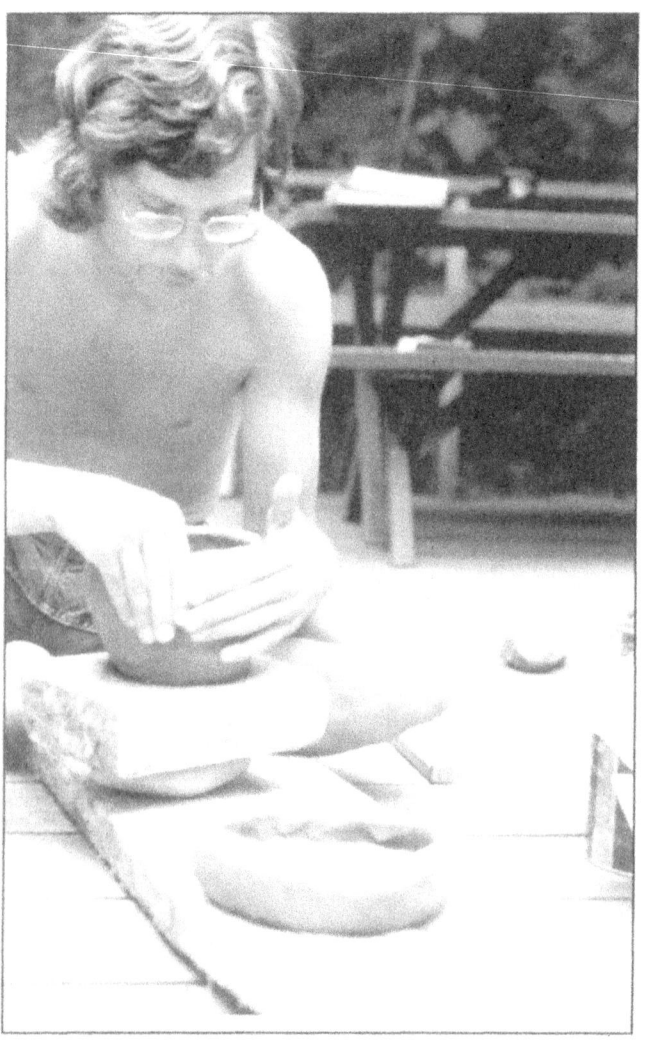

Tom's study of drawing, painting, and sculpture at Alma College had gone well. Little by little, he gained the experience and knowledge needed to narrow and focus his interests. By the end of his senior year, under the tutelage of artist and professor, Ed Jacomo, it all came together in ceramics – a discipline that requires the love of color and form, a blend of painting and sculpture. Needing a few credits to finish his degree, Tom arranged to do an independent study project over the summer at Palisades. The medium would be clay, that was certain, but just how to approach it was not so clear. Where would he find the clay? Moreover, how would it be finished and fired, without a kiln? The answer came from a potter named Hal Reigger who, just a few months earlier, had published a book titled Primitive Potter, in which he explained how one could work with clay in the most basic of circumstances. At the time, living in the back room of the Soda Bar where he worked with his brother Rob, there was no room to set up a studio – his circumstances were indeed basic! But Reigger's book suggested an alternative to a studio. All one needed was the will to explore, imagine, and invent.

On the north edge of South Haven, just next to the Sleepy Hollow resort, is the bed of a river that emptied, long ago, into Lake Michigan. Tom had discovered it by shear coincidence years earlier, during a walk along the shore. The river had long dried up; indeed, the riverbed was situated on a low bluff, well above the current lake level. What remained was a thick deposit of clay which, every time it rained, washed out onto the beach below. There, after the rain, the clay would dry and form into its characteristic bowl-shaped shards. Tom gathered up these shards of pure Michigan clay and took them back to Palisades.

Back behind the Soda Bar, on the small, fenced-in patio, Tom watered down, then filtered the clay by pushing it through a piece of window screen. This process, he hoped, would remove small stones, grass, and twigs that might be in the clay. Once the clay was screened, it was ready for use. He built a variety of objects, mostly small bowls, forming them either by pinching the clay to thin and shape it, or by rolling it on a board, forming long, pencil-thin "snakes" to coil into the shape of a pot. When he was done, the pots were left in the shade to dry.

The final step was the fire. None of the Soda Bar ovens, with a temperature limit of 400 – 500 degrees, could provide sufficient heat to permanently hold the clay together. Something in the range of 1200 degrees, or red heat, would be necessary. What to do? Reigger's book outlined the way a number of peoples throughout time and across the world fired their pots. Essentially, one just had to subject the clay to a gradual increase in temperature in an enclosure that would hold the heat and allow it to build up. If successfully done and a high enough temperature could be attained, the clay particles would actually begin to melt slightly and stick together. The clay then became ceramic, permanent.

On the beach at the north end of Palisades, not far from the new power plant, was a lot of debris washed up by the lake or uncovered by the rise in water level that was then occurring. One of the things revealed was an old sewer pipe, about eight feet long and 15 inches in diameter. Propped up on a 45 degree angle, it formed, in one piece, a lower opening for a fire box, a middle section in which to position the pots, and an upper opening to act as a flue. A primitive kiln! Tom tried several firings, gathering driftwood for the fire, patiently building the fire over several hours until red heat was attained, then burying the whole to cool down slowly. Most things came out broken, perhaps the result of contaminants that had not been fully removed from the clay, or just from building the fire too quickly. But a few pieces survived, charred black or gray-brown, and managed to cling to permanence. Success!

Tom went on to further studies – under more sophisticated circumstances – and earned a Master of Fine Arts degree, concentrating in ceramic. He has been teaching and creating with clay, now, for over twenty-five years.

*Tom's primitive "kiln" on the beach.*

*Carmen Beck at work with paint at age 5. Carmen personifies what Marge Roche said in her introduction to this section: At Palisades, "we are all artists."*

# The Palisades Park Patter
# Park Gossip Par Excellence

From the Patter, July 22, 1939: DOGGEY DAYS – OUR FIRST EDITORIAL AND IT'S GOING TO THE DAWGS — "Every day there are being registered, at this office and elsewhere, complaints about the newfound freedom being enjoyed by our canine pets. A Park rule that specifically states that all dogs be on leash at all times while in the Park is, this year, almost totally disregarded. Seriously and most emphatically, we urge that the Park ruling be accepted by all dog owners as a means of perpetuating this Park as a playground for children."

*Unidentified dog on beach.*

Thus began the Palisades Park newspaper – and the controversy over dogs on the beach, one which, like the Patter, appears every summer. Our Patter, which is now issued two or three times each summer, started in 1939 with "Strolling Through the Park" gossip nailed on trees. It quickly became a newspaper and has continued most summers since, with the exception of the 40's. Mary Lee Tillson, who – with Jayne Mathias – distributed that first gossip on trees – credits Tony Malinowski with starting the Patter. In her interview (printed elsewhere in full) she recalled:

"Tony Malinowski worked at the Lodge for several summers. I think he was a journalism major at Western Michigan, and he worked at the desk at the Lodge. Now I have no idea whether Mr. Quick ever hired him – I don't ever remember him as the director of anything. Well, maybe he ran the tennis tournaments. Somebody had to run them, and he was the type who liked to organize things. He was good at that. He was the one who started the Patter. Well, Jayne Mathias and I really started it. We used to just tack something up on a tree. We thought up "Strolling Through the Park." Then Tony decided it should be a little paper of some kind. He thought of the name "Patter." It was nothing like it is now; it was just a little gossip thing. It was fun."

*Tony Malinowski c. early 40's.*

Tony Malinowski, also interviewed, agreed with Mary Lee that "it was just plain fun." He remembered some of the items in the earliest issues:

"In 1939 I started the Patter with Jeanne Delamarter Best. In the original Patter, we wanted to feature special activities, like the Honor and Glory or some Clubhouse activity. The Patter still has the same opening page. I should have taken a copyright on that – I could've made a fortune by now, five cents a copy. It was just plain fun.

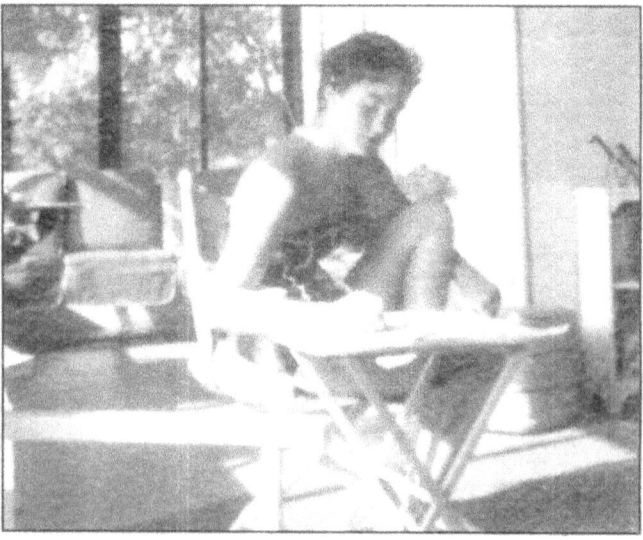

*Katy Beatty (Beck) working on the 1952 Patter, on Mrs. Bishop's porch.*

At first it was sort of a shopping guide and also a news item thing because some of these people didn't know where to shop. And I led them to Mackenzies Bakery. It was all typewritten. Homemade jobs. They looked like it too. I wasn't much of a typist. What was the Shakespeare quote that I revised in there? "What fools these mortals be." So for Mackenzies Bakery, I put down, "What foods these morsels be." I played on Shakespeare a little bit because a lot of these people were educated and college people. They kind of liked that. The purpose of the advertising was to tell these people where they could get some stuff. I wasn't promoting. I wasn't getting anything for 'em either. I just thought I'd help 'em out … and then announcing there'd be events."

From the beginning, quite a few people were involved. "Tony's Scrap Book" in the August 2, 1952 Patter, listed 12 workers from those early productions in the 30's: Mary Lee Cady (Tillson), Virginia Melchert (Coleman), Gilby Mehagen, Betty Muckenhirn, Carol Stone, Ray and Betty Lewis; Dorothy Hagie (typist), Harold Wilson and Joe Anlauf (salesmen), and Mr. Quick and Mrs. Frank Hagie (senior reporters). The grocery store was one of the early advertisers with the catchy blurb, "Bottom of the stairs but the tops in groceries." Another 1939 ad, for Julia Hill's Ice Cream Parlor, reveals the diversity of merchandise then sold: "Whether it's that 10:00 p.m. snack or a bottle of ink, come over to the soda fountain. They handle, in addition to all refreshments, magazines, sunburn aids, some drugs, and tennis balls. Come over whenever you have that yen for a ritzy sundae or for just a coke." (August 5, 1939 Patter) "Strolling Through the Park," 1939 style, included such delicious items as card parties, guests, the Lodge cook, cocktail parties, and even ghosts.

The post-War revival of the Patter, when a teenage staff, helped with a few adults, put out the paper from their office on the second floor of the garage, was "more of a paper," according to Tillson. "Oh, they were good, those Patters were," she continued. Indeed, the post-war Patter was quite an organization. For about four years in the early 50's, Helen Bishop was the advisor to the staff, then mainly teenagers who met in the very hot second floor of the garage. During this time, the teens wrote a ten-section constitution that covered everything from the sponsor, staff, closing hours, and use of keys, to the number of issues, care of equipment, financial records, and annual banquet. Just before Mrs. Bishop retired from position of advisor, she wrote a lengthy article for the August 27, 1955 paper. In it, she discussed subscription count (130) and sale of single copies, circulation editors and first issue salesmen, subscription price (25 cents per season – which included cost of postage) and generous benefactors. A banquet was held at the end of August when each member

*The garage with its upper room that served as the office of the Patter in the early 50's.*

---

(Incomplete) List of Patter Editors

Tony Malinowski (also 1st tennis pro) (1949)
Steve Anderson/Katy Beatty (1952)
Katy Beatty/Jack McDougal (1953)
Alice Beatty/Jim Roach (1954)
Nancy Merrell/Nancy O'Brien (1956)
Nancy O'Brien/Haven Best (1957)
Haven Best/Linda Gates (1958)
Sally Householder/Lambie Borchert (1959-60)
Linda Prange/Cathy Bishop (1961)
Grace Fidler (1964-65)
Louise Beyer (1970 and 1972)
Rick Schreiber (1971)
Betty Householder (1966-69;1973-1987)
Carol Beveridge/Sue Livingston (1981)
Carol Beveridge/Jayne Mathias (1982)
Carol Beveridge/Greg Boothroyd (1983)
Carol Beveridge/Mary Reed (1984-5)
Carol Beveridge/Jim Ellis (1986)
Sue Guirl/Cynthia Rudman (1987-1990)
Carol/Brad Bradford (1991-1992)
Doug Stewart (1993)
Tom Flynn (1994)
Lisa Beyer (1995-1997)
Bruce Beyer (1997)
Bob/Fran McCarthy (1998-1999)
Lori Dillman (2000)
Jim Ellis/Shelly Mason (2001-2003)

of the staff gave reports on the summer's work. The co-editor-in-chief was announced at the banquet, "in accordance with constitution regulations." Her article goes on as follows:

"In line with the general rotation of offices within the Park organization, the present sponsor will retire. Having been on the "ground floor" at the re-borning of the Patter in 1952, it has been a real privilege to stand by while the young folks have magnificently worked out its reorganization and stabilization. Its first editors, Steve Anderson and Katy Beatty (Beck), were followed the second year by Jack MacDougal and Katy. Last year Jim Roach and Alice Beatty took over, and this year Judy Kropp and Alice have headed up the work. From a very large number of the Park families have come the helpers whose names deserve to be recorded. They have either reported or written, typed stencils or mimeographed, stacked pages or stapled, delivered or mailed, collected or kept track of funds for your copies of the "little paper." The Patter created as a project for the young people and by the young people has certainly fulfilled that purpose. Their cooperation and development has been amazing – their achievements remarkable. We hope you agree that the second purpose of the newspaper has been fulfilled also, that of stimulating and uniting the Park residents in thought and interests – through the dissemination of news and ideas set forth in our simple, earnest style. These four years of the Patter's history can perhaps best be described by the word 'formative.'" The foundations have been laid, the pattern set. Now it is ready for 'growth.' We feel especially fortunate to announce that Mrs. Karl Anderson - with her experience in the writing field, her own beautiful creativeness, her love for this Park, her belief in the value of a newspaper as an instrument of progress, and her understanding of the age-group who man this project – will take over the sponsorship of the paper. Her capable guidance will foster that 'growth.'"

By the 60's, the teenage version of the Patter had ended and Betty Householder became editor, a position she kept for many years. She, too, remembered the heat in the office and the "old, messy mimeograph machine"

"In the old days, the teenagers ran the Patter. My daughter, Sally, ran it – let's see, I was just looking it up the other day – she ran it in '59 and '60. With Lamby Borchert and Linda Gates and, of course, they had that old mimeographing machine in their office in the garage. Oh, it was so hot. And they had to ink that machine and then they threw it in the Brandywine after Labor Day, to clean it off. Oh, it was a mess. It was really a mess. And they sold the Patter for five cents in the beginning. Now it's fifty. In the early days, you had to subscribe to the Patter. You didn't get one for free. A circulation director went out and took names. I was editor in 1960 and I remember, the year before I was, Mrs. Peirce and Mrs. Fidler were editors for two years and they sat down there in front of the store and took subscriptions. No, that's wrong. I wasn't editor until 1966. It's in the old history. Then, in 1970 I retired because we were going to go around the world on a trip. We had a big party and Pat Venner, who was in the jewelry business then, got a lovely aluminum pitcher which was engraved with my name on it and it said **"Patter from 1966-70."** Then, of course, since then, I have been doing it ever since."*

Since Betty's tenure, a number of changes have taken place, in the revolving list of editors, the new technology for printing, and the cover. But the spirit of the Patter remains unchanged. Mrs. Bishop said it well, when she identified the purpose as "stimulating and uniting the Park residents in thought and interests, through the dissemination of news and ideas." Yes, we'll admit to an occasional controversy amid the gossip and tennis coverage and ads – and yes, we'll suggest that sometimes even adult editors include occasional divisive comments, rather than seeking to "unite Park residents," – but even so, our little paper is anticipated and read eagerly each time it is published. For the most part, it has a history of which we can all be proud.

*Betty was editor until 1987.*

# *Palisades Park* PATTER

PALISADES PARK, MICHIGAN 49043

**48th Year**
**Annual Meeting Issue**

Issue #2
August 1989

*Crowd at the 1941 Half Mile Swim.*

*Forest Lowrey, who started the Annual Half Mile Swim.*

# A Race with a Purpose

*Since 1939, the Annual Half Mile Swim, originally called the Lake Marathon, has been a tradition at Palisades. Each summer, young swimmers try to prove their stamina by completing the course, and proud parents cheer them on. Often two or three competitive swimmers lead the field and vie for the trophy, but the emphasis has always been on durability, not speed. In the July 30, 1955* Patter, *Ruth Kropp remembered the origins of the swim as follows:*

Today is the glamorously exciting day of the one half mile Lake Marathon. The shoreline of Palisades Park, from Kropp's cottage at the south end to the Sturtevant Lodge, is marked off by red flags bobbing in the gentle waters of the rolling blue lake. (Oh, we do hope our crystal ball is correct in the predictions for warm water and smooth lake.)

Sixteen years ago (1939), Forest Lowrey originated the Lake Marathon with the prime idea of giving the children of Palisades Park the confidence and assurance of being able to swim one half mile. If, at any time, the occasion might arise where the young person would have to swim for some distance, he or she would be able, at least, to be calm till help would arrive.

Arthur Quick, Del Jones, Mrs. William Ward, George Bishop, Gilby Mehagan, Stewart Nelson, and Jack Ott worked with Forest as sponsors for the first lake swim. Leading the entire group of eighteen swimmers was George Rich, followed by Forest Lowrey's daughter, Weensie.

During the war years, like many other activities of our Park, the Marathon was postponed from year to year. Then, in 1952, Lowrey noticed there was an entirely new group of youngsters who had never had the opportunity to prove to themselves that they also were capable of swimming one half mile. So again the red flags were dusted off and anchored in the water along the half-mile course. The Coast Guard cutter with the snappy looking Coast Guard boys arrived at the south end of the Park, where the race started, and followed the swimmers to the finish line. Each contestant was followed by a hand-powered boat with a parent or friend to watch after the safety of the swimmers. The stopwatches were set to coincide at each end of the race. The red starting flag was up. The gun went off and the swimmers started at a good eager rate, but soon settled down to a more steady pace. The parents and friends on shore followed along the boardwalk, keeping pace with their own special contestant until they came to the porch of Sturtevant Lodge where the swimmers came ashore beaming though weary, to receive the prizes.

The boy and girl who came in first received the silver cup, on which their names were to be engraved. These cups they were to keep until the following year when they could again compete to win the race or pass the cup to the next year's winner. Every contestant in the race, no matter where or when he ended the race, received a medal to show himself that he really made an accomplishment worthy of a lifetime momento.

Because of the quiet, efficient way that Forest Lowrey has always run this Marathon, it is hard to realize how much actual time and correspondence has gone into the well planned, well organized swimming Marathon that he has sponsored from year to year. But we are all sure that the thrill our young people receive from their medals and the confidence they have attained for themselves will always be a special joy to Forest. And he will be remembered by the children as the man who proved they could really swim a half mile.

*Ruth Kropp hands Pete Hohman the trophy after the 1952 race.*

*In the ensuing years, many other volunteers have organized this annual event. The Coast Guard no longer joins us, but the children are still eager – perhaps too eager – to compete. As can too easily happen, the emphasis, for awhile, seemed to be on the medal, not the swimming, and for some of the children and their parents, the original purpose – to prove their ability to swim in difficult situations – got lost. However, the report of the 2001 race stated that all had finished and none had touched bottom, thus refocusing on Mr. Lowrey's intent.*

*Dwyer Roche starting the 1979 race.*

# Fishing

By Bill Potter

*Sixty plus perch caught in three hours
at Sturtevant Lodge piling.
Left to right: Jimmy Snow, Rev. Herman Potter, Claude Welles.
Summer 1936*

Seine some minnows out of Brandywine Creek with a fine mesh net, put them in a bucket of creek water to keep them alive, get your bamboo fishing pole with 15 feet of line, two hooks and a sinker, put it all in your boat or canoe, and head for the nearest remnant of pier piling between the first and second sand bars. That usually meant the old piling in front of Sturtevant Lodge. Bait the hooks with minnows, drop the line, feel the tug, and presto – one or two perch waiting to be pulled in.

Well, it wasn't always as good as in the picture, but from the 1910's to early 40's, perch fishing was good. And fishing was simple: no fishing license (Lake Michigan was controlled as federal water then, not State of Michigan), no fancy rods and reels or fish finders, no outboard motors, just oars or paddles. It is not the same anymore.

The lake has had to digest some unwelcome changes. Predators have invaded the lake via ship ballast water. Lamprey eels and alewives from the Atlantic and zebra mussels from the Black Sea in Europe have devastated the perch population by upsetting the food chain. Industrial pollution from mercury and PCB's killed commercial fishing completely by the mid-1970's.

Maybe some day perch fishing will improve again – or maybe not – but even if it does, it will never be the same. Today, fishing is high tech, with license, depth finder, fish finder, GPS locator, rod, reel, motor boat, boat slip or trailer, bait shop, live box – ad infinitum, hardly something for a boy and his dad to enjoy on a lazy afternoon. But we can remember and dream of those days gone by, when fishing was simple and perch fishing was good – very good.

*Don Johnson and Bill Potter perch fishing on the South Haven pier. 1935.*

*Fishing on the South Haven Pier. Note wooden walk to lighthouse.*

## Net Fishing

In the Palisades Park Review 1905 – 1968, Margaret Abbott, then of the Lehigh cottage (now Ryan's Grandpa's Beach #174) wrote:

> In 1926 the fishermen used to come and fish in front of our cottage. They had a big old wooden boat which they left on the beach. The fishermen would bring their families, and the men would row out and set their nets and the wives would cook their supper on the beach. I can still see that coffee pot cooking on the fire. Later, they would go out and bring in the nets. They caught many beautiful fish. They would always sell us a nice whitefish. Often I would have to get up in the middle of the night and go put out their fires.

Several years later, however, during the deep economic depression of the 1930's, net fishing took a more serious purpose of providing basic food for the table. In early evening, once a week or so, unemployed Covert area families would arrive at the Brandywine Beach in their old cars and pickup trucks to fish. If the lake was too rough, they would turn around; otherwise, they parked.

Their two wood spindle windlasses and wooden rowboat were stored high on the beach from week to week, but the net and lines were taken home for drying. After unloading the net, they placed the two windlasses at shore's edge, about 300 feet, and moved the boat to just in front of the south windlass. Then a 300 foot or longer rope line was tied to each end of the heavy and bulky net; net and lines were loaded into the boat. Before launching, they tied one of the line ends to the south windlass spindle, ready for later cranking in.

Two men handled the rowboat, one at the oars, the other at the stern, paying out line that was attached to the south windlass spindle at one end and to the net in the boat at the other end. After rowing straight out from shore until all 300 feet of the spindle line was out, they turned the boat north, parallel to shore. At this point, the stern man began paying out the net, while the boat moved northward. Floats attached to the top edge of the net and lead sinkers on the bottom edge kept the net in a vertical position, with the sinkers resting on the lake's sand bottom. When the net was all payed out, the boat then turned east, back toward shore, and the other windlass rope line payed out. Upon reaching shore, they tied the windlass line to the north windlass spindle. Then hand cranking began on both windlasses to slowly draw the net toward the shore. As cranking continued, the windlasses were gradually moved closer to one another in order to begin closing the ends of the net toward each other, to trap the fish within a circle of net. Except for squeaking of the windlasses, the families and onlookers usually grew quiet; idle conversations stopped in anticipation of what the net was bringing in.

Finally, after a half hour or so of laborious cranking, the ends of the net came together. A team of men at each end then dragged the net on shore, pulling hand over hand. If the tugging was hard and the water began jumping with fish, the catch was good. The families clapped and shouted. If not, the beach was quiet as the sweat of fruitless labor and empty baskets cast their gloom. But that was seldom.

By this time, the sun had usually set and it was dark. Kerosene lanterns were lit so the catch of perch, lake trout, whitefish, pike, catfish, and carp could be divided. If the

*Kay Welles, Bill Potter, Don Johnson, and George Potter on the Net Fisherman's rowboat on Brandywine Beach. June 1935.*

onlookers wanted to buy fish, the men were glad to sell; they divided the money. Then the windlasses and boat were moved and stored high up on the beach, the net was carefully rolled up, the lines coiled and loaded, and the lamps and beach fires extinguished. Fishermen and families slowly headed for home. Onlookers drifted back to their cottages under the canopy light of moon and stars. An ageless ritual had been repeated, almost like at the Sea of Galilee, some 2000 years ago.

## Spring Run of the Smelt

For many years, the annual spring run of smelt, up the Brandywine Creek, was the occasion of a community fish fest. Covert and surrounding area families would come to the mouth of the Creek for a nighttime ritual. Grandmothers tended fires as mothers cleaned and cooked the fish; children and men waded into the Creek armed with nets and buckets and scooped up the running smelt. Many Palisaders, arriving late at night for spring break and opening weekend, found Ravineway and the Circle lined with cars and the beach a scurry of activity. Unfortunately, some spring cottage break-ins cast suspicions on the fishermen – and our locked gate ensued. Recently, Cecil Burrous opined that the smelt were seeking warmer water as they turned into the Brandywine. Now, that warmer water is found in front of the Power Plant and the fish go there instead of up the Creek. Another tradition hit the dust.

## Salmon and Trout Fishing
*From the December 6, 1997, Park Manager's report:*

A man was arrested by Conservation Officer, Zachary Doss, in October, for catching an over limit of fish and possessing undersized fish caught in Brandywine Creek. The man was stopped as he was leaving the Park; he had a total of 11 salmon and trout. Possession limit is five. The arrest stemmed from a complaint that a week earlier, this same man caught 25 salmon and trout and left them along the bank to rot.

## The Latest Problem: Asian Carp
*The Winter, 2002, newsletter, <u>The Lake Effect</u> of the Lake Michigan Federation, reported:*

A new aquatic invader is eating its way north through Illinois and threatening to enter the Great Lakes via the Chicago River, and the last chance to stop them is just 30 miles from Lake Michigan. The newest, but certainly not last, biologic threat to the health of the Great Lakes is the Asian carp. These fish consume huge quantities of small plants and animals called plankton. Most Great Lakes fish rely on plankton as a food source at some point in their life cycle. In turn, small fish that feed on plankton provide food for large predators. A fish that decimates plankton populations could destroy the entire food web. An Asian carp invasion of Lake Michigan has potential to devastate our precious whitefish and yellow perch fisheries. It could turn the Great Lakes into giant carp ponds.

# 1930's By-Laws and Restrictions on the Land

In 1931, Arthur Quick's South Haven Palisades Park Company was changed to the Palisades Park Improvement Association, a "corporation not for pecuniary profit, organized on a non-stock basis" under the "General Corporation Laws of Michigan." Officers would be elected; Quick would be a member of the Board and serve as the Association President. He, in his role as President of the Company, would approve the plans for any cottages to be built, according to the restrictions running with the land. Possibly in 1939, the first elected president was George Duwe.

Article II of the 1931 By-Laws states the objects of the Association "for the general improvement of the entire Palisades Park property, specifically known as the FIRST, SECOND AND THIRD SUBDIVISIONS OF PALISADES PARK and LAKESIDE ADDITION TO PALISADES PARK." It would be responsible for "the maintenance of said tract as a high class private residence park, kept in good sanitary and park-like condition with such utilities, conveniences and services as are necessary and required by the members; the upkeep of such improvements as have been or may be made; adequate caretaker service; the eventual ownership of all the beach, parks, roads, paths, inland lake and stream, dam, bridges, harbor, buildings, tennis courts, and any other lands or property that may accrue to it by gift or purchase; the maintenance, extension and operation of the water system now turned over to this association; and when this association shall eventually become successor to the rights and property of the original South Haven Palisades Park Company it shall have the right to enforce the Restrictions now running with the lands in said park."

(Article III) "Every owner of property in said Palisades Park shall automatically become a member of this association, providing he has complied with all the requirements of this association and the Restrictions running with the Palisades Park lands. Each member shall be given a numbered Membership Certificate, signed by the President and Secretary, said membership being transferable only in the event of the member disposing of his property to an approved purchaser and in accordance with all the Restrictions running with the land." Although we do not have a list of the earliest numbers of the membership list, such names are being collected by Paul Schlacks.

Articles IV, V, and VI cover annual meetings, special meetings, quorum, voting by mail, election of 5 directors, and officers. It is here (Article IV Section 2) that we see that Arthur Quick remained firmly in control. "As stated in the original By-Laws of the South Haven Palisades Park Company, wherein provision is made for the maintenance of the Park property through the organization of this Improvement Association, it is provided that inasmuch as the said Company has the largest individual interest in the proper upkeep of the Park as a whole, therefore, as long as said Company is in legal existence the President of said Company shall also be the President of this Improvement Association, and have an equal voice and vote with any of the other four Directors to be elected annually."

Article VII, after discussing membership fees and the collection of dues, is specific about membership requirements in Section 5. "Realizing the paramount importance of protecting all our members against possible re-sales to undesirable residents by requiring all re-sales of Palisades Park property to be approved before the sale is closed (as to the qualifications of the proposed purchaser), by the approval officials appointed for the purpose, it is mutually agreed by and between all members of this association that each member in accepting membership binds himself, his heirs, administrators, executors and assigns to insert in all re-sale contracts he may make the following clause: *"This contract is made conditionally upon obtaining the **approval in writing** of the South Haven Palisades Park Company, its successors and assigns, as to the qualifications of the purchaser named herein, and failing to obtain said approval this contract shall be null and void, and any monies paid in by said purchaser shall be refunded to him.'*

"Each member of the Palisades Park Improvement Association, by the act of accepting membership, automatically agrees to honor, accept and pay, without contest, any judgment for damages that may be assessed against him by any court of justice for failure to comply with said re-sale requirements and all as stated in Covenant Number Eight (8) of the restrictions running with Palisades Park lands …."

## Section 7 of Article VII:
## "Restrictions Running with Palisades Park Lands:"

(1) That neither the said grantee nor heirs or assigns will use or permit to be used the said premises or any portion thereof for a boarding house, hotel, or for the keeping or sale of merchandise or for any purpose other than residence purposes only.

(2) Nor erect nor permit to be erected upon the said premises, or any part thereof, any store, shop, office or business building, barn or stable.

(3) Nor operate or permit to be operated any public ferry to or from said premises, nor conduct or operate or permit to be conducted or operated, any keeping or letting of boats or other means of transportation by water for hire.

(4) Nor sell or give away nor permit to be sold or given away upon said premises or any part thereof any spirituous or fermented liquors of any kind or description, nor permit the public drinking of any such liquors upon said premises.

(5) Nor permit any drain or sewer from said premises to be discharged in Lake Michigan nor into any of the waters within the boundaries of the Palisades Park tract.

(6) Nor erect or permit to be erected upon said premises any dwelling house costing less that $1500; nor erect or permit to be erected upon said premises any such dwelling house until the plans therefor have been submitted to and approved by the said South Haven Palisades Park Company, by its officers or agent duly authorized thereto; nor permit more than one dwelling house upon each lot.

(7) Nor permit any building to be erected upon said premises nearer to the established street line than the building line established by the said grantor, but this provision shall not apply to steps, piazzas, bay or oriel windows upon houses erected otherwise in accordance with these covenants.

(8) The said grantee further covenant and agree that _____ will not sell, lease or convey said premises to any other person, persons, corporation or corporations without first obtaining the approval in writing of the said grantor of such sale, lease or conveyance.

(9) The said grantee further covenant and agree that all arrangements for the disposal of sewage and garbage and for the sanitation of the premises hereby conveyed and the streets and alleys adjacent thereto shall be and remain under the control of the said grantor and that the said grantee and heirs and assigns will strictly conform to all reasonable rules and regulations respecting sanitation adopted by the said grantor, of which due public notice shall be given.

(10) It is further covenanted and agreed that the said grantee, heirs, administrators, executors and assigns, will pay annually in advance in January of each year, until 1960, to the said grantor, or its successors and assigns for the sole use of the PALISADES PARK IMPROVEMENT ASSOCIATION, the sum of $5.00 for the FIRST vacant lot herein described, or that it now or may hereafter be owned by said grantee in Palisades Park, and $1.00 per year per lot for all additional vacant lots after the first lot owned by said grantee; Provided, however, if said grantee owns one or more lots upon which residences have been built, then he shall pay $25.00 per year on each residence (figuring one residence to a lot) and only $1.00 per year on each additional lot that he may own that is vacant....It is further expressly covenanted and agreed by the parties hereto that the above covenants made and entered into by the said grantee, and each and everyone of them, shall run with the land and be binding upon all subsequent holders of said property, or any part thereof, until January 1st, 1960; except however, that any of the above covenants except that pertaining to the sale, gift, or public drinking of spirituous or fermented liquors may be altered or annulled at any time by written agreement by and between the said grantor, its successors or assigns, and the owner for the time being of the premises above described.

# Tony Canonie

*The obituary for Tony Canonie, in the August 10, 1998 South Haven Tribune, reads as follows:*

Tony Canonie, Sr. was born in Johnston, PA, the son of immigrant Italian parents. He attended Covert Schools. He married Marialyce Welsh during 1942 and had six children. He enlisted in the Seabees in Michigan in March, 1943, and served in Australia and New Guinea. He moved cargo ship-to-ship, overland to airstrips, and to supply depots. He also built roads and camps in the jungle. He was discharged from the Navy in November of 1945.

When he returned from World War II, he started a construction business with one truck and a bulldozer. In 1954, Canonie Construction Company was incorporated and moved to M-43 and Blue Star Highway. Canonie Construction Company grew throughout the years, completing over 160 miles of highways and more than 150 bridges, as well as piling driving, caisson installations, and power plant construction. During the 1970's, he acquired a marine construction business and a hydraulic dredging firm and created a marine transportation company. In 1980, he retired and his son became CEO of Canonie, Inc., the parent organization.

He had a wide range of interests from oil and gas exploration to thoroughbred horse racing and real estate holdings. He sat on the board of Citizens Trust & Savings Bank, belonged to the VFW and American Legion, and was a philanthropist to many community projects.

*A successful businessman, one of South Haven's leading citizens, Canonie once delivered ice to the vacationers at Palisades. Immediately after the War, he built at least one cottage in the Park and at least one seawall – both mentioned elsewhere in this volume. Apparently his first office was in the little gas station at the entrance to the Park. Forest Lowrey's interview tells more of the story:*

Tony Canonie initially handled the ice wagon. Everybody had to have ice. They had no electric refrigeration then…. They were here maybe twice a week. Tony had to carry the ice to the cottages on his shoulder. Where he couldn't get in by road, he had to go down the beach. By the time he got there, sometimes, they'd both be half melted, Tony and the ice. The kids would follow him, hoping he would chip some off, so he got acquainted with everybody. I don't remember how Charley Tunecke came into the picture, but pretty soon they – Tony and Charley - were working together. They did a lot of work and odd jobs for me and everybody else…. Charley was a pretty good carpenter and Tony did the hard work. And then, of course, Tony went to war. He was a member of the Seabees; he learned how to handle heavy machinery. When he came back, he bought a little bit of a bulldozer. It was only

*Park workers gathered at the Circle. Tony Canonie, Charley Tunecke, and Sam Canonie are probably 2nd, 3rd, and 5th starting at the left.*

about four feet wide. And that's the way he started in business. He did all kinds of jobs. In the early 50's, the beach got kind of bad and we had to do something about it. A guy came in, he was a real barnstormer and he was supposed to know something about seawalls. He didn't know anything, but no one noticed it, so he convinced us he could put in a wooden seawall. Tony Canonie had great ambitions and he went to work for this other man. Before he was half done, Tony was running the whole thing, doing more than the other guy did. Tony was just a natural at that kind of thing. So you all know the story about Tony. He's the biggest earthmover in the United States.

*Tony Canonie certainly made a memorable mark on early Palisaders. Almost everyone interviewed who was in the Park before he went into the Seabees remarked upon this young man who started so humbly and whose career led him to immense success.*

# Interviews

## Connie Borchert

Interviewed by Katy Beck
September 17, 1984

I was about eight years old when we first came to Palisades, but, you see, Mother had come here all her life. She was born in Oak Park, Illinois, and came up here as a child. She had relatives in South Haven, and they had a cottage down the beach where the State Park is now. She and her brother used to come down here, when the Clubhouse was still on the beach, and go to dances and hayrides and buggy rides. She knew Vashti Ward and Ernie Wunsch. I'd say that was between 1910 and 1915. She got to know the area, and I think that's why she and Father finally wound up here. They didn't want us around the Chicago area during the summer. Dad courted her up here. She was married by the time she was 19.

I was raised on the beach in South Haven. We'd stay in a hotel or we'd rent a little cottage there. Then we started coming here. One year we couldn't rent the cottage we wanted, so Father got mad and he bought it. We'd stay for the whole summer. Mother and Father just didn't want to be bothered with all the social stuff in the city. Mother was involved in our community but summer was the time she could get away.

We bought the Harding cottage from Marion Harding. The cottage at one time was on the other side of the Brandywine, and in one of the storms, it fell into the lake. They pulled it up on this side. (Now cottage #39.) There were pictures, somewhere, of it in the lake. It was where Malablocki is going to build. (#190)

Father never liked the other end of the Park. I shouldn't say he didn't like it, but this was his end and he wanted to be in this end. You couldn't see this end of the Park at all. There were very few cottages down here. Father liked the corner by the Brandywine. He liked the freeness and the openness of it. He liked this whole area and, as I said, a lot of people didn't know this end was here. They'd get down as far as the garage and not notice the road going around the garage. The Wunsches owned the cottage the Colemans are in now (#45). His sister owned it and they would use it occasionally. Then they bought the McCarthy cottage (#49). Some of these cottages have long, long histories.

They let the Brandywine go and it got to be a mess. It had all sorts of snakes and such. Dad was instrumental in making a meadow out of it. He was going to put the lake back in, but when it came to putting a new bulkhead down by the bridge, it was just too expensive, and he said it wasn't deep enough anyhow, so he just made a meadow out of it. A lot of people didn't want that done, but now that they've got the meadow, they think that's just great. Some wanted it left alone, but it was really a jungle. This was about 25 or 30 years ago. There were frogs, toads, snakes – some said we had bears down here, too. Give me a break! Father thought the mosquito breeding could lead to disease. I think he hoped to dig it out and see what was there. Of course, in those days people came up here because they couldn't afford to go anyplace else. They couldn't afford to put money into an operation like turning the meadow into a lake.

*Connie Borchert and her mother, Marion Lowrey. 1951.*

When you look at some of the cottages people lived in, you wonder how they ever managed. But they were happy; they were out more than they were in, so they didn't need much. I guess Mr. Quick wanted to make it sort of an art-type colony, but that never worked out. The older people brought their kids, and their kids brought their kids, and finally it has evolved into what it is today. I keep looking back to when I was a girl, and there were so few cottages here, I knew everybody in the Park. Now, I don't know anybody, so to speak. Oh, I know a lot of people to speak to, but at that time I knew everybody. Of course, our main groups were here, and when we first came we were told that our beach was right down in front of our cottage, so people didn't go down to the Brandywine if they lived on the south end. If you were near the Clubhouse, you used that beach. But that's all changed now. Because there's no beach!

Another change that's happened in the Park, nowadays all the mothers work so they're not here as a group, or the family isn't up here all summer. So they really don't get to know anybody. Maybe they're here for two weeks and then their time is up and they have to leave. Or maybe they're just here for weekends, which is tough. Whereas, we had the whole bloomin' summer.

I can remember having parties in the house. Mother wouldn't let us go out, so all the kids would come down to our house and we'd do jigsaw puzzles, or Weensie would play the piano and we'd all sit around or, on rare occasions and with Mother as chaperone, we'd go to the movies.

Our biggest event was going out of the Park into town, maybe once a week, to do the grocery shopping. In the afternoons, we'd play on the beach. When we got to be teenagers, we'd play football. Weensie and I were the only girls allowed to play because we were tough. The rest of the girls had to sit on the sidelines and watch – we had a ball. The Hammerschmidts and our family would come up over Washington's birthday for a couple of days; sometimes we'd stay in St. Joe. We'd come here and spend the day. It was marvelous. We had a lot of fun. That was, of course, when we were older. My sister and Chuck Hammerschmidt and another friend and I had a playclass and that took the place of activities at the Clubhouse. We did that for about three years. We'd pick the kids up and take them to the beach. If it was a rainy day, we'd keep them here in Mom's basement. They ranged in age from about five to whenever they would get bored with it.* The Clubhouse in those days was actually more for adults. They used to have bridge parties and dances and things like that.

*The earliest issue of the Patter, July 10, 1939, listed the enrollees in this Play School as Barb and Ben Bishop, Charles Muckenhirn, Sonny Neilson, Johnny Underwood, Judy Best, Jackie Bower, the Hawkins kids, Peter Wunsch, Ray Lewis, and Jackie Draper. Many of them still have family cottages in the Park. According to the Patter, the children "built sand castles, played with toys, and listened to stories. Some of the older children had instruction in canoeing and swimming, took hikes, and had camp-outs. On rainy days everyone went up to the Palisade Park Clubhouse to play pingpong and other indoor games. A small fee of 25 cents a morning or $1.00 a week was charged."

Mouth of the Brandywine showing the Lowrey cottage #39, before the installation of metal seawall.

The Patter was started by Tony Malinowski. He was a Covert boy (working in the Park). That Patter went on until the WWII. It was just a gossip sheet. It was a fun sheet, only a page or two long. Now it's gotten to the point where, with all the ads in it, it's different. It's still fun, but not as much fun as it was then. Kids got involved in it, and after the war, they put the Patter office up on the second floor of the garage. Oh, it was hot in that garage. I can remember being up there with Lambie when she was doing it. She and Linda Gates, I think, did it one year. They worked until three in the morning, putting the darn thing together. Then the kids started taking it over and running it, and now it's involved with the adults. And older adults, I may say. Kids just don't seem interested in doing that kind of thing. The gossip items were half the fun of the Patter. Now it's a group here and a group there – If they could get one person out of each group to write up a little something about what their group is doing, it would make it interesting.

I happened to be here when the plane went down and they cordoned off the whole beach. Once, some silly men left Chicago in a sailboat and got up this far and hit a storm. They anchored the boat out there and one of the men got terribly sick. One of our boys went out and got one of them. He almost died; he almost drowned. They finally beached the boat in front of the Brandywine. The men walked away from it and never wanted to see it again, so we were all delighted. Oh, we've got a prize here! But they came back and took their boat – second thoughts, I guess. I remember the good times, like going to the Crystal Palace at Paw Paw, where they had all the big name bands. That would be a big night out. We'd have dances up at the Clubhouse, such as they were, and we'd have Bunco; mostly it was just family more than anything else. Most of our fun was here in the Park, at the tennis courts or the beach. Tennis was the social meeting place for teenagers, where the parents weren't. Every night after supper, we'd walk the dogs all around the south end of the Park. That's when we smoked our cigarettes so our parents wouldn't know. What a joke! They knew everything. We thought we were so smart. We were at the south end quite a bit. One time, I found a path behind Dr. Mason's place that went all the way to Linden Hills without getting on the road. I knew this Park backwards and forwards at one time. Nothing ever had a name. They were just trails. Of course, when you see Mr. Quick's map and see that he had roads that were named, that's interesting too.

Father ran the swim race for many, many years. His object was for kids to know they could swim a half mile. If they got into trouble they would have confidence to swim into shore. That was his whole reason. It has sort of lost its purpose now. In fact, the half-mile swim is no longer a half mile. Nobody could do it in that time. Not only that, the kids are not always swimming now. I just don't even go down there anymore, because the kids are walking. I've seen them. It's cheating. I don't know why they even run it. Father wouldn't have the race if the Coast Guard could not be here. Every person who entered the race had to have a boat, and they were not in water where they could stand. They had to be out in deep water – that's why the boats. If something happened to a child, he could be hauled out of the water. The Coast Guard really added to the excitement. We'd stand down by the water and shout, "Here comes the Coast Guard" like two-year-olds. It was great. I'm sorry to see that dwindle down.

Father was active in a lot of things. When all this property was for sale around here, he didn't want to let it get into hands that would take it over and do damage to the atmosphere of the Park. So he and some others – called the Nine Old Men - bought it all up. They were the ones that parceled it all out and saw to it that the people coming into the Park would take care of it. Things like that. He was very active when they started the government of the Park. I think he was the 3$^{rd}$ or 4$^{th}$ president. And then he did the meadow and built extra tennis courts and replaced the broken-down bridge out there. He loved it up here. Father was never one to sit around. He put on tacky clothes and a funny hat and he was out and digging.

I have a picture of Mr. Shepherd. He'd come to the door with fresh vegetables and milk and stuff like that. When he'd arrive everyone would shout, "Oh, Jesus is at the door." He had a long beard and all. The Hempys would come around with the garbage wagon. He had a barn out in the woods for keeping his horses. A nice old man – they were both nice, cheerful people – Mother always had a good word for them. I could never forget Tony Canonie carrying the ice. And Charley Tunecke was always around, and Rudy Weber – those old people who worked around here – Dave VanderBoegh's grandfather used to work with Rudy. Joe Putz: you couldn't ever forget Joe Putz! He did odd jobs. If we had plumbing problems, he'd come in, get out a cork, and put it in the

*Forest Lowrey starting the Half-Mile Swim*

hole. He was something else! But he did some magnificent handiwork, carving – woodcarving – and I don't know where that has all disappeared to. He was just a generally nice guy, but he had a sister, Mary, who was a little bit different. I think people who knew the Putzes took care of Mary when Joe died. She really was kind of different. She was warm. One time she was playing with a child out in the water and people thought she was drowning the child, but she wasn't of course, just playing. My memory of her was she wore about five dresses at once, one on top of the other. She had the layered look before it became popular!

Jimmy Overhuel ran the gas station many years ago and his mother, Mrs. Overhuel, ran the store. We couldn't get as much then as we could later, when Helen Packard was there. When Helen was there, we could always go down and order for a week ahead. She'd go to town and get our order and store it for us all week, so we could run in and say, "I want my pork chops for today." She really worked hard. Didn't the Knapps live in the filling station for awhile, and run it? When they took the filling station out, that broke my heart. We could fill our cars up and whoever was running it would take my car and service it for me - the whole bit. It was nifty; spoiled me rotten. For awhile, whoever ran it made the station into a vegetable stand; then it just folded. Then I guess Fred Nichols took it over.

Del Jones ran the Lodge. On Sunday nights, Mother would make us get all dressed up in the best things we owned up here and take us down to the Lodge for dinner. It was awful; it was horrible. Everybody was down there. We'd sit and glower at each other from table to table, wishing we could get the heck out of there. It was too formal and too hot. There was no air conditioning. However, the food was good. Blanche was a good cook; she worked hard at that place. She was quite a jolly woman and a very good baker. The food she put out was out of this world. Her kitchen was well run. One time, Del had a slot machine in the office, remember that? A nickel machine, a one-armed bandit. Oh, that was fun.

*The old dining room at Sturtevant Lodge.*

That was when I was about 18. I loved to pull the lever and watch the fruit come up. However, it was confiscated. One night we were playing it and the police came in. Here were all our nickels in the machine and they said it was illegal, so they took it away. But that was fun.

There was an old Italian couple that used to come to the hotel. She used to play the piano and he was an operatic singer. Every once in awhile, our mother would let us go down to the hotel and listen to her play the piano and him sing. That was a big night out. That was fun, too; they were an awfully nice couple. Later, the hotel business dwindled off. They just couldn't keep the place going. It was just running down so badly. It's too bad, a shame, but that's progress as usual.

In 1941, more tennis courts were built on the north side of the road. I think they added four courts. That year Palisades Park entered the Kalamazoo tennis meets. Dad

ran an Open that drew people from all around. He invited Bob Arkins from South Haven. I have a newspaper article that says that Bob Ott and George Bishop of Palisades beat Arkins and someone from Kalamazoo. I was really rotten at tennis and, in the draw tournaments, I'd often get all these good tennis players. They were very, very nice to me.

I miss some of the old things, like Ballou Inn and people staying there. I always had nightmares about the Inn, kept thinking those upstairs rooms would be all spooky and full of ghosts. It always looked so forbidding from the outside. The upstairs was a hotel and the downstairs the store and post office. The highlight of the day was running down to get the mail, twice a day. Mary Jane and Bud Hill ran the soda fountain for awhile, before Julia Quick. That would be in the early 30's. It wasn't called the Soda Bar then, just an ice cream parlor or something equally old fashioned. I used to go in there after tennis and I'd make Mary Jane so mad – I'd order a nickel's worth of ice cream and a nickel's worth of soda and put them together. Mary Jane would say, "You can't do that; I charge 15 cents for that!" And I'd say, "Why not?" She'd say, "Because I do that and I charge 15 cents for it!" Later, the Sankeys ran the Soda Bar also. They were the ones who instigated the hamburger end of it. Before that, it was always just an ice cream parlor. After the Sankeys, the Neubauers were in there, and the Roaches. I remember that old porch – we'd go sit on the porch and watch - sort of rubberneck - what was going on in the Circle.

Things have changed in the last twenty years. Kids are older than we were at the same age. They are doing things now that we weren't allowed to. If we smoked a cigarette, we were royally tanned. And we didn't have the availability of cars, either. Mother was very strict; she didn't let us out of her sight. Today the parents come up here for their own fun and let their kids run wild, and don't know half the time what they're doing because they are out somewhere. They go out to dinner and off to a movie and leave their kids to their own devices. I think the kids are left alone too much. The place has changed. Our folks knew what we were doing and why. Even boys had to check in. The curfew was eleven at the latest. Even on weekends. After we had a family, we'd start our beach fires about 6:00 and feed our kids down there and bring them home and put them to bed. Then we'd go back. The beach fire would always be close enough so that we could go check on them every half hour or so, to see they were in bed and not in trouble. They never knew when we were coming back, so they didn't dare sneak out. Nowadays parents just don't seem to check on their kids. Maybe I'm wrong. It is very different, but we have a lot more cottages here than there used to be and a lot more people. Gee, if we could get 20 people together to play football, we were lucky. And that was all the kids in the Park who were old enough.

Palisades is my home address, but I go out to Arizona to be with Dad in the winter. Bob and I stayed here about 12 years, year around, but when he died I couldn't handle it alone. Pat Roche stays here all winter. For awhile there were quite a few staying – about seven families - but all of a sudden we're losing that. Well, people can't take the cold anymore; we're getting older. When we were here in winter, if we saw someone we were absolutely amazed. But then people started coming up here to cross country ski. How they stay in their cottages, I don't know, with no heat or plumbing. But now there are quite a few come up every weekend.

## "Partial Memories of Days Gone"
Written By Connie Borchert

Memories of Palisades Park? How does one explain the enchantment, the spell, the magic that brings a person back to fairyland year after year? You don't. You just remember that the summers seemed long and lazy, yet ever too busy!

We, as children, often heard about her little cabin "up the beach" and many times we'd walk the beach and visit it in its tumbledown state to see the "board" where all the visitors carved their names. Oh, how Mom wanted that board – but it was not to be. They finally burned the place down. Mom told of the many times she and Uncle Med would come down here to Palisades Park for dances at the Clubhouse which, at that time, was on the beach. They would meet Vashti Blaney and Marian Ward and Ernest Wunsch and many others.

The long ago memories of Palisades Park are mighty hazy, but the long afternoons on the beach, the herons feeding at the Brandywine at dawn, the walks in the woods after supper, and the occasional trips into town for a day of re-supplying the cottage are among the highlights of these pre-teen days. South Haven seemed another world!

I remember the occasional big Sunday night dinner at the Lodge. We'd dress to the nines (after complaining about having to come up from the beach early) and be there promptly at 6:30. There we'd see the Hagies, the Wunsches, the Wards, the Melcherts, and most of our assorted friends, as well as the Hotel guests. Fun, but also a bore at that age, as we were anxious to get on with the evening activities – such as Del Jones's nickel "one-armed bandit" which was confiscated one night as we were playing it. Then there was always the treat of dropping by the Ice Cream Parlor for ice-cream on the

*Winter on the Palisades Park beach.*

porch – where on occasion we could watch the antics of three Mooney boys at the windows of their rented rooms in the Hotel. A big event was the twice daily trip to the Post Office to pick up the mail and get milk, eggs, and fresh vegetables as well as catch up on the neighbors' news.

As we grew older, we took up tennis and that became the meeting place (always at 10:00 a.m. promptly) for the gang. There we'd plan out the activities for the rest of the day and afterwards drift down to the Ice Cream Parlor (run by Julia Hill and her children, Mary Jane and Bud), for a quick Coke before lunch. The afternoons were usually spent playing touch football on the north side of the Brandywine and we usually could muster up a good two teams with a few replacements. (You must remember that those many years ago there weren't very many cottages in the Park and not many south-siders even knew there was anything beyond the Ballou Inn, the Garage, the Ice Cream Parlor, and the Hotel.) By that time, Mr. Quick's dream of a lake had become clogged with willow trees and other wildlife and obscured the Brandywine from the main road.

The teen years were fun - tennis, the beach, and a gathering at our house for sing-alongs, jigsaw puzzles, and all sorts of games (Mother always talked about the 125 cases of Cokes she went through in one year) – but mainly the entertainment was in the house. Oh, yes, on occasion we'd go to a movie in Bangor or South Haven or to the free shows over in Covert; and the big events were the big name bands over at Crystal Palace on beautiful PawPaw Lake or a trip up to Saugatuck to visit what is now The Crow's Nest for dancing and a beer or two (very daring). Mostly, though, we stayed in the Park and made our own entertainment. A favorite was a late swim; how exciting it was when there was a storm brewing. In those days, who had ever heard of TV? Radio was a big thing with the boxing matches a highlight and the Allstar football games occasions for a gathering of friends for a football party.

Somewhere along in the mid-thirties, Tony Malinowski came into our lives with a smattering of tennis and a great knowledge of keeping the three courts in shape. At that time the Patter was born. What a fun sheet it was – gossip and more gossip. And Tony was its first parent. It was only a typewritten two page "rag" at first and was put out in the basement of our cottage once a week. During the years of the 2$^{nd}$ World War, the Patter was dropped but it came back into existence, at Tony's insistence, with the aid of Helen Bishop as backer and mentor.

The Patter office moved to a room over the garage where there was a rickety old printing press, and the teenagers took the responsibility of collecting news items and printing it. It grew each year, until finally the teenagers didn't want the responsibility any more and "Grandma" Bishop turned it over to the adults. Thank you, Betty Householder, for your many years of devotion and thanks to the rest of you who have made that baby called the Patter what it is today.

The thirties saw big changes in the Park. I believe we installed our first Park President and had a governing board, all with the sanction of that stern old founder of the Park, Mr. Quick - Mr. Quick who wanted this place to be a sanctuary for the arts – another Saugatuck or Interlochen. How we kids loved to irritate poor, proper, prim Mr. Quick. If he wanted the spill gates up to drain Lake Palisades, we'd make sure they were down, and vice versa. He finally tried chaining them in position, but we'd hacksaw the chains. But with all our impishness, our pranks were never malicious. He would forgive us, but give us that impressive cold look that scared us to death but didn't stop us. Only coming before the Board made us think twice before we committed some other prank to get his goat.

Then there was Joe Putz, who was a "jack of all trades." The Hempys collected garbage twice a week with their horse-drawn cart and on those days one could find Mrs. Hempy sorting through the mess to bring out a discarded treasure or two – a busted lamp, a broken chair, or what have you. They owned the Court House #61. Joe was the one whom you'd call to repair the plumbing or do odd jobs of maintenance around the Park. To mend a broken pipe, all he needed was a cork of the right size and it was fixed! He'd guard the entrances to the Park and did some very fine primitive carving. His sister, Mary, was the inventor of the "layered look," but even with her odd assortment of clothing, she was fairly good with children and scrubbed a wicked floor. Joe with his withered arm and Mary with her withered mind. Fond memories of the past.

Back then (in my teens), the Clubhouse was run by Mardy and Gilbey Mehagan and their two sons. There would be bridge for the ladies one afternoon a week. There were fashion shows at least once a season and occasional dances with a real, live band. But the Thursday nights of Bunco for the kids, run by Mrs. Ward, were the most fun; the prizes always made a great hit. Now I can't even remember how to play Bunco, but I do remember that the winners were always the same guys! Did they cheat? They'll never tell!

## Esther Brand and Peg Ingles Brand

Interviewed by Betty Householder
August 30, 1984

I first came to Palisades Park in the mid-30's when we rented Clint Brae. We had to bring all of our luggage by wheelbarrow from the parking lot. We all took turns pushing the wheelbarrow. In those days, we stayed for the whole summer.

We built our own cottage in 1948. My husband, an architect, made the plans. He wanted Rudy Weber to build the cottage but Rudy was busy so we imported a builder from 30 miles away. In those days, they let you build during the summer. George Boyles had just built next door when we started. This lot had been kept for a hotel site for many years; when we were looking for a place, the lot just happened to be released for sale. So that's how we got this choice spot. Then they thought they would build a hotel below the reservoir, but they never got around to doing that. We think the biggest improvement we have made was to enclose our porch. We used to have those big awnings that we had to roll up and down. At one 4th of July family reunion, we put nine people on the porch and put the blinds up and down for sleeping. When the bad weather came, it was a real nuisance to put down the awnings; they made the porch dark while the winds blew the canvas. Now we just live out on the porch.

We love the water. At first we had a wide beach, with another lot on the lake in front of our cottage. However, we have since built two or three walls to protect the beach. Tony Canonie put in the first one, of wood. The next was a cement wall. Now we've had to put riprap in front of the cement. We think that has helped. We enjoyed walking to the North Beach and picnicing. In fact we used to do that almost every day. We had a little boat that we built from a Chris Craft kit; we took that down the beach with supplies for our picnics. Some of the family even camped over night on the beach down there. That was the meeting place of all the gulls and we enjoyed it very much. I think it's a shame that the power plant went in at that lovely spot.

Whenever I was at the Park, I liked to play for the Sunday night services at the Clubhouse. Mrs. Dinsmore was in charge of the services.

*Plaque honoring Arthur Quick.*

My husband designed the plaques of Mr. Quick that are around the Park. He was on the Board with the Pranges and Westons. We enjoyed all the people on it – the Goodriches and the owners of the Ark, the Welleses. We'd do quite a bit of socializing with all the couples.

Joe Putz did odd jobs for us. For years and years, we saved a little wooden Pinocchio that lost its nose – we were always going to have Joe put a new nose on Pinocchio. He made those little square wooden pictures during the winters, with people and furniture in them. We knew he was good.

Last year I had a nice visit with old Mrs. Sarno. She has a wonderful outlook on life – quite a character. Her son told us that one of her children was born in the blueberry patch. Her children have been active in Covert and have done a good job in leadership. I used to get eggs from a lady on the Covert road – Margaret was her name. She did our laundry for us too. I remember her telling about her silo being struck by lightning. A bull was killed too. She had so little money that it seemed sad. She was a sweet person.

I remember Mrs. Ruthie Erickson, from LaGrange, in the last cottage on the beach before the walk up to the dunes. She was a character. We had fun with her. She had a wonderful sense of humor. I think her cottage was hit by lightning twice. Once it came through the corner of the cottage – in one corner and out the other. There was a hole right through. It must have been the Campbell cottage #171. When we were here a couple of years ago, we had a big storm and a tree came down and hit our electrical wire into the cottage. It was flashing – trees were down all over the place. We had to have the fire department here to take care of the wire. The Owenses came out and they knew the thing to do was to throw sand on that kind of arcing electricity. That was very frightening.

*Bill Ingles, Bill Brand, Esther and John Brand. 1947.*

---

Reflections of the Family Cottage On Lake Michigan

The wind is blowing,
The waves are rolling,
A restless world at sea.

But, oh, how soothing,
How fast I'm losing
The cares that bother me.

A place for dreaming,
Like almost seeming
This day will always be.

I'll soon be going,
But peace is knowing
There is this place for me.

By J. F. R.
June 30, 1983 Patter

*Forest Lowrey, age 90, in 1985.*

# Forest Lowrey with Weensie Lowrey Bishop

Interviewed by Katy Beck
September 7, 1985

The first time I was in Palisades Park was in 1913 and 1914, before Mrs. Lowrey (Marion Skinner) and I were married. Her mother had a cottage about two miles north of here, opposite a public park there, just off of Route 31. I came over by boat. I'd never been here before and my instruction was to take the Fruit Belt Line, which was the name of the railroad, at the pier out of South Haven. Every morning a passenger train went out from the pier to Watervliet. I was to stay on the train until I got to a certain road, get off at that road, and follow right to the lake. If I remember, the place that we went to was a farm that had access to the lake. Then I walked down the beach. That was as close as I could get. There were no roads cut through to the lake.

Marion came over to South Haven as a baby, before she could walk, and that's how they came to build that cottage.

*The Fruit Belt Line train.*

They could also get to the cottage from the road through the woods in a public park. They had to carry everything in. When they went to town, they made a deal with the farm to have them fix up the hayrack and haul them in. They'd do their marketing and come back and have that toted in from the farm. They had a pump halfway up the hill and that's where they got their water supply.

For lack of something to do, we walked up to Palisades Park that year. They had a hanging bridge over the Brandywine. There was no access across the Brandywine except by that hanging bridge. That's how we got over. Sturtevant Lodge was running at that time. The Ballou Inn was a hotel. They would take roomers. A soda fountain was at the Ballou Inn. We had just enough money to get a couple of soda waters. We stayed at Marion's folks' cottage before and after we were married.

We didn't come up more than a half dozen times altogether in the teens, because we had to get up here by car by way of Valparaiso and Watervliet and Paw Paw. It was 200 miles from Chicago up here. There were sand roads; you'd get punctures and have to fix 'em. The first time we drove

*The "hanging bridge" over the Brandywine - usually called the "swinging bridge." Cottage #19 in back.*

up here, we left Chicago at 5:00 in the morning and got up here at 9:00 at night. We came to St. Joe by ferry a couple of times, with the car. Every one of these ports along here, starting with St. Joe, had overnight service to Chicago by ship, in the summer months. There was fruit and produce grown all along here, and those boats would haul that back and haul people up here, particularly on weekends. Then they had train service to this little town over here, Bangor. Of course, it was just sand roads from there to the Park – that's all there were. The roads were conducive to punctures. You had to take the casing off the rim, the inner tube out, and patch it. You did that right on the road.

And then, when we had a family – we had three little girls – we came up here, in 1933 as I remember, and stayed over night here at Del's Hotel. We had a cat and dogs we had to leave in the car. But cars in those days weren't closed; they had isinglass curtains, like the old carriages, that snapped all around. We had come over on the boat to St. Joseph. We rented the cottage for a week (the one I later sold to Jack Anderson) and that cottage had been in the lake. It was originally on the north side of the Creek. They had the high water in 1928, I believe. They towed the cottage back in and rebuilt it where it stands now. It wasn't in very good shape, but it did have a bathroom, which was quite unusual in those days. There was a septic tank and kerosene stove. When we went home in the winter, we had to put shutters on or the place would be blown to pieces.

In 1934, the next year, we rented from Mrs. Harding for a month. In 1935, I wasn't very smart and didn't rent beforehand. We came up and Ernie Wunsch had rented the cottage ahead of me. I was disgusted. So that fall, since the family liked it so well, and of course Mrs. Lowrey loved it – she'd been up here since she was a baby, you know – before Wunsch could get ahead of me, I made a deal with Mrs. Harding. I paid her half again as much as it was worth for the summer, the amount to be applied to the purchase price we had agreed upon at that time, $4500.

There are two reasons I didn't buy it right at the time. One was money; it was scarce in those days. Also, there were two lots in front of us and I didn't want the cottage without those two lots; if someone built there, that would have barred the view. They <u>would</u> have built there, too –

*Marion Lowrey, two Bruninga children and Mrs. Bruninga. 1937.*

Mr. Quick would have sold to anyone with the money. I knew if I went to Quick for the lots, I would have to pay the top price. We knew Al Dubuisson in South Haven, so I talked to him. He said, "I'll buy those lots for you; they aren't worth $10 apiece." So he kept trading and finally got Mr. Quick down to $1100 for the two lots. I said, "Buy 'em, Al," and sent him a check. He said, "You're crazy; that's nothing but a sand dune and that's all it ever will be. They aren't worth $10 apiece." I said that if they build on them by the lake, we'd lose our view and that's the only reason I'm up there. So we bought them. We moved in in 1936. By that time, my older daughter married, got pneumonia, and passed on, so she never got there after we owned the place. Weensie was 13.

One Sunday the girls went swimming. I went to sleep on the couch and while I was sleeping, the girls painted my toenails with nail polish. So 5:00 Sunday night, I was due to be home early the next morning for work. They didn't have anything to take that paint off of my toes. I forgot it until I got home. I got up in the morning and thought, "Boy, what if I get hit with a cab." That went on for a week! I'd get up every morning and see my toes, then forget them during the day. By Friday night, when I returned to Palisades, they were still laughing about it. Of course, they had nail polish remover all the time. They let me suffer for a week.

*Tony Malinowski*

Tony Malinowski was the one who started the <u>Patter</u> in the late 30's, with help from Helen Bishop. He started it in our basement, in a little room down there. He lived over near Covert. He was a Polish boy, of course, and he'd be out here. He'd hang out, always hungry, and Mrs. Lowrey would feed him. He worked hard for an education. He wanted to write. I think he coined the name "The Park <u>Patter</u>." Later, Helen Bishop or Betty

Householder had it copyrighted, I believe. But I give him credit for starting it. Later, they had this little office in the top of the garage. Oh boy, was that hot! You had to go up there and strip down to live. I stuck my head up there one time. I didn't even climb the last step.

Tony Canonie initially handled the ice wagon. Everybody had to have ice. They had no electric refrigeration then. Old man Shepherd peddled milk here because the store didn't handle it. As I said, there was no refrigeration. They were here maybe twice a week. Tony had to carry the ice to the cottages on his shoulder. Where he couldn't get in by road, he had to go down the beach. By the time he got there, sometimes, they'd both be half melted, Tony and the ice. The kids would follow him, hoping he would chip some off, so he got acquainted with everybody. I don't remember how Charley Tunecke came into the picture, but pretty soon they were working together. They did a lot of work and odd jobs for me and everybody else. Charley Tunecke was eight months older than me. He knew every inch of this Park.

Charley was a pretty good carpenter and Tony did the hard work. And then, of course, Tony went to war. He was a member of the Seabees; he learned how to handle heavy machinery. When he came back, he bought a little bit of a bulldozer. It was only about four feet wide. And that's the way he started in business. He did all kinds of jobs. In the early 50's, the beach got kind of bad and we had to do something about it. A guy came in, he was a real barnstormer and he was supposed to know something about seawalls. He didn't know anything, but no one noticed it, so he convinced us he could put in a wooden seawall. Tony Canonie had great ambitions and he went to work for this other man. Before he was half done, Tony was running the whole thing, doing more than the other guy did. Tony was just a natural at that kind of thing. So you all know the story about Tony. He's the biggest earthmover in the United States.

The wooden wall didn't hold up. The wood wall went from just here to the Brandywine. Del Jones was so tight, he wouldn't pay for anything. The Pranges were the next cottage, so we had to bring the wall to the south side of the Prange property.

Later, when the beach really got bad, we had to put the metal wall in. Tony did that and he did a great job, I thought. That was from the Prange cottage all the way around here to the back end of my corner cottage. Hammerschmidt wouldn't pay for anything. He didn't believe in that. Because we were in front of him, we were the ones at risk. After we bought the Hammerschmidt place, I brought the wall back to the bridge. Then it was $50 a foot. It had an iron rail from the bridge to the lake and all the way around to Pranges. We had the alley next to our house that was Park property, about 20 feet wide. I was the promoter, so I had to help these people, up and down the line.

Mr. Quick, when he was alive and active, he was a fine engineer, no question about it. And he did this whole thing by format – 25 foot lots, that's all anyone would need. There were no automobiles, so no provision was made for automobiles in his plan. The dam was put in and he could control the level of, as they called it, Lake Palisades. He would dam that up and put a couple of feet of water in there. They had water lilies and bullfrogs and snakes and canoes in there. I don't know what finally happened, but I guess the kids ruined the dam and there was a real jungle in there. It was nothing but a mosquito breeder. It was a nuisance. It brought flies and bats and all sorts of things.

*Repairing the wooden seawall at the Brandywine.*

*Lake Palisades.*

When Mr. Quick died, he still owned a lot of land and left it to Julia, his daughter. It became obvious right away that Julia wasn't interested in the Park; she never had been. She'd sell anything to anybody for any kind of a price. So Mr. Boyles and Ray Kropp got together, initially, and then called me in. The three of us had dinner one night at the Swedish Club in Chicago and we decided - since nobody wanted to take the job on himself because of the criticism that would follow but somebody had to buy her out to protect the place – that ten of us should buy her out. Nine guys came through and we bought out Mrs. Hill (Julia's married name). Everything she had – Clubhouse, Lake Palisades, and on the west side of the bridge, the Harbor Block. We were just trying to bring some control to the thing.

Quick had some scheme to own a lot back from the lake if you owned one on the lake. It was ridiculous, because these cottages were so close together. Anyway, we got some control of the property and held it together. Did you ever see that early map? It showed all the lots. I guess there 800 or 900 or them, maybe a thousand, and they were not a lot bigger than 25 feet, as I remember. He would put a cottage on every lot – and did, on every one he could sell. But we put up the money, the nine of us. We were all getting older, so they called us the Nine Old Men. Really, the only young fellow in the whole group was Ray Kropp; he was probably 20 years younger than me. All the rest of them were my age or older, and they were all very congenial. Everybody's business was nobody's business, so Georgie Boyles and I, we had to carry the load on that thing. It got to a point where everyone got worn out and we'd sold maybe 25 or 30 lots; that wasn't our business. So we decided to disband before somebody died and the land went into an estate. Only one died ahead of us, so we called a meeting. Everybody, for $1 a lot or $100 a lot, would pick out what they wanted before we would deed the rest back to the Park. We didn't mind giving it back to the Park with some restrictions – for instance, you have to have two lots for a house and a place to park two cars off the road for each house. I remember that was a part of the condition. So I bought the Lake and Harbor Block and all those lots up north. I didn't have in mind a real estate promotion. My original idea was to have a duck blind there where the bridge was and have a cute little family confection there. That was an ideal spot for a duck blind. The ducks would have come in on their flights; they land into the wind. The wind is from the northwest; you could kill 'em like nobody's business.

The more I saw of the swamp the madder I got. So that's it. I decided to clean the darn thing out. I got ahold of Tony Canonie and we went in. We couldn't do it today, because the environmentalists, they put signs on the things and everything else. The objectors – the Peats were one family that objected to it. Then there was an old maid up on the hill, I forget her name, she was a little upset about it. It was just a bug infested swamp. I put that road in where there used to be just a path. I sold enough lots to recover my costs. By owning that, I could put some restrictions on it. For instance, that bridge there at the other end, there was a lot of conversation about putting a road bridge across there. I figured the only way to control this Park was to have one outlet. If we had two outlets, we couldn't control it. The bridge had to be redone, so Cecil and I worked on a deal and we put a new bridge in there. Cecil was very, very cooperative. Whatever you

*Clearing the meadow.*

say about Cecil, I'm on his side, I'll tell you that. He acted the real estate agent for those lots and, of course, he had to run water up into all those lots and meet the price to serve them, not only with water, but with roads, and that was all a part of this project. When I sold enough lots to pay for clearing out that jungle, I deeded all the rest of it back to the Park. I had some restrictions in there and they ran for twenty years. If the Park did nothing about them, then they renewed themselves for another ten years. Another restriction was they couldn't put a road through the meadow. There was talk of putting a two-way road there.

We planted grass seeds in there and one of the conditions was that the Park would keep it as a meadow. I wouldn't want to do it again. There was a little danger attached with all that vegetation and it drummed up a big storm when I was burning down there, as it might have caused havoc. The fire department was alerted in Covert and I was insured with everything I could get, but that was the one thing that concerned me – that in burning up that rubbish, and there was a lot of it, we'd start a fire.

Three years before the war (1939), I started the half-mile swim. Weensie was the first girl winner. She won it two years in a row and then Sue DeButts came along and beat Weensie. I never did get to keep the darn trophy. I had more fun with the races than anyone else. I'd get ready for them and I'd build floats and, of course, we had these prizes. I'd get the Coast Guard to patrol. When they'd see the Coast Guard coming, that's what attracted the people, and we had a pretty good audience. The first few years, the Coast Guard men were very cooperative. Then they made some changes, and the last few years they wouldn't come down. We had to quit during the war. Every swimmer had to have a canoe follow them. Connie tells me now the race happens way near shore. She says it's not like it used to be. Of course the sea walls made a big difference. The swim had a real purpose. If you ever got in an accident in the water, if you could swim a half mile you'd have a much better chance of surviving. It had a purpose and that was it. Without an incentive like that, a kid would just splash around. I don't know how many went through the race, probably hundreds altogether who would never have swum that far otherwise. I'm glad they still keep the race going.

And then the swim race got popularized. I remember Nell Hagie. She was determined to bring in someone she knew to win that race. It was despicable. Those things were done for the kids here, not to bring in somebody to steal the prizes. We had – as long as I was running it – three events in the swim: the girls' resident swim, the boys' resident, and the guest boy or girl. Lots of time, we had a guest win the swim, but first prize went to the local boy who won it. That was the only fair way to handle it. I thought that was a real accomplishment. We got the freeloaders out of there.

I was the second president of the Park. When we came here, Mr. Duwe was the first president. Quick ran it for years. Then he got enough people here to set up an organization to take some of the heat off the management of it, the policing of it, and so forth, and they made George Duwe president. (George is president of Mickleberry Sausage Company.) He was in the highest cottage in the Park, by the Water Tower. Nobody wants to be president. They made me president. I'm accustomed to trying to do things. We were trying to get some activities going, particularly tennis and athletic events. I served for a year. I was willing and anxious to serve a second term. I brought my lawyer over to see that things went according to Hoyle. In those days, the nominations were from the floor. The president had to be elected by the Board of Directors. Bang, bang, they nominated five directors and I wasn't one of them. It let me off the hook and I never regretted it. I had some fun after that. Because in an organization like this, and I've been through it two or three times, all you do is make enemies. You never make friends because you've got to disappoint some people. You can't please everybody. You wind up and you make some enemies. You have to spend money anytime you try to do something. People don't want to spend money for anything. They just expect things to happen.

I got Quick to put in those four tennis courts east of that hencoop out there. Up until then, he had two courts on the south side of the road and one on the north. And he put in four nice courts then, at his own expense. Quick kept the taxes down. He did a very good job in that respect. And when I got here, the dues were a minimum. I think they might have been $35 or something like that, and $1 a year for a vacant lot. Didn't amount to anything. The old gentleman, that poor old guy, he never really made

*Lowrey leading 1954 Half-Mile Swim.*

any money out of this Park. He worked so hard his whole life.

Then we spent a little money on the Clubhouse. We'd have events up there and try to raise money. The place was falling apart. I remember we had a Cabaret up there one year. Jeanne Best had a miniature piano and brought that down. Weensie could play the piano and Connie could sing and they'd go around to the tables, and, for $1, they'd sing a song.

One time a friend and I dressed up like girls for one of the tennis tournaments. We painted our lips. I borrowed Weensie's shorts and other clothes and we went out in a car and they called our event and there we were. Neither one of us could play tennis at all. We were dressed up like girls. I can recall a lot of silly little things. We liked to have fun. Now things are more organized. We had to make our own fun. No TV and no cars to go anywhere made a difference.

*The old Palisades Park golf course.*

Quick had put in the golf course in the early days. Sand greens. You knew about those? The greens would be half again the size of my porch. He'd oil them. Just a little oil on them, yeah. And when you got on the green, he had a sprinkler there. Like you push snow off the sidewalk, you'd push sand in the cup and that was it. The 9th green is still out there by the road, right back of the little building . There's a little raised place there. Of course, it's all grown over with grass now. The course wasn't all weeds, but it never had any grass worthy of the name. You'd hit the ball from oiled sand to oiled sand.

One of the funny things that happened was we tried to put in some athletic events and one year we had a golf driving contest. And old man Hempy came out there. He was older than the Lord and he'd never had a golf club in his hand before and he swung it like a baseball bat – and he won the contest! He was the proudest man in the Park. All he ever used to work on the roads was horses. As far as I know, he never owned a tractor. When he left, that ended the horses. Mr. Knapp was his helper for quite a while.

Knapp ran the filling station that Charley Tunecke owned, in the beginning. People didn't patronize it as they should have. It wasn't any great success. Knapp rented it from Charley. Then Nichols got tired of the soda fountain – I forget the reason – and he wanted to buy that station. I knew Tunecke owned it and he couldn't make up his mind. He wasn't a businessman. I advised him to sell it for $10,000 and he did sell it for that. Nichols couldn't pay for it all at once, but he bought it. Maybe Charley talked to others also. I won't say I was the only one. Tony Canonie, when he first got that bulldozer after the war and went into business, built a little office there, maybe 100 feet from the station, on Charley's property. Georgia Underwood was his bookkeeper. That was the Canonie Construction Company – just the two of them. In a little place - I think it looked liked an outhouse. That was his headquarters. Georgia stayed with him until he outgrew here. Which he did after a few years. He was really into big business. Georgia is no longer living, but her husband is – Vernon, the barber. They lived here and he went to town every day to the barber shop. Boy, that was a long time ago.

I can tell you a good story about Joe Putz. He put a tire on my wheelbarrow. The wheelbarrow is about my size – it's especially for me. I still have it. I'm going to have it used for a tombstone! I've got it out in Arizona. Joe Putz worked on that all winter. He got the tire at some second hand store. Charged me $5.00. He was for hire, here, worked by the hour for anyone who would hire him. He'd do anything, any job. People like Rudy Weber would get a cottage job – he built Kropps' and remodeled mine. He would take all winter. I came over one time when he was remodeling Kropp's house and he had ten men around and gosh, it was zero, but it was just like they were having a big picnic. He gave men work all winter. Knapp was

there. Putz was there. Joe Putz, the poor guy, he was not all there mentally, of course, and he would come and sit on our porch at cocktail time until he got a bourbon in a glass. He wouldn't go home until he got that. I worried about that because I was afraid he'd have an accident on the way home. But he had to have his pound of flesh, and that's the way he'd get it. Joe and Mary, his sister, would go to Virginia VanBeuren's and her mother's every day. I don't know if they fed them or what. Or they cleaned or whatever. I don't think they got a drink there. So many of the men that worked here lived over in Covert and they really had small little places there. They were happy. They had work and they liked the people here.

Sturtevant built the hotel. Del Jones was his son-in-law. When Del's first wife died, he married Blanche. He was a character. He was so tight he had a pump box between here and the soda bar. Of course, everyone wanted a drink of water. The pump was out here so people wouldn't go in and use the hotel toilet. He kept that locked. Well, he had to. This was "downtown" and when everyone was here, they'd wear out his toilet. He was so tight, he wouldn't fix the pump when it was broken. He was really something. He had a little ice cream parlor, too, before the Soda Bar. We used to go get ice cream in the dining room, on the side facing the Soda Bar. The kids would go down the concrete walk and get their ice cream cones. There was a little room down there. We ate in the Lodge every night when we first came up here, for at least two years, 1933 and 1934. It was great for us. We'd have guests and take them to the hotel for food. They'd sleep at the house but Mother wouldn't have to cook all the meals.

We only went to Vespers once. But there were a lot of fine women that promoted that thing. Helen Bishop was one of them. She was very interested. Virginia VanBeuren used to go to Vespers all the time. And the Kings.

When I was president of the Park, there was a cottage burned down, right to the ground. And the owner gave it to one of the nearby local residents, but Mr. Quick didn't want him in the Park, for what he thought – nationality – was a good reason. If I told you what nationality, that would tell the whole story. I had to handle that for him. I hated to do it. I kept the guy as a friend, believe it or not. I must have done a good job on that. I was pretty diplomatic. But Quick was particular about that – he didn't want any of that nationality in the Park, and that's all there was to it. He could set all the rules on membership he wanted to, in those days. That's the way he did things. He was a good Presbyterian. I went to his funeral. They can say what they want, Mr. Quick was a fine man. I didn't agree with everything he did, but so what? He had the interest of this Park at heart. But he never modernized his thinking. He never did. He had – you probably don't know, but if you see the map you'd know – out near where Stan's got his house, I don't know the exact spot, he had what was called garage lots. They were 15 foot lots – 15 feet wide and about 20 feet long. He must have had 100 of them in that little block out there. That was the garage lot. Quick was going to keep the cars out of the Park! He didn't want them in here. You were to walk. He'd always walked in. It was good enough for him. They never did put any garages on the lots. It just didn't go over. Had it worked, I don't think there would be as many cottages, with people having to carry all those groceries. But that's the only provision he ever made for the automobiles. I bought that, amongst other things, and I think I sold it to Cecil for a couple of hundred bucks. I don't know what he did with it.

> **Adopted March 22, 1968, by the PPCC Board, was an agreement to "vote Forest Lowrey in as the first Honorary Member of Palisades Park." To our knowledge, he is the only person to be so honored.**

*Forest Lowrey (right) with George Bishop. 1953.*

*"I sat on the Hagie porch (Toplofty #97) in 1939 and heard how Hitler was invading ... Poland. The Hagies had given me carte blanche to use their quarters there and I sat on the porch, overlooking the lake." From interview below.*

# Tony Malinowski

Interviewed by Katy Beck
August, 1986

I was sort of a free-lance here. Apparently, people got to the point where they figured that they'd check me out and they passed me (I don't know if I passed with flying colors, but I passed) so they weren't disturbed when I was around. I took some of the girls to movies, not romantically, particularly, although some of them surely tempted me. We went to Crystal Palace and I sort of played the escort type. The Crystal Palace is at Paw Paw Lake. They had the big bands. In fact, we had a class reunion, a high school class reunion, just last summer about this time of year. And I had made recordings of all the big bands of that era and we used that for dancing. We didn't do too much dancing, but – great memories.

I went to school in Covert. My parents let me have a piece of ground because I was a 4-H type of person. First, I raised chickens and pigs. Then I got interested in raising gladiolas – flowers of all kinds, but gladiolas particularly. In the resort season I'd take them to the resorts in South Haven and sell my gladiolas. Somebody from Palisades Park came into Sinks Grocery Store and I had some gladiolas there. That's when I came to Palisades with my gladiolas. I was in high school. I met Del Jones. He didn't like me. "We don't allow peddlers here." I wasn't a peddler; I was selling gladiolas. His heart was shining gold, but he had to put on this front. And he had actual physical pains too - heart problems – that sort of thing. Nobody knew it.

But that's what made him feel kind of grumpy at times. He ran the Lodge and after awhile he asked me if I wanted to work on busy weeks. He asked, "Do you have a phone number?" and I said, "No, we don't have a phone." So I really didn't start working here until I started college. He softened up on me after that. I'd come around. Then he hired me to work at the Lodge.

He was a little bit dissatisfied because kids would come and just sit around. He'd say, "What are you guys doing here?" "Oh, there's nothing to do," would be the reply. "Well," he would say, "can't you find nothing to do somewhere else?" Finally, [I decided to give them something to do]. The first thing I ever had here was the horseshoe tournament because that didn't take much space.

I grew up in Covert where the farmers would come in on Saturday afternoon and night. And they came in to do shopping, the women. Imagine shopping in Covert. That was a big event, though. The farmers would bring in their produce there, to the loading platform, where trucks would pick it up. Then the farmers would have nothing to do, just waiting for their wives to get through gabbing. And they always had a dry goods store – Palmers – and of course women spent a lot of time in there. That store is no longer there.

Nellie Palmer became the librarian. She said that these farm communities had some brilliant people and they don't like to just work. They also enjoy reading; they enjoy recreational reading and they're very academic. She made quite a case. Somebody has a copy of that letter. Maybe Pearl Sarno.

*Nellie Palmer and the Covert Library*

Anyway, these farmers had nothing to do because their women were there. They'd sit around, smoke their pipes, and tell their fish stories and other lies, exchange. And a couple of them were good horseshoers because next to our home in Covert, the family beyond us had a horseshoe pit or two he'd set up. As a kid, I could hear the clanking of irons. Of course, my ears would perk up. I'd go over and watch 'em. I'd hear their stories and watch 'em throw their ringers and spit their tobacco. And find they were short. One of the farmers, he had to leave early. "Hey kid," that's how they knew my name: "Hey kid." OK, so I'd start pitching. And I became one of the elite. Eventually I worked my way into the varsity. And I was no longer a reservist. Mr. Packard had a special formula of clay for the horseshoe pits. He was my next door neighbor.

Then the township, the township at that time was nothing, but some of them got together and they had constructed six sets of horseshoe pits down at the fruit receiving station. They put in lights so these men could sit there and instead of chewing tobacco and spitting all over the place, attracting mosquitoes, they could pitch horseshoes. They didn't have tournaments then. I organized tournaments later. The farmers, they'd come and shoot, they'd pitch these horseshoes. But my job was to keep the pits covered during the day with tarpaper. And then I had to soak 'em to just the right consistency, so they wouldn't be too muddy and yet when the horseshoe hit, it would stick instead of sliding and bouncing and rolling all over the place. But where they threw it, that's where it stayed. That was honest horseshoe pitching. They paid me a quarter every week. I'd go to Sinks and get a candy bar and that would last me about two days. Take a nibble at a time. I respected that candy bar – I knew that the next one was far off. Anyway, then they'd turn on the lights and it was nice. And then I organized the tournament and it was nicer. I got the idea from a basketball player in Covert. Anyway, they had a lot of fun in those tournaments. They'd team up.

But anyway, the horseshoe pits: in fact I saw Mr. Packard construct them with two by sixes. He'd make a box around each stake. Then he brought in clay and mixed a little bit of sand. At Palisades we found clay. I forget where we found the clay – I think it was somewhere near that swamp. And we used clay pits like we had in Covert. Most of these people never saw clay pits – they'd just slide their horseshoes in the sand or dirt. The pits were right along the tennis courts. I don't know if anybody really complained seriously about the clay and the horseshoes as they were playing tennis. They weren't that critical, but you could hear them clanging and clanging. The sound carried. Horseshoes kind of went out of style when we started

*Tony Malinowski in 1986.*

getting our tennis tournaments. They still pitched horseshoes, but nobody worried about the clay or anything else; kind of deteriorated, in my eyes.

Mr. Jones, of course, tennis was not his business. In fact, he kind of resented the fact that I was spending so much time with the kids. I put in time there, too – in fact, I got up extra early in the morning and did my chores. I was in charge of the office, 'cause he'd go shopping and all that stuff. At first, he'd close the office. I'd have to stay outside and wait for him. Then he kind of figured that I was - that he could trust me. And then he sneaked that slot machine in there. Did you ever hear about the slot machine? In the back room? You could hear the hammer, the wheels, and everything. But a stranger wouldn't know where they were. Anyway, he finally - I gained his confidence. He let me kind of take over there quite often. He spent more time in the dining room, particularly on weekends; that's where he had the most traffic. He cautioned me … I guess what he was trying to tell me was Jews and Negroes were on the verboten list. I was supposed to kind of check 'em out and if I had any questions, to kind of stall 'em off until he could come over and take a look. My usual answer was, "No, we're filled up." Or, "No, we're not taking reservations, we're set for the summer" and all that stuff.

*"The Taj Mahal of Palisades Park."*

Mr. Quick was very suspect of me as he was of any stranger, but boy, he glared and he raised his eyebrows when we wanted to use the Clubhouse. "Oh, no, we can't have that there, playing games … we use that for rainy days." And I had some of the mothers intercede for me. But I got his confidence and we had long talks after that. In fact, I've got a copy, that I typed up, of his history items he'd told me about this area. Quick was very conservative and all that. "No, we'll think about it," and it took him a generation to think. The Clubhouse became a bit of a hot house issue. They didn't want to open it up to the kids. It was a holy temple – the Taj Mahal of Palisades Park. But anyway, he finally came around.

In fact, I did something that probably nobody had ever done, never even wanted to. They gave me a farewell party up there at the Clubhouse when I was going to leave for the Navy. The Hagie kids got contributions. They gave me a beautiful watch which I've never worn. I've kept it in the case it came in, inscribed on it. And Mr. Quick presented me with a $20 gold piece. To him, that was something. But he was leaning over backwards the last few years and I just reached over and I put my arms around him and I gave him a great big Polish hug. I guess he was not the most surprised – everybody else was more surprised. He was probably more confused than anything. I don't think anybody had ever hugged him before. I just fell in love with that guy. Cause I met him head to head out on the trails and the beach and all that stuff.

Once, I wanted to buy the ice cream parlor. Julia Hill owned it. For $3000 I could have had that. And I should have had it. Meaning, I had a little money, not that I could pay $3000, but I could make payments. I was just a year or two out of college. I kind of petered off on it. I should have. I talked with Julia. There were some Poles in the Park. They didn't have "ski" though. Maybe that's the difference.

And then the Honor and Glory – I started that before Lowrey got in the picture. I'll tell you how he got in the picture. I almost changed the name when he got in the picture, because I called it Honor and Glory because Mr. Quick didn't give us any money; I wanted to get some prizes. Anyway, Quick didn't give me any money for prizes. I didn't ask for much. I just wanted some little trinket. So we called it Honor and Glory. I figured then, you see, you played it for the honor and glory, that's all. Lowrey, though, he almost made me change the name of the tournament. Because now we had cups and prizes and plaques. But I kept it Honor and Glory. I'm glad I did, of course. They spread the word that we were running a good tournament and finally it got to the national body or whatever it was. They called me from New York one night and asked me about the Honor and Glory tournments and how long they had been running. I used to take some kids to Kalamazoo. I started the name here – like I said, I should have copyrighted that. Although I haven't heard of anymore Honor and Glories. I was the richest poor man in the world. I was rich in that

I enjoyed that stuff. I was poor because …. The tournament was started while I was working for Del Jones. In '32 or '33 or '34. That helped me. Then I went to Chicago for a year to work. I was going off to earn my fortune. I had a scholarship to Hillsdale College, a science scholarship. They gave me $50.

Mr. Lowrey was the generator here. He got this swim thing going. We also had boat races out here. Power boats, with outboard motors. I remember that because I got in with the Schlacks. They had a beat-up boat. The father said, "No, you better not enter it; it doesn't work well," but I came up here to their landing down there and I worked on it for them. I wasn't a mechanic but I worked on it. And I said "Yeah!" They said, "The only way we can enter is if you go with us." So take your marks – BOOM! – everybody started. The engines were started, so we went about 50 feet and the thing died. I spent the rest of the race with my neck out of joint, my shoulders out of joint. And of course we had to swim into shore. They made me the good Samaritan and I almost wrecked myself for life. The races were only two years and they petered out because they didn't come out and really get serious about racing. But Lowrey got the Patter to put in publicity.

*Forest Lowrey. 1944.*

After the War, I still worked for Del Jones. He resigned himself to sharing me with the Park. I was teaching tennis out of a book. I was no more of a good tennis player – in fact, I didn't know anything about tennis. But I taught it out of a book. I almost had to go house to house to get people interested. "Oh, I don't know how to play," they'd say. I said, "Ok, I'll teach you." Parents, of course, were my assistant coaches; they forced their kids to play. I wasn't hired to do this. I just had this urge to get these kids going. I got a few tips from the parents. They'd give me little envelopes. They'd slip me things and let me use their cars when I took their daughters to the Crystal Palace. They'd have movies. I stopped doing that in 1946. That's when I got my job in Trenton. I may have come back for a year or two after that, a summer or two, because I came back to Covert.

Originally, Mr. Packard and Mr. Quick were combined in the sawmill industry shortly after the Chicago fire. There was a great demand for lumber after the fire. And so Mr. Packard got a lot of woodcutters and they hacked down thousands of trees in the Covert area. And then they would rough saw them. In fact, our property in Covert still had these eight-inch beams out near the creek.

*Del Jones, owner of Sturtevant Lodge. 1951.*

I think they used that creek as a sort of a power source; they would dam it up. Right in town. Well, we live off the town in West Lake Street. If you know where the fire hall is, you turn towards the lake and we're at the end of the first block. That used to have a shop right on the corner there and we still, when we'd be plowing or I'd be tending my gladiolas, I'd pick up screws and nuts and gravel and things. Behind this, near the creek, he had a sawmill. Packard Mill. Anyway, then someone else in Covert had teams of horses and would haul that lumber down here to the lake and float 'em out to the stream, to the boats, and take them to Chicago. They'd float 'em out. They'd come off shore and make a big raft out of these timbers. The original Quick that set this Park up, he was involved. I don't know whether he made any money from it, but that's what he did. He was kind of a – he watched his pennies.

Have you the history of that little swampland behind the hotel, behind the lodge there? At the entrance, that swampy land. I won't get it straight so I won't even start, but that was a project that Mr. Quick said fell through. He had some idea for that piece of land there.

A sawmill was behind our barn in Covert next to the creek as I said, but there must have been a much larger operation somewhere else. They shipped from the sawmill by us down to the Brandywine and sent lumber out by boat. It was a Packard operation. Their lumber was in great demand along the coastline here; they were shipping lumber like mad. In the Upper Peninsula even, they were shipping 'em down here. Packard was a small operator compared to the big ones. But that's how he raised money. It was shortly after the Chicago fire that the sawmill went into action. There was no need for lumber around here, in such quantities

The area once called Paulville became Packard. It was called Paulville before Packard. Packard was one of the original names from Covert. The railroad came from Hartford and South Haven. And they had a station where it was then called Paulville and Packard. There's a school there and an old church. About two miles north of Covert. If you follow the tracks – I had an uncle who lived right there, near Paulville, near Packard. And his address was South Haven. One railroad still runs back and forth through there.* It's right close to M140. You know, the road curves, going to South Haven; instead of following the curve, take the turn to your left and you'll see the railroad sign. On the right is the building that was once the school. It is now a church. I think it's still painted white. But you'll recognize it as a former country school.

*The railroad is now gone and the Van Buren Trail is on the old right of way.*

*Old Paulville School, about two miles north of Covert and one mile east of Palisades Park. The building was in bad repair in 2001 and may soon be razed.*

## Talitha Peat
Interviewed by Katy Beck

My husband's name is Wilbur (spelled with a "u") Peat (spelled with an "a").and my name is Talitha Peat. That is an Aramaic name from the Bible. Shortly before I was born, my grandmother went to church and the minister used the story of Jesus being called to care for a child who was very ill. By the time Jesus got there, the child was already dead. The mourners were all around but Jesus threw everyone out and said, "Talitha, you may arise," and she did. The name was in the language that Jesus spoke everyday, Aramaic Hebrew, so that adds an interesting part of the lesson. The minister suggested it was a beautiful name and wondered why someone had never thought of giving a girl that name. Well, Grandmother sat there and didn't hear any of the sermon because she was thinking, "Now the next girl in the family is going to be Talitha." And so I was it; that's how it happened. I've always loved my name and felt it was something special. I really do. There are a few of us around. I have some namesakes.

When we first found Palisades, we were living in Indianapolis. It was hot in the summer and everyone went to Michigan. Back in those days – I think this was true everywhere – all activities shut down in the summertime. That's not true now. Indianapolis goes on in the summer as heavily as it does in the wintertime. But back then, you just sort of took care of yourself in the heat. It was very disturbing to me to not be able to get out of the city in the summertime. So we came up with a long list of places to visit in Michigan. All of our friends spent their time at the beach – well, actually, four of our friends. They didn't actually own property here. But they thought it was a perfect place and came, year after year. This was the first place on our list. We didn't make any arrangements. We drove in and there was Mr. Quick, right down there on the Circle, practically waiting for us. He recognized us as strangers and welcomed us as he hopped on the running board – we had running boards in those days – and said, "I'd like to show you around." We said, "That's why we're here." And so he did. We landed way back on the south side, as far as the Park goes. The Baker cottage was the one for rent and we drove into the little driveway. Maybe the name wasn't Baker, but the cottage was way back. It had just been built and was not completely furnished yet. The owners hadn't lived in it yet, but for some reason or other, they couldn't come up. It was way in the woods. Way back. Of course, we got out of the car. Patricia was just about three years old and she said, "I like it here" and that did it. We rented it and before we left the Park at the end of that month, we had bought two lots, these two lots that our cottage is on. We wanted to build many times but we had designed a house Mr. Quick didn't approve of and we didn't get it. The living room was slightly higher, with a balcony behind – a two story living room with a porch on one side and bedrooms in the back. The roof was almost flat on two sides. Mr. Quick said the roof was too flat, too much so for snow. This wasn't true; we had an architect who knew what he was doing. But it was too modern. We realized we had met our match here in Mr. Quick and if we wanted a cottage, we would have to change. We would probably build it differently today – certainly larger.

*Peat cottage #27, Tuckaway.*

Buying the lots was an interesting story. We wanted to buy two front lots but Mr. Quick said, "No, they are not for sale. No, you can't have those, but I can sell you two in back of them." The beech tree was on the lot he wanted to sell us and I just love beech trees, so we decided that this was okay and we bought these two lots. Then that fall I got a letter from Mr. Quick – "Wouldn't you like to buy one of the front lots as a Christmas present for your husband?" And my husband got a letter at the office – "Wouldn't you like to buy one of those lots as a Christmas present for your wife?" Of course, that's what he had had in mind all along, that he would sell us those lots. Well, we went back and he said that he would sell us those lots, but this was the Depression and we were not in a position to buy them. We knew perfectly well he wasn't about to sell them to anybody else, so we just went about our business. All the hemlocks and pines Wilbur got up north, and we planted every one of them. We went about taking care of those lots just as though they were our own. Just about the time we decided to buy them, Mr. Quick died. Nine men bought up all the available lots.

The story of the Nine Old Men goes back to Julia, Mr. Quick's daughter. Just what the altercation was, I'm sure I did know - but it has slipped my mind now. Julia got a little disturbed at the Board. She wanted to do something which the Board said was against her father's wishes and against what the Board thought was right for the Park. She threatened to sell the Park to outsiders and that sort of thing. So there were nine men here in the Park who owned property. All of them were well able to do this and they said, "We will buy the property." Which they did. Different spots were allocated to different people of the nine. Eventually, they said, "We'll be very happy to sell you the front lots at the same price that Mr. Quick was going to sell them to you." So we bought them.

Mr. Quick was an interesting man. By profession, he was a surveyor. He was also a better-than-hobbyist as far as botany was concerned. He sure knew his flowers. As you know, he wrote a beautiful book. Before the Civil War this was probably a lumbering camp. All the primeval woods were cut. The Old Pier cottage # 45 down there is where the pier was where the lumber was picked up. Eventually, they really cleared out all the old ancient trees. Oh, that must have been beautiful. Oh dear, there's not very many of us privileged to see that – well, nobody alive now could have seen it. At any rate, then this lumbering area was closed and the piers were washed away. During the Civil War, Covert was one of the underground stations for Blacks. Many of the Blacks who had worked in the lumbering stayed in Covert; that's the beginning of why Blacks are in Covert. From the lumber camp, here.

*Early cement walk, laid out by Mr. Quick, through the Palisades Park woods.*

As far as Mr. Quick's interest in this, he lived in Chicago and was brought over here, I think, to do some kind of surveying. Well, this spot was available and he fell in love with it. Literally fell in love with it. Apparently, he had enough wherewithal so he could invest in some land and he laid out this whole Park – really a tremendous undertaking. You know, just the way the woods grow, to lay it out so that people could move in and have roads and water – he was extraordinary, really. He was a man of very high moral standards. When we bought our lots, we signed an agreement – I don't know whether it is still valid or not though somebody tells me it is (though it is not being adhered to) – of no firearms and no hard liquor. Very definitely, he was not going to have any of that in his Park. We signed our names that we would not do this and for a long time, if there was any hard liquor, it was kept very quiet. There was no such thing as a cocktail party – there just wasn't. Of course, maybe in the 30's cocktail parties weren't quite what they are today. I would say that the people who came here were all pretty much people on the same – what's the word I want? – certainly on the same standard. Most of them were professional people. I would say there were no extremely wealthy people. And there were no poor people, either. But they were all people who loved the same kind of things, behaved the same way, and when we came here we were introduced to everybody. There were get togethers at the Clubhouse and Sunday night church services. There were two or three ministers in the Park who took turns preparing the services. There were no cliques. There just weren't. Everybody was everybody's friend and pretty soon you knew just about everybody and most of them on first name terms. It was a beautiful community. It really was.

*North Beach before the Power Plant.*

Well, change is bound to come and I have my own theories about what has happened. I don't know whether I should say this, but I think there's a thing crept in here: people who had recently acquired a great deal of money. That always changes things. This was always a unique spot. It still is. Our beach went down from here to the road there. People say, "Oh, come on, you are making that up." Not so. It was unbelievable, how beautiful our beach was. You ask any old timer and he'd tell you. Here, on our side, we have had a whole building lot gone – absolutely gone. We've had that much taken by the lake. Nothing of ours. I've always said I wouldn't have a beach lot. I don't want to live on the beach. I don't like the extreme changes. I do love the water, and when we first came here, we could see the lake. Of course, now the trees have grown so, we can't see it anymore. My friend says, "Oh, give yourself a few years and you'll be the beach lot." I'm sure the lake could go back two or three building lots without protection. I'm sure of that. Very easily. But we still would not quite be on the beach. I'm not concerned about that. But I always thought that was a pretty cute comeback – "Oh, you don't want a beach cottage."

I wonder whether anybody had told you about Mr. Shepherd and Mr. Iverson. Once a year, and this went on for many years – certainly the first ten years we were here, up into the 40's – the whole Park would have a picnic together and everybody at the picnic brought something. It was down on the beach. All the little children would play in the creek. I guess there was a committee to plan this. We did it each summer. Anyway, Mr. Iverson would always come over and bring homemade ice cream. He was always very much a part of this big party. So were Mr. Shepherd and his wife. Mr. Shepherd brought us our milk; he had a little farm with vegetables and fruits. He came over in his car and brought all this stuff and went all around the Park. Of course, we were his regular customers. He delivered milk each morning and cream or whatever each of us wanted. He looked more like a college professor. You would never in the world have guessed that he was a farmer. A person of erect stature. A great presence. Mrs. Shepherd was a perfectly wonderful person too. We often went over there. My mother was in 7th heaven to go over to Mr. Shepherd's farm and get raspberries or strawberries. She used to glory in it. He always used to let her come over and pick. He was just darling to let her do that; there was no reason why he had to let anybody come and pick his stuff. We just adored him.

In the 30's we had a dramatic club. We gave plays. I was in two or three of them. We had fun doing them. That would be at the Clubhouse. You're going to catch me on names of the early neighbors because I have a dreadful time remembering. There were the Filkinses on the beach, actually outside of the Park. I would never come to Palisades without making a call on Mrs. Jocelyn; she had the most northern cottage. There were the Peirces; we just loved the Peirces. I used to get so provoked at Mr. Peirce. Patricia was a waterbug; we couldn't keep her out of the water and she would stay in until she was literally blue in the face. I'd no more than get her out of the water and Mr. Peirce would have her back in again. Oh dear, I used to get so provoked with him. Mrs. Peirce was a very lovely person. I'm very fond of her. I remember they were among the very few people who would come up in the wintertime. She used to say, "Well, you know, it was so cold up there that when I took the washcloth out of the dishwater, it would freeze right away." Slight exaggeration, but we all thought they really were stalwart to come to their cottage which was certainly not winterized.

*Winter on Lake Michigan.*

*Wilbur Peat painting.*

The Canonie brothers delivered our ice, Tony and Sam. Tony, actually, was the bigger; Sam, I think, left the state and got himself in trouble. So for quite a few years, just Tony delivered the ice. Right after the war there was a lot of leftover big equipment – government equipment – and Tony bought it for construction. He really went to town with construction all over the country. But he had a very humble beginning.

Mrs. Steele was an interesting lady. Her cottage is the one that the Goldens have now (#48). She did an awful lot of driving back and forth. She lived just outside of Chicago. She had a predilection for picking up hitchhikers and she did a lot of it, though all her friends said, "Don't do it. You're asking for it." Contrary to all her friends, she kept doing it. She couldn't help herself and she picked up a hitchhiker – or it may have been two, that I am not sure of – at any rate, she was beaten up and they took all her money and her car. It was a terrible thing. This wasn't too long before she died. She still owned the cottage at that time, I'm sure.

I remember the little Ballou grandchild because she and my Pat were friends. The Ballous still owned the Inn then and … yes, it was still an Inn then, they rented rooms. Mrs. Packard had the store for a long time. She ran the post office and lived upstairs. She had good meats, and other good things. Of course, you couldn't buy everything there, all your staples and so on, but you could pretty well take care of your needs. And do I remember the red raspberries she would get! When they came into season - she had a special farmer that brought them in - we would just hang out and wait for those raspberries. Me, particularly, because that is my favorite food. In those little boxes. Everyone put the berries into the box by hand. And on top was a green leaf. They were a thing of beauty. As big as my thumbnail. That was ambrosia. We all counted on her.

When we first came – this is our personal story – we bought these two lots and there was nobody on this north side. The only cottage was the Buckners. That was the only cottage in the woods. The Danleys hadn't built yet. (now Kinsey cottage) Of course, that was supposed to be a park and was on the Park map. Nobody was supposed to be building there. How they managed, I don't know. That's very unfortunate. It really is unfortunate. Because it is not the proper place for a big house. There are several other places that Mr. Quick dedicated as parks that were never to be built upon. Of course, we've infringed on those parks quite a bit, I know. But he had the right idea. He wanted to keep this as close to the way Nature made it as possible. People living in it were to be subservient to the property, not the property subservient to the people: that was his idea. I happen to be very much in favor of that. I do not feel that all Nature and all Creation was made for my benefit. When I own a part of it, it is up to me to take care of it. I've got to preserve it. That was his philosophy. He talked about that and you knew what he believed. You couldn't help it, the way he spoke. To him, that was a paradise – a spot where it was a privilege to be. Many of us oldsters, honestly, really feel that way. We really do. I think we feel it a privilege to be here. I don't think that is true of people who come in now. I don't think they have any conception of how this came about. That it is a unique spot. He advertised in Chicago – half of the people came from Chicago or the suburban area – and he said there were 800 lots. But in the back of his mind, he never envisioned one house after another. Absolutely not. I don't think he ever felt that way. He wanted everybody to have the whole environment and he had his little plot in the center of it. No, I don't think he envisioned a community of block cottages. I'm sure he didn't. Being a surveyor, he knew how laying out the roads could be done. The topography of the land lent itself to the roads. He followed the topography rather than changing it. He wouldn't take a hillside down in order to make a road. No. He worked around it. He didn't want the houses to intrude. But they would be accessible. He really wanted it to be so that everyone would have his own little balliwick so that we wouldn't be looking in each other's windows. I'm sure of that.

I've grown 50 years older here, so things seem different – or my attitude is different. As far as I'm concerned, I came up here the first day after school closed. The first year we came up here, Patricia was in first grade. Oh no, she wasn't either – not the first year – now let me get this straight. David was not a year old and she was four, so it would be two years before she went to school. We were all packed and ready to go the day school was out, and the whole time school was out, we were up here. We didn't go back until the day after Labor Day because usually that was the day school started. I just lived up here – and that's what practically all the young mothers did. I mean, they lived up here. And some of the men could stay all summer, but very few of them. Most of them, like Wilbur, had a month's vacation and came up here for the month. We couldn't get him out of this place. He was here and that was it, except he'd go over to get some lumber in Covert. I can tell you some stories about that man! Wilbur Peat built all our furniture here. He was always running over to the lumberyard for something or other, looking as if the cat had dragged him from the garbage can. He just looked terrible. But we liked this place because it was close enough to home so that he could drive up Friday and get here about 9:00 and leave at 6:00 Sunday evening. So he'd have the weekends here. Of course, I would then go to town to get whatever I had to have. I was here without a car during the week. That was the way it was.

Anybody tell you about the Sinks over in Covert? You can't leave the Sinks out of the history. Because their store was part of our life. Absolutely. That was a lovely family. They had a grocery, meat market, department store, a little bit of everything – all together at Covert – a true country store where you could buy your needles, your steaks, and whatever was necessary. You could pretty nearly get everything you needed there at Sinks rather than going into town. It was a big day when you would go into South Haven. There were the elder Sinks and, I think, three boys. Two of them were married and the family took care of the whole thing. It was an experience, for us town people; it was really something to go to a country store. It was truly an experience. Everybody in the Park went to Sinks. You wouldn't dare come to the Park and not patronize the Sinks. Unheard of. They had marvelous meats. Just wonderful stuff. They were just lovely people, truly

*Mary Ferry and Talitha Peat. 2000.*

lovely people. But when the war came along and rationing came along, that got to be trouble for the Sinks. Eventually, Michigan put a tax on. That was shortly after the war. The Sinks were supposed to charge tax. Well, the Sinks being the Sinks, they said, "We're not going to charge our customers anything. We will pay it." According to what they sold – they were meticulous about keeping their sales, I know they were. But you know, the government walked in and put them out of business. They said, "You can't do this. You're not charging enough." Of course, eventually, they had to charge tax

*Sinks Grocery Store in Covert.*

and eventually Mama Sink died – no, he died first and she carried on for a little while with the two sons. Then one son moved to Chicago and before you know it, all the Sinks were gone. A book in our lives was closed.

We loved the library in Covert and, of course, we always went to Sarnos' farm. The elder Sarnos. Of course, the Sarno family is still very much there. The elder Sarnos were very interesting people. They had a stand, not where it is now. It was a very informal thing. They came over. They were Italian immigrants. They are examples of what our country is built upon. Really. There are several around here you could name that are examples of what America is. Tony's people were immigrants, also. I guess the elder Sarnos looked around and they soon found that over here was close enough to their Italian home environment that they liked it and just built things up. They had chickens – we'd always go over and get our eggs there. Mama Sarno, she'd go out in the hen house and get them for us. We knew we had fresh eggs. They had peaches and cherries and corn. We'd go over there and say, "Well, we want two dozen ears of corn." "All right, I'll go get you some." Then she'd go and pull the corn for us. We almost had the water boiling over here when we went to Covert for the corn. I learned from my mother, that's the way to cook corn. She always grew her own corn on her property and she'd have the water boiling before she'd go out and pick the corn. Once you learn how to eat corn on the cob that way, there's never any corn quite that good. We always did that with the Sarnos. They had the grape arbor, which I understand they still have. Oh, that was a thing of beauty. Beautiful grapes. Oh, they <u>are</u> the community over there. That's what they are – the salt of the earth.

We went into South Haven only when there were special things that we needed. Otherwise – well a little man whose name I do not remember made a contract with Mrs. Packard to take orders and deliver meats. He went off the road down here and we had to pick his car out of the hillside. He was a strange little man, but he would deliver the meat. Other people came into the Park. One woman came in often with fruits. She just drove around to sell her things. Individuals would come in with their own products. We really didn't have to go out of the Park.

A road used to be in front and it went all around in front of Peirces and over the hill and back in front of the McWethy/Plain cottage #19. It was one way – you went that way around to go out. There were cottages in front of that road. So now, when I tell you that the building lot is gone – of course, that horrendous thing that is built out there now, that's not natural. But the cottage that is right next to mine here was brought up here. That was a cottage that, one spring, in a terrible storm, half the cottage just fell in the water. That was in front of the road. Beyond the road. There were two cottages there. Do you know where the Welles cottage #7 is? Along in there were two cottages. They and the road were washed away. They just went.

When we first built, we became friends with the elder McWethys, right away. They were old enough to be our parents. Shortly, we met their daughter and son-in-law, Doris and George Plain. We're still good friends. They have two kids and we have two kids and the friendship went on in that generation. Now the grandchildren are best of friends. That doesn't happen very often, a four generation friendship. They are true friends – a real friendship. I value it.

There was no electricity when the Depression was on, in 1933. We applied to the electric company and it gave us the go around. We were told we'd need six poles and we were to pay $100 for each pole, purchase two pieces of equipment, and guarantee 12 months of use at so much every month. It would have cost us $1200 to put in electricity. We said no thank you. We used kerosene lamps, a kerosene stove, the fireplace, and an ice box. We were very happy. It didn't bother us. Several years later, Mr. Muchinhern, who until then had not had electricity either, worked in some way connected to the electric company. So in 1937 or '38, he put in electricity. Pretty soon the company knocked on our door. We got electricity without paying a penny. They were happy to have us.

*Beach north of Brandywine, showing road that used to come down dune on lake side of cottages. Road was washed out in storm.*

## Bill Potter
Interviewed by
Betty Householder

My first trip to Palisades was in 1932, with my mother and father, when I was a very young boy. We stayed at Sturtevant Lodge. I remember walking up the beach north of the Brandywine with my father and being very bored waiting for him while he talked to a gentleman on the beach about a pile of lumber at which they pointed, up the hill on a pathway. I didn't realize it, but my father was talking to Mr. Ballou about buying that pile of lumber – the remains of a cottage, which had gone into the lake in 1929. I learned subsequently that my father did buy the lumber and contracted with Mr. Ballou to construct a cottage (#3), using essentially the original floor plan. We used the same lumber, the same place, the same roof, and the same floor plan as the original cottage. It really hasn't changed much. The cottage had been owned by a Mr. Hayes, an Assistant Superintendent of Schools in Chicago. He had it built in the early 20's. In 1929, when it started to go in, they disassembled it and put it back up on the trail. In the Park 75th Anniversary Poster, it is the picture in the top right corner, showing the men dismantling it. We call it The Driftwood because it drifted away from us. The Welles cottage #7 next to us is called The Ark because it withstood the flood of 1929. Just south of the Welleses, the Crawford cottage was built in 1937 or 1938. It was just about to go in, about 1947, but they were able to hold it up with cables and poles. I think the Starks bought it from the Crawfords and had it moved back.(#25) So we have had a lot of musical cottages in this area.

My mother, Margaret Schoot, married my father, George Potter, in 1926. It is through my mother that our interest in the Park started. Mother was 13 the summer her mother, my grandmother, discovered the then three-year-old Park. In 1968 Mother jotted down her memories of that 1908 summer which led to such a longtime association with Palisades, as follows:

*Mom (age 45) and Frank, my brother, age 15, set out to walk via the Lake Michigan beach to South Haven from Benton Harbor in the summer of 1908. They left at six a.m., leaving my sister and me with the Noe family on Pipestone Street, where we had two rooms. My sister was 12 years old and I was going on 14. Mom wore a long skirt, shirtwaist with long sleeves, long petticoat, and some kind of hat. Where they ate their meals I do not know; maybe they carried sandwiches. All day long they walked, until 8:00 p.m. when my mother saw a person moving in the distance on the beach. This person was Mr. Ballou; the*

*Ballou Inn. July 4th, 1918.*

*place was Palisades Park, a good setting for a future summer resort. They met Mr. Ballou and he gave them permission to stay overnight in a concrete block structure he had erected.*

*They were about eight miles from South Haven and how – or if – they walked there the next day, I do not know. The nearest town was Covert, about three or four miles inland. A train went through Covert, and perhaps they took this back to Benton Harbor.*

*My mother liked the location of this resort along the lake and we returned many times over the years. We had no car, but daily steamer excursions were made from Chicago to towns on the east side of the Lake. As I remember, Mr. Ballou met us at the boat landing to take us to Palisades Park. On the return trip to Benton Harbor, he drove us to the Pere Marquette railroad in Covert.*

Mother also remembered coming from the train on an old farm wagon, with her brother and sister, their feet hanging over the side in the dark, not knowing just where they were going. The vacations she spent here as a young girl were special memories. Then she grew up and went to Northwestern and became a school teacher in Midwestern towns. She met my father; they were both teachers in Davenport, Iowa. That leads us to the summer of 1932, during my dad's summer vacation.

We were on our way home from Washington, and my mother said she would like to go to this place where she spent her childhood summers. My father loved it, too, and was wondering how we could get some property. You wonder, now, how anyone had any money in the Depression. My dad was a WWI veteran from the trenches of France, and he had just received a cash bonus of $600. That was a tremendous amount of money, in 1932. If I remember correctly, Father made the deal with Mr. Hayes and bought the whole package for that $600. The next year, 1933, Dad contracted with Bob Ballou to rebuild the cottage. I don't remember where we were staying, but we were here while it was being built. I remember my father would pay the workmen on the beach each day, $1.00 a day for a ten-hour day. Men walked in every day from Covert. The cottage went up in a hurry.

Then my dad said, "Well, I don't want it to go in the water again," so he built a large concrete wall, patterned after the Welleses'. I remember when the wall went up. I was a young boy, but I knew, even then, that it was not right (I'm an engineer now). I could sense it. I was offended by the way it was constructed. Instead of pieces of mesh, they used junk; it was a junk wall. In 1949, when the water came up, it toppled over. So Dad had a second wall, wooden, put in by Tony Canonie. In the meantime, the owners of the present Roche cottage #1 and the Welleses built walls and we connected with them. That got us through that period of high water. Then we had another cycle. In 1969, we had the next high water period. The wooden wall had rotted by then. It was obvious we were going to need a new wall. We contracted with Tony again – this time for a steel wall. I was living in Pittsburg at the time and, by phone, organized the wall with my neighbors and with Tony. The neighbors above us all contributed except for one who chose not to. If I remember, that contract was $64,000 for the whole length. That July, before we got the wall in, we had a tremendous storm. Nancy was here with the kids and decided it was time to vacate. They moved all of the furniture to the rear and left, spending the night with the Goffs. It looked as if our cottage would take another nosedive like it did in 1929. Fortunately, the storm abated and the next week Tony was able to start the wall. That was a noisy summer for everybody on the north end, with the pile driver, but I think everyone was relieved to see the wall go in.

Tony said he could use 15-foot pieces with a steel cap or 20-foot pieces with no cap. I decided the ice would rip the cap, but the neighbors decided on the 15-foot sections. That was a mistake; the 20-foot wall was long enough to hit the clay but the 15-foot wall just missed it, so our wall has held up through the years without rotation but our neighbors' wall has tipped. We thought that wall would last forever, but in three years, the water had come up over the wall. In 1973 we built our 4th wall – really a retaining wall behind the steel. We called that wall God's Miracle. The Tillson boys took the contract to build it. Tom was just here the other day to look at it – he said he got a sense of pride from it and I said he really deserved that. The wall was built from start to finish, from buying the lumber to building it in frigid water, in less than two weeks. A real miracle. That wall is still in great shape. In 1975 we put in a new foundation for our cottage; we put concrete piers down to water level. Hopefully, that will last. In 1999, we winterized and finished the downstairs. We have an ambition to someday spend a whole year here. This has been more of a home to our kids than any other place we have lived.

I remember a story about Mr. Quick that my father shared with me. My father was a very sharp businessman, and when he and Mr. Quick got together, it was really something. The two men were two sly foxes. In the early days, this was called Dean's Addition. We had to use the Palisades roads for access, though we had our own well. Mr. Quick really had a lock on us. He said, "If you don't contribute to these roads, I'll just barricade them." That was really fair. Finally Mr. Quick said, "You buy a lot in Palisades and I won't bother you anymore." Dad said all right and the lot was $180 – a junk lot which we still own. In return for Dad buying the lot, Mr. Quick was supposed to give us parking down by the Stangers. Then Mr. Quick wanted Dad to start paying dues right away. Dad said, "I bought the lot and now you want dues. You fix up the parking lot and I'll pay the dues." Quick never fixed up the lot and Dad never paid dues.

Mr. Shepherd, the milkman, had a little dairy farm in Covert in the 30's. He was impeccably neat, with a long flowing beard. The first time I saw him coming down the walk, I said, "Mom, here comes Jesus with the milk." He had cherry trees on his farm and gave us permission to pick cherries. Then one summer he became ill. Turned out he had cancer. That summer we made many trips to his farm. My mother cooked some meals for him. He died late that summer.

*North Beach, showing Millikin, Filkins, and Chambers cottages in distance, all later removed by the Power Plant.*

In the early years, there were three cottages on the north beach – belonging to the Milikins family, Mrs. Joslyn, and Mrs. Filkins. A shanty called Sea Breeze was just south of the Filkins cottage; we would go down there as kids and play house. (Sea Breeze and the Milikin and Filkin cottages were bought and dismantled by Consumers when the plant was built.) There used to be a row of poplars about where the north portion of Consumers is and we would watch the sun set and hundreds of gulls there; that was a pristine beach. In those days, people brought their cars on the beach through the state park. Then some would get as far as the Brandywine. We would say they couldn't go farther and they would argue and some would try it, real fast. Some would make it and some wouldn't. A lot would come with motorcycles and terrorize the people on the beach.

In 1938, we bought an outboard motor for a wooden boat that stayed on the beach. My dad got tired of hauling gas from town so he got an old 50 gallon drum and we filled that and drew from there. In the summer of 1941, Dad decided to fill the tank and bury it, right out here north of the cottage. Wouldn't you know, with gas rationing, there was no way we could drive all the way out here from Iowa, so we used to save our A card rationing stamps and we could get enough to get here. Once we got here, we could always use our 50 gallons to drive the 250 miles back home. And that tank lasted us three summers to go home on. Not that we could spend much time here; I was working at the arsenal then. I'll never forget my dad's clairvoyance. The old wooden boat we sold.

Dad would get our car overhauled before the trip to Palisades each summer. We would pack for three months and sometimes we would rent the house back in Iowa. Our car would not have much trunk room so we had suitcases on the running boards and stuff strapped to the top and a luggage carrier on the back. If everything went right, we would get to Palisades in 13 hours – that averages out about 20 mph. Some of the roads were gravel and we would go straight through. We had all the south Chicago roads to start and stop; there was no fast way to go. As cars got better, travel got easier. One year, we broke down near Paw Paw; the car threw a rod and it was 100 degrees with no air conditioning, but Dad somehow or other got a part and fixed the car. We got to Palisades around 2:00 a.m.

In the early days we didn't have any electricity, so we cooked with kerosene and had hanging lamps. Finally, the electricity came as far as Welleses. My dad and Mr. Welles were good friends and Mr. Welles let us run a long extension cord. We had a light in the kitchen and the bathroom and the living room, three 100 watt bulbs. That was a big improvement. Finally, in 1938, we got electricity. It was expensive, but Dad, who had been pumping our water all this time – he had figured it was 50 strokes a toilet flush – decided we needed it, if for nothing else than the pump.

*Donna Chambers holding son Scott, with husband Bruce's two sisters. Sea Breeze in background. c. 1970.*

*The Elsie J, a South Haven fishing boat. 1985.*

*Bill Potter and friend Don Johnson in the Net Fisherman's rowboat on Brandywine Beach. June 1935.*

During the Depression, people were really hungry and would do anything to keep their families fed. Men would come from Covert with their nets and put their gear on the beach, mostly between our cottage and the Brandywine. Mr. Quick had compassion to let these people feed their families. The procedure was, they had nets about 200 feet long and they would have two wooden windlasses on the beach. They'd spread these about 300 feet apart and then row 200 feet parallel with the beach and let out the net and then row back to the beach and attach the net to the other windlass. When all that was done, they would start pulling with two teams on a windlass. It was always a great moment of expectation to see what they got. As the net would clear the first sandbar, we would sort of get an inkling. By this time, both ends of the net were on shore, forming a pocket, and occasionally there would be a mass of fish. They were mostly perch; it was a real treat to see a trout. As a kid, I thought it was a real treat, but to these people, it was a lot more serious.

Remnants of posts from the old pier stuck up between the Lodge and the Brandywine. They were a good place to fish for perch or reference point to swim to or away from. Old Pier Cottage #45 is named after that pier. Then when Consumers went up, they sank three large hulls to form an artificial harbor. That was fun for some of the boaters. Rud Richards was able to get a big hunk off of one – I think the rope is still up there. It was on the deck and the hulls were sunk in 20 feet of water, but part stuck up and we could climb around and go in the wheel house. Consumers intended to leave them there, but they finally had to cut them apart with a torch and haul them out on barges. Which I guess is good, because we blamed our lack of beach after that, for awhile, on those boats. From what we could see, they didn't do anyone any good.

We love sailing and through the years a bunch of us have competed with Linden Hills in various races. That program suffers from the lack of publicity. About five of us manage to hold up the Palisades end pretty well. Two years ago I won the Men's Senior and my daughter, Caroline, won the Women's. Between the two of us, we had enough points to get the team trophy, but we do need more people.

Over the years, the character of the people has changed. Mr. Quick tried to attract educators and clergy here and some musicians – the more intellectual set. Gradually, particularly after WWII, the typical buyer has been more into business. That has meant that people have had less time to spend here – at least for the men. The original deed says no alcoholic beverages will be served – no if's, and's, or but's – which tells us a lot about the kind of people Mr. Quick envisioned enjoying this area. The early strength of the Park was that it was family oriented and did not become honky tonk. So by and large, Mr. Quick had a lot of wisdom.

I missed coming to Palisades one summer in the service, and one summer when Nancy and I were married. Our daughters have never missed a summer; two of them spent their honeymoons here. I figure that is a good omen.

*Bruce Chambers with his Sailfish. c. 1970.*

## Tony and Pearl Sarno
Interviewed by Katy Beck
October 15, 1999

Tony: I knew Tony Canonie at Palisades Park when I basically did odds and ends. The first year I worked down there was in the 30's – about 1937. Ice delivery was an important role at that time. When Tony was too busy with other things, I would take care of the route. That was one thing I had to be real fussy about. He'd tell me so and so and so – he'd be talking about when I'd bring the ice down there, I had to go a long way [without putting the load down] and I thought, "Why me?" Then I'd take a good deep breath and get started and wouldn't ever lay it down in the sand. I thought I could bring it up and before I put it in the house, I could set it down on the steps and pour a bucket of water on it, you know. But, oh my goodness, this one screamed at me. She said, "That's wasting my ice!" It was the very last cottage on the north end; in fact, it isn't there anymore. There were about three cottages there and she had the very last one. Then later Charley fixed up something like a suitcase. Put a bag over the ice, put it on your shoulder. You could lay it down. The bag was all canvas. You just carted the whole block of ice. If you put it down, you wouldn't get sand on it. Anyways, you'd take tongs and place it on the shelf.

Tony Canonie quit school and went to work. He actually worked for Charley Tunecke. Charley and I had fun digging the basement out when [Forest Lowrey] put an addition on his house. We just dropped all the sand over the lakeside of the sea walls. That was in the early 50's. [Tony was the one who built the sea walls in the 50's.] When Tony came back [from the service], he actually went into business. He got seven new trucks, dump trucks, got the job in St. Joe. He had earthmovers. He had the most earthmovers in the State. I keep thinking about the

*Marilyn Henkel, Pearl Sarno, and Katy Beck at Covert Historical Museum, doing research for this book. 2001.*

nationality thing – they had all the other Canonies working there ahead of Tony. Starting with the oldest Charlie, and Pete. Pete worked down there all the time. Pete ran the gas station up there, too. Sam Canonie, too, and Joe.

Charley Tunecke was under Arthur Quick, manager of the Park. He lived outside the Park. Mr. Hempy came after Charley. He also worked there but he was not the manager. Then Mr. Knapp took Mr. Quick's place. Mr. Knapp ran the gas station awhile, also. Tony once lived at the gas station. They had other guys working in there, too. They had a guy named Joe Putz. He didn't have a position that I know of. He had a farm just outside of Covert. He and Mary, his sister, lived simply.

Del Jones had some property behind our farm. He would come over and talk to Dad. He wanted my dad to buy that. He offered it to him at $5.00 an acre. That was real low land back in there. Now there's a big blueberry patch there. Eventually, it sold, but can you imagine -$5.00 an acre?

I haven't been to Palisades in years. Having the fruit stand [in Covert], I see a lot of Palisaders coming there – second generation and so forth. As Covert Fire Chief, I made frequent trips through Palisades to see that they could get the trucks through. I didn't have too many fires there. The thing of it is, down there, the fact is – and I can understand it very well – they wanted their trees all left alone. They didn't want anybody to cut a limb anywhere. Well, when the fire equipment kept getting larger and larger, we had to make sure we could get through. So when the cottages closed up, I'd go down there. I'd make a drill of it and we'd go through the roads and see where we had problems. If there were problems, I'll tell you now we'd trim the small limbs. So if they interfered with truck lights and things, we'd take the small limb and cut that one back. Some of those roads, especially at the south end, are pretty tight. In fact, back then some of the trees had evidence where cars came too close, chewing off some of the bark. But, I haven't been there for years.

Pearl: When I was young, we lived right next door to the Ballou family in town, in Covert, right down the street here. Dad would have things to do at Palisades, and while he did - it must have been two or three years - we lived at Greystone #89. I was about three or four. Dad did a lot of things in the Park. I'm not sure exactly of all the things, but he worked with Mr. Ballou. It was about 1917. Dad had to go into service right after that. He was really in service, but because he called himself a carpenter, they thought he must have been equipped to build barracks for soldiers, so that's what he did.

*The stairs by Ballou Inn, built with the help of Pearl Sarno's father.*

Dad and Mr. Ballou worked together on the stairs [between Ballou Inn #90 and Greystone]. They did a lot of cement work with beach gravel and black sand – that kind of thing. Rather than getting the sand from elsewhere, they've had to mix cement with beach sand. So the steps they made were pretty rough. As I said, we lived there at Greystone for the summers. That's the year my dad told me that he helped build the stairs. I believe they put part of them in one summer and then extended it up a little bit further - because, aren't they irregular? Bob Ballou was a neighbor, you know, in Covert, and he sort of took dad under his wings. Dad also helped A. B. Palmer put in the water line. That was Nellie Palmer's husband – related to Marion Palmer Hamilton, somehow. Nellie was the librarian for a long time. A. B. Palmer must have been G. F. Palmer's brother. G. F. owned Cherry Hill #144 and was Marion's father.

Mrs. Palmer was working at the general store here in town. Right after he died, she did not like to be alone. I was in high school so I went down and stayed with her nights. The general store was right in the middle of town. It had all kinds of dry goods and knickknacks. At one

*Ballou Inn and Greystone. 1909.*

time, they had a lot of furniture. Upstairs was sort of an opera house. They had plays and things up there. When I lived there, it was more of a general store.

Bob Ballou and my brother were friends. He was ten years younger than I. Ballous were such good people. After Bob Ballou died, she was there alone and the house seemed empty. Mrs. Ballou was a schoolteacher. I was going to sleep at her house, anyway. She would always make a great big breakfast. She knew stories about the people in town. I listened to them; I was interested but they didn't stick. I wish I could go back now and get some of those stories. Bob Ballou's daughter, Adelaide, who went to Argentina, was a Beshgetoor. I never heard that the Ballous served meals in Greystone. That was on the second floor of Ballou Inn. Greystone was three stories. We were on the second floor when we were there. The Ballous built those two cottages and the one in front of them, when Mrs. Beshgetoor lived. One year the water was very high and the furthest cottage around the corner, the Bakers' cottage, was washed in the lake in a storm and destroyed that way.

It seems to me Ballou Inn had a place downstairs where you could get ice cream when I was a little girl. There were three stores to the Inn. The Ballous lived on the top floor. The middle floor had the kitchen and dining room. It started just a small place. I don't think they had more than five or six guestrooms, but I can't tell you for sure. That's probably too small. But I remember it getting larger. I don't think they ever had a big crowd. She was very frugal. Downstairs, when I was there, there was just a little store. Helen Packard ran the store and Georgia Underwood had the Post Office. Well, Mrs. Overhuel ran the store before Helen. The Ballous still owned the building then. They just rented the store to her. Georgia once told me her cottage by the tennis courts was where the stagecoach used to run. You should read her stories at the Covert Museum.

There were eight trains that went through Covert, at one time – four that went to South Haven and four that went to Hartford and then back the other way. From Chicago, some people took the train to Watervliet. Then there was a line that went from Watervliet and through Hartford, here [to Covert]. They made a spur around Paw Paw Lake. I haven't studied that much; I just know there was a spur that went from the Covert line. The Covert line went from South Haven to Hartford. So from Chicago they would go to Watervliet where they would pick up the Covert line. They would come here where they met Mr. Shattuck.

Mr. Sink's store had a meat market. Mr. Spellman had a store further on down, and Mr. Burton ran it. The building is still standing. Then, of course, they had another little grocery store that didn't last long, right next to Mr. Burton. The Palisades Park people frequented Mr. Sink's and Mr. Burton's stores. Sinks ran quite a bit longer after the War. During the War, you could give your order one day, and then maybe somebody would bring it the next day – or the next. Spellman had that one store first, evidently, and then Mr. Sink bought it; and then he fixed this other store down the street.

The Shattucks had the taxi service. The early one was a horse and buggy. Later, they had kind of a Model T. I don't know if they had two conveyances or not, because I remember – I just know that they got stuck all the time [going over the sand hills]. They picked up people from the trains.

*The Shattucks' taxi. 1910.*

There were also a couple of hardware stores, you know. Gunsalls carried groceries, too, just right across the street. The Post Office was in there for awhile, early. There was another hardware which had all our school supplies, and the Post Office and the cobbler shop and ice cream parlor, a livery stable – all down there, all along this street – and the hotel on the corner.

Every Saturday night during the summer they would have a free movie, but then that was to get people to come and buy at the stores – the merchants put it on. People would buy their groceries and supplies and watch the free movie. We always laughed because Tony's dad used to tell the kids, "You worked good and hard today so you get a free movie." In a little gas station on the corner, they served all kinds of candy and pop. That was [run by] Bob Jones; he was a sailor.

They put the first mile of tar down on the road in 1917. Then for a long time they kept extending it. The side roads were just all sand. It was so hard because sometimes, the buses would get stuck. In the year 1931, it became paved.

I don't remember too much about an Indian family, the Nesaws, from the Toquin area; they went to the Covert school. Years ago, the different people got along just fine. I remember with my dad, this Mr. Phillips was a really good friend and John Tyler was a good friend. They used to come to the house and have coffee. They'd meet in a social life. In our church, we were integrated.

I remember about Mrs. Sturtevant. My grandmother made pies for her. My two aunts, for summer jobs, worked at Sturtevant Lodge. My mother worked there during the summer, too. They all worked cleaning the bedrooms. I think Mrs. Sturtevant was a pretty good person. It was her nephew that was so miserly. He'd take the tips from the girls. My daughter worked at the ice cream parlor, maybe when Mr. Nichols ran it.

I had a really great childhood. Everyone knew me and my mother, knew what I might have done wrong. I could go to any of the houses. I went by the doctor's office and he grabbed me off the street to give me a vaccination. Of course, he delivered me. Sunday we went to church and Sunday School. Sunday afternoon we went somewhere, you know, and then young people's meetings. School and church were our social life. We had a lot of fun – I think more fun than today.

*Mrs. Iverson.*

Mrs. Iverson was a cousin of my mother's cousin. The Iversons had that little farm out here. They raised vegetables. Of course, there was a big family of Iversons – 10 or 12. We used to pick strawberries, weed carrots, pick currants, all these things we get at the market now. Carefully? Yeah, you're telling me! And I said "I'll never plant carrots in my garden." I went over to see Mr. and Mrs. Iverson in Paw Paw before they sold that farm. She was really sharp. When she died, she was well over one hundred. You know, they also made ice cream.

Our house was three places down from the Township Hall. My father was a construction man. He worked for a foundation company. They sent him all over. They built these round houses for trains. He'd get lonesome, of course. We had this home here, always. He'd send us back here between jobs, and then when he got a new job, we had to change places and everything and we'd move again. So when it got to about the 10th or 11th grade, I stayed with Iversons for a little bit. Anyway, right after that, my mother said, "No more. I'm staying right here." And we didn't travel again, not at all.

When I was little at Palisades, we spent a lot of time on the beach. The Paulville Pier was still there, a little south

*Main road in Covert being paved.*

of the Brandywine. The Brandywine wasn't just a little creek coming through there – it was all kind of marshy. Another thing we liked when we went down there – they had that swinging bridge. Oh, that was fun to get on and shake, then holler. It was lots of fun. The kids liked it.

When I first went to Palisades Park we had a Model T car – my dad's first Model T. We took the lake road down to the blueberry receiving station and then we went north and then west again. We came out about where the road crossed to the entrance to the Park – the road that was closed when I-196 went in. Those roads were all sand. They put down logs up over the hill so that the horses and wagons could get over without sinking down into the sand dune. Called it the Horse Railroad. One of them went from North Mill, northeast of Covert, to Ludwig's Pier. There were funny stories about the fire department – about their first fire truck. When they would get on – of course the roads were so sandy – they'd get stuck. Then the men'd get on the back of the fire truck and the front end would come free.

*Early cars in Covert.*

---

**A Heavenly Show**
By Janette King
Written July 1981 and as her "In Memorium"
From July 1982 Patter

Who could see a more beautiful sight
Than those sea gulls
Fishing
Against the soft yellow stripe
Of the horizon sky
And the greygreen waves
Of this July night?
A lift and a joy.
Come.
Come and see the sea gulls' flight
O'er the wild rough sea.

# Written Memories

## Katy Beck

My family just happened upon Palisades Park by chance. We were moving from Wilmette, IL to Mansfield, Ohio, and my father had not been successful at finding us a place to live. A friend of the family who knew G. F. Palmer, a Park member, mentioned they knew a place where Mom might be able to rent a cottage for the month of July while Dad went to find a house. So we found ourselves at Seagull cottage #181 in the summer of 1937. It couldn't have been a better playground for children – I was four at the time, my brother Bob nine, and my sister Alice an infant. Behind us stretched the seemingly endless dune land and in front the longest, most incredible beach imaginable. It was a time of endless days of sun, sand, and water. I remember the electric storms coming over the lake and Mom sitting with us to enjoy the excitement and beauty of the display. It wasn't until we were much older that we learned she was really terrified by those storms. Thanks to her, the rest of us have loved dramatic weather even since.

There was no road at that time past Campbells' Oasis #171 and Heart's Haven #170. So to get to Seagull, we left our car and carried luggage and supplies over the sand. There were five cottages nearby. The Lowenthals owned the cottage just north of Seagull. They were a wonderful family – very warm and welcoming. Uncle Leo, as we called him, took the family into the dunes and introduced us to the giant Sugar Bowl – behind which we discovered a meadowful of bittersweet. For years after that, we collected a fall bouquet until professional pickers coming off the Blue Star picked the plants bare and one can no longer find any to speak of. The Big Pine, climbed by generations, is still there. Handsome Ralph Lowenthal, their son, taught us kids swimming strokes such as the "barrel roll." He joined the Navy during WWII and was our "hero" in the armed forces. After a few years, Lowenthals sold their cottage. Surprisingly, Uncle Leo told Mom he would not sell to a Jewish family; the Lowenthals were Jewish and had found things at the Park too difficult to put another Jewish family through. They had suffered such indignities as having their water turned off and not being waited on at the Palisades Park store (before Mrs. Packard's time). Mother didn't tell me about that until I was grown up, but she said it made her sad because they were such nice folks.

*The Beattys by Seagull #181. c. 1940*

In 1940, my folks decided to build. Since Kropps had not yet built, they chose a lot that seemed again to be almost part of the dunes – hence Sundune Cottage #176. Of course, the following year the war broke out. How to get to the Park became a problem. One year we saved rationing stamps all year for the trip to Michigan and back. Another method was to leave Ohio by train in the morning for Plymouth, Indiana, then bus to Benton Harbor and, finally, another bus to Palisades. The driver would let us out at the gas station that night and we would

*1930's beach and dunes by Seagull.*

find our way to the south end, each carrying our summer clothes in a suitcase. Since a painted orange crate sufficed as a dresser, we didn't need to bring much.

*Aerial picture of our dunes and the south end of Palisades Park. 1985.*

*Armin and David Beck collecting treasures along the beach. 1960's.*

Despite there being no car for summer use, my mother was not about to forego the library. We took the hike through Linden Hills and down the road to the Covert Library where we could get our books. I well remember Nellie Palmer, the warm-hearted librarian. Her husband did much of the early Park plumbing. She was the sister-in-law of G. F. Palmer, my good childhood friend Jean Hamilton's grandfather. When I knew him, he was a frequent visitor to his daughter at Seagull cottage. He took us along the lake shore and introduced us to geology; his knowledge of rocks and fossils was great and his enthusiasm catching. His love of rocks passed on to me has continued down through my children to my grandchildren. In earlier days, "Grampa Palmer" and his wife were at Cherry Hill Cottage. His daughter, Marion, grew up here. When she was older, she worked with juvenile authorities in Chicago as a social worker. She had the courage to bring guests such as needy children who benefited from a time in beautiful surroundings and a Black Justice of the Court, despite neighbors' criticism.

*Alice and Katy Beatty, Jean and Judy Hamilton. c. 1942.*

Back in the 30's and 40's, Benton Harbor was a very prosperous town with department stores, movie houses, Holly's restaurant, and the Benton Harbor fruit exchange – a vast area set aside for moving Southwest Michigan fruit, a fascinating place. Benton Harbor also had the House of David where we went each year to ride on their miniature railroad. This was a religious colony where all the men had beards; their House of David jams and jellies were delicious and an economic boost for them. They also had a recognized baseball team.

The big Chicago-Michigan passenger boats docked between St. Joseph and Benton Harbor. For my 11th birthday, my mother took me on a trip to Chicago by boat. She snapped my picture by the rail, with my brownie camera. Immediately we were told, "No more pictures." It was still wartime.

*Katy on boat to Chicago. September 1, 1943.*

Those were the days when electricity was not always reliable. A big storm or blow would often mean no electricity. We used oil lamps. Of course we didn't need to worry about the food in the freezer thawing – we had ice boxes. We also had no hot water for some time – teakettles heated were used for the dishes or hair washing if we didn't use the lake.

In preteen years, my time was divided between dunes and lake. Mother loved berry picking and it was a gift to find them right out our back door. Every year we gathered sand cherries for the best jelly you ever tasted, right here in the Park.

With friends, we set up a Clubhouse on Thunder Mountain, buried Jean's little dog in the dunes, and practiced archery on the blowout we dubbed "Bow and Arrow Dune." We had lunch hikes back to the Sugar Bowl and down to Marvin Slide. One night when we were sleeping out on the Sugar Bowl, a sudden storm came up in the middle of the night. There was a deluge. My older brother was in charge of taking care of us but we argued about the best way to get home – and we split up. Some went back over the dune ridges. Two of us walked straight down the dune, up and down the others, until we reached home – visibility almost zero all the way. My brother came back through Linden Hills and Mother was not pleased when the chaperone arrived home thirty minutes later than the rest of us.

*Katy's mother, Helen Beatty, picking berries.*

Another activity we loved was making up plays which we gave for our relatives. In those days, shutters were used to winterize all the cottages. One summer we built a house of shutters, covered the walls and door frame with crepe paper vines and flowers and used it as a setting for fairy tales. When I was a bit older, Jan and Tom Rutherford and I would write radio plays, set up a studio, and put them on complete with sound effects on Egberts' front porch (Wintermutes #183) – no audience but lots of fun.

My dad had an old rowboat we could take out and on calm days pick up the mail at the Post Office twice a day. It was a heavy flat-bottomed boat with a tarred bottom. Every year we had to re-tar. The tar would harden and then get soft and bubble during very hot days. If we were quick, we could flip the boat over in the water, leaving an air pocket; swimming underneath, we could come up for air and enjoy strangely hollow conversations. It didn't take much to keep us entertained.

One day a friend and I loaded ourselves up with magazines, snacks, and lemonade and anchored by the second sand bar to spend the afternoon sunning ourselves. Slowly water began to creep over our ankles; then suddenly it rushed in, floating magazines and all. The next summer Dad got a new boat. Wooden, made in South Bend, shorter than the other, with a 1 1/2 horsepower trawler motor on it. We claimed it drove backward with the motor on. The fastest boat down our way was the 7 horsepower of a neighbor; it could pull a surfboard one could stand on.

*Robert Beatty, in his wooden boat.*

Perch were prolific in the lake (and still healthy to eat). Fishing one afternoon with girlfriends, we sat forever and caught nothing. A few feet away some boys pulled in one perch after another – they claimed 56 – and they loved the one-upmanship. Perch fishing was also a living for professional fishermen. I remember them coming in front of our cottage, for awhile, to cast their nets from the shore. Sometimes they left and came back. Other times their families came to supper on the beach. When they pulled the nets in, they would be filled with silvery, flipping perch.

When I was a teenager things were different than today. Mothers and kids came for the summer, dads for weekends and vacation time. Schools began after Labor Day because sports did not begin in August. Teens walked everywhere and frequently took long hikes. Usually older teens could find work here, giving them time to organ2ize and plan things together. Each year we took turns entertaining. Usually my party would be a Sloppy Joe party and marshmallow roast. One year the party fell on a Friday. My mother suddenly realized that the Catholics could not eat the meal before midnight, so she turned the clocks ahead one hour. Mike Mooney said, "Oh no, my watch says one hour earlier." His brother said he would believe the clocks. Mike became the priest. I also remember having a progressive dinner. Mary McQuig had a fancy grilled chicken dinner by the Brandywine Beach. Since up to two dozen kids would get together like that, we had quite a variety. We didn't have alcohol at the parties; that wasn't a problem. Parents seemed glad to help make them successful. To be sure, every teen felt a part of the social life, we made a point of announcing the gatherings with little cartoons or posters at the Circle and around the Park. The result was that there might be 50 people at a party – everyone was welcome. The range of age might vary four to six years. Kids generally felt differently about bounds and were mostly responsible for their actions. Parents had set the boundaries and stood by them. Actually, the teens became more and more creative about having fun within those parameters.

A special gathering place in the 50's was the pump house on Clubhouse Beach. The roof in back nearly met the sand hill behind, so we could sit on the ground or the roof and be part of one group. Several of us carried around

*Teen beach party. 1951.*

ukuleles and inevitably there would be singing. Probably the biggest problem my folks saw with the teens was the night of a party at Clubhouse Beach when the boys decided to toss the girls into the water. There was no way to avoid the dunking, but it was all in good fun. The second time I came home wet to change, my mother said, "Next time you will stay home."

The tennis courts were not so full of serious, high-achieving players. Today they seem to need programs to make sure kids can use the courts. Then, young people could have pick-up games most anytime. So everyone played. Mr. Bishop spearheaded a lot of the interest in tennis; his son Ben helped encourage many a novice. Ben was an excellent player who played in tournaments (we went to see him play in Kalamazoo) so he did not enter the Park tournaments. Even the poor or mediocre players participated in the Junior Honor and Glory.

When the lake rose and Tony Canonie put in the sea wall, it made swimming more of a challenge. One year in the 50's there were few places to get into the lake on stormy days. One exciting solution was to jump in at one end of the Park, ride the waves for 1/2 mile, and then be pulled out by a couple of strong people waiting at the other end. With the crashing of water against the wall, it was amazing no one was hurt – it was a thrilling ride. The beaches very slowly began to recover from the high water. They became wide and inviting while my children were growing up. Tony's sea wall disappeared under the sand.

The swim meets were big occasions. Younger swimmers who could not legitimately swim 1/2 mile had a shorter race, little ones an inner tube race. Even the men had a cigar smoking inner tube race. But the big race was the 1/2 mile. All swimmers had to be in deep water. If any swimmers wandered into shallow and touched down, the men keeping track called them out. There were many boats and canoes - including, while there was an active station in South Haven, the Coast Guard. It was great to be a winner, but anyone who really swam that 1/2 mile felt like a winner and knew he or she was ready to meet an emergency on the lake. One year, my sister and I tied for first place, which seems impossible. Today, some swimmers are well trained and their times are much faster than ours.

*An inner tube race. 1954.*

Many of us were very active at the Clubhouse. I remember a white elephant sale to raise money for the Clubhouse and teens helped the adults make it a success. Teens participated in fashion shows, planned and carried out entertainment for various events, and took part in plays. There were variety shows planned and executed by teens with the help of Clubhouse directors, costume parties for all ages, the Sadie Hawkins Dance, and plays for adults and young people to take part in.

One year, at a turnabout dance, Dee Prange and I, knowing we had to pick up our dates, decided to be creative. We misplaced the regular wheelbarrow so instead took an available cement mixing wheelbarrow. We managed ok until trying to make the hill by the fork in front of Mooneys. The boys refused to get out. It took much tugging, pushing, pulling, and laughing to make that hill, but we did it – better late than never.

One entertainment we put on for a Cabaret night included using a sheet to set up a silhouette shadow box effect. The scene was supposed to be a group sitting around a campfire and singing with ukes. I made up a song which someone, probably Pete Wunsch, put to music. It went:

> Down by the seashore sitting in the dark
> We're at a beach fire baby at Palisades Park.
> And when the waves come rolling in
> We know the beach has grown too thin
> But we're not stopped by H2O
> We gather round and shout LET"S GO!
> Down by the sea shore singin' all the while
> We're at a beach fire baby, Mi-hi-chi-gan style. Yeah!

I still remember the tune if ever you want to hear it! My sister remembers with amusement that Mother took pictures of the scene. However, she used flash. Of course, no silhouettes showed up; she just had pictures of a large white sheet.

*Kathy Goodrich dancing in Clubhouse children's show. 1954.*

The Palisettes chorus line also made their debut that year and had return performances in later years. At one variety show, we put on a short original play – a melodrama called The Beautiful Princess. With a narrator for the sparse action, it included the king, queen, and manly duke. Everyone died. It was a hit. A few years later, my sister Alice ran the Clubhouse program. She carried on with wonderful musical programs put on by the children.

One day in spring 1952, Tony Malinowski met with a few of us and asked if we would take over the Palisades Park Patter. He started it before WWII and had teenagers assisting him at the time. He began again after the war, but had to relocate for a job so someone needed to take over. Mrs. Bishop would be advisor. We said yes and organized our staff. Since there was no place to meet, we set up on Mrs. Bishop's front porch. We had the worst mimeograph machine you ever saw – the printing was nearly illegible. But it was a start and we had fun. We even wrote a constitution for our paper. In August 1952 we summed up our experience in the final issue with a poem called "A Fond Adieu:"

> The printing press with its old broken handle,
> The Bishops' front porch by the light of a candle,
> Was the scene of the PATTER'S rebirth –
> Constructed with effort by hardship and mirth.
> At this, the last issue, we lay down our pens
> And crow like a rooster, so proud of his hens,
> For those whom we've slighted, for those whom we've praised
> The torch we have lighted, the PATTER we've raised.
> But now as summer doth draw to a close
> We'll quick lay a finger alongside of our nose
> And leave, not by chimney, but Plymouth and Ford,
> To our ivy-clung campus where knowledge is stored.
> The fun has been ours to pass on to all –
> Your interest was fuel like wind to a squall.
> We'll blow out with this and a big thanks to you
> "Till next summer and news – here's a fond Adieu.

The next year someone proposed the staff be given the upstairs room in the garage. This was really a step up because we felt we had become independent. It was a place we wanted to work during the coolest part of the day – it was stifling up there! That year furniture for the office, screens, an electric fan, and better stencil supplies were donated. Ray Kropp donated a new-to-us, second-hand mimeograph machine. I know some of the editors coming after us felt it was a terrible piece of equipment, but they had never used the older one that produced nearly unreadable copy. Our staff included a circulation manager and we sold subscriptions to defray costs. Patters were delivered first hand. Reporters blanketed the Park to be sure to include everyone and all aspects of activities. The Patter gave a positive focus to our teenage summer months, letting us perform a minor Park service that made us all feel rewarded.

*The old garage with its upstairs "office" for the Patter.*

For a number of years around the 50's, the Roaches ran the ice cream parlor. Mr. Roach was a teacher of science in the Oak Park schools and his wife an elementary school teacher. During the summer months, he and six of his seven children were open for business from 10 a.m. to 10:30 p.m. seven days a week. They painted the ceiling red and white stripes and Beth painted an old-fashioned beach scene on the mirror behind the fountain to cheer the place up. They were wonderful to the teenagers. Electronic games were not the draw, although there was a pinball machine. Socializing and holding songfests there were popular ways to spend time in inclement weather.

Palisades Park was a great place to learn to drive. The narrow winding roads and hills were a challenge, and when mastered, one could drive anywhere. The roads were very confusing to many people, since - at that time - the forks and turnoffs were only identified by small square numbers, possibly about 3" x 3". One story told of a young couple just married who came here for their honeymoon. They arrived after dark. Going round and round throughout the Park, they could not find their destination. After a long, long search, they gave up and drove back to Chicago.

Directly across from the entrance began a dusty road to Highway 140 where teens also got driving instruction. Around the first bend on that road a man set up a small stable and took in abused horses to nurse back to health. For very little, we could rent a horse that was strong enough and ride the web of country roads.

Working at Sturtevant Lodge for Mr. and Mrs. Jones was quite an experience. For two years I waited tables under the direction of Blanche Jones. Del, according to her, proposed marriage with "the tempting offer of becoming the hostess of a beautiful Michigan Lodge." As it turned out, he needed a cook. She cooked three meals a day, seven days a week, for all the guests. As she once put it, "Life if just a bowl of cherries – and I got all the pits!"

I tried staying at the Lodge nights, since we had to be there so early in the morning. The bedrooms for the staff were over the kitchen – tiny, stifling rooms. I roomed with Shelby Spelman whom I enjoyed, but we shared a double bed with her very dilapidated and grungy childhood teddy bear in that heat. Before long, I decided that getting up 1/2 hour earlier to commute was a grand alternative.

Blanche also commuted – but from her house next door to the kitchen door. Del lived in a room behind the office at the front lodge. Since Blanche was on a tight budget, she was forever calling Del to tell him, "No more guests this meal; I have already started cooking the needed amount." No matter how strongly she put it, he invariably called to say more guests for dinner. This happened several times a week and often meant two or three extra tables. Needless to say, it did not endear Del to Blanche. And consequently, the meals became pretty slim for the waitresses. One day, Blanche pulled me aside quite upset and said, "Katy, my sister tells me the girls are eating left over food off the trays, after the guests have left." (Blanche's sister was a regular spy for her concerning the waitresses' behavior.) I rejoined that this was for survival. They couldn't get enough to eat at mealtimes. I could eat more at my cottage, but they were hungry and stuck. After that, she put lots of bread, butter, and peanut butter on the staff table when we were short.

I really enjoyed Blanche. Despite her brusque manner, she had a great sense of humor. One day Shelby came to lunch very excited about getting a new goldfish. Blanche encouraged her to go up and get it and show it to us.

*Blanche Jones (right) and Elsie the cook at Lodge. 1951.*

While she was upstairs, Blanche set a frying pan at her place. Her expression on seeing it was priceless. We were all laughing when Del happened in; his face, as usual, had a deep scowl. "What's the joke?" he asked. Blanche winked at us and said, "Come on over some night, dear, and I'll explain it to you" – again providing us with a good laugh and him a quick exit.

*Blanche Jones in the kitchen. 1951.*

One day we were told to be early to set up for a special dinner party. A very particular guest had invited quite a number of people to dinner. We needed to pay special attention to the correct setting, salads were to be brought out after the meal started instead of being in place before. Two waitresses were assigned to the table with others directed to keep an eye out. Well, everything went wrong in the dining room that night. Glasses were broken, someone forgot to put the freeze in the orange freeze and used the wrong juice as well. One guest was forgotten at her table-for-one for 50 minutes; she quietly went up and got a book. Another guest spilled his iced tea all over his dinner. At last the meal was over. We went in and sat down in the kitchen for our meal. Surprisingly, Blanche seemed cheerful. Well, she told us, at least the big dinner party went well. She opened the refrigerator and stared in shock. There sat all the beautiful salads. Looking as if she were about to cry, she sat down; then she began to laugh. That turned out to be the method we all used to unwind. Oh yes, and we had some delicious salads.

Saturday night was the fancy meal of the week. They served roast beef and Del supervised the carving. Guests were known to surmise that he cut it with a razor. He <u>was</u> tight. On Sunday evenings a smorgasbord (of sorts) was served. The highlight was baked beans. However, the beans were truly yummy, a secret recipe purported to have come from Sun Valley Ski Resort. Blanche guarded it with her life. One day she was especially hard on Elsie, an assistant cook. To get even, Elsie shared the recipe with me and it became a family picnic dish for years.

Meanwhile, that summer as in most summers, teenagers gathered in the Circle to go to the ice cream parlor or to play "ditch" until dark. This made Del very angry; he was forever trying to chase them away. On one occasion, everyone was sitting strung along the wall and singing. This led to "Del Jones Del Jones has dry bones," sung with gusto. Before long, a police car pulled around the Circle and two young policemen got out. Everyone just sat quietly and watched them. The policemen said they knew Del Jones was an old grump, but if the kids kept singing, Del would call them over and over and they'd have to keep coming back. "So have a heart, OK?" This approach was very effective. Everyone laughed and immediately began to disperse.

One year Del talked me into becoming a chamber maid. He said I would get a little less pay, but incredible tips, so would actually make more than waiting tables. Barbara Baldwin and I enthusiastically agreed because all the work was done straight through and then we would be free for the day. We cleaned the bedrooms and bathrooms and changed the linens which went to the South Haven Laundry. Del instructed us to change only one sheet on his bed each week. To move the top sheet to the bottom. As time went on, we began to worry about making our college quota. We were puzzled that tips were not coming in. We asked him about it but he said he was sure they would come. Finally Robin Campbell, who was an office boy at the time, said he knew what was happening to our tips. He heard guests say they wanted to reward the girls for taking such good care of their rooms, where could they leave the tip? Del told them not to worry, he would take care of it. When we got the news we quit. I went to Blanche to apologize for leaving and she said she didn't blame me. If I couldn't find a job in South Haven, she would find work for me in the dining room.

*Del Jones in Lodge dining room. c. 1951.*

When I got married in the Park, Blanche opened the Lodge before the season to house my guests and put on the rehearsal dinner and reception meal. I corresponded with her for several years at Christmas when she went to Florida. She was quite a lady.

Although we seldom left the Park, Big Mike's was a frequent draw. Drive-ins were just beginning to sprout up around the country and Big Mike made the tallest and greasiest double burger of them all. The dance pavilions in Saugatuck and Paw Paw were also fun, but beginning to wane in popularity.

The crash of an airplane off the shore of Palisades Park in 1950 during a storm was a grim episode. The waves kept crashing for several days as the wind changed directions. So the debris was scattered for quite a distance north and south. The beach was closed. Some young people helped collect the debris to turn in for analysis. I stayed home during that time to read, but unfortunately was graphically informed of conditions by a neighbor boy who knocked on my window and held up human remains. It was a bit uncomfortable to venture in the water for some time after that. My first week at college I met a girl whose brother had been on that plane. It personalized the event in a very sober way.

One of the warm feelings of Palisades Park was the friendly relations between residents and all who worked in the Park. The workers seemed to sincerely care indiscriminately about everyone. In turn, the workers were admired and included in much that went on. Tony Malinowski, from Covert, was an office boy. He became so involved that he helped organize and supervise activities, becoming a youth leader. Mr. Hempy, Mr. Quick's right-hand-man, fascinated youngsters as he shoveled stones along the beach into his horse-pulled wagon and went about repairing roads with clay and then gravel. He was included in the sports that took place in the fields. Rudy Weber was a visitor to numerous cottages for coffee or dinner. He reciprocated with dinner at his own house.

Joe Putz was a special person. He was born in Bavaria and brought some of his craft skills with him. He carved many of the cottage name signs from wood during the winter months. He also made more complicated three-dimensional pictures. And he worked hard. His sister, Mary, cleaned cottages. She had an accident and became rather child-like, so Joe brought her along when he went on his jobs. My mother would have us children play with her when they came to our house. He took good care of her until she had to be hospitalized. Joe came to work at mealtimes, often, so would, of course, become a dinner guest. He and my father seemed to find a lot to talk about. When I got married, Dad asked Joe to supervise parking the cars. As I arrived at the Clubhouse in my wedding dress, we came upon Joe all dressed up. He reached in the window and handed me a wedding gift – a kitchen clock. It was quite touching. As Andy Anderson wrote in the Patter in 1952:

> Every day from morning to late afternoon and sometimes after dark – Joe Putz can be found somewhere on the job. Anyone who has been here very long is familiar with Joe and his friendly manner, for he has been working in the Park for 30 years … Joe is so ambitious that at times he has more work than time in which to do it. Consequently, his red truck doesn't leave the Park until late at night. The Parkers can never show too much appreciation for the many services Joe has rendered.

Mr. and Mrs. Iverson were also important to the Park for many years and very special to our family. I remember, as a child, going to their farm in Covert for produce. They were by Little Paw Paw Lake while my children were growing up. David and Joel spent one summer working at their farm and discovered why their berries and vegetables were so perfect – Ben was a perfectionist. All my children loved visiting with both of them and one year Tom requested them as his special guests for his family birthday. The last time we saw them, he told about his early days in Covert and demonstrated his original cone maker, giving the kids ice cream cones. He died the following June.

When the Power Plant plans were announced, it came as a shock. One fall an article came out in the newspaper diagramming plans for the State Park to cover that land. By the next spring, a new road had been put in, part of Blue Star cut off, train tracks laid down, and Consumer Power had taken over. A number of us, with Ginny Melchert Coleman leading, formed a committee to fight this development. We wrote many letters after visiting other plants around the lake and did make a difference. Unfortunately, they simply changed a coal-fueled plant that we had objected to - for its smoke, soot, coal yards, and slag – to a "clean" nuclear plant. I received letters in reply to my concerns from Lady Bird Johnson, Secretary of the Interior Udall, and Senator Douglas, all encouraging us to continue our battle. But Senator Douglas said he knew we would not win as all the Michigan lawyers who were experts in the field were helping Consumers. He said not to give up because every protest helps the next fight for the environment. So Consumers' went clean and the plant was built. Sad to say, it has had a checkered safety record. At one point, The Chicago Tribune reported them to have the worst safety record in the country. The demise of the plant was delayed when they were given an extension to operate until 2007. Storage for nuclear waste was built. Again we mounted a protest but to no avail. Tanks were built. When installed, two tanks had hair line cracks and one had already been filled. Concerns continue today. The air and water continue to be tested. The future is a big question mark.

When my children were young, recycling had not yet started around the country and bottles were no longer universally returnable. Carelessness was beginning to show in the litter all over the Park. Several of us at Betty's craft class decided to organize a clean-up day. The youth who volunteered were divided into six groups covering the entire Park, north to south and east through the dunes and golf course meadow. Their motto was "Grab the garbage, trounce the trash, jinx the junk." They spent two hours at the task and swept the Park clean, bringing bags of debris to the Clubhouse. Some comments were as follows: "I didn't think the Clubhouse was this dirty." "You don't even notice it if you don't clean it up." "We sure have messy people around here." "I wonder if they have to go clear to the Power Plant." "Yeah, clean up the radioactive material." Rewards of the day were a beautiful Palisades and pizza at DiMaggio's.

*Six Beck children at their cottage. October, 1968.*

One day while I was on the beach, a couple of teenagers approached me with a problem. They had been told by the then president of the Park that adults were sick of teenagers. The Park was for the adults to rest and enjoy, not for them. They were told also that anyone the people wanted to exclude they could – it was a closed Park and their folks had all agreed it could be kept closed. The teens asked me what they could do about it. I agreed to talk to the president to clarify what he had said. My conversation with the president being dissatisfying, I wrote a letter to the incoming president. The easiest way for me to describe my response is simply to share my letter, which was also signed by my husband:

"Many of us are aware of the concerns both by adults and young people over the problems at Palisades Park concerning late hours and noise, respect for others' property, possible use of drugs, care of the beach and dunes, etc.

"Fortunately for all of us we have a president who seems to have a rapport with the youth in our Park. We began to set the climate for some good communication last August at the south end of the Park in talking together – hopefully a procedure that will be used and expanded in the future. Getting the young people involved in the Palisades Park Patter is another positive step in adult/young people communication and understanding. We need to do much more. We do not need to have a small group of Park members decide the views, philosophies and moral concerns of the members, placing their own biases on others and then instructing the young people that this is the agreed view of all people belonging to Palisades Park.

"This leads to the reason for our correspondence with you. Last summer a situation arose at Palisades Park that we feel must be faced and dealt with by the Board of Directors. A group of young people became involved in a conversation with a member of the Park Board. During the course of the conversation - a heated one concerning youth parties, life styles and race – the Board member told the young people that their views would be different when they are older, that their parents are in agreement with a racially restricted Park, and that they could find this out by asking their folks about the covenant they signed. The stories, of course, went home and many children and parents were quite upset over the incident.

"Mrs. Beck went to see the particular member of the Board to verify the facts of the story. He agreed that the incident took place as reported. When she questioned him about the covenant, he said, of course, there could be nothing written, but that the covenant was taken care of in the personal interviews with prospective members – that people joining the Park membership had to agree that they were in favor of restricting membership from "Mexicans, Negroes, Jews and other undesirable people." His definition of "undesirable" does not coincide with ours. Polluters, racists, thieves, drug pushers etc. constitute "undesirable" to us. While the Board member would most likely agree with many of these, I doubt he would consider it possible to deny membership to anyone who would refuse to say "I agree never to make any decision or take any action that is racist." How then can he insist on people declaring the opposite as a condition for membership?

"Our position, stated simply, is as follows:

1. We never had an interview dealing with racial restrictions in the Park before becoming members and are absolutely opposed to any requirements of a racial nature in the sale of property and in approving membership at Palisades Park.

2. Many of our close friends in the Park have strongly expressed the same view.

3. We know written restrictions where property is bought and sold are unconstitutional whether we would call our

association a country club, a village, a Park, an association or whatever.
4. Any verbal agreement would likewise be meaningless.

"This summer of 1971 is upon us – 'Gentlemen's Agreements' and overt racial discrimination should be in the past. Perhaps it is time we arrested this fear in our midst – the divisive and hate promoting talk of racial exclusion, and had the courage to make a positive statement: Membership is open to all people who would love and help preserve the beauties that are Palisades Park, regardless of their race, creed, or color.

"We cannot, of course, insist on the latter declaration. That must come from the heart and conscience of members of the Board. But we can insist that no member of the Palisades Park Board of Directors speak officially for us in matters of race – either in instructing our children or deciding membership."

The letter caused a great flurry of correspondence between the new president and various people, including judges that he contacted. They, of course, did agree that a closed park was illegal, but the mail was mostly uncomplimentary to us. However, I did receive one letter from a teenager whose father was on the Board. It was a lovely letter that he said I could share:

> Just recently I had a chance to read your letter to the Board of Palisades Park and I would like to give my thoughts to you. I have been very aware of the reputation that Palisades is and has been building over the years as being anti-Black, anti-Jew, and so on. This has never been set down in any by-law. I am ashamed to belong to an association which lets such misconceptions grow. As a younger member of the Park, meaning the Soda Bar group age, I get very upset with what is going on inside the Park as far as drinking and drugs and am even disturbed by the outright racism exerted by certain members of the Park and Board. What I am leading up to is that I think your letter was what the Board needed and what the Park needed. Everyone is so afraid to take a stand on something which is important. My family called your letter beautiful. I wholeheartedly agree.

I remember Mike Mooney, a Franciscan priest active in his order at the time, wondering if he should continue to come here in the face of some negative reaction to his bringing a Black priest friend as a guest. My view, which I expressed to him, was that racism was everywhere and if we wanted to see change, we should stay and fight it through with example – not relinquish the beauty of the place to bigotry. As it has turned out, times have brought positive change to Palisades Park. As Marge Roach, herself Italian, said about the north end, "It's beginning to look a little bit like a U. N. down here." There are now families that include different ethnic background throughout the Park – some owners of cottages, some through marriage, and others through adoption. As these people are bringing their children here, it will be more and more common for diversity in race and ethnicity to become natural and unquestioned. The teenagers of the 70's initiated a change we can all be proud of.

When the water rose again, the old sea walls being of untreated oak, were no longer successful barriers. A couple of neighbors north of us decided to put in a cement-capped wall. At a meeting of the south end lakefront owners, Cecil cautioned them about the problems of the depth of the wall and proper support for the cement. Two owners were adamant about what they wanted and neighbors down to the Campbells were afraid to resist as they knew backwash behind the walls made their places vulnerable. The rest of us on the south end decided to put in a new wooden wall.

The building of our wall was an extremely frustrating experience. The builder left his younger sons in charge of the job and did not personally supervise. As our wall finally went up, it tipped at a great angle, leaving large gaps at the bottom of the wall. After daily calls with the construction company owner, I would sit down and draw a cartoon on the absurdity of each position they took in order to relieve my tension. The wall did break in the fall. We received a call on Thanksgiving day during dinner. My son Joel drove to Michigan and he and Cecil repaired the break in front of Sundune and The Retreat (Kropps) in the frigid water and increasing snow flurries.

As it turned out, we were more fortunate than our neighbors to the north. Our wall then held. Their cement cap fell over. That was followed by various expensive attempts to solve the problem and they lived with the mess until we all finally put in rip rap.

When our children grew older, the cottage felt the pinch. One summer Joel brought up some friends and, with his siblings, proceeded to expand. They built a deck beside

*Moving the wall in Sundune remodelling.*

the porch. Then they sawed off the end wall, complete with glass windows, inched it to the end of the deck, and finally secured it. This was practically an all-day process and an especially tense one when an afternoon wind came up. It made, however, a wonderful extension for family dining. Another year, he spent the winter at the cottage. He and his sisters and brothers dug out under the entire cottage and eventually were able to complete a downstairs that now makes it possible for children and grandchildren to visit here together.

One incident that happened during our downstairs renovation tickled us. Armin was sitting in the gutted out site, smoking his pipe. Suddenly he called, "Katy, come quick and bring your camera." I went down to see the strangest sight. Sitting across from Armin and staring at him was a young Great Blue Heron taking his ease. "Oh dear, I have no film," I said. "Keep him here while I run to South Haven." When I returned a half hour later,

*The Beck family. 2001.*

there he was, plopped in the same spot. I took my picture and asked why the bird hadn't moved. Armin said he got up, but when Armin walked with him, he went right back and sat down. Later, the bird walked up a plank to the sand, across the back yard, up the road, and disappeared. The next day I found him wading in the Brandywine.

Through the years, art has been a big part of our summers. When my children were growing up, Aunt Barbara came each summer to do art projects with them – stone pictures, sand casting, drawing, and painting. Now that the grandchildren come to our cottage, our friend Charlotte Bond has worked with them each summer – clay, silkscreen, tie dye, painting, and so on. This is a place of inspiration and everyone feels success.

Remembering fondly the hours spent with Betty Householder - learning the crafts she shared with us - brings me to the thought of her interest in continuing this history project. She was the spirit behind the attempts to preserve some people's memories of the past. It wasn't until Marilyn and Don Henkel became involved in the 20-year-old task that it looked like it would become a reality. Marilyn, with her drive, her computer ability, and especially her gift for writing, has made all the difference. Without Don and his combination of skills in computer technology and photography, there would be little to show in the way of illustration. They have been single-minded and talented partners whom I admire and cherish as friends.

Now, with 10 grandchildren, a 5$^{th}$ generation of our family is enjoying this bit of dunes, woods, and lakefront. We have been among the fortunate of the world to have a lovely bit of nature's creations to refresh and sustain us in our lifetime in this place we call Palisades Park.

# Pat Peat Dusendschon

## "Palisades in the 30's and 40's"

From August, 1964 Patter Special Edition

Among our many welcomed Palisades servitors of the late 30's and 40's were three in particular who called regularly at our cottage. In those pre-electric days of the kerosene stove (when our fascinated eyes followed the glub-glub of the air bubbles in the glass tank and the burner's pink glow behind the crackled isinglass holders - and the peculiar warm light of the lamps with their smoky chimneys and ever-to-be-trimmed wicks) was the many-doored golden oak ice-box which relied on the scheduled visit of Tony Canonie to keep it in good working order. With dark hair and charming Italian grin, Tony would clump up the back hill steps with a great ice chunk, gripped by enormous tongs, dripping cool rivulets down the canvas shoulder pad and onto his bare back. After he chipped the block down to size, we youngsters could always count on a chunk or two to suck on. Later, after the War, it was with an almost proprietary elation we watched his company trucks and bulldozers build the highways and bridges all around our area!

To have had acquaintance with Mr. Shepherd, the second of our deliverymen, was not only an assurance of regular milk supplies but the pleasure of doing business with a gentleman of the "old school." His bearded dignity, though clothed in immaculate farmer's overhauls, was worthy of a diplomat assigned to some foreign princely court. Furthermore, it was not just milk he brought, but Jersey milk, the bottles already topping with richly thickening cream! He usually arrived with an additional armload of gladiolas, berries fresh from the bush, sweet corn, and eggs still warm from the hens. When this largesse was laid out on the back porch for our approval, it was more like a solemn offering laid out on an epicurean altar by an emissary of the Olympian gods, rather than an ordinary household transaction.

My personal favorites of all, however, were the Hempys. Where they were was sure to be their trusty team. To a horse-crazy child, these glamorous horses were an epitome of delight. The one, a rusty black, the other a dull dapple-grey, Nig and Prince were sure of a handout of dusty roadside weeds and sassafras leaves when the garbage wagon made its appointed stop on our hill. They came to the north end by way of the back road, across the "broken-down-bridge" (in good repair in those days) and though the wagon made no sound in the soft sand, our alert ears could pick up the gentle snorts and harness clinkings long before the entourage came into view. The team came attired in flapping leather-fringed trappings which supposedly warded off the hovering cloud of flies. Mrs. Hempy wore a most re-doubtable sunbonnet and, more often than not, had snapped off the top of a sassafras sapling for her personal fly-chaser. Spry as a monkey, Mr. Hempy would pop off the seat, garbage bound, and on his return and subsequent "toss" into the open wagon, <u>might</u> issue an invitation to ride on the seat with them to the next stop! Sheer delight …

*Mr. R. D. Hempy. 1957.*

Now a cable has made possible an electric stove and lights, hot water, a refrigerator, radio, television and telephone; civilization is ever with us on the dunes. But old friends still pop up in remembrances and one doubts the efficient sanitation truck has half the charm or "character" of the old, open garbage wagon!

# Marty Edwards

From August 16, 1980 <u>Patter</u>

The magic year for the J. Abbott Edwards family was 1934, when we visited Art and Mabel Mason in "A Wee Bit of Heaven," now (1980) owned by Ward and Gert Harris who bought it from the Masons (#139). Mr. Mason had been Ab's manual training teacher in high school in Jackson, Michigan, many years earlier. We rented the cottage in 1935 while the Masons were visiting in California. Upon their return, we didn't want to leave, so we rented a tiny place on what is now route #8. That cottage burned down during the winter, some years later. In 1936, we rented the Manniere cottage on the beach. This is now called Clint Brae, owned by the John O'Connor family (#158). Oh, what a good time we had, a beach that stretched forever, or so it seemed to our bare feet on the hot sand. Everyone had beach umbrellas then, which made the beach quite colorful. There was no road behind the beach cottages, so everything was transported by hand and wheelbarrows along the boardwalk, from the parking area south of us. It was quite a challenge to keep the wheelbarrow from ending up in the sand and dumping everything out. Tony Canonie brought out ice and Mr. Hempy collected our garbage by driving along the beach with his horse-drawn wagon. How the kids would follow him. Someone always rode up beside him. What a treat! (Who remembers the horses' names?) There was a vacant lot next to Clint Brae #158 where the Hi Brazil #159 now stands, but we chose to build our cottage in the woods, for more privacy.

In 1937, in the month of May, our Tree House #163 was built. It is the second log cabin to be built in the Park. The Holmes-Woodhouse cottage #113 was the first. The logs came from the thumb area of Michigan. Ab located an old ice house and laid out each wall on the floor and marked each log for easy cutting and assembling on our lot. They were transported to the Park by his auto transports (he was a transporter for the Packard Motor Company) and then Tony Canonie brought the logs into the Park. With the help of Oren Reid and a friend, Ab built his "dream."

The French doors and windows are from an estate that burned and are oak, with one/fourth inch glass windows. (They are loads of fun to clean.) The children, Shirley (Sentgerath), Marty (Whippen) and Dave Edwards, gave the cottage its name – Tree House – since it was a house made of trees. They also recall the housewarming we had that summer. Ab had spent his childhood summers in Maine and, of course, who can resist a good Maine lobster? We had several barrels of live lobsters shipped in from Maine; each guest picked his own and popped it into the huge tub of boiling water which was sitting over the fire in the fireplace. Everyone sat on the floor along a long piece of oil cloth and used hammers to crack the shells. What a mess, but such a happy time. A ukulele even ended up in the refrigerator, smashed. Someone had sat on it.

Everyone is now aware of the route signs throughout the Park – very fancy. Well, Ab started it all with his small pieces of metal with numbers painted on them and nailed to the trees. Shirley has observed that there are still quite a few of these still visible. We are on route #10, as are the Harold Drapers (now Ray Lewis, Jr.). I will always love this home he built for me and our children. It will always be the gathering place for the second and third generations, and so on and so on, for many years to come.

*The Edwards cottage, Treehouse, #163.*

*(Though Mrs. Edwards passed away in 1990, her great grandchildren do, indeed, still enjoy the cottage.)*

*The "surrey-with-a-fringe-on-the-top."*

# Freida Eldredge

### "Palisades Fifty Years Ago"
July 18, 1980 Patter

Palisades fifty years ago – well, you might have been met at the Railroad Station in Covert, by a "surrey with a fringe on top," and driven to Del Jones's Sturtevant Lodge in the Circle at Palisades Park. At that time, the beach was so wide that you would run fast to reach the water to prevent scorching your feet on the hot sand en route.

There was a general store and post office managed by Mrs. Helen Packard opposite the hotel. The store was well stocked and you could place an order for future needs; and the post office was a meeting place for the community.

The Soda Bar, where Mr. Quick's daughter was always in control, was a great place to visit with your neighbors on the large screened porch. Mr. Hempy collected the garbage and tended the roads. On quiet days, he would drive his team down the beach and shovel up the small stones along the water's edge to use on the roads. These were days of great economy.

Then there were the tennis courts – very popular and maintained mostly by the young people. They rolled and marked, and woe betide anyone who dared to play on the courts before they were dry. There were some very good players who competed with each other and were in local tournaments. They had great mentors in George Bishop and Frank Householder, and wonderful support from the benches!

The community was small, and rarely did you pass anyone on the road whom you couldn't call by name. The roads were not marked because the residents knew their way, but the visitors had a difficult time finding their friends. So the local boys gave directions or jumped aboard to show the way.

We cooked and canned on oil stoves and used oil lamps for lighting, but there was great contentment and a feeling of privilege top be part of the Palisades community. May Palisades continue to be a joy to future generations.

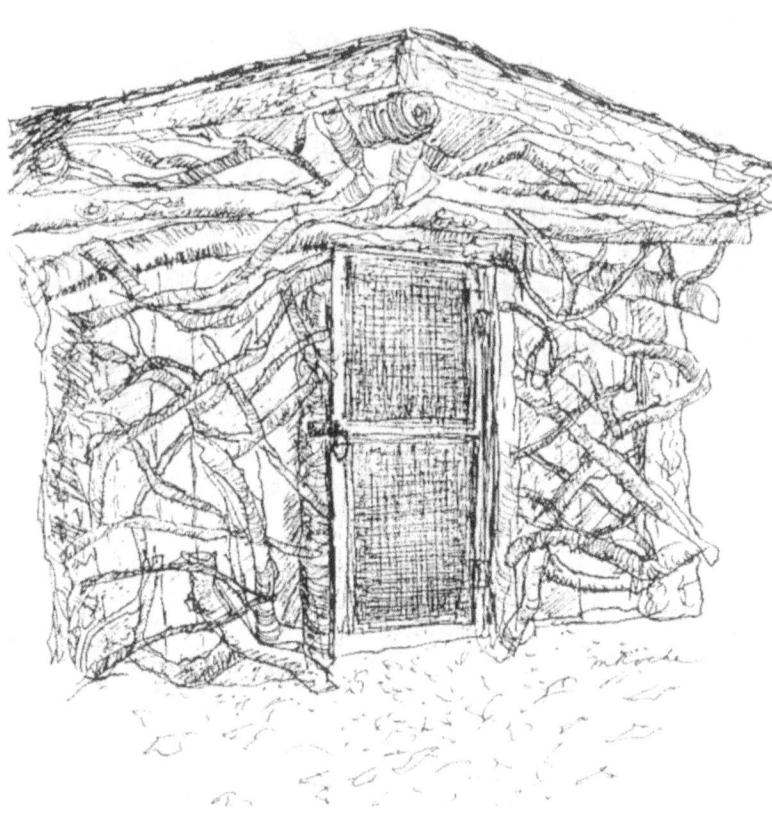

*Grandpa Henderson.*

# Bert Henderson

Written in 2001.

I came to the Park in the summer of 1930 as a one-year-old. We came from Chicago to Covert by train and from Covert to Palisades by horse and buggy. Grandfather Henderson had been in the Park since 1905. My father first met Mardy Mehegan when he was in college. She was still in high school. He sat in the seat next to her on the train and brought her to the Park by the buggy he had hired.

I have fond memories of riding on the Hempy's wagons and horses and playing around their barn. I remember the gas station and its candy at the Park entrance. The dunes, the Sugar Bowl, and Marvin's Slide were favorite playgrounds. Brandywine Creek with its lake was larger, cleaner, and deeper. We could wade up the stream a long way.

The original Hermitage cottage had an "ice" refrigerator, a kerosene stove with three burners, and an oven that fit on one burner. That did not change until the late 50's. This was a vacation home and Mom was not going to do fancy cooking for children or grandchildren. It was not until the late 60's that I put in a phone. When my grandfather, David Henderson, was on up in years and still living in the Park all winter, my father tried to put in a phone for him. Grandpa Henderson ripped the phone out every time it was put in. He liked the isolation.

Change is inevitable, but I would like to return to the slower pace of years past – to the picnics on the beach without trash and to the days when I knew everyone and sat for hours on the beach with different friends, just talking. There were not many renters and the Park had fewer and simpler cottages. Now cottages have become year-round homes with freezers, dishwashers, two or three bathrooms with showers, washers and dryers, and propane furnaces. Cottages have become so expensive that most of my children cannot afford to buy into the Park. To get back to a true feeling of ownership and partnership, we need to enforce our rules. We can't pick and choose which rules to follow anymore. We want to – and need to – protect our traditions.

*Garage and gazebo made by Mr. Henderson.*

## Esmah Orcutt and Clara Strothers

**"Reminiscences from the Hermitage"**
August 22, 1963 Patter

It all started about 1882, when I, now a piece of lumber in the cottage called Hermitage (#120), found myself on the way to Chicago to be used in one of the buildings at the city's first World's Fair. After the Fair, the buildings were dismantled, and I – along with other used lumber – was shipped to Michigan where I became a part of one of the early cottages in a development called Palisades Park, which was a project of Arthur Quick.

Fifty-three years ago (1910), Alice and Guy Orcutt, newly-weds from Chicago, came to the Park with the former's parents, Mr. and Mrs. David Henderson, Sr. They were looking for a place where Mr. Henderson would be able to spend more time in the out-of-doors. There were, at that time, three cottages for sale, but because of its central location, they chose my cottage, THE HERMITAGE, which is probably better known now as the HENDERSON cottage.

Through the years the Henderson clan have made the cottage their summer headquarters. Dad Henderson, whose picture hangs in the Clubhouse, helped Mr. Quick survey many of the trails. He became one of the early caretakers of the Park and some of the products of his artistry may still be seen in the rustic fences, benches, chairs, garages, and rest shelters which he built.

Mrs. Alice Henderson was a familiar figure in the Park. She was well known for her wave and cheery smile to those who passed the cottage on their annual walk to Thunder Mountain. She also always participated in the benefit bazaars which were held at the Clubhouse.

As the family increased, one could often hear the familiar "Honk! Honk!" of Mrs. Shattuck's old Model-T taxi as it bumped and swayed along the winding roads, bringing a new load of summer arrivals from the Covert train. Mr. Shepherd, a near-by farmer with fascinating whiskers and a gentle smile, became a frequent visitor as more of his fresh milk, butter, and cheese were needed. The grocery wagon which brought produce from the surrounding farm area was a welcome sight to the women who gathered around it to do their weekly shopping.

It was a special treat for the Park residents to go to Ballou Inn and chat with friends as they sat in the rocking chairs on the upper porch. Later, when the present Lodge replaced Ballou Inn, some of the rocking chairs from the upper porch became part of the treasured furniture of the HERMITAGE. Another treasured bit of furniture is the old oil stove which still enjoys a prominent spot in the kitchen – although long since replaced by an electric stove. Just so has running water replaced the old green hand-pump and electric lights replaced the oil lamps.

Some happy memories of the Henderson children and grandchildren include: annual hikes to Marvin's Slide; cross country hikes to Forest Dunes, Thunder Mountain, and the Sugar Bowl; gathering and eating choke cherries at the beach; climbing the old tree at the foot of Reservoir Hill; tumbling down the sand bluffs (now prohibited); playing in the first tennis tournament and enjoying a soda at the Soda Fountain afterwards; going with "Dad" Henderson to play golf on the nine hole golf course, the first tee of which was located near the present site of the new tennis courts; visiting the old Ice House, located near Lake Palisades and, nearby, the stable where Mr. and Mrs. Hempy kept the horses that pulled the garbage wagon for the Park; and swimming in Lake Michigan for many delightful hours.

Again this year, members of the Henderson family and their friends gathered for rest, recreation, and renewal of friendships with their summer neighbors of long standing – the Ray Lewises, the Cooneys, the Davises, and the O'Briens.

I, this old board recently repainted, have really enjoyed being a part of the Henderson cottage. I heartily endorse the statement which I hear every year: "Palisades Park has the best beach and the most beautiful sunsets. It is the most wonderful place in the whole world. We love it."

*Henderson porch and furniture made by Grandpa Henderson.*

# The Senior Davy Crockett of Palisades

By Bert Henderson
July 30, 1955 Patter

The editors of the Patter have asked me to write a brief story about my father, David McAllen Henderson, who, because of his great attachment to Palisades Park, I will hail as the Senior Davy Crockett of the Park. As a close protégé of Mr. Quick, founder of the Park, my dad, from 1909 to the year of his death, at 87 years of age, knew and loved every portion of the Park. His loyalty spread to practically all Park patrons, young and old. So devoted was he to Palisades that he was one of the few who lived the winters through at the Park – especially after the death of my mother. He fought several forest fires and rescued two juveniles from possible drowning. In his later years, he became expert at creating rustic signs, rustic fences, and other decorations carved out of sassafrass wood.

Many of us, now fairly adult, will recall the white collie dog that was the constant companion of our Senior Davy Crockett. Dad knew every householder and contributed to the beauty and utility of many of the Park domiciles. He always had a "cheerio" or a story for the young ones whom he loved and by whom he was loved, in return.

Our family notes, with pride, that the management of the Park displays a photo of my dad in the Clubhouse. His face reflects the heritage of love and devotion he always possessed for the Park and for Hermitage Cottage, where he lived for many years. Others will come and go in caring for the Park and its people, but the memory of the Senior Davy Crockett will continue for many years.

*Mr. Henderson's twig "art work" under Treetops cottage # 83.*

*The gazebo in the Henderson's yard.*

*Stairs up to Heisel-Hession cottage, Marjomore #164, on left.*

# Mary Lou Heisel Hession
Written in 2002.

So many wonderful memories come to mind. We had a DeWitt motorboat which we kept for two summers in the Brandywine. We moved it to South Haven Harbor the following summer because the entrance to the lake from the Brandywine would close up and we had to spend much time shoveling sand to get the boat out into the lake.

I remember going to Marvin Slide, a sand dune north of Linden Hills, with the Stoddard family. My father would take the food supplies and a couple of kids in the boat with him and the rest would hike up. One time we spent the night sleeping under the stars. We had many things to do. There was a golf course that my parents played on, but it was not a good one. We played tennis, hiked up to Thunder Mountain, climbed the Sugar Bowl, played Bunco in the Clubhouse one night a week, delivered telegrams for Mr. Jones, and enjoyed ice cream cones at the Soda Bar. Family beach cook-outs were much fun - roasting wieners, toasting marshmallows, making S'mores, and singing around the beach fire.

Once a week we would drive to the Iverson farm for fresh vegetables. Their home was outside of Coloma. They always gave us a bouquet of beautiful gladiolas to take home. One summer they invited my son to spend two weeks with them to help out on the farm. Best of all, he liked driving the tractor.

Marjomore #164, our cottage, was designed by my mother and father. Rudy Weber built the cottage and the lot was purchased from Arthur Quick. Rudy built our dining room table. It was made in two sections – the first seated six and the extension seated six more. As our family grew, we added the extension.

*The hand-made table in the Heisel cottage.*

Mr. Henderson built luggage racks for each of our four bedrooms and a rack to hold logs for the fireplace. He used the Sassafras trees he found here in the Park. Mr. Shepherd delivered the milk. He was a handsome man with a white beard and beautiful, olive-colored skin. There was no electricity at this time. Either gasoline or kerosene stoves were used for cooking and lighting and an icebox for refrigeration. After Tony Canonie retired from delivering our ice, he confessed to my mother that he had taken a piece of fried chicken from the icebox one day. He said our icebox was always filled with the best looking food.

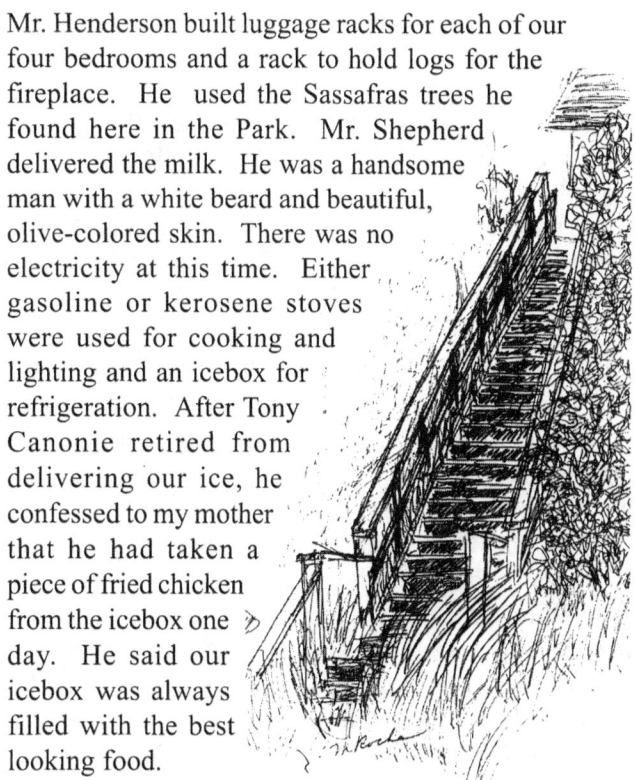

*The Drapers on South Beach. 1935.*

# Nannette Draper Lewis

"Then and Now"
September 30, 1999

I was three years old when I first laid eyes on Palisades Park. What an adventurous place it was — winding roads, beautiful wooded dunes, and a beach that went on forever. A perfect place to explore and delight in everything. Our family lived in Oak Park, and heard about Palisades from our cousins, the Donald Sperrys, who had a cottage in Saugatuck. Mother wanted a summer escape from the heat, so my parents decided to go around the lake to beautiful Michigan beaches.

The first cottage we stayed in was Mrs. Berg's, now Dinnins #133. I remember the long walk down to the Happy Valley beach on long, hot summer days. We would set up the heavy canvas beach umbrella, put out the beach towels, roll the inner tubes (of real automobile tires) down to the water, and jump with the waves, delighting in our surroundings. Very few people were on the beach; the Park did not have a large population. There were few cars and everyone knew everyone. The hiking trails were exciting places to discover. The Park was a magical place for a young child

In 1933, with the help of Orien Reed and his father, from Covert, my folks designed and built their cottage, The Four Winds #165, on a high ridge covered with trees near the Sugar Bowl. It was second nature for my brother and me to scramble over to the dunes with our cocker spaniel, Boots. The Sugar Bowl was a joy to play in — climbing up to the top of the dune, looking out on the Lake from high atop the ridge, then running and tumbling down the hill, head over heels with a head full of sand, shouting at the top of our lungs. Family bonfires with hot dogs and roasted marshmallows were always special times there.

We would leave for Palisades the day summer vacation started. Mother would be in the car at Holmes School, all packed and waiting for my brother and me at 3:00 to drive the long, four hour trip over to the lake. My father would arrive later on for the weekend, as most Palisades fathers did. The mothers and children would stay from early June through Labor Day weekend — with the dads coming from Chicago or Indianapolis for weekends. That's the way it was.

*Fran Draper and visitor on beach near Sandbox #175. 1948.*

*Painting by Wilbur Peat*

# THE PEACE OF WILD THINGS

When despair for the world grows in me
And I wake in the night at the least sound
In fear of what my life and my children's lives may be,
I go and lie down where the wood drake
Rests in his beauty on the water, and the great heron feeds.
I come into the peace of wild things
Who do not tax their lives with forethought
Of grief.  I come into the presence of still water,
And I feel above me the day-blind stars
Waiting with their light.  For a time
I rest in the grace of the world, and am free.

From *Openings* by Wendell Berry
Harvest Books (San Diego, 1980)

Color Photos by
Katy Beck and Don Henkel
(Unless Noted)

# Brandywine

# Lake Moods

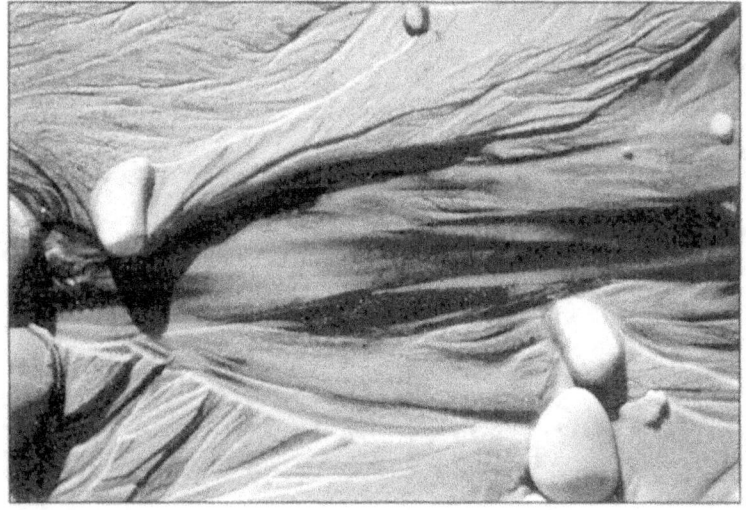

# Nature

# Flowers of Palisades

# Dunes

# Meadow

# Roads

Mary Jones photo

# Old and New

# Palisades Sunsets

We never really had to go out of the Park for any supplies. Mrs. Overheul, and later Mrs. Packard, ran the store at Ballou Inn, with fresh vegetable, meats, and bakery goods – everything we needed. The Post Office was adjoining with Mrs. Underwood, the Postmistress. Park members each had a Post Office Box with numbers identifying the box – and it was always the highlight of the day to peer into our box to see if that special mail we were hoping for had arrived.

The Soda Bar run by Julia Hill (Arthur Quick's daughter) was the meeting place for the kids in the Park. Julia loved children and would make the best cherry and lemon cokes and ice cream cones. We all perched up on the ice cream stools, put our elbows on the counter, and watched her every move. The screened porch off the west side of the Soda Bar was a favorite spot to sit around the table and listen to all the Park news.

*The Soda Bar with flag at half-mast after 9/11/01.*

For trips outside the Park, our parents bought gasoline at the station on the Blue Star Highway run by Charley Tunecke and Tony Canonie, with Gene Howe from Covert as the helper. Charley, with his red hair and mass of freckles, was as friendly as they come. Tony, in his late teens and early twenties, delivered the ice to all the ice boxes in the cottages and he was the heartthrob of the Park. He had a heavy piece of leather that he would throw over his left shoulder and would rest a huge chunk of ice on it, holding it in place for delivery with his big ice tongs.

Although South Haven was a long, long seven miles away, we frequented Mr. Underwood's Barber Shop for haircuts, Birge and Birge for groceries, Tates for books, McDonald Drug Store for all kinds of things, Malbones for hardware, MacKenzies for baked goods, Hollys for food and ice cream sundaes after the movies at the Model Theater, and the South Haven Lumber Yard (now the South Haven Yacht Club) for supplies. Sometimes we shopped in Hales Department Store. South Haven had a Coast Guard Station in the 40's and no family trip was complete without a walk on the pier and a visit to the station to watch the Coast Guard sailors work on their rescue boats, the original of which is now on display at the Maritime Museum.

When we did not want to drive the long distance to South Haven to shop, a dirt road opposite the Linden Hills entrance led to Covert. I learned to drive on that sandy road, past fields of wildflowers to the town, with its meat market and general store called Sinks. My mother always bought a large slice of rat cheese (sharp, sharp aged cheddar) from the huge round of cheese displayed. It was a real treat. Sinks meats were excellent and the store did a thriving business with Park members. Many will remember going beyond Sinks to Sarnos for fresh fruits and vegetables and to Iversons for the same, along with gladiolas.

On weekends all our fathers would arrive in their three-piece suits, hats on, straight from the office, some carrying brief cases. Some arrived in St. Joe on the train from Chicago and were met by their families. I remember sitting on the beach at the south end late on Friday afternoons and seeing Mr. Seymour (from what is now Cheers Cottage #156) pushing his wheelbarrow, filled with his luggage, along the boardwalk to his cottage, still dressed for work. One by one, the fathers would put on their Palisades swimsuits and dash to the beach and get in their canoes or sailboats.

On weekends, to keep the Park secure for it members, the Board relied on Joe Putz (a longtime Park employee who did odd jobs for all of us) to stand guard at the intersection of Route 1 and Ravine Road, where the bulletin board is posted. He would hold a long rope strung from a post or tree. Palisades was a relatively small community of cottage owners at that time and most of us knew each other, so the Board did not issue stickers for our cars. Joe Putz knew many Park faces, and so as our car approached him, and he recognized us, he would lower the rope to the ground and let us pass, giving us a nod as we went by. The system worked quite well. Joe had a sister, Mary, whom many people will remember.

Among the interesting people that came into the Park during that time was Mr. Gervais, who owned a little cottage and sold chickens door to door, always attired in a three-piece black suit. Mr. Shepherd, who was the milkman, came in his pickup truck to deliver milk and cream. He sold his milk (with the cream on top) in narrow necked, thick glass bottles, along with fresh churned butter and fresh hen's eggs. He was a full bearded man, wearing coveralls and a large straw hat and carrying a six-bottle wire milk carrier. He was quite a sight to behold! Mr.

Henderson, Sr., a fine man and a naturalist, carved some of the beautiful twig signs in the Park and built several twig shelters for cars. An early Park resident, he was the grandfather of Bert Henderson. The Underwoods, who lived outside the Park entrance, were a quiet working couple who provided essential services to people. Mr. Underwood had his barbershop in South Haven and Mrs. Underwood was our longtime Postmistress before Mrs. Packard took over upon her retirement. Both were pleasant unassuming people.

*The Sturtevant Lodge. 1945.*

Beach parties were held during the weekend; in the 40's, most parties took place north of Brandywine Beach – where the high school and college kids congregated. Sturtevant Lodge (now Master Lodge) run by Delano Jones was always full of weekend guests, and his dining room (now O'Brien's) served not only his guests, but also many Park families who enjoyed dinner there. Telegrams were used for fast messages at that time, and Del Jones would give us the telegrams to deliver. Our ten cent tip payment we spent at the soda bar.

Mr. Hempy was a delightful "by cracky" character. Everyone loved him and his wife. They would hitch their two horses to the flat bed wagon and go throughout the Park collecting garbage, while swatting the ferocious flies that followed them. It was wonderful to hear the sound of the snorting and struggling horses and the harness jingling as they labored up the hills with Mrs. Hempy urging them on. As they went down the steep and curving road by Harpers' and Masons' cottages, she would have to hold them back with "whoas." The garbage wagon would travel down the boardwalk in front of all the beach cottages and the old pump station on Clubhouse beach. The horses were kept in a barn where there is now a parking area opposite the Village Green.

*Squeak Knapp. 1938*

Mr. Warren Knapp was the Park Manager in the 40's. He was a wonderful person with two sons, Clair and Squeak. The entire Park was saddened by Squeak's tragic death when he was killed in a private plane crash at the age of 21. Cecil Burrous followed in Mr. Knapp's footsteps as Park Manager in 1959 and faced many Park challenges during those years of beach erosion and seawalls. Fortunately for the Park, Cecil was an excellent manager, well liked by everyone. He kept the Park in excellent condition. Cecil retired from the Park as Manager in the 70's to become very involved in construction work in the Park and continues to do that to this day, finally retiring in 2002.

My love of nature and appreciation of life was shaped and nurtured at Palisades. My life-long love of the game of tennis was born at the age of seven on the clay courts of the Park and nurtured under the teaching of Tony Malinowski, the Recreation Director. There were very few girls my age to play with, but somehow Shirley Edwards

Sentergrath always managed to find a racquet to hit the ball with me. There were lots of boys: Ray Lewis, Bill Eldridge, Bill Eifrig, Bert Wilson, Chuck Hammerschmidt, Ben Bishop and others, that played the game and, of course, that was the impetus to learn to play good tennis because they were excellent players and cute, besides. Eventually, Ray and I married in 1954, with Bill Eldridge as a groomsman. Our son, Ray, repeated a Park summer romance when he met Lisa Henry, Diane and Chuck Henry's daughter, at Palisades. In 1994, they were married in South Haven with a reception afterwards on the Village Green. I believe this is a first in the Park for a two-generation Park family marriage.

We've had our share of Mother Nature's fury on our beaches. My childhood was spent on beautiful sandy wide beaches in front of the cottage Hi Brazil #159. We would walk down and up the 100 wood steps by the Heisel/Hession - Harper/Doyle cottages and between Sandbox and Hi Brazil. The beach was so wide that we would have to toss a beach towel down on the sand and stand on it to cool our burning feet, before continuing to the water's edge where we cooled them once again!

We kept our green Old Town canoe on wood horses covered with canvas on the beach with no fear of the lake water reaching it during bad storms. Once during a storm, my brother, Jack, and I came down to check on it and found a young man huddled and shivering under the canoe. His small sailboat had capsized offshore during the unexpected storm. We ran back up to Four Winds to make sandwiches to bring back down to him and also blankets and towels. He was very grateful for our actions; we had done a good deed.

On many afternoons at the beach, some of the kids would make big sandcastles by hand (no plastic molds) with moats in front of the castles to withstand the waves that we knew would be coming from the wake of the steamship Roosevelt, way out in the Lake. The ship made daily trips from Chicago to St. Joe and then South Haven, returning to St. Joe before going back to Chicago. It carried 300 passengers and passed off shore from the Park about 3:30 p.m. It was very exciting to see which sandcastle would not be washed away by the Roosevelt's waves. Whoever was the best builder was treated to an ice cream cone at the Soda Bar! My birthdays were always celebrated at the cottage. All the kids from the south end of the Park were invited to a balloon swim party on the beach where we had swim and inner tube races with cake (MacKenzies) and ice cream (Shermans) to follow. It was a wonderful way to celebrate.

Other things come to mind: the beautiful winding roads of the Park (always challenging the best of drivers) with their unfolding vista of the forest; the constant roar of the Lake during storms; the screeching of the seagulls as they hover over fish in the waters below; the glorious colors of the sunsets that are so reflective of the beauty of God's Nature; the nostalgic feeling I get when I go to the Soda Bar; our very special boardwalk which promotes a sense of community and friendliness in the Park.

Special to me are the hiking trails - so laboriously and generously maintained by several Park members; the clay and hartru tennis courts - so unique to a community of our size - and many tennis tournaments; the wonderful, storybook, ancient, willow tree along the road just past the Village Green on the way to Brandywine Bridge.

*The Draper family in their canoe. 1935.*

323

# Old-Timer's "Memories Way Back"

**August, 1964 Patter Special Edition**
Author Unknown

The Pere Marquette train came to a grinding stop in the little town of Covert, Michigan. We were on our way to Palisades Park for a vacation. A dip in Lake Michigan seemed ideal after the hot, sticky ride from Chicago. Mrs. Shattuck was waiting with her horse and carryall for the trip down to the Lake to our rented cottage on the beach.

That night, we had one of Palisades's famous thunder showers! It thundered! It lightened! It blew! It rained! It poured! Suddenly, we realized the roof was leaking on the bed. We checked on the children. Sonny's bed was wet. We pulled it out from the wall and put a utensil under the leak. Our bed could not be moved. The room was made for the bed or the bed was made for the room. The rest of the night we slept, jack-knifed on the upper half of our bed, listening to the drip, drip, ping, ping, in the dish pan or in the kettle at the foot of the bed. In the morning, we found the water works out of order. No water in the sink. The toilet would not work. We walked to the Hotel. Mr. Jones said his facilities were for his guests, only.

A cottage in the woods, built smack up against a dune, was available. The wall of the cottage next to the sand bank was creosoted to take care of ants, bugs, and insects. It smelt awful. The odor was very strong. With the doors and windows open, we thought it would be livable. We moved in. Next morning, the children were sick to their stomachs and no one cared for breakfast.

A cottage on the south beach seemed "foolproof." Charley carried our bags and baggage down. Meantime, my husband dashed back, out of breath, to the cottage in the woods to retrieve my best, go-to-meeting, blue and white, polka dot chiffon dress. I had left it hanging in the bedroom. It was gone!

Next year we went to the Hotel to be guests of Mr. Jones.

*Old-Timer's "Refuge" - Sturtevant Lodge . 1914*

*Butcher Cottage #151 with stairs to upper deck.*

# Doris Butcher Patterson
"My Favorite Memories of Palisades Park, 1933 - 1975"
November, 2000

In 1933, my family came to Palisades Park for the first time. There were five of us – my parents, Bea and Paul Butcher, my brothers, Dan and Bob, and me. We made the trip in our family car. Some of the luggage went on the car running board. It was held on by expandable metal attachments on one side of the car. We rented a beach cottage just south of the Brandywine Creek. Today it belongs to the Vercillos (#39).

I was two years old and enjoyed running up and down the shore, splashing in the waves, and feeling the warm sand on my feet. That was when I first fell in love with the beautiful Lake Michigan, the great sandy beach, and Palisades Park.

We had such a great time that we returned the following year to the same cottage. That year we came with our new baby sister, Phyllis. When she went into the Brandywine headfirst, my brother, Bob, got great praise for pulling her out. My brothers got some old packing crates and made a raft out of the wood. To help it to float, they tied two inner tubes underneath it. They paddled it around with a board. My cousin and I got to ride on it, too! Everyone enjoyed picnics on the beach. We would bring down a card table and chairs for the adults. All the kids sat on the wooden seawall to eat their hamburgers. When the fire glowed down to coals, we always enjoyed roasting marshmallows.

Evenings are always very beautiful at the Park. While the adults watched the sunset over the lake, the kids would play hide-and-seek. As darkness grew deeper, the stars would shine brightly. The crickets and frogs would begin their songs. The deep croak of the big bull frogs that lived in Lake Palisades was a noise that always scared me. The big old garage on the corner near the Circle scared me, too. My brothers would yell, "Boo!" and the echo came back – "Boo!"

On the other side of the Brandywine Creek was an old cottage foundation. Everyone who looked at it said that the cottage had been washed out into the lake by a big storm. At three, I imagined that whole cottage floating off the foundation out on the lake, just like a big boat.

In the late 30's and early 40's, we rented the Browning cottage, now the Tom Flynns' #152. We had big family gatherings there. The rear sleeping porch could hold a lot of kids. We slept "wall to wall" on cots. When everyone was in bed, we would talk and laugh until, at last, the waves lulled us back to sleep. One night all the boys were hiding under their covers with flashlights. They said they were reading comic books. They would pass them around, joking and laughing, saying, "Oh, that was good!" No one thought much about this until the next day when my aunt found her cookie tin under one of the cots and all of her chocolate chip cookies were gone!

In those days, the kitchen had a big, yellow, wooden icebox. The upper part held the ice and the lower part held the food. The Canonie brothers brought us ice. They pushed a wheelbarrow along the boardwalk, carrying big blocks of ice wrapped in burlap. Then, using big ice tongs, one of the brothers put the ice block over his shoulder and carried it up the stairs to the kitchen. One day, when I was exploring under the cottage, I saw a metal pipe coming through the floor of the kitchen. I realized that the pipe was for the water that dripped from the icebox – down, down the pipe – to land on the sand under the cottage.

The old kerosene stove had three burners. There was a big old oven that went over the burners when someone wanted to bake. My mother was a great cook and could turn out great blueberry pies when company came.

*Building Butcher cottage in 1947. Built by Tony Canonie, the cottage used cement block construction because lumber was scarce after World War II.*

*Dan and Ruth Klunder Butcher, Mrs. Bea Butcher, Bob and Nancy Seymour Butcher, Doris Butcher Patterson, Phyllis Butcher Hartzler*

We had a huge beach in those years. We even had enough room to build a badminton court in front of the cottage. We outlined the court with rocks.

My sister and I enjoyed going to Mrs. Hill's Soda Shop. Her shop was decorated with a Gay 90's beach scene painted on the old mirror in back of the soda counter. She had cute round tables and metal chairs on the porch, where you could enjoy coke, sodas, and sundaes. Mrs. Packard, with her friend Hazel, ran a small grocery store in the lower back of Ballou Inn. Mr. Shepherd had delivered milk to us, but now we could buy it and lots of other groceries from them. This was very handy for everyone. Mrs. Packard ran the Post Office in the front part of Ballou Inn, so you could get your mail and other things at the same time.

My brothers would occasionally go to Sturtevant Lodge to play the slot machine that was on Mr. Jones's screen porch. They were allowed to do this, but my sister and I were too young. However, they would let us join their "syndicate." If we gave them our nickels, we would have a chance to win. It was funny that our nickels never won! We could all go to the Clubhouse to play Bunco. My brother Bob once won a flashlight as his prize.

In the cottage, there was only one bathroom with a john and a sink with one cold tap. Everyone bathed in the lake in those days. Later on, when we built our cottage, we had hot and cold running water and a shower stall. All the girl friends came over to wash their hair at our house.

During World War II, there were many shortages. We had a hard time getting to the Park due to the rationing of gasoline. One year we had to take the Greyhound Bus. We took the train into Chicago and caught the bus - which went along Route 31, now the Blue Star Highway. The bus stopped in front of the old gas station at 29th Avenue. We had to walk, with our suitcases, to Sturtevant Lodge. We enjoyed our vacation that year at the hotel, with its rooms without baths. The bathrooms were down the hall and had cold running water. We ate our meals in the building next door.

Food shortages were common at that time. Butter was almost impossible to find and margarine was difficult to get, also. One summer when we had lots of relatives visiting us, South Haven A&P Market got a shipment of margarine to sell at one pound to a customer. Two aunts, grandmother, mother, and a cousin each bought one pound. So on one hot summer afternoon, five pounds of white margarine sat on the old cottage table. It was illegal to sell yellow margarine in those days, so we had to mix the five pounds with yellow dye. There was much laughter and many greasy hands, but we had "butter" for our bread and corn on the cob. With limited hot water, everyone headed for the lake to clean up.

*The Butchers working on their boat with Browning's cottage #152 behind them. The Browning cottage was later moved to higher ground next door and Butchers built their cottage on this lot. Photo c. 1930.*

We bought our lot, next door to the Browning cottage, but had to wait to build our own place because of the lack of building supplies. Since wood was not well-seasoned, we built our cottage out of concrete. My father designed our cottage and hired Tony Canonie to build it. It was one of Tony's first jobs after he got out of the service. My brother Bob was interested in engineering and building, so he worked with Tony's crew. Bob slept in a tent during that time. When we built, there was no road into that part of the Park. What is now called Ramblewood Drive ended at the curve in front of the Eberts' cottage #149– which was not built at that time. All building supplies and our furniture had to be hauled down to the beach and along the shore and up to our lot. I remember the day that Hempy's horse and wagon came along the beach with my grandmother's old piano. We still enjoy that piano today. That horse and wagon were kept busy by Hempy and his helper, Joe Putz. They collected the garbage and raked the beach, using the horse and wagon all along the beach.

My father always enjoyed art as his hobby. When he retired, he painted pictures quite often. He sometimes made modern paintings that were abstract. That was how we got the idea for the name of the cottage – Up Side Dune. We joked that we couldn't always tell the up side from the down side of his paintings. Everything in our cottage could be upside down and it didn't matter, as we enjoyed just being there. We still have lots of my father's paintings hanging in our cottage. I've always been very proud of Father and his work as one of the "grand old men" (Nine Old Men) who bought up vacant lots in the Park and then donated them back to help preserve the natural beauty and privacy of the Park.

We were all very happy to have our own cottage (#151). My brothers found their wives at the Park in the late 40's. Dan married Ruth Kluender, who lived in the cottage now owned by the Heavrins. Bob married Nancy Seymore, whose family built the cottage now owned by the Stephenses. I learned to drive a car on the old Park roads. We had a great old '39 Ford station wagon with a floor gear shift. Driving that old car gave me lots of shifting experience, so that I passed my driving test in the summer of '49 in Michigan. My husband gave me my engagement ring on the beach in front of our cottage by the wooden sea wall. We were married in front of our cottage fireplace in August '54. Almost every year, we have celebrated our anniversary here. We brought out children – Julie, Jeff, Steve, and Katie – from California each year. Palisades has always been our great family vacation place.

One of our favorite family things to do was to watch the night lightning storms come across the lake. We would all get up from bed and sit on our lake front porch to watch the lightening flashes. One night when we were watching an exciting storm, the lightening hit our cottage, traveled down the electric line and blew out our stove. The stove made a weird moaning sound as it died. Once, when the water level was very high, we left our children with their grandmother when Andy and I went out to dinner. A big storm came up while we were gone and crashed our rowboat into the sea wall. When we got home, the kids said they were sorry they couldn't save it, but Jeff did save one piece. We have that boat scrap today.

Over the years, our cottage has gone through changes. When there were so many grandchildren, there was not enough room for everyone, so my parents added a second story at the roadside entry. They had an upstairs entry only. When my family came to visit, the kids would go up early in the morning to have breakfast and special time with their grandparents. This upstairs addition changed the roof line so we had to eliminate the lake front upper deck. We added a patio below the lake front porch. We often enjoyed barbecuing and eating there, especially when the beach was small.

Changes in the Park, happily, are not swift. The life here in the 1930's was much more primitive; over the years things have become more modern and comfortable. With comforts, more people are spending more time here each year. Since 1998, my husband and I have spent many of the winter months in our cottage. In the future, the Park may become a winter vacation place.

*Walkway down to beach next to Butcher cottage. Bonnie Dune # 150 to right.*

# Paul Schlacks

**The History of Poustinia, Formerly Neverall Inn.**
2002.

I am not sure what year our cottage was constructed, but we do know that it was already built when the sale, dated January 24, 1924, was approved and the property conveyed from Arthur C. Quick to Nellie Harper Marr and Donald A. Marr, a married couple. Upon their deaths, in 1928 and 1931 respectively, the cottage was left to their sole survivor and daughter, Daisy. Daisy, born October 16, 1883, married William John Schlacks in 1904. They had three children – Virginia, William John, Jr., and Henry Proctor. William, Sr. died in 1933, but Daisy and her children came to the Park each summer during most of the 1930's. Daisy's cousin, my father Howard Schlacks, and his wife Clare brought their family to visit during the summer of 1939. They liked the surroundings so much that they arranged to rent the cottage for the following summer.

At that time, we lived in the South Shore neighborhood of Chicago, near 71st Street and Jeffery Boulevard. It took four hours to get to Palisades because my sisters got carsick every five minutes. There was no such thing as air conditioning, so it was always hot and cramped in the car. My dad would just say, "Roll down the window and stick your head out." Yuck! I remember the long trips through South Chicago: passing the huge steel mills; going by the Lever Brothers plant in Hammond, on Indianapolis Boulevard, with its huge box of Rinso on the roof; passing the terrifying fire-belching oil refineries of East Chicago; sharing the street with the large orange cars of the South Shore Railroad along 5th Avenue in Gary. A drive-in food place called Ted's was a regular pit stop on the south side of the street just before the road split. Then the decision to take the road along the lake (U.S.12) or the faster but more crowded four lane U.S.20. This with a car full of five kids – Dan, Dona, Rowena, Paul, Bob, and later the sixth, Billy, when he was born – a dog, Mom and Dad, and enough luggage tied to the running boards, fenders, and top of the old LaSalle to last us the summer. Both routes were scenic and a cheer would go up when we reached the Indiana-Michigan border. There was a State of Michigan tourist stop just over the border, near Grand Beach, where we would stop to use the facilities. From there, we children would ask every few minutes if we were there yet. "How many more gas stations do we pass before we're at Palisades?" Finally, upon arrival at the Park, we had to find the Schlacks cottage behind the Clubhouse. My sisters refused to ride in the car beyond the fork to the Circle because it often took three or more tries up the hill before we finally made it up to the turn. Once at the cottage, we had the task of removing the huge wooden boards covering the windows and airing out the house. There was something wonderful about that musty odor when we entered the cottage for the first time each summer. A fire stoked in the basement furnace soon provided a reservoir of hot water for the taps in the kitchen and bathroom. I recall a two seater out-house up the hill behind the back porch.

During the War, because gasoline and other commodities were rationed, my Dad wasn't able to come every weekend. We would all wait to see him at the Clubhouse. Occasionally, he would surprise us with a huge 25 pound bar of Blommer chocolate (he knew someone at the factory). He would come over to the Clubhouse with a hammer and chisel and cut off a chunk of milk chocolate for each child. It was wonderful. I also remember peeking through the door, late at night (at least eleven o'clock or so) to watch the goings on in the living room. They would roll up the Indian rug and dance, sing to the piano playing

*Paul's grandfather and two siblings on steps and porch of their cottage # 72.*

of Tom Giblin, and listen to Doc Wilson sing solos. Cad and Doc Wilson, Gordon and Alice Tyrrell (parents of Jayne Mathias), Bill and Mary Moran, Tom and Blossom Giblin, Shi and Jim Regan, Betty and Joe Meyers, Buster and Elenore McCarthy (parents of Kathy Foley), Helen and Don O'Brien, and the Berteaus were all regulars at these little get-togethers.

Although the records are sketchy, we believe that when my dad purchased our cottage from Daisy in 1941, he went to Mr. Quick for approval of the transfer at the annual meeting and Mr. Quick asked my dad to serve as Park President. He was an attorney and the Park was in some difficulty as it was unable to raise dues or sell very much property due to the War. That was the summer of 1941. After that, the membership began electing officers at the annual meetings. Mr. Quick was a benevolent old dictator up until that time and pretty much ran the Park with an iron fist. This was the first time that he relinquished any authority to the members. His daughter, Julia Hill, ran the Soda Bar.

*Clubhouse after it was moved next door. 1961.*

The Clubhouse was towed up from the beach to its present location and expanded in the 30's. We were always the first to meet the Clubhouse couples as we lived only a few feet from the building. When I was small, Bob and Gwen Ott ran it and also Mary Ellen Muchenhirn, who taught me to play piano.

During the 40's and 50's, the beach was quite large and had slides and swings out in front of the pump house. We could get a drink of very cold fresh water from the faucet there. A large clock could be seen in the window. We used to wear silly little rubber shoes to the beach to protect tender feet from the hot sand and stones and pebbles. My mom, Mary Moran, and the other women would give us a nickel for an ice cream cone if we would move the stones and create a path to the first sand bar so they could go out in the water to their necks. They would bounce up and down and chat for what seemed to be hours, wearing white rubber caps on their heads. From the beach, all we would see would be the white heads bobbing up and down. Funny. Mrs. Ott, Sr., used to wear some kind of an outfit that looked like a South American Chiquita Dancer to the beach. Mr. Moran owned a trucking company and had the biggest inner tubes you ever saw. We could get six kids on one tube. Ross Bixby had a very strange red object with pointed ends called a surfboard. It had a glass window in it that we could look through and see the bottom of the lake magnified. We just lay on our stomach on the board and paddled it with our hands. Later, a very large raft was anchored to the first sand bar in front of the Clubhouse beach. Dick Danley had a sailboat and a few people like the O'Briens had motor boats but they kept them moored in South Haven.

There were never very many people with automobiles in the Park during the week. Once I stepped on a rusty nail and it took hours to find someone with a car to drive me to South Haven Hospital for a tetanus shot. My mother was quite upset at me and kept telling me I was going to get lock jaw. (She should have been so lucky.)

Sundays were always challenging as we all needed a ride to church in South Haven. If my dad was here, we would all pile into the LaSalle and pick up anyone who was waiting at the fork for a ride. I recall Annie, an Irish woman who worked for the Donahues, usually was there. Joe Putz was always there on Sundays with the rope across the road to keep strangers from coming into the Park. They could go to the Circle; however, after Joe would confront them, most strangers would just turn around and go to Covert Park or somewhere else. I can still picture his toothless smile.

*Billy Schlacks at bottom of hill cleared by Charley Tunecke and two woodsmen to move Clubhouse.*

*A tree fell on roof of Schlacks cottage. 1952.*

On Sunday evenings, Mr. Quick would stop by to remind my parents to keep us quiet during the vesper services that were held in the Clubhouse each week. My dad would give each of us enough to go get an ice cream cone so we wouldn't disturb the peace.

In the early 40's, my dad would drop off the whole family as soon as school was out in June; we were here for three months of summer pleasure. My earliest playmates were Davie Maier and Billy Kirby. We played Indians a lot and had three forts set up along the water reservoir hill. We would roll up dead leaves in newspaper and try to smoke the thing 'til we'd get sick - pretending it was our peace pipe or some crazy thing. Lucky we didn't set the whole Park on fire. We also raided the Ice Cream Parlor in full Indian regalia, feathers and all, shooting arrows and whooping it up. Julia Hill, Mr. Quick's daughter who ran the place, didn't particularly care for this kind of thing and came to see our mothers about it. The result was we were banned from the Parlor for about three weeks. We were marked men. The snazzy wooden Chris-Craft boat we see in some old postcards of the Brandywine was Billy Kirby's uncle's boat and we were allowed to play on it. His uncle was also a pilot who would fly over Palisades and Lake Michigan at a very low altitude and tip his wings at us on the shore. One day he dropped a little box on a small parachute to Billy. I talked with Billy recently and he told me it contained a small pocketknife that he still carries to this day. It was very exciting to see the plane – but then it was gone. When we found out that he went to fight in the War (WWII), we played soldiers instead of Indians.

The Brandywine was quite deep then, as the locks were down, with Lake Palisades on the east side of the bridge and a place to moor boats on the west. We could dive off the bow into the water safely. The Brandywine water always seemed cooler than the lake, so when we came out we would roll in the hot sand, completely covering our bodies. Once we warmed up, we would go jump in the warm lake to clean off. This also served as our bath because there was no hot running water at the cottage. We went swimming every day; I don't ever remember it being too cold to go in. I recall seeing Mr. Lewis walking by the cottage to go swimming and it was never too cold for him, either.

In 1947, the Hohmans began renting the Brown Derby #142 from Leo Sowerby. To this day, I remember my first encounter with them at the tennis courts. Pete and his brother Rich were playing tennis in their bare feet (how improper) and their net broke. I watched in amusement as they pulled the top cable completely out and then tried to rethread it. We spoke and joked and that began a relationship that lasts 'til this day. Pete is my best lifelong friend and our families have grown up here together. Rich and my sister Row were married for 34 years, before Rich succumbed to cancer on June 6th, 1989. Their eight children all visit Palisades from time to time.

As teenagers, we used to have our parties behind the pump house on the beach. We played the game "Ditch." Plenty of kids were here in the 50's, including a wide age range that always seemed to get along well. Pete Wunsch was at the older end of our group that included Rod Lowrey, Linda Young, Sally Zimlick (Davis), Jack McDougall, Mike Mooney, Robin Campbell, Lori Anderson (Dillman), Pete Hohman, Jimmy Roach, Bill and Dick Giblin, Don O'Brien, Dianne McMahon (Jennings), Dave Eifrig, and – of course – the waitresses at the hotel. We once walked to Benton Harbor along the beach and slept in the Beach House at Jeanne Klock Park; we walked back the next day. That is the furthest I've ever walked in my life. I

*Pete Hohman and Paul Schlacks. 1953.*

was exhausted and slept for 24 hours when we got back. As we got older the beach parties went later. It seemed everyone played a guitar, banjo, or some other instrument. We even had a gut-bucket bass. Singing together was in and so were Schlitz, Drewry's and Champagne Velvet. As we grew older, we sometimes would go to the Rose Villa for a drink and dance, go to Big Mike's for a hamburger, and then down to the beach 'til dawn. I also remember going to Crystal Palace over in Coloma on Paw Paw Lake to see the Glenn Miller band (although he had been killed in WWII) in the 1950's.

The biggest physical change in the Park has been the shoreline in the 60's and 70's; vanishing beaches brought the necessity to build all the seawalls and put in rip rap to save the beachfront cottages. Another big change is the number of golf carts in the Park. I believe the Carrs were the first to have one to help Kevin get to and from the beach and after our Peter lost a leg to cancer at the age of seven, we got one for the same purpose. All of a sudden there are about forty or so and now we decorate them and have a grand parade for the Independence Day celebration.

After my dad died in September of 1976, my brothers and I enjoyed the cottage together for a few years, but as our families grew, Bob and Bill decided to purchase their own homes in the Park. Nancy and I now live here full time (except for a stay in Florida in the winter). The

*Jimmy Roach, Rich Hohman, and Paul Schlacks. 1952.*

Park is truly a different place when the snow flies - beautiful and placid.

Our five children and their mates - Erin Campbell, Howie and Meegan Schlacks, Julie and Brian Troch, Peter and Andrew - all come to Palisades regularly, bringing our grandchildren to enjoy all that Palisades has to offer. Of course, the people are the most special part of Palisades. We know several fourth and fifth generation families. Anyone who passes through the gate is cast with a magical spell to forever want to return.

*The meadow in winter.*

## Jim Williams
Written 2002

My grandfather, J. Harry Jones, visited Palisades in 1908 or 1909. He bought a lot and built the first family cottage where Richard G'Sell is now (#157). It burned down one winter and the cottage was rebuilt in the 1920's. My grandmother, my mother, my aunts and uncle used to spend the summers at Palisades. Grandfather used to come on the boat to South Haven and take a horse and buggy ride from there to Palisades. My grandfather died in 1931 and my uncle, Dr. Roland Mathews, bought the cottage.

I start remembering Palisades in the early 1930's when I would spend several weeks with our family. I remember the gas light fixtures which were converted to electric lights. I remember an icebox and the ice wagon with Tony Canonie, who would chip off a piece of ice for us kids. I remember when we got our electric refrigerator That was a big deal. Our milk was delivered by Mr. Shepherd, who looked like he was from the House of David, using a horse and buggy on the beach. We did our shopping at Sinks in Covert and bought all our fruit and vegetables from an Indian family on the road to Covert. The Interstate wasn't there then.

When we were kids there was a gas station at the entrance to the Park and I think Tony Canonie ran it. Mr. Hempy was Park Manager. Often we left our laundry with him and, later, with Cecil Burrous. Mardy Mehagan was running the Clubhouse. One year we had to sell tickets for some program. Mardy gave me a handful and said, "Don't come back until you have sold them all." The smart kids had sold theirs in the Park so I went to Linden Hills and finally got rid of them all.

Once Bill Seymour talked me into taking my old canvas kayak with sail and outriggers out on a stormy day. We tore the canvas and sails. The next day we taped them and tried to paddle the kayak to Marvin's Slide but it kept sinking. We got home as the sun was setting. When my uncle saw us, he ran up and hugged me; then he slapped me so hard he knocked me over. He thought we had drowned.

It's a mystery why we lived through our childhood. My Uncle Roland built a sailboat and my Uncle Dick built a speed boat. Cousin Jack Mathews and I raced them and sank them. One day we tipped the sailboat over, way out in the lake. It took us hours to get it in - and when I did, I was blue from the cold water. My grandmother, who never had a drink, mixed me a hot toddy, which was mostly whiskey with a little lemon juice. When I finished it, I could hardly walk, talk, or see. Often we

*J. Harry Jones on the Palisades beach. C. 1915.*

*First Jones-Mathews cottage (right) c. 1915.
Lightning burned it down in the early 20's.*

would decide to camp out, up near the Sugar Bowl, but invariably it would rain and we would come home with wet sleeping bags in the middle of the night. Great memories – they go on and on.

The character and personality of Palisades has remained constant for almost a full century. It is full of wonderful, friendly, interesting, and exciting people, raising nice kids in a healthy atmosphere. How lucky we are. I would hope my children and grandchildren keep this tradition going and enjoy the unique pleasure that my grandparents, parents, and I have enjoyed.

*Jack Draper and Jim Williams.
1949.*

*L to R: Margaret Jones Williams (Jim's mother);
J. Harry and Mary Jane Jones (Jim's grandparents);
Gladys Jones Mathews (Jim's aunt);
David Reese Jones (Jim's uncle);
c. 1911.*

# Chapter 5

# The 40's

*1941 - Japan attacks the United States naval base at Pearl Harbor and U.S. enters WW II.*
*1942 - South Haven resorts full despite war.*
*1943 - Big bands reign as does the Jitterbug.*
*1944 - Allies invade Europe on D-Day. 1945 - War ends. FDR dies.*
*1946 - $45,000 fire in South Haven destroys McDonald's drugstore.*
*1947 - General Chuck Yeager breaks the sound barrier.*

## The 40's

World War II brought changes to Palisades Park, just as it did to the whole country. Many young men were in the service. Families hoarded their gas rationing cards to enable a summer trip to the lake. The Circle was still very much the center of the Park – with Helen Packard in her Ballou Inn store and post office, Julia Quick Hill in the Soda Bar, and Del Jones running Sturtevant Lodge. Helen Packard took her meat and cheese coupons to "every grocery store or meat market" in South Haven. "People still wanted meat," she remembered, "despite the wartime shortages." In the Park, although four new clay courts were built in 1941, many activities were curtailed for the duration. The Patter was not published during these years. The annual half mile swim was not held. Clubhouse activities were cut back.

After the war, building supplies were still in short supply. At least one new cottage was built of cement blocks. Tony Canonie returned from his stint with the SeaBees and launched his company with war surplus equipment. One of his first jobs was a seawall at Palisades – as lake high water levels threatened beach cottages once again.

On the 12th of August, 1944, the majority of the members of the then Palisades Park Improvement Association voted to change the name to the Palisades Park Country Club. However, this change was not registered with the State of Michigan until October, 1946. The Michigan Corporation and Securities Commission finally certified the Articles of Incorporation and Amendment of Palisades Park Country Club on June 29, 1953.

The biggest change for Palisades Park was the death of Arthur Quick in 1946. His daughter, Julia Quick Hill, replaced him on the Board – but everyone felt the loss of his guidance, presence, and understanding of the Park. Although the Board worried about having enough money to pay a manager, in July of 1946 such position was offered to Warren S. Knapp at $2400 per annum. He declined, countered with $2800 per annum, and that offer was accepted. At that time, Joe Putz was making 75 cents per hour for eight hour days. The Board was able to pay off the Clubhouse and – according to old minutes – "terminate the extra $5.00 per person in dues" previously ear-marked for Clubhouse purchase. However, shortly thereafter, dues were raised to $50 a year for the 132 paying cottages. In 1947, the Board bought the garage from Julia Hill for $4000, each cottage to pay a $35 assessment. That same year, the minutes mention "a discussion of jeeps and tractors for Park work." Horses would have to suffice for 1947, however. Indeed, the July minutes state the "conclusion that mechanical equipment was not practical" and a motion was carried to continue using horses.

A change of organization and leadership is never easy. In the following article, written from the perspective of 10 years later, Mrs. George Bishop reflects upon some of the problems faced and solved during the 40's. (The article was printed in the August 15, 1953 Patter.)

*Then, the Park residents had not banded themselves closely together. Then everybody's shoulder had not risen to the task of keeping the wheels turning efficiently and happily. Then there was criticism, lack of co-operation, misunderstanding, and dissention. Label it Transition, Growing Pains, but it was hard and it hurt. A few good souls tried tremendously to help. The going was tough. The pull was in opposite directions.*

*Two men emerge from the group of doers of this period. Their hands went again and again deeply into their pockets. Their determination to pull this Park through grew stronger in spite of rebuff and disappointment. Their strong belief was that one day this Park would stand squarely on its own two feet ... the men were Mr. Ernest Wunsch and Mr. Forest Lowrey. You will never know how many medals were furnished from them for the tennis tournaments; how much planning, doing, and spending it took to initiate and carry on marathon swims; how many trips to the Park in the fall and spring storm periods were necessary to help and confer with the then new caretaker, Mr. Knapp; how often legal entanglements were solved for our benefit; how frequently deficits were met. Our thanks and appreciation to them – sincerely and earnestly – for the many, many things – both large and small – they have done and are still doing for this Park!*

*Now, since the rebirth of the Park, two other men emerge from the larger group of doers, to whom we give thanks. One is our past president, Mr. George Boyles, whose firm and gracious leadership has guided us to a sound and remarkable reorganization. He has given us stability which we all feel and are grateful for. The other man is our new president, Mr. William Seymour. Already his contribution to our safety and our progress is inestimable. Already his ideals and plans for our next step upward are crystalizing. To him we owe our willing participation and cooperation.*

Another problem faced in the 40's will sound familiar to Palisaders at the turn of the century – that of Park security. The Van Buren County Road Commission gave the Park permission, in a December 16, 1940 letter to Arthur Quick, to "erect a gate … at the entrance of Ravineway Drive." No more Joe Putz and his road! However, the gate was not magic. By May, 1946, Park minutes state the Board "asked the State Police to make frequent tours through the Park, especially at night, to help keep out vagrants." This editor would suggest that the problem remains to be solved.

A further peek at the 40's Board minutes confirms that the Park, which started as blatantly anti-Hebrew, was still making decisions on the basis of race and/or creed. In official Park minutes, their "discussion of finances" considered the hiring "of colored help at 75 cents an hour as against white help at $1.00 per hour." Fortunately for us all, such discriminatory hiring practices would, a few decades later, be illegal.

For all the changes wrought by War and the immediate postwar years, Palisades remained much the same. Mothers and children still spent quiet summers in the Park, joined by fathers on the weekends and for shorter vacations. Families played tennis in the morning and went to the beach in the afternoon. Kids romped in the dunes and built sandcastles along the shore. Wildflowers blanketed the hills in the spring; colorful beach towels and umbrellas brightened the beach in the summer. Families had picnics on the beach and hikes to South Haven, ball games in the new ball field and canoe rides on quiet days. The mornings were filled with the sounds of birds, the evenings with the wash of colors in the Western sky.

*Mr. Wunsch and his son with Mr. Seymour and unidentified woman.*

*This watercolor of the Sugar Bowl during a thunder storm was painted by one of the adult Kowerts who then owned T.L.C. #131, presently owned by Doug Stewart and Linda Sahagian. Thelma Weston won the picture at a money-making raffle back in the late 50's. Thelma's daughter later gave it to Linda and Doug.*

*Boardwalk heading north.*

# The Circle

*Postcard showing the porch of Sturtevant Lodge.*

*From the beginning of the Park, the center of activity has been in the Circle. Among the first few cottages built were Sturtevant Lodge (which then included a store) and Ballou Inn. Many of the vacationers in the early decades took all their meals in the Lodge. Children waited outside the Lodge to deliver telegrams during the day and played ball in the Circle in the evening. Visitors to the Lodge and Inn later bought cottages. A post office was opened – and an ice cream parlor. The porch on the latter became a meeting spot for all ages.*

*Mrs. Sturtevant who built the Lodge has been called a "hustler. She was a wonderful person, small, energetic, and friendly." (Palisades Park Review 1905-1968 p. 12) She and her daughter, a Mrs. Dusenberry, came from Chicago around 1907 and began the Lodge. They and Mrs. Sturtevant's brother, Mr. Nix, also built three other cottages in the Park. In 1923, the Lodge was given to Mrs. Sturtevant's nephew, Del Jones, who ran it with his wife, Blanche. The annex and dining room were added in 1924.*

*As the decades passed, the Circle seemed changeless. Until the 70's. Printed in the August 26, 1977* Patter*, the ensuing article by Donna Henkel Goscinski, tells of what she then perceived as* **" The Death of the Circle:"**

**1963:** "…the old place does seem to change not at all or very little. The roads still run up and down and all around over the old logging trails; the same bumps and ridges at the same old corners; the final bend of the road and the Circle just as it's supposed to be – with thousands of little people milling around the Soda Fountain; the lake just the same, with a couple of old pier ends sticking up out of the water; Mrs. Packard behind the counter in the store as if she's never left it – and those same old fashioned licorice things are on the counter." (from "Changeless" by Rev. William Ferry, Palisades Park Patter, 1964.)

**1973:** The store and lodge only opened on a limited basis. In 1974, the store completely closed. By 1975, the Soda Fountain lay deserted. Now only the skeleton of the Circle remains. The old buildings are tired and still, decaying. One solitary, yellow light bulb hums with the crickets and waves over the old Sturtevant Lodge. In a darkened corner of shadows, the deserted Soda Bar sags and rusts. And it is just Ballou Inn, the old store, that remains somewhat alive, with the sounds of a family living in the upper rooms.

From the Circle's beginning in 1905 to its decline in the early '70's, old timers will paint a picture of a rich, old era. Ballou Inn and Sturtevant Lodge were filled with guests every summer then; the Circle was the lively center of Palisades Park. Even when Helen Packard bought Ballou Inn and changed it into a store and Post Office, the enchantment of an ageless era remained.

In "those days," one could see a young Tony Canonie hauling ice blocks up the stairs by the store. It was then that Mr. Shepherd peddled, from door to door, his fresh

*The Soda Bar in 2002.*

milk, eggs, and the berries or corn when they came into season. Those were days when the snort of horses was a familiar sound as Mr. Hempy's team collected garbage. Generation passed into generation and the Circle stubbornly remained. Julia Quick Hill passed the Soda Fountain through a series of owners, but still it persisted,

*The Soda Bar in 1952 with Jim Roach, who ran it, and his daughter Beth, who painted the memorable mural behind the counter.*

a stubborn remnant of leisure and quality. After 27 years of service, in 1967, Helen Packard sold the store to the Flynns. The store remained. The lodge guests continued to return, summer after summer, as their parents and parents' parents had. Perhaps in 1963 the Reverend Ferry was right in calling the Circle changeless.

What is the reason, then, for the death of the Circle? What turns a lively haven into a ghost town? Those who remember the Circle each have their own theories as to its destruction. Some say that new conveniences, such as giant supermarkets and air conditioned motels, replace old and outdated stores and lodges. Sturtevant Lodge is an antique with its outdoor halls and bathrooms a few rooms down. The thick ivy, lining the walls and the terraces, and the ancient oak that grows through one of the Lodge halls both are obsolete now, unappreciated. The Soda Bar, now completely locked and deserted, perhaps was a dying entity next to the fast-food services of our present time.

Others say that the death of the Circle came with the unusually high cycle of lake level in the early '70's. In April of 1973, the Army Corps of Engineers declared the level of Lake Michigan at 580.5 - the highest it had been

*The Neubauer clan who ran the Soda Bar 1954 - 59.*

since 1886. And it seemed to get worse, with cottages collapsing on eroded lakefronts and damage to the Lodge itself. The summer resorters had no money and no spirit to save the Circle. The individuals that ran the Soda Bar, lodge, and store had their own depression along with everyone else, and perhaps were forced into the desertion of their businesses.

There may be many particular reasons for the ghost town once known as the Circle. Passing through it, one is faced with echoes of lively voices, horse-drawn taxies, children's laughter, family dinners, old fashioned licorice and ice cream sodas – all gone. New centers for activity have risen around the resort, on the beaches (newly returned), or in personal homes. New generations will never know of the old era, and will never care. The changes just continue.

*Donna was right that changes "just continue." She did not, however, foresee the avenue those changes would take. Mary Jo Carr continues the story. Her premise is that, after a decline of many years, there has been a resurgence of activity in the Circle. It has once again become an important hub in the social life of the Park:*

True, the store was closed and Ballou Inn joined the Lodge in private ownership. True, Fred Nichols moved the Soda Bar to the entrance to the Park, on the Blue Star Highway, and sold the Circle building for a cottage. For a few summers kids could not buy ice cream cones in the Circle, though candy and ice cream bars were available from a small store in the Old Garage. Then the Old Garage – which had housed cars, equipment, and the second floor office for the Patter – collapsed under pressure of a heavy snow load in 1979. Bricks were sold to Park members as souvenirs. The idea of the Circle as a magnet for all Park members seemed past.

Yet talk of the Circle's demise was premature. In the early 80's, it came alive again. The Lodge was divided into two cottages and both have been restored, enhancing the old look of the Circle. The Flynns stayed on in Ballou Inn. The Soda Bar was purchased by the PPCC Board, on February 1, 1980, remodeled as it is today. On the site of the Old Garage, the Village Green was created to be used for activities for all Palisaders – ethnic dinners, cocktail parties, square dances, weddings, and – often – some games of pickup basketball. New generations may not remember the old era. Changes continue. But the Circle, as a meeting place for everyone, is alive and well.

*The Circle is still a place where everyone meets. News is shared at the kiosk next to the Soda Bar. It was built by Hal and Mary Lee Tillson.*

*Beth Roach outside Soda Bar in 1954.*

## Signs of the Times

*1935 sign for Sturtevant Lodge.*

Nanette Draper c. 1940's

Rowena Schlacks. 1950.

# Nellie Palmer and the Covert Township Library

c. 1940

Many early Palisades Parkers remember the trek to the Covert Library each week to borrow all those good summer reading books. Part of the enchantment of such a trip was the librarian who would help them – Mrs. Nellie Palmer. Starting in 1942 – at the age of 71! – Mrs. Palmer served as librarian for a number of years. This vivacious, white-haired lady thought nothing of working long hours well into her 80's. "People are living longer today, that's all," she said. Before working as head of the library, she ran a general store in the village of Covert for over a decade.

Mrs. Palmer, who grew up on a farm near Danville, IL, lived in Texas early in her marriage to Alfred B. Palmer. In 1915, the couple paid a visit to Mr. Palmer's sister, Marian Hamilton, who had a cottage at Palisades Park. They liked the area and decided to settle in Covert where Mr. Palmer established his business. The year before her husband died, in 1930, Mrs. Palmer started managing The Village Store. She continued that job until 1942, when she started with the library.

One story Mrs. Palmer enjoyed telling was of the sign, outside the library, which said the first floor was reserved for the library and the second for the use of "Masonic bodies." One day two fourth graders came to her, wide-eyed, and said, "Mrs. Palmer, could we please go upstairs and see the bodies?"

The News-Palladium, on June 17, 1954, in an article honoring Mrs. Palmer's service to the community, put it this way: "Simplicity, a sense of humor, intelligence and a warm friendliness have endeared Mrs. Palmer to practically everyone in the village. Children and adults both seek her advice and look for the friendly smile and the Irish twinkle in her kind blue eyes." No wonder she was so special to all those Palisades Park children who came her way.

# Brandywine Creek

By Bill Potter

## Keeping Our Feet Dry

The <u>Palisades Park Review 1905 – 1968</u> includes a three-page picture history of Brandywine bridges, including a blurry picture of "Brandywine's First Bridge." It bears repeating. A bridge built so strong, with such care and choice of select materials that it was guaranteed to last – at least until the next Brandywine flood.

No surprise, this first bridge did not last long. A better way was needed, a bridge high enough to escape Brandywine's occasional torrential flood waters. And so the Suspension Bridge was built.

*The man on the bridge is Dr. Holmes holding his daughter, Betty Holmes Woodhouse c. 1910's.*

## The Suspension Bridge 19?? – c. 1927

Commonly called the "swinging bridge" because kids loved to get a rhythmic side-to-side motion going, the Suspension Bridge served the beach cottages north of Brandywine. From north to south, these cottages – which faced many problems - were:

| Pre 1927 | 2001 |
|---|---|
| Milliken | Burned while being torn down 1970 for Consumer's Power Plant |
| Filkins's Bonnie Doone | Torn down 1970 for Consumer's plant |
| Dean's Sea Breeze | Torn down c. 1948 to build Olson/Chambers cottage. Torn down again in 1970 for Consumer's Power Plant. |
| Hayes | Washed down 1929; rebuilt in 1933. Now Potters' #3. Renamed Driftwood. |
| Welles | Survived 1929 storm; named the Ark. Cottage #7. |
| McCollum | Washed down 1929. Not rebuilt. |
| Harding | Washed down 1929. Rebuilt on south bank of Brandywine. Now Vercillo, cottage # 39. |
| Crawshaw | Burned down 1959 as McQuigg cottage. New cottage built 1972 by Bill Jennings. Cottage #18. |
| McWethy's Squirrel Hill | Schlobohm (McWethy granddaughter) cottage #19. |

*Above: Harding beach cottage which was washed down in 1929 and rebuilt on other side of Brandywine as cottage #39.*
*Right: Crawshaw cottage which burned down in 1959.*
*c. early 1920's.*

This 150 foot long pedestrian bridge was suspended from two steel cables anchored on each side of Brandywine Creek. Supplies continued to be delivered to the north side cottages by horse and wagon, via the beach, by fording the creek.

*Ready for a "swinging" experience.*
*c. early 1920's.*

# The Combination Automobile Bridge and Lake Palisades Dam

In his original layout of Palisades Park, Arthur Quick included a small inland "Lake Palisades." However, it remained a lake on paper only until the necessary dam was finally built, about 1927. The dam included two adjustable sluice gates and four spillways, so the Lake Palisades water level could be controlled to a depth of 3 to 4 feet.

The dam also provided the concrete foundation necessary for an automobile bridge. More and more people were arriving at Palisades via their personal autos, and the bridge enabled Mr. Quick to cut connecting roads into the woods area north of Brandywine and make available previously unsaleable lots. The roads also made easier access to the existing beach cottages north of Brandywine.

*The new Brandywine Dam and Automobile Bridge looking downstream.*
*Sluice gates are down; Lake Palisades has developed... The Swinging Bridge has been removed. Summer 1929.*

*Dam and Bridge looking upstream. Exceptionally high Lake Michigan water level of 581'4" made possible a "boat harbor" in Brandywine Creek, connecting to Lake Michigan.*
*Inundated boat house at right. Summer 1929.*

*Birdseye view of the Brandywine boat harbor.*
*Crawshaw cottage at bottom; McWethy cottage #19 behind.*
*Horse barn in the distance, above the bridge. Summer 1929.*

*Lake Palisades Summer 1929*

After local complaints about "night sleeping time" noise from rushing water flowing over the dam and dropping into the spillways, and wide complaints about Lake Palisades being a mosquito breeder, the lake was emptied and abandoned in the 1940's.

The overgrown Lake Palisades bottom land was converted into the existing meadow in the spring of 1965. Still later, the dam sluice gates were removed.

*Bridge and dam foundation withstanding the torrential storm of September, 1974.*

About 1974, the bridge underpinnings and concrete foundation were strengthened to handle the ever-increasing weight of concrete trucks and delivery supply trucks to new cottage construction sites north of Brandywine. At the same time, a pedestrian fishing area was added and separated from the bridge's traffic lane by a railing on the west side - providing for safer fishing in the deeper creek water downstream from the spillways.

After the Bittersweet cottage #51 fire of July, 1991, and the shortage of water to fight it, in 1992 a slanting fire hose standpipe was installed at the south end of the bridge. The standpice taps into the deep water next to the spillways. In 1998, the steel deck supports and half the oak deck were replaced.

Arthur Quick designed well. His bridge is now almost 75 years old, and still going strong.

*Brandywine Bridge, showing the fishing area railing, reinforced foundation, the fire standpipe, and sluice gates removed.*
*July 28, 2001. Lake level 577'6".*

ally washed out the connecting boards between the bridge and the creek bank. So until someone replaced the boards, the bridge remained "broken" - which was most of the time.

Finally, a torrential Brandywine flood in the early 1960's just about did the bridge in for good. Much of it was washed away and even the old pilings were left in questionable condition. So the Broken Bridge became the Missing Bridge, and remained so for several years. At the August, 1967, Annual Meeting, it was announced that Forest Lowrey would finance the cost of a new, smaller size foot bridge over Brandywine Creek where the old Broken Down Bridge used to be. To everyone's relief, the Broken Bridge returned from the missing, as it stands today, having been given minor repairs over the ensuing years.

*The new "Unbroken Bridge." Just a shadow of its former size, for pedestrians only. Some of the original "Broken Bridge" piling and supports were still visible in the creek bed in 2003.*

## The Broken Bridge

Who built it? When? For what purpose? It seemed to have been there forever. Located back in the northside woods, it crossed over Brandywine Creek as part of the trail connecting the tennis courts with cottage roads on the north side.

In the 1920's and 1930's, it was common talk that the old bridge was left over from the 1870--1890 logging and large sawmill operation located upstream on Brandywine, or for horse and wagon access to the old ice house which was also located in that area. Could be. Mr. Quick would not have had an economic incentive to build it in the 1910's or 1920's; he didn't even get the automobile bridge built until about 1927. Probably by the time the Park was "born," the bridge was quite old.

What was "broken" about it? Well, the main bridge was structurally OK in the 1920's through 1950's, but the periodic spring flood waters of Brandywine Creek occasion-

*Frank Bruninga on old "Broken Down Bridge." 1937.*

## Brandywine Meadow

*The conversion of the Lake Palisades bottom land into a meadow was due to the generosity of one man - Forest Lowrey. The project was not without controversy, as the following articles from the July 26, 1965 Patter illustrate.*

### "On the Beach, an Editorial"
Grace Fidler and Glyde Bierce, eds.

During this month, blue skies and blue, cold water, white sand, and sunshine provided a good setting for the bouncy little Sailfish and Sunfish, with their blue, red, yellow, and green striped sails. These racy little boats seem to be propagating this year at Palisades. Another color contribution to the scene is furnished by an increasing number of beach umbrellas. In addition to being colorful, they doubtless provide the possessor with a place out of the sun, while in the sun. However, we have heard several husbands complain about carrying them from their cottages to the beach along with other paraphernalia. In fact, we witnessed one of these unfortunate beasts of burden struggling to reach the beach, carrying not only an inflated air mattress, a couple of beach chairs, a beach bag, but also the smallest child in the family.

Another change in the appearance of the Park has been noted and this has to do more with shape than with color. At this time, we are not considering the revelations made possible by the bathing suit designers, but instead have reference to the changes in the landscape which are evident to your right as you enter the Park and which pertain to the area on your map designated as Lake Palisades. This name is, of course, a misnomer at this time, because the lake per se is non-existent. At any rate, the *Hand of Progress* has at last reached out its grasping fingers and has touched Palisades Park. No longer will you see the sylvan glen that was balm to the city-weary traveler, as you enter the Park. In its place you will see a denuded area, churned by bulldozers. However, you can now get a glimpse of the lake. You may take further consolation for the removal of this beauty spot by the knowledge that a popular breeding place for mosquitoes has been eliminated. In time, under the guidance of man, this area will become neat and well arranged. We must admit, though, that we will always retain a nostalgic longing for that rustic, cool, mosquito-infested glen as we entered the Park.

> **W**hen the bulldozers, scoops, and fires are a thing of the past, and the area gently sloped and planted with grass, beauty of another sort will prevail.

### The Rebuttal: "Palisades Park Meadow"
by Connie Borchert

It is with a certain amount of nostalgia that I write this article for the Patter. It seems that everyone is most interested in the past, present, and future history of what was affectionately known as the "Swamp." However, the work that is being done now is to take the swampiness out of the area and make life more bearable and free from bugs.

When I first came to Palisades Park at the age of eight, Lake Palisades was dammed up – but even then there were signs of deterioration. The weeds were beginning to grow up around the edges and the willows were even then beginning to take their toll of the lake. People who came up to the Park long before I did remember the swinging bridge, which has now been replaced, and they remember a peaceful and quiet spot. My first real recollection of the lake in Palisades Park is of a pen full of ducks near the garage – a whim of a Mr. Pond who helped Julia Hill run the Soda Fountain.

Gradually, however, the willows succeeded in taking over, and every year the forest got denser. The sunset, nevertheless, reflecting on the tops of the trees, was a never-ending spectacle, and always different for those of us who face the woods instead of the lake. At certain times during the summer, the fireflies congregated behind the bridge in the evening, making another delightful spectacle. However, for all the beauty, Palisades Park Lake area was becoming a dense, dark breeding spot for all sorts of bugs, including mosquitoes and flies.

So, the over-abundance of willows, underbrush, and deadwood, plus slimy puddles, are giving way to the present. When the bulldozers, scoops, and fires are a thing of the past, the Brandywine straightened out to prevent swampiness, and the area gently sloped and planted with grass, beauty of another sort will prevail.

## Three Views of the Brandywine Meadow

*Bulldozing brush to turn Lake Palisades into the meadow. Spring 1965.*

*Emerging meadow. Spring 1965.*

*Meadow cleared, but dam sluice gates still in place. Glasner cottage #20 at right. July 1967.*

# Brandywine's Meandering Mouth
# And Efforts to Tame It.

*Mid 1920's, looking south.
As it was - untamed.*

*Late 1920's looking west.
An attempt at taming it.*

*1931. Second attempt at taming,
with heavier oak plank and piling
bulkhead wall.
(No treated lumber then, so rot soon started.)*

353

*October, 1960. The ultimate solution? Installing Mr. Lowrey's steel bulkhead wall.*

*Dense overgrowth covers the emptied Lake Palisades's lake bed behind the Brandywine Bridge. (Before the meadow area was cleared in 1965.)*

*August 2001. Meandering south.*

*May, 1997. Meandering north.*

# August 17, 1940 Patter

# Palisades Park PATTER

Vol. 2 No. 5                                                August 17, 1940

TODAY IS THE DAY - TWENTY STARTERS EXPECTED TO START MARATHON EVENT
    Start: South End of Park        Finish: Opposite Lodge.
    George Rich, Jr. and Katherine Lowrey Defending Champs

With all plans completed, twenty Palisades Park young men and women are ready to toe the starting line in the second annual Half-Mile Marathon Swim. Last minute entries may swell the starting lineup. George Rich, Jr. of Battle Creek, Michigan, last years winner, will be challenged by a classy field of contenders which includes; Bert Wilson, who last year finished a close second, John, Bill, and Bob Crawford, David Orcutt, Jack Kautz, George Bishop, Dick Matthews, Richard Hartney, Bud Sherrow, George Hammersmith, and little thirteen year old Jim Williams who is entering the race with special permission.

The Girl's champion, Weens Lowrey, will be busy pushing back challenges from the girl's field that will include; Mary Clark, last years second placer, Maryellen Muckenhirn, Mary Jane Hill, Margaret Sauer, Irene Smith, Barbara Farnsworth, and Betty Dewey.

Other last minute starters are expected to join the above list at the starting line. The late entrants are expected to fill in and sign the official entry blanks before the race. Entries will be accepted up to starting time, which is four oclock.

All contestants are instructed to assemble one half hour before the race, at the starting point - just south of Linden Hills - to check in with the starter, to get their numbers, and to receive further instructions.

At press time the temperature of the water was recorded as being at sixty two degrees - the weather man predicts fair weather. HOWEVER in case of too cold water (it must be at least 65 degrees at noon today) or rough water, the race will be postponed until Sunday, tomorrow, morning, August 18th., at 11:00 oclock. All other rules about the race will be unchanged.

The awards will be presented at the Clubhouse Marine Dance tonight. All first place winners of the three divisions will receive gold medals. The winner of the Boy's division will have his name engraved on the large silver cup that is kept on exhibition at the Clubhouse.

The officials for the race will be its sponsors: George Bishop, Del Jones Forest R. Lowrey, Gilby K. Mehagen, Stewart E. Nielsen, Arthur C. Quick, and Mrs. William Ward. Jack Ott will be the Clerk of Course, assisted by Tony Malinowski.

Any of the above officials will be on hand to answer any last minute questions, or to assist any befuddled entries. Complete program will be on the next page.

# PROGRAM
## August 17, 1940

**3:00 p.m.**   Palisades Park Motor Boat race. Four and a half mile course with a half mile straight-a-way, and three turns. Race will start at bouy in front of the Sturtevant Lodge and finish at the same point after three laps around the course.
Slower boats will be given one or two half-mile laps handicaps, according to speed and horse power.
Entrants and numbers of boats: Frank Hagie, No. 1; Vern Underwood (subject to scratch), No. 2; George Hammersmith, No. 3; Hales, No. 4; Matthews, No. 5; George Danley, No. 6. One or two other entries may be received by starting time.
All boats will begin race from a slow running start and will get the go ahead signal from the down-beat of the starter's flag. A wig-wag signal means a start over. The starter also will signal with a large card, the number of laps each boat must cover as they come around the starting bouy. All boats will be asked to keep on the <u>inside</u> of the course, and any passing must be done on the <u>outside</u>, or to the right hand side of the boat.
The prize to the winning boat will be an Ensign Trophy Flag with the proper inscription. This flag is being contributed by Mr. and Mrs. George Bishop.

**4:00 p.m.**   1940 Palisades Park Half Mile Lake Marathon Swim. The details are announced on the opposite side of this page. In case a contestant finds it impossible to finish the race he must come into shore immediately, report to his parent or host, and then to the official at the finish line.

**4:30 p.m.**   The Married Women's Inner Tube Swimming (?) Race. Mrs. Jack (Betty) Ott is the defending champion. Other entries will include, Mrs. Underwood, Mrs. Mehagen, Mrs. George Bishop, Mrs. Lowrey, and a host of last-minute-persuaded entrants.

---

In case of a postponement, due to adverse weather conditions, the order of the races will be changed to these times: Swim Race at 11:00 A.M., Boat Race at 11:30, and the Tube Race at 12:30.

---

**Private Boats:** All private boats, boats not entered in the race, are requested to remain away from the Swim course and especially away from the Boat race course. All boats in the water at the time of the above events will be subject to orders from the Coast Guard, or from any of the officials. Please co-operate. Boats will be permitted to follow the swimmers, but must in no way help or hinder them in their progress.

**South Haven Coast Guard:** The Coast Guard under the direction of Captain Fisher will be on hand to patrol the activities and to be of any aid necessary. Any courtesy or cooperation that you can show them will be appreciated by all concerned. The announced exhibition of life-saving will not be performed, because the crew is short-handed and cannot be spared from the main station for too long a time.

**Spectators:** There will be plenty of standing room along the course on the beach, of course. But it may be a good idea to bring down a beach chair of some description if you intend to stay for any lenght of time. In case of a hot sun, adequate head covering is suggested. In case of any emergency, spectators are expected to observe common-sense rules.

# Sport Flashes by Thunder

Tonight, at the Clubhouse, you will see the 1939 winners names of the Palisades Park Honor and Glory tennis tournament. The original plaque is filled up with the names of the '36, '37, and '38 winners, so a new plaque has been added to the trophy wall. A separate plaque will be used for each year, from now on. Last year's winners are: Mary Lee Cady in the Women's singles, Hoddy Clark in the Men's singles, Bishop and Mehagen in the doubles, and K. Lowrey and Bishop in the Mixed doubles. A bit belated, but our congratulations - and P.S. - look out for trouble this year from a classy and determined bunch of challengers.

FLASH! Speaking of the year's tennis classic, let's go over the details for those of you who missed last week's edition: the Honor and Glory will begin August 24th, next weekend, with the first and second rounds of the four divisions - Men's and Women's Singles, and Men's and Mixed Doubles. The remaining and the Championship rounds will be played off the following weekend, August 31st.

There will be cups for the winners, and medals for runnersup. Entries for all and each event must be in the hands of Tony Malinowski by Thursday, 7:00 p.m., at which time the draw will be made. Tournament play may begin the next day. Tourney matches will be given preference at the courts throut the week ends of the tournament.

The entry fee for each event, per person, is fifty cents - and must accompany the entry.

The defending champions - singles and doubles - will be seeded as will be the winners of the tournaments held so far this season.

Officials will preside over the semi- and final matches, and it is suggested that officials be used in the prelims wherever possible.

All residents, renters, their guests, guests of the Lodge, and former residents and renters of the Park, are eligible to enter. Any other questions, and other information may obtained from Tony Malinowski.

FLASH! The Horseshoe Tournament will be in it's final rounds over this weekend, with match play scheduled for today and tomorrow. The schedule is posted at four different points: Ice Cream Parlor, Post Office, Hotel, and the Horse courts. Each man will play his opponent once in a fifty point game - the winner advancing toward the final round, the loser dropping out. Ott,Sr., Bendelow, Collier, and Lowrey are seeded positions on the basis of the results of last Sunday's skirmishes.

FLASH! Winners of last week's tennis tournaments: Small Fry - Skipper Bruninga lost to Ted Collier. Junior Boy's - Jack Bendelow beat Harold Wilson in three sets for his second championship.

---

FLASH! The regular advertisors, and friends of the Park whose services are announced on these pages, give up their space this week to allow extra news items to be printed. They all express the desire to be of continual service to the Park people and want to wish all the Swim Marathon entrants a Bon Voyage.

| | |
|---|---|
| MacKenzies Golden Brown Bakery | Tony and Charlie |
| Overhuel's Grocery Store | Mrs. Georgia Underwood |
| Mrs. Hill's Ice Cream Parlor | "Jonesy" - Laundry |
| "The Knapps" at the Station | Sturtevant Lodge |

# PARK PORTRAITS by Rose Ann Stewart
## Mr. Forest Lowrey

In the past issues, "Park Portraits" has attempted to present a composite view of our Palisades Park; to complete the picture, your reporter-camerawoman now focuses her lense toward the future of this southwestern Michigan resort. What is in store for our paradise? What lies ahead? Are we a progressive community, ever seeking improvement?

We could find no better representative to our congress of thought toward-the-future than Forest Lowrey. President of the Park Board, this retiring Napoleon of the battered felt hat has had a literal "finger in the pie" of every Park activity. You see him calling the balls and strikes at the Sunday ball games, you see his name among the sponsors of today's Marathon Swim, you'll see him tripping the heavy fantastic at the forthcoming Cabaret Dance, his own money-making scheme for the support of the Clubhouse, he's among the leaders in the current horseshoe tourney, and has a standing challenge with Mr. Bruninga for a tennis match to determine the Park's worst tennis player.

He is a successful business man, husband, and father. He has been a cottage-owner here in the Park for eight years. He is ambitious energetic, and enters into our activities with an enthusiasm that belies his many respondsibilities. Although only a week-end commuter, he merges his brief but jolly moments on beach and tennis court with anticipation and hopes for the Park's progress.

"Mr. Lowrey," we asked, "what can you tell us of the future of Palisades Park?"

He smiled as he answered, "That's not for me to say. Being no longer connected with the board of directors, I, of course, have little voice in its activity. However, if you would like to hear what we have tried to do, and what I, personally, hope they'll do, I'll confess!!"

He leaned forward in his chair and spoke in an earnest tone, "The Board has been trying to stimulate interest in athletics during the past year. In addition to the shuffleboard courts, which have proved to be immensely popular, we purchased three acres of land (near the entrance of the Park), which the Board hopes to improve in time. Three new tennis courts are in the making there, plus an archery range, and two horse shoe courts, which are finding increasing use. The new baseball diamond will be leveled off, and they have just completed a golf ball driving range on the remaining ground which will have its grand opening tomorrow morning with a driving contest."

"I believe these sports should be put on a self-sustaining basis. The Park Board alone is not in a financial position to support them. Its main concern now is to pay for the Clubhouse. If there is a real interest in the athletics here, I think that those interested will not mind paying a nominal fee for the maintenance and improvement of our facilities." He continued, "The tennis courts are always popular and the current tournaments have been very successful from the standpoint of group enthusiasm. It is my hope that they will set aside one court for match play and initiate a tennis club. Complimentary memberships could be sold for a reasonable amount to those interested. With the money received, the courts could be improved. They need it," he chuckled, "and possibly a tennis clubhouse could be built. I sincerely hope the present Board will consider this."

Mr. Lowrey then expressed his desire to see a similiar plan in connection with the contemplated boat harbor take effect. "It would be an excellent idea for those owning boats to form a corporation and make the harbor. This would have to be done at their own expense, for it would be unfair to assess those who do not own boats."

"At any rate," concluded this genial gentleman of affairs, "Palisades Park has taken rapid steps toward improvement, and the way we are going now, who knows what the future may hold?".

# Fire
# The Big Enemy

By Bill Potter

At Palisades Park, the most frequent fires have been brush fires of dune grass, ignited by careless smokers and fireworks. If caught early, they can be stomped or hosed out, but several have gained a foothold and burned up the dune embankment, endangering cottages above. Fortunately, all have been doused, in time, by neighbors, the Park staff, and/or the Covert Fire Department.

Far more serious are cottage fires. Once started, they can lead to total loss. Several major fires have occurred at Palisades.

## June 12, 1959

The McQuigg cottage on the north bank of Brandywine Creek burned to the ground in June of 1959. (In 1972, the Jennings family built a new cottage on the same site. Cottage #18.)

Firefighters were able to save the neighboring McWethy cottage, although it was scorched. Almost all the trees and vegetation on the dune bluff behind were destroyed, but the Peirce cottage (#14) on top of the bluff was untouched.

On Saturday, June 13, 1959, the South Haven Daily Tribune reported as follows:

*All that remains of a $23,000 home in Palisades Park today is a pile of rubble. A blaze of undetermined origin, whipped by a stiff Lake Michigan breeze, threatened to wipe out the entire summer colony. Only the fact that the wind was in the west kept the blaze from wiping out several dozen homes, firemen said. The Covert fire department was called at 12:10 a.m. by Mike Glasner of LaGrange, IL, who saw flames in the home of J. E. McQuigg of Kalamazoo. Glasner wakened McQuigg and got him from the building safely.....The siding of a cottage next door was scorched and much damage was done to trees.*

*Before the fire, c. 1928; Crawshaw cottage (later McQuigg) on left; McWethy #19 on right.*

*June 1959; McQuigg cottage after the rubble was removed. Carin Potter in foreground.*

*Covert Fire Chief Tony Sarno radioed state police that the fire was out of control and more equipment was needed....*

*McQuigg was at a loss to explain the cause of the blaze. He was asleep in a room at the west side of the cottage and no one had been in the room where the fire broke out for several hours, he said.*

Probable cause was spontaneous combustion from oily rags left during a remodeling project.

*June 1959; McWethy cottage #19 at right.*

## January, 1968

The Milliken cottage at the north end of North Beach was condemned to make room for building the Consumers Power Plant. Cecil Burrous was in the process of dismantling the cottage interior to salvage reusable paneling, cabinets, trim, and the like. The material was stacked inside the cottage, ready for removal the next day. When Cecil returned in the morning, only smoldering ruins remained of the cottage; all the salvage material and his tools were destroyed. No one witnessed the fire, so no fire departments were involved. Arson was suspected, but never proven.

## February 22, 1972

A newspaper article saved from 1972 tells of another Palisades fire. The source of the article is unknown.

### TEENS ARRESTED IN PALISADES COTTAGE BLAZE

*February 23, 1972, Covert – Three Illinois teenagers were arrested on charges involving auto theft, breaking and entering, and arson last night in a case where a summer cottage in the Palisades Park subdivision of Covert township was destroyed by fire and two others heavily vandalized. Covert township police arrested the juveniles, ages 14, 15, and 16, after a cottage, owned by George Brumis of Chicago, was destroyed. Covert firemen said the one–story, six–room building was valued at $13,000.*

*The fire was discovered after the youths were arrested in a car that had been reported stolen from Illinois earlier in the day. Cecil Burrous, caretaker of the subdivision which contains summer residences, said the youths were arrested as he attempted to help them free their car, which had become stuck in snow in the subdivision.*

*Covert police said they were checking the area for the youths after receiving a message from Illinois authorities who said the parents of one of the youths owned a cottage there. The three had been reported missing from home earlier. Burrous's son, Cecil Jr., discovered the fire as he conducted an inspection of an area on a snowmobile.*

*Covert firemen, who responded to the 6:15 p.m. fire with two trucks, said the building was engulfed in flames by the time they arrived. Police said two other nearby cottages were found to have been entered and heavily vandalized. It appeared that an attempt had been made to set one of them on fire but that candle fuses failed to ignite paper spread on the floor. The cottages vandalized were owned by Phillip Kolehmainen of Northbrook, IL, and Rollie Hegwood of Summitt, NJ.*

*Two of the youths were ordered held in the Van Buren County jail and the third to a Kalamazoo County juvenile home by the Van Buren County Probate Court. Authorities said they would determine the extent of formal charges today.*

The Brumis cottage was located next to Kolehmainens (#69). It was not rebuilt.

## July 11, 1991

*Fire trucks in Palisades Park Circle and, below, firemen on roof responding to Kavanaugh fire, July 11, 1991.*

Kavanaugh's Bittersweet (cottage #51), just north of Circle Beach, was destroyed and McCarthy's Seamar (cottage #49) was heavily damaged in one of the worst Park fires of recent years.

A major remodeling of Bittersweet had just been completed and the cottage was as yet unoccupied by its new owners, Tom and Sue Kavanaugh. Fire originated inside the cottage during the early morning hours and was well along when first spotted at 7:00 a.m. The Covert Volunteer Fire Department was called, but by that time, Bittersweet was beyond saving. Virtually all the fire fighting effort was directed at saving the three neighboring cottages, Master's Lodge (#53), McCarthys' Seamar (#49), and O'Briens' (#52). The latter two were badly scorched on the fire side, but otherwise escaped major damage. Seamar, however, was heavily damaged, as its south side and then the interior caught fire. Fortunately, no one was injured. The wind direction kept the fire from spreading further.

After a lengthy investigation, the Fire Marshall determined the cause to be arson by person(s) unknown. As a result of this fire and the shortage of water to fight it, in 1992 a fire hose standpipe was installed at the south end of the Brandywine Bridge that taps into the deep pool of water at the end of the spillways.

## Early September, 1999

Steve and Karen Heavrins' Inn Decision (cottage #140) was damaged by a brush fire. The Heavrins woke up at 4:00 a.m. to what sounded like rain. Upon looking out from their porch, they saw a wall of flame advancing up the sand dune hill from a dune grass fire. Due to a telephone mix up, it took the Covert Fire Department 20 minutes to arrive; they first went to the Palisades Power Plant and then found Park roads narrowed by parked cars. Meanwhile, Heavrins' deck had caught fire.

Once on the scene, the firemen took about 20 minutes to douse the flames and another hour in the dark to extinguish hot spots. Heavrins lost all their trees to the blaze, but the slow burning Wolmanized treated lumber used to build their deck discouraged ignition. According to the firemen, that probably saved their cottage.

Cause of the fire was undetermined, although two previous dune grass fires in their area were started by fireworks. In negotiating Palisades narrow and sharp-cornered roads, the fire truck sustained $6000 in damage to its sides.

*Two views of the Kavanaugh cottage ablaze. July 11, 1991*

*The aftermath. Kavanaugh cottage #51. McCarthy cottage #49 in background.*

# The Covert Fire Department

**By Georgia Underwood**
*Georgia was a Postmistress of Palisades Park; she and her husband Verne lived by the south side tennis courts. Written to Tony Sarno, January 31, 1975*

We spent an hour and a half reminiscing (about early memories of the Fire Department) and had a good laugh. So take this effort as you will ....

Before the two-wheeled pushcart, there was a sort of disorganized bucket brigade. When the Covert Bank caught fire, a bucket brigade was formed, getting water from the pond across from the bank. This would be before 1918. The outfit's cart was kept in a livery stable, located between the old ice-cream parlor and Lynch's poolroom. About 1923 or 1924, a Model-T chemical truck was purchased. This was kept in Carl Shattuck's garage, located just north of Gowen's Filling Station. Thus, Carl Shattuck became the one and only fire chief that we know of in the 20's. This truck had a running board at the back end of the truck upon which two men could stand. More than that number and the front end would come up in the air. The truck had a tendency to buckle at its top speed and would run into a sandbank very easily. It was very hard to start when cold and, of course, had to be cranked. In 1923, it was stored in the town barn, back of Bill Shattuck's filling station .... It had to be insulated to keep the water tanks from freezing.

Firemen received $3.00 for each fire, many of which were started by stills, in Prohibition days. The old school bell was fixed so it "dinged" instead of "dinging and donging," if you know what I mean. There was a hand-cranked siren and a few helmets. The chief's was white. First come first served on the rest....

Verne was driving one time to a fire. Bill Zillman was riding on top of the truck. The truck buckled and threw Bill on top of a clay bank. He climbed down and ran down the road, finally catching up. When he stood on the rear end running board, the front end raised off the ground.

In those more or less happy, carefree days, everyone who could go tagged along with the fire truck. One time the buckets fell off and every car behind ran over them. At the fire – no buckets. One cold night, the truck wouldn't start. Another car was hitched on behind and pushed until the motor started. Another time they had a flat tire. They took the wheel off another Model-T which was along, put it on the fire truck, and went on. One time it was very, very cold and Sherm Tyler hollered to Verne and said, "Hey Verne, did you ever see a white black man?" His face was covered with frost.

One Halloween night, someone set fire to the old Deerfield Hotel, located about where the beautiful fire station is now. We lived in the Braham Brimhall home and the township barn was located no more than 150 feet back of us. About 4:00 a.m. that old bell began to ding. It shocked us partially awake. The light in our living room was blood red and we thought the downtown was all afire. Verne leaped to his feet on the bed, instead of off, ran to the foot, turned around, ran to the top, and stopped and said, "How the hell do you get off this bed?" That night Jimmy Jensen's wife Lucky put her blue smock on Jim and buttoned it to the bottom. The truck arrived at the fire and Dr. Vaughn proceeded to throw the hose off the top of the truck where it was coiled. This didn't help. Verne took the hose and went upstairs and down the hall in the hotel; when the fire was out, it was so dark he got lost trying to get out.

The huge barn on the old Kirby house burned one night and everything in it was lost. It burned to the ground. Carl Shattuck was still running around frantically yelling, "Where's my white hat?" There was a fire out of town one bitter cold time. The last I saw of the truck that night, the men were pushing it over the hill by the school house.

I could go on and on, but things don't sound so hilarious on paper. You have to hear the yarns.... Needless to say, we have had a grand old time talking about that period. Everything told brought back memories of other things.

Rudy Weber once told a story that went way back to the days before the fire department became motorized. One night there was a major fire and the men were hastily summoned to come on duty. The department had gotten a horse drawn cart and it was their first time to use it, so the men were quite excited. When finally all the men assembled had jumped into the cart, the driver flicked the horse to take off. And it did, but without the cart. Someone had forgotten to hitch the horse up and it was gone before anyone could say "Fire."

# Interviews

*The Campbell cottage #171.*

## Dr. and Mrs. Joseph Campbell

Interviewed by Katy Beck
August 23, 1984

Although we bought our cottage in 1941, in earlier years we used to come over here and visit. We'd come in and ride through the Park and maybe have a little picnic. We got lost every time. Some of the first persons we knew were the Van Ripers. They lived up on the hill above here, the first cottage, where the Joys live (#162). We'd come out on the weekends and they'd take us down on the beach. We'd keep asking them about a place for a cottage. This one (#178) was rented for years, by the Sengenbergers, but they did not want to sell. Mrs. Sengenberger's parents first bought the land from Mr. Quick in 1910. The cottage was finished in 1913. There were no roads back up the hill or anything. All of the lumber and everything had to be transported down the beach, in off the road down at the hotel. They brought it down by horse and wagon. In later years, Mrs. Sengenberger became incapacitated and they couldn't come up here very much anymore. She turned over the cottage to her daughter Ella, but they never wanted to give it up. They were holding it for sentimental reasons, hoping somebody in the family would be interested. So, one Sunday – this was in 1941 – we bought a little gas from Mr. Knapp's gas station out on the Blue Star. I got in there talking with him about places in the Park. He knew as much as Mr. Quick did. So I said, "We still have our eye on this little cottage down there by the lake." He said, "You know, I can't be sure but I have a gut feeling that they'll let that go if you contact them." It didn't take much. I went back home and wrote a letter immediately. She sent a very nice letter and said she hated to let the cottage go, but would. We rode down to Indianapolis and completed the deal right down there. Of course Mr. Quick was in all of this too. He did the deed work and the transfers and insurance. That's how we got the cottage.

The name of the cottage was "walk in" spelled backwards – "Niklaw." You can see why we changed it to Oasis. We still have some chairs with "Niklaw" written on the back. We changed it to Oasis because that was where the "camels" came to rest. You don't know how confusing that was, as a young person who was very poor at spelling, ever to get my name straight. That's how they pronounced it in the East, with no "B" - Camel.

The fall after we bought, Ella Sengenberger thought that she'd like to have some of her school friends and herself come up for a weekend. Fine. We got the cottage all prepared and cleaned up and everything nice for her. On the front porch were these big canvas shades with eyelets where you let them down and fasten them on. Lo and behold, the night before they were to come, a big storm came – and I mean a big one – and it blew all the eyelets out of the canvas and soaked the place with water. She didn't think we were very good housekeepers. It was a tremendous storm. We had the shades fixed. Not long after the war, we had sliding wood windows put in by Mr. Wildt. Much later we had them changed to jalousies.

*Dr. and Mrs. Campbell. 1953.*

*Horse and buggy on Ravineway. 1912.*

When we first bought, our cottage had been ransacked during the winter. When we went in, we didn't know what was supposed to be there. We had only been in the place (before we bought it) when it was all dark and closed up and we poked around with a flashlight, but we didn't know what belonged there in the cottage. Someone had come through the Park and helped themselves to things. Probably they took things down the beach to where they had their cars parked. We got a notice from the sheriff's department over in Paw Paw that they had caught somebody who had ransacked cottages all along the lake. They had recovered some of the items and we were supposed to go over and claim them. Well, there were some sheets that said Sengenberger on them, so we could claim those, but there wasn't anything else we could claim because we didn't know what belonged to the cottage and what didn't. That was the only time that the cottage was ever broken into.

The Mehagan cottage was owned by Mrs. Cota. While she lived there, we had an experience. Nancy was three years old at the time and Joe had taken her to Pennsylvania to his folks. My sister was visiting us and we sat on the swing and looked out, just as Mrs. Cota walked out on her little square sidewalk there. She looked over at us and said, "The house is on fire! What shall I do?" My sister, right fast, said, "My car is parked out in the back; I am going to move it." Mrs. Cota called us over to look at it. The fire was downstairs in a water heater and the flames were going right up the wall behind it. I thought, "Uh-oh, that cottage is gone and ours is so close, ours will be gone too." Marion moved her car so she was going to save that even if we couldn't save the house.

Then she started out in one direction and I started out in another, to call for help. Dr. MacDougal was on his porch with his wife, and when I said that Mrs. Cota's house was on fire, he hopped right over and she grabbed a telephone and tried to call Mr. Quick. But she couldn't get him because they were on the same line and she didn't know how to call him on the same line. Dr. MacDougal came over and we had a hose fastened up to our house on that side. He just grabbed the hose, turned on the water, and put out the fire. In the meantime, we'd been running up and down, telling everybody. Then somebody called the fire department from Covert; of course, it took them time to get over. When they came through the Park - all these roads - blowing their whistles, everybody from the Park came down. They came in couples and they all carried fire extinguishers. Later, at the meeting the next time, somebody suggested that it would be a good idea if everybody in the Park had a hose, because nobody had them at that time. People had asked, "Well how did they get the fire out?" And I had said, "Well, they took a hose and turned it on." And they said, "Well, who would think of having a hose at the cottage!" So now everybody is supposed to have a hose.

Mr. Quick didn't think that the lake lots were worth anything. He thought the good lots were back in the woods, that the woods were better. Mrs. Cota told us, when they wanted to buy that lot on the lake, he kept saying, "Oh no, we've got some good ones, don't take that one; we've got some good ones back in the hills." Of course, the Sengenbergers bought this lot with nothing else here. They were number one, at the end of the Park. Why they picked it out, I never did hear; they just did. Everything they wanted – their luggage, everything – they had to walk up the beach. Maybe they got the Shattucks to bring it down the beach on their wagon. In those days, people arrived on the train or by boat and were met by the Shattucks, with a horse and carriage, and brought to the Park.

Ballou Inn was built before the Hotel. That was the only thing down there. They had to have a place like that so that construction people and workers would have a place to stay. Getting back and forth was a major chore. It would take you longer to go from place to place than it did on the job. Then eventually the Hotel was built for a tourist attraction. *(Ed: This may not be accurate. There was an inn during logging days, probably near the Blue Star Highway, but Sturtevant Lodge and Ballou Inn both date from around 1907.)*

Mr. Wildt was a carpenter and painter. He lived outside of Covert. He did, I would say, 90% of the work here in the Park. He was a tradesman and he would come in here and ply his trade.

Tony Canonie brought the ice on a little wagon. The ice was cut from the rivers, you know, and from the lake. It was in little blocks and it had sawdust in between the blocks to keep them from melting; we could separate it. It had been weighed up wherever he stored it.

The Brandywine has shrunk from what it originally was. It was a little lake in there. All the low ground was covered with water. Then they drained it and now it's just a little creek wandering around down there. I think there were mosquitoes – people with cottages around there complained.

For socializing, it was mostly friends and family things with the people here – not so much from back home – with little ones the ages of our children. Joe was working (in Bangor) at the time, so he was gone all day and I watched the kids, in the water. We went swimming with the people right around here. There were kids around on this end and they all got together. Jack MacDougal and our Robin played together – it kept us busy keeping track of our children. The children went to the Clubhouse. Whatever the people in charge thought up was what the kids did. There were different couples every summer.

The store was in the Circle when we first came. It was good for people who came from Chicago and didn't have access to other stores. Later on they ran out to the supermarket. Oh yes, the post office was there. The school bus from Covert used to come down here – I think the Overhuels and Knapps and Underwoods lived here all year. That's where Hempy lived also. He and his wife, they picked up the garbage and did it by horse and wagon. They would come down the beach and walk to the cottage. They also brought other building materials down for people, too. That was an interesting experience for our children. If Hempy didn't have anything else on his wagon, he had a load of stones and he kept putting them on the roads. He was always doing that. Without any engineering qualifications or anything else, with his little stones, he did more to hold back water from washing out the roads than an engineer would. We never had water coming down the hill then. He kept these little stones, took them up and put them in the right place, and that was it. They were a nice couple. Everyone enjoyed them and their children.

Mr. Knapp was caretaker for awhile. He had been living out in the gas station there, and when he got to be caretaker, he built a house because, you see, Hempy still lived in his house. Then when Cecil got to be caretaker, he, too, built his own house. When Stan became caretaker, the Park built the house for him. Mr. Knapp's wife was sick. She died first. And that was the same with Mr. Quick's wife – she was very sick for years and years and he took care of her. She was a nice lady. He was a very sympathetic man.

The changes in the beach break our hearts. In the early days, we had room on the beach out there – it was just heaven. We'd go out there and have a full game of softball and not even the ball would go into the water. And so, to us, to have lost that beach is tragic. It was so beautiful to live here; from our place, the beach just went gradually down. No cliffs or anything, just gradually down to the water's edge, a couple of hundred feet from where those

*Clubhouse Beach looking north. 1959.*

jetties are now. The first seawalls were built around 1949. And then, after a year or two, when the water went back out, then all those seawalls were covered up completely. People couldn't believe when another episode of high water came along that the same thing wouldn't happen. But the beach didn't return. Things became worse and the beach never recovered. It's just as different now as night and day. Of course, the view is always marvelous; that's never changed.

The style of life, both for adults and for children, is different today. Maybe children are given more freedom. We notice that in schools. They are left more to themselves, have more independence, so they have some ideas of their own. They don't always agree with our ideas. And they do more outside of the home, a lot of them, whereas in bringing up our own, we did it inside the home. I suppose that accounts for what we said earlier, how we stayed close-by, socially. All the families were conducting themselves the same way, and we interacted with each other and didn't have to depend on the Clubhouse as much to entertain children. We entertained them at home. It has got to the stage where a lot of mothers are working and they aren't home to keep their eyes on their children all day long. Or when they get home at night, they have so many things to do, they still can't keep their eyes on their children. In other words, the Park was more family-oriented than it is today. At night we got the children all nestled down and then got together with neighbors to play bridge. We were here – we just went back and forth. We took our turn. We always had an eye on our children. Everything was just one ball of wax. I think children kind of looked to the parents whereas now, they look to their peers more. They are afraid if they don't do what their peers are doing, well that's going to hurt their status. Generally, I'm saying. It's been a gradual thing and it's not any one place; it's world wide. Those children bring that attitude into the Park when they come here during the summer – and the same action. They used to go up to the Sugar Bowl and have a picnic, and roast hot dogs and sometimes they'd sleep out all night. But there wasn't such a thing as beer parties. When our kids were all teenagers, they were all working. If there were other things going on, we didn't know too much about it. We had little parties and so forth, with Robin. Mothers in the Park didn't have cars, either. We have Amtrak going from Grand Rapids to Chicago now, and it stops in Bangor. Even years ago, when the train went through, it stopped in Bangor. People from South Haven and Palisades Park used to go to Bangor to get on and off the train. In many cases, father came for the weekend on the train and the family would go over and meet him and then on Sunday night, take him back.

*Children enjoying the dunes.*

One of the interesting events was a plane that crashed in the lake. It was a big jet liner and crashed just a bit north of here. There were 250 people on that plane. If it had all been out there, that would be one thing, but, as the days went one, these things began to wash up on the shore, pieces of bodies, cushions, and things. Then the Coast Guard and the State Police came down and nobody could go swimming or use the beach. They would take their Jeeps and comb the beach, picking up every little item, no matter how small. They thought the plane was struck by lightning. They were trying to identify bodies and I don't know how they could, because I don't think they found anything bigger than a dinner plate. It was the day the Korean War started. Those were the two headlines in the paper – that the plane had crashed in the lake and the War had started.

Echo I and Echo II were satellites that came over. People would get out on the beach at night and when Echo would come over, they'd call, "Here it comes! Here it comes!" They were aluminum – like a space shuttle, only smaller. They were the first things orbiting the earth. They would go over at a specified time and the radio would tell you when they would be going over. Then if you got people provoked, somebody would turn on a porch light outside and that would light up the sky and you couldn't see anything.

Mostly our neighbors were good people we enjoyed. No question about it. Each summer we gave our children a complete turnover of friends. They enjoyed those companionships and we did too.

The story of Mrs. Hamilton and the boys might help to bring forth the fact that people shouldn't be digging in the sand. She had a boy that she knew, a neighbor of hers, and when she wanted to come up and open the cottage, she told him to get a friend of his to come along so that she would have two boys to help. So, they came up one weekend and worked. The next week, the neighbor she knew couldn't come, but the other boy got a friend of his and they, too, worked. Then Saturday afternoon, she told them they could have some time off; she had taken them back and forth between her two cottages. When they didn't come in for supper when it was time, she waited and waited and then she thought, well, they must be working at the other cottage. So she got in her car and went down there and they weren't there. In the meantime, she met Cecil and told him she didn't know where the boys were. He immediately thought of the sand and grabbed the shovel and began digging. Eventually he found them in the sand dunes, right behind the cottage. They had been going to tunnel to each other and both went inside the tunnel. It collapsed and they died. I hope that somebody knowing about that would realize that sand can collapse and fall in.

*Dr. and Mrs. Campbell entertaining Amy Beck. c. 1968.*

# Mr. Ben Iverson

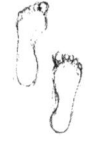

Interviewed by Katy Beck
Fall, 1979

My mother and father both came from Denmark. My father came over from a part of Denmark taken over by Germany. They made Danes learn German. They tried to get the young men to marry German girls, to mix the races. When the young men got to be 21, they had to serve in the German army; they didn't want to, so many left before they were 21. In those days, they could get passes for the U.S. easier than they can now. My father left just before he was 21. His uncle took him over some channel – I forget which – so he could get to America. My mother's sister and brother-in-law were over in Chicago at the time. They had a tailor shop there. I guess my father stayed with them until he got his bearings. He finally got out on a farm and worked. He got $30 a month and board and room. My father was engaged to my mother before he came over here, but she was only 15 years old and they couldn't marry yet. She was still on her farm in Denmark. He worked to get two brothers and my mother's brother over here.

My mother's father had a turf farm in Denmark. It was kind of like this muck they tore out of the ground and dried it in bricks and sold it for fuel. Before he left, my father, in his spare time, would dig it up and pile and dry it. The stuff had probably been there for thousands of years. We used to call them muck fires. When there was a fire in Covert, years ago, south and east of town where all the blueberry farms are, well, the muck caught fire. We had smoke all summer

367

long from that muck fire. They couldn't put it out. Not till the rains came. A dry spell like we had here, it would just keep burning.

I can remember when we first moved to Covert, before they started planting blueberries, they had the muck fires down in there. It took several rains before the fires were put out. There were a lot of wild blueberries that used to grow – they were a lot smaller – and they, of course, died when the fire came. It was just smoldering, smoldering – you could see the red flame down in the ground there. The smoke coming, smoke coming all the time – green smoke. That went on for all summer long. Then after the fire scene, of course, the ground kind of lowered a little, because it burnt some of that out.

We moved to Covert in the fall of 1911 from Bangor. My folks came out from Chicago. In Chicago, before we came to the farm, they practically raised their family. We were all born in Chicago – 12 children – 13, really; one girl died. I was 3rd from the last – born in 1897 – with two younger brothers after me. Anyway, you know

*Main Street of Covert*

if you raise 12 children and work for a dollar or a dollar and a half a day, you can't live very high.

My folks came to Michigan when my uncle said he had a farm for 'em – 160 acres; it had a lot of swamp land on it so it came out 120 acres of good pasture land. My folks rented this farm for two years. When they left Chicago, they took their team of horses and wagon and got on a boat in Chicago and went to South Haven. I guess the boat must have got in about two in the afternoon; then they drove 14 miles out to the farm. That was a long drive. We all sat in this lumber wagon. They brought what furniture was somewhat near good and shipped it out with us to the farm. We took as much as we could on the wagon and went back the next day to get the rest of it.

I can remember we had a long table with a bench all along the outside wall and all us little kids had to sit on that. We never had chairs – just the bench. The older ones would sit on chairs around the rest of the table. Mother bought milk cows as fast as she could afford it. She bought two or three right away. Then she figured, well, we've got the pasture, so we could have some cream to sell to bring a little income. She didn't have much; we had to get along with very little. When she got a little money, she'd buy a little supply of groceries. She had enough flour but she would run out of sugar. Of course, we'd never been on a farm before in our lives. The closest we'd ever been was out to the Chicago forest preserves. So mother had to show the older boys how to milk cows.

A little Italian fella' used to come with a hand cart selling bananas, going up and down the alley saying, "Bananas for sale, bananas for sale." The ladies would come out the back door and go and pick out their bananas. He'd have 'em all laying in rows there. They were very choice in those days. The ones with a little kind of dark spot on 'em, he'd break off the bunch and put them in a little place between the legs of the cart. When he came to our place, he knew my mother'd buy 'em but she had to buy 'em cheap so he'd drag them all out and she'd buy maybe ten dozen, a nickel a dozen in those days. She always baked her own bread; she was very particular on that. We ate plain and simple food – no pastry, no rich food or anything like that. Mother would spread the banana on bread and sprinkle just a little sugar on it. We had milk diluted with water and that was what we'd eat. She'd have a platter this big and load it up with bread spread with bananas and we loved that. I tell you, when you're hungry, anything goes. I still like bananas on bread.

We lived in a jungle out there – just a number of lakes and swamps and brush and everything. You couldn't hardly see there was a lake just over in front of us through the brush. The land wasn't cleared too much, you know. Us kids wanted some milk. But it was so hot we had to blow on it before we could drink it. We had to just sip it – we couldn't go and just drink a glass of milk 'til it cooled off. It would take all afternoon 'til it cooled off.

Once my brother was out plowing and he plowed up a whole bunch of rubber-like eggs. Of course, little kids just think Brer Rabbit lays eggs. When they think of eggs, they think of the Easter Bunny. I said to my brother, "Look at all the rabbit eggs, Emil. Look it." I went behind him and was picking up these eggs but they were rubbery. He looked at 'em – of course, he was older than I was – and he wasn't sure what they were. Then he seen one that was broken. There was a little snake in it. "Oh, those aren't rabbit eggs! Throw 'em down! Those are snake eggs."

Oh, we had a lot of fun – it was an experience for all of us, to be on the farm and see things grow and raise horses. They brought old Tom up from Chicago and a mare named Kit. We had a little colt we called George, named after my brother. It was kind of roan - light and dark colored. Then there was a mare born and when she got older, we raised more colts with her.

*Mr. Iverson on this tractor.*

I had this garden when I was seven. It was on a driveway where there was not grass and stuff growing on it, just bare ground. I thought that was a nice place to plant stuff. It was all coming up beautiful. I had potatoes and beans and some lentils. My mother used to use lentils to make lentil patties, lentil soup, and things like that, so I asked her if I could have a few to plant. I had those in. This road wasn't used, you see. We had a barn right close to the house and another up on the hill, where we kept our cattle and everything, with a straight path up to it. But when it came time to haul hay to the barn, they needed to go over my garden. So here they were, all my stuff growing there. What was I going to do? Well, I had to dig everything up and move it. So I moved it all and my mother felt sorry for me. But I found another place and replanted it. It wilted for a day or so but it all came along nicely. Mother said, "Ben can dig up anything and put it back in and it grows anyway." Once I wanted my mother to see the garden and how big some of the stuff was. "I'll see it when I get time," she said. So I dug up a plant, brought it up to show it to her, put it in the ground again, and it grew right on. I knew enough to dig enough dirt with roots so it wouldn't die.

Our farm was about 1/2 a mile or 3/4 a mile from Bear Lake, the beginning of the Black River that goes into South Haven. The river went through our farm. Us kids used to go swimming there, way back in the woods. We didn't use any bathing suits – just jumped in, in the raw, in the summer time.

After two years, we moved to Bangor and rented a 160 acre farm and started a milk route. We were the first ones to sell milk in bottles. My folks sent to either Sears Roebuck or Montgomery Wards and bought a whole bunch of bottles. We thought we'd try and in three months Mr. Leech (the competitor who sold milk in cans) went out of business and we had all the milk business in Bangor. Then our lease ran out on that farm. We rented another farm south of Bangor for three years. There was no such thing as pasteurizing. We bought a little steam boiler and did the scalding and everything to the bottles. We had cardboard caps. We'd push them down with our thumb. We had what they call an aeriator to cool the milk as soon as we'd pick it up from the barn. We ran it through a strainer into a container and we put clothes pins around and poured it in through the cloth strainer. By the time it got down to the bottom, it was cold. So then we'd just stand there and hold these bottles till they got full. Someone would be there to kind of take it away and put the caps on. We had pints and quart size and half-pints for cream. We bought a separator and we'd separate and sell cream.

The last year we were on the milk route, we bought a two gallon ice cream freezer and we'd freeze up two gallons of ice cream and take it with us. We'd sell it by the quart. The way we measured our quarts, we'd have 16 dippers to a quart; you'd get 16 level balls of ice cream. We didn't have quart containers; we took the ice cream out of that two-gallon can. We had it all packed with ice before we started on the milk route. The milk route was in town – the whole town, the north side and the south side.

We had a parochial school that we kids went to on the south side of Bangor. It used to be the old public school for the whole town, a brick building. The Adventists bought the building and used the downstairs for a church and the upstairs for a school. We had two big rooms; a stairway went down and turned and had a railing. The teacher would watch us. We'd go around the corner in a hurry and get on the railing and slide down. We had a lot

*Joe and Sam Iverson cutting ice in Paw Paw Lake. 1928.*

of fun. We didn't dare do it when she looked at us; then we'd have to walk down.

We sold our milk business to the man we rented from, this Mr. Skinner. He wanted to live on the farm himself because he was married then. Then we bought the farm in Covert. It was half a mile north and three quarters of a mile east of Covert. There's an octagon house there; the next house east was what my folks had. They bought 40 acres, in the fall of 1911. We didn't live there at first, but when we put up ice, we went over there during the week and then back to Bangor on the weekend. We kept horses and sleighs and we just cut the ice. In a little while, we bought what they call an ice plow to cut the ice. It had knives that'd go down through the ice. The farm across the street had a pond and we'd put up ice on it in the winter and go swim there in the summer. Nobody had refrigerators.

There was a big saw mill where the atomic plant is up in South Haven. That was called Ludwig's Pier. Ships would dock and take logs out of there. Also at Palisades Park were two piers and they had two saw mills in Covert at that time. Covert, in logging days, was about 1500 population. When we moved there later, it was only about 500. All those hills were filled with pines. They had a wooden railroad track all the way from Covert down to Palisades Park. There were big sawdust piles, two stories high – must have been several hundred foot long. They were selling sawdust to farmers or anybody who wanted it at a dollar a load. My folks got a lot of sawdust to put up ice. In about three weeks we put up 200 tons of ice. We'd just saw the ice by hand and somebody else would come and saw a cake off, you know. We'd

*Early Packard Mill. It was torn down in 1904. It cut 20,000-30,000 ft of lumber a day and shipped it north.*

saw slits all along and have a whole trench made and we'd float the cakes of ice over to the shore and then slide the ice up on a platform and into our sleighs. We had a hook made with a rope and we'd take a hook behind six or eight cakes of ice and the horse would pull up on this thing until the ice was in the sleigh. We'd pile up the ice in the sleigh and take it over to Covert and put it in the barn. Then we'd put saw dust all around the edge, about ten inches, so the ice would keep all summer long.

The ice plow had like teeth down there. We'd sharpen 'em good and put the horse on the ice, driving the plow down one or two inches and making a narrow groove. When the ice got real thick we'd have to cut it at least 2/3 of the way down. We had a blade with a long pole on it and we could put it down and break off the ice. But we had to leave enough so we could drive a horse on it – at least 6 to 8 inches above the water; otherwise, the horse would go down.

A man on Paw Paw Lake owned a big ice house here where the Lake Shore Club is. It must have been several hundred foot long and maybe 75 foot wide. They used to put up ice there. A company in Benton Harbor owned it. An interurban ran out to Watervliet and a branch here that went to the ice house. They would load up ice and take it to Benton Harbor in carloads and store it in an ice house up there; they'd sell this ice. There were no ice machines in those days, you know.

We had a little stick that would mark the cakes so they would be two feet square. I'd saw in as far as I could and my brother would come and saw the block off. Once he was standing on a cake that he sawed off and he sawed himself off. Down he went. Brr! Up to his neck in ice water. He couldn't get out without help. One of us standing by the side had to give him a hand. We took this pike – a pole that had a little spear like thing – and if we had ice that was floatin' out there where we couldn't reach it, we'd reach out and hook it over here and run it up the channel. We used the pole to reach for him so he could grab ahold of it to get out of the water. Neighbors got him in the house and took his clothes off and put him in bed there. I had to drive the team two and a half miles home to get some dry clothes. My mother couldn't find any drawers. (In those days, we wore two-piece underwear with a top and a bottom.) So my mother sent two tops over, figuring he could put one on below and one on top. She thought that was enough to get him home. When I got back, he put them on, we got our load of ice, and we went home. Of course he changed when he got home.

Then we started makin' ice cream in quantities. We bought a big ten gallon freezer from Smith Ice Cream Company in Watervliet when they bought a more modern freezer. With a great big handle and gears and everything, it would turn a big can in a wooden tub with ice and salt in it. My folks also bought ice cream cone irons. Cast irons. I have one of these original cone irons my folks bought about 70 years ago. They used to make cones to sell on the route. We had an old gasoline stove. My sister would sit there and run the three cone irons and make cones. She had to roll up the cones while they were hot. Boy, that was hot on the hands. She'd roll them on a wooden pin. If she waited too long, then they would break.

*Old cars in the Circle.*

That was when Ford cars were just coming out. You could buy them for $360 apiece. Model T's – little runabouts. We bought several of those and we put a box in the back and made a little platform for our ice cream cones. Then we'd pack it all in ice before we started down on the route. One brother went up here all along Paw Paw Lake. The other brother would go up to the South Haven area. There were a whole lot of Jewish resorts between South Haven and Bangor that would have maybe as many as two or three hundred people resorting. They would have their own swimming pools and everything. We couldn't go in the city limits without a license – we had to stay on the outskirts of South Haven. I was just a kid – about 16 or 17. In the forenoons I would work on the farm. Afternoons I would make ice cream. Chocolate, vanilla, strawberry, red raspberry, lemon – well, chocolate and vanilla were the old stand-bys. My brother would get a whole bunch of this mixed in ten-gallon cans and I'd dump it over into the freezer, filling to about six inches from the top. I had to leave room for it to expand as it froze. All afternoon I'd freeze maybe 60 or 70 gallons of ice cream. We had a great big cement bin made that would hold 12 or 15 five gallon cans. I'd put the containers in there. Then I'd crush a lot of ice (we bought salt by the ton and sugar by the ton) and I'd put some salt on the ice and kind of mix it up a little with a shovel and scoop it over all those cans. It stood overnight and next morning the ice cream was as hard as a brick. My brothers could take it out on their route and it would stay frozen until they got it sold. Some days, in real hot weather, maybe it would start getting soft toward the last.

My folks lived up on a hill next to that octagon house and my wife's mother lived down below. She was a widow with just the one daughter. My wife had been born and raised in that house; that was the only home she ever knew. My house was right down the hill, second house from the octagon. When we got married, and decided to move over here, she cried like a baby. She just couldn't leave that farm.

*The "Octagon House" in Covert.*

I went into the poultry business when we got married. I tried to farm for about a year and I couldn't see any future in that. It just didn't pay. Ordinary farming. You can't do it on a little farm. There isn't enough. We had a 20-acre farm but you can't live on a 20-acre farm. You can only use it to raise enough feed to raise two cows and a horse. You've got to have more than that. I had taken care of the chicken business at home, before I was married. I had kind of promoted that, built that up. I bought several incubators and began selling baby chicks. Then when we got married, I went into it a little bigger. My brother and I saw an ad in the paper that a man over in Fenton, Michigan had a 2400 egg incubator for sale. And it was very reasonable. So we took a train over there and decided to take it. We had him crate it up and ship it back to Covert. When I went home, I dug into the side of a little sand hill and built this incubator cellar. My two brothers and my mother were in partnership together on that farm.

During '28 or '29, the poultry business went to pot. By that time I had bought a 5000 egg incubator and another 2400 egg incubator, so I had three – down in the basement in my barn. Some of the resort people raised chickens and they wanted to buy chicks from me. Well, they were pretty smart, you know. They would get together and have these roundtable meetings and say, "Now how many chicks do you want? How many do you want?" and they'd come and give me an order for 10,000 baby chicks. They expected to get a little better price that way and I give 'em two cents off on the chicks on a 10,000 lot order. And then I could fill it as my batches came out. That didn't quite suit 'em 'cuz they had it all figured this one would get first, that one would get next, and that next. So I could only fill 'em as my hatches came out. Sometimes I had a better hatching than at other times. Sometimes I could fill a 1500 chick order – or 1000 – or 500. Sometimes I could only fill 200 or 250. They weren't quite satisfied because I couldn't fill 'em in the rotation that they wanted. When the crash came, eggs went down eight, nine, ten cents a dozen. You couldn't pay your chicken feed with that. Things got so rough we sometimes had to go to Shirley's little piggy bank to get enough to get a loaf of bread. It really got tough. So I sold the incubators and bought 5000 baby chicks and I built onto my brooder house so I had a building 60 foot long, 26 wide, and two stories high. I put in my own heating system with a lot of old pipes and manifolds and stuff I bought second hand at the junkyard in Benton Harbor. I had to take care of 5000 baby chicks with one heater. I fixed that all up and it worked beautiful, with 2500 chicks on each floor.

Anyway, when the crash came, what could I do? Raise a good big garden so we'd have something to eat anyway. During the WWII days, some of the Palisades Park people would take a ride down our road and they said, "Beautiful garden there." And some of them, stopping, said, "I see that you like gardening." Well, I says "Sure." I figure I was going to go out and do some peddling so I says, "If there's anything that you want …" They says, "What have you got?" "Well, I've got so and so" and they'd take so much of that and so much of this. Then they went back and told some of the other fellas there in the Park. And then more of 'em would come and more of 'em would come and finally some asked, "We don't always have a car. My husband comes out over the weekend with a car, but we don't always have it. Could you deliver sometimes?" Well, I said yes, I'd deliver if the order was enough so it pays. I couldn't go over for two or three dollars. If I had a number of orders so I'd take $15 or $20 worth of stuff down, I'd deliver.

*The Iverson home in Covert.*

Old man Quick down in Palisades Park was kind of a tough one. The people at the north end of the Park there, they lived in what they called Dean's Addition. Well, they had to come across some Park road to get to the main highway. Well Mr. Ballou – I knew him real well, he ran the grocery store there. And Mr. Quick was trying to protect him so no peddlers could come in there. So old man Quick saw me going in there and he stood there by that garage waitin' for me to come out. People out in Dean's Addition – Mrs. Filkins lived way out there – they had asked if I would deliver. When I came back, old man Quick was standing there waiting for me. He says, "I see you were coming here with some vegetables and stuff. You know, these are private roads, don't you?" I said, "Yes. Well," I said, "these people are paying you $25 a year for the use of that road and they're having me deliver to them. I'm not peddling. I'm just delivering some orders." He says, "I don't care what you call yourself, you're a peddler to me. You can't use these roads. We've got to protect the store." So he went to Paw Paw and served an injunction to keep me out of there. Then the Palisades Park people got mad at him. They said, "We'll fix old man Quick. We'll get together and double up in cars and we'll go out and get our vegetables ourselves." So that's what they started doing. And finally cars coming back and forth right down that dust road made my neighbors say, "What's going on down there?" I had 'em standing out by the road, I had 'em in my driveway full of cars.

> There is virtue in country houses, in gardens and orchards, in fields, streams, and groves, in rustic recreations and plain manners that neither cities nor universities enjoy.
> 
> — *A. B. Alcott*

## Helen Packard

Interviewed by Betty Householder
September 14, 1984

I first came to Palisades in 1942 or '43. Mr. Quick pushed us into it. At first, I rented the store from Mrs. Ballou's daughter, Adelaide Beshgatour. Georgia Underwood was the postmaster. She was paid $540 for four months of work, plus 15% for rent; finally she walked out because it was too much work for what little pay she got. I was made acting postmaster. The following year, I was made postmaster. I built up to 94 boxes to begin with, and got up to 134, not counting general delivery for all the renters at the hotel. Mr. Ballou built the regular boxes; later I bought the key ones. We had inspections and once I was scared to death. The inspector was a German guy and he looked and looked, on the second day, trying to find something I hadn't done right. I had to keep everything just so. I forgot to back stamp a darn old COD package with the date but he didn't see that. So I got a perfect score of 100. Now they rate the post office "good" or "excellent" but then they marked us like a report card. We had to get three 100's each year. I never got anything below 96. But I took the Postal Regulations home every winter and read that darn thing from one end to the other and I'd write down all the changes. You know, COD went up, money orders went up, registers went up, box rents went up, everything went up. I opened the post office each June 1$^{st}$ and had everything right in case someone walked in and checked on me. But it was still a lot of fun.

I ran both the store and post office until 1969. I had help. Edith Hardy came in about 1944 and worked for about eight years altogether; she went back to South Haven in 1968. Others who worked for me included Mrs. Appleyard and her two boys, Mrs. Ruth Crumb, the teacher, and her son, and Edith's relative, Pearl. After I bought the store, I fixed up the apartment and did a lot of repair work. The store was so old – with long counters and old iceboxes. Canonie brought ice twice a week and I had to stick everything in the ice- boxes and try to keep it. We didn't have a dairy case or a freezer – we didn't have anything to start with. We went to South Bend to buy a dairy case and you never heard such cussing in your life when it was delivered. My husband, Bob Packard, and Edith's husband, Max Hardy, had to get the windows out of the porch and roll that darn thing in on logs, to get it onto the porch. Oh, they were so disgusted that we hadn't thought of measuring. It could never have gone in through the door. Then we got the freezer and George Haggard had to take all the moldings off the doors to get that it.

Every year little kids would come holding hands, new ones every year. I sold newspapers – over 100 <u>Tribs</u> and <u>Sun Times</u> and <u>Detroit Free Presses.</u> I sold magazines

*Edith Hardy and Henlen Packard outside the store in Ballou Inn.*

*Helen Packard inside the Post Office.*

and toys, too. On the weekends, it was open house – people stopped in before going to their cottages. And the little kiddies got their candy bars and everything. Once a little boy took something. He knew we were watching him so he ran out and down the sidewalk there and dug a hole in the sand and buried it there. We asked him what he had buried out there. Boy, he felt terrible. He brought it back and said, "I'll never do it again. I won't." And he didn't. When the kids would come in from tennis they'd get pop from the coolers – I never knew how many bottles. They'd say "Chalk up 3, chalk up 6, chalk up this many." We never knew just what they drank. We had to get a list made out for them. Every day they came, so it was that extra monkey business we had to do. It was fun. It sure kept our brain working.

I got meat to sell from Swifts and Stones about three or four times a week. People would order what they wanted. I sometimes bought out Stones. People ordered so many steaks, Stones asked, "How many steaks does a cow have, anyway?" I got the best of everything. We had big wheel cheese, Rath cheese, which we got from Bordens. During the war we had all those little tokens and everything. People still wanted meat. I went to every grocery store or meat market in town with my bushel baskets and got whatever I could. Maybe a pot roast, maybe a ground chuck, maybe this, maybe that. Then I had to stop on the way back and park in the woods and sort everything out according to my list and see what I could give to so and so and how much was the cost. I let everybody have the best I could. Mr. Glasner (In Cognito cottage) came in and helped us cut meat sometimes. He was a butcher.

It really was hard work. We had to start in April. We had to pick snow off the steps there to get in and get started cleaning. Then when the store was open, I had to get up at 5:15 in the morning and didn't get to bed until after 10:00 at night. We had to mop the floor and put everything away in the freezer and then make a list of stock that we had on the third floor. And we had to drag things down from there and stock the shelves. But everyone was wonderful. I made a profit every year, but nothing to get rich on.

The toughest part was to take everything home in the winter. We had to drag all our cans to South Haven so they wouldn't freeze. Stores would take back full or half cases; anything else, we were stuck with. All our dried things we gave away, all the sugar and cereals and cake mixes. Everything like that that we didn't want to keep for ourselves. So there went part of our profits. We were well supplied in the winter.

Sometimes Edith and I would go swimming at night after it was dark. But Max stopped us when we got near the fish. I'd rather go beach combing. It was beautiful down there.

There was only one thing I was afraid of – one of the men customers. That's when we had the old ice-boxes. I wouldn't wait on him; when I saw him coming, I'd run for Edith. He was unhapy when someone took his paper. Once I saved it behind the ice blocks and when he came in for it, I'd be darned if I could find it. I thought he was going to break that door down. He slammed that door; I expected it to break to pieces. Well, he was okay. He got real soft. He had an ulcer.

Del Jones ran the hotel. He was good with chess. He had a slot machine. We went over there and put nickels in until the police carried it out. After that, he got some other machine and they carried that one out, too, so then he gave up. I remember when the police came. My family was here. Mr. Hempy and his wife, Mandy, came with a horse and wagon and collected garbage. He was manager when I first came. Mandy was Mother Hardy's cousin. Julia Quick's daughter, Mary Jane, ran the ice cream parlor then.

When I sold to the Flynns (who ran the store and post office for two more years), there were two farewell parties. Mrs. Bishop had that nice big chair I sat in. And we had champagne. And I got a necklace. At the other party, I got a whole bunch of quarters. I did ok. I have a picture of that, out on the lawn, with all the gang down there. My most vivid memory of Palisades is of all the people we met there. We wouldn't even know what their business was or anything. They'd just let their hair down and enjoy themselves, just as nice as anyone could be.*

*Helen, who bought the store in 1958 after renting it for a number of years, retired in 1966. In all, she worked there 27 years. She was preceded by Mrs. Overhuel.*

*Edith Hardy, Helen's partner, inside the store.*

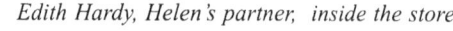

# Memories

## Lori Anderson Dillman
"Palisades Memories"

My memories pretty well cover the years of early 1940's to mid 1950's, though my parents had been regulars in the Park during the 30's. It is hard to imagine how moms coped with infant needs like bottles and diapers in a cottage that had no heat, hot water, or refrigerator. However, we kids were freer than my life has been since, because nothing existed in Palisades about which parents needed to be concerned. From an early age we roamed the woods and the beaches north and south as far as our age and legs would take us. We swung across roads on huge vines entangled in very tall trees and played kickball in the road. We of course did not go in the lake without adult supervision, though my Dad enticed us to learn to swim by placing a silver dollar on the shore. I won it. Before we could swim without being watched, we would beg any adult on the beach (we knew everybody back then) to please watch us if Dad was not in attendance. Uncle Lorry Northrup would show up with interesting things during the Second World War, like a Navy surplus raft that we used a lot.

I don't know how to name the valley that set the boundaries of our early year's habitat. Our neighbors were the Stantons, Frazers, Byers, Lundquists, Leo Sowerby, Northrops, Irwins, Masons, Kleunders, Mrs. Sankey, and later the Smiths who bought her cottage. As mentioned, we knew everybody and often found ourselves in other cottages to have a drink or snack or use the bathroom, even if no kids lived there. Our early playmates were Barb and Roger Smith, the Lundquist kids and Mason grandkids and Judy Easterbrook who lived around the horseshoe curve east of us. Besides the usual play and beach fun, we were free to go to Mrs. Packard's store to fetch the mail or paper. Back then no cars existed in the Park during the week, and we depended on Mrs. Packard for food, mail, papers, and comic books.

On weekends when Dad arrived in a car, a trip to Covert for groceries, fresh produce, and stopping to pick wild berries on the way was a treat. Memories of Covert people we dealt with are gone, but I do remember the store with the huge cheese wheel in it and my love for blackberries found along the way. And wow, trips to South Haven and Benton Harbor, very rare, provided more adventures even if we were only going to purchase cottage necessities. To this day, I don't know how we got five kids, two adults, and a dog in a Ford convertible. That is how we got around in those days. My Dad died before I had the presence of mind or interest to quiz him about WWII days and how he could get enough rationed gas to make those trips to Palisades from Chicago.

Everybody remembers or has heard about Hempy and Joe Putz, such fixtures they were. Hempy and his wife took care of the Park for many years, and a highlight of any day in the Park would be when he stopped his horses during his garbage pickup so we could pet their velvety noses. It was a very big deal that he umpired the annual men's softball game each summer, and any complaining about his calls was done in the most friendly manner. Joe helped with beaches and roads, and could be seen anywhere in the Park. He always smiled at us kids, though I doubt he remembered our names. One special recollection I have of him was on the beach very early one morning carefully watching his sister, simple-minded Mary, run along the shore trailing a scarf behind her. I know he took care of Mary, but I was too young to be privy to details of his home life.

And then there was Del Jones. In spite of his small size, his presence struck fear in our hearts and we gave him wide berth. Occasionally we bravely went on his porch to feed a nickel or two into the slot machine, but one summer it was no longer there. Michigan gaming laws caught up with him, perhaps. Also, from time to time he hailed one of us to deliver a telegram for a coin, a coup to be bragged about among our friends and siblings. In retrospect, I believe he tolerated us kids if we didn't make noise to disturb his guests or use his hotel beach. I do not remember his wife, Blanche, probably because her domain – from which she rarely surfaced – was the hotel kitchen where she turned out excellent fare for guests. The pastry cook, a large lady from Covert, occasionally would greet us from the back porch where she rested between meals.

The Clubhouse was a source of great fun, with bunco nights leading the list for me. We played ping pong and actually used the shuffleboard courts and participated in countless ideas and projects provided by the Clubhouse couple. The bang of that screen door on the south end of the porch stays with me today as a reminder of fun things happening. Thunder Mountain was equally as enticing for a different type of fun. Trips to climb, explore, picnic somewhere on the wooded slopes, and race down the face of the bowl occurred several times a summer, as well as spring and fall. Lack of water or ice delivery for the box did not deter my family from off-season weekend jaunts to the cottage. The bell tower provided yet another kind of challenge, to see who could climb all those steps the fastest. A bell actually used to be there.

The Soda Bar, then as now, provided a gathering place for kids young and old. Once in a while our parents would send us there to eat, and over the summer we were allowed to charge a tiny amount. If the bill went over what my Dad considered tiny, we were cut off for a while. My interest there, however, was the pinball machine that I never mastered. It did not occur to me that my eye-hand coordination lacked the fine tuning needed to win free games, and I was frustrated that others, particularly my brother, seemed to win easily. The old garage behind the Soda Bar was a splendid place to run through, shouting to hear our voices reverberating off the walls. For a time my dad and brother had an old model T parked there. A tiny upstairs room became a publishing empire that produced the <u>Patter</u>.

The Brandywine held many secrets and surprises for us each year. We waded in it, marveling at whatever floated, swam, flitted, or lay at the bottom. It would be hard to imagine this wonderful place before the meadow, but we kids loved it because we could go in it without having a parent present because it was so shallow. We also knew a lot of flowers, because our parents taught us about the woods and what could be picked or not. I remember seeing Arthur Quick walking about the Park from time to time, always in a suit with a long white beard and a cane.

*Steve Anderson, Lori's brother. 1952.*

*Teens and their jeep. 1950.*

During teen years the circle of friends (at least those I remember) widened to include the kids from other areas of the Park. Dee Prange, Paul Schlacks, Chuck Castle, Margaret VonRosen, Dave Edwards, Mary Ruth McCain, Pete Hohman, Mary Ann Dinnan, Mike Mooney, Pete Wunsch, Rod Lowrey, Robin Campbell, Jack MacDougal, Barbara Baldwin, Dick Giblin, Alice Beatty, Katy Beatty, brother Steve and stepsister Judy Best are some of the names that stand out. Activities where we could see these summer pals included the Soda Bar, tennis courts, beach parties, and Clubhouse events. The old pumphouse was great to party behind, though we never built a fire there. The beach fires were just that – beach fires - and we always knew the last to leave would cover the ashes with sand. Sometimes the wood was "borrowed" from various cottages under cover of darkness. I have no recollection of anything other than soft drinks being consumed at those parties. Riding around in Dave Edwards's jeep was great fun. We were not necessarily confined to Park roads in that vehicle. Many of us frequently used the tennis courts or at least went out to see what was going on. Wooden rackets with gut strings in a tennis press were all we had, and a new can of balls meant someone got real lucky asking Dad for money or saved for a long time.

Most of us had curfews, that heinous curtailment of teenage fun, and we dared not abuse the bewitching hour. Scrambling through dark woods and treacherous stone-strewn roads to meet the deadline was touch and go. Carrying a flashlight did not fit the teenage persona of the day, and the light shining down the hill from the front porch helped us speed up those last precious moments before the clock struck the hated hour. My siblings and I despised that curfew, especially the Friday night 11:00 p.m., because the house rules were the family ate together and kids did the dishes and sometimes we didn't complete this onerous task until 9:00 p.m. Parental cocktail hour, you know.

The simple, quiet life of my childhood in Palisades Park is in marked contrast to what we experience today. My own children and grandchildren did not spend days and nights in the Park devoid of noise other than the wind in the trees, an occasional screen door slamming, and the waves expending themselves on the beach. Very little "white" noise that we tune out today existed back then, but our ears caught the creak of Babe and Molly's harness or the clunk of huge blocks of ice delivered for Tony Canonie by those handsome Michigan State football players on summer leave. Some ice days the guys might chip off a small hunk of ice for us to suck on. We were summoned to dinner by a cowbell, and Uncle Leo Sowerby's ship's bell signaled cocktail time for our parents. During the polio epidemic, my mother couldn't wait for us to get away to Palisades summer to escape the potential of contracting that dreaded disease, even if we begged to stay home to spend a summer with our "real" friends.

The tranquility of Palisades Park during those years provided the perfect place for Jeanne DeLamarter (my stepmom during my teen years) to write her poetry and Uncle Leo Sowerby to compose his music, both of whom had their works published. We learned early when to be quiet and not interrupt, but the Park held so many wonders to explore and use that we were not in our valley much at all. My Palisades Park childhood remains a treasured memory, complete with sights, smells, and noises not forgotten.

*Robert Ballou, Sr., Robert Ballou, and Will Smith (Ballou's brother-in-law) sitting on wall beneath the cottages they built and owned - Graystone #89, Ballou Inn #90, and Oceana #91. The cottages were all completed by 1911 or 1912.*

# Eleanor B. DiLuigi

Daughter of Adelaide Ballou
In letter to Ellen Flynn
December 14, 1997
From Covert Historical Museum

Dear Ellen,

First of all, I want to express my appreciation to you for your hospitality this summer when my daughter Nancy and I visited you at your summer home, Ballou Inn, on Lake Michigan. It was very kind of you to let me sit on the porch and remember the happy summers that I spent there as a teenager in the 1940's.

When I was twelve years old, we came to Palisades for a visit. At that time my step-grandmother, Grace Barker Ballou, was running [what is now the Flynn cottage] as an Inn …. My grandfather, Robert G. Ballou, built all three of the houses (Graystone, Ballou Inn, and Oceana) for himself, his parents – my great-grandparents - and his sister and her husband, my great-aunt Luella Ballou Smith and her husband Will. As my mother wrote in the 1968 Palisades Park history, she remembers them mixing the cement, sand, and gravel from the beach and forming the stones that make up the foundations of all three houses. That they have withstood so many Lake Michigan storms over the years is testimony to the fact that they did a good job. My mother would have been 18 years old in 1912, when these houses were built. She waited table at the Inn during her summer vacations from Alma College.

In 1941, my father was transferred back to the United States permanently and we lived in Merchantville, New Jersey. World War II was being fought overseas, and gasoline was very strictly rationed. All year long, my father took a bus to work instead of the car, so we could save the gasoline coupons and the gasoline in cans, in the garage, so that we could drive out to Ballou Inn for the summer. He would drive out with us and come back on the train when his vacation time was up, but my mother, sister, brother, and I stayed all summer and loved it. I waited table at the Inn, and for a number of years was Assistant Postmistress in the little summer post office. These were the summers that I was in college at the University of Pennsylvania. I graduated in 1948 and got a permanent job in Philadelphia.

In 1949, I married John P. Ramsay, Jr., whose family had a lovely summer cottage on a Maine lake. He always wanted to go to Maine, had been overseas in the war, and was totally uninterested in ever going to Michigan, so we always went to Maine. Two of my adult children now live permanently in Maine, and I have a retirement home there also. Last summer (on the trip to Palisades), my daughter Nancy kept asking me, "Why didn't you tell me Michigan was so beautiful and that you can drive for miles right along the lakes?" ….

My mother rented Ballou Inn, first to a Mrs. Overhuel and then to a Mrs. Packard. She sold it in 1960 when it became apparent that neither I nor my brother or sister ever planned to go there again. I would have liked to very much because it is a wonderful place to raise children.

A little more history about Palisades Park. In addition to building the three houses on the Circle, my grandfather, Robert G. Ballou, built many of those large cottages up in the woods behind Ballou Inn. Mr. Quick, who originally owned all the land in the Park, would advertise it in Chicago and Indianapolis newspapers. When people bought their sites, he would recommend my grandfather as a builder. According to my mother, my grandfather was an extremely gregarious, outgoing, honest, popular man in the area. She always remembers that he had a payroll to meet and had a crew of men working for him. I hardly knew him because he died in 1936, when we were in South America. I was very delighted to see that you had Ballou Walk named in his memory. He built those steps, too – quite a stairway. I remember running up them; I'm afraid I couldn't do it now.

…. I can't tell you how much it meant to me to see that your wonderful family has loved and cherished Ballou Inn the way you have. You have certainly taken wonderful care of it. What a great place for your parents to have raised sixteen children over the years in the summer …. I hope you'll be able to spend many more happy summers at Ballou Inn on Lake Michigan.

*Eleanor DiLuigi and Nancy Ramsey visiting Ballou Inn. 1997.*

*Bob Borchert and Bill Eldedge, 1954.*

# Bill Eldredge
September 16, 2003

As best I can remember, I have been coming to Palisades all my life (75 years). Prior to 1946, we rented a variety of cottages – including one that doesn't exist anymore (the Stearns). My aunt, Marie Mahon, knew about Palisades because she had visited Sturtevant Lodge with a friend sometime in the early 20's. From then on, my parents usually rented a cottage for a month every year. It was a five-plus hour drive from our home on the northwest side of Chicago, through East Chicago, Whiting, Gary, Michigan City, and St. Joe. I have a vague recollection of picking up my dad at the train in Bangor. We bought our present cottage (#9) from a family named Roper, in 1946, but I remember visiting it in the late '30's when the Nielsens rented it. I think it was built in around 1935 by Rudy Weber. Rudy was an excellent carpenter and a great guy. He had played some professional baseball in the past, as a left-handed pitcher. Legend was that he had a brief stint with the Cubs, but I can't find him in the Baseball Almanac.

There used to be a cottage on the slope below us, between ours and the beach, owned by the Crawfords. It was moved up the hill during the high water of the '50's; it is now owned by the Fredians (#25). Like others, we then had to build a sea wall – first a wooden one and, when that went, a steel one.

My aunt and uncle, Marie and Joe Mahon built their cottage (now the Cooneys # 6) around 1947-48. Part of it came precut from northern Michigan. The assembler-contractors were Charley Tunecke and Jeff Phillips and his crew from Covert. I knew Charley much of my early life. Legend had it that he was the illegitimate son of an European nobleman – but I don't know.

I imagine most people remember Joe Putz about as well as I do. Joe was the handyman everyone used. He would do almost anything, but he was best with the shovel. My mother soon discovered that the way to keep Joe coming back was to make sure she gave him dinner. I remember one time when Joe repaired a bathroom sink for us. The cold water and hot water pipes were two different kinds. Joe said, "If anyone asks you why it looks like it does, just tell them Joe Putz did it."

I presume the primary social activity was beach fires, but there it would probably be better not to mention that for a period, a <u>real</u> beachfire had wood from Delno Jones's pile.

The South Haven Peach Festival Tennis Tournament went on for several years. Many of us entered it. Ben, Bob Ott, Bill Eifrig, Ray Lewis, Chuck Hammerschmidt, Joe Stewart, Hal and Bert Wilson, myself and others. The finals were always Ben beating Bob Arkins in a close match. I remember playing Art Clarke, the South Haven real estate man, in a marathon match, which he won. After it was over, Art, a real nice guy who was a little rotund, said, "Survival of the fattest!"

*Chuck Hammerschmidt and Ray Lewis. 1951.*

Everyone remembers Betty Householder, but fewer people remember her husband, Frank. He was more low-key than Betty, but equally fine. He used to play tennis with us, but never entered a tournament because he taught at WMU and was a pro. He had a heart condition for several years and I remember going, with Chuck Hammerschmidt, to visit him in South Haven Hospital.

The Honor and Glory. People may not remember that Forest Lowrey sponsored the Honor and Glory. One time, probably in the 50's, 10 or 12 of us got together and bought a trophy of a tennis player and had it inscribed, "**To Forest Lowrey with deepest appreciation from the tennis players of Palisades Park.**" Ben Bishop was easily the best tennis player in the history of the Park, but early on he stayed out of the H & G so as not to dominate it. I played in the tournament for many years and the closest I got was losing, with my brother Don, in the doubles final to Bill Eifrig and Ray Lewis – mainly because I couldn't control my first serve.

*Bill Eldredge in 1951.*

*Ben Bishop. 1950.*

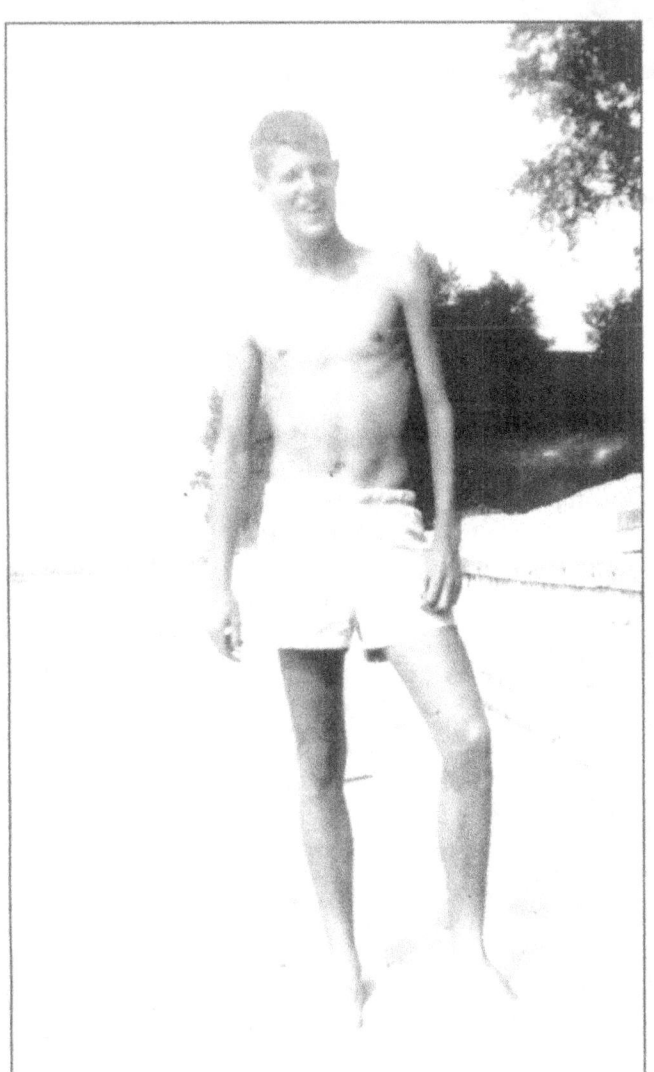

Baseball. Sometime in the late 40's or early 50's, a pickup team from the Park played the South Haven American Legion team. We played two games in the same year or in subsequent years. We played on their field. Ben Bishop pitched one game and Chuck Hammerschmidt pitched the other one. Bert Wilson caught one game and Gene Howe the other. (Gene ran the Standard Oil station at the Park entrance and was probably our best player.) Other players I remember (and I know I have left out many) are Bill Eifrig, Ray Lewis, Frank Hagie, Joe Stewart, and myself. We lost both games. In the second game, we were losing 6-0 with two outs in the ninth. I was on third base. Chuck said to me, "We don't want to get shut out: steal home." I tried – and was thrown out by at least 20 feet.

*Bill Eifrig. 1951.*

*Clubhouse Beach, looking southwest by Brands' cottage. 1959.*

# Sally Davis Ellis

July, 1964 Patter

Palisades Park can mean many things to many people. Palisades is the smell of bacon that seems to linger in the woods on Sunday mornings, and the special stillness of Sunday evenings after a busy weekend. It is the children scurrying off to Bunco on Tuesday night and to the post office to wait for afternoon mail.

To some, it is the joyful cries of children and people with happy faces enjoying the beach and cool woods in the summer. It is the crackle and crunch of dry fallen leaves underfoot in the bright autumn sunshine. Or the hushed stillness of a heavy winter snowfall, drifted and swirled, unmarked except for an occasional wild animal track. It is the lovely unfolding of myriads of spring wild flowers just before the trees break forth with their new leaves.

Yet another person might think of Palisades in terms of the moods of the lake – be it strong and angry in its wind whipped fury; lazy and indolent on a hot, heavy summer day; or flirting and carefree following the caprice of a gentle breeze on a perfect sun-washed day.

Perhaps to someone Palisades is the full moon twinkling through the leaves or casting its shimmering trail on the lake. The quiet dawn light breaking to the accompaniment of the first sleepy chirp from a waking bird. By the time the sun bursts into view, the bird's songs have mounted to a symphony welcoming the new day. Soon the bird sounds decrease and the people sounds begin – the steady plop, plop, plop of the tennis balls, the whir of motors on the lake, the splash as someone dives into the lake, the animated chatter coming from the Clubhouse – these are the daytime sounds played against a background of striped sails bobbing along the lakefront and children building drip castles on the beach. By sunset these sounds subside and once again the quiet lapping of the lake and lullabies of the birds can be heard as the old bull-frog at the Brandywine ker-plunks his appreciation of another day and the whippoorwill sends his evening song echoing through the woods: "Whip-poor-will" "All is well!"

*Wendy Easterbrook, with bangs, and sister Judy standing, plus a group of playmates. Note swings on beach. c. 1946.*

# Wendy Easterbrook Litterst-Day

58 Years Later: My Memories

I started going up to Palisades with my mom and 2 1/2 year old sister, Judy, when I was six weeks old, having been born on July 10, 1942. My grandparents, Joseph "Champ" Gates and Hazel "Del" Gates, owned the cottage now called "Lookout Inn" #130. We called it "Monk's Haven" after the nickname we grandkids called our grandpa. In 1956, my grandparents sold to Jim and Mary Margaret Roach who ran the Soda Bar. They, in turn, sold to Andy Anderson.

My memories of the cottage are still vivid, especially of three items – a sword that hung over the fireplace, the antique organ my grandmother played (she was a concert pianist), and all the wicker furniture that filled the rooms! How I wish I could track down these items – especially the wooden sign on the tree outside identifying "Monk's Haven."

Since we lived far back in the woods, our mom, Muriel "Min" Easterbrook, had to drive to the beach. En route she would always stop to pick a "snowball" blossom to pin in her thick black hair. Those there at the time will most certainly remember that: it was her trademark!

A great group of people were there: the Ray Kropps and their three children (I played with Carol); the handsome Gates boys, Tom and Greg, from South Bend, Indiana; John Ferry, a minister's son from West Virginia; the flamboyant Mrs. Ott, Sr. and her family; and – most special – Jayne Mathias, her husband and four adorable boys (they added a girl years after we were there.)

The Clubhouse was the most popular meeting place for activities, movies, and the ever-popular Bingo. The soda fountain, post office and mini store, hotel and hotel's dining facility were a long walk – over hill and dale – from our cottage.

No such thing as a refrigerator existed as we know it today; we had what was called an ice box. We anxiously awaited the arrival of the horse drawn ice delivery wagon. The driver would let us use ice picks to chip some ice pieces. The shower was an ordeal; showers were in what was known as the basement room outside of the main house. I fought going there as the area always had mice running all around. To this day, I freak out when confronted by those pesky creatures.

Aunt Blannie's visits were special. I slept with her in the couch and enjoyed being part of her morning ritual; applying her creams and makeup seemed to take most of the morning.

# Judy Easterbrook Coker-Green Remembers ...

August 13, 2004

- the boardwalk (miles of it) and our always getting splinters
- balancing and walking on the icy pipes of the water station near the beach
- playing and camping out in the Sugar Bowl
- the winding walk over dirt paths through the woods and down to the beach
- collecting slimy snails clinging to the mossy railings
- seeing many species of butterflies flitting amongst the flowers in the Circle
- luna moths the size of your hand clinging to the screens on special mornings
- the pin ball machine at the post office
- the stairs – 100+ of them, up and over and down to the Circle
- the sound of the hotel bell announcing that lunch or dinner was being served – but only to guests
- cars honking as they went around the corners of the one lane dirt road
- Joe Putz and his wife, keepers of the front gate
- the end-of-the-year half mile swim I completed at age 10
- playing the waves and undertows and being tossed around until I thought I surely would drown!
- family fun of the best kind with grandparents, aunts, uncles, great aunts and uncles, nieces and nephews all summer long
- not being allowed to go in the water until one hour after eating
- having to take naps everyday to prevent polio
- laundry done in South Haven
- fruit-stands along the roads with blueberries and raspberries four pints for a dollar!
- playing tennis on the old tennis courts
- horseback and pony rides somewhere in the Park
- my first kiss ... Skeeter Straka
- playing golf with my dad in South Haven and Benton Harbor
- waiting for our dad's arrival on the weekends; he'd honk at the bottom of the hill (I could barely see his car through the trees) and he always brought bunches of glads "for his girls" as did Grandpa.

Those were truly the endless days of summer; for us children it seemed they would never end! (My mom remembered a lot more work with fewer of the modern conveniences she had at home in Peoria, Illinois.)

*Del Gates playing the antique organ in the Gates cottage #130; husband Joseph "Monk" Gates behind her. 1940's.*

*Judy Easterbrook in middle (with swimming cap) holding brother Randy and Wendy Easterbrook, to her right, holding a cousin. c. late 40's.*

# Betty Lukey (nee Duwe)

"I Remember"
August 17, 1970 Patter

As a child, I spent many winter weekends at Palisades with my family – an enchanted land! White snow that stayed white (no air pollution in those days); brisk, clean air to enjoy as we hiked through the woods (sometimes a deer and other wild creatures could be glimpsed as we wandered over the trails); cutting wood for the fire (Father always said it warmed us three times – sawing, hauling, and burning). Water was a precious commodity. We had no well, so hauled water up the hill in gallon jugs – and believe me, never a drop was wasted.

The most treasured memories of all are of Thanksgiving at Palisades. Mother would have all the food prepared ahead of time and, early on Thanksgiving morning, we'd head for the cottage. As soon as we arrived, the turkey would go into the oven and then, after getting settled and a good fire going, we'd go hiking in the woods. When we returned and walked into the cottage, our nostrils would be greeted by the most glorious aroma of the turkey. Nothing in this world, before or since, has smelled so good to me as that heavenly fragrance of Thanksgiving dinner. It was truly a day of thanks-giving; our own private wonderland to roam through, a snug cottage to come home to, and a feast to enjoy.

# Chapter 6
# The Ensuing Decades

```
1950 – North Korea invades South Korea.
1952 – Coronation of Queen Elizabeth II
1955 – First McDonald's opens; Disneyland opens.
1962 – John Glenn orbits the Earth in Friendship 7
1965 – U.S. enters Vietnam conflict.
1974 – Richard Nixon resigns.
1981 – IBM introduces the personal computer.
1985 – South Haven's Michigan Maritime Museum opens on May 6.
1989 – The Berlin Wall comes down.
1992 – the World Wide Web is born.
2001 – September 11 attack.
```

# The Ensuing Decades

Although significant changes continue each decade, Palisades Park has remained constant in many ways. A visitor in 1950 might have seen a Park quite like that of this new century. Young people spend carefree summers at Palisades; romance is often in the air. Winding dirt roads lead to cottages tucked into the woods – albeit often to bigger and more "citified" summer homes. The summer beach is covered with sand castles and plastic toys, with boats and umbrellas, with tanning (or sunburned) backs, with beach fires and picnics. In the off season, lonely beachcombers search for storm-borne treasures, sharing their solitude with a few remaining gulls. A full system of trails lead nature-lovers deep into the woods and dunes. Crowded tennis courts and frequent tournaments give evidence of the continued popularity of the sport. Clubhouse kids play Capture the Flag and plan their yearly Carnival. Women gather for coffee and fellowship. Families walk down the boardwalk after supper for a Soda Bar treat. Vacationers linger on the beach each evening to watch the splendor of the Western sky. Magic is in the air.

The Clubhouse program in the 50's included frequent plays and dinner dances as well as the Park's first clothes-line art show and fashion show. A new manager, Cecil Burrous, took the reins in 1959. The Patter, which had floundered in the 40's, was reorganized and flourished. The opening of I-196 in the 60's shortened travel time to Chicago and points south. In 1967, the Park attorney filed a request that the County "vacate" the road from the gate to the lake - in essence, making Ravine Way a private road for the first time. In 1979, we lost our Post Office.

Not that the decades haven't brought their problems. In 1951, facing the threat of Julia Quick Hill selling her substantial interest in the Palisades to outside developers, several of the men banded together to buy all of the Hill property. These men – dubbed The Nine Old Men – saved the day. Incorporated as **Palisades Park Properties, Inc.**, they sold some of the property to recoup their investment; later, then deeded the rest to the Park. One chunk of land, what is now called the meadow but had previously been the site of the proposed (and failed) Lake Palisades, caused another controversy when the decision was made to clear and drain the land. A commercial plane went down in the lake, just off our shoreline, closing our beaches as State Police collected what remains were washed to shore.

In 1952, more sea walls were constructed. A letter from Canonie Excavating Company to Mr. A. J. Filkins, dated May 9, 1952, spells out the cost of 336 feet of wall on the north beach. The cost of wall, at $18.00 per lineal foot, equaled $6048, to be divided among three cottage owners.

By 1953, our name had been changed to **Palisades Park Country Club** and our By-Laws revised. These revisions included the definition of both regular and associate membership; annual dues were $60; a quorum at any meeting would consist of the members present in person or by proxy. The number of Directors was raised from five to six, to serve a two-year term. Non-dues-payment meant stopping Park services to owners or their renters. The Article V Section 2 provision for the President of the Company (previously Arthur Quick and then his daughter, Julia Hill) to serve on the Board was eliminated. By 1972, the covenants on the property were revised and reinstated.

Major problems arose on the beaches in the 60's. We had the first of many invasions of tiny aliens – dying alewives piled high the beaches – a recurring problem that still has not been solved. A nuclear power plant was installed just down the beach. That has brought many changes – a visual blight on what had been the pristine gathering place for gulls; lights and noise that destroy what was tranquil; a physical barrier that has stopped the annual family walks to South Haven; the demolishing of three of our cottages on the north beach; and the terrible legacy of nuclear waste stored in casks on the beach. The 60's were also a time of low water levels and a beautiful beach. However, that changed at the end of the decade as high water and resulting storms washed away beaches and previous seawalls. For the next 30 years, beach cottages experimented with a number of protection devices. Some worked fairly well; others were disastrous failures. All were expensive. A resulting mishmash of wood, cement, and steel walls brought chaos to our beaches. High water meant there were few places to access the water. One area's solution became another's problem. Only with the addition of rip rap all along the beach, in the late 80's, did some balance of protection and restoration take hold. By the end of the 90's, of course, Mother Nature took over. The water levels fell, the beaches re-emerged, and the walls and rip rap disappeared under the sand. At this writing, new dunes are forming along the boardwalk. A walk along the water's edge can go for uninterrupted miles.

Presumably, by the 60's the Board had decided that horse-drawn equipment had to go (note that using such equipment was still under discussion in Board minutes of the late 40's), but horses were still to be found in the Park. The August 27, 1966 Patter mentions one popular horse owned by Mr. Vern Underwood:

Horses, Horses, Crazy over Horses!!!

Among the "Old Timers" in the Park is Amber Lad, often called Laddie or Kim. He is a registered half Arab horse and he "owns" Verne "Dutch" Underwood. For 17 years, Lad has been a very real source of amusement and pleasure for the small fry. (Some of those small fry are grown and their young ones are enjoying Lad's company.) "Let's go see Lad," is one of the first things most young ones say in the first sweet days of vacation on their arrival from the city. From the beginning, Lad has loved the kids, too, and never a time was a child harmed by him. We have found as many as six kids inside the corral riding him, using strings tied to his bridle for reins....Lad gets many handouts of carrots and apples from the kids and if the older ones know how to ride, they are often permitted to take turns riding on the old golf course....

One tragic incident in 1975 involved the arrest of one Park member, Dr. Vern Wallace, for "assault with intent to do great bodily harm less than murder" against a man who was then renting in Palisades. The incident took place at a party in the Park. Wallace was tried in December of 1976 and found guilty. On February 7, 1977, he was sentenced to 60 days in the County jail and court costs of $2600. He sold his cottage, Toplofty #97, to the McNamaras in 1976.

Another tragedy occurred in the summer 1983 when Palisades had its second drowning, this time of a guest who got caught in the dangerous juxtapostion of high waves and no beach, and an undertow caused by the waves hitting the seawalls.

On Sunday, September 19, 1976, there occurred a phenomenon called "a sieche." The air pressure pushed water back from the beach temporarily; then it rushed back. The air temperature was in the 80's, the water temperature was 66 degrees. The result looked like the "parting of the seas" as the receding water exposed the lake bottom out beyond the sandbar – a sight not to be forgotten by those who witnessed it.

The Circle has remained as a center of the Park, though it, too, has changed. The store and post office and hotel have long since closed, but the Soda Bar remains a popular enticement for all. To make the best of the collapse of the old garage, a Village Green was instituted where the garage once stood. Starting in the 60's, the Park has gathered each summer for an Ethnic Dinner at the Village Green. The women's coffee group has instituted several cocktail parties each summer at the same spot. These occasions have helped Palisades maintain a friendly atmosphere despite increasing numbers and changing patterns of cottage usage.

One constant throughout the Park's history has been the interest in tennis. New courts were built over these years – and new programs developed for their enjoyment. The Park has always been a place of romance – and through the years many "Park marriages" have resulted. Palisades wedding celebrations are a tradition that has brought substance to the term "picture perfect" - for what picture can be lovelier than that of a bride on our beach?

With more women working, fewer families can spend a whole summer at Palisades before retirement years. That has meant the increased use of the Park for weekends or shorter vacations. Over the decades, car ownership has changed. A pattern of fathers bringing the one car on the weekends has given way to two and three car families. Of course, the toll for all these cars is paid on our roads and on the difficulties of parking. Another result is the continued trend of leaving the Park – for shopping and for other entertainment.

The early years of Palisades were blatantly intolerant of other races and religions. Happily, that has also changed through the decades. Many of the barriers have fallen. However, as the cost of property rises, some concern has been expressed about the financial discrimination inherent in an area that few young people can afford. By-law changes in 2001, raising the membership fees to $10,000, give testament to these rising costs, as do the prices of cottages for sale in 2002, one in the $800,000 price range.

As we approach the 100th birthday of Palisades Park in 2005, we must surmise that Arthur Quick, our founder, and many of the early pioneers would be astonished at what they would see here now. All did not work out the way it was originally planned. However, they might also be pleased to see hills covered with wildflowers each spring; to walk on our many trails or through the dunes (now a part of the Park property); to hear children playing on the beach or watch waves breaking at the sandbar; to see friendship quilts and cottage walks, coffees and parties building the sense of community; or to welcome the many families who return to Palisades Park each summer.

# Clubhouse Plays

Among Betty Householder's papers was a folder containing programs from some of the Clubhouse shows in the 1950's. Because the casts contain so many familiar names, we thought our readers would enjoy seeing some of the playbills.

### Around the World in Eighty Minutes
August 17, 1957

Guest Imitator/Opening: Tom Kelley, Valerie Stevens, Laurie Lehne

Palisades Park: Lambie Borchert, Margaret Golden, Darlene Mundt, Sandy Neubauer, Donna Egbert, James Egbert

Spain: Jim Egbert, John Wintermute, Michael Mathias, Norman Mundt, Jim Wrisley, Robert Borchert, Henry Haude

Germany: Sandy Neubauer, Darlene Mundt, Rachael Bourland

Hawaii: Kathleen McMahon, Diane Hart, Norman Mundt, Jim Wrisley, John Wintermute, Jim Egbert, Robert Borchert

Africa: Lambie Borchert, Fritz Borchert, Jim Haude, Henry Haude, Peter Wrisley, Michael Mathias, Christopher Lehne, Eric Erickson, James Egbert

France: Darlene Mundt, Margaret Golden, Diane Hart, Mary Claire McMahon, Kathleen McMahon, Laurie Lehne, Valerie Stevens, Marilyn Borst, Kathy Goodridge

Palapasadia: Margaret Golden, Jim Regan, Robert Borchert, Kathy Golden, Kathy Goodridge, Carol Heitner, Nancy Heitner, Debbie Lehne, Marilyn Borst

Stage Crew: Pete Ferry, Buck Mathias, John Mathias, Toby Mathias
Directors: Alice Beatty, Margy Lyon
Special Thanks: Mrs. McMahon, Mrs. Beatty, Mrs. Heitner, Mrs. Householder, Nancy O'Brien, Cindy Wintermute, Kathy McCarthy, Mothers of the Cast

*Scene in 1953 Clubhouse play*

### Two One Act Plays
August 23 and 24, 1957

THANK YOU DOCTOR

Cast: Chi Reagan, Al Borst, Armin Beck, Tom Gates, Haven Best
Director: Jeanne Anderson
Stage Manager: Frances Prange

SKITS: Linda Gates, Donna Neubauer, Nancy Neubauer, Cindy Wintermute, Jill Stett, Carhy McCarthy, Karen Weston, Becki Bourland, Sally Householder

CHILD WONDER

Cast: Frank Householder, Katy Beck, Judy Borst, Helen Crise, John Ferry, Talitha Peat
Director: Mary Kay Goodridge
Thanks: Wes and Thelma Weston, Clare Schlacks, Nancy O'Brien

### The Children's Variety Show
August 22, 1959

Beach party: Kathy Golden, Carol Heitner, Nancy Heitner, Monica Joy, Sally McWethy, Sue Mcwethy

Stagehands: Rob Borchert, Jim Egbert, John Wintermute

Supreme Court: Billy Golden, James Speicher, Trippy Bishop, Robin Borchert, Jim Egbert, Pete Ferry, Pat McCarthy, Art Maerlender, Buck Mathias, John Wintermute

San Francisco: Beth Borchert, Ann Golden, Billy Golden, Jimmy Golden, Tom Golden, Sally McWethy, Mike Mathias, Cathy Noff

New York: Pete Ferry, Peter Rossitor, Buck Mathias, Bob Neiman, Susan Rossiter, Jim Wrisley, Pat McCarthy, Mike Mathias, Tom Venner, Margaret Golden

Chicago: Mike Mathias, Billy Golden, Jimmy Golden,

Detroit: Tom Venner, Sally McWethy, Pat McCarthy, Eric Erickson, Kathy Golden, Pete Ferry

New Orleans: Beth Borchert, Mike Mathias, Barbara Golden, Marylin Joy, Sally McWethy, Sue Rossitor, Ann Golden, Tommy Golden, Peter Wrisley, Billy Golden, Cathy Noff, Jim Golden, Erick Erickson, Daniel McCarthy, Tom Venner

Directors: Judy von Rosen; Alice Beatty
Assistant Director: Lambie Borchert
Special Thanks: Mrs. Chi Regan, Fritz von Rosen, Sandy Neubauer, Cathy Bishop, Sue Stoker, Donna Egbert, Jim Regan, Carol Kropp

*A younger Cecil*

```
                        Palisades Park Country Club
                              Palisades Park, Michigan

                                   October 1, 1959

Dear Member:

On October 1st, Cecil Burrous becomes our new caretaker.  As you probably
know, Warren Knapp's retirement was announced at the Annual Meeting,
effective this Fall.

The Board feels fortunate in having obtained a man of Cecil's qualifications
and experience.  A native of Covert, he has been the caretaker at Linden
Hills for the past seven years, where he has done an excellent job.

Cecil is building an attractive home just East of the tennis courts, where
he, his wife Nancy and their three youngster, Lenny, Cecil Jr. and Mia
will soon be living.

Should you wish to reach Cecil by phone, his number is (and will be)
ROckwell 4-1502.  And the next time you are in the Park, stop by and
welcome the Burrous family into our Palisades.

Beginning Monday, October 12, Cecil and Warren will start draining the
water system and cottages.

                                   Sincerely,

                                   Henry H. Prange O.D., President
```

*Letter announcing Cecil's 1959 hiring.*

# Cecil Burrous

Interview by Katy Beck, Tom Beck, and Marilyn Henkel
August 22, 2001

When I first came to the Park, I had been taking care of Linden Hills and working at the Everett Piano Factory. Lou Weston and others walked through Linden Hills and saw what I had done over there with gutters and all and asked if I wanted to come over here. Lou said they were looking for a new caretaker. I said I'd consider it. Then Dr. Prange called me - he was president at the time - and said to come on over and see him. I got down about as far as Trumbulls and there was a "Private Road, No Turn Around" sign. I could see Pranges' cottage but I didn't know it was Pranges' cottage. I said, "I'm getting out of here," so I turned around and I ended up down at the Sugar Bowl by Hamiltons. I stopped and asked a guy, "Do you know Dr. Prange?" and he said no, he was just a renter here. I said, "How do I get out of here?" and he said, "I was just leavin' – you can follow me." So I followed him out. Ok, and I went home and called up Dr. Prange and said, "I don't want the job." Then he said, "What's wrong?" I said, "Well, if I can't find you, how do you expect me to take care of the place?" This was on a Labor Day weekend. I mean they had all the tennis going on there at the courts. This would have had to have been – let see, '59 is when I came over; it had to have been in the fall of '58. He said, "Come on over and meet me at the gate." So I got in his car and he started driving and showing me around. When he got to his house I said, "I got to here, but it says 'Private Road' – that's when I turned back." He showed me everything, you know. I decided, well, maybe I'd give it a try. And here I've been ever since.

Before that I had worked with my dad, Leonard Burrous; he was a contractor. I worked on Kropps' cement there for Rudy Weber and about six or seven other houses in here. Anytime my dad needed somebody to push the wheelbarrow I got a day off from school. I grew up in Covert. I was born there right behind Joe's Mini-Mart. That's on the first crossroad as you come into Covert.

There's a little house that my Dad built right in behind there. The fire station used to be nearby also. My dad made it of stone up to the porch. He must have done a good job; the house is still there.

After I took the job in the Park, my dad got to build houses in here. He built Dr. Keene's (#101) and Sheehans (#21), too, up there. He started working on a lot of them after that. Rudy Weber was getting about to the end of his time and Harry Wildt was getting about to the end of his time, also. Harry turned all of the shuttering and stuff over to me. Rudy and Harry were both from Covert. I used to go to school with Wildt's son. He was a really good ballplayer, Wally. He was going to turn pro.

I had two brothers, Bill and Don. Don took over Linden Hills when I came over here and he's still there. It's been about 50 years now. There are about 50 cottages over there now, but only about 38 when I was over there. They had two cliques there – one in the center. Then you had the people to the north end; they were another group – I think most of them were from the same church. They had a church right there in Linden Hills – the Swedenborgian Church. Down here Happy Valley was a group in the center section.

At the north end, the Park really never got going until Mr. Lowrey put all the water mains up through the north end. The lots were not picked up real quick. Just like the creek was the boundary, you know. That would have been about in the early 60's, maybe. Then Lowrey cleaned out the meadow and got rid of all the mosquitoes and snakes. Anytime he would come back from Chicago he'd get out there with his shovel and start clearing a little spot and that little spot got bigger every time and then finally he had Canonie come down and really do a job on it. Canonie came in with his machine and seeded it and stuff. Lowrey bought all the pipe for the north end and Dave Vanderbeogh and I put it in. Before that, the only water on the north end went across the bridge and north around the lake front road – that road that went along the bluff, up the hill to Potters (#3). There was one loop that came partway around. The first broken down bridge Lowrey paid for. Lowrey paid for all the material and David and I put it together. That had nails that big around – had to drive 'em with a maul. Lowrey did a lot. He got the first lawnmower for the meadow.

Lowrey and Boyles had the Park in mind. They had all they needed. When Boyles owned that whole circle across from the Clubhouse (he bought it so no one could build there), when he was ready, he gave that to the Park. The Big Nine bought all that land from Quick's estate. They picked out some from their area – Seymour picked out some and Kropp picked out some – mainly their theory was just to pick what they didn't want people to build on. Several places now are in dispute – labeled as "park" on the map.

Hammerschmidt (#35) was the first to build big over there across the bridge. Muchinhern (#34) was behind him. Hammerschmidt lived on the south side of the Brandywine but he built the new cottage on the north side, right across from Glasners (#20). He had a fire on the other side, you know. He didn't want to have any more fires. So that was a fireproof house. He had poured slab floors. (Rumor was that he built it that way in case there was an atomic bomb attack – it was during that era. In a house my dad built in Covert they still have the bomb shelter there. During the war my dad poured it – you can still drive by it and see the round top of the shelter.) Hammerschmidts' was built strong and was fire proof, but it looked like a motel. Lowrey bought By-a-Dam-Site (#40) where the fire was and the Borcherts (his daughter's family) lived there. Now Morsches live there. Then Lowrey bought the O'Byrne cottage, after they left, for another part of his family. Across from the concrete house was Glasners, now Kinseys (#20).

McQuigs' cottage also caught fire. It burned to the ground. (Later site of #18.) We had that fire and then the one with the Prange/Schlacks/Kavanaugh cottage (#51)next to the Lodge. Another fire was when the power plant came in. They condemned three cottages and gave one of them to me for a hundred dollars. One Rudy had all redone with nice knotty pine on the inside. I had taken all that knotty pine and put it face to face, wrapped it all up and was going to haul it out. We couldn't haul it out that Saturday. At night it burned to the ground on me.

*Aerial view of the Brandywine after the meadow had been cleared.*

Someone had told me I couldn't build next to my house with used wood. He was right; I didn't. All that was left of the house was the chimney. That was Millikins' cottage. It was a two story house – mysteriously burned to the ground. I was so devastated I gave the next one away to another guy to tear down. That was Filkins' cottage? Or Jocelyns' was the one I had; then Filkins. They gave me two of 'em for $100 apiece. So the second one I gave away to a man from Covert and I said I was done with them.

*Warren Knapp on tractor*

I came in '59; Warren Knapp was before me. He was a nice guy and he was here quite a long time. He just got old. And when you get old you just can't do what you did before. I'm finding that out. Mrs. Packard ran the store when I came. Miss Palmer used to be librarian. Then another one was there – I went to school with her two sons. Mrs. Madeline Bradford – she had a cottage here – was the State head librarian and she got the library bus to stop in the Park until she was replaced.

A man named Charlie had worked with Warren Knapp. Charlie was old and lasted through the winter. Dave Vanderbough was going to school and working for me in Linden Hills. When I came over here, I brought David with me. Then he had to go to the Vietnam War. His grampa had just retired from being school janitor so he took David's place. He was a worker! Frank Empson. He used to run the food mill over in Covert. Then he was the only janitor taking care of both Covert schools. Now they have about 20 janitors.

I knew Tony Malinowski. My dad used to work for him. I almost went out with his niece once. I went to school with her. She came up and lived with Tony's mother – her grandmother. She was Polish. I had to go in there to take this girl out. She said, "You have to ask my grandma." I go in there and I said I'd like to take Carol to the movies. She said, "Are you a good boy?" I said, "Yes, I'm a good boy. She said, "Is he a good boy?" she kept saying that. Finally, I said I'm not going to beg nobody, so I never took Carol out. We had our 50th class reunion this year. She lived real close, but she never came. For 50 years, I thought everyone would have showed up. We only had four boys in our class and only two of them showed; another one lives in Benton Harbor, but he never showed.

The Sunnyside sign I have came from Linden Hills. It was from a cemetery. A man named Kingsley had it. He had a little 12x16 cottage, red and white, a lot of windows, and he was going to put that sign up in the front. Over in Linden Hills you don't own your land. You only get a 99 year lease. Well, he had this little cottage. He had to pay the same amount as all those people on the lakefront with all those big cottages. He went to the meeting and said it wasn't fair. They said, "If you don't like it, sell and get out." He knew I always told him how nice the cottage looked. He came by and said, "You always said you liked the cottage. It's yours." Just like that, you know! I thought, well pay no attention to it. The next weekend he said, "Don't you want that cottage?" I said, "You're joking aren't you?" He said, "No." I said, "You've got a brand new stove in there and a brand new sink." "You're going to have to take them, too," he said, "and it's got to be down in two weeks, because that's when the new bills come out and I'm not going to have any cottage." My dad took a look at it. We got a farmer's great big old flatbed truck. We took the roof down in two pieces, laid it down on the flatbed, took each side down, put that on the flatbed, cut the gable off and put that on there also. We stuck the floor on top in two pieces. The next week I took six guys with me and a bunch of beer and went up north to property I owned. We dug and poured the footing the night we got there and by Sunday night we had that cottage put back together. People came and said, "Where

*Dave Vanderbough, still a mainstay of Park staff. 2001.*

*Grader with long history of use in the Park, above, and its sign telling of its original use with horses pulling it, below.*

*Below: Cecil riding behind grader as he works on roads.*

did you get that?!" That was the start of my fishing cottage. It was a nice little cabin. All my money from selling cottages I put into a special account. As soon as I got money in there, I'd go up and put an addition on.

Over there in the corner [of the meadow] toward Joneses (#55), there's a spring. When I was first starting to mow that area, I went over there and I almost lost a tractor. I was going to dig a trench over there to get that water out of that hole. I rented this tractor. I got it over there and I got that thing stuck. Push it down, get it up – David and I pushed up underneath it, but down it goes again. I got a backhoe and raised it up. We put planks underneath it and then the front would go down. We finally got it out. That's the only spring in the Park I know of, that Charlie Tunecke told me about.

I found the road grader back in the woods – the one that used to be pulled by horses. I put a tongue on it for the tractor. It would really smooth out the road because it had a long space between the wheels. Someone, usually David, drove the tractor and I was on the back. Warren had a tractor when he quit that he took with him. I had my own tractor, too. They paid me $500 a year for my tractor and $500 a year for my truck. The price of gas kept going up. When it came to the point I was going to have to buy a new truck, that was the first time I was going to quit. I figured by the time I took the gas out of $500 a year, I was really making nothing. Goodwillie told them, you've got to buy that guy a truck. They figured a truck would be good for four years. They'd buy the truck and after four years the truck would be mine. I used the old truck to haul gravel so the new truck was in pretty good shape after four years. Then Goodwillie said the contract says a new truck, so they got another truck. My old one was shot. Then when I quit, I had one year left and the truck would be mine and I had first right to buy it after it got over the halfway. So I sent them the $1500 and they sent it right back. When I quit, my lawyer was Ron DeGraw. (The Park wanted him for their lawyer but he said he was mine. We had been partners in remodeling a cottage – his money and my work.) When they sent back the truck money, he wrote and said we're sending back the check one more time. Send it back and the truck is paid for. It never came back again. One year I had taken an insurance policy in lieu of a raise. They told me what good insurance it was; if I died my kids would go to college. When I quit, the insurance policy had built up equity but they wouldn't give it to me. They made it a policy where they got the money if I died. DeGraw gave them five working days to get the insurance policy to me. I had the paper to prove I got the insurance in lieu of a raise. When I gave Ron the paper, he made a copy and sent it to them. He found three pages had been cut out of the Park minutes. He showed that to them as well and the insurance came flying through to me.

One Board member was originally from Linden Hills. He came over and used the tennis courts every morning with his group and our people were waiting to play. Every time I'd go by and see them there, I'd chase them off the court. He said Fred Nichols was a friend of his and he could play. I said when Fred was with him, he could play there; otherwise he couldn't. We had one main court and two across the street – clay courts. (When he moved to Palisades) he wouldn't talk to me for years. So when he was a step away from being president of the Park, I knew my days were numbered and I quit. Mrs. Householder said, "You can't quit" and I said, "I just did." One of the arguments in the final years was over the courts. The Board members wanted them prepared first in the spring. They would call each week over the winter and say they had to talk about this. I said that the water goes on first; there were 160 people waiting for water and only six of them waiting for the tennis courts. "Water is our first and most important thing," I'd say. He would ask that I get one court ready. I would say no, that he should get cement courts if he wanted to play that bad. He said that there would never be cement courts as long as he was here. So Dave and I used to get out there at 5:30 a.m. to prepare the courts before we began our full day of work for the Park.

One guy in the Park was suspected of taking posts and other things from the Park (for his own building projects). When asked by the Park president, he said they floated in from the lake. So then when we had to build new board walks, we got 2x6's. Winkle Lumber brought out a whole load of 2x6's so I put "PPCC" on the ends of them. Then 22 of them were missing. So David and I went to the house building and there they were. I asked where he got them and he said Winkles. I said it was funny that they put the same thing on the ends of them that I did – "PPCC." He took up his hammer and asked if I was calling him a liar. I said, "You're right" – then I had to make about an eight foot jump out his front door to the ground – David and I both bailed out of there. I called the Board president and told him about the 22 boards. He said to lock up the rest with new locks and so that's what we did. (Later) Fred's garage paneling order didn't make it to Fred's garage. A detective came to look and found it down at this same guy's place.

People I remember fondly: I remember Mrs. Abbott. And I remember him. "Toot, too, toot, toot." I knew when he was coming. Then a sign went up saying "No Horns." I remember Mrs. Ott as always dressed in green. She and Mrs. Adams and Mrs. Bishop always had a card game going – bridge or something. Mrs. Harper was great. She was a good person, you know; she was always happy. When her husband died, I told her nobody should try to sell something the first year. Times change. Right off the bat, you're down; just back off and wait two or three years. Then Mardy lived so long. They were good friends. Mardy walked all the way to the mailbox everyday. That's what I'm aiming for.

My worst event was digging the two kids out of the Sugar Bowl, Leonard and I. The kids - they were 15 and 16 year old boys - came up to work for the Hamiltons – they were mentally challenged kids. They went to the dune and were digging. (When they didn't come back) I was asked to go out in my truck with the loud speaker and call them. I went to the dunes and found two pairs of shoes with their glasses there. So Leonard and I started digging. All of a sudden, "thump." I hit one of them. So I went and called my wife to call the sheriff's department. They came and made Nancy drive 45 mph through the Park. When they got there, we had one of them unburied. In Vietnam, you know, they were tunneling, you know how they always had those troops tunneling. Well, the boys dug down and went to tunnel to each other and when they tunneled the sand collapsed on them. There was one more kid there with them and he ran home. The cop said even if he had gone and gotten help it would have been too late anyway – there was no sense getting him all upset. He couldn't have helped them anyway.

When we had high water, Burkhardt's son, Bob Jr., went out with Mr. Hoff. I was down working on Mrs. Molineaux's cottage (#175). It was when they had to move the cottage back. I saw them out there. It was real rough, you know. They went out there in a Sunfish. I thought this was bad news. I got my line out, you know, and put that ball on the end of it. Mrs. Molineaux said, "What are you doing, Cecil?" and I said, "They're going to get in trouble." She said, "Good thinking, Cecil." All of a sudden the boat tipped over and they both went off. You remember there used to be a big post out there. Well, they were banging up against that. Mr. Hoff, he grabbed on to one post and Bob grabbed on to the other. And I mean they were really getting pounded by the waves, you know. I went down there and I threw that ball out and I got it to Bob and I pulled him in. I kept throwing it out to Mr. Hoff and he wouldn't let loose of that post for nothin'! You know, he was hangin' on. Finally, I told him, "Look, next time I get that to you, you better grab it because that's your only hope." That time, I threw it and it went right between him and the pole; he grabbed on to that. And you know, he came back and he said, "Cecil, you're selling me a cottage. I owe you." So he bought Johnson's cottage up there on the north end. The Sunfish got beat up. The waves smashed it.

I was a workaholic. I did three cottages last year. I belong to the boat club down there [in South Haven], you know. The last two years I never even took my boat away from the dock. Too busy. I have built cottages for McCarthys, Speichers, Henkels, and McWethys - and just about rebuilt Andy Anderson's and Phil Kolehmainen's places. I've worked on just about all of the cottages. I don't mind working yet, but I need to get my shoulder back in shape. I've had a lot of guys work for me. Now I have Gary I and Gary II. They're good carpenters. If I didn't have good carpenters, I wouldn't still be working. You have to have good finish carpenters to get it going.

We had some tornadoes go through here. Tore the trees over the tennis court. Once, we were working on Richards' cottage on the north end (#15). We seen the one that hit Kalamazoo. We seen it coming across the lake. We seen a flash of light. We were just putting a roof on there. We had planks up there to hold the (roofing) paper down. We had plastic sheeting on the steps and we seen this tornado coming across the lake. Where do we hide? There is no place to hide. So we got in behind the fireplace. We could see that wood just a rollin' off the roof. Hail was that big – just kept to peppering the sheeting, piling up down below. We all just kinda hung tight to that chimney, you know. When it was all over, the roofing was laying out in the back parking lot.

Then one time we were working down in the Park. David's cousin was working for me. He had a motor scooter. A storm was really coming – we knew it was going to be a bad one. So we raced out of the Park. I mean, it was starting to rain and stuff. We made it through the gate, headed home – and no Bobby. I mean, it was raining down so you could hardly see, you know. Oh, he must have tipped over or something. We all ran out to get in the jeep and he came out this back road. I said, "What the heck did you come out the back road for?" He said, "Well, the trees are down on the main drag." Just between the time we left, he had to go back around through the Park and come back around. It must have knocked down eight or ten trees right there. They were all over the tennis courts – all the big trees were just busted all over.

The first year I was here, we had a tornado come through by the Clubhouse. And I mean to tell you, that took down 22 trees up through there. The electricity was out for four days. That was in the season. I was out there and we worked all night. The electric company was there and we was trying to get the roads open.

When the sea wall broke out here Thanksgiving weekend, Joel Beck and I had to go down there. We had to tear out the old one that was left and put in a new wall there. It was cold. It was icy. That was between Becks (#176) and Kropps(#178). When we put the seawall in down in front of G'Sells (#157) and O'Connors (#158), there were ice balls in the water. Icebergs were forming. We had waders, but we still about froze to death. We'd have to run up and down the beach and warm up, and then get back in there. After the ice storm, we got back in there and finished it up. People don't do anything along the lake until it's too late. Some people (south of the metal wall) came up with the cement idea. So they went with the cement; it lasted through two storms and tipped over backwards. They put a wall jetted down to the sand level. Then they set the front of the cement wall on that – nothing on the back – so as soon as it sucked from the back, it just flipped right on over. If they had had a wall on the front and a wall on the back, the lake would have had a harder job tipping the cement over. Weldon Coates was all worked up about that; that caused him to have his heart attack, I'm sure about that.

Then there were bags filled with sand and some big bags where they pumped in cement. As soon as the sand washed out from underneath, they went out of sight. Then

*By 1987, with walls built and riprap added, the beach protection was in place.*

Ochsenschlagers sold. North of his cottage (#159), they were all going along with the steel there and then a couple of his neighbors talked the next group of cottages into the cement thing. That's when everything went down the tube. Seymour put in a wingback and whenever you put a wingback, the next guy down the seawall is dead, he's a goner. When someone does something next to you, you've got to do something because that swirl is going to get you every time.

The best thing they've ever done is put those rocks out front. Some didn't get enough rocks. But some down by Tillsons (#92) and Warners (#95), they don't ever have to worry. The guys that put that in – they would see a hole and then they would find a rock the size of the hole. (The contractor) – he'd see a hole and he'd find one big enough to cover the hole. When you've got the feeling the (high water) cycle is coming – like right now they could come down these roads with a front end loader and give you more rocks and save you so much money. Now's the time to do it.

When Stan came, they had to spend money for a pole barn and for his tools. I always had furnished all the tools. I think the manager you got now would be a good one - he knows what needs to be done - but I don't see why two guys have to drive the truck– that's the only thing. One of them should be out working. Your job is to see that this park runs. Your job is to see when people come and forgot their key, you give them a key. That's what the keys are there (in the office) for. But that ends in October. You have to have a box on your house so if you have the bug man coming, he can get in there or if you have a cleaning lady coming, she can get in there. They will not pass out any more keys after October. That is what a manager is for. Always on Saturdays there is a changeover (of renters). You always had to be there on Saturdays to pass the keys out; you know that. That's what the people expected.

Yes, I've seen changes in kids' activities. They had the pot thing when they all did that, I think in the 70's. You could walk along the beach and get high, you know, at their beach parties. My brother-in-law was a state trooper; he came and we walked around behind my fence there, in back, and he said, "What are you growing here? That's marijuana." Here was this marijuana growing right behind my fence. It was only about that tall, but he knew what it was. The biggest change I see in the Park is there aren't cottages now, they are homes; it's coming to a year-around Park. They're talking about a new water system. When I was in Linden Hills, the pipes were starting to rust out at the joints. Since my brother's been there, they have changed all those pipes themselves, to PVC. They do a stretch every year. It's not for year-around; it's for summer use. They could do the same thing in here and not worry about putting it down five foot, But I'll bet we have 70 wells in the Park – they put in six to eight every year.

Not any hunters around, though occasionally one will slip through. The smelt (which used to run in the Brandywine) now go up to the power plant where the water is warm. You'd be lucky if you get a mess out of here now. Now they just go up by the power plant. They get a lot of them up there. I'll tell you the God's truth, I been at that boat club down there (in South Haven). Them guys were fishin' and eatin' fish every day. They're no longer here. The group of guys that had fish down there every day – all of 'em are gone. Their wives, too, that would go down there. Boy, you know, they quit eatin' down there – havin' fish every day. Any fish in the lake were bad at the time. Now the zebra mussels are cleaning up the lake.

I will be glad when it's all over but I'll miss it. I've enjoyed all the people. I've had a lot of good times here – enjoyed working here. I'm going to retire next year. I'm going to turn the business over to Bill early. When the phone doesn't ring, it bothers me, you know what I mean? When I'm there and they see my truck in the yard, the phone rings, which is good. But, you know, at my age now – I'll be 70 – I'm ready. I'm going to throw a party for the Park. I'm going to have a pig roast and a fish boil. Let everybody come and thank 'em for all the work. Hopefully I'm going to sell my house and I'm going down to Michigan Beach. My wife owns a house down there. I told her to get (the renters) out so I have time to fix it up and that's where I'm going. I'll have my trailer right there. Friday night I can head north or wherever I want to go.

*Cecil at his retirement party. He intends to move about seven miles away. He will be missed!*

# Park Resident Managers after Mr. Quick

**Mr. Hempy (temporary) - 1946**
**Warren Knapp 1946 – 1959**
**Cecil Burrous 1959 – 1973**
**Stan Severinghaus 1973 – 1988**
**Bob Zimmermann 1988 – 1997**
**Joe Southwood 1997 –**

## Mr. Hempy

*From Patter, August 31, 1946:*

Mr. Hempy, or "Hemp" as he's been known for years and years, has been a familiar figure to the Park residents for many years. He first came here over forty years ago (1904) when the Palisades Park we know today was but a tract of virgin timber on the shores of Lake Michigan. This pioneer is responsible for clearing the land and building the roads which has made it possible for us to spend pleasant summers in this rustic vacation site.

The present Park Manager was born on March 28, 1870, in Mount Blanchard, Ohio. In his youth there he worked on farms in the vicinity of his home. During this time he met, fell in love with, and married Emanda Elsea, who lived in a neighboring town. Together they moved to an 80-acre farm in Covert in 1904. While there, "Hemp" met Mr. Arthur C. Quick who founded Palisades Park. It was largely due to this meeting that Mr. Hempy came here in 1906. After twenty years of clearning land for roads and cutting trees, and yet preserving all the natural dignity of the Park, he and his wife built their permanent home here in 1928. Since then, he has helped Mr. Quick manage the Park, at the same time helping to keep the roads in shape, doing teamwork, scraping sand, and looking after sanitation. Since Mr. Quick's death early this year (1946), he has had his duties doubled.

*Mr. Hempy (left) and Mr. Knapp. 1953.*

*Mr. Knapp (right) with two customers at old gas station at entrance to Park.*

## Mr. Knapp

*From August 31, 1946 Patter:*

Warren Knapp of Covert has been elected to the job of Park Manager, a post vacant since the death of Arthur C. Quick last spring. As a temporary measure, Mr. Hempy, long a Park figure and assistant to Mr. Quick, has been carrying a double responsibility.

Mr. and Mrs. Knapp, along with son Clare, will be remembered by many Parkers. They operated the Service Station for several years before the War. With the station, for awhile they provided a taxi service, also. A younger son, Harold Vernon, was fatally injured while serving as flight instructor in 1941.

Although Mr. Knapp will not assume full duties until early next year, he has already spent much time in and around the Park, getting a line on his future work.

*Mr. Knapp.*

*Cecil Burrous working on seawall.*

*Stan Severinghaus, Mr. Sweetay , and Dave Vanderboegh*

## Cecil Burrous

On October 1, 1959, Cecil Burrous took over the reins of the Park. A native of Covert, he had been the caretaker at Linden Hills for the previous seven years. (His brother still fills that post.) The good work he had done in Linden Hills recommended him to our Board. Cecil built a home just east of the tennis courts, where he has lived ever since and where he raised his three children. He was a "hands on" kind of manager, someone whose work showed his real love for Palisades Park.

On Saturday, August 4th, 1973, the Park Board sponsored a Clam Bake for Cecil and his family to honor him for the good job he did. This was the first of our annual "ethnic" dinners. Upon his retirement as manager, he continued to work in the Park and environs as builder and handyman; his familiar Park truck was still always seen around the Park – but without the "Manager" sign on it. He finally retired for good in 2002. This time, Cecil was the one to give the party. On June 15, 2002, his many Park friends and clients again gathered to honor this man who had spent his life in Palisades. Presently his house is for sale. He will be missed.

## Stan Severinghaus

In the June 25, 1973, <u>Patter</u>, Dwyer Roche's President's Newsletter introduced Stan as follows:

The Board of Directors is confident that we have found a most able successor as Palisades Park Manager/Caretaker in Stanley 'Stan' Severinghaus. Stan comes to us with a long experience as a carpenter with other construction and handyman skills; he has managed a trailer park with about the size of Palisades Park and has other experience that brings him well qualified. As this goes to press, Stan will be commuting from his home just south of Covert.

Stan built a home in the Park and served until 1988. He later retired to Florida.

## Bob Zimmermann
The July, 1988, Patter

*Bob and Betsy Zimmermann*

Twelve years ago, Bob and Betsy Zimmermann were first lured to Palisades Park by the promise of clay courts. They rented "Sandwitch" (#114) from their St. Louis neighbors, the Ankenbruchs. The natural beauty of Palisades brought them back year after year. Now they have succumbed to that charm with the decision to retire here to "B 'N' B." (#119) For this energetic couple, though, retirement will not be long walks through the woods and afternoons spent lazily on the beach for Bob has accepted the job of PPCC manager.

An avid do-it-yourselfer, sportsman, and amateur naturalist, Bob feels he brings enthusiasm, a knowledge of tools, engineering, and management skills to the job. Bob holds a degree in mechanical engineering and is retiring as district sales manager from Babcock and Wilcox in Chicago.

"I'm not afraid of hands-on work," Bob assured, "but I want to do more than that. I think I can improve the use of time and tools to get the job done."

Bob said he'll be concentrating on mechanical improvements at first, such as roads, posts, wires, and the remodeling of the park manager's cottage which requires major foundation repairs. He and Betsy plan to live in the manager's cottage during the season and the winter "both for accessibility and security," he said.

Conscious of the Park's past, Bob would like to restore some of the old grandeur, perhaps by restoring the golf course, or painting park structures in park colors.

Transported Connecticut Yankees, the Zimmermanns consider themselves to be "winter people." Snowmobiling and cross country skiing are among Bob's hobbies. Betsy enjoys quilting, bridge, and knitting in the winter. Bowling, golf, and tennis also keep them busy. Avid nature enthusiasts, the couple like bird watching and have succeeded in luring hummingbirds to their yard. Bob also has an interest in astronomy and mushrooms, "though I haven't had the courage to eat any of the ones I've found yet," he laughed.

The Zimmermanns have been married 34 years .... They have five adult children and have attained grandparent status.

## Joe Southwood

In the July, 1997 Patter, new manager Joe Southwood introduced himself as follows:

> I am delighted to have been chosen as your new resident manager. I have only been on the job a few weeks, and I want to thank everyone who has taken the time to introduce themselves and welcome me to the Park. It's obvious to me that Bob Zimmermann has done an excellent job of management and maintenance, a standard I intend to keep.
>
> I have just ended a 28-year career with the Michigan Department of Natural Resources, Parks and Recreation Division, and accepted the "early out" retirement. My experience comes from working in several Michigan State Parks – from Porcupine Mountains Wilderness State Park to Warren Dunes State Park, where I spent the last 15 years as Park Manager.

# Loyal Workers in 50's and Beyond

*Gene Howe in front of the gas station at entrance to Park*

Above: Bill Shattuck. 1957.

Below: Rudy Weber (right) with Francis Hoffacker.

## Gene Howe

From August 2, 1952 <u>Patter</u>
By Lynda Young and Alice Beatty

Old residents and newcomers alike are welcomed at the entrance to the Park by Gene Howe's friendly wave. He has been working at the gas station for eight years. After graduation from Covert High in 1948, he took over the management. He met his pretty wife, Lorraine, in high school and they were married in 1949. Their son, Davey with a million dollar smile, is first member of the basketball team they hope to have some day.

Besides doing a splendid job here, Gene works at the Whirlpool Washing Machine Company in Benton Harbor. His latest venture is the addition of a gift shop next to the station. Knick-knacks of all kinds can be found there – including many ceramics, such as ash trays and vases. One of the main attractions is a rug, hand woven by Mrs. Howe.

The people of the Park really appreciate all the many favors Gene has – and happily – done for them. He is always ready to lend a helping hand when you need it.

Below: Willard Phillips. 1957

Left: Dave Vanderboegh and Bob Zimmermann rebuilding boardwalk. June 1996.

## Joe Putz

August 29, 1952 Patter
By Andy Anderson

*Joe Putz in 1954.*

Joe Putz ... was born in Bavaria in 1904, but came to America with his family before he was a year old. He lived on the north side of Chicago until after the WWI Armistice; then he came to Michigan. He began working for Mr. Quick back when – staying on the job from April until November, doing maintenance work and helping to build two or three new cottages every summer. Joe says that the cottages now being built or remodeled are becoming more like homes. Every Sunday, Joe is on his post at the entrance to the private roads, keeping outsiders out. Due to the glare of the sun, he sadly reports that he sometimes detains residents, while he ascertains their identity.

.... He is rushed during the season, but during off-season he will gladly take on jobs for you. He is skilled in all kinds of property improvement and cottage work – including electrical and plumbing work. Satisfaction is guaranteed – so if you have anything for Joe to do, let him know before you leave....

## An (Incomplete) List Of Soda Bar Managers

Julia and Mary Jane Hill
Archie Allen
Carmen Sanke
Lou Pletz
The Roach Family
The Neubauer Family (1955-1959)
The Nichols Family (1966 - 1968)
Bill Colbert (1970)
The Venner Family (1971 - 1972; 1980)
The VanCampen Family (1969)
The Owen Family (1974)
Beth Kowalski (1981 - 1983)
Phil Kowalski (1984 - 1985)
Colleen Schlacks (1986-1988; 1991-1992; 1995)
Kathy Aliotta (1989)
Mary Reames (1990)
Keri Heavrin (1993)
Karen Gubbins (1994)
Tim Bell (1996)
Neil Smith (1997)
Bobby Schlacks (1998-1999)
Vica Southwood (2000-2001)
Seawolf Restaurant (2002)
Jay and Julia Marcoux (2003)

## Tragedy at Palisades

By Jean Hamilton Keller

One summer after my sisters and I had grown up and were no longer living at home, Mother (Marion Hamilton) and Daddy (Jim Hamilton) invited two neighbor teen-age boys to go to Palisades Park with them. The boys would help with cottage maintenance in the mornings and have afternoons to play.

One afternoon, Mother saw the boys playing on the Sugar Bowl, running up and down the dune. Later she called them in for supper – but she got no response. She waited a while and called again. They didn't answer. Then she and Daddy started searching. They asked the neighbors to help – and finally, the state police. The police searched up and down the beach with no success and then asked Mother where she had last seen the boys. "There on the dune they call The Sugar Bowl," she answered.

The police examined the dune and noticed that the sand at the base was disturbed and jumbled, not smooth and blown like most dunes were. With sad, anxious, and almost knowing looks, they started to dig. The sand was loose, not heavily compacted. With each shovel full of sand, the outcome seemed more certain. They found the boys' bodies, buried in the sand.

How did it happen? Unaware how unstable sand is, the boys had each dug a deep hole and thought it would be fun to tunnel between. Their tunnel had turned deadly – the sand had collapsed, burying them alive.

Mother said later that the saddest day of her life was the day she went to two funerals. But she never talked much about how she and Daddy and the two families got through the days and weeks and months that followed. Now we've always cautioned our children about digging holes in the sand and not burying someone up to his or her head without an adult present. Sand is wonderful and warm and fun – but it can be deadly.

*Amy Beck admiring the excellent produce offered by "The Umbrella Lady," Mrs. Sweetay, on the Blue Star Highway.*

*Left: Fred Nichols lived and ran a shop at the entrance to the Park, where we used to have a gas station. c. mid-70's.*

*Below: Covert police confiscating marijuana growing in the dunes.*

*Wally Uajkovitch and Glenn Daisey, our trash collectors over the past 23 years.*

*Our gatehouse, new and old.*

# Hats Off To The Nine Old Men

From July 18, 1980 Patter

In this issue we are saluting nine loyal, enthusiastic men of Palisades. Several of them have served as president of the Park and all have served, at one time or another, on the Board. When Mr. Arthur Quick died, his daughter, Mrs. Julia Quick Hill, wanted to dispose of his Park property, including such items as the roads, Lake Palisades, Harbor Beach, parking areas, the old golf course, and the tennis courts. She offered it to the Park, but the treasury at the time could not finance such an acquisition.

To preserve the property from promotion by outside interests, nine of our summer cottage owners organized Palisades Park Properties, Inc., in 1951, and purchased all of the Park properties owned by Julia Quick Hill. These nine men were: **George Boyles, George Duwe, George Hammerschmidt, George Bishop, Paul Butcher, Ray Kropp, Forest Lowrey, William Seymour, Jr., and Ernest Wunsch.** After Mr. Wunsch's death, **Gerald Hatch** purchased a proportionate interest in the Corporation, and became secretary and board member.

To all these men go our thanks and salutations for their generosity and foresight from which Palisades continues to benefit. Fortunately, all of the men have children or grandchildren still coming to the Park in 1980 and enjoying the advantages which have been preserved for them and us.

Palisades Park Properties, Inc. was dissolved on November 24, 1972.

---

**We honor these "Nine Old Men" whose generous actions made the Park what it is today. Unfortunately, we have not located pictures of all of them. Instead, we will repeat their names. May each generation of Palisaders remember the debt we owe them.**

**George Boyles**

**George Duwe**

**George Hammerschmidt**

**George Bishop**

**Paul Butcher**

**Ray Kropp**

**Forest Lowrey**

**William Seymour, Jr.**

**Ernest Wunsch**

*Nine sets of footprints to follow*

# A SALUTE TO SERVICE AND LEADERSHIP – OUR PAST PRESIDENTS OF PALISADES PARK

Starting years: **Palisades Park Country Club**

The group of Palisades families which owned the Clubhouse had their own officers until the Clubhouse was sold to the Park.

|  |  |
|---|---|
| 1915 | Charles Allen |
| 1916 | A. C. DeSouchet |
| 1917 | A. W. Fleming |
| 1918 | A. W. Fleming |
| 1919 | D. A. Anderson |
| 1920 | E. J. McCarthy |
| 1921 | Martha Braun |
| 1922 | Seymour Nelson |
| 1923 | Dr. A. W. Stilliaus |
| 1924 | Alma Nellis |
| 1925 | Leo Sowerby |
| 1926 | Leo Sowerby |
| 1927 | Mrs. D. A. Anderson |

In the early years, Arthur Quick served as President of the South Haven Palisades Park Company. In 1931, the Palisades Park Improvement Association was instituted, again with Quick serving in the capacity of President. If the list of presidents below is complete, we can guess that sometime in the 30's, elected presidents were instituted. If the first six served one year terms, their terms would have started in 1939. If they served for two years each, they would have started in 1933. It is also possible the pre-1945 list is incomplete. Unfortunately, definitive records are not available.

1st President George Duwe
2nd President Forest Lowrey
3rd President George Boyles
4th President C. Mukenhirn
5th President Don O'Brien
6th President George Hammerschmidt

|  |  |
|---|---|
| 1945 | Karl Anderson |
| 1946 | Philip Fraser |
| 1947 | Ernest Wunsch |
| 1948 | Charles Wood |
| 1949 | Wm. J. McCarthy |
| 1950 – 52 | George Boyles |
| 1953 – 54 | William Seymour, Jr. |
| 1955 – 56 | Milton Young |
| 1957 – 58 | William Heitner |
| 1959 – 62 | Henry Prange |
| 1963 – 65 | Lou Weston |
| 1966 | Hal Tillson |
| 1967 – 68 | Bill Sheehan |
| 1969 | Jack McArdle |
| 1970 – 71 | Weldon Coates |
| 1972 | Dwyer Roche |
| 1973 | Brad Piper |
| 1974 – 75 | John Anderson |
| 1976 | Hayden Bradford |
| 1977 | Tom Eley |
| 1978 | Phil Kolehmainen |
| 1979 - 80 | Robert Burkhardt |
| 1981 | Sue Schlacks |
| 1982 – 83 | Joe Kirk |
| 1984 | Jack Flynn |
| 1985 – 86 | Don Beveridge |
| 1987 | Boots Duesing |
| 1988 – 89 | Gil MacNeill |
| 1990 – 92 | Joe Jansen |
| 1993 | Tom Flynn |
| 1994 | Betty Nelson |
| 1995 | Dillon Reed |
| 1996 – 97 | Bert Henderson |
| 1998 | Sharon Kirk |
| 1999 | Jack Gubbins |
| 2000 | Rick Venner |
| 2001 | Tom Morsch |
| 2002 | Jim Richmond |
| 2003 | Andy Anderson |

*Two girls watch onstruction of the Palisades Nuclear Power Plant.*

railroad spur were built to accommodate equipment. Steel and concrete dominated the scene for years, as did the many hundreds of workers who came to work on this massive project. It would become one of the earliest of the many nuclear power plants to be built in this country in the early 60's and 70's.

Shoreline communities along the lake joined Palisades and Linden Hills and fought in vain to keep Consumers from building this nuclear power plant, citing its dangerous proximity to the fresh waters of Lake Michigan, along with radiation concerns. This was early in the days of a building boom of nuclear power plants across the country, and little was known then about their effects on the environment, spent fuel and its storage, let alone eventual decommissioning of the plants. The general public was uninformed on this subject and the press had given it little attention. The lawyers hired by the communities were hard pressed to fight a huge utility company on these issues at that time. Thus, Palisades Park eventually had to accept the reality of having a nuclear power plant as its neighbor.

The impact of the plant on the Park has been significant and long lasting. Before the plant was built in 1967, one could walk along the beach from Palisades all the way to South Haven, seven miles north. Pristine forests and beautiful sand dunes graced the shores as one walked along the beach. Palisades had literally no boundaries to the north or south. Upon completion of the plant, all that changed. A massive concrete and steel structure and gigantic cooling towers dominated the area where once dunes stood. At nighttime, extensive illumination of the area turned night into day and the plant could be seen from as far away as St. Joseph. When the power plant is operating on line, the sound generated from it is evident.

In the early 1990's, the plant had safety and management problems and the NRC levied fines against them. The Nuclear Regulatory Commission Agency in the Department of Energy is charged by Congress with responsibility for overseeing the nuclear power plants in the country. However, the plants themselves are owned and operated by the Utilities, not by the NRC, which licenses them. (Utilities have comprised the biggest donors to members of Congress – thus, perhaps, the reluctance of some to get tough with the NRC.) The safety concerns at the Consumers Plant continued to be very troubling to those in the Park who were keeping a close watch. Because of persistent and dedicated efforts by Park members, along with other watchful groups who enlisted the press in their cause, pressure was brought to bear by the NRC on officers with Consumers Power Company. The outcome of all this was a management shake-up in 1994.

The issue of "dry cask storage" was raised in 1993, when Consumers decided that this was the route they were going to have to take with the spent fuel from the reactor. As a result of their decision, activist groups and others concerned about the safety issues of the casks took action in order to stop the proceeding and enlisted the assistance of Tom Kelly, the Attorney General of the State of Michigan. The NRC would not hold public hearings on the casks, only accepting written comments, so Attorney General Kelly – representing the people of the State of Michigan – became involved. In 1993, he filed suit in the 6th circuit Court of Appeals, in Ohio, with the Lake Michigan Federation and the organization called "Don't Waste Michigan," co-founded by

*Plant from the water.*

nationally known nuclear researcher, Mary Sinclair, Ph.D., of Midland, Michigan. The suit, brought to court by them, contended that Consumers Power Company and the Nuclear Regulatory Commission had erred in licensing the storage casks without a public hearing and an environmental impact statement. In January, 1995, the United States 6th Circuit Court of Appeals permitted Consumers Power to continue loading the casks at the power plant. Despite that ruling, the plaintiffs took the case to the United States Supreme Court, where on June 27, 1995, it upheld the ruling of the Circuit Court of Appeals. The decision was based, not on the issue of safety, but on a rejection of the technical legal issues that were sent on Appeal.

Today, Consumers Power Plant stands on the shores of Lake Michigan to operate under its license until 2007, at which point its future will be determined.

*One of the Park members actively involved in opposing the plant was Virginia Melchert Coleman. Her memories of this time are below:*

When word of the impending construction of a nuclear power plant filtered into the Palisades Park community, most people seemed apathetic. A nuclear power plant … So? PR people from Consumers Power spoke at the annual meeting. The plant would be beautiful, clean, and safe; it would provide cheap electricity to General Motors in Kalamazoo. Consumers had tried to buy additional land by taking over Van Buren State Park, but that Park was buttressed safely by unbreakable laws. Hence, Consumers turned its gaze southward toward Palisades Park, and offered highly inflated, unbeatable prices to cottage owners on its boundaries. The owners sold immediately. No problem.

The impact and dangers facing the Park seemed so apparent to me and to Joan Glasner Stewart that we could not understand why others couldn't see them. I took pictures of the Consumers plant in Charlevoix, showing how ugly and sloppy it was, with old timber, rocks and other detritus. I made copies and sent them to all Park members, with an accompanying letter delineating the dangers of a nuclear plant, and pointing out where Consumers Power had already misrepresented itself to us. I asked for donations to help ally ourselves to other environmental groups. All this – pictures, postage, letters, and time – was done at my own expense. In all, we raised about $3600. I turned the money over to the Board with careful instructions about how it was to be spent. Before much time passed, I learned that the Board had spent the money to buy property

*View of the cooling towers in action.*

adjoining the Park near the highway. I felt betrayed and deeply concerned for the people who had entrusted me with their money. But what was done was done.

We ultimately allied ourselves with the Sierra Club, but not until after the plant was up and running. The Sierra Club pursued the cause of cooling towers, so that the plant would not dump thousands of gallons of hot water into the lake, killing the fish and enhancing the growth of algae. The Sierra Club won the legal battles and Consumers was forced to build the cooling towers. These decisions did not enhance my popularity with Consumers Power.

In the many years (twenty-five or twenty-six) it has been there, the plant has been "off line" almost half the time. The plant is now old and "brittle," and increasingly dangerous. The ConEd plant in Zion, Illinois, was built the same year and has been permanently "mothballed" for the same problems that Consumers has at Palisades. However, in many ways it is better to have it running than off, because it gets better inspection from the U.S. government.

The dangers from the poorly-constructed silos for the storage of spent nuclear fuel are legion. Palisades Park had better keep a close watch. Thanks for keeping that watch go to Nan Draper Lewis and Jane Kipp Gardner, who have assumed that responsibility. Meanwhile, buy a gieger counter.

Several of those interviewed for this history have noted, with sorrow, the changes on our North Beach. The loss of a favorite picnic spot, or a quiet haven for gulls, or a family cottage are all mourned elsewhere in this volume. For years, the area where still-warm water from the cooling towers is returned to the lake (thus raising the temperature of the oft-cold Lake Michigan) became a favorite "swimming hole" and party spot for many South Haven boaters. On weekends and holidays, hundreds of boats docked in front of the plant, only yards away from the casks of spent fuel. Only in 2002 has plant security sent the boats elsewhere – no doubt to a more picturesque spot even though it lacks the plant's "hot springs."

Over the years, Consumers Power Company has been anything but straightforward with their relations to Palisades Park. One of their early statements, reproduced in the July 26, 1965, <u>Patter</u>, gives proof that their word was not always to be believed. In the statement, Arthur H. Lee, Division Manager, Kalamazoo Division of the Power Company, assured Palisades that Consumers had "no immediate plans for the 600 acres south of South Haven" which had been recently purchased. He continued, "No plant has been designed for the site and we do not know when it will be put to use." When decisions would be made he could not say – nor "what sort of a plant it will be." (Of course, construction on the plant began soon thereafter.) The letter concludes with Consumers promise to maintain the beauty of the site:

> It can be assumed, however, that any generating plant built on this site will occupy only a minor portion of the acreage. The site is not exceptionally large – some of our existing plants are on larger sites – but there will be plenty of unoccupied space around the plant buildings. With its sand beach, its hills, and its heavily wooded areas, this site has great scenic attractiveness. Consumers Power Company is keenly interested in keeping Michigan beautiful. When the time comes to make use of the site, preservation of its natural charm will be a major purpose of the company.

A boat ride past the plant may disenchant anyone who believes that "preservation of its natural charm" was a consideration in the design of the "Monster down the Beach."

September 11, 2001, brought a new urgency to concerns about our safety, so close to a nuclear plant. Would terrorists ever strike such a target? Could the unthinkable be, now, a dreadful possibility? The spent fuel stored on the beach looks more menacing than ever. True, some increased security can be observed – with Coast Guard and Sheriff Patrol presence at some point each day, plus better monitoring, new signs, and a NO ENTRY zone. But the stakes are so high – with our beautiful Palisades Park only one small part of what might be destroyed in an attack on the Plant – that even these security measures are not much reassurance. A new world was ushered in by 9/11, to be sure!

*North Beach - changed forever.*

# Holiday Celebrations

Palisades has always enjoyed celebrating the July 4th and Labor Day weekends. For many years, the annual Married Men vs. Singles softball game was an eagerly anticipated part of the 4th. In his interview, Forest Lowrey remembered sprucing up the baseball field for these annual games:

*Well, people – you have to stimulate their interest. For instance, we had this baseball game every 4th of July. Fathers and sons is it? Married men vs. singles. Well, I remember spending $100 one year to get a bulldozer in here. Sam Canonie got it. That field used to be a golf course, you know, and it was full of brambles and briars and everything. Sam scraped the outfield clean. Boys had been falling down and all that. Little things like that, without spending very much money, we could really make it fun. They have kept the ball field in pretty good shape. It was the last time I saw it. They still have the game on the 4th and young people use the baseball diamond, as part of the Clubhouse activities. The field is kept very well and used for all kinds of things.*

Howard Beyer and his sons helped organize the game for many years. Howie remembers "getting out of bed early, when everything was peaceful and inviting another hour of sleep; there was a baseball game to be played. I remember Don Henkel playing 2nd base or right field, John Reed playing center field, Dick Martin 3rd base, Steve Heavrin 1st base, Doc Wallace pitching, and myself playing short stop. We all had a great time working out the middle-age kinks and scoring a few runs. But, along about the 5th inning, there appeared these young unmarried studs, who resembled tree trunks, and they showed us how to hit the home run. We usually lost those games, but the refreshments and laughs at Doc Wallace's place, Toplofty (#97), after the game was well worth the effort. As I remember, 'the young studs,' they included the Mathias, Fitzgerald, and Flynn boys."

Ray Lewis mentions a team c. 1936 – 37 that included both Sam and Tony Canonie and Squeak Knapp. Their field was out by Blue Star at our present burn area. They played in a league with teams from South Haven and Covert. Ray remembers a good group of 20-25 rooters who would cheer the team on to victory. Bill Eldredge remembers a similar Park team after the war, about 1946 – 49. Bennie Bishop was the pitcher. It too played in a league with surrounding teams. One year, the Schlacks family had a reunion that was so large that they had their own baseball tournament.

Another July 4th memory came from Ralph E. Nelson, previous owner of Heart's Haven (now Sandpiper #170). He remembers that "the Lodge originally had outdoor toilet facilities. After indoor plumbing was installed, a group of boys played a trick on the owner of the Lodge. On the 4th of July, a "cherry bomb" type firecracker was placed in a porcelain toilet. When the firecracker exploded, the toilet was blown into several pieces. The boys were scared and escaped to the woods. Twenty years later, Ralph Nelson was visiting with the owner of the Lodge and confessed to the 4th of July bombing. The owner told Ralph he had always suspected him of the mischief. They both had a good laugh."

For many years, the 4th celebration included fireworks, Ralph Wenham – then owner of Sturtevant Lodge – providing them for many years. David Peat also provided fireworks after Wenham sold the Lodge. However, a dune grass fire in the 90's brought about our present ban on fireworks. Vacationers had to be content with the fireworks in one of the surrounding towns. Not to let the holiday go unnoticed, however, the golf cart parade was started at about the time that fireworks ended. This parade has grown each year since; clever decorations and costumes abound.

*Above: The 2002 July 4 gathering at the Circle for what has become an annual golfcart parade and picnic.*

*Jon Beck celebrating July 4th, 1974.*

## Blood and Guts Spilled Each Labor Day

When a Palisades Parker thinks of Labor Day weekend, he thinks of the Honor and Glory Tennis Tournament; this tradition is discussed elsewhere in the book. However, basketball also has its place in the traditions of the Park, and the Honor and Glory Tournament is played along side another tournament – the Blood and Guts Four on Four Basketball Tournament.

No polite tournament this – no talk of honor or glory; the annual Blood and Guts Labor Day Basketball Tournament rivals any Park event for intensity and history. The summer of 2001 found two families spearheading a drive to replace the wobbly basketball backboard with a high-tech version. It may not be coincidental that these families are from Indiana – a state known for basketball mania. For whatever reason, the Flynns and Dinnins promised that a new backboard would be in place for the annual Labor Day tournament - and it was.

Basketball has not always been a high priority in the Park. At first, there was just a grass field in front of a backboard, out by the tennis courts. By the end of the 60's, the grass was gone and only clay remained. Players found themselves covered with dust when they used the court. But play they did, with enthusiasm, despite the dust. In about 1971, a bunch of the players – including Gene Warner, the three Tillson boys, and four of the Flynn brothers - helped Stan Severinghaus, then Park manager, hand-dig a half-court area and set forms; the Park then poured concrete. Two years later, Hal Tillson paid for concrete for the full court.

Meanwhile, the Labor Day "four on four" tournament had evolved. The rules allowed a three- person team to enter the competition after picking a fourth member from the pool of those who entered as singles. A double elimination tournament was played, giving teams more than one chance to demonstrate their skills. At first there were scheduling conflicts with the Honor and Glory. As Tom Flynn remembers, most of the basketball players were eliminated in the first rounds of tennis, so the conflicts were solved by starting to play basketball on Sunday, the second day of the Honor and Glory. About 1975, Tom Tillson built the first Blood and Guts trophy. Tradition has been to add something to the trophy each year. The present version is – well, shall we say outlandish? Not exactly the epitome of beauty, the trophy was bitterly contested among the winning team members (who got to keep it over the winter?) whose mothers secretly hoped they would <u>not</u> have to display it for the ensuing year.

*The Blood and Guts trophy is "improved" each year. Mothers of winners are not always thrilled at the prospect of displaying the trophy for the ensuing year.*

About the same time as the trophy started, Mike Mathias painted the famous (infamous?) Puma on the court. That, too is a tale worth telling. In 1974, Mike, a master of creativity, had planned a fall party for the college age group at Palisades around the theme of a high school Homecoming party for the "Palisades Park Pumas." The party, complete with hayride, went down in the annals of "things to be remembered" at the Park – and the Puma was painted on the court to celebrate that memory.

Steve Tillson remembers that the Blood and Guts started as a "one hour tournament" – a statement about the full weekend devoted to Honor and Glory tennis. The basketball players could compete for the one hour and then get back to the *real* business of the weekend, on the beach. However, Steve continued, "Like anything else, it has turned 180 degrees. Now it takes two days of Blood and Guts."

The first year of the tournament, Murray Dawson, Jr. and friends met the Flynns in the finals. A number of families have remained loyal to the tournament over the years, including Tillsons, Flynns, O'Connors, Forsees, Huffines, Goldens and Vanas, Mathiases, Gateses, Connors, Masons, Roaches, Mooneys, Stangers, Klebs, Ferrys, McCulloughs, and Nelsons. In the 80's, a Covert team was active in the tournament when Jim Sarno, who was a 6'10" player on the Northwestern University team, joined by two Canonies and John Spanos (who now owns Captain Lou's in South Haven), challenged the Palisades teams. Needless to say, Sarno and company usually reached the finals and often won.

The original court had posts on each end that were a problem when kids ran into them. When Bob Zimmermann was Park manager, he modified the backboard by bringing it forward to avoid the posts. That

*Basketball reigns each Labor Day weekend.*

modification was falling apart in 2001 when a new fiberglass backboard replaced it.

Memorable moments remain. Jody Flynn remembers when her brother, John, made the first slam dunk, in 1982 or 1983. For a few years, a Junior Blood and Guts was held for younger kids. The original participants now have sons playing – and still the beat goes on. Many Palisaders come up to the Park for Labor Day weekend just to play basketball. The year 2001, with its new fiberglass backboard, saw an especially big celebration. Maybe not the "Real Honor and Glory Tournament" – but the Blood and Guts has more than its share of tradition, ritual, and fond memories, an honor and glory of its own.

*2002 Blood and Guts tournament.*

# The Era of Labor Day Theme Parties

By Mike Mathias

While the "Hawaiian Luau" is sometimes remembered as being the first of the annual "Labor Day Theme Parties", this series of end-of-summer blowouts spanning eight years actually originated as a theme-less event that can best be referred to simply as "The Fruit Party". The idea for this first Sugar Bowl spectacle began innocently enough on a late August afternoon in 1967 as I sat on the Circle Beach discussing the lack of creativity in Palisades' night life, which consisted pretty much of beachfires 'n beer 'n beachfires 'n beer 'n beachfires 'n beer. It struck us that the simple addition of food - any food - might serve to make a beach party actually more of a beach party, especially since the beverages of choice usually made everyone hungry anyway. The concept was pretty basic at first, and we began preparations for normal stuff, like hotdogs, buns, chips, and corn on the cob (great after soaking in water and roasting still in the shuck on the coals of a fire!). Plans began to mutate quickly, however, when we decided to make things a little more exciting by having a "spiked" watermelon or three. One debauched idea led to another, and we figured why stop at watermelons? Couldn't we spike other fruit as well?!

The first party was quite a success. People had handed over $2.00 on the simple promise of plenty of food, some alcohol (beer was still BYO for several years), and a few surprises… and surprised they were! The Sugar Bowls were filled with cries of "Try one of these plums!", "Whoa! How 'bout these nectarines!!", "Mmmmff, this orange is GREAT!", and "Da(ng), give me another handful of those blueberries!!" Cecil Burrous' cleanup crew must have been more than a little curious about the next morning's debris, which consisted mainly of watermelon shells, banana peels, peach pits, orange rinds, and empty bottles of some toxic looking substance called "Cactus Jack"…

While the second version of the "Labor Day Weekend Party" in summer 1968 was equally as wild and successful as its predecessor, it really wasn't all that different from the inaugural event with the exception of the "Hawaiian" flavor. Island libations had been prepared, assembled, and sampled in a nearby cottage, and were carted down ceremoniously in boxes to the Sugar Bowl scene by costumed volunteers (Hawaiian shirts, grass skirts, leis, etc.) with tiki torches at an appropriate time in the revelry. The pageantry itself was a big hit, and another step was taken in the evolution of this "end of summer extravaganza"!

Probably the most memorable of the Labor Day Theme Parties was its third rendition in the closing days of Summer 1969 - the fabled "Greek & Roman Toga Party", a.k.a., "the Roman Orgy". The most wonderful aspect of the whole thing was the incredible scope of participation, enthusiasm, and creativity demonstrated throughout the Park by young and old alike; it took on a life of its own. Soon, we were planning a chariot race to take place in the Circle, gladiator fights to be staged at the Sugar Bowls, the roasting of a whole pig, and more. Almost daily up to the event, carloads of Parkers kept descending on the Blue Star Junkyard (oops, "antiques"), affectionately known as "Gruntly's," in order to purchase props and bits and pieces that could be creatively joined together into "period costumes" appropriate to the theme. Old rubber doormats soon became "spiked" gladiator apparel, while junk pieces of leather and discarded cookie sheets were transformed into armor for the Roman guard.

By the time that the day of the event arrived, the energy and excitement level in the Park seemed almost palpable. The party was to start just before sunset with a Chariot Race in the circle, and the crowd that turned out to watch (and even participate) far exceeded any expectations - the Circle was packed (much like today's 4th of July Golf Cart Parade)! The stage was set: the chariot teams had gathered near the Stewart cottage (#20); I sat in the tall judge's chair from the tennis court which had been placed in the Circle's central flower garden as the Emperor's throne (hey, as main organizer of these things, I had the egotistic duty to assign myself whatever title the theme called for); Praetorian guards stood ready; and a colorful "cast of thousands" of Greek & Roman characters, from gods to commoners, awaited to cheer on their favorite charioteers. Suddenly, a toga'd figure came running from the woods behind Graystone with a home-made Olympic torch ablaze; with the crowd yelling its approval, he set fire to the Olympic Flame (i.e., a bucket of oily rags) at the Emperor's feet - which in turn served as the signal to start the race (a signal which was relayed to the anxious competitors by a series of strategically placed shouters). The mad dash of eight chariots trying to get across a

Brandywine Bridge only wide enough for two and a half was spectacle enough, but the Park is unlikely ever again to see the amazing scene of the surviving chariots roaring around the Garage (now the Village Green) and into the Circle to the raucous shouts and laughter of an excited crowd of friends and neighbors of all ages bedecked in sheets, rubber doormats, leather straps, cookie sheets, and various forms of indigenous plant life twisted into wreaths; yet, somehow - and this is the real PPCC magic - it all seemed unbelievably…normal! The incredible spectacle continued as the chariots were pulled round and round the Circle by their determined, but quickly tiring, teams. As anticipated, there were a few impressive "wipeouts" of Ben Hur-ian magnitude, but in keeping with miraculous Park traditions, no one was hurt. I don't remember who eventually won the race, but I do remember their reward - a bottle of Cactus Jack for each of the victors!

Several of our stronger youth attempted to carry me all the way from the Circle to the Sugar Bowl on one of those shoulder-born platform chairs you always see the Emperor being taxied about with in old Cecil B. DeMills' movies; they tired out about Tillson's cottage, and I walked indecorously the remaining way with the rest of the costumed throng. The Sugar Bowl party area was ablaze with numerous home-made torches, and off to one side was a huge fire pit where a whole pig (complete with apple-in-mouth) was roasting on a spit made from young sassafras trees. Wood for several smaller fires had been laid out in several locations, so that the dune area looked much like a Roman army encampment. From time to time, several self-designated "Gladiators" would get up in a specified "arena" area and stage a mock battle with a selection of cleverly-made weapons, shields, and nets.

A two-year hiatus ended in late summer 1971, when the Labor Day Theme Party was enthusiastically brought back in its newest version as the "Barbarian Party", also fondly remembered as the "Viking Orgy" (a clear pattern of "pagan" themes seemed to be emerging, but after all, it was the Dawn of the Seventies and disco was only a few years away!). Once again, creative Parkers embraced the theme, and paid daily visits to "Gruntly's" to gather old furs, leather scraps, shag rugs, or just about anything else they could envision fashioning into barbarous outfits and mock weapons.

This time, the "pre-party" Circle event was to be a Viking Funeral. A Viking ship would be needed, and for this rather ambitious prop, an abandoned, busted-up, seam-split old aluminum row boat was found half-buried in the sand near Brandywine Beach. After excavating this relic, we duct-taped a deflated plastic raft to the side like a huge patch to hold the seam together, and haphazardly repaired a few of the larger remaining holes. We didn't have to make it terribly seaworthy; the vessel only needed to float for a few minutes – long enough to carry a shrouded dummy on top of a blazing pile of kindling several yards into the lake, where, undoubtedly, it would sink rapidly. We then fitted it with a tall mast (i.e., a sassafras pole), from which we hung a large square sail (i.e., a bedsheet spraypainted with a large black eagle and several rune-looking symbols). We filled the shell with dry wood, and voila! we were good to go! The effect of this floating Viking Funeral Pyre would be brief, but magnificent!

As evening began to fall that Labor Day Thursday, the Circle filled with a myriad throng of Vikings, Huns, Visigoths, Vandals, Mongols, Saxons, Jutes, Renters, and assorted other Barbarian representatives. Creative costumes were de rigeuer, with fur vests and leather accessories being the most popular fashions (the "chapeau du jour" seemed to be a salad bowl with protruding aluminum foil horns). At a given signal, a solemn procession began from the Willows parking area, with several costumed tribesmen shouldering a wooden pallet on which lay a wrapped "dummy mummy". Escorted by several torchbearers and a circle of wailing women, the parade moved slowly through the mourning horde that had gathered for the spectacle, and made its way to the edge of Circle Beach, where the makeshift Viking barge awaited. The wrapped "body" of the "fallen warrior" was ceremoniously placed on top of the woodpile in the vessel (which had previously been soaked with lighter fluid for a guaranteed burn), and several Viking comrades pushed the boat out into the lake in a generally westward direction. I stood thigh-deep in the water with a small torch, ready to set flame to the pyre once it was set adrift, but the launching shove had been strong, and the boat zipped by so fast I didn't have time to light it as it passed. This accidentally turned out for the better, however, as I now had to throw the torch several yards at the quickly fleeing target; Thor must have guided my aim, for the incredibly lucky shot saw the torch lob end-over-end in a rainbow arch only to land smack dab in the middle of the floating pyre, which was immediately set ablaze to the crowd's thunderous approval. But now an odd thing happened, typical of those minor miracles the Park has played host to over the years: instead of burning rapidly and sinking within a hundred feet from shore, the flaming ship kept plodding outward against the current and through the breakers, as if being pulled by some invisible rope. Caught up in the theatrics of the moment, the Barbarians at the Lake began roaring with shouts of "Odin! Odin! Ooohh-DEEEEEEEN!", and gazed in wonder as the fiery craft, with flames engulfing the mast and painted sheet, continued sailing swiftly toward Valhalla (or Milwaukee; I'm not sure which). Like the Energizer Bunny, it just kept going, and going, and going... Eventually, it was just a brightly lit ball on the horizon, but as the ecstatic fur and leather crowd began to disperse toward the Sugar Bowl to continue the Barbarian festivities, some of us saw a Coast Guard cutter headed toward that flickering light, obviously investigating a report of a burning boat.

As Labor Day Weekend approached in summer 1972, the wheels were put in motion for an "Arabian Nights" theme party. A costumed crowd of pseudo-Arabs began to congregate in the Circle for the usual meet & greet and pre-party activities. Flowing robes, turbans, sashes, veils (i.e., sheets, beach towels, and rags creatively employed), and the occasional fez made up the apparel of choice for most attendees, who, after a few libations, gathered to witness the "Slave Market" taking place on the Flynn's lawn at the edge of the Circle.

A "Cowboys & Indians" theme was next up for Labor Day Weekend 1973 ( "political correctness" was far in the future, so we never shrunk away much from celebrating stereotypes in those days). This festivity began, not in the Circle, but in the still-standing garage, which had been temporarily transformed into the "Golden Fugget Saloon". Cowpokes, wranglers, barmaids, dance hall girls, gamblers, Indians, and other assorted Shane Gray characters could "mosey on up" to a make shift bar and get a shot of whiskey, tequila, or – surprise, surprise! — Cactus Jack (finally a theme befittin' this foul firewater!)! Once we were all in the "proper mood", the next event was staged back on Flynn's lawn at the other side of the Circle — a Cowboys vs. Indians pie-eating contest! There were no real winners (most of the competitors had to wash off in the lake and change clothes before continuing down to the Sugar Bowl), but the struggle was fierce, leaving both sides generally covered (appropriately enough) in bloody-looking blueberry stains. (Chief Buzz Blackett tried to claim victory for his tribe, but was easily outnumbered by the White Eyes, who simply took his land.)

The series of Labor Day Theme Parties culminated in 1974 with the "Knights of the Round Table" (a.k.a. King Arthur Party). That evening brought a colorful collection of knights, damsels, squires, courtesans, lords, ladies, and assorted peasantry into the Circle to begin this final year's pageantry. The opening event was to be a Jousting Competition - on roller skates! First up would be the Black Knight, who had brazenly challenged the King (me, who else?!) to a combat. The pure theater of this event would have been great entertainment, except for one thing - it's physically impossible to "roll" on roller skates across a sandy, stony surface like the Circle's. We clomped in the general direction of each other a few times, even traded a few glancing blows with our wooden swords, but quickly agreed to a draw before we bored each other to death. The crowd barely noticed. Knights, ladies, and the whole motley crew soon regrouped at the Sugar Bowls for the real celebration. A roast pig provided the culinary atmosphere this year, along with mead (i.e., wine), ale (i.e., keg beer), sumptuous fruits, and a few flagons of Sir Jack for the unschooled serfs. Several colorful pennants furled while torches flickered in the late summer breeze, enhancing the Arthurian ambiance in the dune encampment. And so legends are forged.

While the epic Labor Day Sugar Bowl Theme Parties of the late Sixties and early Seventies may be a thing of the past, the likes of which may never be seen again, it cannot be said that the creative spirit and energy which fostered these events has also disappeared. For several years after that last end-of-summer blowout, the void was filled with

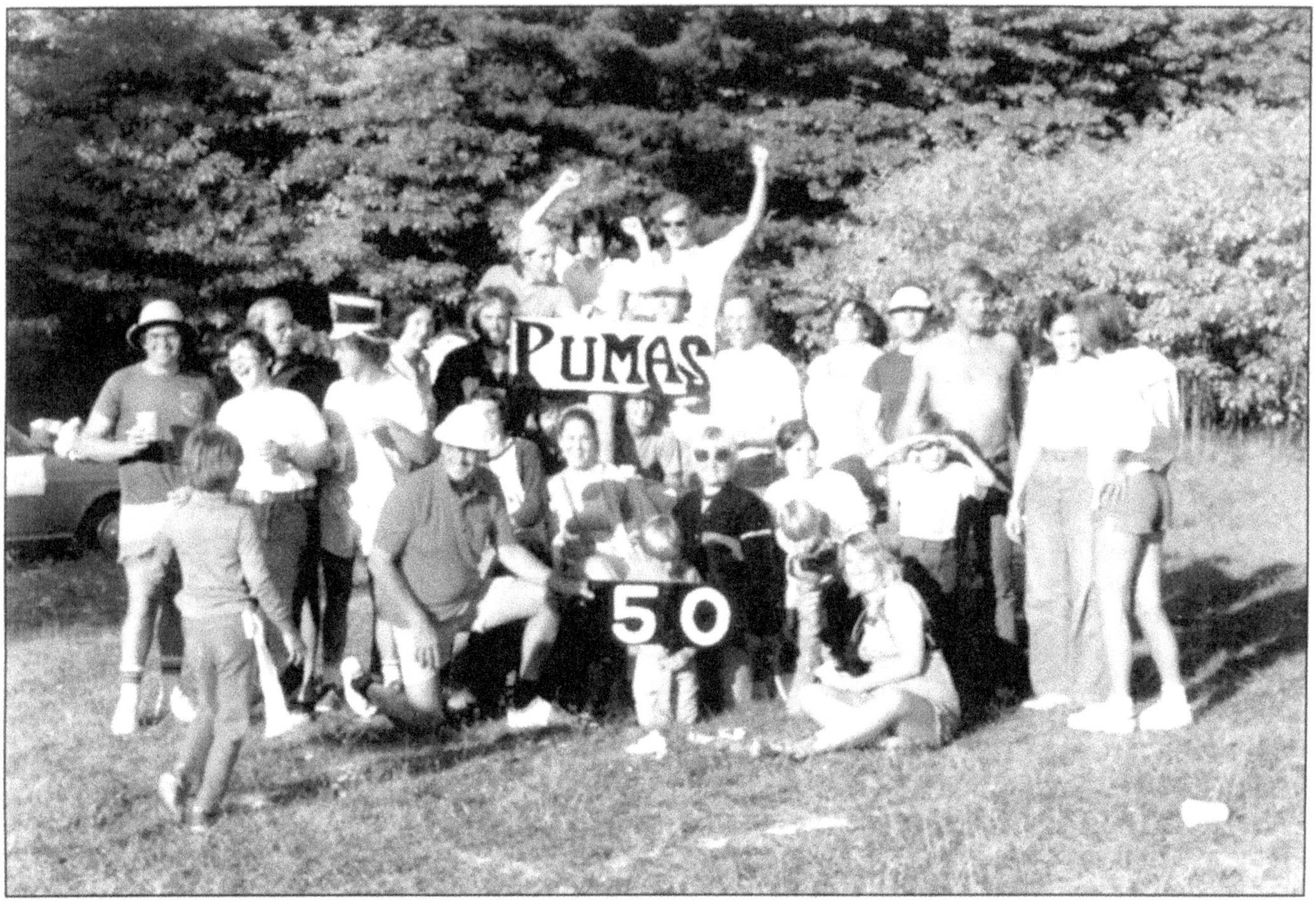


*An announcement of "Homecoming Weekend"*

PALISADES PARK
PALISADES, MICHIGAN
HOMECOMING
WEEK-END
September 26 & 27
A gathering of Palisades Park High School
Classmates and Friends
Homecoming Festivites
Friday, Sept. 26 - 10:30 p.m. JOE PUTTS MEMORIAL STADIUM
BON FIRE & PEP RALLY
HAY RIDE following Bon Fire
- - SATURDAY - -
HOMECOMING PARADE -- 2:00 p.m.
FOOTBALL GAME -- Kickoff 2:30 p.m.
Palisades Park Puma's
vs. Covert Tech
VICTORY SOCK HOP
In the Helen Packard Room
of the Clubhouse

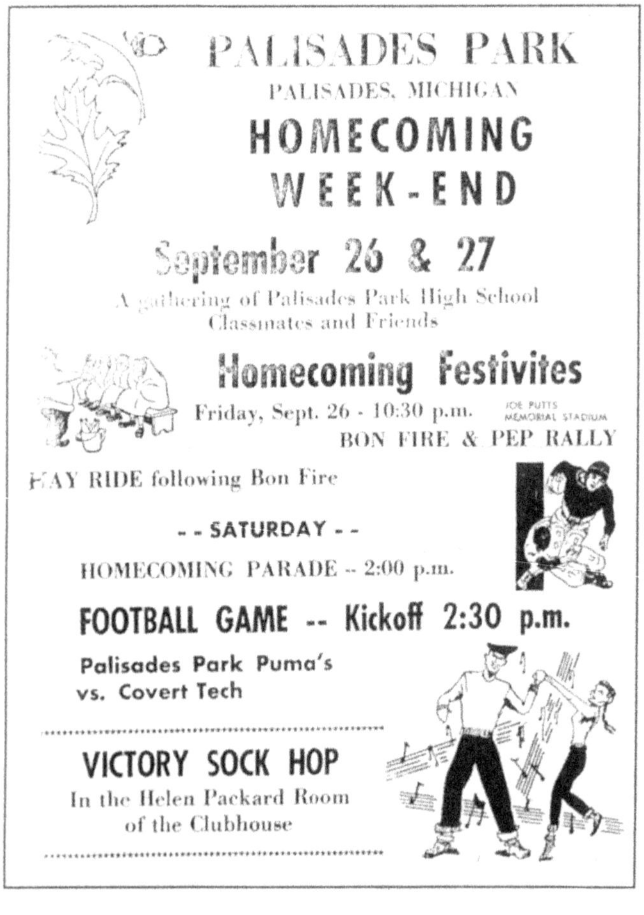

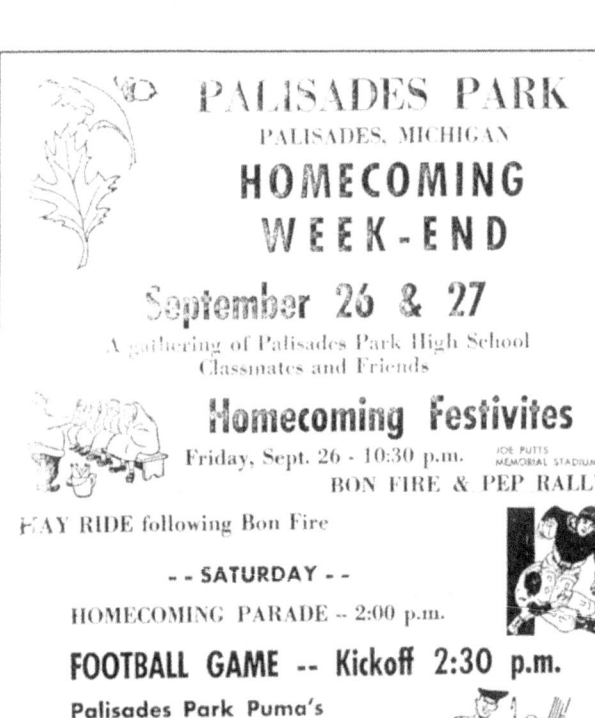

October "Homecoming Weekends" for the students and alumni of the fictitious Palisades Park High School, home of the "Fighting Pumas"! It might possibly be (although arguable) that the Park's somewhat tamer, yet more inclusive and always wonderful Annual Ethnic Dinner evolved from the Labor Day Theme Party. The participation and pageantry of the Fourth of July Golf Cart Parade has grown steadily each year! There is no shortage of imaginative good times here in PPCC. Nevertheless, from time to time, I find myself back at the fabled dune area, standing in the hollow that fronts Baby Sugar Bowl, scene of all those glorious magical nights, and it feels like sacred ground. The air is so thick with memories, they are almost palpable. With little effort, I can see the torches and the campfires, smell the roasting pig, and hear the shouts and laughter of my friends as they engage in mock combat, pass a Mai Tai pineapple, or set fire to a covered wagon. In my mind, the sands still echo with "My gawd, have you tried the blueberries!" Those of you who were there and lived it too, I think you know what I mean. It truly is a bygone era, and I miss it.

# Ethnic Dinners

The Ethnic Dinners more or less evolved over the years. Mike Mathias may be right that the Labor Day Theme parties led to something for the whole Park. At any rate, when Cecil Burrous retired as Resident Manager in 1973, he was honored with a Clam Bake. That was so popular that the idea was expanded the next year into an Old German Festival - and Palisaders have gathered each summer since. When the garage collapsed in January, 1979, the "Village Green" was instituted on its remaining cement floor; the dinners have been held there ever since. Listed below are the themes that have been used.

1973 – Clam Bake for Cecil
1974 – Old German Festival – had "Snack and Stein Hour" with German cheese and crackers, beer, brats, German potato salad, sauerkraut – and danced the polka!
1975 – Hosted by Don Goodwillie
1976 – Greek Night
1978 – Italian Night
1979 – Epicurean Delight Night
1980 – Heritage Dinner and Pageant (75th Anniversary)
1981 – Luau
1982 – A Night at the Casbah
1983 – Country Western
1984 – Renaissance Fair
1985 – Carnival
1986 – Fiesta Mexican
1987 – Tahitian Luau
1988 – French Night
1989 – Fiesta Night
1990 – Country Western
1991 – Barbecue Dinner
1992 – English
1993 – Italian
1994 – Jamaican
1995 – Gay 90's
1996 – New Orleans Jazz
1997 – Irish
1998 – Hawaiian Luau/Pig Roast
1999 – Disco
2000 – Asian Pig Roast
2001 – Summertime Blues
2002 – The Big Night
2003 - Mardi Gras

*Circle area in August, 1974. Note garage still standing. Also note telephone booth. Many cottages did not yet have phones.*

*Celebrating the new millennium in the Clubhouse. December 31, 1999 - January 1, 2000.*

## Frances Prange and Memories of Happy Valley

Henry and I and our children, Linda and Bill, came to Palisades as property owners in 1954. Henry's mother, Elizabeth Prange, was the owner of Bittersweet Cottage (#51) by the hotel for many years. (That cottage burned to the ground and was rebuilt by present owners Susan and Tom Kavanaugh.) Thinking it time to strike out for ourselves instead of staying with Henry's mother, we rented Miss Miller's cottage (Bonnie Dune, now owned by Marilyn and Don Henkel) for two weeks. We had miserable weather and I didn't care if I ever saw Palisades again. Two years later we rented the Potter's cottage on North Beach and had a wonderful time. During that time, Henry found two lots up in back of Bonnie Dune with many trees and a beautiful view of the lake. We decided to buy the lots and build. We purchased the lots from the Nine Old Men, a group of men who purchased several lots to protect the Park from undesirable growth and development. We worked with Mr. George Boyles and I remember Mr. Seymore's name on some of the legal papers. At the same time we were buying, the cottages down in front of our lots, on the lakeshore, were negotiating to buy land to install a road that would go in back of their cottages, taking a few feet of our lots. They needed this road badly; they had a long walk carrying everything from the fork in the road of routes 2 and 9 – where at that time they had to park. This was all settled in due time, and we spent the winter working on the plans for our cottage.

We hired Rudy Weber of Covert to be our builder; he started in March to clear the space for the cottage. We thought it was very slow going, but of course it wasn't; we were just so anxious and excited. We camped in the cottage over July 4th and took possession in late summer of 1954. Palisades Park became the focal point of our lives from that time on. Living in Kalamazoo made it very accessible for us. We moved out to stay on the day school was out, returning on Labor Day. Henry drove back and forth every day. Our Chicago neighbors were envious of his proximity to his work. In the early spring and late fall, we could make use of weekends as much as school activities allowed.

Henry was approached to serve on the Board of Directors the next year. He served two two-year terms as president (1959–1962) and enjoyed every minute, even though he was sometimes awakened at 2:00 a.m. because of loud beach parties, barking dogs, and the like. In desperation, he sometimes put his sailboat in the lake at 6:00 a.m. on Sundays in order to have a quiet time to sail.

Our area was always a very friendly and fun place to live. The other families made us welcome at once. As time went on, we shared our friends and families. We enjoyed Saturday night potlucks, followed by games of charades, sing-alongs, or card games. There was that glorious, big beach on which to spend hours - reading and talking and taking long hikes with a bag lunch to collect all those unusual stones and beach glass. The girls played bridge and golf during the week. We were aware we needed a name for our valley but just couldn't come up with one. One fall, Henry and I were on our way West to spend the winter. Driving through New Mexico, we saw a sign saying *HAPPPY VALLEY*. The perfect name for our Palisades valley! The following spring, it met with everyone's approval. We all became residents of Happy Valley in Palisades Park. The Park as a whole accepted the name; Betty Householder, who wanted everything in the Park named and identified, thought it was just fine.

One annual event, the 4th of July beach picnic, became a highlight of every season. We set up tables, beach chairs, and umbrellas and shared great food, year after year. One year, the alewives were so plentiful it was impossible to use the beach, so the party was held at our cottage on our patio. We had a mob but it worked fine.

Time marches on. Linda and Bill became permanent residents of California. Henry died in 1986 and I, too, moved to California, returning to Palisades for summers. Henry and I had spent ten years as "snowbirds," spending winters in Florida, Arizona, and California. After five more years continuing this pattern, I made the wrenching decision, with the consent of my family, to sell the Happy Valley cottage and become a full time resident of California. At this writing, April, 2002, Gert Harris (who owned what is now Feldman's cottage #139) and Vivian Erwin (who owned what is now Pomeroy's cottage #138) and I are the only survivors of the original Happy Valley group. I know they treasure the memories of those years as I do. It will always occupy a very special place in Linda's and Bill's and my hearts.

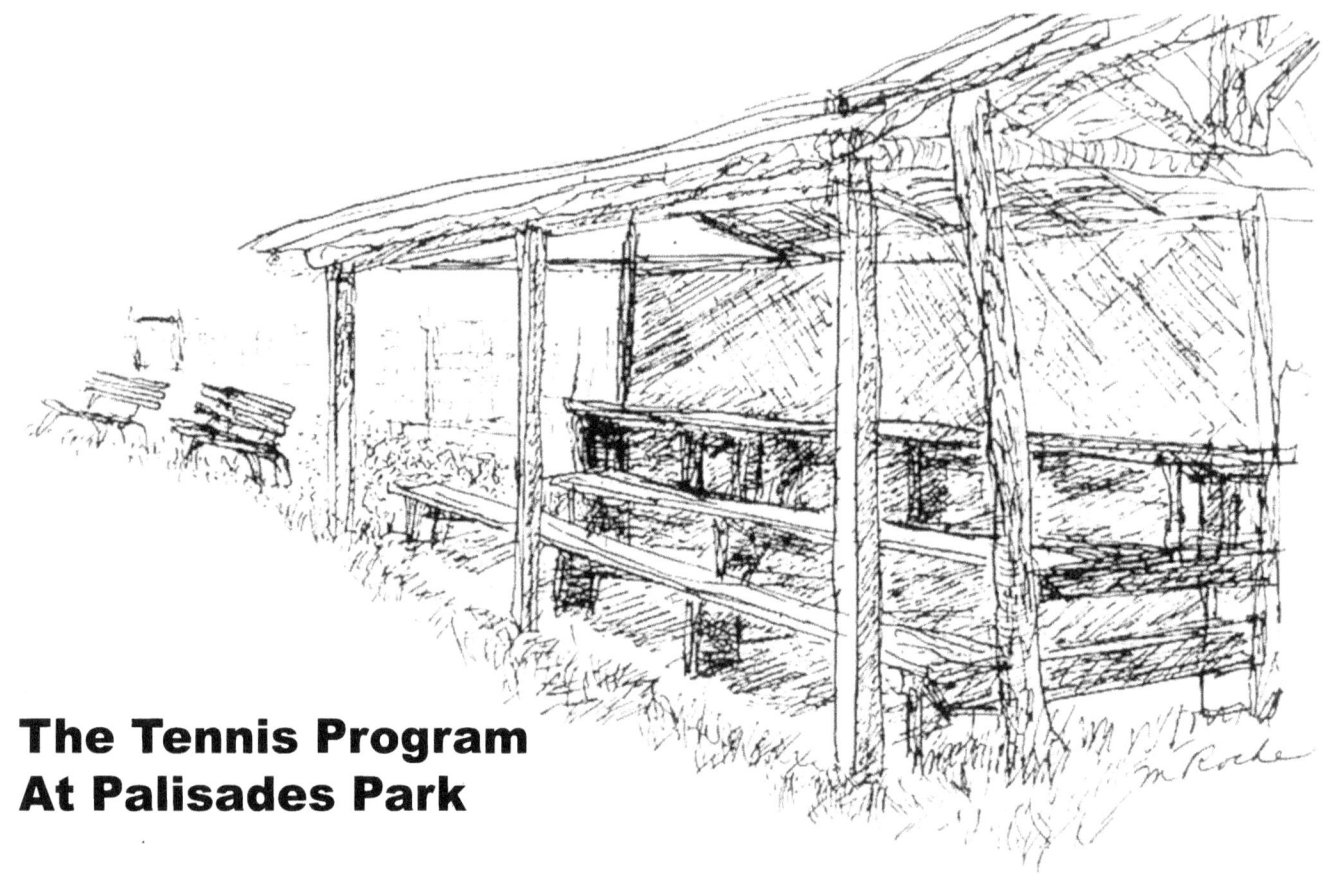

# The Tennis Program At Palisades Park

Tennis has been a popular sport in Palisades from the Park's inception. Mr. Quick's earliest advertisements mention the inclusion of tennis courts. Apparently the first two courts were built on the north side of Ravine Way. Sometime in the 20's, a third court was built across the road.

One of the early tennis enthusiasts was Tony Malinowski, a young man from Covert who worked at the Lodge and was something of a recreation director for the youth in the 1930's. Tony recalled, in his interview, going door to door, instruction manual in hand, to recruit kids for tennis lessons. A 1972 Patter article tells of his involvement in the first Honor and Glory tournament, in 1937:

"Born of necessity and perpetuated by popular demand, the first Honor and Glory tennis tournament came into being in 1937. Some climax to the tennis season was needed – to settle once and for all the question of who was who in the tennis Blue Book. While working at the Lodge, Tony Malinowski dreamed up the five-ring tennis circus and also (while sleeping on the job) dreamed up the title which has lived on. Since it was an individual project, and individuals going to college had no money to spare, Tony figured that the HONOR of winning and the GLORY of playing were enough reward for the court antics. There also was no entry fee, and of course, no prizes. At the Recognition Dance after the tourney, Mr. Quick surprised the promoter by slipping him a five-spot, and announced publicly that a fund for athletics in general - and the Honor and Glory in particular – would be set up for the following year. The idea was swiftly accepted. Mr. Forest Lowrey was appointed godfather – an anonymous and fairly costly title he has retained since – and the tourney became the annual high-point ever since. Wooden plaques with winners' names used to hang in the Clubhouse – but have disappeared, somehow. However, Mr. Art McCain, no mean racqueteer himself, has collected for and bought beautiful silver plaques which will be inscribed during this winter and hung in the Clubhouse, bringing up to date the Honor and Glory winners since its first year."

The Honor and Glory "godfather," Forest Lowrey, no tennis player himself, always believed in the importance of the game at Palisades. In his interview, he twice stated tennis was "the best thing that ever happened here." He continued: "The tennis program was encouraged by the Bishops. George's father - George Bishop, Sr. – was a very great tennis fan and he was good enough so Benny got into the Junior Davis Cup and he stimulated interest in tennis. He brought a pro up for a couple of years. They had contests and he'd bring players over from Kalamazoo and South Haven. They encouraged a lot of the kids to play. I think that was the greatest thing that happened. Up until that time, they had this Honor and Glory tournament with no prizes at all. We budgeted and had prizes the Park didn't have to pay for. I'd give them

and George would give them and we'd just have people who were interested donate money so we could give the winners cups and nice things. That stimulated the interest. When I first came up here I used to get so angry; one fellow came up here once a year – the father of someone we all know and love – just for the tennis tournament and he'd beat the kids and take the prize home. That just burned me up. Some people are funny. They want to beat the game, some way, so they bring these winners in. We've had some pretty good tennis players up here. I built the umpire stand out by the tennis courts. After Benny Bishop, John Ferry's wife, Vickie, took over the tennis program and had a program for young children. She and John are still playing and she is doing a wonderful job with the program. Tennis is extremely active. I think that's the best thing that ever happened here."

From the 30's on, both facilities and tournaments have grown. By 1941, four more clay courts had been built. Tennis players reached out to surrounding areas, competing in South Haven and Kalamazoo. The Honor and Glory tournament and its junior counterpart remained a climactic event of each summer's tennis season. Families, cars packed and ready to go home, didn't dare plan to leave the Park before their children finished playing in the tournament. A second chance to compete, the Blind Bogey Tournament, was instituted in 1946. The Ladies Buttercup was started in 1969; the George Gates "Over 40 Charming People" Tournament in 1978.

The first all weather courts were built in 1974, under the leadership of George Brumis, Bill Carr, Vernon Wallace, and Bob Ott, Sr. This was at a time when the Park had many seawall expenses, so no Park funds were used. The courts were financed entirely by private contributions.

Brad Bradford wrote the history of these courts in an article entitled, "Hard Courts Built 15 Years Ago" in the July 1989 Patter:

"Rain-out of the clay courts during the 1988 Honor & Glory Tennis Tournament recalled to many onlookers the building of the two hard surface tennis courts in the Park 15 years ago. George Brumis, Sr. initiated the project. After rejecting a contractor's bid of $20,000, Brumis turned to Stan Severinghaus as his advisor and saw them built for less than a third of the contractor's price. With his two sons, the late Bob Ott, and a number of volunteers doing physical work, the courts were completed in 1974. Brumis, Bill Carr, and Dr. Vern Wallace made the outlay of $6000 in capital for the project. Funds were then solicited from park tennis players who were asked to contribute $300 per family. There were considerable donations and no players were pressed for full payment. As a result, Brumis said the three were paid back their outlay of $6000 plus six percent interest."

Diane Henry recalls the next addition to the tennis domain – the building of the HarTru Courts. According to Diane, "the HarTru Courts were constructed in the early 1990's. Permission to use the land on which they were built was received from the Lowrey Land Trust. The money was raised through donations from the membership. The courts have become the favorite of hundreds of Park members and visitors who play the courts each summer." Chuck Henry, who engineered the project, shared his enthusiasm in the July, 1991 Patter:

"Come run your Reeboks through the gravel … Palisades's new Har-Tru courts are in action. After more than six months of planning, nickel-and-diming contractors, lugging gravel, and soliciting your support, the courts are ready for your tennis comfort. The project kicked off last November, as contractors laid a 400-ton base of country road gravel on the north side of the existing hard courts. The base set through the winter, and after some springtime rain delay, a second layer was laid and graded in April, this time 200 tons of 3/4-inch gravel. A third layer of 260 tons of trail mix followed. Finally, with the help of "superintendent" Bill Carr, "foreman" Bob Hladic, "mechanical engineer" Stan Severinghaus, electricity expert Bill Trumbull, and volunteers Sal and Barbara Grigola, Ray Waldron, Earl Kirsch, Bill and Maureen Henry, and Jim Williams, we painstakingly laid and rolled to perfection 80 tons of HarTru surface.

"Now lines are down, and some of you have tested the new surface. In no time, we'll have fences installed and windscreens hanging. We've also installed some additional amenities: a well to provide for a sprinkling system and a water fountain; and we've redone the road for those who store boats down at the courts. And if we may say so ourselves, the courts blend beautifully with the existing tennis facilities. Now Palisades can boast a full complement of quality playing surfaces – a real draw for tennis enthusiasts and a significant enhancement to Park property values."

Finally, the addition of quality tennis instruction has brought further change to the Palisades program, particularly for Park youngsters. Boots Duesing, who has been instrumental in developing our present Junior Tennis Program, reminisces about this aspect of the sport:

"In the spring of 1960, Doris suggested that we should take a family vacation and go to Palisades Park. The lure that she used to get me interested was that there were six clay tennis courts. This started my odyssey with this beautiful haven; we have been back every summer since then.

*Anna Goscinski at Junior Tennis lesson. 2002.*

"I remember telling our oldest daughter, Donna, age eleven, that there was a junior tennis tournament and that she was going to play in it. No, I'm not! Yes, you are! No, I'm not! Yes, you are! – This went on all the way to the tennis courts as I held her tennis racquet in one hand and her hand with my other, pulling her along in spite of her resistance. I remember this well: the little girl who was Donna's first opponent had been taught that if a ball goes beyond the service line, it is out. This little girl mistakenly thought that this applied to every shot, not just the serve alone. Every time Donna would hit a deep shot over the service line (but within the court), it would be called out. I did not want to interfere and correct her because I was afraid it would intimidate her, so I walked across the road. I could not bear to watch. Donna was not strong enough to hit many shots beyond the service line, so she ended up winning the match. But this illustrates how unstructured tennis was in those days. At the same time, the youngsters enjoyed it.

"In about 1963, tennis underwent a change when Phil Dillman started spending summers in the Park. Phil was an outstanding all around athlete – football, basketball, and baseball. He also had worked at River Forest Tennis Club under its professional, Cap Leighton, and while at Kalamazoo College had tutored Vic Sunderland, who was perhaps the top collegiate tennis player in the Midwest. Vic, to pay for his tutoring, worked with Phil on his tennis game. To supplement his income as a teacher, Phil began giving tennis lessons in the summer. This helped improve the quality of tennis at Palisades Park.

*Left: Junior Tennis class. 2002.*

"Over the next twenty year, tennis expanded in the Park with the addition of two all weather courts and two composition courts. But although interest in tennis was very great, it was predominantly so with the adults. The youngsters were not very high on the totem pole when it came to the right to play on a court. In fact, sometimes they were discouraged from playing if adults were present. It was only through the tireless efforts of Nancy Menconi and Cindy Wintermute Kearin, who ran the Junior Tennis Tournament in July and the Junior Honor and Glory in August, that junior tennis was kept alive.

"In 1994, Nancy and Cindy decided to let someone else run these two tournaments. At the July meeting, the Board asked for a volunteer to handle them. When none appeared, I unwittingly raised my hand and volunteered. My eyes got opened when I saw the enthusiasm of the youngsters in these tournaments – and also how unprepared they were in both playing ability and knowledge of the rules. A Junior Tennis Committee was formed which led to the hiring of Doug Gruber, tennis professional from South Haven. We now have one of the finest free junior tennis programs that can be found in the entire country."

In the summer of 2001, plans got underway for a Junior Tennis pavilion, to be called Pat'z Place, in memory of young Patrick Zimmermann, who lost his life the previous winter. The pavilion was completed the next summer, 2002. Built by volunteer labor, it has added one more feature to Palisades Park's continuing tennis mania and shifted the focus of playing and tournaments to the courts nearby. Finally, in the spring of 2003, two new courts were constructed to replace the hard surface courts built in the 80's.

*Above: Two new courts. 2003.*

*Above: Some of the volunteers constructing Pat'z Place.*

*Left: Pat'z Place, built in 2002*

*An enthusiastic crowd at the Honor and Glory Tennis Tournament.*

## PPCC HONOR & GLORY TENNIS TOURNAMENT WINNERS

| YR | MIXED DOUBLES | SINGLES | MEN'S DOUBLES |
|---|---|---|---|
| 2002 | Martha & Peter Hanson | Co-Champs, Toby Mathias/Tom Jeffers | Co-Champs, Toby Mathias/Mark Stephens |
| 2001 | Jody Flynn & Mark Stephens | Mark Borge | Bill Dinnin/Bryan Robinson |
| 2000 | Jane & Rey Meadowcroft | Jeff Lauterbach | Bill Henry & Steve Jones |
| 1999 | Vicki Ferry & Bill Trumbull | Toby Mathias | Vicki & John Ferry |
| 1998 | Diane Henry & Jeff Lauterbach | Mark Nightingale | George & Mark Borge |
| 1997 | Vicki Ferry & Bill Trumbull | Dave Branding | Vicki & John Ferry |
| 1996 | Trish & Jeff Lauterbach | Jeff Lauterbach | Dave Branding & Steve Jones |
| 1995 | Kathleen & Tom Jeffers | Jeff Lauterbach | Bob Murphy & Tom Jeffers |
| 1994 | Rosie & Graham Rogers | Graham Rogers | Dave Branding & Steve Jones |
| 1993 | Donna Joy & Tom Kersten | Jeff Lauterbach | Chuck & Bill Henry |
| 1992 | Kathleen & Tom Jeffers | Dave Branding | Bill & Bryan Henry |
| 1991 | Kathleen Conroy & Bob McNamara | Tom Jeffers | Dave Branding & Rey Meadowcroft |
| 1990 | Jane & Rey Meadowcroft | Bob McNamara | Bob McNamara & Toby Mathias |
| 1989 | Kathleen & Tom Jeffers | Dave Branding | Dave Branding & Toby Mathias |
| 1988 | Jane & Rey Meadowcroft | David Fleming | Paul Bruning & Jim Williams |
| 1987 | Kathleen Mooney & Tom Jeffers | John Ferry | George Brumis Sr & Geo. Brumis Jr |
| 1986 | Jane & Rey Meadowcroft | Joe Anlauf | Dave Branding & Steve Jones |
| 1985 | Jamie Williams & Peter Wood | Dave Branding | Vicki & John Ferry |
| 1984 | Jane & Rey Meadowcroft | Dave Branding | Dave Branding & Steve Jones |
| 1983 | Jennie Replogle & John Wintermute | John Ferry | Dave Branding & Steve Jones |
| 1982 | Jennie Replogle & John Wintermute | Dave Branding | Dave Branding & Steve Jones |
| 1981 | Christy & Ben Bishop | | Dave Branding & Steve Jones |
| 1980 | Jane & Rey Meadowcroft | Dave Branding | Vicki & John Ferry |
| 1979 | Carol & Bob Replogle | John Ferry | Vicki & John Ferry |
| 1977 | Beth Baer & Eddie Owen | Tom Tillson | Mike Dinnin & Mike Ferguson |
| 1976 | Ann Aliotta & Steve Buschman | John Ferry | Vicki & John Ferry |
| 1974 | | John Ferry | Vicki & John Ferry |
| 1973 | Janet Kohelmainen & Steve Tillson | John Ferry | Vicki & John Ferry |
| 1969 | | | Toby Mathias & John D. O'Connor |
| 1968 | Judge & Mrs. Phillip McNagny | Toby Mathias | Toby Mathias & John D. O'Connor |
| 1966 | | John Ferry | |
| 1965 | Laurie Bishop & Jeff Stewart | Tony Mathias | Toby Mathias & John D. O'Connor |
| 1964 | Mary Lee Tillson & Art Maerlander | John D. O'Connor | Toby Mathias & John D. O'Connor |
| 1963 | Anne Householder & Peter Ferry | Greg Gates | Toby Mathias & Trip Bishop |
| 1962 | | | Jeff Stewart & Ray Lewis |
| 1958 | Nan & Ray Lewis | | Bob Ott & Ray Lewis |
| 1957 | | | Bob Ott & Ray Lewis |
| 1949 | | | Ray Lewis & Bill Efrig |

### WOMEN'S DOUBLES

| | | | |
|---|---|---|---|
| 2002 | Marie Roche & Martha Hanson | 1998 | Donna Joy & Jamie Williams |
| 2001 | Jamie Williams & Jody Flynn | 1997 | Donna Joy & Mary Lynn Hladik |
| 2000 | MaryBeth Cunningham & Jamie Williams | 1996 | Donna Joy & Vicki Ferry |
| 1999 | MaryBeth Cunningham & Diane Henry | | |

Note: No records for missing years

# Memorials in the Park

| | | | |
|---|---|---|---|
| **John Anderson** | Birch tree in meadow | **Henry Prange** | Prange deck |
| **Vashti Blaney** | Rose of Sharon bushes by tennis courts | **Mr. Arthur Quick** | Plaques and Arthur Quick Circle |
| **Bob and Connie Borchert** | Pine trees in meadow. | **Rud Richards** | Flag |
| **Mary Ellen Colbert** | Tables and umbrellas at Soda Bar | **Colleen Schlacks** | Stone in Circle garden |
| **"Bucky" Coleman** | Anchor in Circle | **Hal and Mary Lee Tillson** | Hand hewn bench and kiosk |
| **Sally Ellis** | Buttercup Tennis Tournament | **Betty Wintermute** | Plaques for Jr. Honor and Glory |
| **Jack and Nancy Flynn** | Lilacs in Connors' yard | **Pat Zimmermann** | Pat'z Place |
| **Jack Gardner** | Tulip poplar tree at entrance (since died) and trails | **All** | Weather vane at Soda Bar – (put up by Jayne Mathias and Mary Lee Tillson) |
| **George Gates** | Over 40 Tennis Tournament | | |
| **John Heisel** | Benches along stairs | | |
| **Nancy Heitner** | Yews in Circle planter boxes | | |
| **Betty Householder** | Garden, bench and Betty's Club | | |
| **Janette King** | Trees and benches by Clubhouse stairs (since washed away) | | |
| **Judy Kinsey** | Trees in meadow | | |
| **Forest Lowrey** | Meadow | | |
| **Jack Mathias** | Baseball bench | | |
| **Mardy Mehagan Mavor** | Cocktail party | | |
| **Bob Ott, Sr.** | Trophy cup for most improved player and blue spruce by tennis courts | | |

Donations in memory of Mary E. and John Gardner, Janette King, Gerald and Belden Hatch, Ruth C. Bartle, Genevieve Kearns Ball, Kevin Egan, Arch King (plus the generosity of an anonymous Park member) made possible the Memorial Garden at the entrance to the Park.

Donations in memory of the following are listed on the Memorial Plaques in the Soda Bar: Betty Householder, Mary Lee Tillson, Jack Mathias, Larry Joy, Jane Joy, Kirby Roche, Hazel Harper, Cliff Harper, Virginia King Van Bueren, Helen Beatty, Frances Draper, William Ferry, Jack Flynn, Nancy Flynn, Joseph King, Hal Tillson, Mary Lou Tombaugh, Thelma Weston, Lucius Weston, Ab and Mary Edwards, Marion Hamilton, John Heisel, Diane Jennings, Jack Gardner, Dorothy Parshall, Colleen Schlacks, Dr. John Mason, George E. Owen, Jr., J. Harold Draper, Myron Osth, Carol Osth Doumas. Some of these memorials went toward beach benches and wooden trash containers; others toward trees at the entrance.

Not exactly a memorial, but pine trees in Circle are from Mrs. Bishop and Jeanne DeLamarter Anderson, bought with Patter money.

Thanks to Ginny Coleman, the story behind the anchor in the Circle can be told. Sometime around 1927, Ginny's father, Ernest Melchert, found the anchor and a ship lying on its side in front of the Kavanaugh's cottage (#51). Either the ship had been uncovered by the waves or during the construction of a seawall. The conjecture is that the ship dated to the lumbering days when the two Paulville Piers ran out into the Lake at about this area. Probably it had gone down in a storm. At any rate, Mr. Melchert claimed the anchor and took it to his cottage. Mr. Quick, believing the anchor belonged to the Park, had other ideas about where it belonged, however; he "rescued" the anchor from the Melcherts and put it in the Circle for all to admire. Not to be daunted, Mr. Melchert "kidnapped" it back and chained it securely at his cottage. There it remained until the late 80's.

In 1988, the son of Ginny and her husband Randy Coleman, Randolph Buck Coleman, was killed in a tragic bicycling accident. In Bucky's memory, the Colemans moved the anchor back to the Circle where it stands as a tribute to the shortened life of this well-loved Palisades Parker.

*Spectators at baseball field enjoy bench in memory of Jack Mathias.*

# Pal-Hill Sailing Races

By Bill Potter

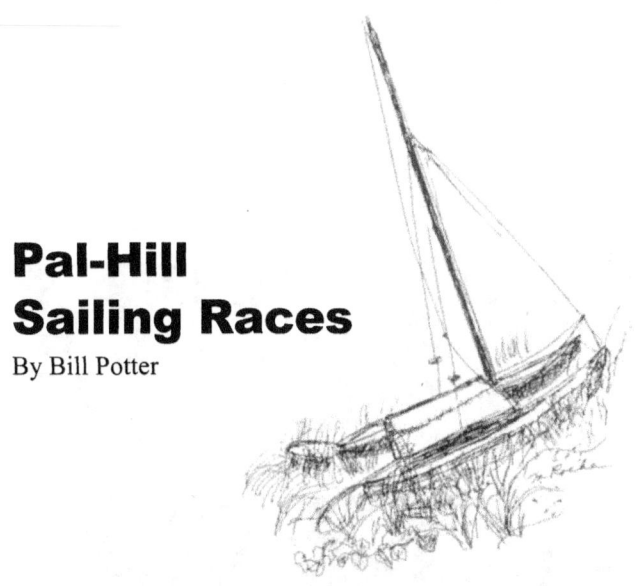

The earliest Palisades beach boats were canvas-covered canoes and wooden rowboats that could be dragged and safely stored on the beach at day's end. Almost immediately, some of these craft were rigged for sailing, with improvised masts for sails, removable side-boards for stability, and paddles or rudders for steering. But most craft were one-of-a-kind, which – other than "my boat can beat your boat" – left little room for a real race between identical craft. This changed in the 1950's when aluminum and fiberglass became the hull materials of choice.

The molded fiberglass single-person Sailfish hull was introduced as a "beach-type" sailboat. Similar sailboats in size and sail area - the Porpoise, Firebird, and Super Sailfish – also appeared. Soon, an improved two-person Sunfish hull was also introduced, and Sunfish sailboats blossomed all over Palisades and Linden Hills beaches. Some twin-hulled catamarans, like Hobie Cat, also appeared on the scene; their larger sail area led to breath-taking speed. However, higher initial cost, lack of size uniformity, heavier weight, and difficulty in beaching and storage kept their numbers small and prevented "class boat" sailing.

By the early 1960's, impromptu race challenges were happening between PPCC and Linden Hills Sunfish owners. This led to the formation of a Labor Day weekend Regatta. The Linden Hills – A History of Covert Resort Association of 1979 describes this beginning: "Finally, on September 5, 1964, the First Annual Pal-Hill Regatta was held with races for junior boys, junior girls, women, and men. Trophies were awarded to the winners and ribbons to the second and third place finishers, as well as a traveling trophy to the winner of the men's race. During the first few years, several different volunteers bought the trophies and the refreshments. The refreshments were free to all spectators and to our guests from Palisades Park."

---

**Regatta Competition**

**Boat Class**

Up to 75 square feet of sail area (Sunfish were just that).

**Course**

Triangular, about one mile long, with two starting buoys about 100 feet apart some 300 feet off shore. The race went south to 1st buoy, then northwest to 2nd buoy, northeast to 3rd, back south to finish between the two starting buoys.

**Races**

1. Men's 1st heat
2. Boys
3. Girls
4. Men's 2nd heat
5. Women
6. Men's 3rd heat
7. Trophy and ribbon presentation

**Some Rules**

Crossing start line ahead of horn blast – turn around and start over.
Touching a course buoy – turn around the buoy and try again.
Disqualifiers: touching another boat while overtaking it or failure to give right-of-way.

---

Excitement ran high among both racers and spectators. On the water, racers congregated behind the starting line. At the three minute warning horn, jockeying for starting position began – at a leisurely pace. At the two minute horn, the pace picked up; still more at the one minute horn. The final 60 seconds were a frenzy of judging wind direction, boat speed, nearness to the starting buoys, boat right-of-ways, and intimidation. Adrenaline soared; many a race was won or lost at the starting line.

*Sunfish on the Linden Hills beach - impatient to get the races started. August 30, 2003.*

*Men's race, 2003.*

At the final horn blast, the race was on – in slow motion compared to the pre-start frenzy. Being distant from other boats while rounding the buoys was a major goal to minimize chances of touching the buoy or another hull. Novice sailors tended to copy the course and sail setting of the leaders, but it was often the invisible fine-tuning of the sail loft or the exact moment of changing course that made the difference in who moved ahead. On shore, as boats rounded the 3rd buoy and headed toward the finish line, spectators moved along the beach, shouting encouragement and cheering the winners. Linden Hills boaters were the permanent hosts, as their shoreline usually included some beach during years of high lake levels when waves lapped directly on Palisades sea walls.

The John Andersons lived and sailed for Linden Hills through 1966. In 1967, they moved to cottage #39 in Palisades. When sailing for Linden Hills, John recalls huddling with Ben Platt and Marsh Miller on how to beat Bill Mooney, Jr., of Palisades in the Men's Race. In 1967, John huddled with Bill Mooney on how to beat Ben Platt. John soon became unofficial "Commodore of the Palisades Park Yacht Club;" thereafter, Palisades began winning races, including the Men's Race four consecutive years, 1969 – 1972.

*Above: Bill Potter and daughter Carolyn holding all the Palisades victory trophies. September 4, 1982.*
*Below right: Men's race traveling trophy.*

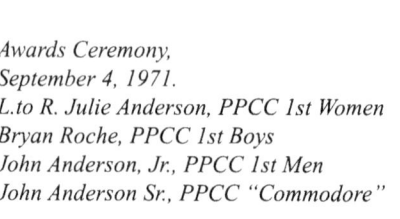

*Awards Ceremony,*
*September 4, 1971.*
*L.to R. Julie Anderson, PPCC 1st Women*
*Bryan Roche, PPCC 1st Boys*
*John Anderson, Jr., PPCC 1st Men*
*John Anderson Sr., PPCC "Commodore"*

**Palisades Winners, 1966 – 1987**

| | Girls | Boys | Women | Men |
|---|---|---|---|---|
| 1966 | 2nd Sarah Keehn<br>3rd Kathleen Roche | | | |
| 1967 | 2nd Paula Anderson | | 1st Haas Anderson | |
| 1968 | 2nd Wendy Anderson | 1st John Cordell<br>3rd Dave Cordell (tie) | 1st Julie Anderson<br>2nd Haas Anderson | 2nd John Anderson<br>3rd Bill Buick |
| 1969 | 1st Paula Anderson<br>3rd Carin Potter | 1st Dave Cordell<br>3rd Brian Roche | | 1st Bill Potter |
| 1970 | | 2nd Dave Cordell<br>3rd John Cordell | | 1st Bill Potter<br>3rd Claude Welles, Jr. |
| 1971 | | 1st Brian Roche (tie) | 1st Julie Anderson | 1st John Anderson, Sr.<br>3rd Bob Kellet |
| 1972 | | 1st Rick Venner<br>3rd Steve Keehn | 1st Paula Anderson<br>3rd Inger Kirsten (tie) | 1st John Anderson, Jr. |
| 1973 | 3rd Gretchen Potter | 2nd Rick Venner | | 2nd Dave Cordell |
| 1974 | | | 2nd Barb Bauman | 2nd John Anderson |
| 1977 | | 2nd Bruce Beyer (tie) | 3rd Haas Anderson | 1st Rick Venner<br>2nd Dave Cordell |
| 1978 | | | 3rd Jerry Suarez | |
| 1979 | | 2nd Bill Kleb | 2nd Gretchen Potter | 3rd Bill Potter |
| 1980 | | 2nd Bill Kleb | | 3rd Bill Potter |
| 1981 | | 2nd Bill Kleb (tie) | | 1st Rick Venner |
| 1982 | | 1st Bill Kleb | 1st Carolyn Potter | 1st Bill Potter<br>3rd Rob Venner |
| 1983 | | | | 2nd Bill Potter (tie) |
| 1987 | | | | 2nd Bill Kleb |

The high lake levels of 1975 – 1976 and 1984 – 1986 "grounded" the Palisades contenders, as there were no beaches and, thus, no places to store sail boats. Andersons moved away in 1980 and the Park lost its "Commodore." Interest waned and Palisades Parkers did not contend after 1987, although Linden Hills continued the Regatta each Labor Day weekend. However, 2003 brought a sudden flicker of renewed interest in the Regatta. Bill Potter and his daughter Carolyn Thompson, as the lone entrants from Palisades, attempted to topple the supremacy of Linden Hills. It was a clear and windy day, almost too windy for some sailors. Alas, hopes for victory were soon dashed, as boats collided and capsized in the chaos of starting. Clearly, the time has arrived for a younger generation to hone their sailing skills, challenge the "Hill People," and restore the honor and glory of Palisades!

# A Toast To Summer Romance

Summer romance has always been celebrated, whether by teenage magazines, standup comedians, or dime novels. Palisades Park has had, one supposes, more than its share. For vacationers of all ages and throughout the decades, summer has meant "love is in the air." Jack Gardner proposed to Jane Kipp on the Kipp cottage's front porch; Andy Patterson to Doris Butcher on the beach; Lou Goscinski to Donna Henkel at the water tower – and on and on. The Park even produced a two generation wedding family when Ray Lewis, Jr. and Lisa Henry married, having met in the Park, just as did Ray's parents, Ray, Sr. and Nanette Lewis.

The August 18, 1982 <u>Patter</u> celebrated the marriages of couples who had met here in the Park. That article got us to thinking. Besides the couples mentioned above, our still-incomplete-no-doubt list of such couples includes Mary and Hoddy Clark (previous owners of Reed's cottage #148), Julie and John Mathias, Connie Lowrey and Bob Borchert, Mary Jo and Bill Carr, Marti and Bill De Butts, Ginny Melchert and Randy Coleman, Jeanne DeLamarter and Carl Anderson, Joan Glasner and Joe Stewart, Weensie Lowrey and George Bishop, Ro Schlacks and Rich Hohman, Lori and Phil Dillman, Betty Boyles and Jack Stott, Jane Trumbull and Scott Henkel, Dorothy Coates and Gordon MacQuaker, Colleen Roche and Bob Schlacks, Kittie Wissom and Arthur Quick, Nancy Seymour and Bob Butcher, Ruth Klunder and Dan Butcher, and Kim Buchanan and Bruce Rakowski.

These editors could not take on the daunting task of chronicling all such romances – be they faded or blooming – but we do want to give the subject of summer love its due. Consequently, we have chosen to celebrate, in pictorial form, a much more manageable list of Park weddings. Even here, we know our photos are incomplete. However, we trust you will agree, based on the evidence we have discovered, that Palisades affords a picture-perfect setting for many different kinds of wedding ceremonies.

*Above: Doris Butcher and Andy Patterson in the Butcher cottage. 1954.*
*Top right: Jenny Mailander and Jerry Foust on beach by King cottage. 2001*
*Right: Stephanie Trece and Jeff Ebert on Circle Beach. 2002.*

A WEDDING AT PALISADES PARK
From July 1, 1964 Patter

On Saturday, June 13, Anne Light, daughter of Ralph and Virginia Wenham, was married to Tom Siegler at the Trinity Lutheran Church in St. Joseph, at 4:00 p.m. Following the ceremony, a reception was held at Sturtevant Lodge where about 150 friends gathered to congratulate the young couple. The dining room was beautifully decorated and the colorful punch bowls were kept very busy. Later on, an elaborate buffet table was arranged and the guests enjoyed a bountiful and delicious feast which had been prepared by Mrs. Wenham and the famous Melzara.

## Palisades Park Weddings

*Counter-clockwise starting at top:*
*Jane Trumbull and Scott Henkel and*
*wedding party on Village Green. 1981.*
*Chairs for Ebert wedding at Circle Beach. 2001.*
*Kandra Riddle and Chris Kolehmainen*
*toasting on the beach. 1994.*
*Lisa Henry and Ray Lewis arrive at*
*Village Green Reception. 1994*
*Jessa Kolehmainen and Chris Zimmerman in*
*Clubhouse. 1991.*
*Mary Lynne and Bob Hladik's flowers waiting*
*to decorate the Clubhouse.*

*Right Column starting at top:*
*Kandra Riddle and attendants on Palisades road. 1994.*
*Bob and Mary Lynne Hladik attended by Mary Jo Carr. Clubhouse.*
*Frannie Roche and Michael Mitrano on walkway. 1998.*

*Left Column starting at top:*
*Village Green awaiting Trumbull/Henkel reception. 1981.*
*Kari Heavrin Donavan and friend celebrate on beach. 1996.*
*Armin Beck and Katy Beatty with their parents, at Clubhouse. 1955.*
*Center: Annie Owen and David Bartley at Clubhouse. 1993.*

*Clockwise from top:*
*Kimeri Swanson and Tom Beck beside the Beck cottage. 1989.*
*Andrew and Jacqueline Schlacks on beach. 2003.*
*Carolyn O'Connor and Peter Ferry in reception line at Ferry cottage. 1999.*
*Jamie Williams and Charles Sloan at the Brandywine. 2001.*
*Frannie Roche and Michael Mitrani on Brandywine Bridge. 1998.*

### Children's smiles never change.

*Top: unidentified girls in 1900.*
*Left top: Anna and Marilyn Goscinski and Steve Rakowski. 2002.*
*Left bottom: Chester Beck, Miles Henkel and Theo Beck. 2002.*
*Below: Norma Jordan, 1927.*

# Chapter 7

# Lake Michigan
## Our Untamed Treasure

# Lake Michigan
# Our Untamed Treasure

Cottages in the woods, meadows, tennis courts, a Soda Bar – indeed, much of what we love at Palisades – could be found in other locations. One thing makes *this* location unique - being on the shores of Lake Michigan. That is what gives us our dunes; that is what gives us our beach; that is what gives us our sunsets. Who can return from a walk along the edge of the water and not feel refreshed? Who can enjoy the waves on a windy day and not feel exhilarated? Who can watch the sky as night falls over the lake and not feel a sense of wonder? "Great" in name and in reality, Lake Michigan provides a magical setting for our beloved Park.

And yet, there is another side to the story. A love affair with Lake Michigan is not always an easy relationship. The lake has its ups and downs - quite literally - and our beaches come and go. The fury of its storms has cost us several million dollars in bluff and cottage protection. Sometimes, inexplicably, unwanted visitors - like alewives or zebra mussels - litter our shores.

Bill Potter has gathered pictures and information to highlight our history on the shores of Lake Michgan. Some of that history has been happy; some quite the opposite. We think you will agree it is a tale worth telling.

# The Beach

### In Spring

*Sprouts of dune grass shadow the beach.*

### In Summer

*Mrs. Chatfield and the Welles family c. 1925.*

### In Fall

*Gone to seed: October*

### In Winter

*A cold beach south of South Haven c. 1912.*

# The Beach, A Place For ...

## Infants Children

*Kay Goff, Nancy Potter, and Goff, Potter, and Sturgeon kids. July 1959.*

Sunshine,
sandy diapers,
sand in the mouth,
sand in the ears,
sand between the toes

Sand buckets,
sand castles, sun lotion,
sea gulls, sand pipers, swim races,
stone skipping, picnics, sandy hot dogs,
sandy marshmallows.

*Donna Goscinski and son James, taking a break.*

*Sam and Jim Beatty.*

# The Beach, A Place For ...

## Teens and Young in Heart

*Left: North Beach, Aug. 2001.*

*Above: South Haven's North Beach. c. 1913.*

*Right: Connie and Weensie Lowery. 1939.*

*Left: Katy Beatty and Dee Prange with group of youngsters.*

# The Beach, A Place for ...

## Young Adults

Beach umbrellas, coolers, sandy diapers, sand buckets, sand castles, sun lotion, seagulls, sand pipers, beach picnics, sandy hot dogs, sandy marshmallows, sunsets.

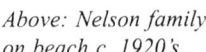

*Below: A stroll on the beach. 1913.*

*Above: Nelson family on beach c. 1920's.*

## From A Gift From the Sea
## by Anne Morrow Lindberg
In June 16, 1975 Patter

The beach is not a place to work; to read, write, or think. I should have remembered that from other years. Too warm, too damp, too soft for any real mental discipline or sharp flights of spirit ....

Rollers on the beach, wind in the pines, the slow flapping of herons across sand dunes drown out the hectic rhythms of city and suburb, time tables and schedules. One falls under their spell, relaxes, stretches out prone. One becomes, in fact, like the element on which one lies, flattened by the sea; bare, open, empty as the beach, erased by today's tides of all yesterday's scribblings ....

The sea does not reward those who are too anxious, too greedy, or too impatient. To dig for treasures shows not only impatience and greed, but lack of faith. Patience, patience, patience is what the sea teaches. Patience and faith. One should lie empty, open, choiceless as a beach - waiting for a gift from the sea.

*Below: A beach picnic in front of Sundune #176. Don and Marilyn Henkel with Henkel and Beck children. August 1967.*

# The Beach, A Place For ...

## **Empty Nesters**

Beach umbrellas, coolers, conversation, reading, cards, boat launchings, boat landings, beach walks, beach combing, snoozing, sunsets.

*Beach comber c. 1930*

*Robert Beatty in his old rowboat with tar bottom. 1946.*

*Roy and Zula McWethy and unknown couple by Cottage #7. 1930s.*

# The Beach, A Place For ...

## Grandparents

Beach viewing, beach walking, beach combing, beach sunsets, more snoozing.

*Genteel Harold VanBueren on beach by Anchorfast #43. Harding cottage in background. c. 1927.*

*Bill Eldredge, Sr. (in his 90's) at right, and George Potter (in his 80's) sitting on the bench of Juniper Pass - a picture of serenity and shared love for Palisades. September 1, 1969.*

# And, Unfortunately, A Place For ...

## Alewives and Other Invaders

The headlines read: ***Dead Fish Clog the Shore*** and ***Billions of Alewives Attack Our Shore.*** Perhaps the second is the most accurate – it seemed like an attack. In the mid-60's and several times over the years since, these small silver fish died and washed up on our shore by the thousands in June or July. Our beaches and others clear around the southern periphery of Lake Michigan became smelly battle grounds. Possibly connected to the demise of the hungry lake trout – or the temperature of the water – the alewives had arrived through the St. Lawrence Seaway and quickly became a huge percentage of the bulk of fish in the lake. The mystery as to why they die off every few years has yet to be solved.

The August 10, 1965 Patter discussed this mystery in an article written by Frederick Graves which appeared in The Chicago Sun Times, July 13, 1965, entitled **"The Lake's Yearly Fish Death Mystery."**

> To paraphrase the poem "Who Killed Cock Robin," - "What killed the alewives?"
> Alewives are silvery fish, usually 7 to 10 inches long, that are related to the herring family. Each year in June and July they die by the thousands and are washed up on Chicago area beaches. The smell takes a lot of the joy out of swimming.
>
> The exact reason for the death of these fish has not been determined, although there are several theories. The most accepted is that the alewives are not able to adjust to the temperature changes that occur as the water rises from a cool-and-comfortable 65 degrees to anything over 68 degrees. A second theory is that there is a poisonous plant in Great Lakes waters that causes the death of the fish. A third theory is that the water is polluted.
>
> The alewife is a native of the Atlantic Ocean that made its way to the Great Lakes through the St. Lawrence Seaway. It was first noted in northern Michigan in 1949. By 1954, it was abundant in the lower lake region.
>
> In addition to discouraging swimmers, the presence of the alewife causes a problem for Chicago Park District. It reported that last year more than 80 truckloads of the dead fish were cleared off city beaches by daily clean-up crews. With two strikes already against it, the alewife managed to get a third – it clogs up the water crib intakes at filtration plants.
>
> The alewife has one enemy – the lake trout. But the trout has been decimated by the lamprey eel. So until the lamprey is disposed of – which will take about another two years, according to the Bureau of Commercial Fisheries in Ann Arbor, Michigan – the trout will not overwhelm the alewife.

Perhaps the worst season for alewives at Palisades was in 1967. A bulldozer was hired to dig deep trenches on the beach at several hundred foot intervals. Tens of thousands of maggoted rotting fish that had been raked and shoveled into piles were gathered and dumped into the trenches and covered with sand. Despite everyone's best efforts, 1967 was an "off" summer for the beach. Not many people wanted to serve fish for supper that summer, either.

The alewife problem, though most severe in the 60's, has continued through the years. The lamprey eel was, indeed, controlled so that lake trout could return to the Lake. The coho salmon was sucessfully introduced to Lake Michigan and it, too, preyed on the alewife. Yet as recently as 1998 alewives littered the beaches of Palisades. Why? No one is quite sure.

## Zebra Mussels

Another foreign species which arrived in Lake Michigan in the 1980's is the zebra mussel. It has been causing havoc ever since. Eating tiny shrimplike creatures called "diporeia," the zebra mussels are upsetting the food chain in the lake. Scientists believe the diporeia are part of the diet of many kinds of fish in Lake Michigan. Scientists are studying the effects of the disappearance of this important food substance. The zebra mussels are also responsible for clogging the water intake systems all up and down the lakeshore – a recurring and expensive problem. Finally, they seem to be connected to a very pretty change in the color of the water. This, at first glance would seem benign, but scientists warn that though the filtered water looks pretty, its clarity is affecting the growth of plant life in the lake – again causing a basic change in the ecosystem. Mussel shells collect on the beaches after each storm; their edges are sharp on bare feet. Not as nasty as the alewives, they are nonetheless harbingers of future problems.

## Beach Trash

Our beaches are sometimes under siege from careless people. Cans, bottle caps, bottles, broken glass, cartons, wrappers, cigarette butts, litter, hot embers, abandoned fires – all are found all too often. Careless, thoughtless beach-goers of all ages – will they ever find the trash barrels, only a few feet away? In the summer of 2001, 19 stitches were required on a young lad's bleeding foot – cut on a broken glass bottle.

## Sand Puzzles and Little Monsters:
"Mysteries of the Beach"
July 8, 2002 Newsweek

Scientists are always telling us about things we can't possibly understand ('dark matter,' anyone?). So why can't they explain everyday things? Consider the sand under your toes. Each grain is shaped slightly differently. Put thousands, millions, billions of them together and they jostle and bump with unspeakable complexity. Ever notice how a pile of sand tends to 'avalanche' until it attains a certain slope, which is always the same? Know why? Neither does anybody else.

> Once the beach could have been called the Palisades Park Speedway. Cars, Jeeps, and motorcycles driven by "outsiders" were less than welcome as Palisades beach visitors. They entered at Van Buren State Park and many rode fast on the hard sand by water's edge. Some sank to their axles trying to cross Brandywine Creek. Construction of Consumer's Power Plant in 1968 blocked and ended the sport.

## DOGS ON THE BEACH

High on the list of annual problems that come up for discussion every summer is that of dogs on the beach. The rules say **"No Dogs Allowed."** However, the reality is that owners often want Fido to enjoy a romp on the beach. Some people take offense, complaining that children are frightened and dog owners often do not clean up properly after their pets. Linden Hills, our neighbor, allows pets on the beach early in the morning and late in the evening. Some think that is a good plan. However, at this writing, though the issue has been addressed over and over, no solution has been suggested for Palisades.

The more experiments physicists do, the less sand conforms to their expectations. Here's a cutting-edge problem: make one pile of sand with a funnel and another with a sieve. They look almost identical, but they aren't. The pile formed by the funnel has less weight at its center than its edges. The sieve distributes the weight uniformly, mystifying scientists.

Each time your foot sinks into the sand, you're squashing perhaps 30,000 animals. They'd scare your pants off – if only you could see them. Many look like worms or shrimp, but most resemble nothing else on this planet. Tiny Loricifera has two legs, a hairy mouth and a springlike body. It hides in its shell until a bacterium wanders by, then pops up and snatches it. Tardigrade, also called 'water bear,' has eight legs and sticky pads that cling to dead plants in the sand.

These beasts, called meiofauna, are the smallest of multicellular organisms, about the size of a (single-celled) ameba. They live anywhere there's sand and water. Amazingly, there are as many different species of meiofauna – about 3 million – as of all other earthly creatures combined, says biologist Paul Montagne of the University of Texas. Scientists suspect the creatures form a crucial link in the food chain, but they're only beginning to find out what that might be, and why there are so many different kinds.

## Beachcombers
By Anne Fuller
From August 13, 1966 Patter

Palisades Park is producing a host of curved-backed beachcombers and some are in danger of developing crinoiditis. There are at least two ways of classifying beachcombers: by collecting technique and by selective tastes. There are three breeds according to collecting technique: those who sit and sift, those who walk erect and challenge their bifocals, and finally the curved-backed species who roam the wave margin in a perpetual stoop.

One hesitates to say how many categories we have according to selective taste. There are those who specialize in etched glass. Mrs. Ward Harris has two huge jugs full, which catch the sunlight on her patio. ... Some use it in designs with grout on tabletops ... (or for) a beautiful mobile. We've heard of one collector who is using it for a translucent wall. Dunewind shows its possibilities in a decorative cottage sign. ...

Then there are those who collect beach stones, any stones as long as they are pretty. I am in this class. I climb the hill with pockets and beach bag laden with loot. But it soon dries and the bright colors are lost. It lies around a day or two and then is dumped to make room for the next load. Mrs. Mae Sankey used to line her patio wall with stones and kept a sprinkling can handy to water them before guests arrived.

We interviewed Frank H. Demski, Jr. at VerDunk's Paint Store in South Haven about keeping the shine on our stones. He and his father use a motor-driven tumbler to polish beach stones as well as imported gem stones for jewelry which they sell. He cautions that the tumbler must rotate very slowly for five or six weeks…. However, he recommended an inexpensive substitute for the tumbler. Simply soak your stones in a metal container with mineral oil, linseed oil, motor oil, or what have you, keeping the container setting in the sun for several weeks until the stones have soaked up as much of the oil as they will take. Then coat with nail polish, lacquer, or clear varnish. Or, if you need more activity, buy a couple of grades of emery cloth from Mr. Demski and polish while you watch TV.

But to get back to tastes in beachcombing, we mustn't forget the driftwood fanciers. If there is anyone in the Park who can advise on the care and nurture of driftwood, the Patter editor would appreciate an article. Have you seen the beautiful driftwood specimen on the outside wall of the Peat cottage (#27)?

And then there are the fossil hunters. Some spurn all but Petoskey stones, so called because they are especially abundant in the limestone quarries near Petoskey. Mr. Demski has a beautiful specimen on display. They are a species of colonial coral, which lived in the warm seas of this area in the Devonian period some 300 million years ago. Other colonial corals found on our beach are honeycomb coral and chain coral, and there is also a horn coral made by a solitary coral animal. Mrs. Don Marshall picked up a fossil horn coral last week in front of Broadview (#93) beautiful enough for a ring setting without any polishing.

But it's the crinoid hunters who are most in danger of developing crinoiditis. Crinoids or sea lilies are animals related to starfish but they look like a flower on top of a segmented stem. The mouth of the animal is in the center of the flower with a circlet of waving arms to pull in food. Arm and stem are encased in a segmented limestone skeleton - which breaks up into the circular disks, like doughnuts. Legend has it that these holed disks were the wampum of the early Michigan Indians. Mrs. John Gardner has a string of wampum dating from probably 40 years of beach combing. But the prize for crinoid collecting the last three years goes to Mr. Fitzgerald of Fitz-Inn. Of course he bribed all the great nephews and nieces and neighborhood kids to collect for him.

*Barbara Beck collecting rocks. June 1974.*

... When I do get to steal a few days away and head from the lake, I revel in the beauty of nature, the sunsets and the ribbons of beach. However, my mind always seems to wander back to reality, to what I have to do in the "real world." When I was a child, the greatest care I had was whether my sand castle would be there the next day, or be washed away with the tide. I lived for the moment, from adventure to adventure. As I have gotten older, I have grown envious of the little children I see playing on the beach. I want to go up and whisper in their ears and urge them to enjoy their innocent and carefree days, for with their sand castles, their carefree youth will be washed away someday.

*Written while Katie was in college. She is now married to Paul Filbin and building sand castles with her own three young children, Maeve, Owen, and Emmet.*

## Sand Castles Washed Away

Excerpt from paper by Katie Foster, February 27, 1990

... As I have gotten older, I have noticed that the Park has changed. The Soda Bar has been remodeled; Pac-Man has replaced the pinball machines and Madonna outplays American Pie. You can still get a Green River, but it somehow doesn't taste the same. The lake has risen and taken over much of the beach, and the family that used to run the general store has all married and only visits on weekends with their own children....

# The Lure of Warm Sand ...

*Above: A quartet of sunbathers;*
*Right: Girls digging in the sand,;*
*Right below: Couple playing chess on beach.*
*Below: Bill Henkel and Tom Beck*
*ready to have an adventure in the dunes*
*with their "snurf boards" c. 1972.*

# Ever Changing Lake Levels

By Bill Potter

Our beaches come and go. Some years they are wonderfully wide; some years they are buried under water. Lake Michigan calm water levels have varied from an all-time low of 576.4 feet in March, 1964, to an all-time high of 582.4 feet in October, 1986 – a difference of six feet. The newcomer to Palisades may well ask, "Why?"

## Long Term Changes

The U. S. Army Corps of Engineers' chart below illustrates calm lake levels over the past 85 years. Two primary influences determine lake levels – which in turn determine whether or not we will have a wide beach, or any beach at all:

1. Precipitation in the collective Lake Superior, Lake Huron, and Lake Michigan drainage basins over a period of years.

2. Evaporation rate from the three lakes, which depends on lake surface temperature, air temperature, and humidity.

Thus, consecutive cloudless drought years, which decrease precipitation runoff into the lakes, and direct sunshine, which increases lake water temperature and evaporation rate, both result in a lowering of lake levels. This happened in the mid 1920's, most of the 1930's to mid 1940's, late 1950's to mid 1960's, and – most recently – since 1999.

Conversely, consecutive wet, cloudy years increase lake levels, as in the late 1940's to mid 1950's and much of the 1970's and 1980's. All this is beyond man's control.

The effect of long term lake level changes on the width of our beaches is dramatic, a story best told with the series of pictures following. Although these pictures only illustrate changes in the Clubhouse and Brandywine Beaches, all of Palisades feel the effects. Sometimes our beaches are wide and wonderful; sometimes they are so-so; sometimes they are completely flooded. Although there is occasional talk of a 20-year (or some other) cycle, the reality is that no one can predict when the swing from high to low will take place.

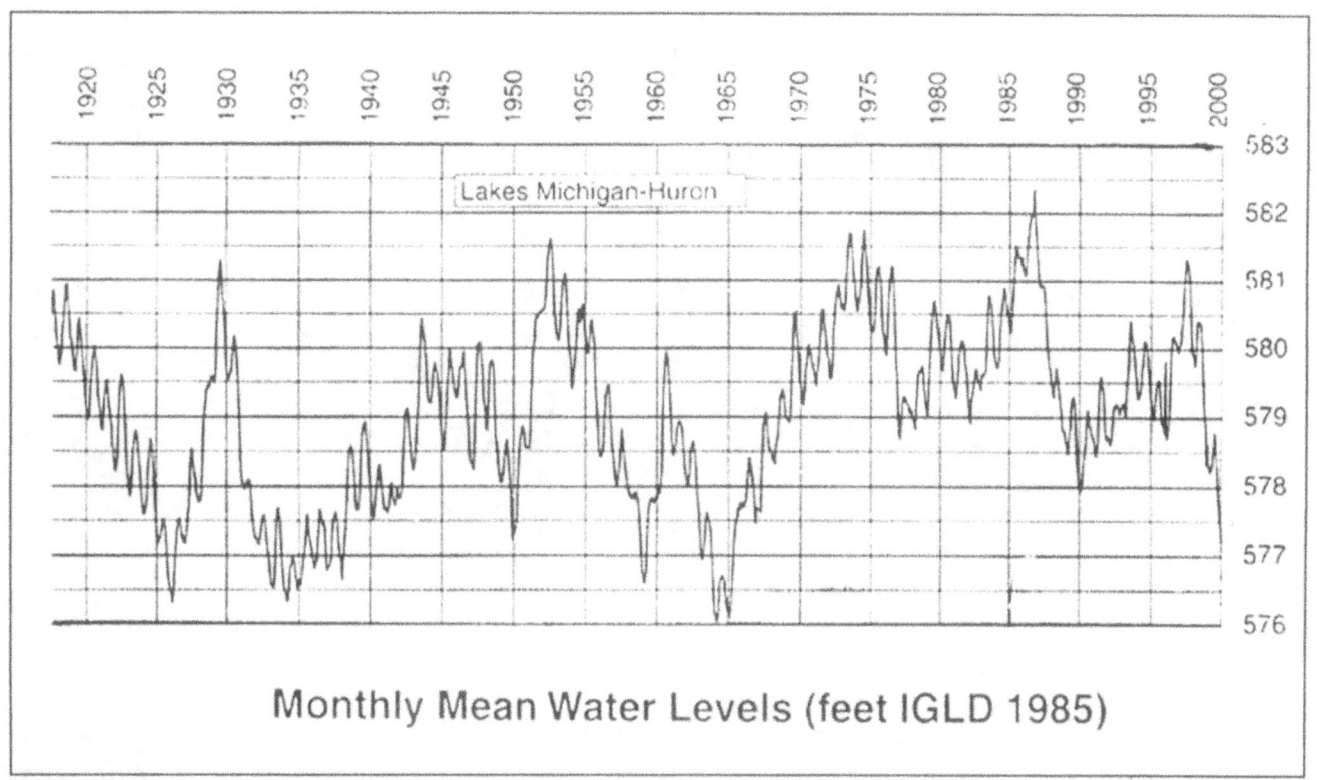

Monthly Mean Water Levels (feet IGLD 1985)

# Clubhouse Beach

*No beach. August 1984.*
*High lake level 580'11"*

*(Below) A bit of beach.*
*July 1993.*
*A bit lower level 580'4"*

*Above: More beach July 1982.   Medium level 579'8"*

*Below: Magnificent beach July 2000.   Low level 578'9"*

## **Brandywine Beach**

*September 3, 1973.*
*Near all-time high lake level, 581'6"*
*Beach covered with water almost back to Brandywine Bridge.*

*October 15, 1977.*
*Medium lake level, 579'1"*
*Water level receding and beach reappearing.*

*July 27, 2001.*
*Low lake level, 577'9"*
*Mammoth beach.*
*Cottage #190 in background.*

## Seasonal Changes

Seasonal variations of one to two feet each year result in lowest water levels and widest beaches in February and March. Highest levels and narrowest beaches usually come in July and August. This variation results from three sources.

1. Evaporation rates are highest in the fall when lake temperature is warmest and the air humidity is dry. Occasionally, during a clear, calm, cool and dry fall morning, it is possible to actually see the evaporating moisture rising from the lake surface. During the frozen winter months, snow accumulation and water runoff into the lakes is considerably reduced. Lake levels continue to drop.

2. Spring thaw water runoff from accumulated winter precipitation, together with spring rains, cause the lake level to rise one to two feet in just three or four months.

3. Seasonal outflow control from Lake Superior to Lakes Huron and Michigan, at St. Mary's River near the Soo Locks, usually amounts to a few inches of change. This is regulated by the International Joint Commission (IJC) of the United States and Canada.

## Short Term Changes

Short term lake level changes, measured in hours or days, are usually minor. However, occasionally they turn violent, and level changes of four feet have been recorded as recently as 1985. These include:

1. On Lake Michigan, twice daily lunar tides, of 1/2 to 1 1/2 inches, are usually masked completely by wind and waves.

2. Storm surges from strong sustained north winds, pushing water over a 200 mile fetch from northern to southern Lake Michigan, can increase south lake levels one to two feet over a period of hours. They may also produce a drop if the strong winds blow from the southeast. The August, 1984 Patter (and reprinted in the August 29, 1986 edition) included this short explanation of the storm effects on water levels:

   Winds, particularly of storm velocity, and sharp gradients in barometric pressure have pronounced effects on lake levels and can cause a wide range of fluctuations. As wind blows over the surface of a lake, it creates a "stress" on the surface water particles, and starts these particles moving in the direction in which the wind is blowing. Thus, a

---

*U. S. Army Corps of Engineers Monthly Bulletin of Lake Levels – October 2002*
*Water levels for the previous year and the current year to date are shown as a solid line on the hydrographs. A projection for the next six months is given as a dashed line. This projection is based on the present condition of the lake basin and anticipated future weather. The shaded area shows a range of possible levels over the next six months dependent upon weather variations. Current and projected levels (solid and dashed lines) can be compared with the 1918-2001 average levels (dotted lines) and extreme levels (shown as bars with their year of occurrence).*

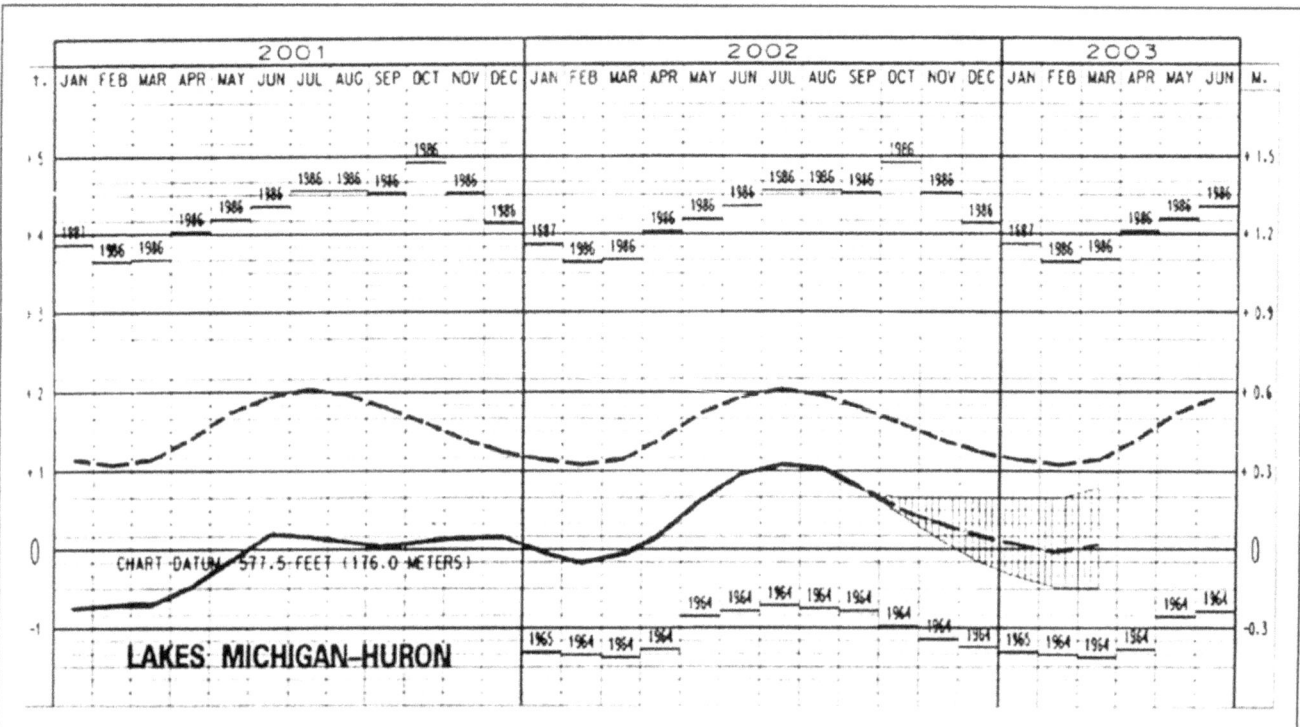

surface current is created causing an unbalancing or tilting of the lake surface as shown in the chart below. For a severe storm, the temporary rise at a particular locality may be two or three feet above the monthly average lake level for the larger deeper lakes (such as Lake Michigan). *From the Michigan Department of Natural Resources booklet, "A Plan for Michigan's Shorelands," 1973.*

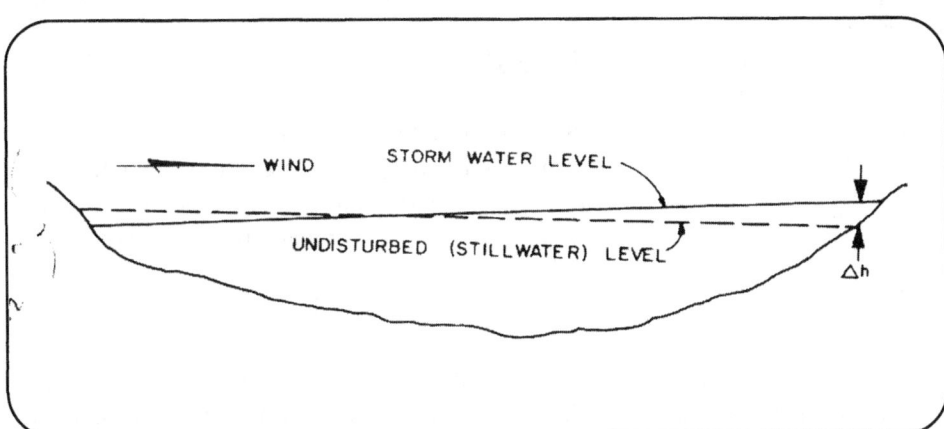

3. A seiche, caused by differences in atmospheric barometric pressure between the Wisconsin and Michigan sides of the lake, can set up an oscillation movement of lake surface water. Normally, seiches affect lake level by only a few inches and are indiscernible due to wind and waves. Yet, on a calm day, a shallow sand bar can – in a matter of minutes – become uncovered, stay that way for several minutes, then rapidly be covered again. The oscillation of lake level continues, moving from the Michigan shore to the Wisconsin side and back again, increasing or decreasing in amplitude, depending on increase or decrease in the barometric pressure differences.

Palisades experienced a devastating seiche during the storm of Sunday, December 1, 1985. Don Beveridge, who was Park President at the time, described this rare event in his December 16, 1985 letter to Park members:

> Besides the near all-time-high lake level and strong winds which whipped up 20 foot waves, another factor was at work. This was a freak, once-in-a-century condition when the atmospheric pressure on the Michigan side was a very low 28 inches of mercury, while on the Wisconsin side it was 31 inches. This caused the water in the lake to rise on the Michigan side by an average of four feet. Thus the water was forced above the top level of the seawalls in most places, even before the incredible waves were taken into account.

The resulting damage was extensive and costly.

Perhaps the "Grand-daddy" of all seiches in this area occurred when Palisades was only a few years old. It was May 6, 1909, when a seiche reported to be ten to twenty feet high swept into South Haven, sending small craft up on the river flats and destroying the bath houses on the beach. If another one like this arrives at the Park during the summer boating and swimming season – WOE!

*Devastation caused by 1909 seiche in South Haven.*

The South Haven Tribune told the story as "**The Day the Big Wave Rolled In,**" by Kristin Hay:

> Cassius Edgertop peered out from his lookout tower the night of May 6, 1909, and saw a wave as high as the station sweeping towards the shore. A flash of lightning illumined the big wave as it rolled relentlessly towards South Haven's waterfront. The wave was eight feet high cresting two feet above the South Haven Pier. When it hit the shoreline, the crushing wave carried off bath houses and cottages and ripped boats from their moorings all along the Black River to the Dyckman Bridge.
>
> The Tribune Messenger, the local newspaper at the time, called it a "tidal wave," but it was actually a seiche. The attraction of the sun and the moon, which causes the tide on oceans, does not affect lakes. A seiche on a lake is usually caused by high winds, small earthquakes, or changes in atmospheric pressure.
>
> "The buildings along the north bank at the foot of Black River Street were shuffled up and redealt along the marsh," the newspaper account says.
>
> One man whose house was engulfed by the wave lit a lantern and signaled for help. The life saving crew rescued him by boat. His house was carried almost 400 feet by the rushing water from its original location. The lifesavers were busy all night rescuing boats sent adrift.
>
> "The big wave caught up the heavy life car of the life saving crew and tossed it like a cork, carrying it into the launchway and out into the lake. Guided by flashes of lightning, three crew members retrieved the life car, catching up with it a half mile out in the lake," says the newspaper account of the disaster.
>
> Fortunately, no one died. At the time, the storm was one of the most severe and destructive in South Haven's history. No single wave has equaled it in size or destructiveness since that night when Cassius Edgerton spied the wall of water rushing towards the sleeping lakefront town.

## Lake Level and Beach Width Summary

**High level**   Approximately 580'6" and above.

Virtually all of our beaches are flooded and disappear.

**Mid level**   Approximately 578' to 580'6".

Most lake front property beaches in front of the seawalls, from Brandywine Creek to south of the Clubhouse, are still covered with water. The Clubhouse, Brandywine, and North Beaches reappear and are useable.

**Low level**   Approximately 576' to 578'.

Just about all lake front property has some beach, even where sea walls have been built well forward towards the water, as from Brandywine Creek south to the Clubhouse Beach. The Park community beaches are extremely wide.

Ross Kittleman, Army Corps of Engineers, Grand Haven, MI, expressed it another way – that for every foot of lake level rise, about 20 feet of beach is lost (flooded) in the area of Michigan. Our experience at Palisades is more like 40 feet of Clubhouse, Brandywine, and North Beach is flooded for every foot of lake level rise – probably due to the more gentle slope of our beaches.

## Lake Level Measurement

Lake Michigan monthly average lake levels are measured at three locations: Mackinaw City and Ludington in Michigan and Milwaukee in Wisconsin. All the Great Lakes are measured against a standard datum plane elevation established at Rimouski, Quebec, on the St. Lawrence River, near the Atlantic Ocean. Periodically, this datum plane is revised to correct for the earth's crustal movement in the Great Lakes basin. A correction was made in the 1960's and adopted as the 1955 International Great Lakes Datum (1955 IGLD). More recently, effective January 1, 1992, the 1985 IGLD was adopted, which added 0.72 feet to all prior 1955 IGLD Lake Michigan readings. So it is easy to be comparing apples and oranges if one refers to one chart labeled 1955 IGLD and another labeled 1985 IGLD. To eliminate this potential confusion, all lake levels in this chapter are reported as 1985 IGLD, including all levels dating back to 1918. According to the Army Corps of Engineers, another change in IGLD should not be necessary until about 2020.

## Recent Lake Levels

On May 1, 2000, the South Haven Tribune reported that lake levels were then the lowest since 1965. Rivers needed dredging, a problem for boaters, but beautiful beaches had reappeared, a plus for sun lovers and beach walkers. By the summer of 2002, blowing sand had buried our boardwalk and 95% of Park riprap was covered also.

The Tribune article explains some of the problems accompanying what is, for the Park, a wonderful bonus:

> The Great Lakes are at the lowest water levels since 1965 and may reach new records this year unless there is an extremely wet spring and summer, according to Commerce Secretary William M. Daley and NOAA scientists. "The lakes have not been this low since March, 1965, and I'm concerned that recent growth in the Great Lakes shipping industry might evaporate with the water levels," said Daley. "The near record low lake levels hurts shipping, but recreational boaters and marina operators suffer too."
>
> According to the Lake Carriers' Association, an organization that represents 11 companies operating 60 flag vessels on the Great Lakes, the lower levels mean each vessel forfeits between 70 and 270 tons of cargo for each one inch reduction in loaded draft. The association reports a 6.5 percent decrease in shipments of iron ore, coal, and stone in 1999 compared to 1998....
>
> "Lake Michigan and Huron have set records by dropping nearly three feet in two years. While this will have major adverse impacts on commercial and recreational boating, on the plus side, there will be the biggest beaches in 35 years and considerably less erosion. However, we may be seeing some new record lows on lakes Michigan and Huron in the late fall and winter," said Frank Quinn, senior hydrologist at NOAA's Great Lakes Environmental Research Laboratory in Ann Arbor, Michigan.
>
> Lakes Michigan and Huron have experienced a drop in levels of 2.9 feet over the past two years, the largest such drop in 140 years of record. Quinn noted that the unprecedented drop in levels over the past three years ended a 30-year run of above average and high lake levels. During the summer of 1986, Lake Michigan spilled over its banks and washed some lakefront homes off of their foundations.
>
> A long-term cause of the drop in water level, according to NOAA climate experts, is that despite recent La Nina climate patterns, the region has experienced an overriding long-term warming trend, which means less ice and more evaporation in winter months. Contributing more recently are hotter temperatures and lower amounts of rainfall, said Quinn.
>
> Last winter's warmer temperatures and below average precipitation meant that there was less winter snow, which the lakes require for the normal spring lake level rise. In addition, the hotter temperature increased the lake evaporation and reduced the runoff in the tributary streams.
>
> "Many of the streams have also been at record low flows for this time of year, so not as much water is going into the lake from those sources," Quinn said.
>
> The little snow that did fall in the region melted in late February and early March and is already in the lake system. NOAA's outlooks are for normal to dry conditions this spring and summer. Since the lakes are at low levels – in the case of lakes Huron and Michigan, as much as 18 inches below average – recreational boaters may have difficulty finding docking space, especially if the craft has a deep fixed keel.

## Summary

The July, 1975 Patter contains an interesting article "explaining" lake levels. Park member George Owen had found a document in the library of the University of Illinois entitled: **An Inquiry Into the Causes of the Rise and Fall of the Lakes Embracing an Account of the Floods and Ebbs of Lake Ontario as Determined by a Long Series of Actual Observations and an Examination of the Various Opinions in Regard to the Lake Unprecedented Flood Through the Chain of Great Lakes.** (Phew!)

The book, by Edward Giddins of Lockport, NY, was written in 1838 and covered data collected by Mr. Giddins over the previous 50 years, back to 1787, far antedating the official figures later collected by the U.S. Army Corps of Enginers. Apparently, most of the present popular conceptions as to the causes of the rise and fall of the Great Lakes were also current then – and all of them of only limited use. Giddins proved that "the cyclical theory had no basis in fact." His study led him to discount such influences as precipitation, drainage, or evaporation. "**It appeared to Mr. Giddins, as it appears to many recent observers, that the changing levels of the lakes are a natural phenomenon still beyond man's complete understanding.**"

# Big Storms, Big Damage
## 1913  1929  1951-52  1969-74  1985

By Bill Potter

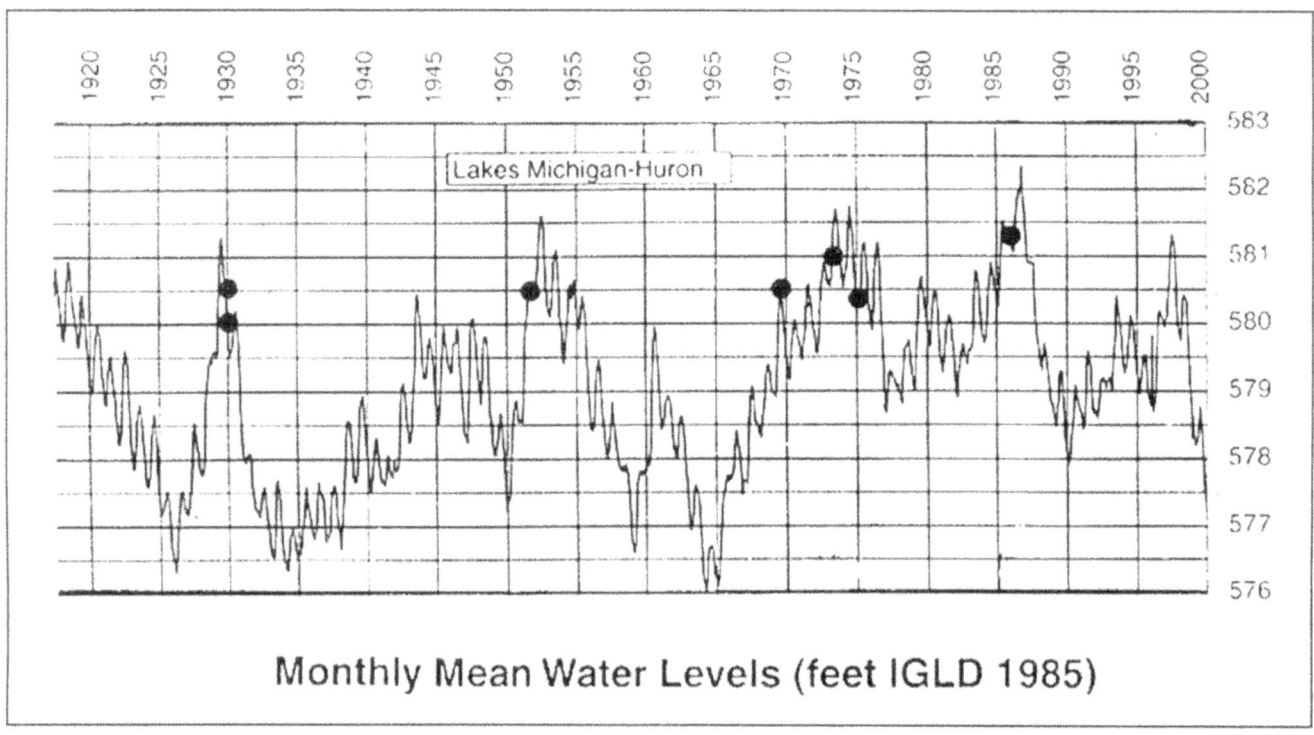

*From "Living with the Lakes"*
*U.S. Army Corps of Engineers*

There have been years that beach cottage owners would rather not remember:

**1913, 1929, 1951-52, 1969-74, and 1985.**

These were times when already high lake levels combined with "once in a decade" storms to create beachfront havoc at Palisades. On the chart above, those storms are indicated by large dots. This examines the effect of such storms on Palisades Park.

During calm weather, high water levels in themselves haven't caused shoreline damage. True, they flooded our beaches, just as a rising river floods its banks; however, add prolonged gale winds to already high lake levels, offshore waves of 14 to 20 feet, and a storm surge of up to two feet, and then both unprotected Palisades sand bluff lines and beach cottages begin to crumble.

### Sunday, November 9 to Tuesday, November 11, 1913

Lake Michigan Water Level 579'6"

This storm is not recorded on the chart above or in our local history, but on the combined Great Lakes, it was the costliest storm ever. Between 250 and 300 lives were lost; 12 major ships went to the bottom and 25 others were seriously damaged. The huge storm raged over a period of four days as it moved from Lake Superior to Lake Ontario, from Duluth, Minnesota, to Western Pennsylvania. It was the worst early November snowstorm in Cleveland's history. According to Robert Hemming, in Detroit, the barometer dipped to 28.35," the lowest ever recorded there, *

*Hemming, Robert J., Ships Gone Missing: The Great Lakes Storm of 1913, Chicago, Illinois: Contemporary Books, Inc. 1992, p.59-60.

Closer to Palisades, the storm took two days to pass through. Beginning early Sunday morning, November 9, the southerly winds abruptly changed to the northwest and within 30 minutes reached 55 mph. As morning dawned in Milwaukee, the new municipal breakwater project began to crumble from the tremendous seas. Hundreds watched in the bitter wind and cold as 1500 feet of breakwater were systematically destroyed and the floating pile drivers wrecked.

In Muskegon, factory smokestacks blew over, store windows smashed, house rooftops blew away, and debris-filled gale winds reached a reported 80 mph. Along the Chicago lakefront, Lake Shore Drive was flooded and a twelve-foot high pier was breached from a storm surge that may have reached ten feet. In Lincoln Park, a newly created landfill was washed out into Lake Michigan. All up and down the shoreline, piers and docks were washed away, hundreds of boats were smashed, shoreline buildings were damaged and destroyed. Hundreds were injured.

Fortunately, at Palisades, so early in our history, beachfront cottages were relatively few in number. Whatever damage may have occurred locally is not recorded. The once-in-a-century storm was a good one to miss.

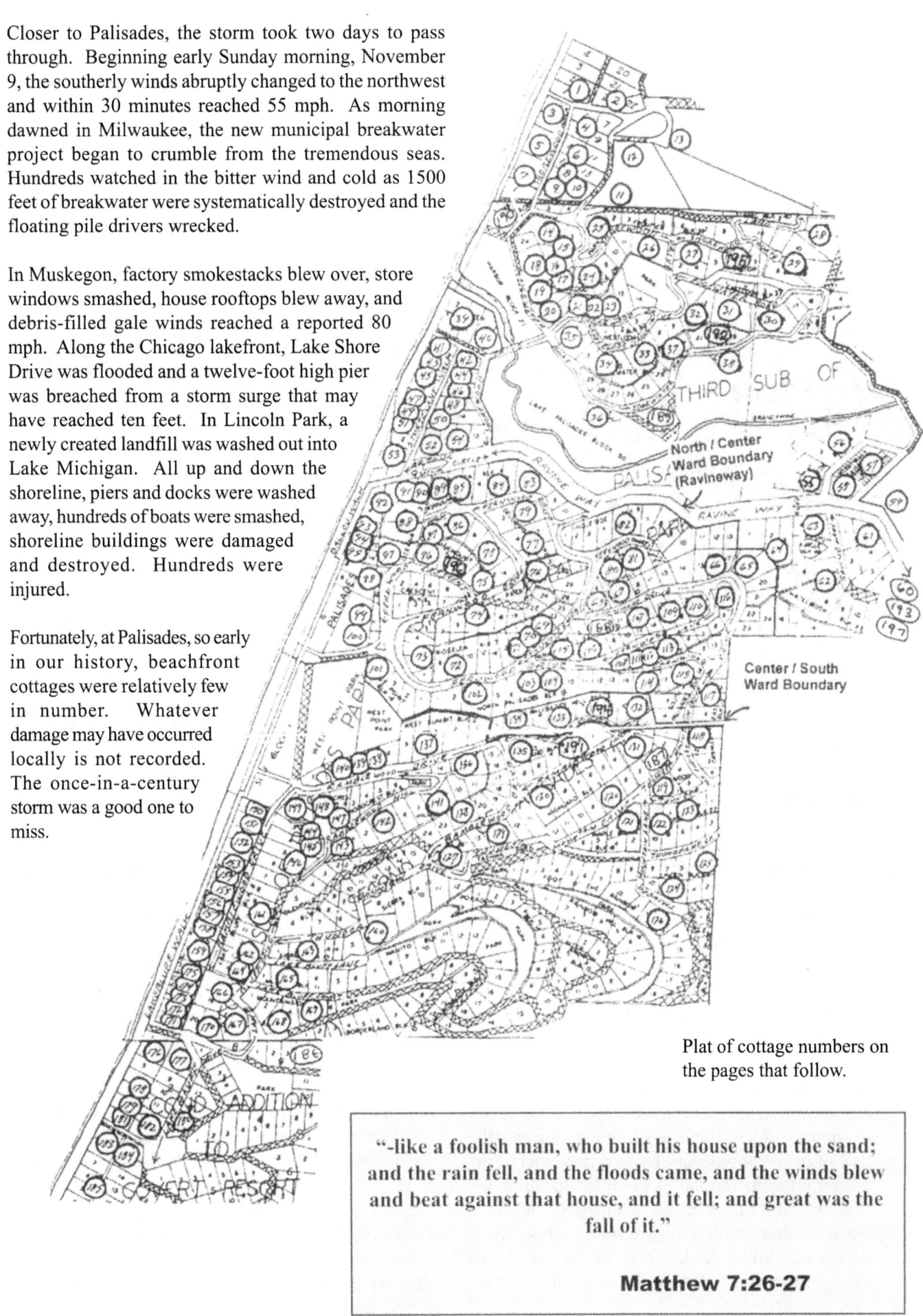

Plat of cottage numbers on the pages that follow.

> "-like a foolish man, who built his house upon the sand; and the rain fell, and the floods came, and the winds blew and beat against that house, and it fell; and great was the fall of it."
>
> **Matthew 7:26-27**

*Brandywine Beach after December 1929 storms.*
*Lake level 580'*

## **1929 Storms**

October and December, 1929, was a bleak period in Palisades history. That fall, two storms, just two months apart, devastated the Park beach front. Two factors contributed to this disaster.

1. Low water levels and wide beaches during the early to mid-20's had encouraged a flurry of beach cottages to be built – and maybe roaring Twenties prosperity helped. The new buildings were sited on the forward "shelf" part of the sand dune, in front of the natural bluff line.

2. Although water levels changed rapidly from a near all-time low in 1926, rising almost five feet to a high in summer of 1929 and flooding our beaches, the lack of major storms during this period masked the dangerous situation that was rapidly developing. Clearly, sea wall protection was needed, and some sea walls were built. Most were of flimsy wood design that failed the test that was to come. An exception was the Ark #7 which enjoyed a massive new concrete sea wall.

Then the gales blew! Details of the storm, as reported in Chicago, were:

**October 21-22, 1929: 37 hours of north winds up to 58 mph, a storm surge of two feet above the already high Lake Michigan level of about 580'6" (1985 IGLD).**

This storm destroyed most of the little sea wall protection that existed at Palisades and began undermining the forward "shelf" of the dunes. But the worst was yet to come.

**December 17-18, 1929: 34 hours of north to northeast winds up to 50 mph, a storm surge of 1'10" above a slightly lower lake level of about 580'0" (1985 IGLD).**

Though a "milder" storm, by comparison, it struck when virtually all shore line defenses were gone. Erosion of the dune shelf continued until at least four beach cottages collapsed into the pounding waves. Many others were severely damaged.

## North of Brandywine: Aftermath from the December 17-18, 1929 Storm

*Above: Hayes cottage. Rebuilt 1933; now Potters' Driftwood #3.*

*Below: Welles cottage, The Ark #7, still standing "after the Flood." Massive concrete sea wall is visible, tilted but intact. Hayes cottage in background.*

*Harding cottage, 1929.
Later moved to south side of Brandywine Creek
and was rebuilt. Now Vercillo cottage #39.
A new cottage (#190) was built in 1988 on
the Harding site.*

Dr. McCollum's cottage was undermined and destroyed and not rebuilt. No photo is available. The McCollum site was just north of present cottage #190.

## South of Brandywine: Aftermath from the December 17-18, 1929 Storm

*VanBeuren's Anchor Fast; now Joseph Kings' #43.*

*Mick's cottages #93 and 94.
Baker cottage collapsed in background.*

*Baker cottage, present site of Hong Kong Hilton #95.*
*Bakers relocated in the woods. 1929.*

*Sturtevant Lodge, now Master Lodge #53. 1929.*

## Lull of the 1930's – Mid 40's

After the high water levels of 1929, the lake provided a pleasant surprise by suddenly dropping some two feet during the next 18 months. It then continued to drop. The beaches reappeared, growing dramatically in width during the early 1930's. Dune grass flourished; dune buildup accelerated; wide beaches were the norm throughout the decade.

However, beginning in the early 1940's, lake levels gradually rose up to 580' and the shoreline slowly receded. Soon, even during "routine" storms, waves would reach the old "shelf" dune line. Dune erosion began again. By 1948, dune erosion was nearing the front of many beach cottages. Although the lake level receded to the 578' range for three years, dune erosion continued.

It was time for beach cottage owners to install some kind of storm protection. Fortunately, many wood sea walls were installed during the fall of 1950 and spring of 1951. Then, abruptly, through the summer and fall of 1950, the lake level began a swift rise.

*March 28, 1948. Claude Welles Sr. viewing dune erosion. Potter cottage #3 in background. Lake level 579'6."*

*December 2, 1950. Storm driven erosion against unprotected dunes continued slowly during the next 2 1/2 years, even though lake level dropped a foot to 578'6." Cottages #1 and #3 in background.*

## November 6-7, 1951.

By November 1951, the lake level had risen two feet, to 580'6," the same as 1929. Starting November 6 and for 31 hours, northeast to north winds blew up to 42 mph, creating a storm surge of 1'9" above the 580'6" level. (As reported in Chicago in the February, 1952, <u>Midwest Engineer.</u>)

Unlike the 1929 storm when sea wall protection was mostly missing, this time only one cottage, the Crawfords' cottage north of Brandywine, was lost. The new wood sea walls had saved the day, even though dune shoreline damage in unprotected areas was severe.

Besides the Crawford cottage, the Park lost the pump house that had been on Clubhouse Beach. One-way Shorewood Road, north of Brandywine, was washed out along the front edge of the bluff.

*Ruins of the old pump house.
November, 1951.*

*Left: Clubhouse Beach.
Dune line badly eroded.
No sea wall protection.
No beach.
November 1951.*

*Below: The water-covered Clubhouse Beach
after the new wood sea wall was installed.
Remains of the pump house and debris in foreground.
Spring 1952.*

*Washout of one-way Shorewood Road north of Brandywine. The portion of road was abandoned and traffic north of Brandywine subsequently became two-way. Photo spring 1952.*

*Crawford lot and the remains after the cottage and debris were removed. The cottage was saved from collapse by temporary support poles on the water side and steel cables in the back. Later, the cottage was moved from its beach location back about 300 feet into the woods and became cottage #25. Cottage #7 at left. Photo spring 1952.*

Following the November 6-7 storm, on Friday November 9, 1951, The Chicago Tribune ran an article with the headline: **Lake Hits Peak Level Since '29 Storm.** Reporting the costly damage from the storm, the article ponders the wisdom of greater diversion of Lake Michigan waters:

> The highest Lake Michigan level since 1929 was reached during this week's storms which caused damage estimated at a quarter of a million dollars along the lake front from Waukegan to Michigan City, lake experts reported yesterday.
>
> Horace P. Ramey, Assistant Chief Engineer of the Sanitary District, said the lake reached a level of 583.2 feet Wednesday. It was the high mark for the year, and the highest in the last 22 years. The lake is heading for an average level of 581 feet this year, or 1.65 of a foot above the 1950 level. This year's average level will exceed any since 1929, when the lake rose to 581.4 feet above sea level.*
>
> Ramey and other Sanitary District officials view the high levels as effectively removing the objections of lake states that greater diversion at Chicago would lower the lake and interfere with shipping and harbor facilities.
>
> North winds were the chief cause of the storm and resultant property damage, Ramey said. If Chicago was permitted to divert 10,000 cubic feet a second as it used to do, the lake level would be lowered only four inches. (Indeed, it would take five years at this diversion rate to lower the lake these four inches.)
>
> Anthony A. Olis, president of the District, said the rising lake levels should spur Congress to act on proposed bills to allow greater diversion here. Olis has obtained promises of Congressional support for a bill to increase diversion from 1500 to 3500 cubic feet a second.

*Lake levels in the above article are the prior IGLD 1955 datum.

## 1952 Lake Level Rise

Lake levels continued to rise during spring of 1952, reaching an all time peak of 581'6" in August. Through the spring and summer of 1952, wood bulkhead sea wall construction continued at a furious pace across almost all unprotected dune shoreline.

## July 1969
Lake Level 580'6"

Up to now, the destructive storms had occurred during fall months, when the Park was mostly unoccupied. That changed in 1969 when a big storm hit late in July. People had their cameras ready.

Events leading up to the high-water-levels of summer of 1969 were almost a duplicate of those in November 1951. For some 12 years, lake levels had generally decreased, reaching an all-time low of 576'0" in March, 1964. Beaches were magnificently wide – 250 to 350 feet at the Clubhouse, Brandywine, and North Beach areas. Then, as in the 40's, a slow but steady rise in lake levels brought a gradually receding shoreline. By summer 1969, the lake had reached its dreaded level of 580'6". Most of the beaches had disappeared, flooded by the high water. Waves lapped at the old wood sea walls built 17 years earlier – and now mostly rotted, with little strength remaining, some almost completely rotted away. The wave action uncovered their remains.

Once again the clarion call sounded for new protective sea walls. This time it would be walls of steel. Walls that wouldn't rot. Walls "that would last for 100 years." But before actual construction could begin, the lake's fury struck again.

### A First Hand Report

The storm began on July 27, the day before steel seawall installation north of Brandywine was to begin – on July 28. Nancy Potter and four daughters – Carin 14, Kris 12, Gretchen 9, and Carolyn 7 – were in their Driftwood Cottage #3 whose 17-year-old wooden sea wall had rotted to near uselessness. Husband Bill was back home in Pittsburgh, PA, oblivious to events at Palisades. At two p.m. on Monday, July 28, Nancy's phone call to Bill who was at work in Pittsburgh, as reconstructed from telephone notes, had these highlights: **"Lake storm at the height of its fury, continued all night with no sign of abatement. Existing old sea wall disintegrating rapidly and water penetrating both side walls, eating into the sand dunes. Worried about sleeping there tonight and what furniture to remove. Bill advised Nancy to get as many photographs as possible, particularly as the cottage starts to go in."** At 5:45 p.m., Bill called back. Again the conversation is reconstructed from notes: **"Storm

**continues and whole cottage is shaking with each wave. Furniture all moved to back rooms. Nancy and the children will sleep elsewhere and will call Bill if cottage goes. Contractor for steel wall visited the site this afternoon and indicated his opinion that the cottage would survive the night. Nancy was less than reassured."**

Just 50 feet north of Driftwood, people were sitting on the concrete steps of Juniper Pass that lead down to what was left of the dune. They had been waiting for hours, cameras in hand, for that dramatic moment when the cottage would take its plunge.

It was an odd kind of storm. Sometimes during the day, the sun shone brightly, then was obscured by moving clouds. There was no rain – just the unceasing waves and the storm surge higher and higher. Onlookers seated on Juniper Pass steps were in an ideal outdoor viewing stand. Some people would leave after a while, as others arrived, cameras in hand, to take their place.

At sunset, about nine p.m., the cottage was still standing. It was time to leave and let the cottage fend for itself through the night. Everything that could be done under the circumstances was done. The furniture might survive in the back rooms. The power had been shut off. On the first night of the storm, Nancy had little sleep, fearing that something awful was going to happen to the cottage as in 1929. On the second night, exhaustion set in and a sense of sadness that Driftwood might be gone by daybreak. But Driftwood survived the night. The storm's fury and waves finally subsided. Construction of the steel wall began just two days later.

As the steel sea walls were installed and completed north of Brandywine, sea wall construction continued south of the Creek, past Circle Beach, Clubhouse Beach, and onto the south end of the Park. Some walls were steel; some were wood. All were installed to replace the rotten wood walls which mostly dated from 17 years earlier.

By spring of 1970, seawalls were completed and Palisade's shoreline was rather well protected again – or so it was thought. Not all newspaper articles were so reassuring. A. F. Mahan, an Associated Press Writer, expressed doubts about the coming year in an AP Press Release:

*Waves pounding at the rotted sea wall of the Potter cottage #3. Before noon, July 28 1969, from Juniper Pass.*

*Canonie ConstructionCompany installing steel wall. Cottage #3. Photo July 30, 1969. Lake level 580'6"*

**Great Lakes at Record High, May Wreak Havoc During 1970.**

DETROIT (AP) – With damages mounting and levels already near or surpassing high water records for this century, the Great Lakes are expected to wreak more havoc along their 10,000 miles of shoreline in 1970. Waves eating away embankments, particularly the high bluffs along eastern shores of lower Lake Michigan, are threatening to topple scores of homes and vacation cottages. Whole front or back yards have already vanished. Once high and dry private docks now are awash, waiting for a storm to carry them away. Where sandy beaches once stretched outward, there now is water. Nearby low-lying areas once above water level now are marshes.

No figures are available for 1969 damages, but the Lakes Survey District of the Army's Corps of Engineers estimated somewhat similar high waters did $61.2 million damages in the springs of 1951 and 1953. And the three lakes over which man has virtually no control – Michigan, Huron, and Erie – are expected to start their annual spring rises next year at levels considerably higher than they did this year. Experts attribute the high waters to above normal precipitation in all of the five lake basins this year and last …. Last month, Michigan, Huron, and Superior were less than an inch and a half below their highest levels for this century ….

The Great Lakes are tremendous bodies of water. If the contiguous 48 states were level, had a rim around them, and all the water in the Great Lakes were dumped over them, it would form a lake nine feet deep from the Atlantic to Pacific and Gulf of Mexico to Canada, according to Lake Survey engineers.

High water is not unwelcome by all who use the lakes. It means money to ship operators. For each inch of water above the so-called low-water datum line, a freighter can take on an additional 100 tons of cargo. Last month, the lakes ranged up to 47 inches above the low-water datum line, and all were above both their average levels for the last 10 years and for the 1860-1968 period. And the Lakes Survey forecasts all except Ontario will exceed their 10-year and long-term average levels for the next six months.

Sure enough, with the lake level still at 580'6," Weldon Coates, Park President, reported in his December 18, 1970 letter to members:

**And now for a little bad news. There have been some terrific storms at the Park this fall and there has been further erosion of the beach, particularly on the north side. The water has gone over the sea wall at The Ark #7 and is 50 feet behind the sea wall in spots. Unless there is a freeze and an ice barrier develops soon, some of the cottages could be in danger. The old wooden sea wall is exposed to Dr. Campbell's cottage #171 on the extreme south end of the beach. Extending the sea wall is being studied.**

The words, **"The water has gone over the sea wall,"** were the first indication of three major flaws in the new sea wall designs. First, many were not built with tops high enough above the 580'6" lake level. With no beach, the high waves and storm surges broke over the top, and the wave action continued its eroding action behind the walls. Second, a scouring effect in front of the steel walls meant sand could not build up; waves actually carried sand away and water depth in front of the walls increased. Finally, any unprotected property at the end of a section of wall felt the brunt of all waves racing along the wall – and faced increased sand erosion.

> The words, "The Water has gone over the sea wall," were the first indication of three major flaws in the new sea wall designs.

## 1972-73 Storms

The 580'6" lake level of the summer of 1969 was only the beginning. The lake continued rising, reaching a new all-time high of 581'6" during the summers of 1973 and 1974.

The Thanksgiving storm of November 1972 - plus a follow-up storm on March 17, 1973 – created a new problem. Two cottages behind Brandywine Beach – the Jennings newly built cottage #18 and Plains' cottage #19 – were threatened, as the unprotected north bank of Brandywine Creek crumbled under the battering of the waves. Portions of Edgewater Road were washed out, right up to the foundations of these cottages.

The same two storms breached the old 1950's wood sea wall at the north end of the Clubhouse Beach, eroding the bluff and threatening cottages #98, #99, and #100. The storms also breached the sea wall south to Henkels' cottage #150 and deeply eroded the Clubhouse Beach bluff. The continuous but decayed wood sea wall, from cottage #157 south to Beck #176, was breached in many places.

Thereafter, even minor storms were causing beach front property damage and further dune erosion. This forced a new round of wall construction, to install a second tier of treated wood retaining walls behind the new steel and concrete sea walls, and to replace sea walls that were no longer effective.

The aerial photograph below, taken on May 4, 1973, shows the aftermath of the November 1972 and March 1973 gale-level storms. Brandywine Beach is totally flooded; Sturtevant Lodge's front porch is collapsed as the wood sea wall failed. The inadequate steel sea wall height and lack of secondary retaining walls between Lowreys' #39 and the Lodge caused washout right up to the front of cottages. This is also true from Tillsons' #92 south to Hong Kong Hilton #95. Clubhouse Beach is flooded and bluff erosion is apparent. At this time, the lake level was 581'4."

*Detail of Lodge damage. Cottages #49 and 51 at left.*

# December 1974 Storm Damage

Lake level 580'3"

From the Park Board membership letter of June 30, 1975:

> **The damage to the lake front on the south end of the Park from Campbell's (#171) to Kowalski's (#159) is severe. The winter storm took out the cement seawall and broke up most of the secondary wall. There has been erosion of the bank sufficient to threaten five cottages.**

*DeGraw cottage #159 teetering on the edge. April 18, 1975.*

*Erosion of dune by cottages #157-159. April 18, 1973.*

*Looking north, O'Connor #158 to Duesing #154. December 1974.*

*Looking south toward Beck cottage #176. (See p. 293)*

### November 10, 1975:

A tragic storm struck the Lake Superior area with gale winds and gigantic waves. The ore carrier Edmund Fitzgerald, largest ship on the Great Lakes, broke in two and sank in minutes, taking its entire crew of 29.

Palisades escaped, exposed only to the storm fringes.

## December 1, 1985 Storm Damage
Lake level 581'3"

In 1985, the lake was very near its 581'8" all-time high level of 1973 and 1974. On December 1, a storm hit Palisades head on with gale force winds, up to 20 foot waves, a storm surge of at least two feet, and a "once-in-a-century" seiche that added four more feet to the level for short periods of time. Collectively, these pushed the lake level up toward 587 feet, plus whatever the waves added on top of that. Park President Don Beveridge best described the devastation in his December 16, 1985, letter to the membership:

> At this time of year, I would like to be sending you a cheery holiday message. Instead, it is my sad duty to tell you that the Park suffered heavy damage from a storm on the night of Sunday, December 1. For reasons that will become obvious as you read further, we're enclosing the 1986 dues notice with this letter.
>
> Fortunately, no cottages went into the lake, although much beach frontage, steps, decks, and other outside structures and a dozen or so boats were lost. The most serious loss for the Park was the hill in the Clubhouse Beach area. What beach there was is gone plus a 240 foot section of retaining wall and a huge portion of the dune up to within a few feet of the concrete block pump house. The water mains which emerged from the pump house and went north and south to the water distribution system are completely destroyed.
>
> South of the pump house, some of the wall and dune remain but then another large section is gone, including the stairs and the Henry Prange Memorial Deck. In their place is a 30 foot drop to what is left of the beach.
>
> To continue with the depressing list:
>
> – Tillsons #92 lost their entire front yard and O'Connors #158 lost all the sand and the new deck from in front of the cottage.
>
> – The road along the Brandywine in front of Kinsey's #20, Plain's #19, and Jenning's #18 was destroyed.
>
> – The strip of beach behind the concrete wall below the Heitner's #98, Owens's #99, and Brand's #100 cottages lost a tremendous amount of sand when the retaining wall to the south gave way.
>
> – All the owners from Henkels #150 to Tombaugh #156 lost their stairs except Butchers, but theirs now stand 30 feet away from the bluff.
>
> – The wooden wall between Becks #176 and Wintermutes #183 at the far south end was breached in at least two places and some sand was lost. However, it's widely agreed that without the riprap installed this fall, it's likely most of these cottages would be in the lake.

*Clubhouse Beach, December 6, 1985*

*Sand being trucked in to reconstruct beach between cottages #150 and #156. Damage to Clubhouse Beach bluff can be seen. Photo spring 1986, looking north from #150.*

*Steps to nowhere.*
*Cottage #151.*

**Three views of December 1, 1985 storm damage.**

*Above: Cottage #176.*
*Below: South of Clubhouse Beach.*

**From <u>South Haven Tribune</u>**
**Tuesday, December 3, 1985**

Flooding, power outages, and blizzard conditions plagued the South Haven area Sunday night and Monday as high winds swept across Lake Michigan and slammed through the region. City officials may apply for state and federal disaster aid to help repair the damage caused by the storm.

Lake Michigan waves battered the shore with 12-15 foot waves causing erosion. Some shoreline residents lost as much as 100 feet of property near Ganges to the ripping waves. South of South Haven, near 18th Street, 30 to 50 feet of shoreline disappeared. Trees fell like matchsticks as the bank under them was gouged away by waves. Many shoreline protection structures were battered to pieces. Debris could be seen floating in the rushing waves all up and down the shoreline ….

"It looks like the water is 16 to 18 inches above the previous flood plain," said Robert Giesler of All-Seasons Marine, located on hard-hit Black River Street. "All of us involved with shoreline properties will suffer moderate to heavy damage." The extent of the damage will not be known until the waters recede ….

## February and March 1987
Lake level 580'11"

On February 8 and again on March 8-9, two 1987 storms, as reported in The Chicago Tribune, both developed 60 to 70 mph, near-hurricane force, north to northeast winds. The blow traveled down the full length of Lake Michigan and created waves off shore of 14 – 20 feet together with a storm surge that flooded sections of Chicago's Lake Shore Drive. Although the lake level was exceptionally high, the northeasterly wind direction spared Palisades beach cottages from major damage. Beach damage was confined mostly to south end boardwalks.

## June 17, 1992
Lake level 579'2"

Bob Zimmermann, then Park Manager, reported, in the July, 1992 Patter:

> About six p.m. it started to rain. By seven it was raining and so windy you could see only about 20 feet. By eight, it stopped and the sun came out. Almost two inches of rain fell in less than two hours. The temperature dropped more than 20 degrees. Winds were reported gusting about 60 – 70 mph in our region.

The storm did no appreciable damage on the beaches, but in the woods, over 100 trees of all sizes were blown down in the Park alone. The Beveridge cottage #136 lost seven large trees on the property. Power was off from downed lines from Wednesday, June 17, until fully restored on Saturday, June 20.

> Miraculously, no cottages, vehicles, or people were seriously injured. Minor damage occurred to several cottages, power wire connections pulled off, gutters or eaves bent, but we were spared overall.

## March 9, 1998
Lake level 579'11"

Reported in The Chicago Tribune, this storm's gale winds reached 60 – 70 mph. Wave heights of 14 – 20 feet and the storm surge again flooded sections of Chicago's Lake Shore Drive. Fortunately, at Palisades, winds were mostly from the northeast, so shore wave action was somewhat muted, and no beach cottages suffered more than minor damage. However, beach boardwalk, lake access stairways, and benches were battered, and fallen trees and branches littered the roads and woods cottages.

## November 9–10, 1998
Lake level 578'10"

This is the storm that spawned the famous picture of South Haven's lighthouse engulfed in gale driven spray. The photo was picked up by Associated Press and printed in most major U.S. newspapers on November 12, 1998. Winds exceeded 50 mph when the picture was taken.

Unfortunately, the Kalamazoo Gazette did not give us permission to use its picture. However, Don Henkel was in South Haven during the same storm and caught this wave - admittedly not quite the size of the one in the Gazette photo, but quite dramatic, nonetheless.

This "granddaddy" storm, covered a huge area similar to November 1913, some 85 years earlier. The Chicago Tribune reported:

> **The National Weather Service noted the storm's central pressure dropped to 28.48" mercury over Duluth, MN – a pressure which in the hurricane world, would rank as a Category 2.**

The lake, at 578'10", was down to "average" level, and was in a receding cycle. Some beach existed from the north end of the Park to the south end, even in front of the sea walls. Despite the gale force winds, very little beach front damage resulted.

In the woods, however, it was a different story. Trees and branches were blown over everywhere, and most roads were completely blocked. Chain saws roared, and the debris temporarily tossed aside to clear a path. Electrical power lines were downed and power was out from Tuesday, November 10, until late Friday, November 13.

Five woods cottages were damaged from fallen trees and limbs. Among them, Lori Dillman's Valkommen #134 had its roof pierced by a large, wind-driven tree limb. Osths' Osthaven #75 had chimney and roof damage from a falling tree. Speichers' Happy Hollow #104 was so wracked by a big tree falling on the roof, the cottage had to be rebuilt.

> A wailing, rushing sound, which shook the walls as though a giant's hand were on them; then a hoarse roar, as if the sea had risen; then such a whirl and tumult that the air seemed mad; and then, with a lengthened howl, the waves of wind swept on.
>
> Charles Dickens.

*Speichers' Happy Hollow #104 after the November 1998 storm.*

# Shore Protection

By Bill Potter

## Introduction

This is the comforting, exasperating, frustrating, and extravagantly expensive history of shore protection at PPCC since the late 1920's. The pages that follow contain more detail, dates, and lake level references than most non-beach cottage owners will want to know.

Be patient, as all beach cottage owners have learned to be. This is intended for future PPCC Boards and beach cottage owners —a written history of what installations have worked as protection and for how long, as well as what has not worked, even for a short time, regardless of expense.

No shortage of ideas, creativity, or varieties of installations has entered our repertoire of experience. We have tried all of the below.

> No sea wall protection (1920's)
> Wood walls in many heights and variations
>   (used in the 1930's - 1950's)
> Concrete walls (1920's - 1974)
>   Concrete-filled 50 gallon drums (1951)
>   Concrete-filled tires (1972)
>   Precast concrete blocks (1970's)
>   Jacking up and moving a cottage (once)
> Steel walls (1960-1973)
> Beach Building Attempts
>   Groins and jetties (1947, 1976)
>   Gabion baskets (1974, 1986)
> Stone rip rap (1984-1990)
>   Concrete-filled bags (c1989)
>   Sand bags (1985)

The dates, lake levels, heights, and lengths given in this section are reasonably accurate, gleaned from many sources. Sometimes they conflict with one another but most times are corroborated. Beach cottage owners, both old-timers and new, have been generous with their time, sharing of recollections, photos, and construction documents. Thanks to all of you.

Over the last 80 years of Park history, shore protection has had various meanings, depending upon one's viewpoint, upon lake level, and upon beach width at the moment. In these 80 years, lake levels have varied by six vertical feet. When lake levels are low and beaches wide, thoughts of shore protection seem a distant distraction, even to old-timers. At the same time, newcomers to the Park arrive with little or no understanding of the relationship between lake level and beach width, nor how they change from year to year. Some have virtually no concept of the need for high water shore protection.

Conversely, during periods of high water, beach cottage owners are interested in property protection; bluff cottages owners are interested in dune bluff protection; and woods cottage owners and the Park Boards are interested in Clubhouse, Circle, and Brandywine beach retention.

Sometimes these interests have worked together; sometimes they have been at loggerheads. Gradually, over the years, we have learned what works and what does not work.

## No Sea Wall Protection

Until 1930, Palisades Park lake front cottage shore protection was lacking, with the exception of a concrete sea wall built in front of The Ark #5 in the late 1920's. The high lake level and two gale-force storms of October and December, 1929, ended this "age of innocence." Storm damage to beach cottages was severe (as already pictured in the section **Big Storms, Big Damage**.) Four cottages were destroyed and virtually all remaining beach cottages needed major repairs to restore foundations, porches, and steps.

What follows is a history of Palisades sea and retaining wall protection beginning in the late 1920's.

*Note: all lake levels in this chapter are corrected to the 1985 IGLD (International Great Lakes Datum) standard.*

Cottage numbers in the text that follows refer to this map.

Owners and names may change from year to year, but cottage numbers remain constant.

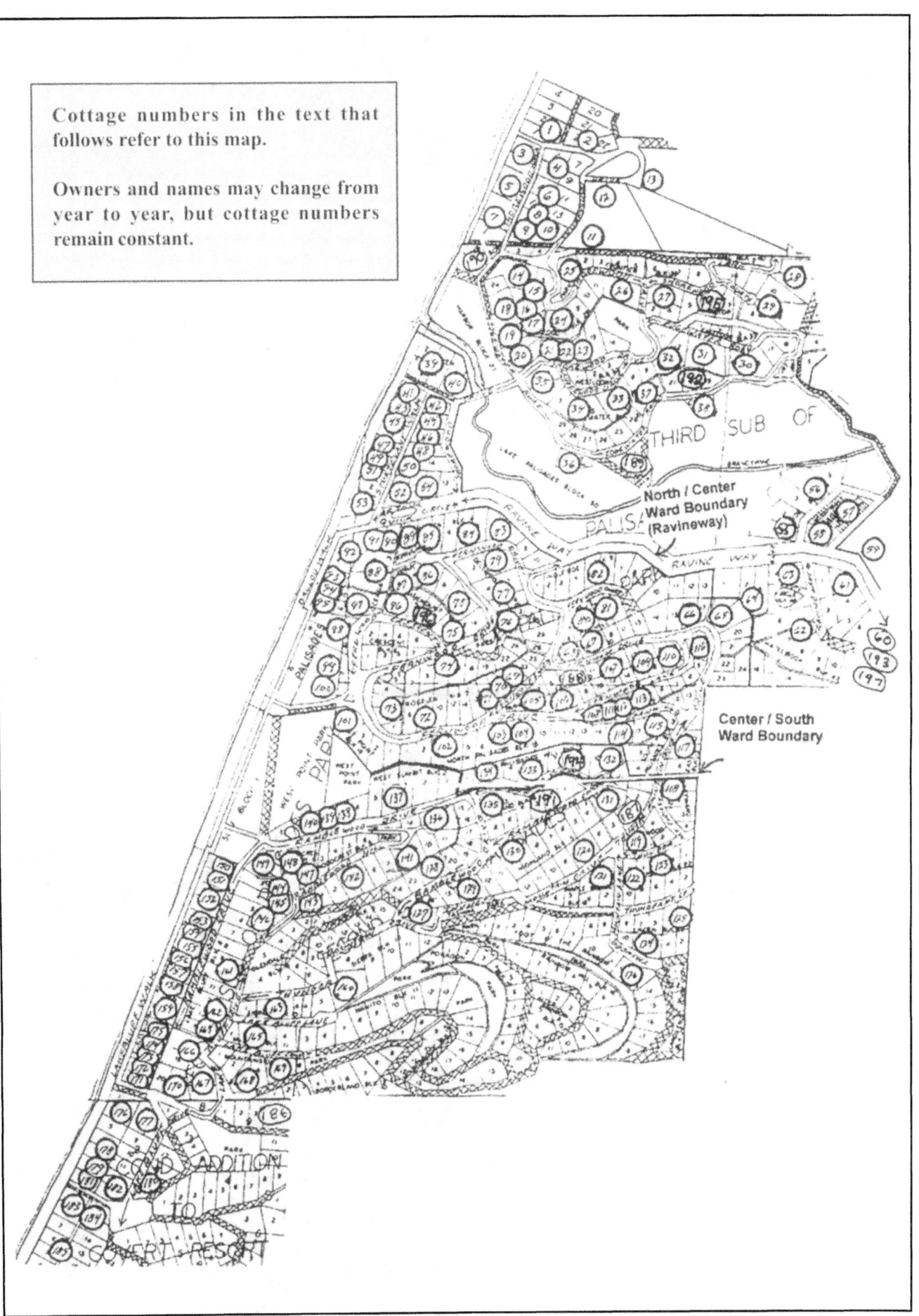

## Failure Costs

Palisades sea and retaining walls - of concrete, wood, or steel - all include examples that have failed due to inadequate foundations or inadequate height and/or lack of continuity. Wood, of course, has a limited life; many other failures have been of design. The failure costs have been high, not only in original cost of the failed wall, but also in property and bluff damage resulting from the failure and in cost of the replacement protection.

*Collapsed PPCC wood retaining wall, installed 1971 to protect Shorewood Walk, north of Brandywine. Poor design failure. Piles 40 feet long descending to 30 feet at south end, spaced 6 ft. on centers. Boards 3"x10" by 18'6" long. Cottage #9 in background. Photo c. 1972.*

## Wood Walls

The early Palisades sea walls, through the 1950's, were built almost universally of two layers of staggered oak planks, typically 2 inches thick by 12 wide, sunk vertically into the sand with 2 x 12 inch horizontal oak "wales" for lateral strength. Logs were sunk vertically at 6 to 10 foot intervals in front of the wall -and sometimes also in the rear - as reinforcement against leaning or tipping.

The old "rule of thumb" for oak plank length was three feet below the sand for every one foot projecting above the lowest expected sand level. Thus, if five feet of wall height was desired above the lowest expected sand level (usually during periods of high lake level and minimum beach) then 15 feet of length would be needed below the sand, requiring 20 foot long planks. The vertical reinforcing logs were usually several feet longer.

These walls were strong, yet easy to install without heavy equipment, by using a jet of high pressure water driven vertically deep into the sand to form a sand slurry. Then a single wood plank was lifted high and sunk, or "floated," vertically down through the slurry into place. The process was repeated for each vertical plank, with planks staggered between the front and back rows, to form a sand-tight wall.

*Right: An early crew at work. The tall tripod supports two pulleys. One pulley raises the water hose and its attached jet pipe, which is lowered vertically into the sand to make a slurry. The second pulley raises the oak plank that is then lowered down into the slurry. As the pipe is withdrawn, water leaves the slurry and the remaining sand grips the plank tightly.*

*Until portable gasoline driven pumps became available in the 1930's, high pressure water for the jet was created using an old horse-drawn coal-fired steam pumper. When not in use, it was stored in the old garage building. Here it is, below, drawing water from Lake Palisades to build the Brandywine Creek south retaining wall. c. 1931.*

*Completed Brandywine Creek south bank wood retaining wall. c. 1931.*

## WOOD WALLS

Although strong to begin with, the untreated oak soon began to rot, and in seven to ten years, its strength was considerably reduced. After 15 years, disintegration advanced to a point where a wall was almost useless against the battering of storm waves and winter ice slabs.

*Typical untreated wood sea wall, installed 1951-52. Cottage #1 and #3, north end. Photo June, 1953. Lake level 581'1"*

*Same wall, 17 years old. June 1969. Lake level 580'6"*

*New untreated oak wood sea wall.
Looking north toward Clubhouse Beach.
Photo 1952. Lake level 581'7"*

*Remains of the same sea wall 21 years later - battered, bowed, and a Clubhouse Beach hazard. Gas engine powered high pressure water slurry pump bottom left, being used to build new treated wood bluff retaining wall at right.
Photo June 1973. Lake level 581'7"*

Treated (wolmanized) pine wood planks and posts became available in the 1960's, with claimed 20 year resistance to rotting. Thus, pine became the wood of choice almost immediately for sea and retaining walls, as well as for outdoor deck construction. The treated wood wall installation technique, using high pressure water jets to form a sand slurry and floating down of one board at a time, remained the same. A number of properly designed and installed, treated-wood <u>retaining</u> walls in the Park, constructed in the early 1970's, are still in sound condition in 2001, after almost 30 years service.

Treated wood <u>sea</u> walls, however, in direct contact with lake and storm waves and ice slab battering action, have not lasted much longer than their untreated ancestors. Not that they rotted, but after eight to ten years of continuous battering, the wood and its nail and bolt fastenings simply splintered and cracked and finally broke in areas of weakness. Once a hole or breach developed, failure to adjacent areas followed.

*A hodge-podge of poorly designed and ill-located wood and treated-wood sea walls with lack of continuity along the south beach shoreline, after December, 1974 gale storm.
Photo spring 1975. Lake level 580'10"*

# WOOD WALLS

*South end continuous untreated wood sea wall, cottage #150 at left to #183 at right, installed early 1950's. Breaches through the wall had developed in front of cottages #150 – 152. Clubhouse Beach 1952 untreated wood sea wall at left.*
*Photo April 4, 1961.*

Left: Completed 1973 treated-wood 400 ft. sea/retaining wall at base of Clubhouse Beach bluff. Double 2" x 12" 16 ft. long vertical boards and 20 ft. long posts staggered on 5 ft. centers. Double 2" x 12" horizontal wales.
Contractor: Leonard Burrous. Cost $51/ft. This wall was breached in the storm of December 1985 and was replaced with a new treated wood sea wall in 1986.
Photo September 22, 1973, looking north. Lake level 581'3"

Below: 1973 treated-wood sea/retaining wall already beginning to rotate one year later due to scouring away of sand, upsetting the (3 ft. down, 1 ft. up) ratio, before cottages #176, 178, 179, 181, and 183. Skeleton of 1950's untreated wood wall at right.
Photo summer 1974, looking south. Lake level 581'9"

## Table 1

### Wood Sea and Retaining Wall Installations
(North to south, by year)

| | Cottage #/location and PPCC R.O.W. (Right of Way) | Sea=S Retaining=R Dual Function=SR | Wood Type Untreated=U Treated=T | Approximate length |
|---|---|---|---|---|
| **1929 Storms** | | | | |
| Early 1930's | #39 South bank of Brandywine | R | U | 300 ft. |
| | #39, PPCC R.O.W., #41- 51 | S | U | 650 |
| | #92-95 | S | U | <u>300</u> |
| | | | | 1250 ft. |
| **Storm November 6-7, 1951** | | | | |
| 1950-52 | #1,3 | S | U | 250 ft. |
| | #53 and PPCC Circle Beach | S | U | 150 |
| | #92-95 | S | U | 250 |
| | #98-100 (bluff cottages) | S | U | 300 |
| | PPCC Clubhouse Beach | S | U | 400 |
| | #150-159, 171-183 | S | U | 1275 |
| | and 2 PPCC R.O.W.'s | S | U | <u>40</u> |
| | | | | 2665 ft. |
| **Storms 1970, 1972, 1973** | | | | |
| 1971* | PPCC Shorewood Walk between #9 and Edgewater road | R | T | 175 ft. |
| 1972 | Edgewater Road and #18 | R | T | 150 |
| 1973 | #3 | R | T | 100 |
| | PPCC Clubhouse Beach | SR | T | 400 |
| | #157-159, 171-175 | R | T | 450 |
| | 2 PPCC R.O.W.'s | R | T | 40 |
| | #176-183 | S | T | 400 |
| 1974 | #157-159, 171-175 and PPCC ROW | Low ht. front protection for new concrete sea wall | T | <u>465</u> |
| | | | | 2180 ft. |
| **Storm December 1974** | | | | |
| 1976 | #157-159,171-175 | SR | T | 450 ft. |
| | #157-159,171-175 | Sand trap low lattice wall | T | <u>450</u> |
| | | | | 900 ft. |
| **Storm December 1985** | | | | |
| 1985 spring | #49, 51, 53 | R | T | 175ft. |
| 1986 | #1,5 | R | T | 200 ft. |
| | #98-100 (bluff cottages) | R | T | 300 |
| | PPCC Clubhouse Beach | SR | T | 400 |
| | #150-156 | R | T | <u>400</u> |
| | | | | 1475 ft. |

*collapsed within a year

# CONCRETE WALLS

> **Failure Lessons of Treated Wood Walls**
>
> <u>Retaining walls</u> for dunes and bluffs, not in contact with the lake:
>
> The most common error is violating the 3 foot down, one foot up "rule of thumb." Maximum available plank lengths are usually 18' to 20', limiting useful wall height to four or five feet, based on the three foot down, one foot up rule of thumb. Exceeding that height has often resulted in the wall tilting or collapsing forward after a period of time. If the rise is greater than four or five feet, a better solution, often, is to build two lower height parallel retaining walls in stairstep fashion.
>
> <u>Sea Walls</u>:
>
> Treated wood is not a good long term choice for sea wall protection; the pounding of waves and battering from floating logs, tree stumps, or early spring ice slab breakup usually limits useful life to less than eight or nine years of direct wave contact.
>
> The maximum exposed wood wall height of four or five feet above high lake levels means such a wall will not provide protection during gale storms when high waves and storm surge are driven over its top. A wood sea wall should usually be backed up by a secondary higher retaining wall located closer to the cottage or bluff base, with its top four or five feet higher than the sea wall in front of it.

## Concrete Sea Walls

The history of beach cottage concrete sea walls in Palisades includes a few successes and some spectacular failures, scattered along the shore line. Beginning at the north end:

### 1933-1951 Failed Concrete Sea Wall

The picture at the bottom of the previous column is in front of the Potters' cottage #3. What one sees lying on the sand at base of the wood sea wall are the remains of a 12 inch thick concrete sea wall built in 1933 without reinforcing steel, foundation, or front support "sleepers." It collapsed forward and broke into pieces in a matter of hours during the storm of November 1951. Remains were exposed by the gale storm of December 1, 1985.

The treated wood retaining wall behind the slabs, built in 1973, is in precarious condition of rotation forward, as the 12-1-85 storm washed out almost four feet of sand. This was later corrected by back filling with trucked in sand. The wood wall was still in good condition in 2002.

### 1920's – 2004
### The Ark's Success Story

This massive concrete sea wall was built 21 feet in front of the Welles cottage (#7), with some concrete buttresses extending back, to prevent tipping.

*Above: As built, summer 1929, with steel railing. 62 feet long with 15 feet return wall toward the dune at the south end. Top 21" wide, sloping at the rear to approximate 36" base. Height about 5'.*

*Left: Cottage #3 Photo December 8, 1985.*

# CONCRETE WALLS

*Above: After the October and December 1929 storms, the Ark's concrete wall tilted backward. Storm waves crashed over the top due to inadequate height, but the cottage survived. Both adjacent cottages were destroyed. (Hayes cottage #3 shown collapsed in background.) Photo December, 1929.*

*Below: Next door to the Ark, the Crawford cottage's undermined and overturned concrete sea wall is visible at left. The Ark's tilted, but still intact, concrete wall at right saved the cottage for a second time. A concrete cap was later added to restore the wall's original height. After the 1969 steel sea wall was installed, the concrete wall serves as a backup retaining wall.*
*Photo November 1951.*

## 1951 - A Design Failure

The Crawford cottage was located just south of The Ark. As the lake level rose alarmingly in the summer of 1951, the family hastily constructed a wall of hand-mixed concrete-filled 50-gallon steel drums, arranged in a row along the narrow beach to form a wall. Without a foundation or back support, the wall was undermined and fell forward almost immediately during the November 1951 storm. The cottage was left dangling in mid-air and later moved back to Shorewood Drive. It is now Friedian's cottage #25.

> **1972 – Brandywine North Bank - Another Folly**
>
> The August 10, 1972 Patter announced: "Cement loaded tires have been placed in Brandywine to help restore the beach." The tires soon sank out of sight. Let's not ever repeat this idea!

## 1973 – Brandywine Creek: Unique North Bank Concrete Contour Slab Retaining Wall

In 1972, a torrential flood eroded much of the creek's north bank, west of the auto bridge, destroying some of Edgewater Road and threatening three cottages - Jennings #18, Plain #19, and Glasner #20. A treated wood retaining wall was built in front of cottage #18 and back-filled to restore the road.

Later in the year, with the lake already near all-time high levels and covering the Brandywine Beach almost back to the bridge, a November storm further eroded the north bank and again washed out much of Edgewater Road – and again endangered cottages #18, 19, and 20.

In front of cottage #18, sand fill was trucked in and piled on top, in front of, and in back of the treated wood retaining wall, which was still standing. Both front and back of the fill were sloped downward about 45 degrees; then an eight to ten inch thick concrete slab was poured over the contour of the front fill, extending over the top, then down over the back fill, forming an inverted "U" of concrete. Finally, more fill was trucked in to restore Edgewater Road.

*Pumping the concrete contour retaining wall directly on to Brandywine's north bank. Jenning cottage #18 left; Plain cottage #19 at right. March 1973.*

In front of cottages #19 and 20, back to the Brandywine Bridge, the north bank was much less eroded, so the concrete wall was extended in front of these two cottages by laying down segments of old telephone poles directly over the contour of the sloping sand bank, then pouring the concrete slab over the poles.

The approach proved to be a quick and lower-cost alternative compared to the steel retaining wall of Brandywine's south bank, built in 1960. More than a few doubted the contour concrete's ability to hold up as a retaining wall.

*The complete wall, cottage #19 at right, #18 at left. West end of the wall connects to vacant beach lot 's 1971 steel bulkhead wall at left. Now site of cottage #190.*

*Massive concrete cap added November 1986, on top of the original concrete retaining wall. Steps to the Brandywine Beach also added. Cottage #190 at left, #18 at right.*
*Photo August 13, 2001. Lake level 577'7"*

The test came 12 years later, in 1985, with the lake again at near all-time high level (581'6"). Brandywine Beach was totally covered and the lake's direct wave action pounded the contour concrete month after month. Finally the raging storm of December 1, 1985, pushed water over the top of the contour, further eroding the sand bank behind, and once again washing out Edgewater Road in front of cottages #18 – 20. Early in November of 1986, a massive concrete cap was poured on top of the original concrete contour slab in front of cottage #18 to provide added height and to transform the contour slab into a protective sea wall.

Almost 30 years later, in 2002, the original 1973 concrete contour slab is still in remarkably good condition, cracked here and there, but still protecting Brandywine's north bank.

### 1973 – Bluff Protection North of Clubhouse Beach

After the November 1951 storm, bluff cottages Heitner #98, Owens #99, and Brand #100, above the north end of the Clubhouse Beach, were threatened by the eroded bluff below. In 1952, an untreated wood sea wall was erected to prevent further erosion. By 1972, this wall had rotted above the water line, but was still solid where it had been buried in sand. The Thanksgiving storm of November 1972 further eroded the bluff, but the remnant of this old 1952 wood wall would serve as foundation for a new concrete sea wall, built in 1973.

*New untreated wood sea wall in front of bluff cottages #98 – 100.*
*Photo spring 1952.*
*Lake level 580'7"*

# CONCRETE WALLS

*Bluff washout of November 1972.
Hong Kong Hilton #95 at left;
bluff cottage #98 at right.
Photo spring 1973. Lake level 581'0".*

*Completed 1973 concrete sea wall with backfill,
looking north near Brand cottage #100.
1952 wood sea wall remnant visible at wall's base.
Hong Kong Hilton #95 in background.
Contractor: Root Construction.
Photo October 13, 1975. Lake level 580'6".*

In spring of 1973, the three bluff cottage owners were included in a PPCC plan to build a new concrete sea wall that would extend 350 feet in front of their three properties, then south across the Clubhouse Beach, ending with 35 feet at Henkels' cottage #150. However, when construction was scheduled to start on the Clubhouse Beach segment, rising lake levels flooded the foundation area, making concrete construction impractical. Thus only the segment in front of the three bluff cottages was actually built – at the owners' expense.

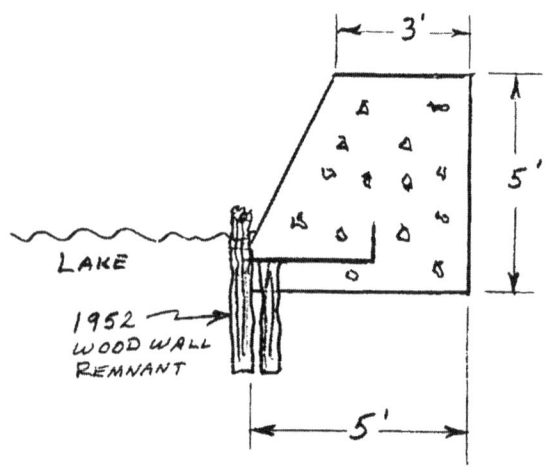

*Figure 1:
Cross section of the 1973 concrete wall utilizing 1952 wood wall as base of its toe and tied to the wood wall by steel straps embedded in concrete.*

The Park opted instead for a treated wood sea/retaining wall located further inland at the base of the Clubhouse Beach bluff, with a wing extension connecting at the north end with Brand's new concrete wall. In hindsight, the decision to locate the wooden sea wall at the base of the bluff was fortunate – as it eliminated what would otherwise have been a permanent concrete barrier to bathers and boaters at the edge of Clubhouse Beach.

The rising lake level and wave action of 1983-84 took its toll on the deteriorating 1952 sea wall remnant, and the concrete sea walls' toe was being undermined in some areas. It was decided that the toe could be protected from wave action by trucking in broken concrete paving and other rubble. By 1985, the rubble had largely slipped and settled to the lake bottom and the undermined toe of the concrete wall was again exposed. Finally, in 1986, many truckloads of rip rap stones were installed in front of the full 350 foot wall length.

*Pushing rubble over the edge of the decayed toe. Clubhouse Beach 1973 wood wall at base of the bluff in the background.
Photo April 18, 1984.
Lake level 580'.*

CONCRETE WALLS

**A Sorry Mess!**

*The completed job. Sand and lightweight rubble dumped on top and west of the concrete wall.*
*Photo May 3, 1984. Lake level 580'3"*

**A Sorrier Mess!**
*In a month, the sand was all gone and nothing but rubble remained.*
*Soon even the rubble disappeared.*
*Hong Kong Hilton #95 concrete capped steel wall in background.*
*Photo June 11, 1984.*
*Lake level 580'6"*

# CONCRETE WALLS

## 1974 South End - A Disastrous Failure

In 1974, a group of eight cottages decided to protect their property with a concrete sea wall which would connect on the north to the steel sea wall at the south end of cottage #156 and extend about 450 feet south to the PPCC beach access path just north of Becks' cottage #176.

Previously, these eight cottages - #157, 158, 159, 175, 174, 173, 172, and 171 - had been protected by a continuous untreated-wood sea wall erected in the early 1950's. (See aerial photo dated 4-4-1961, earlier in this chapter.) By the early 1970's, this 20-year-old wall had decayed to a point of near uselessness. The Thanksgiving 1972 storm administered the coup de grace, and a replacement was necessary.

A continuous concrete sea wall design was chosen, similar in size and shape to the concrete wall built in 1973 in front of bluff cottages #98 – 100, except the entire wall would rest on sand. It would have no tie-in to a new, short-height treated wood wall immediately in front. Instead, it was reinforced with continuous embedded lengths of steel rebar.

The wall was built. Its life was short.

In December 1974, disaster struck. The winter gale storm waves washed over the top of the concrete wall and filled the area behind with water; this in turn undermined the wall's rear base. Eventually, as the storm continued, almost the entire wall fell over backwards. The new back-up wood retaining wall also failed in areas where sand washout destroyed the "three foot down one up ratio." The unprotected dune then eroded further, and five cottages were damaged. The concrete wall has since sunk into the sand and is no longer visible exept for a glimpse at its north end.

*Above: Concrete forms in place on the beach. 1974.*

*Completed concrete sea wall, without backfill, and new treated wood dune retaining wall in foreground. Summer 1974. Lake level 581'6"*

*Left: David and Joel Beck and unidentified girl sitting on the new wall. Summer 1974.*

# CONCRETE WALLS

*North end of the wall, now on its side, with the concrete connector to the neighboring cottage #156 steel wall – sticking up in the air.*

*South of above picture: Showing the 1974 concrete wall and damage to the 1974 treated wood retaining wall. As a result of these damages, cottage #175 was jacked up and moved back on its lot – east of the shoreline. December 1974. Lake level 580'6"*

**Table 2**

**Concrete Sea and Retaining Wall Installations**
(North to south by year)

| Year | Cottage # | Sea=S Retaining=R | Approx. Length | Fate |
|---|---|---|---|---|
| 1929 | #7 The Ark | S | 62 ft. | Still standing |
| 1933 | #3 Driftwood | S | 60 | Collapsed Nov. '51 storm |
| 1951 | Crawfords' Next to #7 | S | 50 | Collapsed Nov. '51 storm |
| 1952 | #7 The Ark Concrete cap added | S | 62 | Still standing |
| 1973 | North shore of Brandywine Cottages #18, 19, 20 | R | 350 | Still standing |
| 1973 | North of Clubhouse Beach, bluff cottages #98, 99, 100 | S | 350 | Still standing |
| 1974 | South end cottages #157-159, 171-175 | S | 450 | Collapsed Dec. '74 storm |
| 1986 | North shore of Brandywine, Cot. #18. Concrete cap added to convert retaining wall to sea wall. | S | 150 | Still standing |

## Steel Bulkhead Walls
### North to South

The steel sea walls in PPCC are built of individual steel sheet piles in one of three cross section shapes, all with interlocking edges:

Type 1: Industrial heavy duty; 16 inches wide with a corrugation depth of 10 inches.
Type 2: MP 115; 19 inches wide with a corrugation depth of 7 inches.
Type 3: 13 inches wide; flat sheet.

Sheets are all 3/8 inch thick, in 15, 20, or 25 foot lengths. To keep costs down, second hand sheet piles were installed on some projects in the Park; these had been removed from pier or jetty projects elsewhere.

Steel walls are installed by pile-driving – first lifting each sheet high in the air, then engaging the bottom end interlocking edge into the previously driven sheet, and finally pounding it down until its top is at the desired elevation. The wood wall "rule of thumb" (three feet of wall below the sand for every one foot above) is also used for steel walls.

Before signing a contract, the contractor and cottage owner have a number of decisions to make: choice of sheet pile cross sections, sheet lengths, and wall height, plus the option of either a decorative steel cap (to be welded on top) or a concrete cap. Both the latter are intended to hide the raw top edge of the completed wall.

Canonie Construction Company of South Haven was the installing contractor on many, if not all, of the steel walls in the Park. The first steel walls were built in 1960 at Brandywine creek, then south to Sturtevant Lodge. After 1960, steel sea walls became the favored choice to protect beach cottages; most were installed by 1973. A review of these several projects – plus the Park's one pre-cast concrete block wall – follows, presented in geographical order, from north to south.

### 1969 Steel Sheet Pile Sea Wall - North End

Built in August – September, 1969, of Type 2 steel sheet piles, this sea wall extends about 475 feet from the north return wall of the Roche cottage #1 to, and including, the vacant beach lot in front of Eldredges' bluff cottage #9. In 1972, a north end extension was added across the toe of the bluff line of Vandersalms' cottage #2, using Type 1 sheets.

For the 1969 wall, Canonie Construction Company offered 15 foot or 20 foot sheet pile lengths. The 15 foot length, with a steel decorative cap welded on top, was the same price as an uncapped 20 foot length. However, the "rule of thumb" (three feet down to one foot up) meant the top of the 20 foot sheets would rise 5 feet above the lake level (then 580'6") to 585'6" while 15 foot lengths would top out 18 inches lower at only 584'0". Installed cost for the total 475 foot length was about $100 per frontage foot.

*Sand scouring effect behind the short-height steel wall across PPCC Juniper Pass right-of-way and cottage #1 vacant lot. Decorative steel cap still surviving on top of high steel wall at right. Photo 1998. Lake level 580'3"*

Cottage owners Roche #1 and Potter #3 installed 20 foot sheets across a frontage of 150 feet, while the remaining 325 feet of the wall utilized shorter 15 foot sheets with the decorative steel cap. This shorter length, with its shortened height above water, proved to be a sorry choice. Within a few winters, block ice had popped welds on all but one of the decorative caps, dropping them into the water where they disappeared. The high-water storm of spring 1973 pushed waves right over the top of the short walls and scoured sand from behind the higher walls of cottages #1 and 3. This necessitated building secondary treated-wood retaining walls during the summer of 1973 – with the added expense of trucking in backfill sand. It also convinced cottage owners that the top of their short steel walls was too low. Hence, later in 1973, to raise the top of short sheets to the same height as neighboring 20 foot sheets, 18 inch steel extensions were welded to the top of the steel wall in front of cottages #5, 7, and 9. This upset the ratio of three feet down/one up and made a bad situation even worse. By 1975, these heightened walls, particularly in front of cottage #5, began to rotate, with their tops tilting down and outward toward the lake.

# STEEL WALLS

By 1985, the tilt approached 35 degrees in front of cottages #5 and 7; this required complete removal and reinstallation, just as the gale storm of December 1985 struck. The storm scoured out up to four feet of sand in front of cottages #3 and 5 which poured out through the low PPCC wall in front of Juniper Pass – for the second time.

In 1986, after the steel sea wall repairs were completed, rip rap stone was placed in front of the sea wall, across cottages #5 and 7 frontage, in the hope of adding protection for the sea wall. However, the wall's inadequate height remained.

Cottages #1 and 3, which selected the longer 20 ft. sheet piles, were fortunate enough for the bottom of their longer sheet length to penetrate into a clay strata below the sand when the piles were driven into place. The clay locked the lower edges firmly, and in over 30 years, the walls have not rotated. They still stand straight and have withstood the high-water level gale storms of 1972, 1974, and 1985 without rip rap protection, and without hindering beach reformation when high lake levels have receded.

*Maloblocki new 1971 steel sea wall. Brandywine Beach mostly under water. In the background, PPCC is building a wood retaining wall to protect the eroded bluff and Shorewood Walk, both of which were washed out in the storms of 1970-71. The wood wall violated the three down/one up ratio and collapsed in 1972. Eldredge bluff cottage #9 in background. September 6, 1971. Lake level 580'5"*

## 1971 Steel Sheet Pile Sea and Retaining Wall - Brandywine North Bank Area

In 1971, the new owner of vacant beach lot #190, Richard Maloblocki of Canonie Construction Company, installed a Type 1 steel sea wall. It connected on the north with the Eldredge #9 steel wall already in place, extending south about 150 feet, across the PPCC right of way, vacant lot #190 frontage, and the dead end of Edgewater Road. Finally, the wall turned 90 degrees, extending east about 100 feet as a retaining wall along the south edge of flooded Edgewater Road.

This wall was very well built, with a top edge some two feet higher than the neighboring sea walls to the north or the walls on the other side of the Brandywine. The steel sheet pile length is unknown, but is probably at least 25 feet, with its bottom edge embedded in clay strata. Regardless, the wall has withstood direct storm wave action and winter ice battering for over 30 years, including the monster storm of December 1985 and high water of 1997 – all without stone rip rap protection. It still stands straight, without damage to the wall or to cottage #190, built in 1988, which stands only 20 feet behind. Nor has its lack of rip rap frontal protection hastened or hindered the reformation of sand beach as the lower lake levels reoccur.

## 1960 Brandywine Creek
## Steel Sheet Pile Retaining Wall

The very first steel wall in PPCC was installed in early fall, 1960, as a retaining wall along the south bank of Brandywine Creek, between the bridge and the lake, adjacent to Lowrey cottage #39. The wall is about 225 feet long. It used heavy duty Type 1 sheet piles immediately in front of a decayed wood retaining wall built in the 1930's. A concrete cap walkway is included on top of the wall, 24 inches wide and 12 deep, extending three inches above the steel top and nine below, reinforced with one inch diameter rebar welded to the steel wall. The top of the cap is at 584'1" – about 5 ° feet above the lake-creek level of 579'6" in October of 1960. The cap also featured a steel pipe railing on the creek side of the walkway.

This wall was not only the first steel wall in the Park, but even to this day survives as the "Cadillac" of all steel walls built in Palisades Park.

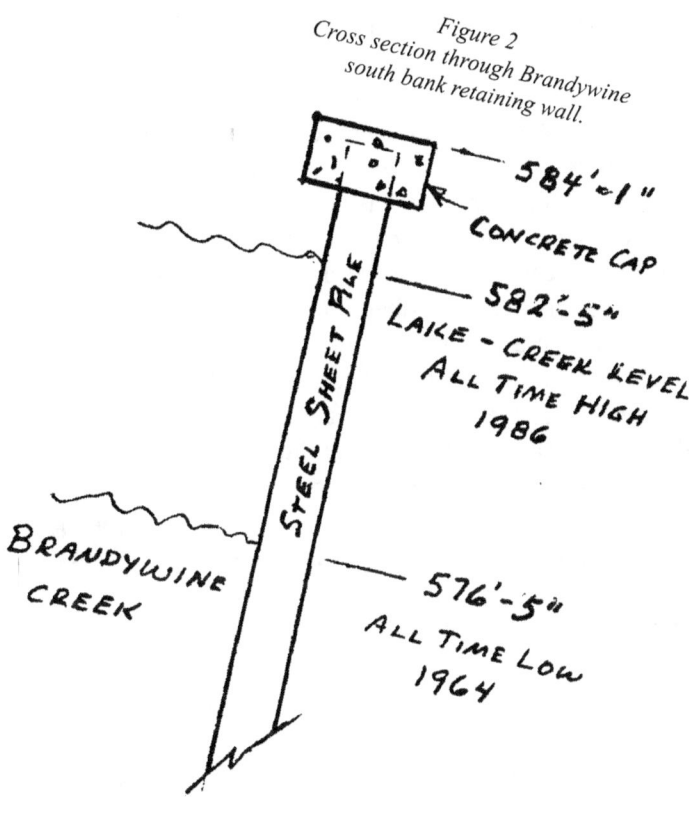

Figure 2
Cross section through Brandywine south bank retaining wall.

*Installing Brandywine steel retaining wall, October 1960. Lake level 579'6"*

## 1960's Steel Pile Sea Wall - Brandywine to Sturtevant Lodge

The 1960 Brandywine Creek steel retaining wall was followed immediately by a new connecting steel sea wall extending south 567 feet across the frontage of seven cottages – Lowrey #39, PPCC Sunset Drive right-of-way, Donahue #41, VanBeuren #43, Melchert #45, Haude #47, Wunsch #49, and Prange #51. It was constructed with Type 2 steel sheet piles, each 16 to 18 feet long, and placed a maximum of six feet in front of the decayed 1930's wood sea wall, visible in the October 1960 aerial photo and illustrated in Figure 3. The cost with concrete cap was about $58/linear foot; the handrail added another $3/foot. Top elevation of the cap was about 584'4". The cap is still visible near the Brandywine, but has been damaged by the elements through the years.

In spring of 1975, a horizontal "U" channel steel wale was welded to the front face of the steel wall for added strength, across the frontage of cottages #47, 49, and 51.

*Newly installed 1960 steel sea wall lakeside of decayed 1930's wood wall. Longitudinal rebar is welded in place, prior to pouring a concrete cap. Skeleton of 1947 jetty in background. Looking north along Lowrey #39. Photo October 1960. Lake level 579'3"*

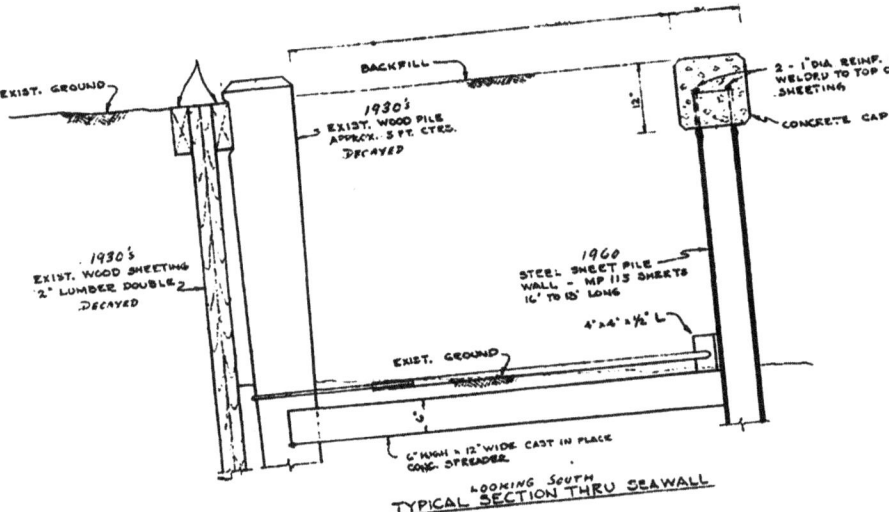

*Figure 3*
*Section through 1960 sea wall, looking south.*

*Pile driving steel sea wall sheet piles into place. Contractor: Canonie Construction Company. Looking north. October 1960. Lake level 579'3"*

# STEEL WALLS

*A variety of walls by cottages #49 and 51. Precast, concrete-block retaining wall and steel cage retainer are visible at left, in front of cottage #47. Type 3 steel sheet wall visible at right, by Sturtevant Lodge. Photo April 1985. Lake level 581'*

The short, 16' – 18' sheet pile lengths later proved inadequate as portions of the wall began to rotate; one portion in front of cottages #49 and 51 failed completely during the winter storms of 1984-85.

*Detail of Cottage #51 collapse.*

## 1973 STEEL RETAINING WALL SOUTH OF BRANDYWINE

Figure 4 illustrates a secondary Type 2 steel retaining wall constructed, in spring 1973, 20 feet behind the 1960 steel sea wall. It extended 228 feet, across the PPCC Sunset Drive right-of-way, Anderson cottage #41, VanBeuren #43, and Coleman #45, as further protection. Cost was about $100/linear foot. The sheet piles varied from 13 to 23 feet long, depending on the topography. The shorter length proved inadequate, as parts of the wall later began to rotate.

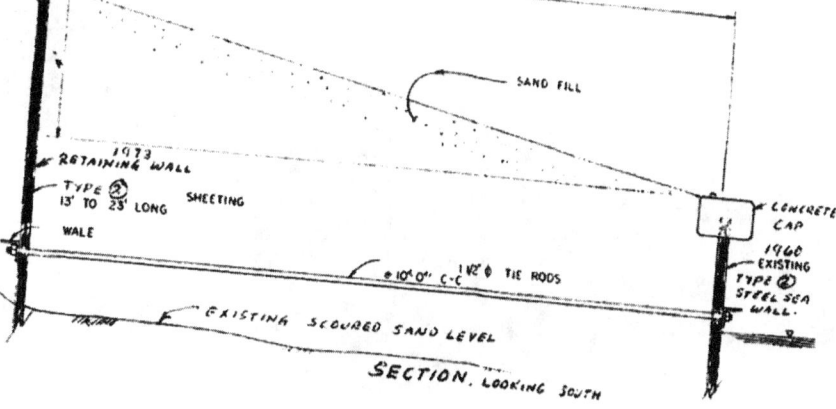

*Figure 4*
*Cross section of 1973 steel retaining wall installation south of Brandywine Creek, looking south.*

STEEL WALLS

### 1970's Precast Concrete Block Retaining Wall

Some time in the 1970's, a one-of-a-kind (for Palisades Park) 50 foot long retaining wall was built in front of cottage #47 north of Circle Beach, consisting of large pre-cast concrete blocks four feet wide, one foot high, and three feet deep. The blocks were placed two rows deep and held in place by a prior built treated wood retaining wall in the rear. In front, they were held by a welded steel "U" channel frame attached to 14" I-beam steel pilings sunk deep in the sand at ten foot intervals.

When the steel sea wall in front of cottage #49, next door, failed during the winter of 1984-85, the concrete block retaining wall helped protect cottage #47 from damage. See aerial photo on previous page.

*Exposed precast concrete blocks at right. Rip rap installation under way in background for cottages #45, 43, and 41 to the north. 1973 steel retaining wall at right of crane is beginning to rotate. Looking north. Fall 1986. Lake level 581'8".*

### 1970's Steel Sea Wall - Sturtevant Lodge and PPCC Circle Beach

Some time in the 1970's, a Type 3 flat sheet pile steel sea wall was installed across the 150 foot stretch of beach in front of Sturtevant Lodge and Circle Beach. It is partially visible at right in the aerial view on the previous page. The wall was reinforced on the front with a continuous horizontal welded steel "wale." Although the Type 3 flat sheet pile is not as strong as the corrugated cross sections of Type 1 and 2 sheets, whatever sheet length selected was adequate to prevent wall rotation in accordance with the "rule of thumb." It still stands straight.

A modest amount of rip rap stone was placed in front of the wall in 1985, as added protection.

## 1960'S Steel Sea Wall South of Circle Beach

A 250 foot sea wall, built in the 60's, extends from Circle Beach to the south end of Hong Kong Hilton #95. Constructed of Type I sheet pile with exposed steel top edge, it was located about six feet forward of an earlier decayed wood sea wall. Sheet pile length is not known.

The gale wind storm of November 1972 proved that the top of the sea wall was too low to prevent wash-over and sand scouring behind, so early in the spring of 1973, a 12 inch high by 13 inch wide concrete cap was added to increase its height.

In the long run, the concrete cap proved counterproductive, as it disturbed the "rule of thumb" ratio. Battering from the high water level wave action and winter ice continued during 1974-76, 1979-81, and 1983-84. By spring of 1984, the top-heavy wall had rotated forward significantly and sand scouring behind was severe. As the failing steel sea wall was no longer providing adequate storm protection to the four cottages involved, in the fall of 1984 stone rip rap was added in front, on top of, and in back of the wall to restore protection.

*Newly installed concrete cap near Hong Kong Hilton #95. Looking north. Sturtevant Lodge in background. Photo March 1973. Lake level 581'0"*

*Sand scouring has disturbed the ratio on the recently constructed wood retaining wall; it has already begun to rotate. Rotation of the steel wall and skeletons of prior wood walls can also be seen. Sturtevant Lodge at right. Photo May 3, 1984. Lake level 580'3"*

## 1969 Steel Sea Wall South of Clubhouse Beach

This steel sea wall, built in 1969, extends about 400 feet, from the south end of the Clubhouse Beach, across the frontage of seven cottages, from #150 to #156. The wall utilized Type 2 steel sheet piles. Built in front of a decayed wood sea wall installed about 1952, it is one of the best examples in the Park of a single design, continuous steel sea wall, with adequate sheet length, installed at one time by contiguous beachfront neighbors.

Other than losing its decorative cap, the wall has held up well, remaining straight except for some rotation in front of cottage #154, after the storm of 1972-73. In 1975, wood tie back bracing was added behind the steel wall, from cottage #152 to and across #156, to provide additional strength.

In 1986, after the previous winter's gale storm which caused some washout of sand behind the steel wall, a continuous 400-foot long treated wood retaining wall was built about 30 feet behind the sea wall for added cottage protection. In the spring of 1990, quarry stone rip rap was added across the full 400 foot frontage as further protection to both the steel sea wall and the wood retaining wall behind.

This group of seven contiguous beachfront cottage owners have worked collectively for their long-term shore protection: in 1969, to install the original steel wall; in 1975, to add tie back bracing; in 1986, to add the treated wood retaining wall; and in 1990, to add stone rip rap in front of the steel sea wall.

*North end of the 1969 steel wall showing the decorative welded steel cap, installed only on the Henkel cottage #150 segment. One section of the cap already missing. Photo August 1982. Lake level 579'7"*

*Winter ice pounding away, in the process of breaking the decorative steel cap welds and dropping the cap into the lake. Photo Winter 1985-86. Lake level 581'6"*

## Table 3

### Steel Sea and Retaining Wall Installations
(North to South, By Year)

| Year Installed | Cottage # and location and PPCC R.O.W. | Sea=S Retaining = R | Sheet piling type | Approx. length |
|---|---|---|---|---|
| 1960 | #39 south bank of Brandywine Creek from bridge to lake | R | 1 | 225 ft. |
| | #39, PPCC Sunset Drive #41, 43, 45, 47, 49, 51 | S | 2 | 567 |
| Early 1960's | #92 - #95 | S | 1 | 250 |
| 1969 | #1, 3, 5, 7, 9 | S | 2 | 475 |
| | #1 north bank return | R | 1 | 40 |
| | #150 – 156 | S | 2 | 400 |
| | | | Total 1960's | 1957 ft. |
| Early 1970's | #53 and Circle Beach | S | 3 | 150 ft. |
| 1971 | #190 and PPCC ROW and part of #9 | S | 1 | 150 |
| | PPCC Edgewater Road | R | 1 | 100 |
| 1972 | #2 (bluff cottage) | S | 1 | 50 |
| 1973 | PPCC Sunset Drive | R | 2 | 28 |
| | #41, #43, #45 | R | 2 | 200 |
| | | | Total 1970's | 678 ft. |

## Beach Building

### Attempts at Shore Protection

A recurring hope appears, when lake levels are high and beaches are disappearing, that some method of beach building will solve our problem of protecting beach cottages and restoring use of the PPCC Clubhouse and Circle Beaches. Palisades has been involved in three attempts at beach building – twice with jetties and sand traps and once with gabion baskets. These attempts were not successful, to say the least. A review of these efforts follows.

# BEACH BUILDING ATTEMPTS

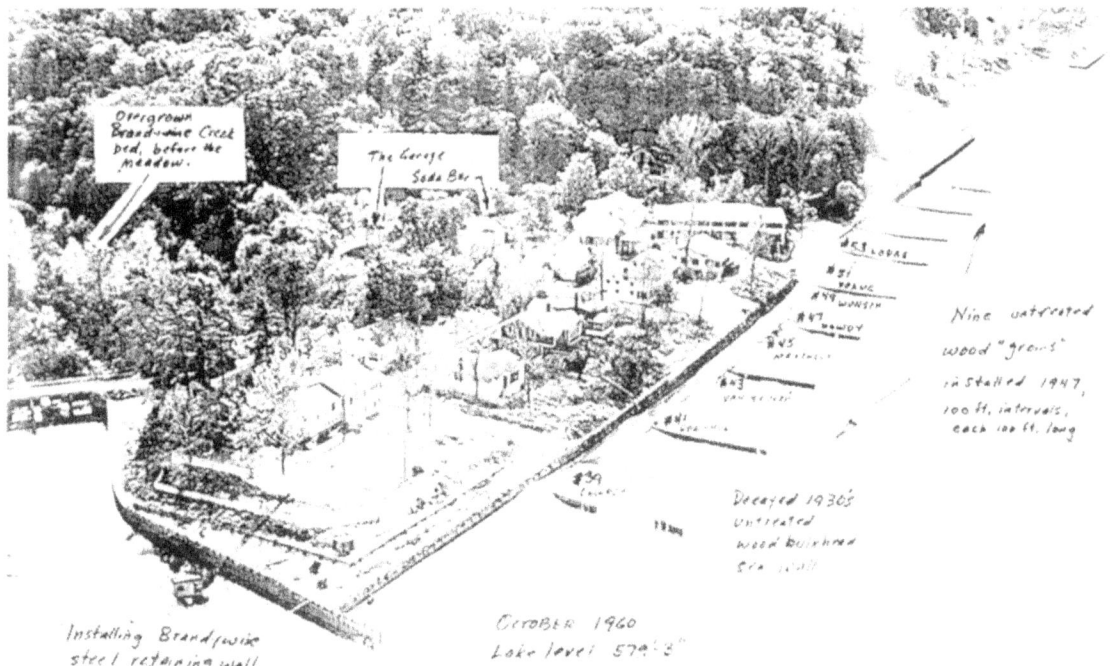

## **Jetties, Groins, and Sand-traps**

When a projection, such as a pier or jetty, is built on the southeastern shore of Lake Michigan, a sand beach tends to build on the north side of such projection; conversely, beach is subtracted on the south side. The slow-moving general flow of eastern-shore water from north to south, called the "littoral drift," carries with it suspended sand, scoured from the lake bottom by wave action over the sandbars. This can be seen in aerial views of the South Haven pier; the pier's interruption of the littoral drift has caused the suspended sand to drop out on the north side of the pier, thus feeding the north beach and starving the south. The U. S. Army Corps of Engineers finally responded to this problem they had created and have since re-fed South Haven's South Beach with trucked-in sand, at considerable cost to taxpayers.

Building on the concept of littoral drift, the idea of sand-trap jetties was born. The theory was that a continuous series of low-level wood walls projecting into the lake, and spaced at intervals apart, would collect more sand than would be lost; thus a sort of serrated beach would form. As a further refinement, a continuous low-level wood "sand trap" wall, built to connect the jetties near the shore line, would – in theory – collect sand pushed over the wall by wave action and trap the sand behind to form a beach. Thus, the "sand trap" wall. Sand-traps, it was said, could protect shorelines during periods of high lake levels, when beaches are flooded and waves lap at the lower edge of sand dunes and/or cottage foundations.

The first attempt at beach building at PPCC consisted of nine sand-trap jetties built of untreated wood about 1947, positioned from the Brandywine south to the site of Hong Kong Hilton #95, at 100 foot intervals. They extended about 100 feet into the lake, measured from the continuous wood sea wall. Their battered remains are clearly visible in the October, 1960 aerial view above. At that time, the lake level was relatively low at 579'3'. Any evidence of sand trapping or scouring in this photo is masked by the back filling of sand in front of the wood sea wall, from Brandywine to Sturtevant Lodge, in preparation for installing the new steel sheet pile sea wall across the same frontage.

Little conclusive evidence can be cited that the jetties either assisted or hindered the accumulation of sand within their boundaries – or at either end – over a period of time. But for many years, these nine jetties continued to be a hazard to beach walkers, swimmers, and boaters who collided with their skeletons – above and beneath the water. The aerial photo shows the above-water portions of eight remaining jetties in 1969, some 22 years later. (By 1978, four still remained.)

Such a less-than-resounding success in shore protection and beach building, with its continuing hazards over its 30 year life, might be expected to lead Palisades Park to want no more jetties – ever. **That would ignore our collective amnesia whenever lake levels drop, our beaches are wide, and frustration over past problems are a distant memory**.

Concern began to grow with the rise of lake levels in the late 1960's; steadily, more and more of our beach width was flooded. The first beaches to disappear, between 1969 and 1972, were those in front of our beach cottages where owners had built sea walls at considerable distance lakeward from the natural dune line. By 1973, as the lake continued to rise, even the Clubhouse, Brandywine, and North Beaches were completly flooded.

So what good is a vacation at Palisades without a beach – without swimming and without boats? That was the question the membership asked over and over – to themselves and to the PPCC Board. Beach front cottage owners and PPCC collectively had already spent over a million dollars on sea and retaining walls to save their property and dunes. High lake levels continued. By 1975, six years had passed without beaches. Some sea and retaining walls had failed and been rebuilt. The mood at Palisades was <u>FRUSTRATION</u>.

Meanwhile, in 1974, Linden hills, our neighbors to the south, had begun to install wood jetties perpendicular to the shore line, with latticed low-profile sand-trap wood walls parallel to the shore line, between the jetties. The apparent intent of these jetties was to retain what little beach remained and to enhance beach growth, even in the face of the high water levels of 580'6" beginning in late 1972. In contrast to Palisades Park's beach cottages, which are built well out toward the lake in front of the bluff line, Linden Hills cottages are, for the most part, built behind the bluff toe line. This allows for more natural beach width at Linden Hills, in any given lake level, much like our Clubhouse Beach, for example. As Palisades faced increasing problems, the Linden Hills installation was maintaining some semblance of sand in front of their bluff line.

Thus began PPCC's second attempt at beach building.

During the 1974 storms, eight PPCC south-end beach cottages had suffered the catastrophic loss of their new concrete sea wall and much of their new secondary wood retaining wall. Five of the cottages were on the brink of toppling over the edge. The situation in early 1975 was beyond frustration; it required <u>ACTION.</u> The PPCC Board took action, as explained in a May 28, 1975 Membership Letter from the Chairman of Buildings and Grounds, Hal Minick. First, the letter said, Professor E. F. Brater, of the University of Michigan's Department of National Resources Coastal Zone Laboratory – an established authority on shore erosion problems – had been contacted and asked for recommendations. Second, Donald Cluchey of Cluchey Marine Construction Company in Pentwater (who had worked with Professor Brater on similar problems and had built the Linden Hills installation) agreed to visit our site the first week in June. Minick concluded with the following:

*It is my <u>hope</u> that we will be able to resolve a definite plan for the problem area and that this plan will not adversely affect adjacent property owners. It is <u>hoped</u> that such a plan will be economical, <u>hopefully</u> less than the $200 to $250/linear foot for conventional steel seawalls .... It is also <u>hoped</u> that the proposal will build beaches.*

Minick's letter, full of "hope," clearly suggests that the first intent was for shoreline protection; the second – to build beaches. Professor Brater was hired and visited the south end on June 4, 1975. His report followed, on June 11, 1975 and recommended the following:

1. *Fill in front of the endangered houses with sand or gravel to create a beach extending out to the location of the shore line to the north and south.*

2. *Protect this beach by building impermeable groins from the present bluff line out to the line of existing walls to the north and south. A reasonable spacing for these groins would be 100 feet.*

After discussing other possible additional protection measures (such as a new sea wall or a copy of the Linden Hills design), his recommendations ended with "the most satisfactory and permanent type of protection would be a rubble revetment placed at the toe of the bluff." He thought the cost would be at least $200 per foot. Although his report didn't provide much help in reaching a decision, he did call for action.

On June 30, 1975, the Board advised all PPCC members of its decision:

*The Board unanimously agreed that the Park participate in a pilot effort to build beach by helping in the installation of a groin and sand-trap system similar to that which was successful at Linden Hills last year. (See Figures 5 and 6.) The resolution states: The Board recommends the adoption of an assessment not to exceed $50 per cottage for one-half the cost of construction of groins and sand traps from Campbells to and including Kowalskis .... Seven groins, extending 40 feet into the lake, were proposed at a cost of $28 per foot, total cost $7840. 450 feet of sand-trap wall was to be constructed at $18 per foot, total cost $8100. One-half of the combined total of $15,940 was to be borne by the property owners. In addition, the owners would pay for the primary sea wall, making their total cost $2690 plus the cost of the sand fill, estimated between $1000 and $2000 per property.*

## BEACH BUILDING ATTEMPTS

*Jetties and latticed sand-traps one year after installation and backfilling, and after lake level had dropped two feet. Photo spring 1977. Lake level 579'2"*

*Jetties, in upper right corner, two years after installation. Lake level receded from 1973-76 highs. Clubhouse Beach reforming. Beach reforming in front of concrete and steel bulkhead sea walls. Photo April 1978. Lake level 579'1"*

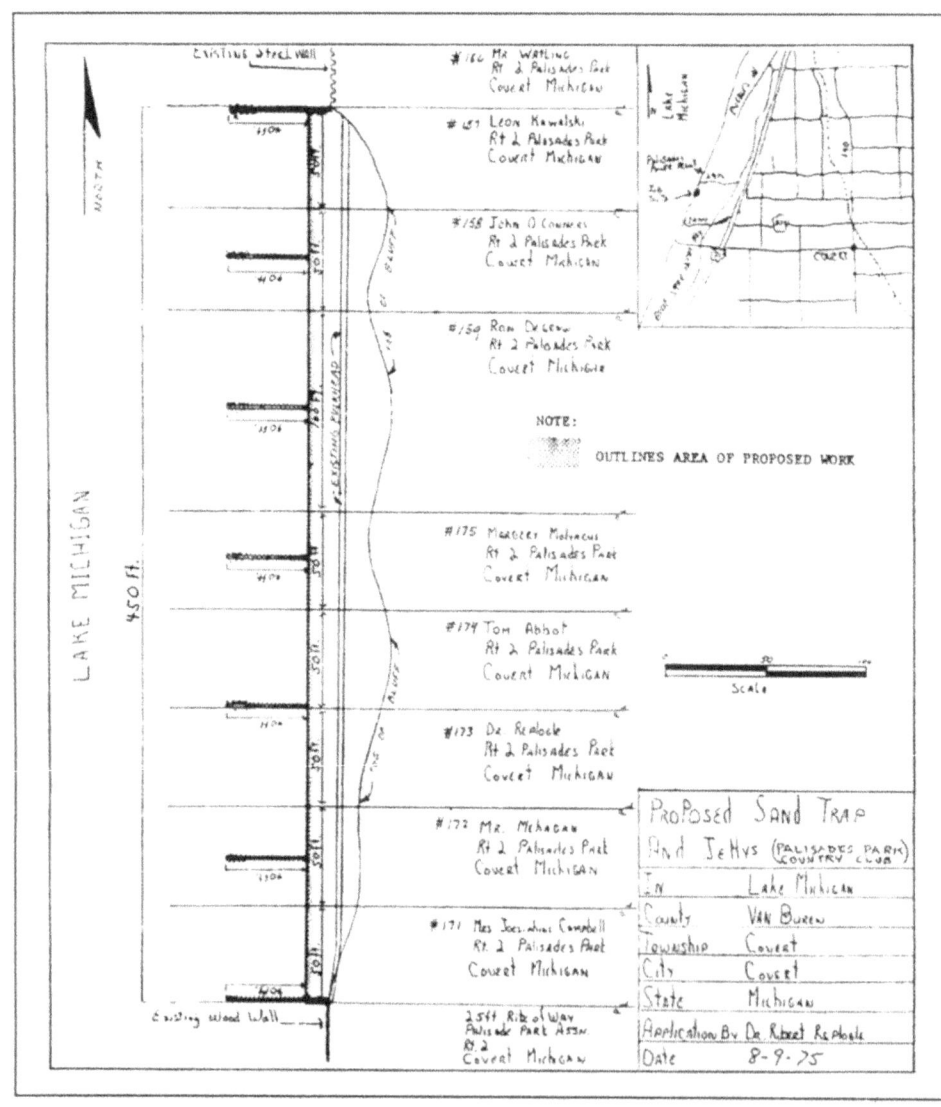

The role of jetties and sand traps, portrayed in the Brater report as shore protection, were now interpreted as "building beach." Brater was the least optimistic that jetties and sand traps would collect sand in the already deep water situation in front of these eight cottages. Nevertheless, in 1976, the seven jetties were installed at 75 foot intervals – across frontage of the eight cottages, #157-159 and 171-175. Lake level was about 581'.

*Figure 5*
*Plan of 1976 450-foot Jetty Sand-Trap Installation, as submitted to Army Corps of Engineers for approval.*

506

# BEACH BUILDING ATTEMPTS

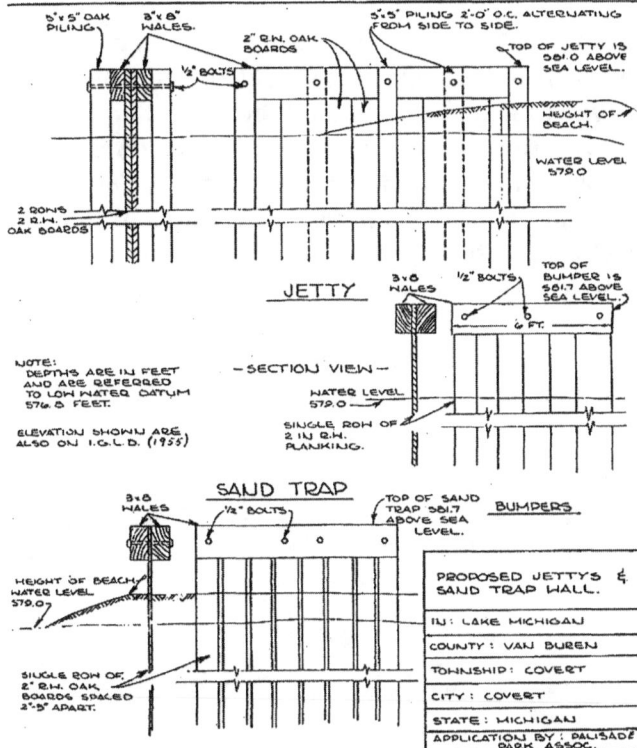

*Figure 6*
*Design cross section of 1976 sand-trap/jetty installations.*

Hopes for this new system ran high. Excerpts from the February, 1976, Board President's letter to members:

> *Ideally we shall (1) end up with a model for the restoration of other beach areas; (2) alleviate the pressure of crowds on the North Beach, and (3) thereby enhance property values of the entire Park.*

The jetty and sand-trap installation was completed in 1976, just as the lake level began a steep two foot drop in less than six months. Beaches began reforming everywhere, and the back-filled sand behind the sand-trap wall stayed in place.

*Four years after 1976 installation. With lake levels rising again, water level deepened both east and west of the sand-trap walls.*
*Photo September 1980. Lake level 580'3"*

## 1978 – The "Final" Solution

By 1978, even though aerial photos indicated a lack of collected beach sand behind the then two-year-old experiment with a jetty and sand-trap system - and even at the then "average" lake level – a grandiose plan to extend the system was presented at the August 5, 1978 Park membership meeting. The plan was to continue the 1976 installation northward, about 2000 feet, from cottage #156 to the Brandywine. It passed by a majority of those present (but representing only 1/3 of the total Park membership), at a proposed cost of $92,000. This plan raised an immediate outcry from those beach cottage owners who had no interest in a jetty or sand-trap wall potentially blocking their beach. A similar objection was raised concerning potential blockage of the Clubhouse Beach. A move was spearheaded by member Ron DeGraw, to scale down the size of the project. He outlined his reasons in an August 21, 1978 letter to the Park membership. A special meeting was called for September 2, 1978.

DeGraw's letter starts by admitting his and his neighbors' personal opposition to sand-traps: they don't want sand-traps in front of their cottages. Since one can guarantee neither their success nor their failure, he suggested proceeding on a limited basis this year. His reasons:

> *First, we are considering an expenditure of $92,000 which is almost twice our annual budget at the Park. To some, the proposed special assessment of $390 is insignificant. To others, it is monumental.... The second reason for a limited construction program at this time comes from an examination of the relative gains or losses from attempting the entire program at one time. In the event the program fails, we will be left with no central beach. We will have a wall extending two feet above present water levels, 20 feet out in the lake .... A barrier to boating and swimming. It would be impossible to get a boat over the wall on any but the calmest day, and then only for those who are strong enough to lift a boat over a two foot structure. In addition, the area behind the wall will become a collection area for dead fish and other flotsam, making it undesirable for swimming .... As compared to this loss, the gain, if the project works, would be a full beach. However, in the event the limited project works, we can always add the additional sand-traps, and we will only be delayed a year or two in our ultimate goal of having a beach in front of the entire Park.*

DeGraw ends his letter by noting that Professor Brater had "nowhere in his letter" called the proposed construction of a groin system "anything more than protection." The system may catch some sand, but to make the sand-traps effective, it would be necessary to periodically fill them with sand. **"The traps themselves do not build beach."**

The proposal to downsize was adopted with some amendment at the September meeting, making beach front cottage participation optional and eliminating the Clubhouse Beach. In July, 1979, PPCC signed a downsized contract of $47,000 with Cluchey Marine Construction Company, which had installed the 1976 system. Construction of jetties, sand-traps, and bumpers was to begin August 15, 1979 with completion in 60 working days. The section from the Brandywine south to Hong Kong Hilton #95 was to look like Figure 7 below:

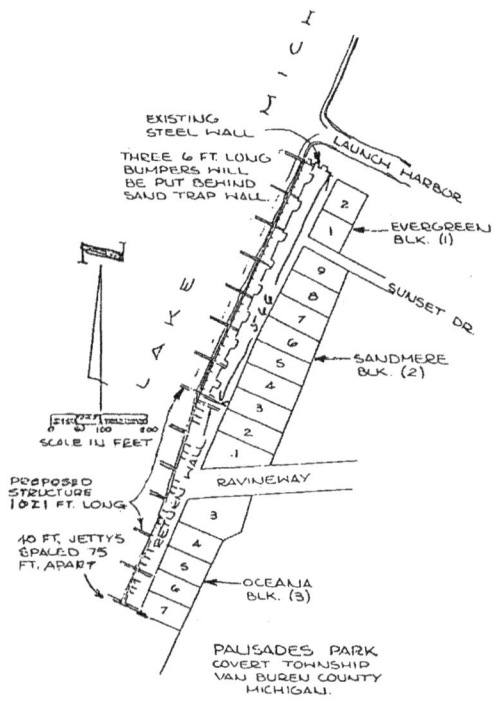

*Figure 7*
*Plan View of Proposed 1979 Jetty-Sand Trap Installation*

By September 12, 1979, PPCC had paid some $12,000 for lumber. Construction lagged and was discontinued during the winter months. Much of what was constructed was damaged by winter storms. Relationship with the contractor then deteriorated, and in the spring of 1980, construction did not restart. Fortunately lake levels declined from the 1979 highs; as beaches reformed, the perceived need was shelved and the project was abandoned. But that wasn't the end.

**1980 Shore Protection Study**

On July 16, 1980, PPCC entered into a contract with Burke Association of Park Ridge, Illinois, for $4950 plus expenses. Their report would, **"if appropriate, recommend a lower-cost form of protection which will take care of the short range problems and which will serve as a holding action until the present high water levels return to average or lower water levels. The report will also include a recommendation for a long-term permanent solution to the shore protection problem. Naturally, the permanent solution will be more costly."** The report recommendations included a plan for sea wall repair, rip rap, and a series of jetties. After reviewing the report and the estimated cost of its recommendations, the Board shelved its recommendations.

*By spring 1983, beaches reformed, but the 7 year old jetties had been damaged by the lake. Looking north, starting at Cottage #171, at the cluttered beach. Photo April 1983. Lake level 579'6"*

**1984: A Fresh Look?**

In the fall of 1984, with lake levels again rising, the PPCC Committee to Study Shore Protection and Beach Restoration recommended to the Board that Edith McKee be retained, for $2000 plus expenses, **"to make a geological survey of lakefront conditions extending 1/2 mile north and south of the Palisades Park shoreline and to include recommendation as to the most appropriate installations for our specific situation to protect property and reestablish a beach."** No record was found whether the Board proceeded with this study. However, in the same progress report, the Committee summed up the Park membership's mood rather well:

*Whether it be due to recent events, e.g. damage to wall just south of Quick Circle and installed or planned rip rap projects; general disappointment in this year's lack of beach; or safety considerations ranging from last year's drowning, several close calls this year, and a broken arm from the torn up condition just south of Quick Circle – based on comments and sentiments expressed individually and publicly at the two above August meetings - the Committee feels that the membership is more inclined to coordinate an overall Park action than it has been in recent years.*

# BEACH BUILDING ATTEMPTS

## Gabion Baskets

Gabion baskets have been successfully used as retaining walls in highway culvert construction, as seawalls on small inland lakes, and as retaining walls on creeks and smaller rivers. In each case, those successes have been in areas where heavy wave action and winter ice floe battering are absent. Unfortunately, that is not true of the conditions at Palisades.

Gabion installations consist of placing empty, hinged-top wire mesh baskets side-by-side to form a wall. Each basket is filled with rocks and/or rubble before the top is wired shut; the process is repeated for additional layers and height. Each basket is six feet long, four feet wide, and 18 inches high. The wire mesh is either galvanized to prevent rusting, or galvanized with a plastic coating to minimize rock abrasion.

### 1974 – North End

Gabion baskets were first installed at north end of the Park, across the frontage of PPCC's 15-foot Juniper Pass right-of-way and Cottage # 1's 50 foot vacant lot. They were installed as back-up behind the low-height 1969 steel sea wall which had allowed storm waves to wash over the top and scour away sand from behind the neighboring higher-top sea walls of cottages #1 and #3. The use of gabions was intended, according to the July 13, 1974 Patter, to "break the force of the waves. They are not retaining walls. There is a gravel bed underneath the baskets to prevent waves from sucking up the sand."

After 28 years, the plastic-covered wire gabion baskets are still intact. On the other hand, the baskets are almost impossible to walk on with bare feet. Furthermore, as installed they added little effective height to the low sea wall; sand scouring has continued behind the adjacent high walls.

### 1986 – South End

Twelve years later, gabion baskets were considered for installation in four locations at the south end of the Park: across the Clubhouse Beach shoreline; at the north end of the steel sea wall by Henkel #150; at the south end of the same steel sea wall by Tombaugh #156; and south of Wintermute #183.

### 1986 – 1989: Clubhouse Beach - A Disaster That Wouldn't End

In 1985 lake levels were again rising. At their August 31, 1985 meeting, the PPCC Board authorized up to $20,000 "to build a 'low-profile' treated wood sea/retaining wall across the Clubhouse Beach shoreline." Designed to help capture sand, it was also intended to shore up the 1973 treated wood retaining wall at the toe of the Clubhouse dune.

Later, at the October 12, 1985 meeting, "Park Manager Stan Severinghaus described a proposal to instead install rock filled baskets (gabions) behind the decayed 1950's sea wall, with a proposal from ADD Construction to do the work for $7,900. **It was believed that the prospects of building a beach were greater with gabions than with a solid wall.** If necessary, sand bags could be put down for access to the water." The Board agreed to the proposal.

*The north end's 1974 plastic-coated gabion baskets behind low-height steel sea wall.
Photo October 1985.
Lake level near all-time high of 581'5"*

## BEACH BUILDING ATTEMPTS

The gabions were to extend the 400 feet from Cottage #100's concrete wall, across Clubhouse Beach, south to Cottage #150's steel wall. The cost would work out to about $20/linear foot, compared to $50/foot for a low-profile treated-wood wall.

The baskets were laid end-to-end, directly on the shore line sand. As reported during the April 19, 1986 Board meeting: **"The contractor is tardy in constructing the gabions ... They will be installed one foot above the water line."**

Finally, by summer 1986, the installation was complete. The baskets were made of galvanized wire, without the plastic covering used in 1974 at the north end of the Park. Soon the direct wave pounding and the 1986-87 winter ice battering caused the rocks to abrade the galvanized coating. Rust weakened the wire and many baskets broke open, spilling and scattering the relatively small gabion rock and rubble, covering the beach behind. The hundreds of broken wires presented sharp points that made barefoot passage across the baskets impossible. By the summer of 1987, with its high water level, what little Clubhouse Beach remained was like a minefield.

On July 11, 1987, volunteers tackled the sharp wire problem. From the August 1, 1987 Patter: **"At the other end of the beach, an effort was made to remove the wire debris from broken gabions. Unfortunately, despite the best efforts, the available tools weren't up to the task and the wire removal effort was not successful."**

The problem wouldn't go away. Excerpts from Joe Fitzgerald's letter to the editor in the September, 1988 Patter: **"Our Clubhouse Beach is in a shambles, despite a dramatic reduction of the lake level .... Consideration should be given to the removal of the rock, brick, block, and gabions, which are presently disintegrating, and then cutting off the (old) wood sea wall."**

In 1989 the problem was finally put to bed. In that summer's July Patter, Bob Zimmermann, in his Park Manager's Update, said, **"At the Clubhouse Beach we've cut off the posts at sand level and trimmed protruding wires on the remaining gabions to make the beach safe for swimming."**

In hindsight, the decision to protect the Clubhouse Beach's 1973 treated wood retaining/sea wall "on the cheap" by once again trying to build beach - with yet another untried and unproved method – resulted in an expensive failure. When the PPCC Board decision to use gabions was made, in their October 12, 1985 meeting, the Circle Beach rip rap stone installation to protect the Circle Beach 1970's steel sea wall had already been completed the previous spring. Had the Clubhouse Beach's 1973 wall been similarly protected by rip rap

*Clubhouse Beach with split open gabion baskets in background. Kaleb Cargin "enjoying" the beach of spilled rock and rubble. Photo Oct. 4, 1987. Lake level 580'.*

that spring, the wall may well have survived the December 1, 1985 storm. Instead, that storm destroyed over half the 1973 wall as well as a huge portion of the Clubhouse Beach bluff.

A replacement treated wood sea/retaining wall was built immediately in spring 1986; it was further protected that fall by adding quarry stone rip rap – thus finally duplicating the Circle Beach sea wall protection.

The three attempts to build beach – first in 1947, again in 1976, and last in 1986 – by almost any evaluation proved to be costly failures that also created long lasting impediments to beach safety and enjoyment. The basic lesson was relearned three times over: **When lake levels are rising or are already high, trying to retain or build a beach is futile. The lake always wins. The focus should always be on saving bluffs and cottages and their protective sea walls.**

### North in front of #150 and South in Front of #156

At the two ends of the steel wall constructed from cottage #150 to #156, galvanized gabion wire baskets were used as rip rap type protection for the new, 1986 treated wood "wing" walls extending back from the steel wall. The wood walls provided backing to the baskets and the oblique direction provided some protection from direct wave action and ice battering of rocks against the galvanized wire. These baskets are still in place, but buried deep in the sand.

### South of #183

In this installation, galvanized wire gabion baskets were used as a retaining wall, not in direct contact with waves and winter ice. The installation has been and continues to be successful. Presently, the baskets are buried in the sand.

*Lou Goscinski examines damaged galvanized wire gabion basket at south end of Clubhouse Beach, connecting with steel sea wall in front of cottage #150. Note the steel cap on top of the sea wall, bent up by battering of winter ice.*
*Photo August 1987. Lake level 580'*

---

## Stone Rip Rap Revetment:
## The Sea Wall Protection of Choice

In the fall of 1984, with lake levels rising and with a damaged steel sea wall, the four beach cottage owners south of Quick Circle (#92, 93, 94, 95) started the Park's first rip rap project. That installation was completed in November 1984. Concurrently, the PPCC Committee to Study Shore Protection and Beach Restoration sent an interim progress report, dated December 19, 1984, to Board President Don Beveridge. He forwarded the letter to all Park members in February, 1985, suggesting that rip rap might be the answer to PPCC's two problems – protecting shoreline and saving a large number of failing beach cottage seawalls. In part, the report stated:

> *In high water periods, sea walls have a wave rebound which keeps the sand in suspension and prevents beach building. This can also cause scouring along the base of the wall and may lead to undermining. Also, the rebound effect could cause problems in areas where there is no wall because of the turmoil in the water.*

> *Rip rap may be a solution to the rebound effect. It allows the wave to run up an imitation beach. It dissipates the force of the wave and allows sand to deposit. Several different rip-rap sites were visited with various material (two-ton concrete blocks, massive sand and concrete bags, boulders, etc.) and the results seem to be the same. The force of the wave is spent before it hits the seawall. This allows sand to deposit and eliminates rebound. In all cases viewed, the water has shallowed and sandbars have formed. However, only in cases where there was enough setback did beaches form and cover the rip rap. In high water, it seems the seawalls themselves and the rip rap remain showing, but the water is shallow and the property protected. The rip rap project requires proper preparation, material, and construction to be effective. Otherwise, not only the property itself, but the adjoining properties can be adversely affected. So far, the Palisades project from the Tillsons to Warners seems to show the same result.*

## Table 4

### Rip Rap Installation

(North to South by Year)

| Year | Location, Cottage # | Seawall Type | Stone Type | Approximate Length |
|---|---|---|---|---|
| 1984* | #92, 93, 94, 95 | Steel | Boulder | 250 ft. |
| 1985* | (May) #47, 49, 51, 53 | Steel | Quarry | 250 |
|  | (May) PPCC Circle Beach | Steel | Quarry | 50 |
|  | (Fall) #176, 178, 179, 181, 183 | Wood | Quarry | 375 |
|  | (Fall) PPCC right-of-way between #181 and #183 | Wood | Quarry | 15 |
|  |  |  | Total | 690 ft. |

<u>December 1, 1985 Storm</u>

| Year | Location, Cottage # | Seawall Type | Stone Type | Approximate Length |
|---|---|---|---|---|
| 1986 | #5, 7, 9 | Steel | Boulder | 300 ft. |
|  | #39 next to Brandywine | Dune | Quarry | 175 |
|  | PPCC Sunset Drive between #39 and 41 | Steel | Quarry | 15 |
|  | #41, 43, 45 | Steel | Quarry | 200 |
|  | #98, 99, 100 | Concrete | Boulder | 300 |
|  | PPCC Clubhouse Beach | Wood | Quarry | 400 |
|  | #157, 158, 159, 175 | Wood | Quarry | 250 |
|  | PPCC right-of-way between #159 and 175 | Wood | Quarry | 15 |
|  | #174, 173, 172, 171 | Wood | Quarry | 200 |
|  | PPCC right-of-way between #171 and 176 | Wood | Quarry | 25 |
|  |  |  | Total | 1880 ft. |
| 1987 | North Beach (Consumers Property) | Sand bluff | Quarry | 100 ft. |
|  | Consumers lot in PPCC | Sand bluff | Quarry | 50 |
|  | #2 (installed by Consumers) | Steel | Quarry | 50 |
|  |  |  | Total | 200 ft. |
| 1990 | #150, 151, 152, 153, 154, 155, 156 | Steel | Quarry | 400 ft. |
|  |  |  | Grand Total | 3420 ft. |

*The monster gale storm of December 1, 1985, with the lake level near its all-time high, provided a maximum test for these 1984-85 rip rap installations. Though there was some damage to frontal areas, most agreed that without the rip rap protection, at least some of the cottages would have been in the lake.

## Installation and Uses

The installation of stone rip rap in front of so many Park beach cottages testifies to its ability to protect our varied sea walls – treated wood, steel, and concrete – many of which were inadequately designed and installed. Since 1960, rip rap has been:

1. Added in front and on top of failed sea walls, in effect to create a new sea wall.
2. Added in front of treated wood sea walls as protection against wave action and winter ice battering of the wood, to extend its useful life.
3. Added in front of poured concrete sea walls to protect their underwater "toe" from erosion.
4. Added in front and on top of low height treated wood, cement, and steel sea walls to protect the walls, to increase their effective height, and to increase cottage protection during high water.
5. Placed against the toe of bluffs to protect them from further high water wave erosion.
6. Added in front of "wing" walls to strengthen the transition connection between adjacent but differing style and height sea walls.

Rip rap "cover" stones are typically 500-4000 pounds each, either granite boulder fieldstones from Northern Michigan, which have been glacier-smoothed and are variegated in color, or quarry limestone, which is light gray and with rather jagged edges from being blasted loose. Boulder fieldstones are virtually weather impervious, as they have already been exposed to eons of time. Quarry stone, having been blasted loose, can be distressed with fine cracks that allow moisture to enter. Freezing and thawing may then gradually split the rock into smaller pieces. However, this is a long term process and may take many years to become significant. Much of the quarry limestone used in PPCC originated from the Chicago area and was transported by truck in 20 ton loads. Many hundreds of truck loads were required to satisfy the Park needs. All these trucks either maneuvered through our roads to dump their loads near the beach or deposited the stone at a staging area on the old PPCC golf course.

Installing rip rap calls for first removing and leveling the sand in front of the distressed sea wall, down to the level anticipated during periods of highest lake water level. This forms a bed for the rocks; its width is in proportion to the height of the distressed wall. The higher the wall, the greater the width of the boulder field. Next, a heavy-duty filter fabric is placed over the entire flat sandy area. This is crucial. Otherwise, the stones would eventually sink out of sight. If the installation is in the water, the filter fabric is weighted down with small "mattress" stones to prevent floating; then a row of heavy toe stones is placed across the full length of the filter fabric's outer edge.

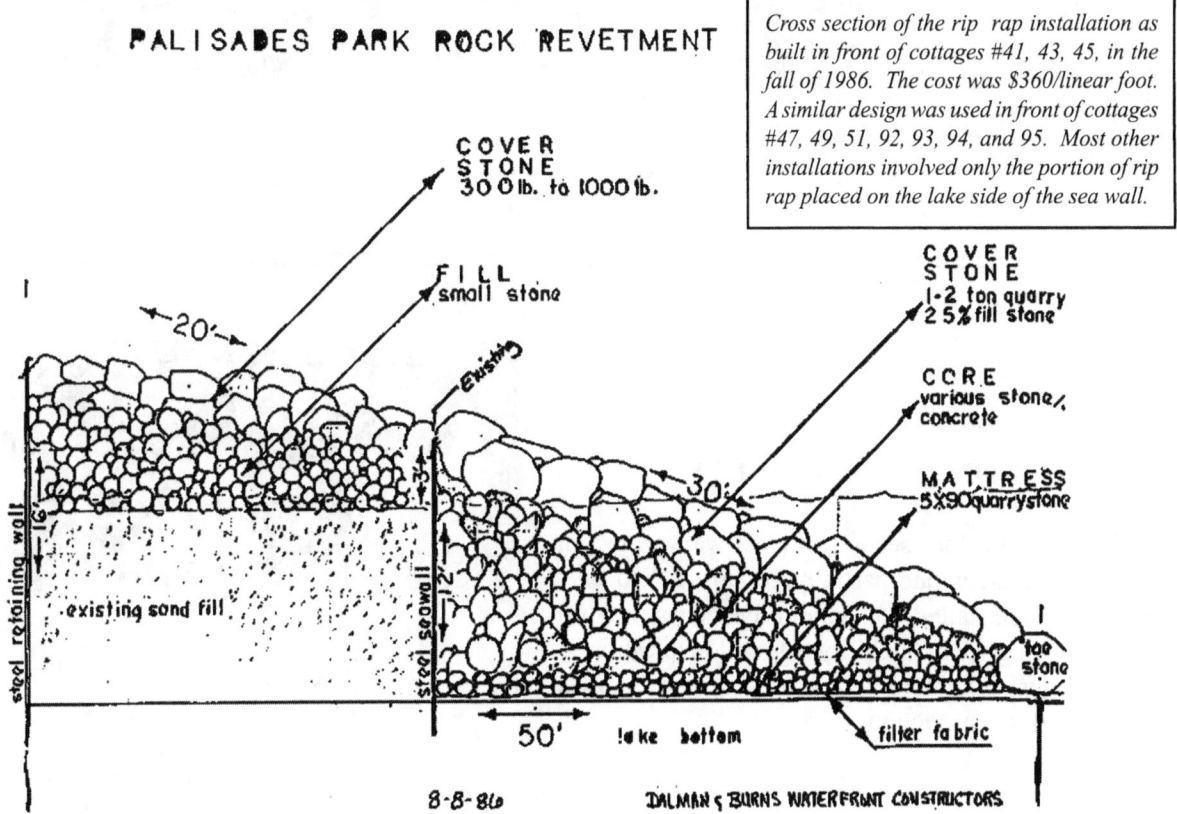

*Cross section of the rip rap installation as built in front of cottages #41, 43, 45, in the fall of 1986. The cost was $360/linear foot. A similar design was used in front of cottages #47, 49, 51, 92, 93, 94, and 95. Most other installations involved only the portion of rip rap placed on the lake side of the sea wall.*

Figure 8

The following survey of the Park's installation of rip rap is presented geographically, from north to south.

## 1976 – Consumers Power Plant

Though not in Palisades Park, Consumers Power was the first in the area to install rip rap in a 1386 foot long massive project designed to protect the plant from any conceivable lake level threat, should the extremely high levels of 1973-75 continue. The gale storm of December, 1974, had eroded much of their unprotected shoreline, and the lake had advanced toward the plant. The project was completed in 1976.

During the next period of rising lake levels in 1985-86, Consumers received a permit to extend the rip rap 400 feet further south to protect their two cooling towers. That project was completed in July of 1987. At the conclusion of the project, the Plant had a considerable number of quarry stones left over. Minutes of the July 25, 1987 PPCC Board meeting, report that Mr. Dave Hoffman, Consumers' Plant Manager, indicated that *"Consumers is willing to cooperate with PPCC to the best of their ability and indicated they had large (1500 pound) stones left over from their shoreline project, which could be made available to the Park."* Because our North Beach bluff area had eroded from the high water of 1985-86, the left over stone was used to fill the corner junction of Roche #1 and VanderSalm #2 steel sea walls, and then to cover the base of the North Beach bluff northward as far as the stone lasted. That project was finished in the fall of 1987; the stone extended sufficiently to protect about 200 feet of North Beach bluff base. Give Consumers credit for being a good neighbor on this one.

*Consumers quarry stone rip rap installation at base of North beach bluff at left, and piled up at the Roche-VanderSalm steel wall junction. Cottage #1 in background.*
*Photo September 30, 1988.*
*Lake level 579'*

## 1986 North End Cottages #5, #7, and #9.

Although the 300 foot section of steel wall protecting these three cottages had partially collapsed, had been removed and reinstalled, and had survived the gale storm of 1985, its long-term durability was still in question. In 1986, a modest amount of field stone rip rap was placed in front as added protection.

*Rip rap installed in front of reinstalled steel sea wall of Cottages #5 and #7 at right.*
*September 4, 1987. Lake level 580'*

# RIP RAP

## Cottage #39, A Rip Rap Exception

This cottage accounts for about 100 feet of frontage at the north end of the 567 ft. 1960 steel sea wall. However, cottage #39 did not join the 1973 steel retaining wall project of its neighbors to the south and left its dune line unprotected. By fall 1986, the dune had eroded some 25 feet. Quarry stone rip rap was then added for protection at the toe of the dune. This is the only example in the Park of a bare exposed sea wall with rip rap protection at the dune line behind.

*Looking north across cottage #39's newly installed rip rap. Contractor Dalman and Burns. 1960 steel wall barely visible at far left. Brandywine Beach underwater in background. Maloblocki (later site of Cottage #190) steel wall, well above the waves, in background. December 9, 1986. Lake level very high at 581'2"*

## Cottages #41, 43, and 45

The 1960 steel sea wall crosses 15 feet of PPCC Sunset Drive right-of-way and 200 feet in front of cottages #41, 43, and 45. By 1986, its concrete cap showed further signs of distress. Furthermore, its top height proved inadequate to prevent wave wash-over during high lake water levels. That fall, quarry stone rip rap was installed, completely burying the front and back of the sea wall. The rip rap in effect became the primary sea wall, adding about two feet of effective height. (See cross section as illustrated in Figure 8.)

*1st stage of building the rip rap protection by placing stones west of the steel sea wall. Contractor Dalman and Burns. Looking south from Cottage #43. Fall 1986.*
*Lake level 581'2"*

### Cottages #47, 49, and 51

The 150 foot section of the 1960 steel wall, in front of cottages #47, 49, and 51, partially rotated forward during the winter of 1984-85. That next spring, quarry stone rip rap was installed across the front of the wall, over the top, and about ten feet back – to the retaining wall built behind. Rip rap above the top of the steel wall added one to two feet of effective height. The design was similar to the cross section in Figure 8, but differed in dimensions.

By the early 1990's, the front portion of rip rap stones had begun to settle; the lake level was again rising. In 1995, field stone rip rap was added across the frontage of these three cottages, restoring the rip rap's height. Hence, a mixture of quarry and field stone is presently visible along this frontage.

### 1985: Sturtevant Lodge and Circle Beach

The 150 foot frontage across Sturtevant Lodge and Circle Beach was further protected in the spring of 1985, by installing quarry stone rip rap in front of the existing steel sea wall. The rip rap was installed only part way up toward the wall's top. The steel wall still stands straight and appears in good condition, but the sea wall's inadequate height remains.

### 1984: South of Circle Beach, Cottages #92, 93, 94, and 95

These four cottages, Tillson #92 through Hong Kong Hilton #95, pioneered the first rip rap installation in the Park. By the spring of 1984, their 250 foot steel wall was failing; sand scouring behind the wall was severe. Installation of rip rap was completed late in 1984, using a massive amount of boulder placed in front of the steel sea wall, over the concrete cap, and 10 to 15 feet further back. The rip rap depth added at least two feet to the effective height of the wall. Its design was similar to the cross section illustrated in Figure 8 earlier in this chapter.

*Completed rip rap by Hong Kong Hilton #95, looking north. In this case, the rip rap extends back to the cottage's cement and steel retaining wall.*

*Completed rip rap covering both sides and rear of the distressed 1960's steel sea wall. Cottage #92 concrete walk and railing at bottom. Looking south.*

**1985: Cottage #176 South Across #178, 179, 181, and 183**

After severe dune erosion from the storms of 1984 – 85, several of the five cottages from Beck to Wintermute were left perilously unprotected. Sand bags were used for temporary protection. That fall, quarry stone rip rap was installed in front of their breached treated-wood sea walls – and just in time, before the gale storm that December 1, 1985.

*Cottage #176.
Temporary sand bags below.
April 1985. Lake level 581'*

## A 60 YEAR SUMMARY - 1985

So, finally, by trial and error, PPCC has evolved into a shoreline protection mode that protects cottages and bluffs during high lake levels and reforms the beach when lake levels subside. Board President Beveridge sent a letter to Park members on June 20, 1985, summarizing some 60 years of Palisades shore protection experience:

*I've been asked frequently how the members in general feel about the beachfront. The President always hears from a vocal minority and this small sample may not represent the large block of members we never hear from. A few thoughts have emerged. Obviously the lake front owners are most concerned. I do sense a growing realization among the "woods people," as those of us not on the lake were dubbed at a long-ago membership meeting, of what the beachfront means to the Park. It's something we tended to take for granted until one day we found it was gone.*

*Over the years we've seen many failed beachfront projects, both large and small. There's a very definite feeling that no one wants to pay any money for a solution that doesn't have a strong probability of success, either for property protection or beach building.*

*At the same time, there's a faction that feels there must be some "magic" solution and we just haven't looked hard enough to find it. A year ago, I tended to think that way but after many hours of meetings and discussions, I'm convinced there is no such magic.*

*Another point that's been frequently mentioned is that not only have we had failures but many are "fifty foot failures," i.e., individual owners have attempted individual solutions. The point has been driven home to many that we need to cooperate on solutions as much as possible.*

*We can finally point to some successes. The Tillson/ Bishop/Nebendahl/Warner rip rap project completed last fall survived some especially brutal storms in the early winter and spring and came through intact. Now the area inside the seawall has been topped with small stones and Stan and Dave have installed an attractive and sturdy boardwalk. We'd all prefer to see sand but if you have to look at rock, this is about as nice as you can get and it's doing the job.*

*This spring Livingstons, Andreas, McCarthys and Haudes carried out a similar project to the north of the Circle but with quarry limestone instead of fieldstone. It was completed about a week ago. The owners and others I've talked to are quite pleased with the results. The same specifications were followed as for the Tillson – Warner job so there's every reason to believe it will protect their property. (As owners of the Circle Beach area, the Park shared in the expense of both these projects.)*

*The homeowners involved with these projects spent large sums of money, typically $15-20,000. This has been the traditional way. Including the inlet at the Brandywine, we have about 4650 feet of lakefront of which about 950 feet (roughly 20%) belongs to the Park. With one exception, the owners of the other*

# RIP RAP

*3700 feet have footed the bill for their piece of property. The exception was the sand-trap project of the early '70's in front of eight cottages toward the south end of the Park. Those eight owners split 50% of the cost and the other 160 or so owners split the other 50% via a special assessment.*

*We've heard suggestions that this be changed, that the Park should somehow assume a bigger share, perhaps in the ongoing maintenance of some of these areas. The sand-traps, for example, are only partially effective because not all owners of this or other areas have maintained them. Should the Park assume the maintenance of this or other areas to insure they remain intact? I don't have an answer for this but it's something we need to think about.*

The answer to the question of Park maintenance of the deteriorating jetties and sand-traps came quickly when the December 1, 1985 storm destroyed whatever effectiveness they may have had. Their vestiges were soon cut down to clear the beach area for installation of rip rap protection in front of the surviving 1975 wood sea wall.

*Aftermath of the gale storm of December 1, 1985, which destroyed much of the deteriorated jetty-sand trap installation. Looking north from Cottage #158. Photo December 1985.*

### Table 5

### PPCC Beach Frontage Held in Common
(From North to South)

| Name | Beach Location | Approx. Sea Wall Length |
|---|---|---|
| Juniper Pass | Between cottages #1 and 3 | 15 ft. |
| Right-of-Way | Between cottages #7 and 190 | 15 or 20 |
| Edgewater Road | Between cottage #190 and Brandywine Creek | 25 * |
| Edgewater Road | Brandywine Creek north bank and road south of cottages #190, 18, 19, and 20 | 400 ** |
| Sunset Drive | Between cottages #39 and 41 | 15 |
| Circle Beach | Between cottages #53 and 92 | 125 *** |
| Clubhouse Beach | Between cottages #100 and 150 | 400 |
| Right-of-Way | Between cottages #159 and 175 | 15 |
| Right-of-Way | Between cottages #171 and 176 | 25 |
| Right-of-Way | Between cottages #181 and 183 | 15 |
| | Total | 1050 ft. |

\*The 25 ft. PPCC steel sea wall was built at cottage expense in 1971.

\*\*The west 80 ft. of PPCC steel sea wall was built at cottage #190's expense in 1971. The east 320 feet of PPCC concrete sea wall built at cottage #18, 19, 20 expense in 1973.

\*\*\*The south 50 ft. of cottage #53 beach frontage was deeded to PPCC, increasing PPCC Circle Beach frontage from its original 75 ft. to 125 ft. PPCC assumed sea wall responsibility.

## What Have We Learned?

By expensive trial and expensive error, PPCC has evolved into a shoreline protection mode that protects cottages and bluff lines during high lake levels and reforms the beach when lake levels subside. Our history seems to provide the following guidelines for the future:

### Adequate Sea Wall Protection

Over time, a cost-effective system points to a steel bulkhead sea wall with sufficient sheet pile length to prevent rotation during maximum lake levels. Test borings can determine the clay strata depth, or lack thereof, for selecting adequate sheet pile length. To protect against storm surge, this option also requires a back-up steel or treated-wood retaining wall. Finally, backfill is needed between the sea and retaining walls.

### Preferred Protection

More costly - but more effective - would be full-height rip rap in front of the steel or treated-wood bulkhead sea walls. If the bulkhead wall is of inadequate height to provide high water surge protection, rock height can be increased.

The "ultimate solution" is illustrated in Figure 8, with rip rap covering the sand area between sea and retaining walls.

### Future Counsel

PPCC has unparalleled experience in what works and doesn't work as our shoreline protection. We have paid dearly for the lessons. No outside consultant or contractor can match our experience. As future needs may arise, the best counsel regarding our shoreline may well be gleaned from the history of our own 80 years of experience.

Based on our history, it makes sense to do the following:

1. At the North Beach bluff line, keep the existing rip rap in good repair.
2. At the Brandywine Beach, if the concrete contour sea wall begins to weaken, install rip rap protection.
3. At the Clubhouse Beach bluff line, maintain full rip rap height against the wood sea wall. Raise the rock height or add retaining wall height as needed to protect the bluff line.
4. Avoid all jetties, sand-traps, low-profile shore line walls, gabions, or any other obstructions which interfere with beach use when low lake levels return.
5. Work collectively with contingent groups of neighbors, remembering that protection is no more effective than its lowest height segment.
6. Violate the three feet down/one up ratio for bulkhead walls only at the risk of great expense for repair or replacement.
7. Remember that no "magic solution" has been found to date to grow beach along the Palisades shoreline during periods of high lake levels. Conversely, when high levels recede, our beaches have always reappeared, regardless of shore protection method.
8. Keep experiments small; monitor and record periodic conditions and accurately report the test results.
9. Consider stock piling rip rap rock on the old golf course in time of low lake levels. When levels are high, demand and prices rise and availability decreases.
10. Deal with reputable and financially sound contractors.
11. Never stop looking for better solutions.

### In Retrospect – An Expression of Thanks

The 19 years from 1969 – 1988 were probably the most difficult in the history of Palisades Park. It was a period of never ending high water. For some 16 years we had little or no beach in front of our cottages. At least six of those years, we had no beaches at all, anywhere, in the Park. Of the six major gale storms that savaged the Park in the last 80 years, four occurred during this 19 year span. Property damage and sea wall construction cost us collectively many millions of dollars.

Those who served on the Palisades Park Boards and guided us through those turbulent years, especially the Chairs of Buildings and Grounds and those who served on the various Shoreline Protection Committees, deserve thanks. The challenges faced were unprecedented; circumstances often forced quick decisions with only fragmentary information. Budgets were more than tight and Park members were often discouraged, impatient, second-guessing, and angry. Some of you spent countless hours, days, weeks, months, and years to serve us, without pay, and too often without thanks. Many volunteers led PPCC through those 19 years of storms to a safe port, and we are all the wiser for it.

The biggest thanks, however, must go to the 38 beach and six bluff cottage owners who, by far, have borne the lion's share of financial and emotional sacrifice in preserving bluff and beach frontage. Without a beach, values of all Park property decrease. The Park's debt to these 44 families is monumental.

# The Park in Winter

# Chapter 8
# Nature Programs

*Marge Roche, right, leading nature walk to Big Pine, her favorite spot in the dunes - the place to which "she takes everyone." Ann Kennedy, Marilyn Kleb, Carol Beveridge, and Katy Beck (l. to r.) enjoying this beautiful spot.*

## Our Sanctuary

How does one go about describing "Nature Programs" at Palisades Park? The Park itself is our teacher; it presents its own "program." Hillsides bursting forth with wildflowers, sunshine sparkling through the leaves, storm clouds gathering over the water – all offer us lessons if we but have eyes to look and ears to hear. From the beginning, Palisades has been marked as a "sanctuary" - according to Webster, a "consecrated place," a "place of refuge and protection," even "holy." Arthur Quick's Wild Flowers of the Northern States and Canada (18-21) spells out his dream of "sanctuary," as follows:

> I have always been a lover of nature and a wild flower enthusiast. In most parts of the northern states we have wild flowers – a few; but not a great variety in any one locality. Rarely have I seen more than a few different sorts at any one time. So you may imagine my elation when I accidentally discovered this Eldorado of wild flowers. While the entire dune country of Indiana and Michigan is famous for its wild flowers, yet but few localities are favored as we are here; for within the compass of our few hundred acres at Palisades Park we are fortunate in having nearly all soil conditions, and all gradations of shade and sunlight. We have them all. And what a galaxy of flowers! On a single day last May I found here in Palisades Park and near vicinity *seventy-four species of wild flowers actually in bloom.* Can anyone beat it? I verily believe there can be found more species of wild flowers here in these wooded dunes in Michigan during spring, summer and autumn than in any other spot in the northern states. This is truly a *wild flower sanctuary.*

> America, thanks to nature lovers, has many wild life sanctuaries – for birds, for animals, for fish. Why not one for wild flowers? With this in mind I bought this tract of wild land immediately after I discovered it, some years ago. Here my wife and I have had built a cozy, roomy bungalow, among the pines and maples, with a regular old-fashioned six-foot fireplace, wide eaves, and broad porches overlooking Lake Michigan and miles of wooded dunes along the shore. Here we spend a delightful seven months every year. Each spring, with the disappearing snows, we looked forward to going to "Seavista Cottage" at least by the first of April, in time to catch the first hepaticas, spring beauties, and adder tongues; but invariably some of these early risers beat us to it, and smile their welcome when we arrive to brush aside the dry leaves or perchance a little patch of April snow.

> Quite a number of our nature-loving acquaintances have also built summer homes here among the dunes, and together we have a congenial little community with all the modern conveniences one could wish, and yet quite isolated from the public. Still we are only six miles south, along the shore of Lake Michigan, from the thriving little city of South Haven.

> Before telling more about our *flora*, let us have a simple word picture of this most unusual spot. Unusual, because the sand dune formations in America are quite limited, and most of these are in process of formation; that is, the wind year after year is blowing the dry sand from the beach into hills and ridges, grotesque in form and outline,

and constantly shifting, changing in form and moving inland. Many of these sand hills in the limited dune country of Michigan, which comprises only certain points along the western coast of the state, are comparatively bare of vegetation, having only here and there clumps of underbrush and small trees, and scattered patches of wild beach grass – marram and sand reed grass. Also, most of the dunes are small – from thirty to fifty feet in height, many of them from seventy to a hundred and fifty feet, with occasional peaks running up to two hundred feet. Finally, with the aid of the rapid growth of the beach grasses covering the surface and holding it in place, the sands ceased shifting and settled down to permanency.....

That our particular section of the dunes is older by hundreds of years is fully attested by the depth of this top soil covering the pure sand, as well as by the heavy growth of virgin timber – standing trees with a stump diameter of twenty to thirty inches or more being not unusual. Even on the highest peaks we have some of these large trees, while plenty of ancient pine stumps, that seem never to decay, show that these fallen trees were big ones, and old.

After seeing the high and beautifully wooded bluffs that confront the shore of Lake Michigan at this point, no more suitable name could be thought of, in our estimation, than "PALISADES PARK," and this we called it. These wooded dunes straggle off inland a half-mile or so in the most careless, irregular manner, in the form of rising and falling ridges that twist about in tortuous shapes, winding around, joining together, separating again, losing themselves and their identities in fan-shaped, sloping plateaus, and finally making their way back again to the shore apparently augmented in stature and ending at the lake side in towering palisades and miniature mountains....

With such a maze of winding tortuous mountain ranges, fully twenty or more of these ridges to the mile, yet all mountains in miniature, a most fitting appellation would seem to be "Michigan's Miniature Switzerland." Instead of Mt. Blanc, we have within our grounds old Thunder Mountain, around which the Pottawatomie tribe of Indians associated a number of interesting legends. Rising about two hundred feet in height,

the highest peak in the park, the view from the summit is well worth the climb. Every turn in the circuitous road opens up new pictures of lake and country, hills and glens. And from the summit an unobstructed panorama for 20 to 30 miles.

While the grounds were an almost impenetrable thicket when we took it over, we now have all this underbrush and briers removed, giving the trees and vines, the ferns and wild flowers a better chance. But still it is as wild as one could wish, and has every appearance of having always been just as it is, except the trails. These we have made to make it more accessible – fully eight miles of winding bridle paths, Indian trails and autoroads, reaching every part of the grounds, even to the summits, yet with easy grades. While I maintain that walking is the pleasantest way to take in all these woodland scenes and pleasures, still - considering the distances - a carriage or motor, or a saddle trip is sometimes a welcome change.

*A welcome place to read.*

Yet dreams are hard to maintain. A "sanctuary" involves a total ethos. As early as the 7/20/68 Patter, Anne Fuller, one of our nature-loving pioneers about whom you will hear more presently, wrote in her "Nature Notes: Wyndune Road Revisited:"

It's such a dilemma, how to keep Palisades Park the sanctuary for wild flowers Mr. Quick envisioned when he bought this tract. ... The bridle paths and foot trails are again a maze of catbrier. Few of us today ever take the old map and explore them – Tennessee Trail, Fairview, Fairmount, Mountaineer's, Ke-Ka-Ba-Sic (boys') Trail, or Ke-Kea-Qo-Sic (girls') Trail. Some are

*Anne Fuller, center, and Jack Gardner, right, examining a discovery made on a Nature Walk while Marilyn Henkel looks on.*

not to be found. How amazed Mr. Quick would be at our beautifully constructed and well-drained roads. But still the dilemma, how to save the hillsides where the wildflowers and ferns are holding on? Perhaps we could revamp our driving habits to a suitable style for a wildflower sanctuary – be willing to "inch" along narrow roads, pause at every curve, and limit ourselves to 10 miles per hour when we enter the gate. We come for peace, quiet, relaxation, change of pace. What a good way to "let down" at the gate and thus take the pressure off our hillsides.

And so the dilemma has continued – how to maintain the reverence of "sanctuary" in this place that has become, for many, a multi-use area? How, even, cling to the idea of "refuge" and "protection" in lieu of the carelessness of the moment? There are no easy answers. However, several Park members must be singled out in this battle. Anne Fuller with her Nature Walks and writings; Betty Householder who spent untold hours marking the trails with her macrame cords; Rob Venner who picked up the torch, constructed a new trail along the Brandywine, and dedicated his lifework to Nature studies and leadership; Jack Gardner who, in retirement, became the new Park guru of Nature, refining and expanding our trails and leading many a walk; Jim and Lois Richmond who produced A Botanical Survey and Guide for Palisades Park Residents and Guests; and Marge Roche who is always ready to lead a family walk or work with the children. Marge and her grandson even started a new "club" in the summer of 2003 for anyone who completes the hiking of ALL our trails in one day – a notable feat.

This section, then, has two goals - to remind us of some of the precious things that make up this "sanctuary" and to celebrate those special people who have fought to keep alive Quick's dream.

# Through the Eyes of Anne Fuller and Friends:

## A Reminder of Some Precious Things We Too Often Take for Granted

For many years, Anne Fuller, owner of Treetops #83, served as the Park's nature specialist. She faithfully led several Nature Walks each summer and wrote delightful pieces for our Patter which she entitled **"A Rambler's Random Notes"** or just **"Nature Notes by Anne Fuller."** As a part of the history of her cottage, she wrote, *"Of course, the fact that Mr. Quick had started this colony in an effort to preserve an unusual collection of Michigan flora was an added attraction. His book ... was one of my prized possessions. What fun to follow Mr. Quick's botanical rambles through Palisades Park dunelands and his week by week report of the plants in bloom from the time of his usual arrival, the first week in April, and for seven months – his book closes with the fourth week of October."*

It is hard to choose from among Anne's writings; luckily many are preserved in our Patters. On the following pages are a few of her observations (and, as noted, those of fellow nature-lovers,) on some of the precious things in the Park about which she wanted us to know and care.

### Dunes

The history of our dunes is told elsewhere in this volume. Perhaps a few pictures will remind us of their beauty – and their fragility. Even Mr. Quick wrote about some of the changes in the dunes our Park brought about:

*Sand cherries in the sand dunes.*

*Surely, where these dunes were being formed by the winds hundreds of years ago there must have been abundant crops of pokeberries here, and thousands of birds to eat the juicy berries and drop the seeds promiscuously all over the area. This part of the story happened years and years ago, and only now we read the sequel: In grading our miles of roads, trails and bridle paths all over the several hundred acres of dunes that comprise Palisades Park, much soil was overturned and moved to one side in order to make wide, terraced roadways along the steep sides of the hills. The following season we always found all these freshly graded roads green with a heavy growth of young pokeberry and velvet mullein plants. The seeds had remained buried in the sand for no one knows how many years; yet they retained their vitality, and when brought to the surface of the ground and the sunlight they commenced their long delayed growth. (Wild Flowers of the Northern States and Canada p. 268 – 9.)*

Anne Fuller embellishes the story of our dunes with the legend of Thunder Mountain in "Anne Holmes and Thunder Mountain Rumblings."

*According to Anne Holmes "Memorabilia," the rumblings which were heard in Thunder Mountain, up to 15 or 20 years ago, were caused by a limestone fault which runs out into the lake. That is why the Indians called the high dune in the Park Thunder Mountain. "Many times pans rattled in cupboards, windows shook, and on occasions hanging lamps would sway; our back screen door would open and shut with a tremor." How much more exciting than today's bull horn and steam blowout at the Consumer Plant. Let's have another Thunder Mountain rumble!*

> Lament
>
> I long to hear once more
> Old Thunder Mountain's roar,
> But all I seem to get
> Is Consumers Power's jet.

*Postcard showing Vinemount - a vine-covered early pathway near Mr. Quick's cottage.*

## Vines

Again quoting Mr. Quick's book (436–7): *"No one could spend a day here in the dunes at Palisades Park without noticing and commenting on the thousands of wild grape vines creeping over the ground, climbing over the shrubbery until the weight bends the shrubbery so low that they seem almost like Indian mounds, or hay cocks, half covered with the dense foliage of the grape. They climb trees 40 to 60 feet high and hang down in long leafy festoons. They climb up younger trees 10 to 12 feet high, that often grown near together in little groves, and then spreading out in wildest abandon from tree to tree until the little grove is transformed into a densely covered arbor. One long ridge-like dune near our house was such a wilderness of wild grape vines, festooned over trees and shrubbery in such abundance that we named it "Vinemount;" and for 500 feet along the crest we built a long, rustic arbor, covering one of the numerous trails through the woods, trained many of the vines over it, and within a year it was completely roofed over with the vines, loaded in October with a wealth of ripe, purple wild grapes – a delight to all who like wild-grape jelly. Our friends are carrying home great basketfuls of the ripe fruit."*

## Trees

"Review Your Trees on the Bridge Trail"
By Anne Fuller
July 30, 1966 Patter

Thanks to Mr. Sherrow's sign-making skill, Beth Haynes and the Clubhouse Gang, and Betty Householder, you can review your trees as you walk our beautiful Bridge Trail – from bridge to bridge. Note, we have abandoned the old name of Fallen Bridge Trail; Cecil's repair job last year guarantees a safe journey over the Brandywine. But you may decide to retrace your steps rather than crawl under the fence of Mr. Underwood's enlarged paddock to reach Ravine Way.

The most interesting variety of trees will be right at the beginning of the trail because of the plantings of Mr. Muckenhirn many years ago. Fortunately, the new Edgewater Road (projected on Mr. Quick's map) bypasses the Ginkgo, Russian Olive, and Larch which he planted along the meadow bank. The Ginkgo, or Maidenhair Tree, with the fan-shaped leaves, dates back to ancient geological times. In terms of ancestry, it is the Park's most venerable tree. Our specimen is growing very slowly but looks healthy and should be guarded from fill from the new road. The Russian Olive, popular with birds for its olive-shaped fruits, didn't come through the road building too well, but with care should survive. The Larch or Tamarack is our only deciduous conifer in the Park and although it looks stark and dead in winter, it is now most beautiful with its clusters of soft green needles.

Charles Muckenhirn says his father planted 68 species of conifers on his property many years ago. Showing from the road are fine specimens of Colorado Blue Spruce, Ponderosa Pine (I would have called it Austrian or Black Pine if Charles hadn't come along to set me straight), and a pyramidal Red Cedar.

At the beginning of Edgewater Road you will find the only Ironwood on the trail. It is also know as Hop Hornbeam because the fruits are bladder-like sacs resembling hops. The bark is distinctive for its narrow scaly plates, which shred off in curling strips.

Before you reach the bed of white cushion moss west of the new Cordell Cottage, you will have passed several of the Park's huge trees, spared by the early lumbermen: White Oak, Red Oak, Beech, and Hemlock. Slender second growth Red Maples, a typical maple of Michigan lowlands, is fairly common, but the Sugar Maples are just in the sapling stage above the giants. There's a Tulip

*The white ash, reputed to be 3rd largest in State of Michigan, in winter of 2003.*

## White Ash – 3rd Largest in Michigan
(Note by Betty Householder)

Have you seen the 3rd largest white ash tree in the State of Michigan? Johnny Golden took the Clubhouse Gang to his cottage at the end of their tree labeling hike and showed us his tree. It is big enough to get the 11 Goldens in the tree house they have made. Johnny says there is a fire escape in the tree house too.... Our nature expert, Miss Fuller, says the tree must have been injured when it was young to account for the unusual shape. YOU MUST GO SEE IT!!!

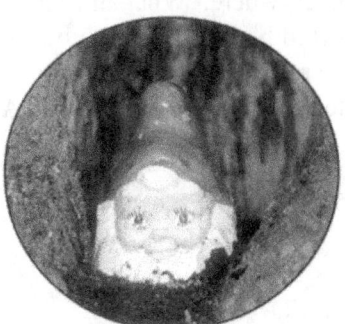

*Some of our trees are said to be magical homes of gnomes and elves.*

## Natural History – 1776 – Give or Take A Couple Hundred Years
By Rob Venner
1976 <u>Patter</u>

tree here and there and a few Tulip seedlings we hope will survive. White Ash saplings are everywhere along the trail.

At the end of the new road beyond the second cottage, you come to the old trail at its most precarious, across the face of a steep hill. The Clubhouse Gang has cleared it a bit for you and put a toe notch in the fallen tree lying across your path, but a walking stick is recommended for this area.

Once over the "slope hazardous," you arrive at the loveliest Hemlock forest primeval we have in the Park. If this isn't community property, can't we save it through a special Park assessment? It should be preserved for posterity as long as the hemlocks and beeches will renew themselves. A few regal clumps of royal fern border the wet spots in this hemlock grove. The white bells of the wintergreen are in bloom today. The trailing vines of the partridge berry should have some twin red berries before autumn. And the Brandywine runs brown-red under the bridge.

Can you find 19 tree species from bridge to bridge? They aren't all labeled. If not, better retrace your steps. Who will make it 20?

I think it only fitting in this historical year to put forth a note of natural history for Palisaders to ponder. There's an element of history in everything, but maybe the story of the lowly Sassafras may spark some interest. It was not always looked upon as just a pleasant-looking tree or shrub, good for holding the sand dunes. There was a time when the French were exploring the Louisiana territory and found the Indians "bringing a wooded root of a tree that grows in these parts, of great virtue and great excellence that healed grievous and variable diseases." (<u>The Natural History of Trees</u> by Donald C. Peattie.) This tree was called "Pauame" by the Indians. The French men called it Sassafras. They said it cured malaria fever and comforted the liver and stomach. In 1602 the English sent explorers down the New England coast to fill their ships' hulls with the roots and bark of these trees. The price in England for Sassafras was L336 sterling a ton.

Sassafras was one of the first exports sent by Captain John Smith from Jamestown Colony even as late as 1610. Finally disillusionment of its powers grew to the point where Sassafras was just a tonic. Pioneer children suffered the annual spring tonic of which Sassafras was a large element. So, next time you are walking along a path and you pluck a Sassafras seedling to smell the root-beer roots, remember that with inflation since the 1500's, that little root is probably worth a week's wage. (Don't I wish!)

# Flowers

**"Nature News"**
By Bill Haywood
August, 1978 Patter

An early Fourth of July nature walk proved most rewarding. The balmy weather coupled with a weekend of rain produced a burst of natural color. The old Palisades Golf Course appears to provide the perfect environment for the Prickly-Pear. The large, yellow, waxy flowers were everywhere. What an irony that a plant as thorny and forbidding as this member of the Cactus family should produce a flower of such delicate beauty. Be sure to watch for the pulpy red fruit in August.

*Prickly Pear found in the old golf course area.*

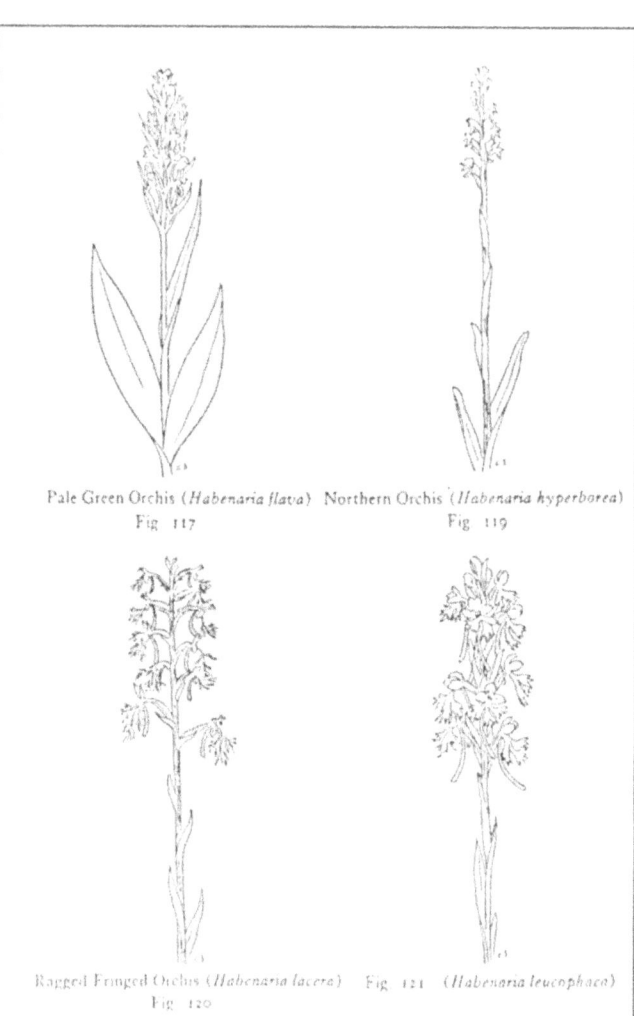

*Page 232 of Mr. Quick's book.*

## Green Orchids
By Anne Fuller
August, 1970 Patter

While a wet summer increases the mosquito population and the problems of mildew in damp cottage corners, there are enjoyable compensations on our woodland trails. In nine years I have never seen the green orchid so tall, vigorous, and handsome. They are scattered here and there along Route 1, beginning at Wee-A-Bode and following along inland to the point where Route 8 forks off. I counted 17 in the Wee-A-Bode stand, not as sturdy and tall as in some other spots. Perhaps they have trouble surviving too heavy a leaf pile. Strangely enough, they seem to like the sun of the very roadside and are seldom as numerous or sturdy back in the shadier spots of the woods. Between Bradfords and Happy Hollow I counted 14, but the prize stand this year lies between the Hermitage and Ray Lewis's cottage where there were 22 plants along the west side of the road, some two feet tall, with a spike of as many as 30 blossoms topping the leafy stem. Then, returning along the outbound Route 7, I found two more plants in Sally Ellis's garden.

Quick calls this the Bracted Orchis (see his book, p. 232). The "bracted" refers to the tiny leaves below each individual blossom. It's almost finished with the best bloom now, but there is still time to get down on your knees and look full in the face of one of the greenish white blooms. See its three pale green sepals, and the lower petal which has a greenish-white inflated sac, purple inside, called the spur. It reminds one of the lady slipper of spring in miniature. The sac is tipped with a curled lip to serve as a landing field for an insect. Some year – one with less mosquitoes – I hope to have time to sit by a plant and find out exactly which insect carries the pollen away.

Of the nine members of the Orchid family Quick says are here in Palisades, I have only found three species. This may only mean the failure to hike in the right places. One of the three, the small purple-fringed orchis, lived in the meadow when I found it in 1962. Perhaps it will make a comeback, as the cardinal flower has.

# Ferns

**"To the Fern Fanciers"** By Anne Fuller
1973 Patter

Some years ago a New Jersey naturalist friend and I made a survey of the ferns of Palisades Park. At that time, we found ten species, described them for identification, and gave their location in the Park. Since then there's been a loss of one species and a gain of two. The two fragile plants of the Maiden Hair Fern on Route 1 between Michigan House and Kirk of the Dunes has completely disappeared. My hunch is, a thorough survey of the deep ravine on the other side of Route 1 at that point might reveal other Maidenhairs, but there never seems to be the time to do the scouting. "The longer I live, the less it takes to keep me busy."

One of the recent discoveries is the Ostrich Fern alongside the steep public steps north of Brandywine next to Sheehans' Inn Orbit. How many times I have descended those steps and yet never noticed these two handsome plants until '73. It is one of the most beautiful and largest of our Michigan native ferns with its ostrich-plume-shaped fronds growing in basket-like tufts. It is more commonly found along streams and riverbeds and I wonder when it was planted in its present location. Am waiting to learn more about it from the Sheehans.

The other recent find, the Marsh Fern, is probably a 'come-back' in the meadow along the Brandywine rills. Sometimes in sunny, moist meadows such as ours, it is almost as common as the grasses. It is thin and delicate with new fronds appearing all summer spaced along a creeping root stock rather than growing in circular clumps as does the Ostrich and our abundant Marginal Shield Fern.

The fertile fonds of the March Fern are interesting to examine closely – note how the upper leaflets appear constricted as the margins curve back covering the fruit dots.

*Barbara Beck caught in the wonder of the ferns.*

# Birds

**"Pileated Woodpecker"**
By Anne Fuller

Tom and Julie McCullough reported seeing one early in the season. Then in early July Arch King reported seeing one up on the Householder hill. That's exciting bird news, although the Pileated has been increasing in numbers along this coast of Lake Michigan during the past decade. We have seen the rectangular and oval holes in a number of dead trees, standing and fallen, and the large chips hacked out by a powerful beak. Ask any of the clubhouse gang who went nature hiking a few weeks ago to show you the evidence on Ravine Way.

The Pileated Woodpecker is crow-sized and has a conspicuous red crest. (The only woodpecker with a crest.) It is mostly black as you see it against a tree except for a white streak down the side of the head and neck. But in flight it exposes the flashy white wing patches and a huge white expanse on the under side of the wings. If you hear a rapid series of "kuk-kuk-kuk" like a flicker, look again and you may glimpse the rarer and shyer bird.

**"Wanted: Hawk Watchers
Near Juncture of Route 1 and Route 2"**
By Anne Fuller

Stan reports two large hawks this past week in the area where Route 2 leaves Route 1. From Stan's description they are undoubtedly one of the large Buteos (hawks with broad wings and broad fan-shaped tails). But which one is the question. If anyone sees or hears them, please report. The most likely in our woodlands would be either the Red-Shouldered or the Red-Tailed. It would be most gratifying to know that either species finds our woodlands acceptable for nesting. They often return to the same nest year after year, adding to its bulk of coarse twigs and sticks as needed. Their nest will be high, 30' to 70' from the ground. They nest very early, even in February, and it takes the young about six months before they are on their own. But it takes a year or more for the young to attain the distinctive markings of the adult. For sightings, let Peterson be your guide:

Red-Tailed Hawk:   Adult: Rufous tail.
                   Immature: (and adult) Light chest, streaked belly.
Red-Shouldered Hawk: Adult: Rufous shoulders; narrow white tail bands.
                   Immature: Streaked on both breast and belly.

Better still, listen to the call. The Red-Tailed's usual note is a long-drawn squealing and slurred whistle. The Red-Shoulder's usual call is a 'two-syllable piercing 'kee-yer' with a dropping inflection," says Peterson.

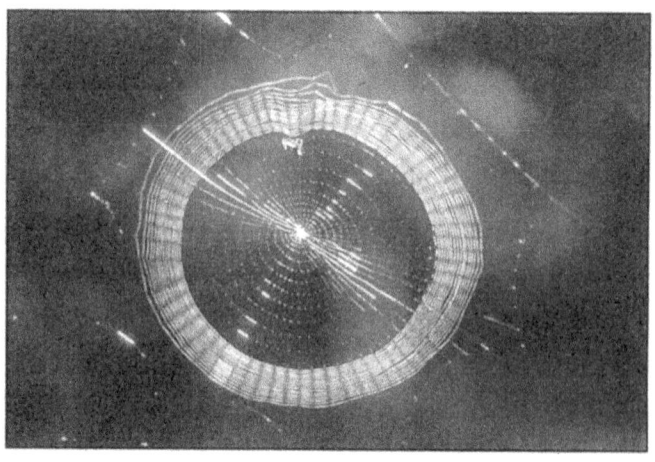

## Critters
"It's Garden Spider Time Again"
By Anne Fuller

One of our interesting late August happenings is the report of a descendant of Charlotte (in <u>Charlotte's Web</u>) out by the tennis courts. Charlotte belonged to the family of Orb Weavers or Garden Spiders. There are several species in the family. The most common in our meadow and in the tall weeds anywhere along our roads and tennis courts will be a large silver, black, and yellow one. They all will be mending their beautiful orb webs by night to be ready to catch the unwary grasshopper or other insect by day, resting on their stabilimentum (remember how Charlotte wove the name of "Horace" into her stabilimentum?) in the center of the web with a foot on eight radiating spokes to catch the message of any invading morsel for dinner.

<u>**Flying Squirrels**</u>: At this time of year the Flying Squirrels live in communities and share common feeding grounds. At least one has taken over the wren nesting box for the second year. It is difficult to know how many are "flying" into the bird feeder each night at about 9:45 – late dusk at the edge of night. They're partial to sunflower seeds but will gingerly try a variety of fruits and table scraps. An old stale angel-food cake was popular this week.

# Trails

Anne Fuller was a fount of knowledge, determined to share what she knew and loved with everyone in the Park. A hard act to follow – but the wonder of her story is that other equally dedicated people have followed in her **footprints**. This is particularly clear in the development of our Park Nature Trails.

One of Anne's cohorts in clearing and marking trails was Betty Householder. In her 1985 interview, Betty remembered their efforts.

> Nature trails were in existence from the beginning, set up by Mr. Quick. All the roads and trails are on our map. Enough people took those paths to keep them open, like up to Thunder Mountain. There was always a tree house up there at the top, in back of Mrs. Edward's house. Sometime after 1948, Anne Fuller and I had signs printed on pointed pieces of wood, like "Thunder Mountain Trail." My brother, Jack Gardner, fixed up some of those paths. He's started new ones, also. He's built two new ones this summer. Anne Fuller and I used to mark things with clear plastic signs. We identified the names of trees and plants. We had "leaflets three, leave it be" to identify poison ivy. But the kids would take our signs and put them on hopwood, which had three leaves but wouldn't hurt a thing. So it wasn't very satisfactory because the signs got moved all the time. When Jack retired, at the age of 58, he had too much energy and he had always been interested in nature – he had been a Boy Scout – and so he started making these trails. Then we used my macrame cords to mark them. The birds took them and they got dirty. It was an awful chore to keep putting them on every year, so this year, we used little dots of paint. There's yellow and red and orange. From one tree, as far as you can see, there's a dot on the next tree, so you don't get lost. Coming and going. The trails are all named. There's the Fern Trail and the Sassafras Trail and the Maple Trail because there are predominantly all those trees on those trails. There is a Hemlock Trail also. But now, next year we're going to have trail walks on Sunday, because so many of the men want to go. We've had three this year on Sunday, but just by private parties asking to have them. Next year, we're going to have one on Thursday and two on Sunday. They are very popular and people – even if they only go once – are getting impressed with the fact that Palisades Park is more than just the beach. As Mr. Quick said, it is remarkable that we have marsh and dunes and all these plants. Rob Venner did one trail thoroughly and Anne Fuller helped him finish it – the first Brandywine Trail. And then Jack has taken over and is doing the rest. Now they all have been printed in the Patter so they are on our maps. That's a nice addition to the Park. But Mr. Quick started the trails.

*Anne Fuller teaching in the rain.*

The Patters of the 70's continue the story of the trail system.

June 25, 1973 Patter: "Some trails and other public right-of-ways as indicated on Mr. Quick's original map have just disappeared by encroachment. But there are some trails that would give you a happy few hours of hiking ... Back in 1962, Betty Householder and Ann Fuller analyzed the condition of a number of the trails and small parks. Later they experimented with replacing some of the signs remaining from days of Mr. Quick." *(A later Patter reports those signs were vandalized; however, in the 90's wooden signs made by Dave Vanderbough were put on trails and have remained in place.)*

June 25, 1973 Patter: "Robert Venner, a student in the School of Natural Resources at University of Michigan has just completed a study on Nature Trails and is willing to make practical application of his studies on the proposed trails in the Niners' Bird Sanctuary. We have agreed to begin with clearing a Brandywine trail in the Red Maple lowland, keeping close enough to the Brandywine to have glimpses of animal tracks in the Brandywine mud, and with a crude bridge for the venturesome giving a circle route to the tennis court area. Work was begun this month ... When this trail is passable, Robert will assume leadership in exploring the rest of the Sanctuary and directing the layout of a more extensive trail deeper into the Sanctuary."

The August, 1978 Patter reported that Anne Fuller, Brian Peat, Ted, Don Jr., And Don Scheel Sr. rerouted Brandywine Trail around fallen trees.

## Jack Gardner

The August 30, 1980 Patter reported that Jack Gardner and family (4th generation) worked on a new trail, "up a hill and a hill" in Niner's Bird Sanctuary – "a bit more rugged than the Brandywine trail." And that leads us to Jack Gardner – and our present system of trails.

In 1997, memorial funds for Jack Gardner underwrote A Botanical Survey and Guide for Palisades Park Residents and Guests. Its "Dedication" introduces this man who spent his retirement years "blazing our nature trails."

*Jack Gardner and Anne Fuller on a Nature Walk.*

Jack Gardner blazed our nature trails, chaired the nature program, led nature walks, and studied the flora of Palisades Park for many years. Jack first came to Palisades Park as an infant. The Gardner family rented several cottages at the Park, then bought Sunset. Jack and the whole family became very involved in all the Palisades activities and events. Early on, both Jack and Jane (his wife) grew up as regulars here at the Park. It was one of those special Palisades romances. Jane's family, the Kipps, had once owned the Donohue cottage. They met there in 1941. When Jack retired, they bought that very cottage, Piccadilly Circus.

Jack was never idle. When at Palisades, he was on-the-go every day…. Everyone will remember Jack for his diligent work in boosting the nature program here at Palisades. He physically poured himself into the program. Almost single handed, he blazed six miles of nature trails throughout our 748 acres. His constant pursuit of botanical species identification was culminated in the added research, preparation, and publication of this booklet. He was a friend to everyone at Palisades and daily shared the fruits of his labor and reams of knowledge about the natural world with us all.

In Jack's memory, the trail system that he worked so diligently to develop was named the Jack Gardner Nature Trails.

Mention must be made of the contributions of Jim and Lois Richmond, who picked up the torch after Jack's death. They are especially to be commended for the Palisades Botanical Survey – an Herculean task on which they did much of the work. They also led nature walks for several years, arranged for outside experts to join us, and initiated the signed trail by the Brandywine, with its guide and identified species. Boots Duesing, for many years, was seen with clippers in hand as he cleared the trails each summer. At this writing, Marge Roche continues the tradition, working closely with the Clubhouse children's program. Given our rich heritage, we are sure that other nature-lovers will come forth and remind us, anew, to carefully and quietly cherish this place we call Palisades Park.

*Jack's widow, Jane Kipp Gardner, cutting the ribbon on the newly named Jack Gardner Nature Trails.*

# Trail Selection, Direction and Use Guide
## Jack Gardner Nature Trails at Palisades Park

| Trail No. | Nature Trail Name | Blaze Color | Degree of Difficulty | Starting Point | Finish Point | Length in Miles | Comments |
|---|---|---|---|---|---|---|---|
| | **NORTH SIDE TRAILS** | | | | | | |
| 1 | Brandywine to Fern Loop to Brandywine. The "Self Guided Nature Trail" Guide sheets in cedar box by "Info-Post" No. 1 | yellow | easiest | Woods Bridge | Woods Bridge | 0.4 | A trail for all ages with no climbs. Visit 15 "Info Posts" in route |
| 2 | Oak Loop to Brandywine | yellow | moderate | north off Edgewater | Woods Bridge | 0.6 | Tough finish down a steep slope to connect with Brandywine Tr. |
| 3 | Brandywine to Upper Sassafras and return | no blaze on Brandywine | easy to moderate | Woods Bridge | Woods Bridge | 1.2 | Assumes you double back. Must climb short dune each way |
| 4 | Oak Loop to Upper Sassafras to Brandywine | yellow to red to Brandywine | moderate | north off Edgewater | Woods Bridge | 1.4 | Steep decent to Brandywine |
| 5 | Oak Loop to High Point Loop to Lower Maple Loop to Brandywine | yellow to orange to red | moderate | north off Edgewater | Woods Bridge | 0.6 | Steep decent to Lower Maple Loop |
| 6 | Oak Loop to Upper Sassafras to Lower Maple Loop to Brandywine | yellow to red to Brandywine | moderate | north off Edgewater | Woods Bridge | 1.2 | Moderate decent to Brandywine Trail |
| | **SOUTH SIDE TRAILS** | | | | | | |
| 7 | Stage Coach to Hemlock Loop to Stage Coach | yellow on Hemlock | moderate | Stage Coach | Stage Coach | 0.9 | Gentle ups/downs on Hemlock Loop |
| 8 | N. Sugar Bowl Trail - return thru N. Sugar Bowl | orange | moderate | Mason Cottage 168 | Lake Bluff Drive | 0.4 | Short steep uphill-long downhill |
| 9 | N. & E. Sugar Bowl Trails | orange to red to Sugar Bowl | moderate | Mason Cottage 168 | Lake Bluff Drive | 0.6 | Short steep uphill-long downhill |
| 10 | No. Sugar Bowl Trail to Red Pine Loop to East Sugar Bowl Trail to No. Sugar Bowl Trail | orange to yellow to red to orange | moderate | Mason Cottage 168 | Lake Bluff Drive | 0.7 | No major slopes |
| 11 | N. Sugar Bowl Tr. to Red Pine Loop to Big Pine Tr. to Big Pine Ridge to N. Sugar Bowl Tr. | orange to yellow to red to orange | moderate | Mason Cottage 168 | Lake Bluff Drive | 1.1 | Long moderate downhill |
| 12 | N. Sugar Bowl Tr. to Red Pine Loop to Big Pine Trail to Big Pine Valley | orange to yellow to red to yellow | more difficult | Mason Cottage 163 | Thunder Mr. Lane | 1.2 | Long steep downhill |
| 13 | Stage Coach to Ravine Way near tennis courts | no blaze colors | easy | Thunder Mt Court | Ravine Way | 0.3 | Moderate downhill |
| 14 | N. Sugar Bowl to Red Pine Loop to Big Pine Trail to Big Pine Link Trail to TOP of Sugar Bowl coming down, walk toward Lake Bluff Drive | orange to yellow to red to yellow | more difficult | Mason Cottage 168 | Lake Bluff Drive | 1.2 | There are return trails along the north & south rims of the Big Sugar Bowl |
| 15 | Thunder Mtn. Path to So. Thunder Mtn. Ridge to No. Sugar Bowl Trail | yellow to orange | more difficult | Lehmann Cottage 127 | Mason Cottage 168 | 0.5 | Steep beginning |

Copyright © Palisades Park Country Club 1999

**Plants to look for during your nature walk**
Refer to your "Botanical Survey and Guide" for more details

**TREES:**
white & red pine—hemlock
alder—beech—hop hornbeam
red, white & black oak
water & green ash—basswood
tulip tree—sassafras
black & pin cherry—black locust
cottonwood—red & sugar maple
flowering dogwood—red cedar

**SHRUBS:**
spicebush—serviceberry
spirea—maple leaf viburnum
red osier & grey dogwood

**VINES:**
riverbank grape—Virginia creeper
dewberry—nightshade—greenbrier
poison ivy—bittersweet

**PARASITES:**
squawroot—beech drops

**SAPROPHYTES:**
indian pipes

**FERNS:**
bracken—Christmas—cinnamon
hay—intermediate wood—marsh
interrupted—marginal wood
New York—ostrich—sensitive
polypody common—royal
spinulose wood—rattlesnake

**FERN ALLIES:**
horsetails—grape fern—clubmoss
ground cedar

**WILDFLOWERS:**
cucumber root—solomon's seal
trillium—moccasin flower—sweetflag
ginger—boneset—Joe Pye weed
cardinal flower—purple fringed orchis
chickory—fleabane—knapweed
snakeroot—wormwood—yarrow
pokeweed—bearberry—wintergreen
herb Robert—evening primrose
partridge berry—bergamot—betony
heal all—mullein—hairy puccoon
Pitcher's thistle (endangered list)
sarsaparilla—lambs quarters

Check your Botanical Survey and Guide for complete listing

Published November 1999

*Rob Venner and Marge Roche on a meadow walk.*

# Robert Venner

*Robert Venner, now Director and Naturalist at DeGraaf Nature Center in Holland, grew up in the Park and has a story to tell of its influence on his career choice. Rob has led many of our walks and worked on our trails. He wrote the following:*

It is interesting how the things that fascinate us as children, tend to remain with us through life. As a young boy, exploring the dunes and forests of Palisades, I was attracted to places "off the beaten path" and I still am today. In fact, leading people into wild places to discover wild things is how I make my living. Years ago, my brothers, friends, and I would often head out from our cottage, first on the south end and later on the north, and go back into the forested dunes and blowouts. If we saw a large hill we would say, "let's go up it" or "let's see what's in the next valley". In the wintertime, we would escape the winds and blizzard conditions of the lakeshore by climbing down into the bottom of two intersecting dunes. At the base of the hills, there was no wind. Only songbirds and the sound of snow landing on the ground could be heard. I often wonder if it is still quiet enough to hear a snowfall with many other sounds intruding in our lives.

One of my favorite journeys as a young boy of seven or so was to venture into the woods and find where pirates had buried their treasure. It was always very exciting to first figure out where they would have come ashore and then how they would have secretly marked the spot in the forest where the pieces of eight were hidden. "Treasure Island" had its effect on us.

Most often, I followed the Brandywine Creek as my starting point for adventure. By exploring the creek with small boats, on foot by walking right up the waterway, or most times by finding my way along its banks, I found many wonderful things. The sight of a scarlet tanager poised on a low branch of a forest tree; a row of grouse on a branch hanging right over the stream; pileated woodpeckers "wick, wick, wicking" their way across the river valley; woodducks flushed with the sound of flying pigs and the never ending quest for the giant silk moths that come at night.

My many youthful experiences at Palisades and other locales convinced me of the value of wild places. Just to know that there is a place to go where the hand of man is not so evident, that there is balance and great power in wild places, gives me the strength to continue to explore and teach about the wild things.

It is out of this belief in the power of wild things (and that others would enjoy these places too if they could be led into them) that the trails were initiated at Palisades. The first and only trail I had a hand in making was in the "doorway" of my favorite stomping grounds, the Brandywine valley. In the early 1970's, I started at the bridge in the woods and running alongside the stream; I cleared and cut to make it easier for others to enter this wonderful spot. When I got to the stream-cut bank, I ran the trail over the creek by felling two small trees to help in completing a rustic bridge over the Brandywine that led up to the old golf course (the area east of the tennis courts). It was a beginning. Of course, later, Jack Gardner spent much more time and effort in creating more trails for the residents of the park to enjoy. Some of my best nature shots were taken along the Brandywine. I hope they will bring back some memories for those that like to venture into wild places. They may also tempt some to explore, as I have, to take hold of a natural moment and make it their own. There is nothing like discovering something first hand. It stays with you a lifetime and makes life a real experience.

A teacher ...

and his students.

# Chapter 9
# Cottage Histories

# Cottage Histories

For many years, Betty Householder, a long time Palisades Park resident, collected information about the history of individual cottages. As long ago as August, 1964, in a special edition of our Patter, Betty told of a visit to Julia Quick Hill, Arthur Quick's daughter, who had spent many years at the Park before selling her interests in the Park after her father's death. During the visit, Betty and Julia shared stories about early cottages. In fact, Julia first lived in a tent at Palisades:

> In 1906, when Julia was ten years old, her folks put up three tents on the ridge where Dr. Marshall's cottage is (#98 -presently Jim and Lois Richmond) and they lived in the Park that summer. She remembers the lumber camp that was housed on the old golf course. The Rev. Schreck visited the Park and fell in love with the place and built the first cottage – Treetops (#83) …. Then she remembers Ballou Inn (#90) being built. It was a rooming-boarding house …. Then Vashmar(#92) – Mary Lee Tillson's cottage – was built by her grandparents, the Wards. At the same time, the Sturtevants built the Lodge (#52 & #53). Mrs. Sturtevant's sister built Broadview (#93) and Lakeside (#94) …. Mrs. Monroe, a millionaire from Joliet who owned a bank and a hotel in Joliet, built Sunset Cottage (#88) …. Mrs. Monroe's chauffeur lived in Nichol's house (#63 - now McNamara's Gate House) …. The Wunsch's cottage(#49) was one of the early ones and was built by a Mr. Cota who worked for the C.B.&O. Railroad in Chicago. The Old Pier cottage (#45) … is another old one.

Betty continued this kind of conversation about cottages throughout her summers at Palisades. Often she could be heard asking Park owners to research this history. Many did and gave their information to Betty. At one point, she had a committee look into records in the County Court House. Upon Betty's death, her daughters donated her files to the Betty's Club (which she founded and which honored her memory by naming the club after her). Much of the following information comes from her files. The editors believe that Betty would be pleased to know that at least this much information finally has been printed.

# PALISADES PARK COUNTRY CLUB – COTTAGE HISTORIES - 2003

| PRESENT OWNERS | | # | | COTTAGE NAME | PREVIOUS OWNERS-YR SOLD / TRANSFERRED |
|---|---|---|---|---|---|
| Alsterda | John & Terry | 85 | | Sp'eyeglass<br><br>Sea Vista | John Slater 1985<br>Creighton Sherman<br>Dr. Don/Ev Marshall<br>Arthur Quick |
| Anderson | Albert | 130 | | Lookout Inn<br>Happy Daze<br>Monk's Haven | <br>Jim/Mary M. Roach<br>Joseph/ Hazel Gates 1956 |
| Ankenbruck | John | 193 | * | | Built in 1996 |
| Ankenbruck | Lisa | 197 | * | | Built in 1999 |
| Ball<br>  Kearns<br>  Egan | Tom<br>Peggy<br>Mary Kay | 144 | | Dublindoon<br>Cherry Hill | Gen Ball/Kathy Kearns<br>Monica Brown<br>G.F. Palmer |
| Bartley | Janice | 171 | | A Summer Place<br>Oasis<br>NI-KLAW | <br>Joe Campbell 1982<br>Nel Sengenberger 1941<br>Built in 1913 |
| Bates | James & Eleanor | 183 | | Breezy Hollow | 3 Wintermute children 2001<br>Roy/Janet Wintermute 2000<br>Donald/Elizabeth Egbert 1967<br>Dr. Woodard 1946<br>Built 1922 for 3 Bielenberg sisters |
| Bates | Michael & Patricia<br>Stephen & Nancy | 70 | | Just Inn Time<br>Kalihiwai<br>Playhouse | <br>Lawrence/Sharon Hussey 2001<br>Ralph/Janet Hegwood 1984<br>Built in 1942 |
| # Beck | Katy | 176 | * | Sundune | Robt/Helen Beatty 1968<br>Built in 1942 |
| # Bendelow | Shirley | 74 | * | Balgownie | Tom Bendelow II 1986<br>Tom II/Bruce Bendelow 1967<br>"Ernest, Jack, Mae Bendelow 1930"<br>Tom & Polly Bendelow 1919 |
| Beveridge | Don & Carol | 136 | | The Other World<br><br>Hillcrest | Clay/Ruth Johnson 1979<br>Jean Delamarter 1959<br>Alice & Eric Delamarter 1939<br>Built in 1928 by Harry Wildt |
| Beyer | Howard & Patricia | 135 | | Exit Inn | Irv/Louise Beyer 1980<br>Hubert Stoddard 1960<br>Built in 1928 |
| Bishop | George & Weensie<br><br>Benny & Elaine | 93 | | Broadview | George & Helen Bishop<br>Dr. Frank Hagie<br>Mr. Nix (brother of Mrs. Sturtevant) |

# indicates five generations have owned or vacationed at PPCC.  * indicates cottage owned by only one family.

| | | | | | |
|---|---|---|---|---|---|
| Borchert | "Robert, Beth" | 44 | | Bum's Rush | Connie Borchert |
| | Marion (Borchert) Foster | | | | Forest & Marion Lowrey |
| Dembs | Howard & Barbara (Borchert) | | | | |
| | | | | | Grandma Bourland |
| Borge | George & Renee | 175 | | Sandbox | M. Molyneaux 1990 |
| | | | | | Built in 1909 |
| Bradford | Brad & Carol | 103 | * | Cedar Nook | Built in 1968 |
| Brand | John & Marion | 100 | * | Dunewood | M/M Herbert Brand |
| | | | | | Built in 1948 |
| Branding | David & Karen | 61 | | Court House | Dorothy Branding 1988 |
| | | | | | Lori/Phil Dillman 1969 |
| | | | | | Mr. Hempe |
| Breen | Mike & Sally | 194 | | The Dugout | Doug Van Boven 2002 |
| | | | | | Built in 1995 |
| Brumis | George & Marge | 33 | | | Clare Fletcher |
| | | | | | Built in 1967 |
| Buchanan | Sally | 141 | | Windridge | Esther Lundquist 1972 |
| Burkhardt | Robert & Hazel | 167 | * | Sand Castle | Built in 1970 |
| Burrous | Cecil & Nancy Enos | 60 | * | Sunnyside | Built in 1960 by Leonard Burrous |
| Canonie | Jody | 5 | | Our D.I.G.S. | |
| | Bill Sylvester Family | | | Cabbat | Carol Feltes 1999 |
| | | | | | Harold Minick 1975 |
| | | | | | Built in 19773 |
| # Carr | Mary Jo | 102 | | | Horace Brewer |
| | | | | | E & Lou McWethy |
| | | | | Wee Abode | Ethel Bodeweese |
| | | | | Gwa-Si-Ka | "Gwartin, Siefker, Kagie" |
| Claffy | Ed & Margaret | 29 | | Peggy's Place | W. Jensen 1993 |
| | | | | North Fork East | Built in 1981 |
| Colbert | Bill | 115 | | Colb's Cozy | |
| | | | | Sunnyside | Fidler |
| | | | | | Anne DeBlois |
| Coleman | Virginia | 45 | | Old Pier | Ernest/Marg Meichert 1943 |
| | | | | | Edith Wunsch |
| | | | | | Henry Wunsch |
| | | | | | Built in 1908 by Dr. Schreck |
| Compernolle | Tom & Mary Pat | 106 | | LaCasita | Gwen Ott 1993 |
| | | | | | Mildred Adams 1960 |
| | | | | Ta-Kit-E-Z | "Marion ""Bo"" Bosier 1930" |
| | | | | | Built in 1928 |

# indicates five generations have owned or vacationed at PPCC.  * indicates cottage owned by only one family.

| | | | | | |
|---|---|---|---|---|---|
| Davis | Gerald & Sally | 124 | | Casa Loca | Constance Zimlich<br>Chas./Ruth Apostol 1951<br>Chas./Helen Jansen 1942<br>Fred/Vicky Nunneley 1939<br>Grover/Matilda Perry 1935 |
| DiKlich<br>Zacharko | Milan & Dolores<br>Frank & Gina | 122 | | The Sand Trap<br>Bond-Fire<br>Halcyon | Michael/Joyce Bleuher 2001<br>Jim Scholley |
| Dinnin<br>"Breen, Forsee, Huffine, Lezon" | Michael & Irene | 89 | | Graystone | Six O'Connor Children<br>AK-SAR-BEN<br>Mrs.Wm. O'Connor (1952)<br>Harry Long<br>Built by Robt. Ballou |
| Dinnin | Wm. & Elizabeth | 133 | | Tucked Inn<br>The Chalet | M. Dawson Jr. 1990 |
| Dobbelaere | Arthur & Eileene | 79 | | Valley Haven | Burrous & Beck (1989)<br>Dr. Carl Boothby<br>John/Kay Smith 1953 |
| Donovan | James & Jane | 192 | * | Ichiban Ryokan | Built in 1993 |
| Donovan | John & Patricia | 38 | | Brandyville | Clare Fletcher 1979 |
| Doyle | Michael & Trudy | 105 | | Betwigst<br><br>Dow's Gazebo<br>R Dream | John/Nancy Jung 1996<br>Jean Penny 1994<br>Kolehmainens & Speichers 1994<br>George Dow 1991<br>Alice Ott 1972 |
| Duesing | Boots & Doris | 154 | | Pottawatomie | Duesing/Wells 1983<br>M. DeSouchet 1966 |
| Ebert | Bob & Dianne | 149 | | Focus Inn<br>Rainbow's End<br>Port o'Call | Errol/Lynn Kirsch 1992<br>Henry/Fran Prange 1990<br>Built in 1953 |
| Ebright<br>Edwards<br>  Sentgerath<br>  Whippen | George & Patricia<br>Dave<br>John & Shirley<br>Marlin | 195<br>163 | *<br>* | The Briars<br>Tree House | Built in 1996<br>Abbott/Marty Edwards<br>Built in 1937 by Charley Tunecke |
| Eisenberg | Barry & Susan | 160 | | Beechwood-Bee's Knees<br>Michigan House | Rich/Betty Pollack 1993 |
| Eldredge | Family | 9 | | | Wm. Eldredge<br>Mrs. Roper 1944<br>Built in 1935 |
| Ellis<br>  Slater | Jim & Katie<br>Tim & Susan | 116 | | The Lost Weekend<br>Happiness<br>Friendship Lodge | Bob /Sally Davis Ellis<br>Davis Family<br>Built by Dr. McCollum |

\# indicates five generations have owned or vacationed at PPCC.   * indicates cottage owned by only one family.

| | | | | | |
|---|---|---|---|---|---|
| Farrell | Liz and Greg | 137 | | Water Tower Hill | Cathy Stanton 2003<br>Betty Duwe Lukey/Dorothy Duwe Stanton 1984<br>Built for George/Dora Duwe |
| Favor | Arsenio & Erika | 180 | | | Henry/Francis Adema 1998<br>Built in 1983 |
| Feldman | Rich & Deb Walsh | 139 | | Ups'n Downs<br>Wee Bit O' Heaven | Ward/Gert Harris 1983<br>Art/Mabel Mason 1930 |
| Ferry | Mary | 65 | | Up Country<br>The Snow Cottage<br>Oak Hill | Dr. Asa Ferry 1948<br>Dr. Ruth Vail Snow 1928<br>Built in 1911 for Dr. Vail/Hedger |
| Filkins | David & Mika | 12 | * | | Built in 1983 |
| Filosa | Matthew & Mary-Ellen | 198 | * | White O'Mornin' | Built in 2000 |
| Fitzgerald | Joseph & Jean | 23 | * | In-De Inn | Built in 1963 |
| Fitzgerald | Joe | 177 | | Traylside<br>Kilkare Cottage | Helen Beatty<br>Armin/Katy Beck 1968<br>Robert/Helen Beatty 1958<br>Sheldon/Virginia Spellman 1955<br>O.B./Loretta Spellman 1942 |
| Fleming<br>Aliotta<br>Zigmond | Mary<br>Ann<br>Sally | 88 | | Sunset | Betty Householder 1998<br>John/Mary Gardner<br>Jesse/Esther Shuman 1948<br>Geo. Munroe 1911<br>Built in 1910 by Mr. Phillips |
| Flynn | Family | 90 | | Ballou Inn | Jack/Nancy Flynn 1995<br>Helen Packard 1967 (Store)<br>Built by Mr. Ballou/Inn 1907 |
| Flynn | Tom & Jody | 152 | | Slieve Liag<br>Fun Harbor | John Thornton 1987<br>Browning |
| # Foley | Dan & Kathy | 118 | * | Foleys' Follies<br>Elk's Lodge | W.J. McCarthy |
| Fort | Dea | 82 | | Casa Giallo | Molinaro/Doyle 2001<br>Mooney Family 1989<br>Mrs. Wm. Mooney<br>Built by R.G. Ballou for Mrs. Brown |
| Foster | Francis & Maureen | 145 | * | Summer Hill | Built in 1972 |
| Fredian | Alan & Dorothy | 25 | | | Joe Starck 1975<br>Rebuilt in 1954<br>Weakened by storm in 1953/moved<br>Mr/Mrs. Crawford<br>Built in 1938 |

# indicates five generations have owned or vacationed at PPCC.   * indicates cottage owned by only one family.

| | | | | | |
|---|---|---|---|---|---|
| Gardner | Jane | 41 | | Piccadilly Circus | Virginia VanBeuren 1977<br>Isadore Donahue 1967<br>Harry Kipp 1944<br>Mary Field 1938<br>Harriet Fry 1915<br>Built in 1908 |
| Garvey | Maurice & Marie | 143 | | Eldamar<br>Read's Retreat | Greg/Kris Boothroyd 1984<br>John/Jeannine Read<br>Larry/Char Northrup<br>Built by Charles Allen in 1910 |
| Gerity | Family | 10 | | Sonnblick | Don Lemoin<br>Built 1968 |
| Goeppinger | John & Kathleen | 113 | | Blueberry Hill<br>Hemlocks | Robt/Betty Holmes Woodhause 1991<br>Anna Holmes<br>Log cabin moved to Park about 1908 |
| # Goff | Harvey & Kay | 8 | * | | Built in 1963 |
| Golden | Margaret<br>Tom & Carolyn | 48 | | Better Here<br>than There | Barbara Golden 2001<br>Mrs. Steele<br>Mrs. Ewing |
| Grigola | Sal & Barb | 129 | * | Griggy's | Built in 1970 |
| Gryzwa | Ken & Joanne Kearns | 132 | | Grave Decision | Charles/M.K. Goodridge 1996<br>Bakers - Built in 1930 after 1928 storm destroyed their beach house |
| G'Sell | Richard | 157 | | Michigan Split<br>Wind Song | Leon Kowalski 1978<br>Dr. Matthews 1972 |
| Gubbins | Jack & Karen | 67 | | Brigadune<br>Kumback | R. Matteson 1991<br>R. McConnell 1976 |
| Guirl | David & Nadine | 62 | | Innwood | Dorothy Guirl 1994<br>Dutch/Georgia Underwood 1968 |
| Gustafson | Robt & Judy | 107 | | | M.Bradford 1978<br>McCain/Felgen 1972 |
| Halpin | John & Helen | 109 | | The Back Door<br>Blarney Inn | Mary Ann Moran 1995<br>Mrs. Mary Moran<br>Built in 1925 |
| # Hamilton | Jeryl | 125 | | Whippoorwill | Marian Hamilton<br>George Owen<br>"Fannie, Louise Anna Palmer"<br>Built in 1910 |
| # Hamilton | Judy | 181 | * | Seagull | Marian Hamilton<br>Built in 1928 |
| Hartman | Edith & Jane | 111 | | | Kenneth Hartman 1979<br>Built in 1951 |

# indicates five generations have owned or vacationed at PPCC.  * indicates cottage owned by only one family.

| | | | | | |
|---|---|---|---|---|---|
| | Hauber<br>Doyle | Tim & Martha<br>David & Mary Paula | 166 | Bunker Hill | Hazel Harper 1997<br>M/M Thomas Harper<br>Built in 1927 |
| # | Haude | Betty | 47 | Owl's Nest | Martin Roefer/Betty Roefer Haude<br>Henry Roefer's daughter 1950<br>Henry Roefer 1937<br>Olive Cota McClair/Bernice Cota Timmons 1931<br>Olive Cota 1927<br>Marion Cota 1924<br>Built in 1910 |
| | Heavrin | Steve & Karen | 140 | Inn Decision | Lou/Thelma Weston<br>Beth.Luth.Home 1967<br>Paul Kluender 1967<br>Built in 1935 |
| # | Heisel<br>Hession<br>Heitner | Janine<br>Mary Lou<br>Mary | 164<br><br>80 | *MarJoMore<br><br>Happy Time | Margaret Heisel 1991<br>Built in 1929 for Elmore Heisel<br>Irene Timen/Bernice Anthony 1953 |
| # | Henderson | Bert & Thelma | 81 | Hermitage II<br>Retreat House | Peter Gahala 1987<br>Easley 1976<br>Dr. Borchert |
| | Henkel | Don & Marilyn | 150 | Bonnie Dune | W. Paulsen 1966<br>H.Blakemore/G.Volsch 1964<br>Marg.Miller/Emma Klein<br>Built in 1909 |
| | Henry | Chas & Diane | 13 | * | Built in 1983 |
| | Hladik | Bob & MaryLynne | 84 | Honey Do<br>Seavista | Ted/Jan Williams<br>Gordon Ross |
| | Hoff | Wm. A. & Glenda<br>Wm. W. & Julie | 26 | Happy Days<br>Weekend Pass | D. Johnson 1976<br>Built in 1964 |
| | Hohman | Pete & Sue | 142 | East o' the Lake<br>Brown Derby | Bert/Gen Hohman<br>Leo Sowerby |
| | Hoskin | John & Patricia | 78 | Highlands<br>Hi-Up | Kathryn Harriman 1999<br>Isabel Larson<br>George/Catherine Wilson<br>Valentine Scheppers 1924<br>Built in 1913 by Mr. Phillips |
| | Huffman | Mary & Chuck | 57 | | Joel & Jo Parshall<br>Dorothy Parshall 1996<br>Mike Hill<br>Built in 1978 |
| | Jansen | Joe & Colleen | 187 | *Morewood | Built in 1985 |

\# indicates five generations have owned or vacationed at PPCC.   * indicates cottage owned by only one family.

| | | | | | | |
|---|---|---|---|---|---|---|
| | Jennings | William | 18 | * | Shorewood | Built in 1971<br>J.E. McQuig 1970<br>Cottage burned in late 50s<br>Ralph Dempsey 1941<br>Cranshaw 1940<br>Rebuilt in 1971 after cottage burned<br>Built in 1930's |
| | Jones<br>Vanna | Chas. & Ann<br>Roy & Barbara | 50 | | Family Thais<br>Wee Gates | George/Thai Gates 1989<br>Built in 1907 by Sturtevants |
| | Jones | Ross & Mary | 55 | | The 19th Hole | Ralph/Virginia Wenham 1968<br>Built by Ralph Wenham |
| | Joy<br>Karney<br>Rhomberg<br>Joy | Dennis & Donna<br>Monica & Tim<br>Jennifer<br>Marilyn | 162 | | Enchanted Hill | Richards<br>Giblon<br>VanRiper<br>Built in 1936 |
| | Kavanaugh | Thomas & Susan | 51 | | Bittersweet | "Burned in 1991, rebuilt in 1992"<br>Matt/Char. Andreas 1988<br>Bill/Sue Schlacks<br>Dee Mundwiller/Don Prange<br>Horace/Elizabeth Prange<br>Mrs. Duesenberry |
| #  | Keehn<br>Keller | Bill & Marian<br>Jean Hamilton | 101<br>182 | * | Above & Beyond<br>Grapevine | Built in 1964-65<br>Marian Hamilton<br>Carpenters 1940 |
| | King | Barbara Warner | 95 | * | Hong Kong Hilton | Built in 1967 on lot where<br>Baker cottage washed away 1929 |
| # | King | Joanne<br>John & Sally | 77 | | Buckeye King | Built in 1911 for Dr. Bergman |
| # | King | Joseph & Janice | 43 | | Anchor Fast | Virginia VanBeuren 1999<br>VanBeurens<br>Harry/Estele King<br>Built in 1924 |
| | Kinsey | Chas & Hollis | 20 | | Inn Cognito | Francis/Rosie Glasner<br>Built in 1940's Danley |
| | Kirk | Joe & Sharon | 161 | | Wyndune | Richard Lewis 1968<br>W. Paulson 1966<br>Built in 1961 by Rudy Weber |
| | Kittredge | Sallie | 146 | | Waukwin | Dr. Robt. Holmes 1980<br>Built in 1978 |
| | Kleb | Oscar & Marilyn | 153 | | Little Brown Jug | Betty Hard 1968<br>Mrs. Roy Harlow 1957<br>Ward/Blaney/Tilson 1946<br>Mrs. Mary Ward 1944<br>J. Stockwell 1929<br>Built in 1912 |

# indicates five generations have owned or vacationed at PPCC.  * indicates cottage owned by only one family.

| | | | | | |
|---|---|---|---|---|---|
| | Kline | Scott | 71 | Diamond Inn the Rough ThistleDoMe | Bud/Lura Lotts 1995 Art Mailander Dermilton/Woods Built in 1925 |
| | Kolehmainen | Philip & Janet | 69 | Sugar Hill | Lou/Thelma Weston 1969 Built in 1945 |
| # | Kropp | Ray Jr & Tori | 178 * | Retreat | Ray/Ruth Kropp Built in 1952 |
| | Lehmann | Audrey | 127 * | Lehmann's Haven | Built in 1964 |
| | Lewis | Ray Jr. & Lisa | 165 * | Four Winds | Ray/Nanette Lewis 1999 J.Harold/Frances Draper Built in 1933 |
| | Lewis | Ray & Nan | 159 | Hi-Brazil Vid Sjon | Duncan King 1994 Arch King 1993 Ochsenschlagers Holmstrom |
| # | Mailander | John & Joan | 46 * | Innisfree Gopher | "Jo. W. King, Jr./Janice 2000" Joseph W. King Sr. 1994 Mary King Shepardson Built in 1960 |
| | Marks Sharpe | Natalie Ryan Rosemary Ryan | 112 | Cher-Oak-Ee | Elsie Ryan 1987 R.J. Hartman |
| | Mason | Phyllis | 168 | To Each His Own Whistle Stop | E. Henningan 1969 W. Chamberlin 1958 Built in 1932 |
| | Master | Lynne | 53 | Master Lodge Sturtevant Lodge | D. Livingston R. Wenham D. Jones Built as LODGE by Sturtevants Replacing Dr. McCollum's cottage |
| | Mathias | Jayne | 96 | Crest Haven Hy-Up | G. Tyrrell Tyrrell-Wilson 1921 P. Holmstrom 1910 Built in 1909 |
| | Mauer | Don & Bonnie | 86 | Gazebo Villa Mendadh | Pat Warren 1999 John/Estella Gahala 1981 Elsa Smith 1974 |
| | McArdle | Jack | 32 * | Chalet-Leigh | Built in 1964 |
| | McCarthy | Ed & Sheila | 49 | Seamar | Ernest Wunsch 1973 Dr. Timmons "Wickiup" Henry Wunsch |

# indicates five generations have owned or vacationed at PPCC.   * indicates cottage owned by only one family.

| | | | | | | |
|---|---|---|---|---|---|---|
| # | McCarthy | Robert & Fran | 188 | * | 6th Generation | Built in 1985 |
| | McCullough | Rudy & Julie | 117 | | Hillside | Mrs. Beirce 1974 |
| | McMahon | Alice | 169 | | McMahon Emelia | John/Jeannine Read 1980<br>Glenn/Dewey Rogers 1973<br>Anna/Erwin Sprouth 1962<br>Built in 1940 |
| | McNamara<br>Skrine<br>Stratton | Robert & Suzy<br>Steve & Mary Rita<br>Brent & Maureen | 63 | | Gatehouse | Tom/Rita McNamara 1998<br>Tillson/Blayney 1992<br>F. Nichols<br>W. Knapp<br>G. Monroe<br>Built as Munro Lodge in 1910 |
| | McNamara<br>Wentzien | Tom & Rita<br>Paul & K | 97 | | Top Lofty | Vern/Mary Wallace 1976<br>Hagie Family<br>Built in late 1930's |
| | McWethy | Lee & Sandy | 121 | | Lexington Ave<br>Ye Nooc | Torn down/replaced in 2000<br>F.Cooney 1975 |
| | Meadowcroft | Reynar & Mary | 128 | | Sticks & Stones<br>The Little Worlde | Richard/Dolores Martin<br>K. Anderson |
| | Mehagan | Michael & Brenda | 172 | | | John/Nancy Mehagan<br>Art Warner 1966<br>Mrs. Cortes<br>Built between 1915-1920 |
| | Menconi | Bill & Nancy | 28 | | Trail's End | Henry LeFever 1985<br>Art Maerlender 1969 |
| | Menconi | Bill & Nancy | 31 | * | Log Cabin | 1969 |
| | Morsch | Tom & Jackie | 40 | | Edgewood Too<br>Happiness Is | Connie Borchert 1985<br>Hammerschmit<br>Built in 1937 |
| # | Nelson | Al & Betty | 76 | * | | Alvin Nelson 1978<br>Built-1907 for Seymour/Alvin Nelson |
| | Nickerson | Ralph & Audra | 37 | * | Bauhaus | Built in 1965 |
| | Oberlin | Paul & Mary Carol | 58 | | Home Port | S. Severinghaus 1991<br>Built in 1988 |
| | O'Brien | Terrence | 123 | | Beats Working | Donald/Helen O'Brien 2002<br>Fleming |
| | O'Brien | Terry & Laura | 155 | | Port St. Louis<br>Point of View<br>Breezy Nol | Steve Buschman/Tammy Boehm 2003<br>Henry & June Buschman 1999<br>Mary Louise Tombaugh (1980)<br>T. Longley & J Anlauf 1972<br>Mr. DeSouche 1964 |

# indicates five generations have owned or vacationed at PPCC.   * indicates cottage owned by only one family.

| Surname | Name | # | | Cottage Name | History |
|---|---|---|---|---|---|
| O'Brien | Thomas & Joan | 52 | | Castlemaine Kerry<br>Sturtevant Lodge | Dave Livingston<br>Ralph Wenham<br>Del Jones<br>Sturtevants-Annex & Dining Room<br>Built - 1906 or 1907 |
| O'Connor | Anne | 189 | * | Carpe Diem | Built in 1990 |
| O'Connor | Elizabeth | 158 | | Clint Brae | Whitfield Alley<br>Mrs. Hare 1967<br>Mrs. Ward |
| Orr | Bret | 16 | | The Pour House<br>The Prosecution Rests<br>Timber Lake | Marilyn Orr<br>James Kowalski 1995<br>Leon Kowalski 1972<br>Ed/Marian Arey 1971<br>James Spence 1961<br>Built in 1923 |
| Osth | Billie | 75 | | Osthaven<br>Trail's End | Sue Sweet 1983<br>DeButts |
| Owen | Edward & Mary Ann | 196 | * | | Built in 1998 |
| Owen | Josephine | 99 | | Holiday House | Geo. Boyles |
| Owen | Josephine | 68 | | Fern Hill | Kitty Wisson |
| Patterson | Andy & Doris | 151 | * | Up-Side-Dune | Paul/Bea Butcher 1987<br>Built in 1945 by Tony Canonie |
| Peat<br>Wehrheim | Brian & Linnae<br>Joe & Ann Peat | 27 | | Tuckaway | Talitha Peat 2002<br>Built in 1933 |
| Petrulis | Walter & Crystal | 126 | | Rainbow<br>Livin End | Blatchford 1978<br>Elmer Owen 1972 |
| Pierce | Pat | 110 | | Acadia<br>Pegasus | Wade Brill |
| Piper | Brad & Jean | 170 | | Sandpiper<br>Hearts Haven | Alvin Nelson 1969<br>Judge Sprowl 1912<br>Built in 1911 |
| Polizzoto<br>Hennin | Dominic<br>Beth | 186 | | Point of View | Scott Proctor 2002<br>Ed/Jamie Zarling 2001<br>Don Henkel 1985<br>Built in 1985 |
| Pomeroy | Paul & Edy | 138 | | The Apple<br>LaVivienda | Vivian Erwin 1985<br>Ira/Georgia Erwin<br>Built in 1935 |
| #Potter | Bill & Nancy | 3 | * | Driftwood | Geo/Marg Potter 1957<br>Into Lake 1929/Rebuilt 1933<br>Built in 1923 by Mr. Hayes |

\# indicates five generations have owned or vacationed at PPCC.   * indicates cottage owned by only one family.

| Surname | First Names | # | | Cottage Name | History |
|---|---|---|---|---|---|
| Reed | Dillon & Mary | 148 | | Halfway House | John/Elaine Smith 1983<br>Mae Sankey 1945<br>J.T. Manierre<br>David Storrs - Built in 1912 |
| Richards | Virginia | 15 | * | Richards Roost | C.A. Pierce<br>Built in 1933 |
| Richmond | Jim & Lois | 98 | | Wayside<br>Chalet | J.Heitner Lloyd 1993<br>Heitner Family 1948<br>Kirby O'Malley<br>Built in 1928 |
| Robins | Norm & Sandy | 87 | | Robins Nest<br>Hill House<br>Hi Time<br>Rest More | Joe/Mary Gormley 1980<br>Arch/Janette King 1977<br>Pierce Jensen 1949<br>A. Edee<br>Built in 1910 |
| Roche<br>Hoo | Brian & Emily<br>John & Marie | 199 | * | | Built in 2000 |
| Roche | Dwyer & Marge | 1 | | North Beach<br>Mother's Dream | Harry Sherrow 1969<br>Built in 1938 |
| Roche | Pat | 42 | | Beach House | Clarke |
| Rudmann | Larry & Cynthia | 83 | | Treetops | Anne Fuller<br>Kendrick 1960<br>Glassner 1954<br>Mary Ward 1943<br>Rev. E. Schreck 1928<br>First Cottage in Park |
| Ryan | John & Suzanne | 174 | | Grandpa's Beach<br>Lehigh | Katy/Armin Beck<br>Tom/Margaret Abbott 1976<br>Built between 1915-1920 |
| Saraceno<br>Henk | Steven<br>Sharon | 119 | | B'n'B | Bob/Betsy Zimmermann 2002<br>Ray/Marjorie Lewis 1978<br>Chas/How/Jen. Hoffman 1933<br>Carrie Jensen 1932<br>Josie Cheney 1917<br>Built in 1912 |
| Sauer | Margaret | 64 | * | | Rev. Paul Sauer 1956<br>Built in 1925 by Mr. Phillips |
| Schlacks | Bob | 34 | | Owl B'Darned | Muckenhirn<br>Built in 1936 |
| Schlacks | Paul & Nancy | 72 | * | Neverall Inn<br>Poustinia<br>Never All In | "Bob, Bill, Paul Schlacks 1982"<br>Howard/Clare Schlacks 1939<br>Daisy/Wm.Schlacks 1928<br>Don/Nellie Marr 1924 |

# indicates five generations have owned or vacationed at PPCC.  * indicates cottage owned by only one family.

| | Family | Members | # | | Cottage Name | History |
|---|---|---|---|---|---|---|
| | Schlobohm | James & Sally | 17 | | Windjammer | Cleo Kowalski 1997<br>Marilyn Miller 1991<br>VanCampen |
| # | Schlobohm | James & Sally | 19 | * | Squirrel Hill | George / Doris Plain<br>J.A./R.E. McWethy 1972<br>J. LeRoy McWethy<br>Built in 1922 |
| | Sheehan | Bill & Nancy | 22 | * | SheeInn | Built in 1961 |
| | Sheehan | Fran | 21 | * | Inn Orbit | Built in 1961 |
| | Sheehan | Terry | 200 | * | | Built in 2003 |
| | Shortridge<br>Schwartz | Mike & Mary<br>Dick & Anne | 120 | | Hermitage | Bert Henderson/Orcutt 1990<br>David Henderson 1976<br>Built in 1910 |
| | Sitterly | Mike & Nancy | 35 | | Far Niente<br>Not A Care | Hammerschmit 1992<br>Built in 1960 |
| # | Speicher | John (Spike) & Linda | 104 | * | Happy Hollow | Rebuilt in 2000 after 1999 storm<br>Harold/Jean Speicher<br>M.L. Bosier<br>Built in 1930 |
| | Stanger | Richard & Joan<br>Ronald & Helga<br>Juel | 11 | | Waldameer | Mr. Binna 1961 |
| | Steiner | Patricia | 4 | | High Tor<br>Top Deck | Michael/Kathy Goggin 1995<br>Rich/Pat Venner 1989<br>Built in 1967 |
| | Stephens | Mark & Mary Lee | 156 | | | Mary Lou Tombaugh 1993<br>Henry/June Buschman 1980<br>Carl/Anita Watling 1979<br>William Seymour 1967<br>Built in 1934 |
| | Stewart<br>Sahagian | Doug<br>Linda | 131 | | TLC | Tom Dawson 1978 |
| | Stracke | Bob & Maria | 66 | | HiView | Zita/Katherine Mahoney 1988<br>Messner<br>Built in 1908 |
| | Tamm | Gregory & Mary Beth | 24 | | Wit's End<br>Escape Hatch | Gil/Marian MacNeil 1996<br>Gerald Hatch 1976<br>Built in 1962 |
| # | Tillson | Jim & Skipper,<br>Steve & Lucie,<br>Tillie, Tom" | 92 | * | Vashmar | Wm. Ward<br>Built in 1907 |

\# indicates five generations have owned or vacationed at PPCC.  \* indicates cottage owned by only one family.

| | | | | | |
|---|---|---|---|---|---|
| Trezise | Wally | 108 | | Bozeman | Tom/Salli Eley 1994 |
| Petty | Mary Lou | | | Hi Lo | Owens 1970 |
| | | | | | Gervais |
| | | | | | Built by S. Baker in 1940s |
| Trumbull | Bill & Barb | 147 | | Set Point | "Carol, Lori, Steve Anderson 1985" |
| | | | | Anderson Cottage | Karl Anderson 1970 |
| | | | | | Art Olaf/Mary Storrs Anderson 1946 |
| | | | | Villa Vista | David Storrs 1919 |
| | | | | | Built in 1912 |
| VanderSalm | Harold (Bunkie) | 2 | | Bunk-In | Consumers 1968; moved to present site |
| | | | | | Ted Little |
| Venner | Richard & Gail | 114 | | Valhalla | |
| | | | | Sandwitch | John/LaVerne Ankenbruck 1996 |
| | | | | Merrikot | Mrs. Marie Vierow 1976 |
| | | | | | Leota/Orion Reed |
| Vercillo | John & Tracy | 39 | | | |
| | | | | Haas and Andy | John Anderson |
| | | | | NotByaDamSite | Forrest Lowrey |
| | | | | | M. Harding |
| Vujtech | Gertrude | 190 | | Lakehaus | Malablocki 1992 |
| Grist | Alice | | | | Built in 1990 |
| Carr | Beatrice | | | | |
| Waldron | Vivian | 14 | * | Spindrift | Jim/Viv Richards |
| | | | | | Andrew/Jane Peirce 1979 |
| | | | | | Built in 1925 |
| Welles | Peter & Anita | 7 | * | The Ark | Welles Family 1988 |
| | Cameron & Anne | | | | Claude A.Sr./Ines Welles 1965 |
| | | | | | Built in 1920 |
| Whitney | Frank & Susan | 134 | | Valkommen | Lori Dillman 2000 |
| | | | | | B.Becker/M.Lancaster 1996 |
| | | | | Mac's Shack | Gordon MacQuaker |
| | | | | Silvercrest | Frasers |
| | | | | | Built for Mrs. Sturtevant |
| # Williams | Jim & Pat | 173 | | Windsong | Robt/Carol Replogle 1988 |
| | | | | | Weldon Coates |
| | | | | | McDougal |
| | | | | The Mary Lee | Ward |
| Wilson | James & Maureen | 56 | | Sunset Grill | |
| | | | | Key North | Richard/Pat Venner 1994 |
| | | | | | Key North |
| | | | | | Peters |
| | | | | | Built in 1968 |
| # Wintermute | Bob & Nancy | 184 | * | | |
| Kearnin | Tom & Cindy | | | | Built in 1979 for Roy/Betty |
| Zimmermann | Bob & Pam | 191 | * | Bedford Falls | Built in 1992 |

\# indicates five generations have owned or vacationed at PPCC.   * indicates cottage owned by only one family.

"Cottages bought, demolished or moved by Consumers in 1969 for new power plant:"

| | | | |
|---|---|---|---|
| | #1 | | Helen Joselyn Scott<br>Dr. Irene Joselyn<br>Built by Milikens |
| | #2 | Bonnie Doone | Arthur/Jessie Filkins<br>Built in 1926 |
| | #3 | Sea Breeze | Bruce Chambers<br>Nellie Olson 1960<br>Built in 1920 |
| | #4 | Ted Little's Cot. | Moved to VanderSalm's |
| Additional Building:<br>SODA BAR | | Managed by: | Built by Arthur Quick<br>Quick's daughter & granddaughter<br>Archie Allen<br>Carmen Sanke<br>Mary /Jim Roach<br>Laura Neubauer<br>Mary Ellen/Bill Colbert<br>Pat/Rich Venner<br>Fred Nichols<br>Colleen Schlacks & Family<br>And Others |

**Chart compiled by Barbara Trumbull**

## Above and Beyond #101

Above and Beyond was built in 1964-65 by Cecil Burrous and his father, Leonard, for Bill and Marian Keehn. Fran Hoffacker, from Covert, and his crew did the carpentry work. Bill first came to Palisades in 1928, at the age of six, with his parents, Roland and Marion Keehn of Oak Park, Illinois. They stayed at Sturtevant Lodge. Bill brought Marian to PPCC while they were engaged – and they have returned every summer after that, first staying at the Lodge, then renting various cottages, before hearing about the land where the cottage stands.

*Remodeled Anchor Fast #43. 2001*

## Anchor Fast #43

Joe and Janice King, the present owners of Anchor Fast, have the contract dated May 21, 1924, between Arthur Quick and Harold and Estelle King Van Beuren, to build their cottage. Harry Wildt was the contractor; the cost was just over $3000. They also have the bill for the sod put around the cottage – including 41 hours of labor at 35 cents per hour, for a total of $14.35! The cottage was passed to the Van Beuren's daughter, Virginia Van Beuren, who owned it for many years. Upon her death, the present owners (Joe is a cousin of Virginia) extensively remodelled the cottage in 1990.

## Ankenbruck's # 193 and 197

John and LaVerne Ankenbruck built their lovely home in the woods south of the entrance road to the Park, in 1996, as their retirement spot. They had previously owned a cottage in the Park – Venners' Valhalla (#114). Their daughter, Lisa, and friend Christine Kasperzak built another lovely home across from John and LaVerne in 1999.

## The Ark #7

The Ark was built by Claude A. Welles, Sr., and Ines Welles, in 1920. In 1965, ownership was transferred to their five children – Emerson, Leonard, Jeanne, Claude, and Kathryn. Since 1988, the Ark has been in the capable and loving hands of Cameron and Peter Welles, sons of Emerson Welles.

*The Ark in winter. 1971.*

## The Baker/Goodrich Cottage #132 and #95

From the August 3, 1966 <u>Patter</u>, we learn that Mrs. Katherine Baker was the third person to own land in Palisades Park. (The first was Rev. Shreck, who built Treetops and one other cottage; the second the Nelson family who still own that cottage.) For two or three years they camped in tents on what was called the "Camp Grounds." There was a pump installed to pump water to drink. This was located in a big blow out, somewhat protected from the weather, on the grounds where Jo Owens and the Brands now have cottages. The Bakers did a lot of fill before they built, where Cottage #95 now stands. Mrs. Katherine Baker's son, John, and his sisters were the owners when the cottage was washed away in

*Mrs. Wunsch at the VanBeuren cottage #43, calling her son Peter to lunch. 1937.*

the big storm of 1929. The Bakers at that time opted to leave the beach and move to a new cottage (#132) in the woods. John's daughter, Mary Kay Goodrich, and her husband Charles owned that second cottage for many years. In 1996, they sold it to Kenneth and JoAnn Gryzwa.

### Balgownie #74

Balgownie was built for Tom Bendelow, Sr., in 1919, by Mr. Quick. Tom was introduced to Palisades Park by Mr. Quick, who wanted him to build a golf course (eight holes) in the park. This he did, but it proved too expensive, in those days, to bring water to the grounds, so it no longer exists. At Tom Bendelow, Sr.'s death, around 1930, the cottage went to his three children, Ernest Bendelow, Jack Bendelow, and Mae Mizen. In 1967, the cottage was sold to Ernest's sons, Tom II and Bruce. In 1973, Tom purchased Bruce's share. In 1986, Tom passed away and the cottage is now owned by his wife, Shirley, and children T. Craig Bendelow and Nancy Jean Zmuda. The cottage was named by the senior Tom Bendelows. There is a "Bridge of Balgownie" in Scotland where Tom Sr. proposed to his bride, Polly, many years before they came to the United States.

### Ballou Inn # 90, Graystone # 89, and Ambivalent #91

These three cottages were among the earliest built at Palisades. On the Arthur Quick Circle, they were built by Robert Ballou and his family. The three buildings, originally somewhat alike, were built of cement block construction. The cement blocks were made in hand operated molds right on the spot, using sand and gravel brought up from the beach. The first cottage, nearest to the lake, then called Oceana (#91), was owned by Mr. Ballou's father; the second – Ballou Inn (#90)– by Mr. Ballou; and the third, now named Graystone (#89), by Mr. Ballou's sister and husband, Dr. and Mrs. W. R. Smith of Pawnee City, Nebraska. The Smiths called it Aksarben – Nebraska spelled backwards.

Robert Ballou built a number of other early cottages. He and has wife ran Ballou Inn as a guest house. The Inn also offered a store and, for much of its history, a Post Office. See the article on Robert Ballou and the letter from his granddaughter, Virginia Steinbacher, elsewhere in this volume.

### Bartley #171

From Dr. Campbell's interview elsewhere in this volume: "Although we bought our cottage in 1941, in earlier years we used to come over here and visit. We'd come in and ride through the Park and maybe have a little picnic. We got lost every time. Some of the first persons we knew were the Van Ripers. They lived up on the hill above here, the first cottage (#162), where the Joys live. We'd come out on the weekends and they'd take us down on the beach. We'd keep on them for a place for a cottage. This one was rented for years, by the Sengenbergers, but they did not want to sell. Mrs. Sengenberger's parents first bought the land from Mr. Quick in 1910. The cottage was finished in 1913. There were no roads back up the hill or anything. All of the lumber and everything had to be transported down the beach, in off the road down at the hotel. They brought it down by horse and wagon. In later years, Mrs. Sengenberger became incapacitated and they couldn't come up here very much anymore. She turned over the cottage to her daughter Ella, but they never wanted to give it up. They were holding it for sentimental reasons, hoping somebody in the family would be interested. So, one Sunday – this was in 1941 – we bought a little gas from Mr. Knapp's gas station out on the Blue Star. I got in there talking with him about places in the Park. He knew as much as Mr. Quick did. So I said, "We still have our eye on this little cottage down there by the lake." He said, "You know, I can't be sure but I have a gut feeling that they'll let that go if you contact them." It didn't take much. I went back home and wrote a letter immediately. She sent a very nice letter and said she hated to let the cottage go, but would. We rode down to Indianapolis and completed the deal right down there. Of course Mr. Quick was in all of this too. He did the deed work and the transfers and insurance. That's how we got the cottage.

The name of the cottage was "walk in" spelled backwards – "Niklaw." You can see why we changed it to Oasis. We still have some chairs with "Niklaw" written on the back. We changed it to Oasis because that was where the "camels" came to rest. You don't know how confusing that was, as a young person who was very poor at spelling, ever to get my name straight. That's how they pronounced it in the East – Camel."

Janice Bartley and family bought the cottage from the Campbells and still own it.

### Bauhaus #37

Ralph and Audra Nickerson were first introduced to Palisades Park while they were dating, as guests at the Wunsch family cottage (#49) on the beach. Later, with daughter Deborah, summer vacations were spent as guests of Gerald and Belden Hatch at their northside cottage, Escape Hatch (#24). Gerald Hatch, Audra's brother, was one of the "Nine Old Men." His abiding love for Palisades continues within the family.

Purchasing lots and eventually building at Palisades Park was a "dream come true" for the entire family. The lots were bought in 1966 from Forest Lowrey when the Edgewater section of the Nature Trail was developed. Herman Stremler, of Ganges, Michigan, built the cottage, based on a design by Audra and Ralph. It was completed in 1968. The cottage, built of full-thickness cedar planks in board and batten construction, was designed so that there would be a view of the meadow in any season. Ceilings are open beam style, rising from eight feet tall in the back to twelve feet tall on the screen porch and front deck. Clear story, floor to ceiling windows across the front bring in lots of light and access to the wonderful vista from almost anywhere in the cottage. The feeling that we are living up among the treetops inspired the cottage name. The Bauhaus (pronounced Bough House) is also a reference to the architectural style.

### The Beach House #42 and North Beach #1
A Short History of the Roche Family in Palisades Park

Pierre Roche operated an advertising agency in Chicago and had a summer home in Paw Paw, Michigan. A commercial papers sales representative who called on him kept telling him about this "great place I have on the lake and you ought to come over to see where we are." The sales rep was Ernie Melchert (father of Ginny Coleman/Old Pier cottage - #45). In 1947, Pierre came over and, within two or three weeks, purchased the Clark cottage – the second cottage south of the bridge on the road. He renamed it The Beach House.

The cottage was little used until Pierre's older son, Kirby, got married and started using the cottage, in the summer of 1952. Pierre's other son, Dwyer, married Marge in 1953 and started using the cottage as well. Marge's sister, Katie Cordell, and her family shared in the use of the cottage also, until the middle 60's when they built their own cottage (Meadowview #36), the first cottage on the meadow going east from the bridge.

In 1969, Kirby bought out Dwyer's half of the cottage. Kirby's widow, Pat, and son, Kerry, still live there. Marge and Dwyer bought the Sherrow cottage (#1) at the far north end of the Park on the beach. The family named it North Beach. To make room for the six Roche children, a second floor was added to the original one-bedroom cottage over the winter of 1969-70.

Since then, three more cottages have come to be in the family. Kirby's daughter, Colleen Schlacks, and her family bought the Muckinhern cottage (#34) in 1979 and named it Owl Be Darned. In 1993, his other daughter, Mary Pat Compernolle, and her family bought Gwen Ott's cottage (#106), La Casita. In 2001, Marge and Dwyer's son, Brian, and daughter, Marie, and their families jointly built a new cottage (as yet unnamed) at the back of the meadow (#199).

All of which shows that efforts of the sales rep, Ernie Melchert, back in the 40's, led to six of our Palisades cottages belonging to the extended Roche family. What a legacy!

### Bedford Falls #191

Bedford Falls history starts with the family of Bob and Pam Zimmermann. Their cottage was built by Dave Hope during the '92–'93 winter season. Prior to that time, they vacationed with their children, Pat and Pete, at Bob's parents' cottage, B 'n B. Bob and Pam first came to the Park in the 70's, when Bob's parents were renting the Ankenbruck's cottage (#114 - now owned by Rick and Gail Venner). They spent a weekend here or there while working during college summers. They soon decided a few days a summer was not enough for them. In the fall of 1992, they broke ground on the lots they had purchased a few years earlier. The cottage was finished in May of 1993. Pam adds: "We have been blessed with many beautiful memories. Pat would have been the first to say, 'It's a wonderful life!'"

### Blueberry Hill #113

This log cabin predates the Park. It was, during the late 1800's, first an office for the logging company, located near the present Blue Star Highway. In the first years of the Park's existence, it was moved to its present location. Extensively remodelled since, it nonetheless retains one log wall both inside and out.

### B 'n B #119

This cottage was built in 1912 by Josie R. Cheney of St. Louis, MO. In 1917, Carrie Mathilde Jensen of Chicago bought the property from the Cheney estate, for $500. In 1932 ownership passed to Jennie C., Charles L., and Howard A. Hoffman of Chicago. At this time, dues were

$25 per year for a house, $5 for the first undeveloped lot, and $1 for each additional vacant lot. In 1938, the property taxes were $13.56. In 1933, Raymond and Marjorie Lewis purchased the cottage. In August of 1978, Bob and Betsy Zimmermann purchased the cottage from the Lewises. They named the cottage B 'n B for Bob and Betsy. Two of their sons managed the property until the summer of 2002, when it was sold.

## Bonnie Dune #150

Bonnie Dune was one of the first cottages built on the beach south of the water tower. Appearing on the earliest map of the Park, it was built by Miss Margaret M. Miller and Miss Emma B. Klein, both teachers at McCosh School in Chicago. They enjoyed it for many years and left it to Miss Miller's niece Hazel and her husband, George Volsch. In 1964, the Paulsens (who at that time owned what is now Kirks' cottage - #161) bought and remodelled Bonnie Dune. Two years later (1966), they sold it to Don and Marilyn Henkel, who had been renting in the Park. Marilyn had first come to Palisades with her parents, Ruth and Jim Bartle, and her brother, Bill, in the 30's.

In a letter to Katy Beck, Marilyn's mother, Ruth Bartle, who had stayed at the hotel and rented several cottages over the years, remembered the drive to Palisades from Oak Park, in the early years. "My, what a job it was to drive up there when we had to drive through Gary and all the other towns along the way. Then the thruway was built and there was no speed limit and I sure drove my car fast in those days! Now, I can't even walk fast." The most famous yarn about the cottage dates from the 30's when John Dillinger supposedly broke in and hid there, after escaping from an Indiana prison. This was shortly before his final date with the FBI; Dillinger and a girlfriend reputedly waited out the manhunt for him in

*Bonnie Dune. c. 1940's.*

Bonnie Dune. Police traced items left behind to Dillinger when the cottage was opened in the spring.

## Brandyville Cottage #38

John and Pat Donovan purchased their cottage from the Fletcher family. The cottage was built, with the help of Cecil Burrous, in 1962. The Donovans liked it because it was relatively new, when they bought in 1979, and had a beautiful view facing the meadow and the Brandywine. They added a porch and used the deck in the sunlight and the porch when it rained and was dark. Their pleasure in the cottage was complete when their son and his wife, Jim and Jane Donovan, built a cottage across the road.

## Breezy Hollow and Generation Four #183 and #184

In 1912, the Covert Resort Association deeded the lot where Breezy Hollow now stands to Robert Ballou. That same year, Ballou sold the lot to Frida, Emma, and Henriette Bielenberg, of Chicago, Illinois. The Bielenberg sisters built the cottage in 1913-14. They, in turn, sold to Herbert B. and Helen A. Woodard in 1923. The Woodards also bought a second lot, next door, from the Covert Resort Association. The records are a bit confusing, but it seems the cottage ownership passed, in 1938, through Edwin Dvorak (a relative?? a lawyer??) to Helen, Eldon, and Herbert L. Woodard. About this time, the Woodards also bought a lot within Palisades Park, enabling them to use Palisades Park roads, walks, and other services for a membership fee of $25.00 a year.

*Breezy Hollow #183 right, Grapevine #182, above, Seagull #181 left.*

Betty Wintermute's parents, Donald and Betty Egbert, rented Potawatomie (#154) from 1924 to 1938, with their three children – Donald, Betty, and Louise. Then they rented Marjomore (#164). In the fall of 1947, the Egberts bought Dr. Woodard's cottage, Breezy Hollow. Their daughter and her husband, Betty and Roy Wintermute, raised their three children there. The family grew so that Betty and Roy built a second cottage, called Generation 4, with the money left to her from her mother. Though

Roy and Betty are both now deceased, two of their children and their spouses, Bob and Nancy Wintermute and Tom and Cindy Wintermute Kearin, still enjoy Generation Four. Breezy Hollow was sold, in August, 2001, to Jim and Ellie Bates.

## The Briars #195

George and Patti Ebright had their cottage built in 1996. They named it The Briars because there were so many briar bushes on Knolltop, the name of the lots they purchased from the Hammersmith estate. Coincidentally, The Briars is the name of a famous resort hotel in Sutton, Ontario, Canada, the place from which Patti's family came.

*The Briars #195.*

## Buckeye King #77

Isadora King Donahue built the first Buckeye King cottage around 1933 or 1934. This cottage was destroyed by fire not long after. She had the present Buckeye King rebuilt and completed by 1936. That summer, she invited her brother and his wife - Robert Ahimaaz and Winifred King – and two nieces - Shirley King and Joanne Mailander King – for a visit for a "grand opening." This was Joanne's first trip to Palisades Park – a visit that has occurred every year afterwards (minus one). Aunt Iz was married to William F. Donahue, a member of the M. A. Donahue Publishing Company in Chicago. Isadora's sister was Estelle King VanBeuren of Evanston, Illinois. Both sisters loved Palisades. The VanBeurens lived among beautiful trees in Evanston. The Donahues lived on Sheridan Road, right on Lake Michigan. Therefore, each sister selected a view she did not have in Illinois. Aunt Stell chose Anchorfast (#43), on the beach, and Aunt Iz chose Buckeye King in the woods.

Ultimately, Buckeye King was inherited by J. W. King of Kings Mills, Ohio - and passed to his daughter, Joanne Mailander King. It is enjoyed by her children - John, Jody, Jeff, and Jenny - their spouses, and four grandchildren.

## Bunkahill #166

In 1927, before Thomas Harper and his wife, Montana, could begin construction on their cottage, the road which is now Route One, Lake Bluff Drive, had to be built. Horses were used, not only to cut through the woods and make the road, but also to bring in all of the building supplies. The design of the cottage was based upon the inn in the book Seven Keys to Ballpate. The cottage always belonged to the Harper family until Hazel Harper's death in 1997, when it was purchased by co-owners Tim and Martha Hauber and David and Mary Paula Doyle. See Harper interview earlier in this volume.

## Bunk-In #2

The VanderSalm family started coming to Palisades Park in the mid-50's. They would drive to the parking area by Pierce's cottage, walk the boardwalk to the end, then picnic and swim on their lake front lot. Usually they would bring guests from Kalamazoo. Very few people were on the North Beach at that time. The Sherrows (now Roche cottage #1) were their neighbors. In 1969, Consumers Power Company purchased all cottages and land north of their property for a buffer zone. Three cottages were to be demolished. The Company contacted Harold VanderSalm regarding the Ted Little cottage (which was then about five years old) and agreement and terms were reached. Assured that the cottage could be moved over frozen ground, Harold purchased it from Consumers. The Van Allen Contractors of Delton, Michigan, were engaged to move the cottage. Harold chose the location and designed the foundation, which was to become the lower level of the cottage. The original owner and builder was the Ted Little family of Kalamazoo, Michigan. It was not part of Palisades Park; a private entrance from Blue Star Highway led to the site.

They were delighted when they saw their new summer home in the spring of 1970. On May 22, 1970, they escorted a moving van filled with furniture to the cottage. A new road had been built. The van proved its worth. Upon arrival, they were greeted by one of the beautiful but violent wind and lightening storms. Each person and each piece of furniture was properly soaked, then put under cover. A tired, rain-soaked crew returned to Kalamazoo, accompanied by claps of thunder and flashes of lightening. The cottage was named Bunk-In.

The bluff on which the cottage now stands was quite devoid of vegetation. Harold VanderSalm, with a crew of workers, terraced the dune and planted many pine trees, spirea, and ground covers, to hold and beautify the dune and to make a garden spot. The VanderSalms now enjoy a beautiful pine grove with its many birds, flowers, rest areas, and path to the beach.

### Burrous Home #60

Cecil Burrous built this house when he was hired to be Park manager, in 1959. With the help of his father, he built a place to live just outside the Park. Staying on at Palisades as a builder after he resigned as manager, he has found the location a good one through the years, adding rooms and outbuildings as his family and professional needs demanded. In 2002 Cecil retired; the house is presently for sale.

### Casa Loca #124

In October of 1935, the property was purchased by Grover C. and Matilda J. Perry, of Chicago. A house was built on two lots and the garage/servants' quarters on two lots across the road. The latter became a separate residence in later years (Rainbow #126). The house was sold to Frederick and Victoria Nunneley of Peoria in August, 1939. In August of 1942, it was purchased by Charles and Helen Jansen of Indianapolis. Charles and Ruth Apostol, friends of the Jansens, bought the house in 1952; they later handed it down to their daughter, Constance Apostol Zimlich, and her husband Ray Zimlich, of Tipton, Indiana. The present owners are Constance's daughter, Sally, and her husband, Jerry Davis, of Muncie, Indiana.

### Castlemaine Kerry #52

Tom and Joan O'Brien bought what had been the back half of Sturtevant Lodge and turned it into a home for their large family. The Lodge was one of the first buildings in the Park. Mr. and Mrs. Sturtevant ran it for a number of years, followed by their nephew, Del Jones. Del was followed by Ralph and Virginia Wenham. However, by the time the Wenhams tried to sell, the repairs needed to bring the buildings up to code were so expensive that a decision was made to divide the property and turn it to private use.

This northern two-story section of the building was built in approximately 1907 by Mrs. Sturtevant. Sometime prior to 1924, this original lodge was put on logs and pulled by mules to its present location at the rear of the building. The original front south section now faces west. The first floor of the original lodge served as the kitchen after 1924 and the second floor had eight bedrooms, primarily for summer employees. The present three-story addition was then built in front of the original lodge and attached to it. The first floor of this new addition served as the living room and the two upper floors contained 18 guest bedrooms for summer rentals. Del Jones was given control of the Lodge in 1923. The oak tree by the front door was mentioned in Palisades Park documents as early as 1907.

The present name – Castlemaine-Kerry – is the name of a small town and County in southwest Ireland which was the birthplace of the O'Brien direct ancestry as early as 1850. The original homestead is still retained today by their descendants.

Mr. Quick noted, in the July 29, 1939 Patter, that the oak tree now standing "by the hotel dining-room door was a little sapling" when he first knew it. "East of it, there was a high sand hill ...and directly beyond that a deep bayou." Apparently the sand was later used to fill in the bayou.

### Cedar Nook #103

Contractors Woodley and Shine built Cedar Nook for Brad and Carol Bradford, who still make it their summer home. The Bradfords had rented in the Park for two years – cottage #107 which belonged to another Bradford family (no relation) in 1966 and what later became Colb's Cozy (#113), in 1967. In 1968 they decided to build their own cottage. In 2002, the cottage was enlarged by contractor Dave Hope who moved the west wall out three feet and roofed and screened the deck.

### Chalet-Leigh #32
From September, 1996 Patter
By Jack and Pat McArdle

"We had always dreamed of having a summer place. In 1963, Bill and Fran Sheehan invited us to Palisades to see their new summer cottage. The moment we drove through the gate, we fell in love! We bought our lot in 1964 with the intention of building sometime in the future. We couldn't wait; our cottage was completed in July, 1964, and we moved in. Ours was the second A-frame in the Park, the first being the Van Campen's (#12) on the lake. This is our 32nd summer at Palisades. Our children spent every summer of their young lives here and returned often during high school and college. Now our grandchildren are enjoying the beauty and great fun of Palisades."

### Cher-Oak-Ee #112

The original owners built Cher-Oak-Ee between a cherry and an oak tree. The Ryans loved the name and, when they bought the cottage, have never changed it. From a small cottage with the ice box placed half in and half out of the small kitchen, it has been made into a lovely, knotty pine interior. The pine came from Rainy Lake, Wisconsin.

Mr. and Mrs. Ryan hauled it into the cottage, piece by piece. Cecil Burrous helped by enhancing it with a scalloped trimming. The cottage has been kept as antique-looking as possible, with furnishings all bought in the Michigan area. Elsie always loved Palisades. Her son, Jack, and his family own a cottage on the beach. Natalie Ryan Marks has owned Cher-Oak-Ee since 1987.

### Colb's Cozy #115

The first owners listed on the October 5, 1912 deed were William and Alice Tucker. When George and Bessie DeBlois tried to buy the cottage, it took eight years in court to settle their case, but they finally received title on October 1, 1928. In 1961, Dorothy and Ann DeBlois sold to Wendall and Grace Fidler for $6500. Wendall Fidler was a professor at Western Michigan University. Grace Fidler helped Mrs. Bierce (Julie McCullough's mother) put out the Patter for three or four years. In March of 1968, Bill and Mary Ellen Colbert purchased the property. They added a deck, put in a well and electric heat, glassed in a porch, did over the bathrooms, and added a lower level. When Bill bought the property, his lawyer called him and said, "You don't want to buy this property! The original covenant with Palisades Park Country Club does not allow alcoholic beverages."

### Cresthaven # 96

Built in 1910 by Robert Ballou for the Homstrom family, Cresthaven was later sold to the grandparents of present owner, Jayne Mathias. Jayne tells a bit about early days in her cottage in her interview, printed elsewhere in this volume.

### Driftwood #3

This cottage really has a history of "driftwood." Built in the early 20's by a Mr. Hayes, then Assistant Superintendent of Schools in Chicago, the cottage fell into the lake in a 1929 storm. It was carefully dismantled and the wood piled together. In 1932, Margaret and George Potter bought the lot and the pile of wood. They then rebuilt the cottage in the same spot, using the same wood and the same plans, and naming it – appropriately – Driftwood. Their family has enjoyed the cottage ever since – albeit with frequent additions of protective seawalls. Bill and Nancy, the present owners, remodeled the downstairs area into an apartment they can enjoy while the younger generations stay upstairs.

### Dunewood #100

Herb and Esther Brand, from Western Springs, Illinois, brought their children – William, Margaret, Martha, and John – to Palisades Park in the mid-1930's. They rented Clint Brae cottage until about 1941. After vacationing near Ludington during the war, the Brand family decided to purchase property in Palisades Park and build a summer cottage of their own. In 1948, Herb purchased 60 feet of Lot 11 in the Oceana Block in front of the Clubhouse for $1800, from Arthur Quick's daughter, Julia Hill. In September of the same year, he purchased 60 feet of Lot 10 directly west of the first parcel for another $600.

Dunewood Cottage was built with the first floor exterior walls of cinder block, floors of yellow pine and wall paneling of knotty pine; it had a screened porch overlooking the lake, a small kitchen, full bath, living room with fireplace, and two bedrooms – one with a small sink. The sleeping loft for the children was accessed by climbing a ladder. In 1949 a stairway was built and a half bath installed on the second floor. In 1952, Herb purchased the remaining portions of Lots 10 and 11 for $1000 and installed a wooden sea wall. A dormer was added in 1969 to create a third bedroom on the second floor to help accommodate the 16 grandchildren at that time. In 1991 John Brand purchased the cottage and added a combination kitchen and living room. The old kitchen was converted to a laundry room.

*The Brand Cottage #100 after remodelling.*

### East of the Lake #142

The Hohman cottage was originally owned by Dr. Leo Sowerby, a world famous composer and one of the first Pulitzer Prize winners for music, in 1946. The then "Brown Derby" was rented to Burt and Gen Hohman and their four sons, from 1945 to 1964, when the Hohmans bought the cottage from Dr. Sowerby. Dr. Sowerby died in 1968 and left his cottage, a studio, and several lots to Gen Hohman. Dr. Sowerby's two cottages were torn down around 1970. Pete and Sue Hohman purchased the Brown Derby from Pete's mom in 1983 and renamed it "East of the Lake," Pete, Sue, and their children and spouses –

Peter and Kelly, Wendy and Jame, Matthew and Veronica, Kevin and Margaret, Chris and Monica, and Nancy and Tony – now share their enjoyment and love of Palisades with the 4th generation. They are, at the time of this printing, Tim, Peter, Ryan, Colin, Lily, Anna, Abby, and Aidan.

## Escape Hatch (now called Wit's End) #24

George and Mary Beth Tamm bought this cottage in 1996 from Gil and Marian MacNeil. The MacNeills said the following, in the July 18, 1980 Patter: "We have done little to Escape Hatch since we became its owners four years ago except to enjoy it! With heat and our own well, we do enjoy weekends during the fall, winter, and early spring seasons very much. … We bought the cottage from Gerry and Belden Hatch and we've asked them to tell its history." The Patter continues with the Hatch report as follows: "Escape Hatch was built for us, at my design, in the spring of 1961, by Hermen Stremmler. Stremmler was a builder from up near Ganges. The cottage was built originally with the idea of retiring there, and therefore it was planned to be enlarged by a wing to the south and west, with a large living room up and a large bedroom and bath beneath – making it a tri-level, with a large foyer between the two wings. The cottage was originally named Hoch Haus, a name taken from days living in Vienna, Austria. We got so tired of overhearing, from our terrace, the pronunciation "Hock House," we decided to change it. It was never in "hock" and we didn't like the sound of it. So, at the suggestion of a friend, we named the cottage Escape Hatch – which it was – along with being a lifesaver all the years we owned it. Travel we loved, so we never got around to enlarging the cottage. All in all, we have had much fun with our drinking and eating terraces. And all our guests could never get over the Palisades effect when entering the Park. The roads used to terrify our guests. One got as far as the cottage back of us, turned around, and went home. The drinking terrace was the setting for the organization of the opposition to the Palisades Atomic Plant. If you do not know that story, ask Ginny Coleman. We were defeated in the end, but it would make an interesting book, and at least we had the pleasure of trying to do something about it.

Most of our iris came from Belden's iris farm, called Windridge Farm. As for the wild flowers – for the first ten years after building the cottage, we never drove anywhere but what we took a box or two with our shovel in the trunk of the car. With the result we brought the hepaticas – from white to blue to purple to pink – from along the Kalamazoo River, west of Battle Creek; the bloodroot and the myrtle from outside Battle Creek; many of the asters and the trailing arbutus from northern southern Michigan; and the trilliums from along the highway. Also there were Turk's caps, bergamot, cardinal flower, and spider wort from the roads towards Covert. The Dutchman's britches, wind flowers, scilla sibrica, trout lilies, and dogtooth violets came from woods south of Covert near Watervliet. The pink columbine is natural in the Park. The dark purple came from my Dad's garden in Marshall. Growing the ivy on the terrace banks was a job. We are very pleased that you have kept the name Escape Hatch. It was truly that for us and we hope it is for you. Our best, Gerry and Belden Hatch."

## Exit Inn #135

Exit Inn is owned by Howard Beyer and located in Happy Valley, at 79904 Ramblewood Drive. Erwin and Lousie Beyer, Howard's parents, bought what they named Exit Inn in the mid-40's from the Hubert Stoddard family. (Hubert was Ruth Kropp's grandfather and Ruth's interview elsewhere tells of her early visits to this cottage.) The Beyers enjoyed it for many years until failing health prevented them from making the trip from Chicago. The elder Beyers sold to son Howard in the late 80's. Howard reminisces about his life in Palisades as follows:

> My father and mother, Mr. and Mrs. Erwin Beyer, brought a very young me to Palisades Park in the late 30's. Dad was a member of Dr. Leo Sowerby's church choir in Chicago and my parents always drove to Palisades to attend Dr. Sowerby's cottage parties for his choir members every 4th of July. The Sowerby cottage was located in what is now known as Happy Valley. After Sowerby's death, his cottage was torn down; so was his very small, adjacent studio cottage, in which certain members of his choir had stayed. My family always stayed at Sturtevant Lodge. Later, they rented the Stoddard cottage, buying it in 1957. The cottage has remained in our family ever since. My father was a member of a barbershop quartet and therefore knew many "sing-along" type songs. He always led a group of Happy Valley Palisaders in songs at beach parties. They had a great time drinking their favorite beverages and singing those vintage songs. However, as the years passed, those Park members have moved on.

## Fifth Generation #188

Bob and Fran McCarthy designed and built their cottage in 1985. Bob served as general contractor and Cecil Burrous was the builder. The cottage is called "Fifth Generation" because five generations of the McCarthy family have been in the Park, starting in the very early days of our history. Indeed, the family may have to change the name to "Sixth Generation" soon.

### The Filkins Cottage #12

David and Mika Filkins built this cottage in 1983. They bought the lot from the Vandersalms. It was not in Dean's Addition and had not been part of the original survey. David's family had owned one of the cottages that Consumer's Power tore down when they built the power plant north of Palisades. David, having grown up in the Park, wanted his children to do so also.

*Filkins Cottage #12.*

### Focus Inn #149

Built in 1953–54 by Rudy Weber for Henry and Frances Prange, this cottage was originally called Port O'Call. Henry's mother owned Bittersweet #51, near Circle Beach, so Henry and Fran were no strangers to the Park when they decided they wanted a place of their own. They loved Palisades, and Palisaders loved them. They and their children, Linda and Bill, enjoyed the cottage for many years but sold, in 1990, after Henry's death, when Fran moved to California. The second owners were Oak Parkers Errol and Lynn Kirsch, who – with their three

*Original Prange Cottage #149. Dublindoon (Cherry Hill) #144 on hill above.*

children - called the cottage Rainbow's End. They, too, had many great times at Palisades. In 1992, they sold to fellow Oak Parkers, Bob and Dianne Ebert and their children Sue, Jeff, Jennifer, and Dan. Bob, being a professional photographer, changed the name yet again. It is now called Focus Inn. The Eberts did an extensive addition to accommodate their growing family. The cottage no longer resembles the early version, but the love of Palisades remains for its owners.

### The Four Winds #16

The Four Winds was designed and built in 1933 by Frances and Harold Draper of Oak Park, Illinois. The builder was a long time Park carpenter, Arin Reed, who himself owned a cottage in the Park. The cottage has been occupied by the family every summer since it was built. The Draper children, Nanette and Jack, spent all of their summers growing up at Palisades. Nan married Ray Lewis, also of the Park. Ray and his sisters also spent childhood summers at the Park. The ownership of the cottage passed to Nan and Ray upon the death of the Drapers. They, in turn, passed ownership on to their son, Ray Jr., and his wife, Lisa Henry Lewis. Theirs is a second generation Palisades romance, Lisa's parents owning a cottage at the north end of the Park.

### Fredian Cottage #25

The Fredian cottage has, perhaps, the most unique history in Palisades Park. It was originally built in 1938 by the Crawford family on the lake front, just south of the Ark. It didn't stay there. In 1953 the lake rose and a severe storm weakened the foundation of the Crawford cottage. In 1954, it was moved, with amazing skill, over 200 feet, up to the top of the second level of dunes east of the original site. It was then repaired and rebuilt. It has remained there safely since then. In about 1955, Joe and Margaret Stark purchased the cottage. After Margaret died, Joe sold it to Alan and Dorothy Fredian in 1975. The Fredians made a number of improvements to accommodate their growing family. Three generations of the Fredian family have enjoyed it since then. Long may it stand!

### G'Sell #157

*First Jones-Mathews cottage. 1912-1915. This cottage burned and was replaced by G'Sell cottage #157.*

### Gatehouse #63

The Gatehouse is now owned by the McNamara family - Bob and Suzy McNamara, Brent and Maureen McNamara Stratton, and Steve and Mary Rita McNamara Skeine. It was once owned by the Warren Knapps. Mr. Knapp was an early Park manager and owner of the gas station at the entrance to the Park. Later, it was owned by Fred Nichols who had the Palisades Party Store out on the Blue Star. McNamaras bought from the Tillsons who had added on for Aunt Vashti Blaney. Recently the McNamaras added a porch and made the garage into living quarters.

In Betty Householder's interview, elsewhere in this volume, the house is described as first built by the Monroes who also built the Householder cottage in 1910. Betty suggested that the Monroes' chauffeur lived in the cottage in those early years. Also, in the Pauline Sauer memoirs, mention is made of "Monro Lodge" as being "on the south side of the road at the entrance to Ravineway" – again suggesting the Gatehouse was then called "Monro Lodge."

### Goff Cottage #8

The Goff cottage, which is located north of the Brandywine on lots 12 and 14, block 1, Dean's Addition to Palisades Park, was constructed in 1964 by Leonard Burrous, assisted by Fran Hofacker, both Covert, Michigan residents. The interior was finished by the owner, Harvey C. Goff, Jr. Kathryn Welles Goff and Harvey Goff had been residents of the Park for many years prior to building their own cottage, having shared the Welles cottage, The Ark, with Kay's family. The Goffs and their children and grandchildren are regular visitors to the Park.

The area known as Dean's Addition was sold to Edward P. Deacon by the United States government on May 1, 1839. It was divided and sold about 24 times until it was purchased by Merrick Dean in 1909. Over the years it was called Dean's Addition. Other property owners included Emma Hays in 1915, Marion L. Adams in 1933, and Joseph S. Mahon in 1947. Goffs purchased the property in 1963.

Kay Goff wrote: "It was interesting for us to read Emma Hays's building code for the property from 1915 to 1933: '…. (4) Nor to sell or give away, nor permit to be sold or given away, upon said premises any spirituous or fermented liquors of any kind, nor permit the public drinking of any such liquors upon said premises.' My, how times have changed!"

### Grandpa's Beach #174

Mr. and Mrs. Lobenstein built LeHigh in 1925. When Mr. Lobenstein died, his wife Margaret married Tom Abbott. Lehigh was sold to Katy and Armin Beck in 1976 when the lake was almost lapping at the cottage door. It was then improved by their son, Joel Beck, and sold to Suzanne and Jack Ryan. The Ryans closed in the porch, added a second level and changed the name to Grandpa's Beach.

## Graystone #89

Graystone was one of the early cottages constructed by Robert Ballou and his family. In a note (8/20/03) to Katy Beck, Mary Ann Forsee wrote of its recent history as follows:

> My grandmother, Eleanor O'Connor bought Greystone cottage on the Circle in 1951. She had eight children. For the three years prior, she had rented the Tillson's cottage. Grandmother's oldest child was Eileen Dinnin; now Graystone is owned by the families of three of Eileen's children – the Huffines, the Dinnins, and the Forsees.
>
> My childhood memories include the Soda Bar where we met and gathered, the fun beach parties we had, the Clubhouse and tennis courts – and all the wonderful people I have had the pleasure of meeting. A good memory involves you, Katy. Our family was renting the Tillson cottage and you came knocking at the door and invited my sister Eleanor to a beach party. I think that is why my grandmother bought Graystone. She saw what a friendly place the Park was.

## Happy Days #26

One October day in 1975, after a long walk from the south end of the Park with their friends, Bill and Glenda Hoff found a large, weathered tree stump on the North Beach which provided seating for a good rest. After that rest, they wandered up through the woods behind them where they saw a cottage for sale. It looked good to them, on the hill overlooking a deep ravine, surrounded by large oaks, maples, and various evergreens. The many evergreens had been planted by a Palisades neighbor, Harold Vandersalm, when the cottage was new.

The Hoffs spoke with Cecil Burrous, the agent, who prepared a contract to give Christine and Richard Johnson – who had purchased the cottage new in 1963. What a job it was to lug that weathered tree stump up through the woods to their yard – where ever since it has been a special reminder of the day they found a cottage for their family, all of whom, like Bill and Glenda, love Palisades.

## Happy Hollow #104

John Speicher's grandparents, Marion and Nina Bosier of Bangor, Michigan, built a cottage in Palisades in 1927. They called it "TA-KIT-E-Z" (#106). That cottage now belongs to Tom and Mary Pat Compernolle. Mr. Bosier owned the Bangor Lumber Company and was his own contractor. Then, in 1930, the Bosiers built Happy Hollow, which John's parents, Harold and Jean Speicher, inherited. Even though present owner John now lives in California, he and Linda and their three children, Leigh, Ted, and Jill, still spend time in Palisades. In 1999, the cottage was severely damaged by a falling tree. Except for one corner, it was almost entirely rebuilt by Cecil Burrous.

## Hartman Cottage #111

Kenneth and Edith Hartman had a cottage built on Lot 111, Fernwood Drive, in 1951. That year much of the beach and the pump house were washed away from the heavy storms. Kenneth Hartman died in 1979. Edith will someday leave the cottage to her two daughters, Jane Hartman and Sue Hartman Ward.

## Heart's Haven/Sandpiper #170

The cottage currently owned by Mr. and Mrs. Brad Piper (Sandpiper) was previously known as "Heart's Haven." Built in 1909, the cottage was purchased by George Nelson in 1911. George and his family resided in Chicago when not in residence at the Park. George's wife, Matilda Gunderson Nelson, had a wish to have an organ at the cottage. George secretly purchased one from a church in South Haven as a gift for his wife. A team of horses and wagon pulled the organ down the beach from

*The organ pulled to Heart's Haven by horse and wagon. Marge Nelson Gibbs, George Nelson, and Olga Nelson.*

Sturtevant Lodge to the stairs of the cottage. (At that time, there were no roads into the cottage. Everything came from the Lodge area by canoe or along the beach.) Mr. Nelson played for his wife, "When You Come to the End of a Perfect Day" to announce the arrival of the organ. The organ remained at the cottage with the Nelson family until 1969, when it was shipped to the home of the then owner of the cottage, Marilyn Gibbs, of Maderia Beach, FL. Marilyn was the grandaughter of George Nelson, the original owner of the cottage. The organ today remains in the Nelson family with Great Grandson Michael L. Nelson of Orlando, Florida. The picture shows the organ in about 1914, with elder the Nelson's children, George M. Nelson, Marge Nelson Gibbs, and Mrs. George M. (Olga) Nelson.

*Sandpiper today.*

Marilyn Gibbs was the third generation of her family to own Heart's Haven. Her grandparents, the George Nelsons, were in Palisades when Mr. Quick started the Park, the Sturtevants started building the Lodge, and Mr. Henderson was the manager. The family had the cottage over 50 years and sold to the Brad Pipers.

At one time, Danny Kaye visited the Park as a child. During his visit he met Ralph E. Nelson and the two of them organized a vaudeville act. Danny provided the entertainment while Ralph took care of the advertising and financing. The admission fee was $.10.

*Early picture of Heart's Haven #170, on hill. Abbott Cottage #174 (now Ryan) below.*

### Henry Cottage #13

Built for Chuck and Diane Henry, the cottage is on a lot that was annexed to Palisades through the Vandersalm property.

### Hermitage #120

From July 24, 1976 Patter
In "Strollin' Thru the Park" by Esmah Orcutt

"Who made all the wood tea houses and garages in Palisades?

"Answer: David MacEllen Henderson. He lived in the cottage called Hermitage, which had Henderson ownership from 1910 to 1976. His descendants in the cottage (in 1976) were Mr. and Mrs. Albert Dean Henderson, Jr., and their four sons; Miss Esmah Orcutt and father Guy H. Orcutt. Esmah has two brothers, Guy Henderson Orcutt and David Allen Orcutt (11), British Columbia.

"The Hermitage, located on Route 1 at the top of the hill leading toward the south shore cottages, is one of the older cottages in the Park. I do not know the date, but I recall my mother saying some of the boards used in the original cottage were floated to Palisades from boards brought from the first Chicago World's Fair. Remember, those boards probably originated in Michigan, as the last push of the lumbering days sent Michigan lumber to Chicago for the Fair. The Hermitage was purchased by Mr. and Mrs. David MacEllen Henderson, with the down payment being made by their daughter, Alice Henderson, with money given to her as a wedding gift at the time of her marriage to Guy H. Orcutt in June of 1910. The Henderson family - Alice Orcutt, Bell Summers, Bert, Norman, and David Henderson and their families - have spent many wonderful summers at Palisades.

"Grandpa Henderson would come early in the spring and stay late in the fall and for several years he served as Park Manager. Using the trunks and branches from the many lovely slender sassafras trees in the Park, Mr. Henderson built the wood houses, garages, and fences, many of which can still be seen today on a walk through the Park. One of the best preserved examples is "Heritage, Jr.", a little house used by Mr. Henderson to escape the noise of the many grandchildren who descended upon Grandma and Grandpa each summer. It was refloored and screened (in 1974) by his grandson Bert Henderson and (was) used by "Dad" Henderson's four great-grandsons.

"Upon the death of their parents, Alice Orcutt and Bert Henderson became co-owners. The cottage (was then) owned by Mr. and Mrs. Albert Dean Henderson, Jr., of Glenview, Illinois, and Miss Esmah Alice Orcutt of Lumberport, West Virginia, and her father, Guy H. Orcutt of Wyandotte, Michigan." In 1990 the cottage was sold to Mike and Mary Shortridge.

## Hi-Lo

*Early picture of Hi-Lo #108, now called Bozeman and owned by Wally and Mary Lou Trezise.*

## Hi-Up #78 (now Highlands)

In August 13, 1966 Patter: "George Graham Wilson, the grandfather of Kathryn Larsen Harriman, bought Hi-Up cottage (now named the Highlands) and was one of the founders of the Old Palisades Golf Association. His son-in-law, E. E. Larsen, designed and engineered the bridge and dam over the Brandywine." The cottage was sold in 1999 to the Hoskins family; they remodelled it extensively and renamed it "Highlands."

## Hi Brazil #159

According to present owner, Nanette Draper Lewis, "Hi Brazil"is a metaphor for Shangra La – a place of dreams, which the cottage has been for all these years, for those who have graced its presence. Built by a Chicago architect, it has had a succession of owners, including Lambert Ochsenschlauger, Cecil Burrous with Ron DeGraw in 1975, and Jeanette and Arch King, in 1977.

Situated on the south beach, perched up on a dune, the original bright red color served as a beacon for pilots of small planes flying overhead. Purchased and remodeled in 1994 by Nan and Ray Lewis (former owners of Four Winds #165), Hi Brazil took on a new look, still keeping the original charm.

Nan ends: "Hi Brazil is, indeed, a Shangra La – as is our Palisades Park."

## HiView #66

Bob and Maria Stracke bought HiView from Zeta Mahoney and Kay Berta, the Mahoney sisters, in 1988. The Mahoneys told the Strackes that someone else had built the cottage and their parents had purchased it – probably in the early 20's. The Mahoneys did at least two additions, the most recent being in 1937. Part of the first addition was a second floor room called the "Lookout," – so named because of its good view of the lake. The last addition was an enlargement to the living room plus the additions of another bedroom. Zita was proud to relate that in the early years, neighbors would gather at the top of the stairs, between HiView and the Ferrys' cottage, to view the sunset. The Strackes have tried to enhance the arts and crafts quality of the cottage and maintain the early 20$^{th}$ Century look. They have had several trees topped so that the lake can again be seen from their "Lookout."

## Holiday House #99

Built by George and Myrtle Boyles in about 1948, this cottage is on land originally reserved for a hotel. When Arthur Quick died, in 1946, his daughter, Julie Hill, abandoned ideas for another hotel and sold the three lots so reserved. This ridge had also been the site of the original "tent city" used by Quick and others in 1906, before any cottages had been built. George and Myrtle sold to George and Jo Owen. Jo still owns the cottage which is enjoyed by her children and grandchildren.

## Homeport #58

Stan and Veon Severinghaus were living in the Park manager's house when Stan decided to build his own cottage. He purchased the property next to the manager's office and started to make plans on what kind of cottage to build. After working for the Park all day and on his days off, Stan would go over to his new place and build. Needless to say, it took several years for him to complete his own cottage. He finished some time in the late 1970's and after retiring as manager, Stan and Veon lived there. In the summer of 1991, the Oberlin family was looking for a cottage to buy. They decided that the house that Stan built was perfect for them. In the middle of July, they took possession of their cottage and have come up in both winter and summer to enjoy the Park and all it has to offer.

## Honey Do #84

Present owners, Bob and Mary Lynne Hladik, report that their cottage was built by someone by the name of Ross in the early 60's, at about the same time the Bradfords' Cedar Nook #103 was built. Cecil Burrous's father built the cottage, with the assistance of Cecil. The plans for a "California cabin" were from Popular Mechanic Magazine. It was built of California redwood. In 1976, it was sold to Ted and Janice Williams who, in turn, sold to the Hladiks in 1988.

### Hong Kong Hilton #95

Built by Art and Barbara Warner in 1966, this cottage stands on the lot from which a previous cottage was washed away, in 1929. The Warners used a variety of materials – steel beams, concrete, and riprap – to protect their new cottage from sharing the fate of its predecessor.

### Ichiban Ryokan #192

Jim and Jane Donovan built this cottage in the 90's. It was moved into the Park on trucks, in several pieces. Within days, the two story house looked like it had always stood on that spot. The most difficult part of the project may have been moving such big trucks across the bridge – which had to be temporarily widened – and along the narrow, sandy roads. However, success was theirs.

### Inn Decision #140

(by Karen Heavrin) "In 1967, my parents, Lucius and Thelma Weston, purchased this cottage from Bethany Mission, a retirement home in Wisconsin, that had been deeded the cottage from the Kluender family. Before this purchase, the cottage had been vacant many years.

"Rudy Weber, who built many of the cottages in Palisades, told us this was one of the first cottages he built, probably in the late 20's or early 30's. The physical construction must have been an amazing feat for the time and equipment available since the cottage is built on a 60 degree angle high up the bluff overlooking the lake. Cement pillars were placed in strategic places and wooden stilts placed on top, which support the weight of the main building. Since 1967, Cecil Burrous and/or his father have raised the cottage twice, each time over 14 inches. Natural erosion caused some of this problem but the majority of the slippage was created by commercial and heavy-duty equipment vehicles using the roads, something never envisioned by the founders of the Park.

"The original floor plan shows three bedrooms up and one downstairs, a four by eight foot bath with basin and toilet (no need for shower or tub since bathing was done in the lake), and a combination dining room/living room exiting through French doors to an enclosed porch on the lakeside. The kitchen with its manual water pump was at the back of the house, attached to a screened-in eating porch. This room must have been a great retreat from the blazing late afternoon sun until the trees matured enough to shade the cottage. My mother immediately set about renovating to make her dream cottage. Cecil did the work. The kitchen was moved to where the front bedroom had been. A large pass way was cut into the wall and made into a snack bar so she could see the sunset while doing dreary kitchen work. The back room became the Indian bedroom. Mr. Kluender, a minister, had collected Indian artifacts on his trips; many of these items are displayed in this room. A small undersize bathtub was added upstairs and a new shower stall and toilet downstairs. An outside staircase was added to the front of the cottage, going to the new kitchen. My father and I lugged hundreds of cinder blocks up the hill to build a 30 x 20 foot patio. In the 80's, when the cottage was raised a second time, a fifth bedroom was added downstairs to help support the structure from slipping.

"In the late 80's and early 90's, Jim Tipton, the son-in-law of Stan Severinghas, insulated the dining room/living room, kitchen, and porch. He also replaced old cupboards and installed new sliding glass windows and door. A wooden deck was built across the front porch to the large pine tree on the bluff. This beautiful tree that shaded the house was lost in our fire of September, 1999. Tipton also enlarged the downstairs bath.

"Dave Hope became our contractor in the mid-90's. He completed insulation of the bedrooms and designed built-in closets, drawers, and platform beds for each room. The bathroom upstairs was extended outwards and remodeled, adding shower and jacuzzi. The screened-in porch became the laundry room. The only other renovation is the rebuilding of the wooden deck which was burned in the 1999 fire. It was never determined what caused the fire – perhaps a spark from a beach fire or tossed cigarette."

### Innisfree (formerly Gopher) #46

Cottage #46 is currently owned by John and Joan Mailander, of Mount Prospect, Illinois. John is a member of the King family from Kings Mills, Ohio. Two of his great aunts were among the original members of Palisades Park. The cottage was built sometime in the late 1950's by Mary King Shephardson. Ms. Shepardson was the niece of Isadora King Donahue and Estelle King Van Bueren. She built her cottage on land given to her by her aunts. Mary named the cottage "Gopher" in honor of the University of Minnesota. Her father was a lifelong professor at the university.

Ms. Shepardson owned the cottage for a number of years, commuting every summer from Minneapolis. When she passed away in 1970, her cottage was passed to Joseph Warren King. By this time, he had also acquired Buckeye King (#77), so for many years, his family shuttled between Gopher and Buckeye King. Grandson John Mailander, the current owner, remembers most of his high school and college years were spent at Gopher. Some of his favorite memories are of spending time there in September, while waiting to go back to Miami University.

In 1994, Joseph King passed away and the cottage went to his son and namesake whose family enjoyed the cottage for a number of years. In 1998, ownership of Anchorfast (#43) passed from Virginia Van Beuren to Joe King; at that time, he sold Gopher to John, Joan, Peter and Joe Mailander. The Mailander children are the 5th generation of Kings to enjoy Palisades Park. John's mother, Joanne King, currently owns Buckeye King.

The Mailanders recently changed the name of the cottage from Gopher to Innisfree. In one of their family's favorite movies, "The Quiet Man," Innisfree is the name of the small town in Ireland where John Wayne settles down after moving to Ireland. It is also the name of a poem by William Butler Yeats.

## La Casita #106

Originally named Tak-It-E-Z, La Casita was built about 1925 by Marion (Bo) Bozier, who at the time was the Mayor and Fire Chief of Bangor, MI. Mr. Bozier also owned the Bangor Lumber Company. About the same time he built Tak-It-E-Z, he built another cottage across the road to the southwest, called Happy Hollow. Bo and his wife Nina had three daughters, Jean Speicher (John Speicher's mother), Marjorie Zook, and Ruth (Earl) Snyder.

Circa 1927, Mr. Bozier sold Tak-It-E-Z to Mildred Adams. Mildred loved traveling to Mexico and renamed her little cottage La Casita. Mrs. Adams spent summers there until the 1960's. In the early '60's, she sold La Casita to Bob and Gwen Ott (children Bobby and Pam). Bob taught tennis and worked on the tennis courts for years. Gwen was the Park's treasurer in the 1980's. Bob died about 1979 and as Gwen tried to keep up with the maintenance of La Casita, it got to be too much for her. She sold the cottage to the Tom Compernolle family in October, 1993. Gwen died in the spring of 1996 at the age of 76.

Tom, Mary Pat, Tim, and Carolyn Compernolle have made some changes to the cottage through the years, but have tried to keep the memories of La Casita's previous owners alive for generations to come.

## Lakehaus #190

Three friends – Trudy Vujtech, Alice Grist, and Beatrice Carr – bought Lakehaus in 1992 from Mr. Malablocki, who had built it in 1990. The cottage has an interesting and controversial beginning. The land on which it is built, at the northern edge of Brandywine beach, was reclaimed from the lake when Mr. Malablocki put deep steel walls around it. For several years it filled in with sand and, gradually, vegetation. Finally, in 1990, Mr. Malablocki decided to build. Apparently he did not go through the Park for approval – as required in the covenants on the land – and the argument he and the Park had ended in court. Soon thereafter, he sold to the present owners. However, at this writing, the cottage is for sale once again.

## Lehmann's Haven #127
By Audrey Lehmann, October, 1979

"Our family's acquaintance with PPCC came about through the family of Richard Pollack, who had purchased their cottage a few years prior and graciously invited us to visit. Needless to say, Palisades was such a pleasure that we had to spend more time there and decided to buy lots near the Pollacks, in the woods. Betty Pollack and I, Audrey Lehmann, have known each other since the age of 10.

"We planned to build the cottage ourselves, but since it was to be on top of a hill and we had no conception of how to begin building on stilts, Rudy Weber and his buddy George Packard built the shell for us in 1963. Rudy was 72 years old at the time. His will reigned when he insisted the deck be creosoted, leading to painful hands. Also, the 3/4 inch plywood purchased for the floor was put on the roof, leaving 1/2 inch plywood for our forever flexing floor. He was concerned with snow load. And he was right – the roof has never caved in. The tile on the kitchen floor has cracked to pieces, however!

"The children elected to name the cottage 'Out-House' since we were always out (and perhaps for a private joke of theirs); however, the cottage has remained 'nameless" with only our surname posted for some years now. That's what maturity will do for you.

"The family tried to complete the cottage while living in it over the summer. All hands were needed and used for nailing down the floor, putting up plasterboard, taping and painting. I am sure this is part of the reason for our great love for the place. The project took us two years. At the very beginning, our bathroom was a framed-in closet shielded by a green plastic sheet, the kitchen sink a dishpan on a piece of plywood, and beds all mattresses on the floor. Our city-bred kids soon learned to whisk away the daddy-long-legs with nary a thought as they crawled over their sleepy bodies. The children finished their own dressers, one of which has the names and dates of all visitors painted on the bright blue finish." At some point, the name Lehmann's Haven was posted on a cottage sign.

## Little Brown Jug #153

In the fall of 1968, the Oscar Kleb family of Aurora, Illinois bought Little Brown Jug. Marilyn had first visited the Park some 37 years earlier, with her friend Vi Hautau (Mrs. Murray Dawson), a longtime Park member. In 1968 there was a small beach but in '69 the old wooden seawall, built in the early 50's, was exposed. Canonie Construction installed a metal seawall of 20 foot sheeting. In 1976, this metal wall was buttressed by Clutchey Marine and sand fill added. Next a wood retaining wall to hold the sand bank was added by Lenny Burrous. In 1985 a freak difference in atmospheric pressure from the Wisconsin side to the Michigan side of the lake caused the lake level to reach the top of the steel seawall; the resulting high waves washed out about 20 feet of the bank in front of the cottage, Finally, in 1986, A.D.D.Construction installed large pieces of stone riprap in front of the '69 steel wall. Also that year more sand was added to the front of the cottage and Cecil Burrous replaced the damaged breast wall. Since then the lake level has gradually decreased and the beach enlarged.

Prior to the Kleb purchase, the cottage was owned by Betty Hard (Mrs. Wm. H.) of Elgin, Illinois, who had inherited it in 1957 (at a value of $4750) from her mother, Mrs. Roy Harlow. The Harlows had purchased it in 1946. The 12 foot road easement behind the cottage was built in 1953. Previous to the Harlows, the cottage was purchased in 1929 by Mrs. Mary B. Ward of Riverside, Illinois. Upon her death, the cottage was inherited (at a value of $3750) by her husband, William H. Ward, her daughter, Mrs. Wilson Blaney, and her granddaughter, Mary Lee Cady Tillson. Mrs. Ward had purchased the cottage from John Stockwell, a bachelor of Philadelphia. He, in turn, had purchased it from Arthur and Kitty Quick in March, 1912, for "$1 and other valuable considerations." At that time, the Park yearly membership fee was $1. In 1909, the covenants on the land did not allow stores, hotels, businesses, barns, "public use or sale of fermented spirits," ferries, or boats for hire. The covenant also stated that the dwelling must cost more than $300. In 1960 this covenant was changed to $2500.

Over the years the Klebs have added a new kitchen, laid concrete block for back and front patios, cleared sand out of the basement for head room, installed a basement bathroom, and windowed the screen porch. The big project was in 1992-3 when they added a second floor with three bedrooms and two baths, electric baseboard heat, a deck, and new windows and bath on the first floor. Cecil Burrous did that work.

Through the years the Kleb family has enjoyed sunsets, swimming, Sunfish sailing, windsurfing, canoeing, hiking, water skiing and tubing. They enjoy the visits of family and friends at this very special place.

## The Lowrey Cottage #39

Now owned by John and Tracy Vercillo, this cottage started its life on the other side of the Brandywine. After the storm of 1929, it was moved to its present site and rebuilt. Forest Lowrey owned the cottage for many years.

*Lowrey cottage c. 1937.*

## Marjomore # 164

Marjomore was built by and has remained in the hands of the Heisel family. Mary Lou Heisel Hession and her sister-in-law, Janine Heisel, are co-owners. Mary Lou tells of her parents' first visit to Palisades:

"In July of 1929, Margaret and Elmore Heisel and their children, Mary Lou and John, planned to take a trip around Lake Michigan. A friend suggested they stop at Palisades Park on their way, for it was such a beautiful resort. We did – and stayed at the Lodge for our vacation. Before we left Palisades for home (Peoria, Illinois), my parents purchased a lot overlooking the lake on a bluff at the south end of the Park. They chose this lot so we would have a beautiful view of the lake and access to the beach, with the woods to our back. Our only neighbor was the Harper cottage, which had been built the year before. Cement steps coming up from the road to the bluff and wooden steps going down to the beach were already there."

The name was chosen as a combination of Mary Lou, John (her brother), and Elmore.

## Master's Lodge #53

This cottage has had an interesting history. The earliest map of Palisades shows that one of the first cottages in the Park was built on this lot by Dr. Sally Josephine McCollum, an M.D. and Miss Mary Vincent, a nurse. Anne Holmes, in Palisades Park Review 1905-1968, suggests it was "built or brought in from the lumber camp." (9) Several oldtimers referred to it as "temporary" – but we do not know if that meant the cottage was something along the lines of a tent or was only there a few years, hence temporary. At any rate, about the time Dr. McCollum built, possibly 1907, Sturtevant Lodge built its first building next door. Before 1912, the McCollum cottage was removed and the Lodge added its second building. Mrs. Holmes added, "They say you can still find the old foundation under the Lodge." The Sturtevants ran the Lodge many years, as did their nephew, Del Jones. Eventually it was sold to Ralph and Virginia Wenham who also ran it as a Lodge. When the Wenhams sold to the David Livingstons, the cost of updating the facility was prohibitive so it became a private cottage. Subsequently it was sold to Lynne Master who still owns it.

## Meadow Chalet #36

In the 1950's and 60's, Forest Lowrey and Dick Cordell spent many hours organizing the sand around Lowrey's cottage (#39) and the Roche's Beach House next door (#42). (Dick's wife Katie is the sister of Marge Roche whose in-law's owned the Beach House.) Mr. Lowrey always talked about how he would like to clean up the swamp which used to be Lake Palisades. By 1964, he had acquired the land surrounding the area and was ready to roll. He hired Tony Canonie and Rudy Weber to remake the swamp into the beautiful meadow we have today. During the process, Dick Cordell was on hand with his shovel to help.

The Cordells were fortunate to be able to purchase the west point on Edgewood Road. In the winter of 1966, Leonard Burrous, Cecil's dad, laid the cement block for a cottage designed by Dick and Katie. The building was brought up on a truck from the Libertyville Lumber Company and was erected over the 4th of July weekend. Back in the "good ole days," one could pound nails all summer, so in August of 1966, Dick, Katie, John, David, Margaret, and their dog, Heidi, moved into their not-quite-finished chalet. Many of their Palisades Park friends and neighbors gave them lots of help in completing it.

The years 1966 to 2002 represent wonderful times for all the Cordells and Jamisons - winter and summer! The family of five is now fifteen: Dick and Katie; John and Cyndy and their three - Jonathan, Chris, Allie; David and Sue and daughter Jackie; and Mike and Margaret Jamison and their children Phil, Riley, and Avery.

## Meadowview #30

The Dannenbergs were first introduced to Palisades Park through Wendall and Grace Fidler. They rented their cottage for a week one summer and fell in love with Palisades. They soon began looking at cottages or lots to buy and, in 1965, chose two lots high on a hill overlooking Brandywine Creek, on what is now Edgewater Road. The plotted road to the lots was undeveloped at the time, but by the following summer a road had been opened which looped around and back to the Brandywine bridge. In the summer of 1967, they had their cottage built by Casey DeMink of Kalamazoo, in that lovely, sparsely settled area. The whole family pitched in to stain and paint and do the finishing. That was the year of the alewife fish die off. The stench was so potent that the builders could hardly stand it and thought the Dannenbergs were real optimists.

The most unique thing about the cottage is the sunken seating around the Franklin Stove. The cottage continues to be enjoyed by Dannenberg children and grandchildren, nestled in the woods, close to the birds and wildlife.

*Dannenbergs' cottage # 30, Meadowview.*

## Menconis' Trails End #28 and Log Cabin #31

The Menconis' first cottage, Log Cabin, was built in 1969 by the Michigan Shore Lumber Company of South Haven. The family came up on the 4th of July weekend, with all their furnishings in a U-Haul trailer. That spring had been very rainy, causing a delay in construction and a huge crop of mosquitoes. Although the cottage looked complete from the outside, there was a hole in the wall where a fireplace was to be, and there was no plumbing or electricity. The two young children and Nancy stayed in the cottage, with the dog, until it was completed.

In the mid-80's, Nancy and Bill bought Trails End. Nancy says that it had the amenities they didn't have in Log Cabin – a porch, washer/dryer, second bath, well, and heat – but she couldn't bear to sell the Log Cabin. So she and Bill settled for "his and hers" cottages. As their family grew, they have been glad to have more space. Also, they have since remodeled Log Cabin, adding two porches and an outside shower.

## Natty Bumpo #35

Owned by Mike, Nancy, Thomas, John, L.C. and Anneliese Sitterly, cottage #35 was built in approximately 1959 by George Hammerschmidt, Sr. Its second owner was Chuck Hammerschmidt. The Sitterlys purchased it in January, 1993. There are several myths about its concrete block and cement construction. One is that the wife of George did not like mice and thought they could be kept out of this new cottage. Her son remembered that she was afraid of fires, again to be prevented by the cement. (That version is supported in the interview of Cecil Burrous, to be found elsewhere in this volume.) Perhaps it was simpler – the Hammerschmidts were and still are in the concrete business. At any rate, they had owned a cottage on the other side of the Brandywine (# 40) previous to building their new "bomb shelter." Apparently there was a fire in the first cottage; it was subsequently sold to the Lowreys. For many years the Hammerschmidt cottage, which looked a bit like a motel, sat unused, until it was purchased by the Sitterlys. They remodelled it completely, softening the stark appearance – and also the excuse for all the nicknames. Now it is called Natty Bumpo, after a primitive character in James Fenimore Cooper's Leatherstocking series.

*Early picture of living room and porch in the Nelson cottage.*

## Nelson Cottage #76

In 1907, the Nelson cottage was the second cottage built in the Park, by two brothers, Seymour and Alvin E. Nelson. Seymour and Alvin had been very involved with Mr. Quick in helping to get Palisades Park started; donating money to pay for the bridge, they were repaid with lots on which they built their cottage. Alvin E. Nelson is the present owner's grandfather. The cottage was held in their wives' names and never legally passed down until 1948. At that time, the children of Alvin E. decided to skip a generation and pass it on to the 2nd generation heirs. Finally, present owners, Alvin and Betty Nelson, cleared all the hurdles from the 22 plus family members involved and assumed ownership in 1978. A guest house was added later for the many relatives who visited Palisades.

One family story, from 1910, is of Aunt Dot who – as a seven or eight year old – contracted a serious disease while she was at the Park.

*Nelson family gathering by their cottage.*

The family curtained off a corner of the living room for her sickroom – and to keep her more or less quarantined. Her little sister, Bea, having listened to the adults discussing the "awful disease" Dot had contracted, went upstairs, opened the curtains, and said to Dot, "You're going to die." Dot replied, "I am not!" Grandma Nelson, seeing her determination, bribed her to eat and be a good patient by offering her Palisades Park memorial plates as rewards. Three of these plates are on the wall of the Nelson cottage and are reproduced elsewhere in this volume.

## Neverall Inn #72

We are not sure what year this cottage was constructed, but we do know that it was already built when the sale, dated January 24, 1924, was approved and the property conveyed from Arthur C. Quick to Nellie Harper Marr and her husband, Don A. Marr. After their deaths in 1928 and 1931 respectively, the cottage was left to their sole survivor and daughter, Daisy. At that time, the cottage faced the lake and the Clubhouse was still on the beach, so they had a beautiful view. Supposedly there was to be no building on those lots in front of the cottage because that area had been designated as a park by Arthur Quick. However, Mr. Quick had a surprise for Daisy. Sometime in the 1930's, the Clubhouse was moved up to its present location when the lake threatened its safety on the beach.

Daisy (b. October 16, 1883) married William John Schlacks on June 4, 1904. They had three children – Virginia, William John, Jr., and Henry Proctor. William Sr. died in 1933 but Daisy and her children came to the Park each summer during most of the 1930's. Daisy's cousin Howard Schlacks (father of Paul Schlacks, the present owner) and his wife Clare brought their family to visit in Palisades during the summer of 1939. Howard liked the surroundings so much that he arranged to rent the cottage for the following summer – 1940. He later bought the cottage from Daisy.

At that time, the Howard Schlacks family consisted of six children: Dan, Dona, Rowena, Paul, Bob, and Bill. After the death of both parents, the cottage seemed too small for the six children, their spouses, and their growing families, so Bob and Bill each purchased his own cottage. Nancy and Paul are the present caretakers at Neveral Inn. Their five children all come to Palisades regularly, bringing the grandchildren to enjoy all that Palisades has to offer. Of course, the most special thing about Palisades is the people. Several Park families are fourth or fifth generation and anyone who passes through the gate is cast with a magical spell to forever want to return. Paul ends this mini-history with a question to ponder: What changes have you witnessed (both good and bad) here at Palisades and what do you think is important to perpetuate for future generations? As he says, "Let's talk about it." The editors hope that this volume – in some small way – does just that.

## Osthaven #75

In doing research, we have found the short history of a very old cottage. Osthaven was renamed in 1984 when Myron and Billie Osth purchased Trails End from Sue Sweet. The DeButts family was the original owner of Trails End, built in the early days of the Park. It first consisted of a porch, living and dining room, two bedrooms, and a small kitchen. There was also an attached garage. Laurene (Bool) and Cary DeButts were from Oak Park. They had two children, Bill and Sue. After marriage to Mr. Sweet, she spent most of her life at Palisades. When she began living in Trails End year round, she made many changes to the original cottage, adding a bedroom suite on the first floor and an entire upstairs with full bath for her son, Bradley. After Brad got married, Sue decided to sell.

Myron and Billie bought the cottage after renting in the Park. They enjoyed the cottage for one summer before Myron succumbed to a stroke. He was able to make a few trips up to Palisades before he passed away in 1995. Carol, Mary, and John, with their spouses and children, spent many weeks at the cottage during the early years of ownership.

Dick and Mary Kilburn have made some changes to Osthaven. High winds and flooding have determined some necessary remodeling. The November winds in 1999 were so fierce that they blew a tree down which snapped off the chimney. After having the chimney repaired, the Kilburns added a larger deck. Osthaven evolves to keep up with the ever-changing events in the lives of its owners. But the joy of arriving and the sadness of leaving never changes. Fond memories of the people in our lives are always present in the cottage.

## Theotherworlde #136

As written by Jeanne DeLamarter Bonnette:

> Theotherworlde, formerly 'Hillcrest,' was the cottage built in 1928 by Dr. Eric DeLamarter, my father. It stands on lots ten through eighteen in the Hillcrest subdivision of Palisades Park. Harry Wildt of Covert did the actual construction, and, when he had the frame up in two-by-fours, I stood in the center of the cottage and did not dream that one day it would belong to me.
>
> After the death of Alice Main DeLamarter, my father's second wife, he married Pegeen Healy, a capable Irish

lady of charm. Then he found that the cottage – long since completed, lived in, and loved – held too many ghosts for him. One summer day when I was grown, Father came to me. "Dutch (his name for me), have you a dollar bill?" Puzzled, I replied that I did and gave it to him, whereupon he handed me the deed and keys to Hillcrest. I was astonished and thrilled to find that this lovely "second home" was now my own. I also felt that it must be renamed to fit me, my lifestyle, and the life-styles of my young. I recalled that an English Poet Laureate had used the name 'Theotherworlde' for his ivory tower, and it was the perfect name for my retreat.

I was to live in that cottage from the end of May until the fall of each year for the next twenty years, during which time three marriages changed my names, but Theotherworlde remained, containing my roots as well as those of my daughters and my part-time stepchildren.

I commissioned Mr. Wildt to put skylights into the roof over the living room and kitchen, and, that first summer, they saved me the magnificent sum of $20 (a fortune then!) in electric bills. Over the years, the bedroom off the kitchen, former quarters for Arthur and Bessie, my father's servants, was enlarged to house four girls: Judy and Haven Best, and Lori and Carol Anderson. The downstairs room under the south porch, which had been my father's composing sanctuary, now became Steve Anderson's hide-out. Mr. Wildt also enclosed the back porch and made it into a large glassed-in dining room with sliding windows, a long table, and built-in benches on three sides. I appreciated this change for I never knew how many people might be there for a meal. Since the cottage site was atop a hill, it was as though we were dining in a treehouse. When my husband, Arthur Bonnette, and I moved to New Mexico, we thought it best to sell Theotherworlde.

In 1959, Jeanne sold the cottage to Clay and Ruth Johnson who enjoyed it for 20 years. Then, in 1979, to complete the circle, Carol (Anderson) and Don Beveridge bought this same cottage where Carol grew up, from her infancy into her teens.

### Owl's Nest #47

Owned by William and Betty Haude, Owl's Nest, built in 1907, is the third cottage on the beach north of the Lodge. Betty said her folks, Laura and Henry Roefer, were introduced to Palisades by George and Ella Hammersmith. They rented cottages for years. In 1931, after the big storm, they bought their cottage and moved it back 100 yards. It was pulled back by horses and put up on props. The cottages on either side were owned by Ernest Wunsch. The Wunsches lived in the cottage to the south of Owl's Nest and rented what is now the Old Pier cottage owned by Ginny Melchert Coleman. All three cottages were moved back to escape the high water.

*Sketch by Martha Conlin Haude, drawn on train trip en route to Palisades with one of the grandchildren.*

The names on the title deed include Mr. Quick, the original owner of the land; Marian E. Cota, who bought the land (with other lands) January 31, 1910; Olive Marian Cota, November 21, 1924; Bernice Cota Timmons and Olive Cota McClain, August 22, 1927; Henry A. Roefer, May 26, 1931; and Mr. Roefer's daughter (Betty Roefer Haude's mother) in 1937. After Betty Haude's mother died in 1950, Betty and her brother Martin H. Roefer became joint owners. Betty bought out Martin in 1956. Charlie Tunecke held a $600 mortgage on the house when Betty's mother bought it.

### Palisades Park Soda Bar #54

For most of its existence, the Soda Bar has been just that – a place to buy ice cream, a hangout for the teens, a safe destination for little kids who walk down the beach clutching their coins for buying candy. At least once the Park Post Office was in this building, also. At one time, a large garage was behind the Soda Bar; it collapsed during the 70's and the Village Green came into existence where the garage had stood – ushering in an era of Park gatherings at this central spot. Briefly, just before the collapse of the garage, a family tried to turn the Soda Bar into a cottage. Ice cream was sold in the garage, at Sturtevant Lodge, or at Fred Nichol's store on the Blue Star. However, the Park quickly realized the importance of this meeting place and purchased the building, remodeling it once again into our present Soda Bar.

The Soda Bar was built and run by Arthur Quick's family, especially his daughter, Julia Quick Hill. A list of other early proprietors is found in Chapter 6.

### Piccadilly Circus #41

The Gardner cottage has been in Jane's family much of its life. Her parents, the Kipps, owned it from 1938 to 1944. When Jack and Jane Gardner retired, they rebought the cottage in 1977.

*1937 picture of Gardner Kipp cottage #41.*

## Pottawatomie #154

Doris and Boots Duesing closed on the purchase of Pottawatomie on August 6, 1966. They purchased it with Doris's brother and sister-in-law, Marsh and Sue Wells, and immediately remodeled it. Lenny Burrous was the contractor and he had them in pretty good shape by the summer of 1967. The month of July of that year, the Duesings lived among the workmen, but by August (when Marsh came up), it was put together. The purchase price was $11,500! By 1983, Marsh and Sue were using it less and the Duesings wanted to use it more, so they bought out the Wellses' interest. They had a very agreeable turnover as they went along with the assessment that Cecil did for them. Now the cottage is in a residential trust and the Duesings' four daughters will take it over at a specified time. Originally the cottage was purchased from William and Aimee DeSouchet (Boulder County, CO), Helen Cann (Alameda County, CA), and Jessie Lord King (Cook County, IL). Doris and Boots assume these are the children and spouse of the original owner – Mr. DeSouchet – as he built the cottage next door after his first wife died and his new wife wanted a different place. According to the records from the County Court House in Paw Paw, the lot was purchased in 1910 and the cottage was probably built shortly after that time.

## Pour House #16

In 1893, the land was sold from Alfred S. and Clara O. Packard to Arthur C. Quick. In 1923, the South Haven Palisades Park Company deeded the property to James and Miriam Spence of Chicago and a cottage was built. When Mr. Spence died, in 1944, his wife owned the property. She sold it to Edmund Arey and his wife, Marian, in 1961. Ten years later, the Areys sold to Leon Kowalski. Leon, a prosecuting attorney from St. Joseph County, Indiana, aptly named the cottage "The Prosecution Rests." Leon, in turn, sold to his brother, Jim Kowalski, in 1972. The name changed twice - to The Poor House and then The Pour House. The Kowalskis sold to Marilyn Orr in 1995. Her son, Bret Orr, now owns the cottage.

## Reed's Cottage #148

This cottage, built in 1912, has had four transfers of ownership. On September 16, 1912, the South Haven

*Reed's Cottage #148. 1938.*

*Mrs. Bruninga, "Grandma" Lee, and Mrs. Sankey on Cottage #148 porch. 1937.*

Palisades Park Company sold the lot to John T. Manierre and Mary Foster Manierre. 25 years later, the Manierres sold to May Taylor Sankey on July 3, 1937. On August 29, 1945, the cottage got its third set of owners – Edgar M. and Katherine M. Smith. Edgar's second wife, Elaine Smith was the owner in May of 1983 when it was sold to Dillon and Mary Reed.

### Retreat #178

Ruth and Ray Kropp built their cottage in 1952. The builder was Rudy Weber. The cottage is now owned by their son and his wife, Ray, Jr. and Tori Kropp. The cottage – as with all beach front cottages – has faced a number of problems because of high water and storms. These have been solved with break walls and rip rap. It is on property that originally belonged to Linden Hills. When the Kropps bought, they arranged for its incorporation into Palisades Park. Ruth tells this story in her interview, elsewhere in this volume.

### Richard's Roost #15

Richard's Roost was built in 1933. Andy Peirce, the owner's son, Rudy Weber, and Rudy's helpers finished it that Labor Day. Originally called the Dog House by the Peirce family, it was the smaller of two cottages owned by the C. A. Peirces of LaGrange, Illinois. In the 60's, the property was divided and Rud and Ginny Peirce Richards and their family remodelled to its present condition. The larger cottage was sold by Andy Peirce to the Jim Richards family (Rud's brother), in 1979. The Peirces were alone on the dune for a long time. Now Ginny has many nice neighbors.

### Robins Nest # 87

From a Guest Book started in 1946 and found in the cottage: **The History of Dr. Pierce and Gretchen Jensen's Cottage.** Gretchen and Pierce Jensen and their three sons lived in Oskaloosa, Iowa. Mrs. Jensen's mother and father built the cottage in 1910. Her mother, Minnie Maud Comfort of Spring Lake, Michigan, married Allen Barnett Edee, of Omaha, Nebraska. Mr. Edee's family came from Alsace Lorraine. The Edees were good friends of Mr. Robert Ballou's sister, who had married Dr. Willard Smith, a dentist, and had built one of the early cottages at the Park Circle. The Smiths told the Edees about Palisades Park, so Minnie and Allen came over and rented Graystone. Mrs. Edee didn't like living in Graystone as the kitchen was on the ground floor, the dining-living room on the second, and the sleeping quarters on the third. In 1910 they hired Bob Ballou to build a cottage for them to the east of the cement stairs on lot 2 of Vinemount Block. At the same time, Mr. Ballou built a cottage for the Holmstroms (now the Mathias cottage #96) next door. Below the cottage, a Mr. Phillips, a contractor from Covert, was building Sunset cottage for the Joliet, Illinois senator, Mr. Monroe (now owned by the Householder daughters # 88), as well as Elsa Smith's cottage and Isabel Larson's cottage." The first entry in the Guest Book was by Frances Edee who said "Restmore with stairs to climb! But what a good, good time!" Also on that page was written, "Palisades Park formerly called Paulville – Ludwig's Pier where lumber was loaded. The 'Bluffs' as the dunes were called in the early days were favorite exploring grounds – strange plants on windy sands and in the dark swamps behind Brandywine Creek."

The cottage has had many names. Mrs. Edee called it Restmore, then the Jensen boys liked Lazy Livin'. By 1949 it was called Hi-Time. In the fall of 1973, it became Hill House when the cottage changed ownership, from Gretchen Jensen to Janette King. Janette had come to Palisades as a child with her parents, Mary and John Gardner, of Riverside, Illinois, her sister Elizabeth and brother Jack. Janette lived in Palo Alto, Caifornia with husband, Arch. Her sister Elizabeth was Betty Householder who owned Sunset cottage just across the stairs. At that time, Jack lived in London and visited Palisades each year. On his retirement, he and his wife, Jane, bought Piccadilly Circus #41 – the cottage her family had owned when Jane was a child. In 1980 Norm and Sandy Robins bought the cottage and the Kings moved to Hi Brazil #159 on the beach. The name was changed once again to Robins Nest.

The Guest Book tells of reunions, parties, friends and even recipes used over the decades. Guests' remarks indicate what a special spot this is – "Out of this world! It leaves me speechless. Beautiful place – grand vacation. Hurrah! Never a dull moment – love it!" and on and on. In 1951, the painting of the cottage was recorded, as well as this remark: "Lake two feet seven inches higher than last year.

Highest it has been since 1929 when it washed out three cottages. Cement block foundation of Baker cottage washed up for first time since '29 when it washed out." A real treasure trove of cottage history.

### Roche/Sharpe/Hoo #199

Brian Roche and his wife, Emily Sharpe, and four children – Clara, Jabob, Andrew, and Leah – share their new cottage with Brian's sister, Marie Roche, and her husband, John Hoo, and their children – Max, Melissa, and Charlotte. The cottage was built in 2001. Brian and Marie grew up in the Park, their grandfather having bought Beach House in 1947, and their parents North Beach in 1969.

*Sandpiper #170 on left; Sand Castle #167 above.*

*South Beach cottages.*

### Sand Castle #167

After renting the Sandbox #175 from Miss Molyneaux for ten years, Bob and Hazel Burkhardt bought a piece of property on a high dune from Mr. Hennigan who lived across the road in what is now the Mason Cottage #168. The property looked totally unbuildable. They hired an architect, J. Gale Brown, from Evanston, IL, and had him spend a weekend in the Park to look over the property and see how they could preserve most of the trees and terrain and still build a house with a lake view. Brown advised them to start the living space on the second floor, with a carport below and a third floor loft with a deck. LaMar Construction out of Holland, MI bid on the project as they were starting construction on the Hope Reformed Church in South Haven; they could keep their men busy at both jobs during the winter. They broke ground right after Labor Day, 1969. The contractor soon decided they needed to build a concrete drive and retaining wall in order to get heavy equipment and laminated wooden beams up the dune (an added expense they hadn't counted on). By May of 1970, they had a livable shell of a house.

The interior was completed over the years by their good friend, Edgar Ebner, a general contractor from LaGrange, working a couple of weeks at a time in the spring and fall. At times they felt they were always a "work in progress" – but they were still able to enjoy the beauty of the Park, the lake and the dunes.

Both of their children, Bob and Barbara, have grown up in the Park and now Bob's wife and three sons also are enjoying the Sandcastle. They hope this will continue for future generations.

### Sandpiper #170 – See "Heart's Haven"

### Sauer Cottage #64

Paul Sauer purchased Lots 1, 2, and 3 (Hazelnook Block) in 1915-1923 from Arthur C. Quick; Lot 13 (Ingleside Block) in 1936 from J. W. Stockwell; and Lot 1 (Circle Block) in 1945, in payment of a loan. The cottage was constructed, in 1924 –1925, by Eugene Phillips of Covert, for $1647.50. Designed by the owners, it is roughly square with a large front porch and a rear eating porch. For the ten summers prior to building, the Sauers rented Munro Lodge at the foot of the hill, east of the Park gate. Certificates of membership in the Park were issued to Paul Sauer, in 1931 (#100); to Minnie Sauer, in 1953; and to Margaret Sauer, daughter, who purchased the property and cottage in 1956 and is the present owner. Rev. Paul Sauer (1874 – 1952) was pastor of First St. John's Evangelical Lutheran Church in Chicago, a lecturer in the Music Department at Northwestern University, a recognized authority on the works of Johann Sebastian Bach, and founder and president of the Chicago Bach Chorus. His wife, Minnie Klein (1883 – 1966) was a graduate-music teacher and concert pianist. They had four children, one of whom still owns the cottage.

The cottage is located on a hillside above the Park entrance gate. The lots run east to west about 400 feet, 250 of them fronting Ravineway Drive. The view from the cottage is northwesterly, across the Drive and Brandywine meadow to Lake Michigan. The property is on the eastern and northern side of a moderate-sized Nipissing dune, having an elevation of about 680' (about 100' above mean lake level). The north side of this dune descends steeply toward the Brandwine Creek basin, which forms an opening in the series of Palisades Park dunes. The opening provides an avenue for winds from the northwest, which shaped the dune about 3000 years ago and which today affords air circulation and cooling effect on hot summer days. The occupants built many paths across the property, opening the beautiful vegetation to view.

Vegetation consists of climax northern hardwoods (among the southernmost found on pure sand) such as red oak, sugar maple, and beech – and including red maple, black cherry, eastern hemlock, white pine, white ash, sassafras, witchhazel, and ironwood. The common shrub is maple-leaved viburnum. Group cover include True Solomon's-seal, False Solomon's-seal, Lily-of-the-valley, aralia, goldenrod, asters, wild orchids (formerly), partridge berry, wintergreen, sedge, beechdrops, Indian pipe, ferns, mosses, and mushrooms. Botany classes from Michigan universities have come to study vegetation on this hill. An analysis of soils on and near this property (a graduate thesis research 1966 – 1972 by the present owner, for Northern Illinois University) showed that the characteristics of this soil are similar to those of Rubicon sand found on shoreline dunes in Muskegon County, 50 miles north of Palisades, and similar to those of Rubicon sand in northern Lower Michigan and in the Upper Peninsula. The soil has a black surface layer, gray subsurface layer, strong acidity, absence of carbonates, evidence of intense weathering, and organic matter content.

## Seamar #49

Presently owned by Ed and Sheila McCarthy, this cottage was badly damaged in the 1991 fire that destroyed the cottage next door. The McCarthys had to do extensive rebuilding.

*Carmen Sanky Platz and Jane Conway sunbathing by Wickiup#49 in 1937.*

## Set Point #147

The lot was purchased from the Palisades Park Company in 1912 by David Storrs of Chicago. The property next door (now owned by Mary and Dillon Reed) was purchased at the same time by another family and "twin cottages" were built. David Storrs left the property to his daughter, Mary Storrs Anderson, in 1919. She and her husband, Arthur Olaf Anderson, owned this and other nearby properties for a number of years. They sold the cottage in 1946, to another Anderson - Karl W. (no relation). Karl was introduced to the Park in the 1930's by Leo Sowerby, the noted composer and organist, who owned the cottage east of Set Point for many years. Karl was active in the Park until the 1950's, when he moved to Connecticut. He died in 1967, leaving the cottage to his three children, Steve, Lori, and Carol. In 1970, Barb and Bill Trumbull purchased Lori's 1/3 share. In 1979, Carol and her husband, Don Beveridge, purchased "Theotherworlde" cottage and sold their 1/3 share to the Trumbulls. In 1984, Trumbulls purchased additional land for a parking area just east of Set Point. The next year, they purchased the remaining 1/3 of the cottage and are now the sole owners. Major improvements over the years have included a cement block south wall, insulation, paneling, a well, two decks, rewiring, and new appliances. In 1986, Mary Anderson Clark, the daughter of Arthur Olaf Anderson and wife of Hoddy Clark, wrote the following in a letter to Carol

*Wickiup #49, then belonging to the Timmonses. 1937. (Now McCarthy's Seamar)*

Beveridge: "Hod and I met at Palisades on the tennis court and we are still playing every day but one, every week. I remember my mother telling us about her father, David William Storres, taking the boat from Chicago to South Haven and walking from South Haven to Palisades with his suitcase. He built our cottage and friends of his built close next door in order to share the cement steps between the two cottages with a well between and a pump at the top of the stairs. Of course there was no electricity and my brother and I used to clean the lamp chimneys out in the sand by running the sand through them. Peter and I loved it there and so did our sister, Helen. Later, Leo Sowerby used to come to visit and finally had his own cottage built. He was like another member of our family."

*McQuig Cottage which burned down in 1951 on right (later site of Shorewood 11 #18); two cottages on left were washed away in 1929 storm. Note young trees. Probably Peirce cottage on hill. Photo c. 1920's.*

### Shorewood 11 #18

The first deed to this land was recorded on February 23, 1904, by Moody Emerson and James Lord, from Berrien County, Michigan. In 1905, the land was sold to Arthur Quick. One year later it was deeded to the South Haven Palisades Park Company. Then, for a period of time, it passed from a George Munroe to a Francis Gardner to a Fred and Willa Cranshaw. In the early 30's, the Cranshaws built a cottage and occupied it until 1940 when it was purchased by Ralph and Gertrude Dempsey. A year later, the cottage was purchased by Mr. and Mrs. J. E. McQuig.

The McQuig cottage burned to the ground in the late 50's and the land remained with the McQuig family. Interestingly enough, the present cottage is built exactly over the old cottage, even to the point that the old sidewalk on the north side leads up to the present door. Also, the old back steps lead up to the back patio built over the old cement porch. Because of the fire, the dune above the cottage was left without trees or growth. This caused the dune to lose sand and the roof of the neighbor's cottage was damaged.

The land remained vacant and was sold to Harold and Grace Logan in 1970. The present owner, Bill Jennings, bought it and constructed the present cottage in 1971. He built the cottage himself, with the help of the carpentry expertise of his brother, Jim. As the cottage was being finished, erosion ate away the sand dune back to the bottom step of the cottage. A seawall was installed. In 1985, a second wall was built to further protect the area.

The cottage is named "Shorewood 11" for the 11 members of the Jennings family. So far it has withstood the rigors of both nine children and Lake Michigan.

### Slieve Liag #152

Tom and Jody Flynn bought their cottage in 1987 from Mr. and Mrs. John Thornton. The Thorntons bought it from the original owners, the Brownings, who had built it as one of the first beach cottages in Lakeside Addition. In fact, it is on the map (reproduced elsewhere in this volume) that shows the first 21 cottages. The map probably dates 1909. At first, the cottage was in the lot next to Bonnie Dune (#150), where Patterson's cottage (# 151) now stands. However, at some point before the mid-40's, Mr. Browning – concerned about its closeness to the water – moved it back a bit and higher up on the lot next door.

*Browning cottage #152 before it was moved to lot next door, on right. Henkels' Bonnie Dune #150 (then owned by Miss Miller) on left. Both cottages were among the earliest to be built, probably by 1911. Again, note lack of trees.*

*Cottage #85 built by Arthur Quick as his summer residence.*

*Winter scene of Cottage #14. Note small trees in early years.*

### Sp'eyeglass #85

Owned by John and Terese Alsterda, this cottage was built by Mr. Arthur Quick – one of the first few cottages to be built. (The Quicks stayed in a tent prior to their cottage.)

### Spindrift # 14 and Richard's Roost #15

Vivian and Jim Richards purchased their cottage from Andy and Jane Peirce in the spring of 1979. They named it Spindrift after a ship whose engraving in a rare book in Mystic, CT, attracted them. They later found out that many cottages and boats in the New England area were similarly named.

Andy Peirce is the brother of Virginia (Ginny) Richards of Richards Roost cottage (#15). Their parents originally built Spindrift about 1925. The father of Cecil Burrous constructed it for $850. When the parents, Agnes and Cap Peirce, retired, they built a small guest cottage, now Richard's Roost, next to the original cottage. They could stay in it and come and go independently while allowing Andy and his family a month's vacation, followed by Ginny and her family the next month. Later on, the parents decided to divide the property between Andy and Ginny. Rud, Ginny's husband, skilled at renovation, took the small guest cottage and enlarged it to three stories. Andy received the original cottage and preserved it in an "as is" condition.

Rud died in 1979 at age 56 and never knew that soon after, his brother, Jim, bought the larger cottage from Andy Peirce. Andy and his family, though living close by in Benton Harbor, had other interests. The following year, Vivian and Jim made some extensive renovations (with the help of Cecil Burrous). In 1982, Jim died, also at age 56. Four years later, Vivian married Ray Waldron. They enjoyed over ten summers in Spindrift. Ray died in 1998. Vivian's three children spend very little time at the lake as they have diversified interests. She still enjoys her summers here, as long as tennis can figure in as a main feature.

### Squirrel Hill # 19

This cottage was built by and is still owned by one of the Park's five generation families - the McWethys. It was built in 1922.

*McWethys' Squirrel Hill # 9 on right; swinging bridge.*

### Stanton Cottage # 137

Built by Cathy Stanton's grandfather, George Duwe, this is a cottage that remained with one family throughout most of its history. Duwe was one of the Nine Old Men and active and influential in Park affairs for many years. The cottage is on one of the highest spots in the Park, near the present water tower. The cottage was sold to Liz and Greg Farrell in 2003.

### Sugar Hill #69

The central area of the cottage was built on a single lot by Lou and Thelma Weston in 1945. Due to the postwar shortage of conventional lumber, half-logs of Michigan white cedar joined by hardwood splines were used. Similar materials have been used in the later additions. The Westons built the stone fireplace themselves.

About 1950, the room addition on the west side of the cottage was built on an additional half lot acquired by the Westons. The original front door was near the door of this addition, now the master bedroom. The door now leading to the deck became the front door.

The Westons bought another cottage in the Park and sold the cedar log cottage to Janet and Phil Kolehmainen in January, 1969. The name "Sugar Hill" was given to the cottage in 1970, from an old 5-string banjo tune. During the next several years, the original interior was replaced by the present bedrooms, loft, bath, and kitchen. In the early 1980's, a screen porch was removed from the front of the cottage and the present entry, porch, sauna, dressing room, and deck were added. This structure was designed by Duane Sohl, who later designed the Willis Jensen cottage at the north end of the Park. In 2001 it was further remodelled to meet the needs of the expanding Kolehmainen family.

### Summer Hill #145

Built in 1972, by Hamill Homes of Grand Ledge, Michigan, the Foster cottage stands high on the bluff overlooking the south end of the Park. Frank and Maureen Foster and their children and grandchildren have owned and enjoyed it throughout its history.

### Sundune #176

Sundune cottage was planned by the Robert Beattys in the fall of 1941 and built in the spring of 1942. Although the cottage construction was contracted just as WWII began, the building supplies had been already purchased just before a moratorium on building was put in place. Those were the last construction materials available until after the war's end. The contractor was Arthur Quick and the building was done by Rudy Weber. Mr. Beatty died in 1957. In 1968, his wife, Helen Beatty, traded the cottage for Traylside, then owned by her daughter Katy and Katy's husband, Armin Beck. The Becks glassed in the porch. Their son, Joel – with the help of his siblings - extended the porch, built a deck, and dug out the basement to provide more room for a growing family. Throughout, the effort was made to maintain the feeling of the original summer cottage. After the death of Armin, Katy became the sole owner.

### Sunset Cottage #88

Mary and John Gardner bought land in Palisades Park in 1924, but for many years thereafter rented cottages for the summer. Then, on the 4th of July, 1948, Sunset cottage was up for sale. They looked at it in the morning; at 4:00 that afternoon they bought it. The cottage overlooks the lake and is situated on two large lots of Oceana Block 3. Their daughter, Betty, married Frank Householder, an English teacher and tennis coach at Western Michigan University in Kalamazoo. Because of their proximity to the Park and because they had the summers off, Betty and Frank spent all summer at Palisades. The other Gardner children, Jack - and his wife Jane Kipp - and Jeanette - and her husband Arch King - would bring their families for three weeks at a time until they each bought cottages of their own. Mr. and Mrs. Gardner lived into their late 80's. Frank Householder died in 1979. For many years thereafter, the cottage was owned by Betty Householder. Now it is owned by her three daughters.

The cottage was built in 1910 by a Covert, Michigan contractor by the name of Eugene Phillips, for Mr. and Mrs. George Munroe of Joliet, Illinois. Mr. Monroe was an Illinois State Senator in the 1890's. In 1911, he died, leaving the property to his daughter and her family – Jesse and Esther Shuman and their two daughters, of Pittsburg, PA. The Shuman girls, after selling the cottage to the Gardners, retired to California. When George Munroe built Sunset, he also built the cottage by the gate for his chauffeur and family, now owned by the McNamara family. That cottage was called Munro Lodge.

*Sundune Cottage #176.*

## The Nineteenth Hole #55

Ralph and Virginia Wenham and sons built this house in the 1960's. Mary and Ross Jones, present owners, think that would be a story in itself. (The antenna for the TV was at the top of a tall pine tree in the meadow.) It was a "Gold Medallion" home – no gas, oil, or coal, all electric.

Mary and Ross Jones purchased in May of 1968. They continued to raise four children between Kalamazoo and Palisades Park. Boys Rick, Steve, and Chuck worked as busboys at Sturtevant Lodge, through high school and college, and for maintenance in the city of South Haven. Carol kept up her high school/college tennis. She became a successful teaching pro in California. Mary and Ross were golfers; thus the name 19th Hole. They entertained 12 to 16 players every year. They played all the local public golf courses, one time or another.

Ross and Mary doubled the size of the house in 1980-81 to add more space and better accommodations. The additions in 1981 were made while they were on a Circle Pacific Cruise, travelling the equivalent of the distance around the world at its circumference. Among their prize possessions are albums of snap shots and photographs taken in Palisades Park, South Haven, and all over the world.

Many improvements in lighting and ventilation, inside and out, have been made since 1981. Two large dead oak trees plus a lightning-struck cherry tree have been removed. Bob Zimmermann counted 100 rings on one oak tree.

## The Tiki Room #155

The Tiki Room, initially known as Breezy Knoll, was formerly owned by the DeSouchet family. According to Mardy Mehagan Mavor, Billy DeSouchet and his wife owned Pottawatomie #156, the cottage immediately north. After his wife passed away, Billy remarried. His second wife would not stay in Pottawatomie, so he built Breezy Knoll right next door.

In 1964, Don Longley bought the cottage and totally remodeled it, adding a lower floor that made it twice as large. It was at Breezy Knoll that he and his wife, Terese, told their six children of his terminal cancer. The cottage was a heritage for his children. A few years after Don passed away, Therese met Joe Anlauf. A romance blossomed and they married. Joe had five children; the cottage was where the two families came together. They renamed the cottage Longley-Anlauf City, Population 13.

When Joe was transferred to California, they sold the cottage to Mrs. Mary Lou Tombaugh who was widowed and had two grown sons. After spending several summers at the cottage she renamed Point-of-View, she decided it was too large for her. She swapped cottages with Henry and June Buschman, who lived next door in the cottage now called Cheers #156. The Buschman family occupied the cottage, which they renamed Port of St. Louis, until the spring of 2003, when they sold it to Terry and Laura O'Brien, of Indianapolis. The O'Briens, with the help of their three young children, named the cottage The Tiki Room; they plan for a lifetime of memories.

## To Each His Own #168

In 1931, Jessica and Wells Chamberlin of Villa Park, Illinois, purchased the property from the Palisades Park Company. They built the cottage in 1932. Jessica sold it in 1958 after the death of her husband. The second owners were Marguerite and E. D. Hennigan of River Forest, Illinois. The Masons purchased the property from them in 1969 and doubled the size of the cottage in 1973 after the birth of their eighth child. Phyllis Mason continues to enjoy summers at Palisades and visits from her children and their families.

*Toplofty # 97, above right, with Wards #92, Bishop #93, and VonRosen # 94, left to right, on beach. Hong Kong Hilton was built some years later. 1944.*

## Top Lofty #97

Rita Rigney McNamara first came to Palisades in the late 40's to visit Dona Schlacks, a high school friend. When she and Tom McNamara married and had their family, they came again, renting Potters and Balgownie. They all loved it here so much that they bought Top Lofty with their friends, K. and Paul Wentzien, in 1976. Top Lofty had been built pre-war for the Hagie family. The McNamaras-Wentziens bought from the Wallace family. They have had many happy times since 1976. The

McNamara family grew so they bought a second cottage, Gatehouse, in the 90's to house the overflow and give them a cozy place to come in the winter. That has led to more fun times.

## Top Deck #4

Pat and Richard Venner started coming to Palisades Park in 1953 when son Tom was two years old and Robert six months. They were introduced to the Park by Frances and Henry Prange who were building a new cottage on the point in Happy Valley. They rented many different cottages in the Park throughout the early years, especially Traylside from Katy Beck when the boys were all grade school age. In 1967 they built "Top Deck" #4 on the North Beach above Potters and remained there until 1989 when they bought a lovely "home" #56 behind Ross and Mary Jones. They remained there five years and reluctantly left the Park in 1995 to return to hometown, Kalamazoo, so Rich could be closer to his job, working at son Rick's Marina on Gull Lake.

The Venner family participated in many aspects of Palisades life. Richard served on the Board under Weldon Coates as membership chair and was instrumental in heading a committee to see that a retaining wall was put at the base of reservoir hill to hold back the serious erosion. That wall is still in place and vital protection for the dunes. Tom and Rob ran the Soda Bar in 1971 – 1973 while they were in college. Pat and Rich ran it for one year when it was renovated and reopened after having been used as a cottage for a short time. Rob and Rick both helped Stan Severinghaus on clean up crew one spring in the late 70's.

Pat was interested in tennis and participated in the tournaments, winning both singles and doubles in the Buttercup in the 70's. Pat was also active in the Women's Clubhouse group, serving as treasurer and chair of the Fashion Show and House Walk. Rob, Director of DeGraff Nature Center in Holland, still loves to give nature walks in his old haunts. He was instrumental in starting some of our trails. Rick recently purchased his own cottage, served on the Board and as President of the Park. Now Pat and Rich enjoy staying in Rick's cottage and seeing their grandchildren play on the beaches. The Venners all share a love for Palisades.

## Traylside #177

First named Kilkare, this cottage was built and owned by O.B. and Loretta Spellman. It was built of lumber from the family lumber yard in Covert. It was next owned by Virginia and Sheldon Spellman; they, in turn, sold to Helen and Robert Beatty in 1955. In 1959, after Mr. Beatty's death, it was sold to his daughter and her husband, Katy and Armin Beck. The name was changed to Traylside. The Becks traded Traylside for Sundune cottage, directly in front of it, with Katy's mother, Helen Beatty, in 1968. She sold it to Jean and Joseph Fitzgerald in 1978. They have renovated and slightly expanded the cottage, retaining the sense of the original cottage.

## Tree House #163

Tree House was built in the spring of 1937 by J. Abbott and Marty Edwards. The workers were Charlie Tunecke and others from the Covert area who worked for many years in the Park. The name was given by the children of Mary and Ab. It is unclear whether it means built from trees (which it is) or built in the trees (which it also is). The Edwards family had spent two summers renting when Ab decided he wanted more privacy and bought the lot in the woods. The cottage is built of cedar logs from the thumb area of Michigan. The plans were chalked out on the floor of an old ice house; then the logs were cut to size and numbered, then transported to Palisades on auto trailer trucks that belonged to Mr. Edwards's company at that time. They were then carried to the cottage site on smaller trucks. When finally erected, to the amazement of all, only one log had been cut wrong and that was about two feet short.

Ab drew up the plans for the first route system in the Park and made the first signs of four inch square tins, painted in black figures. A few of them can still be seen. He and one of the Ferry boys were the instigators of the first softball teams. He wanted the cottage to be the gathering place of his family and heirs; it has been just that. He died in 1959 and his wife in 1990. His three children, grandchildren, and now great-grandchildren still enjoy the cottage.

*An early picture of Treetops.*

## Treetops #83

Treetops is the first cottage on the right as one leaves Ravine Way on Route 1. The name "Tree Tops" is easily seen on the side of the cottage above the rustic foundation trim. In August, 1909, the lot was purchased by Rev. Eugene and Mrs. Frances Schreck of Chicago. There is no record of the date when the cottage was built, but old-timers insist it is supposed to be the oldest cottage in the Park and built in 1909. (See page 10 of Palisades Park Review 1905 – 1968.) Dad Henderson of the Hermitage, which was built soon after Treetops, probably built the rustic foundation cover of the cottage.

In 1928 the Schrecks moved to England and gave the power of attorney to Henry and Edward Wunsch, of Detroit, to handle the cottage. In November of that year, it was sold to Mary B. Ward of Riverside, Illinois (Mary Lee Tillson's grandmother). In 1943 the cottage was sold to Francis Glasner of LaGrange, Illinois and in 1954 to John and Carol Kendrick, also of LaGrange. In 1960, it was sold to Anne V. Fuller of Kalamazoo, Michigan. The present owners are Cynthia and Larry Rudmann. The cottage has lots of charm and a tiny view of the lake from the porch. Many internal changes and improvements have gone over the years, but the cottage still appears much as it must have looked in the early years of the 20th century.

Ruth Raschke Innes wrote of her family's ownership sometime in the 30's. Possibly her family bought the cottage from Rev. Schreck. She reminisced as follows:

> I can't recall or know the exact year Grandpa Innes (F. L. Innes, my father-in-law) bought the cottage we called "Treetops." I don't know anything about the costs nor building of the cottage, but it was completely furnished with beautiful furniture, linens, dishes, and kitchen supplies. As I understood, the original owners probably bought or built everything and then the Depression hit in the 1930's. My first visit was in 1936 when my daughter, Ruthie, was two years old. The Inneses had four children; we all took turns, as our families grew, to stay certain weeks in the summer, sharing the cottage. Sometimes there would be 14 – 17 of us there at the same time. The noise of happy children and activities rang through the woods.
>
> I remember a Mrs. Mehagan who was active in planning social parties and events for children, expecially Bunco games and cards. Grandpa was the chief grocery shopper and I remember the wonderful

platters of corn on the cob we would have from Covert country farmers. And the peaches! I remember Joe Putz who stood at the entrance up the hill and kept non-members or strangers from ever coming into the Park. Mary, his sister, used to help Grandma clean the cottage. Then there was the ice cream parlor, the little post office and a sort of hotel at the end of the road down by the beach. How do you expect me at 86 years old to remember all these things?

Whenever a storm would change the beach there was an old gentleman with a team of horses that would drag the beach and clean it up and level it off. We had to walk over and down to the beach. I remember some cottages right on the beach. And the Peirce family. Andy was a classmate of mine. I remember the beautiful sunsets, the sand beneath our feet, and the waves and cool evening breezes.

## Tuckaway #27

Wilbur David Peat and his wife, Talitha Rasmussen Peat, first came to Palisades Park in 1929 and rented a cottage on the south side. In 1932, they built on the north side with Arthur Quick as the general contractor. Though Wilbur had detailed blueprints for the cottage he desired, Mr. Quick convinced him that the local carpenters would be better with a simpler design. Most of the furniture was made by Wilbur, giving him a pleasurable outlet for sawing wood. At that time, and for several years, electricity was not available and they were the only folks in the north side woods. After the Depression, the Muckinhern cottage was built and then electricity became available.

Palisades Park was home all summer, every summer, for Talitha and the children. Wilbur spent the summer weekends and the month of August at Palisades for the rest of his life. The usual routine for that month was one year of landscape painting and the next two years for cottage improvements and maintenance. He mixed his own concrete with sand and gravel from the beach one summer. With his father Jacob (Puzzy), he dug out the basement. Another summer was spent building an eating porch, with the help of son David.

Wilbur died in 1966 and his wife, Talitha, at age 96, in 2001. Her interview can be found elsewhere in this volume. The cottage is still used by their son David and his wife Mary, their two children and four grandchildren.

## Up Country #65

This cottage has belonged to Rev. and Mrs. William Ferry since 1947 when they purchased it for "almost nothing" at today's prices from Bill's parents, Dr. and Mrs. Asa J. Ferry. Its name then was the rather prosaic Oakhill, named for the block on which it stands, but old timers may remember it best as "The Snow Cottage," taking its name from the woman doctor from Chicago who built it in 1909. It stood then all alone on the top of the second highest dune in the Park, on the ridge which runs downward toward what is now the Mooney cottage, built by Dr. Snow's sister, Dr. Brown. The cottage was named by default. When search for a more romantic name ended in a deadlock, it occurred to someone that the family has always said, whether in Chicago or Wichita, Ohio or West Virginia, "Let's go up country." Dr. and Mrs. Ferry first came up around the lake, or across it by boat to South Haven or Benton Harbor, in 1926, with their three sons – Jack, Bill, and Alan. For three years prior to that date, they had rented one of four cottages still standing on the grounds of a well-known summer hotel at Sleepy Hollow, which had burned to the ground some years previously. For five years, they rented Snow Cottage, but bought it in 1931. Ever since, it has been the focus of family summer activities, Bill and Mary's sons, John and Peter, growing up with the next generation of Palisaders, the process now being repeated by John and Vicki's son, Chris, and Pete's son, Asa. Olive Lewis, Mary's sister, spent many summers here, as well, after her retirement from the Department of Library Science of West Virginia University.

Most exciting time: one Easter vacation in the 50's when, following yearly custom, Mary and Bill, John and Peter, had come to apprise the ravages of winter – and almost lost the cottage in a pre-dawn fire from an overheated fireplace kept burning all night against a particularly cold spring. This family will always be grateful to the Covert Volunteer Fire Department, here in 15 minutes over icy roads, in response to a phone call from the then Park Superintendent, Warren Knapp, then one of the few claimants to phone-power. Incidentally, that was our first meeting with the Sarno brothers, members of the Covert Fire-Fighters.

*The Ferry cottage, Up Country, #65.*

*Concrete-block built Upside Dune when it still had the deck over the porch.*

### Upside Dune #151

The Patterson cottage was built for Mr. and Mrs. Paul Butcher by Tony Canonie, in 1945. Their son Bob camped out on the nearby dune and helped with the construction. Their daughter, Doris Patterson, and her husband Andy are the present owners. The Butchers bought the lot from Mr. and Mrs. Browning, who owned three lots and the house that is presently owned by Tom and Jody Flynn. The Browning cottage was originally on the Butcher lot, but had been moved during a high water season.

### Vashmar #92

One of the earliest cottages at Palisades, Vashmar was built for Mr. and Mrs. William Ward. It is one of the cottages on the earliest map we have, showing the first 20 cottages. And it has been in the Ward's family ever since, passing to granddaughter Mary Lee Tillson and, at Mary Lee's death, to her children, the present owners. Originally it had no kitchen and the Wards and their guests ate all their meals at Sturtevant Lodge. Over the years it has been enlarged and remodeled. Built on the water, it has had its share of problems with storms and high water; walls and riprap have saved it from going in the lake, though it has often been damaged. Several of the interviews in this volume tell of life in Vashmar over the decades.

### Waldameer #11
Reminiscences by Joan Stanger
In September, 1991 Patter

"Ron and Dick Stanger spotted a garage in a valley of the Dean's Addition, adjacent to Palisades Park. They had rented Merrikot (later Ankenbruk's Sandwitch and now Venner's Valhalla #114) for many years. Leota Reed, the owner, was the organist of Brewster Pilgrim Church in Detroit, where Dr. Robert C. Stanger was the minister of Bethel Evangelical and Reformed Church. Dr. Robert, his wife Juel, Ron and Dick began coming to Palisades in the summer of 1940. Now twenty years later, this solitary garage was for sale, and they had the vision of a Stanger Cottage.

"In 1961, the garage was converted into a well constructed knotty pine cottage which was the summer place for three generations of Stangers, including Ron's wife Helga, Dick's wife Joan, and the three children who spent every summer here until their high school years, using the Clubhouse facilities, roaming the Park, and playing along the Brandywine on North Beach. The children have grown up, but holidays bring all of them together, and the reunions with their Park friends are memorable. The cottage was expanded in 1988.

"When the cottage was built, there was a post office and grocery store run by Mrs. Packard. How convenient it was to walk to get milk, bread, meats, and cheeses. In the corner of the store were the beckoning pinball machines. The Sturtevant Lodge offered a lovely buffet. There were fewer tennis courts, but they were well maintained. The spirit of the Park was wonderful.

"Today we have the power plant at the end of the beach; we have perky golf carts quietly traversing the roads. There are the well marked hiking rails and the peaceful woods for those of us who come here to retreat from activities carried on the rest of the year. I hope the Park never gets too 'gussied up' and retains what drew the two young renters with a dream to that garage thirty years ago."

### Waukwin #146

The cottage now owned by Sallie Kittredge was built in 1978 by Robert and Grace Holmes of Kalamazoo. It is one of three or four Hamill built homes in Palisades. Robert was Dean of Fine Arts at Western Michigan University. He and Grace moved to California where he became head of the Idlewild campus of the University of California. He went from there to be the head of Music College of the Pacific in Santa Barbara.

Sallie Kittredge purchased the cottage in July of 1980. The only addition has been a very narrow walkway deck on the lower level. The Park trail along the top of the dune had to be adjusted to go behind this cottage and the Foster cottage to the north. Considerable sand was moved and shored up to create a drive into the cottage. It was named Waukwin, which means "The World Beyond" in Algonquin Indian. Sallie's four children were grown and geographically distant, so they have been here very little.

# Wayside #98
By Joyce Heitner Lloyd

As I remember the story of our cottage, it was built in 1928. In 1929, the gentleman who owned it lost his money in the stock market crash and died shortly after. The woman lived for a long time in a retirement home so the cottage was boarded up during that time. In 1947 or so, Dr. Richard Kirby, her nephew, inherited the cottage. He used the cottage at least part time that summer. On Memorial Day weekend of 1948, my family rented the Larson cottage up the hill from Wayside. My parents, Bill and Florence Heitner, noticed a 3x5 card nailed to the side door of Wayside, read it, discovered that it was a For Sale sign, and copied down the information. When we returned to Chicago, they called and made an appointment to meet with Dr. Kirby the next evening, at which time they purchased the cottage. My parents had seen the cottage when it was being built, had liked it at the time, and felt they didn't need to see the inside before making the purchase. Dr. Kirby retired to California.

When we saw it for the first time the next weekend, it was quite interesting. It still had the 1928 furnishings, which were painted a very dark green and bright orange. The floors were painted the same bright orange. The living room had a small projection – about 12 feet wide - toward the water. This had two French windows. The projection and the screened porch surrounded a tree and there was another set of French windows in the west end looking at the tree. That first summer, my family added a picture window in the end of the projection, using half of the French window on each side.

When we bought the cottage, the name was The Chalet. The name came from the crossed fascia boards on the gable ends that gave the cottage an Alpine flavor. Those were cut off in time because of maintenance problems. Another cottage shared a similar name, so my father named ours "Wayside" rather than entering a name fight.

As was true of a lot of cottages at that time, the cottage had an icebox instead of a refrigerator. The iceman delivered large blocks of ice every day during the summer. It had a three gallon water heater, which made taking a bath a challenge. It had wooden shutters on the screened porch all the way around. Because the cottage had been closed and with no maintenance for so many years, the spiders thought they owned the property. I used to throw back the covers on my bed completely every night to make sure I didn't have an eight-legged bed partner. My father spent that first summer putting new posts and footings under the cottage and leveling it because the doors wouldn't open and close. He also painted it each summer with creosote. He spent a lot of effort over the next several years to caulk and seal it from intruding insects and my dreaded spiders.

"We purchased the cottage near the end of a long period of low lake levels. There was a path to the beach that began just south of the garage. It was a gentle slope and reached the beach many feet further west than the cement seawall. Then there was a long stretch of beach before the shore. A huge cottonwood tree grew by the path close to the beach; two smaller ones grew further up the hill. When we purchased the cottage, it wasn't waterfront. Two lots were in front of us, one directly in front and one to the north owned by the Baker sisters (the later site of Hong Kong Hilton). In 1950 or '51, when water levels started to threaten the safety of the cottages, my father purchased the lot in front of us to put in a sea-wall. George Boyles, our neighbor to the south, and my father purchased the two lots between us and split them lengthwise so they could connect their two sea walls. We had a well in our front lot for years so we could spend winters there. It finally succumbed to the high water.

"During our years of ownership, we put in different versions of seawalls for protection from high lake water levels. The first was a wooden wall built about 1951. The second was cement, using the piling from the wooden wall as foundation. It had to have fabric and sand added behind it to keep it from tipping. The next wall was the wooden one at the toe of the bluff to keep storms from jumping the concrete wall and tearing out the bluff.

"About 1954 we removed the tree in the offset in the living room, increased the size of the living room, and put in a second picture window, making the living room more usable and more enjoyable. My father purchased bead board paneling for the rest of the cottage, but stored it in the basement until sometime in the 70's when my husband installed it and insulated the living room. We

*A mystery: Can anyone identify the people and cottages in this picture?*

had the remainder of the cottage paneled in the mid-80's. Sometime along the way, my father painted the cottage a deep red on the lower half with white above.

"I spent many lovely summers at the cottage, joined by my husband Ross and my children, Kathy and Todd. Father died in 1968 and mother, at the age of 91, in 1988. Selling the cottage in 1993 was one of the most difficult things I have ever done, but we all lived in the Pacific Northwest by then.

"Rumor was that there were mob connections to the cottage. A minor mobster, who called himself Lord Buckingham, built the cottage for his mistress. Mrs. Wilson, who was Jane Mathias's aunt, used to say she saw someone burying something in the foundation while the cottage was being built. We used to speculate whether it was a body or a pot of gold. At one time, the area along our ridge was planned to be another Circle, with a resort hotel planned for the two lots to the south of us."

Joyce sold the cottage to Jim and Lois Richmond, the present owners. The Richmonds have replaced windows, roof, siding, and shutters, adding a new kitchen, carpeting, and their green and yellow sunflower motif. Jim's sculptures add to the décor. Lois says they donated the old dishwasher to a museum in Galesburg which has a reproduction of an old kitchen; they still have the portable clothes washer.

## Whippoorwill, Seagull, and Grapevine #125, 181, and 182

In 1910, Marion Palmer Hamilton first came with her parents to the cottage she later owned, Whippoorwill, which was built by her three aunts, Fannie, Louise, and Anna Palmer, great aunts of the present owner (Marion's daughter, Jeryl). Aunt Fannie Palmer was a schoolteacher, Aunt Louise Palmer was a nurse, and Aunt Anna Palmer was a housekeeper and took care of the family. Mrs. Palmer's sisters sold the cottage to Mr. and Mrs. George Owen, some time after Mr. Palmer bought Cherry Hill. When Mr. Owen died in the early 50's, Mrs. Owen gave the cottage to Marion Hamilton. At that time, it had no plumbing or electricity.

Marion bought Seagull in 1928. Her father, Mr. Palmer, had bought the lot for her some years previously. She used to bring her friends from the Juvenile Court (where she worked) to her cottage. They would take the train to Bangor and then go by wagon to the cottage. Once, during a lightning storm, lightning hit the cottage and broke off a large splinter of wood which went through a visitor's leg. Apparently, he recovered.

Marion and her husband bought Grapevine sometime in the 40's from the Carpenters. When Marion died, her three daughters inherited the three cottages.

## Wyndune #161

Waldemar E. Paulsen and Elvira M. Paulsen purchased lots 8, 9, and 10, Lake Bluff Block, in Palisades Park 2$^{nd}$ Subdivision, on August 19, 1959, from Palisades Park Properties, Inc. Lot 11 was purchased by the Paulsens September 16, 1961, from Richard C. and Bertha L. Stuckmeyer. The Paulsens' primary residence was in Glen Ellyn, Illinois.

Rudy Weber, a builder of many cottages in the Park, erected the original two bedroom ranch style structure sometime in the late 1950s or early 1960s. The Paulsens lived there until the property was sold, August 4, 1964, to Richard L. and Catherine W. Lewis, of Parkersburg, West Virginia. Shortly after purchasing, the Lewises added a 16' x 18' dormitory style bedroom with an attached 24' x 11' screened porch.

September 14, 1968, Joseph C. and Sharon L. Kirk purchased the property from the Lewises. At that time, the Kirks lived in Jackson, Michigan, later moving to Ada, Michigan.

During the spring of 1995, the screened porch was converted to a three-season porch. Beginning in the spring of 1999 and ending June, 2000, the north side of the cottage was remodeled. A second story was added above the dormitory style bedroom and the main floor was extended about twenty feet to accommodate additional bedrooms. A well was drilled in the fall of 2000 and a central forced-air furnace was installed in the fall of 2001. In 2001, the Kirks sold their primary residence and established "fulltime" residence at Wyndune. Their intention is to spend the majority of the year in the Park, but the deep winter months somewhere in a warmer climate.

It is unknown whether the Paulsens had named the cottage, but the Lewises christened it "Wyndune." The Kirks, after calling it "Kirk's Kottage" for several years, decided the original name was more appropriate and renamed it "Wyndune."

*Bruce and Donna Chambers and child by their cottage which Consumers Power Company bought and destroyed shortly thereafter; April 1970.*

*Olson cottage with Miss Olson on porch; also later destroyed by Consumers.*

*Old Pier cottage #45 – one of the Park's earliest cottages.*

*Ebert cottage #149 as it was being remodelled.*
*Right: Same, upon completion.*

*Old postcard looking Northward from Palisades Pier" before building of Sturtevant.*

# Afterword

## Changing or Changeless?

By Marilyn Henkel

In an August 11, 1963 Vesper talk at the Clubhouse, the Reverend William M. Ferry spoke of the changeless qualities he and his family found in the Park. His talk was excerpted in the August, 1964 Patter and was alluded to earlier in this volume, in the articles on our Circle. What he said forty years ago still seems apt in 2004:

> There's a litany recited by our family on entering the Park each summer for the first time, quite unrehearsed and spontaneous. Some one of us will say, "The same old Park! It never changes!" The rest will respond: "It's always the same. It never changes!" And so, I'm sure, for many of you as you come back, year after year, to find the Park so little changed in such a changing world.
>
> I'm not quite sure what we actually expect to find in way of change – the roads blacktopped, an escalator up the hundred steps, pink and charcoal trees, Lake Palisades all dredged out and full of water, high-rise apartments instead of Sturtevant Lodge. It isn't that we really expect any such miracles. It comes only out of a kind of wonder, our spontaneous litany, **that in such a fast-changing world, the old place does seem to change not at all or very little.** The roads still run up and down and all around over the old logging trails - the same bumps and ridges at the same old corners; the final bend of the road and the Circle just as it's supposed to be – with thousands of little people milling all around the Soda Fountain; the lake just the same with a couple of old pier ends still sticking up out of the water; Mrs. Packard behind the counter in the store as if she's never left it – and those same old fashioned licorice things on the counter. **Once again, with wonder and relief, one chants: "At least one place on earth remains, today as it was yesterday, tomorrow as it is today, forever and forever! Amen."**

Well, okay, the old pier ends have disappeared as has Mrs. Packard and the store – but the licorice still remains in the Soda Fountain and the roads – need we mention their "bumps and ridges?" So the story has run through much of this volume. That may be why this history has turned into a love-fest of sorts – so many of you having testified to the unique, enduring, almost-mystical qualities of **this place we call Palisades Park.**

And yet, if we faithfully follow the **footprints** in this volume, we do see significant changes. Patterns of Park usage and of entertainment would be high on that list - along with the problems and challenges of growth. We have opened our gates and hearts to friends and family of differing ethnic backgrounds. The emphasis on artistic and professional people has given way to those who can afford our high prices through business successes. All these matter.

Why, then, do the changeless elements outweigh the changes? The picture on the next page - of Mr. Hempy walking down the beach ( just the right way to end this book) - may provide an answer. Look closely. No longer do we see the horse and wagon with its cluster of children – nor the pier remnants in the background. But the water remains – and the people enjoying it - as do the dunes and trees. The boardwalk is wider but still important to us all (remember the Boardwalk Rebellion of 2002?) The **footprints** could be our prints as they lead into a new century of Park history.

Yes, there is something almost mystical about this place. It is more than the sum total of its parts. All who come to Palisades share one of Nature's beauty spots, as Mr. Quick understood 100 years ago. We also share a history – most of it positive but some that meant sore lessons learned. Most of all, we share a love for this area – a belief in the importance of retreat and reflection and quiet, of friends and family, of the beauty surrounding us, of an escape from the dizzy world in which we find ourselves. As we turn off the Blue Star for each visit, may everyone know Bill Ferry had it right: **Once again, with wonder and relief, we all chant: "At least one place on earth remains, today as it was yesterday, tomorrow as it is today, forever and forever! Amen."**

# Appendix

# The Editors

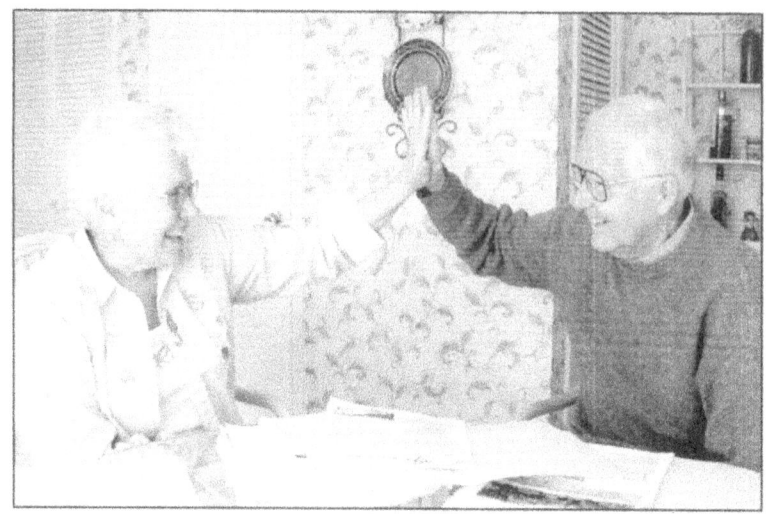

*Bill and Marilyn celebrating the completion of one section. 2002.*

*Marilyn and Katy. 2003.*

*Bill Potter, Nancy Potter, Marilyn Henkel, and Katy Beck sorting pictures. 2001.*

*Below: The complete staff - Bill Potter, Marge Roche, Don Henkel 2nd row; Katy Beck and Marilyn Henkel 1st row.*

# The Future Editors
(Beck, Henkel, and Potter Grandchildren)

# Cottage Names, Numbers, Owners

| Name | # | Owner |
|---|---|---|
| 5th Generation | 188 | McCarthy |
| A Summer Place | 171 | Bartley |
| Above and Beyond | 101 | Keehn |
| Acadia | 110 | Pierce |
| All Decked Out | 94 | Cunningham |
| Ambivalent | 91 | Connor |
| Anchor Fast | 43 | King |
| B 'n 'B | 119 | Zimmermann |
| Balgownie | 74 | Bendelow |
| Ballou Inn | 90 | Bradshaw / Cornelius/Flynn / Jefferson/Luedeman / McCowan/Phillips |
| Bauhaus | 37 | Nickerson |
| Beach House | 42 | Roche |
| Beats Working | 123 | O'Brien |
| Bedford Falls | 191 | Zimmermann |
| Beechwood-Bee's Knees | 160 | Eisenberg |
| Better Here Than There | 48 | Golden |
| Betwigst | 105 | Doyle |
| Bittersweet | 51 | Kavanaugh |
| Blueberry Hill | 113 | Goeppinger |
| Bonnie Dune | 150 | Henkel |
| Bozeman | 108 | Trezise |
| Brandyville | 38 | Donovan |
| Breezy Hollow | 183 | Wintermute |
| Brigadune | 67 | Gubbins |
| Broadview | 93 | Bishop / Vogt |
| Buckeye King | 77 | King / Koller / Mailander |
| Bum's Rush | 44 | Borchert / Dembs |
| Bunk-In | 2 | VanderSalm |
| Bunker Hill | 166 | Doyle / Hauber |
| Carpe Diem | 189 | O'Connor |
| Casa Giallo | 82 | Doyle / Molinaro |
| Casa Loca | 124 | Davis |
| Castlemaine Kerry | 52 | O'Brien |
| Cedar Nook | 103 | Bradford / Fyk |
| Chalet-Leigh | 32 | McArdle |
| Cher-Oak-Ee | 112 | Marks / Sharpe |
| Clint Brae | 158 | O'Connor |
| Colb's Cozy | 115 | Colbert |
| Court House | 61 | Branding |
| Crest Haven | 96 | Mathias / Taylor |
| Curtin's Cove | 179 | Curtin |
| Diamond Inn the Rough | 71 | Kline |
| Driftwood | 3 | Potter |
| Dublindoon | 144 | Ball / Egan / Kearns /Mulvaney |
| Dunewood | 100 | Brand |
| East o' the Lake | 142 | Hohman |
| Edgewood Too | 40 | Morsch |
| Eldamar | 143 | Garvey |
| Enchanted Hill | 162 | Joy / Joy-Karney/ |
| | 162 | Joy-Rhomberg |
| Exit Inn | 135 | Beyer |
| Family Thais | 50 | Gates / Jones / Vana |
| Far Niente | 35 | Sitterly |
| Fern Hill | 68 | Owen |
| Focus Inn | 149 | Ebert |
| Foleys' Follies | 118 | Foley |
| Four Winds | 165 | Lewis |
| Gatehouse | 63 | McNamara / Skrine /Stratton |
| Gazebo | 86 | Mauer |
| Generation 4 | 184 | Kearin |
| Gopher | 46 | Mailander |
| Grandpa's Beach | 174 | Ryan |
| Grapevine | 182 | Keller |
| Graystone | 89 | Breen / Dinnin / Forsee/Huffine / Lezon |
| Griggy's | 129 | Grigola |
| Happiness | 116 | Ellis |
| Happy Days | 26 | Hoff |
| Happy Hollow | 104 | Speicher |
| Happy Time | 80 | Heitner |
| Hermitage | 120 | Schwartz / Shortridge |
| Hermitage II | 81 | Henderson |
| Hi-Brazil | 159 | Lewis |
| High Tor | 4 | Garvey / Steiner |
| Highlands | 78 | Hoskin |
| Hillside | 117 | McCullough |
| Hiview | 66 | Stracke |
| Home Port | 58 | Oberlin |
| Honey Do | 84 | Hladik |
| Hong Kong Hilton | 95 | Warner |
| Ichiban Ryokan | 192 | Donovan |
| In-De Inn | 23 | Fitzgerald |
| Inn Cognito | 20 | Kinsey |
| Inn Orbit | 21 | Sheehan |
| InnDecision | 140 | Heavrin |
| Innwood | 62 | Guirl |
| Kalihiwai | 70 | Hussey |
| La Casita | 106 | Compernolle |
| Lakehaus | 190 | Carr / Grist / Vujtech |
| Lehmann's Haven | 127 | Lehmann / Soch |
| Lexington Avenue | 121 | McWethy |
| Little Brown Jug | 153 | Kleb |
| Log Cabin | 31 | Menconi |
| Lookout Inn | 130 | Anderson |
| MarJoMore | 164 | Heisel / Hession |
| Master Lodge | 53 | Master |
| McMahon | 169 | McMahon |
| Meadow Chalet | 36 | Cordell |
| Meadowview | 30 | Dannenberg |
| Michigan Split | 157 | G'Sell |

| | | | | | | |
|---|---|---|---|---|---|---|
| Morewood | | 187 | Jansen | Whippen | | |
| North Beach | | 1 | Roche | Treetops | 83 | Rudmann |
| Old Pier | | 45 | Coleman / Trotter | Tuckaway | 27 | Peat |
| Osthaven | | 75 | Kilburn / Osth | Tuckaway | 27 | Wehrheim |
| Our D.I.G.S. | | 5 | Canonie / Sylvester | Tucked Inn | 133 | Dinnin |
| | | | | Up Country | 65 | Ferry |
| Owl B Darned | | 34 | Schlacks | Up-Side-Dune | 151 | Patterson |
| Owl's Nest | | 47 | Haude | Ups 'n' Downs | 139 | Feldman |
| Parshall's Post | | 57 | Parshall | Valhalla | 114 | Venner |
| Peggy's Place | | 29 | Claffy | Valkommen | 134 | Whitney |
| Piccadilly Circus | | 41 | Gardner | Valley Haven | 79 | Dobbelaere |
| Point of View | | 186 | Zarling | Vashmar | 92 | Tillson |
| Port St. Louis | | 155 | Boehm / Buschman | Waldameer | 11 | Stanger |
| | | | | Waukwin | 146 | Kittredge |
| Pottawatomie | | 154 | Duesing | Wayside | 98 | Richmond |
| Poustinia | | 72 | Schlacks | Wellfleet West | 6 | Cooney |
| Rainbow | | 126 | Petrulis | Whippoorwill | 125 | Bost |
| Retreat | | 178 | Kropp | Windjammer | 17 | Schlobohm |
| Richards Roost | | 15 | Richards | Windridge | 141 | Buchanan |
| Robins Nest | | 87 | Robins | Windsong | 173 | Williams |
| Sand Castle | | 167 | Burkhardt | Wit's End | 24 | Tamm |
| Sandbox | | 175 | Borge | Wyndune | 161 | Kirk |
| Sandpiper | | 170 | Piper | | | |
| Seagull | | 181 | Hamilton | | | |
| Seamar | | 49 | McCarthy | | | |
| SetPoint | | 147 | Trumbull | | | |
| SheeInn | | 22 | Sheehan | | | |
| Shorewood | | 18 | Jennings | | | |
| Slieve Liag | | 152 | Flynn | | | |
| Sp'eyeglass | | 85 | Alsterda | | | |
| Spindrift | | 14 | Waldron | | | |
| Squirrel Hill | | 19 | Plain | | | |
| Sugar Hill | | 69 | Kolehmainen | | | |
| Summerhill | | 145 | Foster | | | |
| Sundune | | 176 | Beck | | | |
| Sunnyside | | 60 | Burrous | | | |
| Sunset | | 88 | Aliotta / Fleming / Zigmond | | | |
| Sunset Grill | | 56 | Wilson | | | |
| The 19th Hole | | 55 | Jones | | | |
| The Apple | | 138 | Pomeroy | | | |
| The Ark | | 7 | Welles | | | |
| The Back Door | | 109 | Halpin | | | |
| The Briars | | 195 | Ebright | | | |
| The Dougout | | 194 | Van Boven | | | |
| The Other World | | 136 | Beveridge / Dillman | | | |
| TLC | | 131 | Stewart | | | |
| To Each His Own | | 168 | Mason | | | |
| Toplofty | | 97 | McNamara / Wentzien | | | |
| Tree House | | 163 | Edwards / Sentgerath / | | | |

# Cottage Numbers, Addresses, Owners

| # | Address | Owner |
|---|---------|-------|
| 1 | 27842 Shorewood Walk | Roche |
| 2 | 27901 Shorewood Drive | VanderSalm |
| 3 | 27856 Shorewood Walk | Potter |
| 4 | 27859 Shorewood Walk | Garvey / Steiner |
| 5 | 27868 Shorewood Walk | Canonie / Sylvester |
| 6 | 27869 Shorewood Walk | Cooney |
| 7 | 27884 Shorewood Walk | Welles |
| 8 | 27875 Shorewood Walk | Goff / St. John |
| 9 | 27895 Shorewood Walk | Eldredge / Gabriele / Goetzinger / Heck / Welles |
| 10 | 27882 Shorewood Drive | Gerity |
| 11 | 27947 Shorewood Drive | Stanger |
| 12 | 27921 Shorewood Drive | Filkins |
| 13 | 27909 Shorewood Drive | Henry |
| 14 | 28300 Shorewood Drive | Waldron |
| 15 | 28308 Shorewood Drive | Richards |
| 16 | 28316 Shorewood Drive | Orr |
| 17 | 28324 Shorewood Drive | Schlobohm |
| 18 | 79231 Edgewater Road | Jennings |
| 19 | 79251 Edgewater Road | Plain |
| 20 | 79261 Edgewater Road | Kinsey |
| 21 | 28370 Shorewood Drive | Sheehan |
| 22 | 28360 Shorewood Drive | Sheehan |
| 23 | 28350 Shorewood Drive | Fitzgerald |
| 24 | 28330 Shorewood Drive | Tamm |
| 25 | 29303 Shorewood Drive | Fredian |
| 26 | 28310 Shorewood Drive | Hoff |
| 27 | 28315 Shorewood Drive | Peat / Wehrheim |
| 28 | 79462 Shorewood Lane | Menconi |
| 29 | 79500 Shorewood Court | Claffy |
| 30 | 79301 Edgewater Road | Dannenberg |
| 31 | 79287 Edgewater Road | Menconi |
| 32 | 28327 Shorewood Drive | McArdle |
| 33 | 28331 Shorewood Circle | Brumis |
| 34 | 28345 Shorewood Circle | Schlacks |
| 35 | 28363 Shorewood Drive | Sitterly |
| 36 | 79735 Edgewater Road | Cordell |
| 37 | 79690 Edgewater Road | Nickerson |
| 38 | 79537 Edgewater Road | Donovan |
| 39 | 28312 Sturtevant Walk | Vercillo |
| 40 | 28390 Shorewood Drive | Morsch |
| 41 | 28386 Sturtevant Walk | Gardner |
| 42 | 28410 Shorewood Drive | Roche |
| 43 | 28400 Sturtevant Walk | King |
| 44 | 28420 Shorewood Drive | Borchert / Dembs |
| 45 | 28410 Sturtevant Walk | Coleman / Trotter |
| 46 | 28430 Shorewood Drive | Mailander |
| 47 | 28430 Sturtevant Walk | Haude |
| 48 | 28440 Shorewood Drive | Golden |
| 49 | 28440 Sturtevant Walk | McCarthy |
| 50 | 28435 Sturtevant Walk | Gates / Jones / Vana |
| 51 | 28450 Sturtevant Walk | Kavanaugh |
| 52 | 79940 Arthur Quick Circle | O'Brien |
| 53 | 79880 Arthur Quick Circle | Master |
| 54 | | PPCC SODA BAR |
| 55 | 79424 Ravine Way | Jones |
| 56 | 28604 Ravine Circle | Wilson |
| 57 | 28595 Ravine Circle | Parshall |
| 58 | 79390 Ravine Way | Oberlin |
| 59 | 79336 Ravineway | PPCC OFFICE |
| 60 | 79229 Ravine Way | Burrous |
| 61 | 79339 Ravine Way | Branding |
| 62 | 28960 Ravine Lane | Guirl |
| 63 | 79427 Ravine Way | McNamara / Skrine / Stratton |
| 64 | 28880 Ravine Lane | Sauer |
| 65 | 79964 Fernwood Drive | Ferry |
| 66 | 79970 Fernwood Drive | Stracke |
| 67 | 79990 Fernwood Drive | Gubbins |
| 68 | 79994 Fernwood Drive | Owen |
| 69 | 29042 Fernwood Road | Kolehmainen |
| 70 | 29050 Fernwood Road | Hussey |
| 71 | 79809 Fernwood Drive | Kline |
| 72 | 79893 Fernwood Drive | Schlacks |
| 73 | | PPCC CLUBHOUSE |
| 74 | 79867 Fernwood Drive | Bendelow |
| 75 | 79856 Fernwood Drive | Kilburn / Osth |
| 76 | 79857 Fernwood Drive | Nelson |
| 77 | 79843 Fernwood Drive | King / Koller / Mailander |
| 78 | 79842 Fernwood Drive | Hoskin |
| 79 | 79735 Fernwood Drive | Dobbelaere |
| 80 | 79991 Fernwood Court | Heitner |
| 81 | 79985 Fernwood Court | Henderson |
| 82 | 79988 Fernwood Court | Doyle / Molinaro |
| 83 | 79738 Fernwood Drive | Rudmann |
| 84 | 79752 Fernwood Drive | Hladik |
| 85 | 79835 Fernwood Walk | Alsterda |
| 86 | 79845 Fernwood Walk | Mauer |
| 87 | 79843 Fernwood Walk | Robins |
| 88 | 79955 Fernwood Walk | Aliotta / Fleming / Zigmond |
| 89 | 79919 Arthur Quick Circle | Breen / Dinnin / Forsee / Huffine / Lezon |
| 90 | 79929 Ballou Walk | Bradshaw / Cornelius / Flynn / Jefferson / Luedeman / McCowan / Phillips |
| 91 | 79939 Arthur Quick Circle | Connor |
| 92 | 28925 Ballou Walk | Tillson |
| 93 | 28935 Ballou Walk | Bishop / Vogt |
| 94 | 29845 Ballou Walk | Cunningham |
| 95 | 28955 Ballou Walk | King |
| 96 | 79840 Fernwood Crescent | Mathias / Taylor |
| 97 | 79848 Fernwood Crescent | McNamara / Wentzien |
| 98 | 79856 Fernwood Crescent | Richmond |
| 99 | 79864 Fernwood Crescent | Owen |
| 100 | 79870 Fernwood Crescent | Brand |

| #   | Address                   | Name                        |
| --- | ------------------------- | --------------------------- |
| 101 | 79882 Fernwood Drive      | Keehn                       |
| 102 | 79876 Fernwood Drive      | Carr                        |
| 103 | 79914 Fernwood Drive      | Bradford / Fyk              |
| 104 | 79922 Fernwood Drive      | Speicher                    |
| 105 | 29043 Fernwood Road       | Doyle                       |
| 106 | 79931 Fernwood Lane       | Compernolle                 |
| 107 | 79985 Fernwood Drive      | Gustafson                   |
| 108 | 79943 Fernwood Lane       | Trezise                     |
| 109 | 79980 Fernwood Lane       | Halpin                      |
| 110 | 79974 Fernwood Lane       | Pierce                      |
| 111 | 79947 Fernwood Drive      | Hartman                     |
| 112 | 79951 Fernwood Lane       | Marks / Sharpe              |
| 113 | 79955 Fernwood Lane       | Goeppinger                  |
| 114 | 79338 Fernwood Drive      | Venner                      |
| 115 | 79948 Fernwood Drive      | Colbert                     |
| 116 | 79965 Fernwood Drive      | Ellis                       |
| 117 | 29187 Thunder Mtn. Drive  | McCullough                  |
| 118 | 29305 Thunder Mtn. Circle | Foley                       |
| 119 | 29355 Thunder Mtn. Drive  | Zimmermann                  |
| 120 | 29428 Thunder Mtn. Drive  | Schwartz / Shortridge       |
| 121 | 29427 Thunder Mtn. Drive  | McWethy                     |
| 122 | 29435 Thunder Mtn. Lane   | DiKlich / Zacharko          |
| 123 | 29347 Thunder Mtn. Circle | O'Brien                     |
| 124 | 29635 Thunder Mtn. Lane   | Davis                       |
| 125 | 79525 Thunder Mtn. Ct.    | Bost                        |
| 126 | 29634 Thunder Mtn. Lane   | Petrulis                    |
| 127 | 29584 Thunder Mtn. Drive  | Lehmann / Soch              |
| 128 | 79881 Ramblewood Drive    | Meadowcroft                 |
| 129 | 79882 Ramblewood Drive    | Grigola                     |
| 130 | 79862 Ramblewood Circle   | Anderson                    |
| 131 | 79876 Ramblewood Circle   | Stewart                     |
| 132 | 79884 Ramblewood Circle   | Gryzwa                      |
| 133 | 79902 Ramblewood Circle   | Dinnin                      |
| 134 | 79910 Ramblewood Circle   | Whitney                     |
| 135 | 79904 Ramblewood Drive    | Beyer                       |
| 136 | 79921 Ramblewood Drive    | Beveridge / Dillman         |
| 137 | 79934 Ramblewood Drive    | Stanton                     |
| 138 | 79986 Ramblewood Drive    | Pomeroy                     |
| 139 | 79994 Ramblewood Drive    | Feldman                     |
| 140 | 80012 Ramblewood Drive    | Heavrin                     |
| 141 | 79905 Ramblewood Hill     | Buchanan                    |
| 142 | 79941 Ramblewood Hill     | Hohman                      |
| 143 | 80003 Ramblewood Hill     | Garvey                      |
| 144 | 80014 Ramblewood Hill     | Ball / Egan / Kearns / Mulvaney |
| 145 | 80018 Ramblewood Hill     | Foster                      |
| 146 | 80024 Ramblewood Hill     | Kittredge                   |
| 147 | 80009 Ramblewood Drive    | Trumbull                    |
| 148 | 80015 Ramblewood Drive    | Reed                        |
| 149 | 80021 Ramblewood Drive    | Ebert                       |
| 150 | 80024 Ramblewood Drive    | Henkel                      |
| 151 | 80030 Ramblewood Drive    | Patterson                   |
| 152 | 80036 Ramblewood Drive    | Flynn                       |
| 153 | 80042 Ramblewood Drive    | Kleb                        |
| 154 | 80048 Ramblewood Drive    | Duesing                     |
| 155 | 80054 Ramblewood Drive    | Boehm / Buschman            |
| 156 | 80060 Ramblewood Drive    | Stephens                    |
| 157 | 80066 Ramblewood Drive    | G'Sell                      |
| 158 | 80072 Ramblewood Drive    | O'Connor                    |
| 159 | 80078 Ramblewood Drive    | Lewis                       |
| 160 | 29659 Thunder Mtn. Drive  | Eisenberg                   |
| 161 | 29794 Lake Bluff Drive    | Kirk                        |
| 162 | 29821 Lake Bluff Drive    | Joy / Joy-Karney Joy-Rhomberg |
| 163 | 80020 Lake Bluff Lane     | Edwards / Sentgerath / Whippen |
| 164 | 29818 Lake Bluff Drive    | Heisel / Hession            |
| 165 | 80018 Lake Bluff Lane     | Lewis                       |
| 166 | 29826 Lake Bluff Drive    | Doyle / Hauber              |
| 167 | 29842 Lake Bluff Drive    | Burkhardt                   |
| 168 | 29847 Lake Bluff Drive    | Mason                       |
| 169 | 80017 Lake Bluff Court    | McMahon                     |
| 170 | 29860 Lake Bluff Drive    | Piper                       |
| 171 | 29869 Lake Bluff Drive    | Bartley                     |
| 172 | 29886 Lake Bluff Walk     | Mehagan                     |
| 173 | 29844 Lake Bluff Walk     | Williams                    |
| 174 | 28936 Lake Bluff Walk     | Ryan                        |
| 175 | 80084 Ramblewood Drive    | Borge                       |
| 176 | 30018 Lake Bluff Drive    | Beck                        |
| 177 | 30010 Lake Bluff Drive    | Fitzgerald                  |
| 178 | 30034 Lake Bluff Drive    | Kropp                       |
| 179 | 30048 Lake Bluff Drive    | Curtin                      |
| 180 | 30059 Lake Bluff Drive    | Favor                       |
| 181 | 30066 Lake Bluff Drive    | Hamilton                    |
| 182 | 30056 Lake Bluff Drive    | Keller                      |
| 183 | 30078 Lake Bluff Drive    | Kearin                      |
| 184 | 30092 Lake Bluff Drive    | Kearin                      |
| 185 | 30100 Lake Bluff Drive    | Cunningham                  |
| 186 | 29853 Lake Bluff Drive    | Zarling                     |
| 187 | 29342 Thunder Mtn. Drive  | Jansen                      |
| 188 | 79993 Fernwood Drive      | McCarthy                    |
| 189 | 79641 Edgewater Road      | O'Connor                    |
| 190 | 79210 Edgewater Road      | Carr / Grist / Vujtech      |
| 191 | 79899 Ramblewood Circle   | Zimmermann                  |
| 192 | 79544 Edgewater Road      | Donovan                     |
| 193 | 78898 29th Avenue         | Ankenbruck                  |
| 194 | 79890 Ramblewood Circle   | Van Boven                   |
| 195 | 79538 Shorewood Court     | Ebright                     |
| 196 | 79xxx Fernwood Crescent   | Owen                        |
| 197 | 78967 29th Avenue         | Ankenbruck                  |
| 198 | 28xxx Shorewood Drive     | Filosa                      |
| 199 | 79xxx Edgewater Road      | Roche                       |

# Early Sales

Names identified in County Court House records as constituting the earliest sales from South Haven Palisades Park Company, 1905 – 1914. For some reason, the earliest date found was 1909, although evidence suggests cottages were built starting in 1907. One surmises that Mr. Quick (or the Courthouse) postponed the paperwork on these first sales. At any rate, quite a number were listed on 8-27-09. Also note that the record in the County Court House was not completely in time sequence. Possibly errors were made. More likely, the sequence indicates that a number of deeds were given, all at the same time, to the Court House. It is interesting to note the number of females represented on this list. Finally, some of these names represent people who turned around and sold the lot to someone else before any cottage was built. No attempts were made to check on subsequent sales, only those from South Haven Palisades Park Company.

| Sold To | Lot | Block | Date |
| --- | --- | --- | --- |
| Marian E. Cota | 4 & 5 | Sandmere | 8-13-09 |
| Samuel K Markman | 2 | Oceana | 8-13-09 |
| Raymond V. Lewis | 11 & 13 | Fernwood | 8-27-09 |
| Clara Sturtevant | 2, 10, 15 | Sandmere | 8-27-09 |
| Frank Sturtevant | 3 | Sandmere | 8-27-09 |
| Katherine Baker | 7 & 8 | Oceana | 8-27-09 |
| Tekla Bergman | 7 | Dellwood | 8-27-09 |
| George W. Munroe | 16 & 17 | Oceana | 8-27-09 |
| Annie and Helen F. Nelson | 26, 27, 29, 30, 31 | Ridgelea | 8-27-09 |
| Ellis Nicholl | 10 | Seavista | 8-27-09 |
| Kate W. Nicholl | 9 | Seavista | 8-27-09 |
| Wilford M. Tubbs | 7 & 9 | Fernwood | 8-27-09 |
| Mary B. Ward | 3 | Oceana | 8-27-09 |
| William B. Ewing | 16 | Sandmere | 8-27-09 |
| Eugene Schreck (Sold to Henry Wunsch 8-21-12) | 7 | Sandmere | 8-27-09 |
| Frances A. Schreck | 8 | Seavista | 8-27-09 |
| Dr. Josephine McCollum/ Mary A. Vincent | 1 & 5 16 | Sandmere Fernwood | 8-27-09 8-27-09 |

| | | | |
|---|---|---|---|
| Thomas O. Browning | 16 & 17 | Lakeside Ad. | 8-27-09 |
| Willard R. Smith | 1 | Seavista | 8-27-09 |
| Valentine Scheppers | 15 | Lakeside Ad. | 8-27-09 |
| Emma B. Klein et al | 18 | Lakeside Ad | 8-27-09 |
| George C. Monroe | 1 | Oceana | 10-27-09 |
| Augustus C. DeSouchet | 13 | Lakeside Ad. | 9-2-10 |
| Nellie Sengenberger | 2 | Lakeside Ad. | 9-2-10 |
| Bertha M. Hoeck | 10 | Lakeside Ad. | 9-2-10 |
| Wilford M. Tubbs | 5 | Fernwood | 9-2-10 |
| Asman C. DeSouchet | 12 | Lakeside | 9-2-10 |
| Minnie M. Edee | 2 | Vinemount | 9-2-10 |
| Olcott H. Nix (Sturtevant brother-in-law) | 6 | Oceana | 9-2-10 |
| Hattie W. Nix | 5 | Oceana | 9-2-10 |
| P. T. Barry | 14 & 15 | Oak Hill | 9-23-10 |
| Valentine Scheppers | 10 | Vinemount | 10-6-10 |
| Dora Heuermann | 4 & 6 | Vinemount | 12-28-10 |
| Annie McNaughton | 22 | Fernwood | 12-28-10 |
| M. Angie Baker | 1 | Shadyside | 12-28-10 |
| Mary B. Ward | 4 | Oceana | 12-28-10 |
| Edward Gaidzek | 20 | Oak Hill | 12-28-10 |
| Christense M. Nelson | 15 | N. Palisades | |
| Mary E. Noyes | 6 | Fernwood | 3-7-11 |
| Mary L. Gervais | 13 | Oak Hill | 3-7-11 |
| I. .C. Taylor | | Seavista | 4-27-11 |

| Name | Lot | Section | Date |
|---|---|---|---|
| Ruth Vail Snow | 18 | Oak Hill | 5-15-11 |
|  | 6 | Shadyside | 5-15-11 |
| Reas L. Eitel | 8 | Oak Hill | 6-9-11 |
| William D. Watson | 5 | Lakeside | 9-13-11 |
| Eloise M. Willard | 10 | Oak Hill | 9-13-11 |
| Harriet Wayne Fry | 4 & 6 | Oak Hill | 9-13-11 |
| Minna S. Heuermann | 8 | Vinemount | 9-13-11 |
|  | 8 | Lakeside Ad. | 9-13-11 |
| Thomas H. Chase | 7 | Lakeside Ad. | 9-13-11 |
| George W. Leslie | 18 | Fernwood | 3-11-12 |
| John W. Stockwell | 14 | Lakeside Ad. | 3-11-12 |
| Edgar R. Smith | 2 | Dellwood | 3-11-12 |
| David W. Storrs | 2 | Woodcrest | 9-26-12 |
| Minna S. Heuermann | 7 & 9 | Beechwood | 9-26-12 |
| John T. Manierre | 1 | Woodcrest | 9-26-12 |
| Robert S. Lindstrtom | 3 | Mountainside | 9-26-12 |
| William H. Tucker | 1 | S. Palisades | 9-26-12 |
| Samuel T. Baker | 8 | Foothills | 9-26-12 |
| John W. Stockwell | 3 | Lake Bluff | 9-26-12 |
| Josie Cheney | 2 | Oakwood | 9-26-12 |
| Charles H. Smith | 9 & 10 | Linden | 9-26-12 |
| Louise E. Palmer |  | Linden | 9-26-12 |
| Effie B. Cortis | 3 | Lakeside Ad | 9-26-12 |
| Charles W. Carr | 1 | N. Palisades | 9-26-12 |
| Ezra T. Sturtevant | 1 | Sandmere | 9-26-12 |
| Louise K. Hawkinson | 3 & 5 | Beechwood | 9-26-12 |

| | | | |
|---|---|---|---|
| Ada B. Huber | 8 | Foot of the Rainbow | 9-26-12 |
| Wilford R. Sproul | 19 | Lake Bluff | 9-26-12 |
| Charles A. Aldrich | 7 | N. Palisades | 9-26-12 |
| Mary McGowen | 1 & 2 | Eastwood | 9-26-12 |
| C. DeWitt Wines | 23 | Oak Hill | 3-13-13 |
| Hattie A. Bush | 3 | Eastland | 3-13-13 |
| Fayette S. Cable | 3 & 4 | Vinemount | 3-13-13 |
| Nellie D. Arzner | 9 | Foot of the Rainbow | 3-13-13 |
| Edward F. Stearns | 2, 4, & 6 | Beechwood | 7-21-13 |
| Harriet Wayne Fry | 8 & 9 | Sandmere | 8-15-13 |
| Alma M. Vos | 5 | W. Summit | 9-15-13 |
| Ruth Vail Snow | 10 | Fernwood | 10-11-13 |
| South Haven Palisades Park Company | 6 | Shadyside | 10-11-13 |

## Associate Members
### (Incomplete)

| # | ISSUED TO | DATE | YEAR | NOTATION |
|---|---|---|---|---|
| 1-A | MRS. HELEN R. PACKARD | April 01 | 1953 | BECAME REG MEMBER |
| 2-A | CLAIRE STURTEVANT BOOTH | April 01 | 1953 | |
| 3-A | MIRIAM E. SPENCE | April 01 | 1953 | |
| 4-A | HARLEY M. & MARIE L. McDONALD | April 01 | 1953 | |
| 5-A | HENRY H. PRANGE | October 22 | 1953 | BECAME REG MEMBER |
| 6-A | MARK E. MUNWILER | July 27 | N/Y | |
| 7-A | GERALD B. HATCH | October 17 | 1959 | BECAME REG MEMBER |
| 8-A | HAROLD VANDER SALM | December 01 | 1960 | BECAME REG MEMBER |
| 9-A | RICHARD L. STANGER | DEC 3 1960 | 1953 | |
| 10-A | MR. JOSEPH F. FITZGERALD | May 15 | 1961 | BECAME REG MEMBER |
| 11-A | MR. ELMER C. FITZGERALD | May 15 | 1961 | |
| 12-A | MR. WILLIAM J. SHEEHAN | May 15 | 1961 | BECAME REG MEMBER |
| 13-A | MR. LOUIS A. BERTAUX | May 15 | 1961 | BECAME REG MEMBER |
| 14-A | MR. EDMUND J AREY | May 15 | 1961 | |
| 15-A | R. R. JOHNSON | September 04 | 1961 | |
| 16-A | VAUGHN SHUTES | September 04 | 1961 | |
| 17-A | GEORGE E. OWEN JR. | July 04 | 1963 | BECAME REG MEMBER |
| 18-A | VOID / BLANK | | | |
| 19-A | JOHN F. McARDLE | July 07 | 1953 | BECAME REG MEMBER |
| 20-A | GORDON R. ROSS | November 02 | 1963 | |
| 21-A | ROGER BRANE (SP?) | November 02 | 1963 | |
| 22-A | BURTON R. HOHMAN | January 07 | 1964 | BECAME REG MEMBER |
| 23-A | DR. WILLIAM KEEHN | February 17 | 1964 | BECAME REG MEMBER |
| 24-A | RICHARD T. VENNER | May 25 | 1964 | BECAME REG MEMBER |
| 25-A | FRANK S. HINES (SP?) | August 01 | 1964 | |
| 26-A | RALPH D. & AUDRA M. NICKERSON | April 14 | 1967 | |
| 27-A | T.H. STANFORD (SP?) | September 27 | 1967 | |
| 28-A | VOID | | | |
| 29-A | HAZEL E. & ROBERT BURKHARDT | March 13 | 1968 | BECAME REG MEMBER |
| 30-A | WILLIAM MENCONI | March 19 | 1969 | BECAME REG MEMBER |
| 31-A | ARTHUR J. GNEUHS | October 08 | 1969 | |
| 32-A | WILLIAM SEYMOUR JR. | December 03 | 1969 | |
| 33-A | JOSEPH W.. KING | March 02 | 1970 | S/B REGULAR CERT |
| 34-A | ROBERT J. SCHLACKS | July 07 | 1970 | BECAME REG MEMBER |
| 35-A | WILLIAM A. SCHLACKS | July 27 | 1970 | |
| 36-A | ANDREW W. PEIRCE | February 08 | 1971 | |
| 37-A | HAROLD D. MINICK & JACQUILINE A. MINICI | May 22 | 1971 | |
| 38-A | FRANK W. BLATCHFORD III | April 16 | 1972 | BECAME REG MEMBER |
| 39-A | DR. ROBERT HOLMES | November 01 | 1977 | |
| 40-A | VOID | | | |
| 41-A | VOID | | | |
| 42-A | VOID | | | |
| 43-A | VOID | | | |
| 44-A | VOID | | | |
| 45-A | WILLIAM J. JENSEN | December 14 | 1981 | REG |
| 46-A | BRADLEY & PAMELA SWEET | March 31 | 1982 | |
| 47-A | MISS LISA M. ANKENBRUCK | April 20 | 1982 | BECAME REG MEMBER |
| 48-A | CHARLES J. HENRY | October 21 | 1982 | BECAME REG MEMBER |
| 49-A | RICHARD FELDMAN & DEBORAH WALSH | | 1983 | BECAME REG MEMBER |
| 50-A | DAVID M. & MIKA I. FILKINS | January 10 | 1983 | BECAME REG MEMBER |
| 51-A | MICHAEL MEHAGAN | May 26 | 1984 | BECAME REG MEMBER |
| 52-A | LAWRENCE K. HUSSEY | May 26 | 1984 | BECAME REG MEMBER |
| 53-A | A. MYRON OSTH | May 26 | 1984 | BECAME REG MEMBER |
| 54-A | PAUL G. POMEROY | May 26 | 1984 | BECAME REG MEMBER |
| 55-A | VOID | | | |
| 56-A | VOID | | | |
| 57-A | VOID | | | |
| 58-A | BARRY & SUSAN EISENBERG | April 02 | 1992 | BECAME REG MEMBER |
| 59-A | VOID | | | |
| 60-A | VOID | | | |
| 61-A | VOID | | | |
| ? | BRUCE & DONNA CHAMBERS | | 1970 | |

# Photo Credits

The alphabetical list below indicates the source of the photo image(s) on each page number. The source listed is either the photographer or his/her collection, or a separate collection as indicated. Photos listed under "Palisades Park Collection" are from unknown photographers. Every effort has been made to verify the accuracy of some 78 sources and close to 1,000 photo images in this publication. We apologize in advance for such mistakes that were inadvertently made due to the complexity of keeping so many images straight. However, the Palisades Park Archives Committee would appreciate corrections or additional information.

Each image is also listed by position on the page. Abbreviations are used as follows: *t(top), m(middle), b(bottom), l(left), r(right)*. For example, a photo image in the lower right corner of page 436 would be "436br" for bottom right. If all the images on one page are from the same source, they are listed by page number only. - *DH*


Anderson, Stephen: 28m, 222, 226, 227
Appleyard: 457b
Archaeology Atlas of Michigan: 29, 36, 61
Baker/Goodrich: 98, 160br
Bartley, Janice: 436mr
Beatty, Robert: 592
Beck, Katy: 12, 31, 40, 42, 43, 44, 45, 46, 65, 67, 84br, 84t, 87, 101tl, 106tl, 107br, 116, 120, 121br, 121tl, 125br, 126tl, 127bl, 129, 130br, 170m, 171m, 172, 174, 175, 178, 179b, 185ml, 186, 192b, 206, 231br, 232bl, 232br, 232t, 233tl, 233tr, 233tl, 235bl, 235br, 235tl, 237t, 238b, 239, 242, 249b, 252b, 257t, 258m, 261, 263, 264, 265, 267mr, 275, 276, 282t, 283m, 285bl, 285br, 286bl, 286br, 287, 288bl, 288br, 289, 290b, 291, 293, 294, 295b, 305, 307m, 307tl, 307tr, 308mr, 308tl, 308tr, 311b, 311mr, 312b, 312mr, 313br, 314bl, 314mr, 314tr, 315, 316b, 317br, 323m, 324, 329b, 330b, 330t, 331t, 340bl, 341b, 343br, 343tl, 363, 366, 367, 369, 372, 374b, 375, 376, 378, 379, 382, 383, 392, 393tl, 396b, 396t, 399, 400bl, 400br, 401tl, 401tr, 403tl, 404, 405, 411b, 412, 426b, 427br, 437tl, 442br, 443bl, 446bl, 450, 451, 452bl, 452br, 452m,, 474b, 483tr, 484br, 492b, 492m, 493, 499m, 499t, 502m, 506tl, 507b, 508mr, 516bl, 518t, 519, 520, 523, 531t, 532br, 533b, 535t, 538b, 561, 563ml, 565b, 581, 585, 589b, 589tr, 595
Bendelow, Stuart: 118t, 161
Benton Harbor News Palladium: 472br
Beyer, Bruce: 233mr
Beyer, Howie: 233br
Brand, John: 34tr, 90tr, 256, 329m, 365, 384, 467tl, 488b, 489b, 490b, 490tl, 491, 501, 509, 517
Bruninga, Hank: 55b, 126tr, 136t, 168, 258b, 342br, 350b, 355, 356, 358, 443br, 570m, 575, 576, 578
Cargin family: 510
Chambers, Bruce: 166t, 278b, 279b, 589tl
Clark/Phillips: 52br, 78, 108bl, 283b, 284, 346t, 364, 368, 579b
Connor, Toni: 169, 171b, 381
Covert Museum: 10, 32, 48, 50m, 51b, 52bl, 53, 54b, 54tl, 57, 58, 71, 79, 86, 90, 94, 97t, 99, 100br, 102b, 103, 111br, 117tl, 123, 125bl, 127br, 131ml, 134b, 137b, 138t, 142m, 144, 145b, 149t, 152, 164, 182t, 193, 210mr, 210tr, 211t, 212, 248, 251, 257b, 273b, 282t, 344t, 370, 372, 373, 380, 425, 438br, 438t, 480t, 488t, 525, 567, 590b
Dannenberg, Ray: 571
Ebert, Bob: 434br
Ebright, Patti: 559

Ferry, Mary: 437m
Foust, Jerry: 434mr
Frencheck, Anne: 16t, 216b, 217, 218, 219
Goeppinger family: 557
Goff, Kay: 165b, 205, 220, 257m, 441tr, 470bl, 486br, 555mr
Goscinski, Donna: 595
Hann Photo Service, Hartford, MI: 472bl
Hasmer, William Morrell: 53b
Haude, Betty: 574
Heavrin, Kari: 124br, 436
Heisel/Hession: 207bl, 207br, 207m, 303m
Henkel, Don: Cover Jacket (except front), 1, 3, 4, 5, 6, 9, 11, 13, 14, 16, 25, 50b, 51t, 54tr, 69, 76b, 77, 80, 88tl, 89m, 89b, 93bl, 118tr, 131mr, 131br, 140, 148, 151, 157, 160bl, 195, 196, 234, 235tr, 240, 255m, 266, 268, 280b, 287t, 299tr, 300b, 300t, 302, 306, 307b, 308b, 309, 310, 311ml, 311t, 312t, 312ml, 313bl, 313tl, 313m, 313tr, 314br, 314ml, 314tl, 316t, 317t, 317b, 318, 319t, 319br, 320, 325t, 327, 331b, 335, 339, 341t, 342t, 343tr, 354m, 389, 393m, 395b, 396m, 398, 402b, 403bl, 406, 407, 414m, 415, 416, 421b, 426t, 427mr, 430b, 435t, 435ml, 436tl, 438, 439, 440, 441bl, 441tl, 442bl, 449bl, 452t, 454, 474m, 476, 511, 516br, 518b, 522t, 522m, 522b, 526, 528b, 529mr, 529tl, 530m, 531bl, 532t, 534b, 537, 539, 558b, 580tl, 583mr, 593, 594, 595
Hladik, Bob: 435mr, 436mr
Householder, Betty: 75, 97b, 122b, 124br, 223, 225, 231t, 270, 349tr
Jones, Mary: 319bl, 361m, 361t, 401br, 477
Kalamazoo Gazette: 473t, 473ml
Keehn, Bill: 253, 502b
King, Janice: 119, 301b, 353b, 447t, 462, 463b, 464, 465, 487t, 555ml
King/VanBeuren: 498t, 498br, 500, 515
Kleb, Bud: 524t, 570t
Kline, Keith: 104tl
Kolrmainen, Philip: 435br, 435bl, 436tr
Lewis, Nanette Draper: cover, 19, 70, 76t, 112, 182b, 304, 321, 322ml, 323b, 333m, 336, 338b, 343bl, 401bl, 413, 428, 435br, 449, 483tl
Litterst, Wendy (Easterbrook): 385, 386
Lowrey family: 22tr, 60, 82, 101br, 106br, 113m, 114tl, 124ml, 158bl, 158br, 180, 183b, 188, 199, 200bl, 210b, 238m, 239m, 241tl, 241tr, 259bl, 267ml, 296, 340br, 346b, 352m, 352t, 394, 395m, 403br, 403m, 403tr
Mathias, Jane: 183t, 400t, 420b
Mathias, Mike: 420t
McCarthy, Sheila: 360m, 361m
Mehagan, Mike: 115, 492t
Michigan Maritime Museum: 91t, 113b, 141, 194, 279tl
Michigan State Archives (with permission): 33, 49
Nelson, Betty: 15, 18t, 23, 67b, 82, 91b, 92, 93br, 96br, 102tl, 105br, 126br, 139b, 143, 145m, 150b, 154bl, 189, 204b, 213, 224, 228t, 238t, 244t, 259br, 271b, 337, 442ml, 444tl, 524b, 527, 528t, 565m, 566, 572, 584t
O'Brien, Tom: 109
Palisades Park Collection: 12, 17, 22, 52t, 56t, 60, 62, 81b, 85bl, 85tr, 88br, 100bl, 107bl, 108ml, 111t, 114br, 128br, 135br, 137, 142b, 147, 162, 166b, 177, 181, 185br, 192t, 198, 204m, 211m, 215, 262m, 273t, 274, 286tl, 290t, 295m, 298t, 328b, 345, 348, 353m, 354t, 371, 388, 414b, 421t, 435mr, 436bl, 436mr, 437br, 438br, 442mr, 446t, 463t, 467b, 480b, 481t, 484bl, 484t, 497b, 504, 506tr, 540, 577m, 587
Patterson, Doris: 187b, 205, 229t, 325b, 326, 434bl, 586
Peat, David: 18b, 229b, 269b, 271, 272, 359mr, 481b
Peterson, Roger Tory: A Field Guide to the Birds: 532bl

Piper, Brad: 32, 473b, 475, 483b, 577t

Potter, Bill: 66, 150t, 173b, 173m, 211bl, 243, 244b, 278t, 279tr, 347, 349br, 352b, 353t, 354b, 359bl, 409, 411t, 431b, 432, 442tr, 443tl, 447b, 453,455, 456, 457t, 460, 461, 466, 470br, 470m, 479, 482, 486bl, 487b, 489t, 490m, 495, 496, 497t, 498bl, 499b, 506b, 507t, 508ml, 513, 514, 531br, 595

Prange, Fran: 393tr

Quick, Arthur, Wildflowers of the Northern States and Canada: 530t

Reed, Mary: 563b, 590t, 590m

Richmond, Jim: 536

Roche, Marge: 36b, 74, 84bl, 88bl, 96tl, 104br, 105t, 108tl, 122tl, 130tl, 135tl, 138b, 139t, 155, 163, 165t, 167, 170t, 176, 179t, 184, 187t, 191, 195t, 197, 203, 208, 212t, 214, 249t, 252m, 255t, 262b, 269t, 275, 277, 280t, 285t, 297b, 298b, 299tl, 303b, 323t, 328t, 332t, 340t, 342bl, 344b, 349bl, 349m, 349tl, 350m, 374t, 377,387,397,410,422,423,424,429, 430t, 431t, 436br, 437bl, 443tr, 444tr, 445t, 533t, 534t, 535b, 563mr, 564b, 575m, 583ml, 584m

Saugatuck-Douglas Historical Society: 56br, 63, 64, 68, 95, 200mr, 245, 441br, 443m, 444b

Schlacks, Andrew: 437tr

Schlobohm, Sally: 81tr, 250, 359ml, 446br, 579m, 580m, 580tr

Sentgerath, John: 89tr, 117mr, 128bl, 133, 303t, 421m, 467tr, 468

Stewart, Doug: 338t

Stieve, Jeanette: 110, 149b, 154br, 209, 281, 558mr

Trotter, Jane: 230, 231bl

Trumbull, Barb: 402t

Venner, Rob: 350t

Venner, Tom: 236, 237b

Williams, Jim: 114br, 211br, 332bl, 333, 438br, 442tl, 445b, 473mr, 564t

Wood, Julia: 72, 146

Zimmermann, Pete: 427bl

## My Memories

# MAP OF
## THE FIRST SUBDIVISION OF
# PALISADES PARK
## SEC'S 7 & 8, COVERT TOWNSHIP
## VAN BUREN COUNTY, MICH.

APRIL 25, 1909.   WARREN H. GOSS, SURVEYOR

SCALE
ONE INCH = 100 FEET

### DESCRIPTION OF LAND PLATTED

The land embraced in the annexed plat of The First Subdivision Of Palisades Park, is described as follows:— Beginning at the Southeast corner of the Southwest quarter of the northwest fractional quarter of Section 8 in Covert Township, T.2.S, R.17.W. Van Buren Co. Michigan. Thence by Metes and bounds South on eighth line 300'; Thence S 87½° W 260.5'; Thence N 24° W 109'; Thence S 84° W 206'; Thence S 71° W 364'; Thence N 72° W 53.8'; Thence N 80° W 51'; Thence N 85¼° W 100'; Thence S 63¾° W 107.7'; Thence N 34° W 118.1'; Thence N 57¼° W 61' to the west line of Section 8 at a point 171' South from the north eighth post between Sections 7 and 8. Thence in section 7 N 57¼° W 23'; Thence N 9¾° E 78.5'; Thence S 75¼° W 63.6'; Thence S 99° W 135.5'; Thence N 14¼° W 65.8' to the shore line of Lake Michigan. Thence N 18½° E along said shore 105' to the north eighth line of section 7. Thence N 18½° E 722.3' to the east line of section 7 at a point 68' North from the north eighth post between sections 7 and 8. Thence in section 8 N 18½° E 175'; N 23½° E 363'; Thence S 66½° E 152'; Thence S 18° E 127'; Thence S 40° W 68.5'; Thence S 11° W 126'; Thence S 32½° E 85'; Thence S 11½° E 152'; Thence N 75½° E 44.8'; Thence N 84½° E 47.8'; Thence S 71½° E 50'; Thence S 48° E 183'; Thence S 67° E 83'; Thence S 79° E 38'; Thence N 86° E 127'; Thence S 55° E 146'; Thence N 76½° E 154.5' to the east line of the west one crowed half of the northwest fractional quarter of section 8. Thence South on the eighth line 100'. Thence on the northeast quarter of the northwest fractional quarter of section 8 N 87½° E 100'; Thence S 42½° E 80.5'; Thence South 287.2'; Thence S 87½° W 150' to place of beginning.

### PALISADES PARK WITNESSES

| | | | | | |
|---|---|---|---|---|---|
| A | Red Oak | 11" in diameter | N 67° E | 34.5' |
| | Double White Oak | 13" " " | N 47½° W | 41.' |
| B | Red Oak | 10" " " | S 79° W | 13' |
| C | Beech | 12" " " | Corner | |
| D | Sassafras | 4" " " | S 62½° E | 87' |
| | Red Oak | 8" " " | N 72½° E | 129.5' |
| E | White Ash | 18" " " | N 48° E | 2' |
| F | Red Oak | 13" " " | S 49° W | 8' |
| G | Red Oak | 11" " " | South | 4.0' |
| | | 21" " " | S 88° E | 9.5' |
| H | Sugar | 11" " " | South | 8' |
| I | Red Oak | 6" " " | Corner | |
| K | Hemlock | 17" " " | N 52° W | 5.4' |

### SURVEYORS CERTIFICATE

I hereby certify that the plat hereon delineated is a correct one and that permanent monuments consisting of iron pipe 1.5" in diameter and 24" long have been planted at points marked thus "O" as therein shown at all angles in the boundaries of the land platted, and at all intersections of drives or avenues, and walks and all lot corners.

Warren H. Goss
SURVEYOR.

Examined and Approved
JUL 16 1909

Deputy Auditor General.

## DEDICATION

KNOW ALL MEN BY THESE PRESENTS that we the SOUTH HAVEN PALISADES PARK COMPANY, a corporation organized under Act No. 232 of the Public Acts of MICHIGAN for 1903, as proprietors, have caused the lands embraced in the annexed plat to be surveyed, laid out and platted, to be known as "THE FIRST SUBDIVISION OF PALISADES PARK" and that the drives, walks, parks and beaches, as shown on said plat, and also easements are not hereby dedicated to the public but are hereby dedicated to the joint use and benefit of the members of the corporation, and the owners of lands in said PALISADES PARK.

SOUTH HAVEN PALISADES PARK Co,

By Arthur C. Quick PRESIDENT

And By Edwin C. Wyman SECRETARY

State of ILLINOIS } ss
County of KANE

On this 28th day of June 1909 before me William F Lynch a clerk of a court of record in and for said County personally came the above named Arthur C. Quick President and Edwin C. Wyman Secretary of said corporation, known to me to be the persons who executed the above dedication and acknowledged the same to be their free act and deed as President and Secretary of said South Haven Palisades Park Company, and the free act and deed of said Corporation

Wm F. Lynch Clerk of County Court.

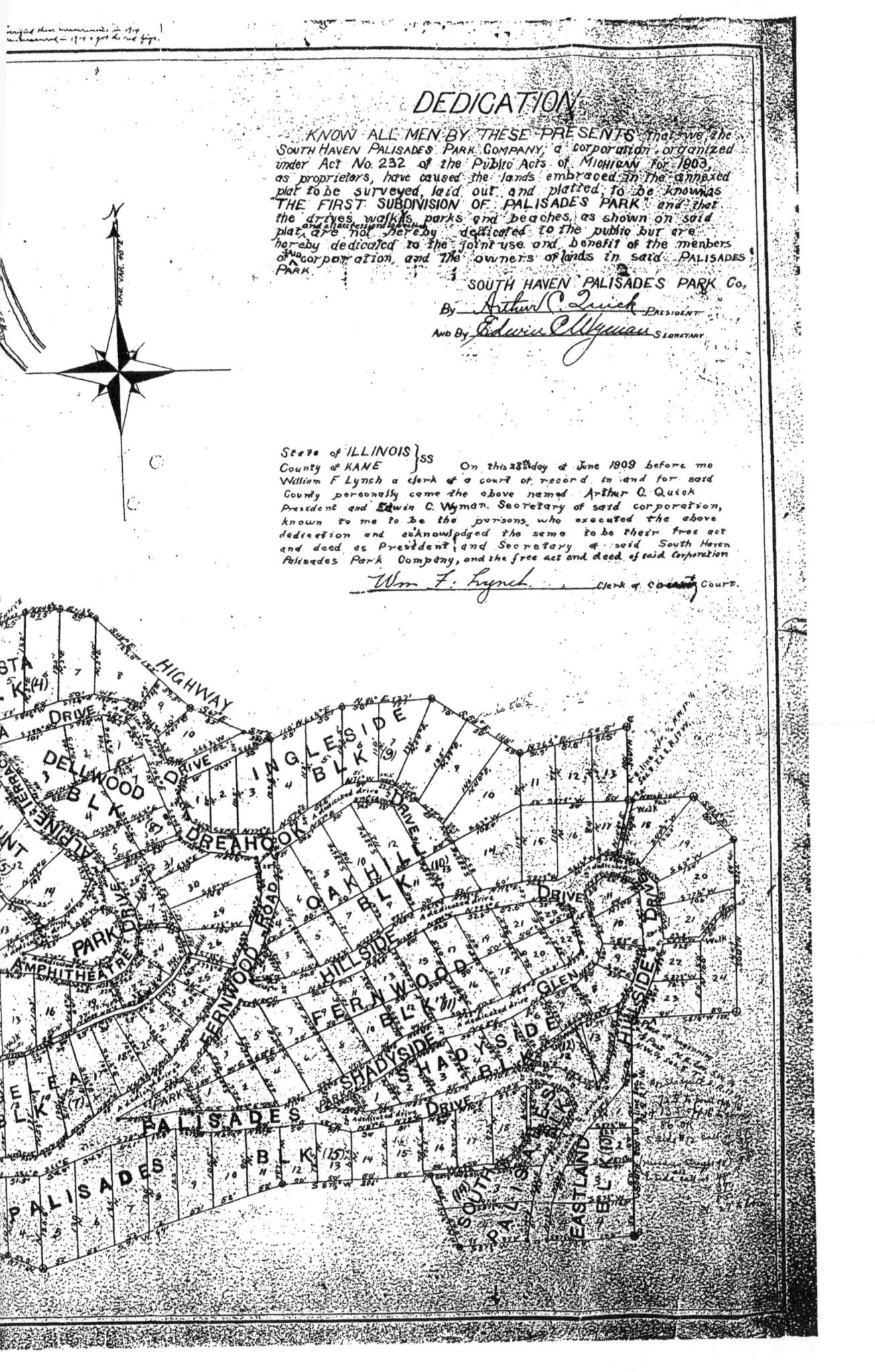

www.ingramcontent.com/pod-product-compliance
Lightning Source LLC
Chambersburg PA
CBHW080921300426
44115CB00018B/2910